Tolley's Guide to the Pensions Act 2004

A complete update of law and practice

by

Alec Ure
Pension & Taxation Consultant, Author
Alec Ure & Associates

Gavin Moffatt
Senior Technical Adviser
SBJ Benefit Consultants Ltd

Members of the LexisNexis Group worldwide

United Kingdom	LexisNexis Butterworths, a Division of Reed Elsevier (UK) Ltd, Halsbury House, 35 Chancery Lane, London, WC2A 1EL, and RSH, 1–3 Baxter's Place, Leith Walk Edinburgh EH1 3AF
Argentina	LexisNexis Argentina, Buenos Aires
Australia	LexisNexis Butterworths, Chatswood, New South Wales
Austria	LexisNexis Verlag ARD Orac GmbH & Co KG, Vienna
Benelux	LexisNexis Benelux, Amsterdam
Canada	LexisNexis Canada, Markham, Ontario
Chile	LexisNexis Chile Ltda, Santiago
China	LexisNexis China, Beijing and Shanghai
France	LexisNexis SA, Paris
Germany	LexisNexis Deutschland GmbH, Munster
Hong Kong	LexisNexis Hong Kong, Hong Kong
India	LexisNexis India, New Delhi
Italy	Giuffrè Editore, Milan
Japan	LexisNexis Japan, Tokyo
Malaysia	Malayan Law Journal Sdn Bhd, Kuala Lumpur
Mexico	LexisNexis Mexico, Mexico
New Zealand	LexisNexis NZ Ltd, Wellington
Poland	Wydawnictwo Prawnicze LexisNexis Sp, Warsaw
Singapore	LexisNexis Singapore, Singapore
South Africa	LexisNexis Butterworths, Durban
USA	LexisNexis, Dayton, Ohio

© Reed Elsevier (UK) Ltd 2006
Published by LexisNexis Butterworths

A CIP Catalogue record for this book is available from the British Library.

ISBN for this volume

ISBN 10: 0 7545 2730 1

ISBN 13: 978 0 7545 2730 5

Typeset by Letterpart Ltd, Reigate, Surrey
Printed and bound in Great Britain by Hobbs the Printers Ltd, Totton, Hampshire
Visit LexisNexis Butterworths at www.lexisnexis.co.uk

Preface

The *Pensions Act 2004* is having a major impact on the regulation of occupational pension schemes and the protection of member benefits. Although the main provisions of the Act came into effect on 6 April 2005, a great number of regulations and orders have been made under its provisions since that date. This book has been produced in order to help scheme managers, trustees, advisers, employers and members understand those far-reaching developments. This is a complex field, and I am delighted to have been joined in writing this book by a valued ex-colleague, Gavin Moffatt. Gavin is Senior Technical Adviser at SBJ Benefit Consultants Ltd.

The main intent of the Act is to provide increased security for members (primarily of defined benefit pension schemes), introduce revised administrative and compliance procedures, and accommodate many of the proposals of the December 2002 Green Paper by the Department for Work and Pensions (DWP) *Simplicity, Security and Choice: Working and Saving for Retirement*. It was estimated by the DWP that there are over 10m members of defined benefits schemes in the United Kingdom. It is therefore of great significance that the Act contains details of the Pension Protection Fund (PPF) to protect the benefits of members of such schemes which have insolvent (or departed) employers.

The PPF is not restricted to schemes of companies which became insolvent after its commencement date of 6 April 2005, as long as the pension scheme has not yet gone into wind-up. The compensation scheme of the PPF is funded by a composite levy on schemes, and a significant part of this levy is risk-based. However, certain schemes, including schemes with fewer than 100 members, are exempted from the risk-based levy. Full details of the PPF are given in Chapter 4.

The *Pensions Act 2004* also contained details of the Financial Assistance Scheme (FAS), for the purpose of offering protection for many of those persons who are not covered by the PPF. The FAS applies to persons who suffered loss from their defined benefit schemes when their schemes were wound up, or began winding up, within a prescribed period, with an insolvent, or non-existent, employer. The prescribed period is between 1 January 1997 and 5 April 2005. Unlike the PPF, the FAS is not funded by levies; it is funded out of public monies. The cost to the taxpayer is likely to considerable, based on recent government estimates. The FAS is described in Chapter 8.

The *Pensions Act 2004* is not only concerned with compensation, but also with regulation. The objective is to protect member benefits for the future. These matters are the responsibility of the new Pensions Regulator, which replaced the Occupational Pensions Regulatory Authority (Opra). The Regulator had considerable powers conferred on it by the Act, some of which are under attack as being too extensive. Among other things, the Regulator has to ensure that monies are not misappropriated or misdirected from schemes. It is empowered to investigate and take control of underfunded schemes, and to require them to wind up if it considers it in the best interests of the scheme members. In addition to such matters, the Regulator also has an important role in providing education, assistance and information to those persons who administer or advise on pension schemes. A description of the role and powers of the Regulator is given in Chapter 3.

Another significant aspect of the Act, and a major consideration for trustees and scheme sponsors of defined benefits schemes, is the new scheme-specific statutory funding objective, which has replaced the minimum funding require-ment (MFR). The government had first declared its intent to replace the MFR in December 2002, partly because of the need to take into account, by 23 September 2005, the provisions of EU Directive 2003/41/EC on the Activities and Supervision of Institutions for Occupational Retirement Provi-sion (the 'IORP Directive'). In the event, matters were delayed. The new method applies to most actuarial valuations from 22 September 2005. The cost implications are significant, and further information is given in Chapter 5.

The Act also addresses certain overseas matters. The *Occupational Pension Schemes (Cross-border Activities) Regulations 2005 (SI 2005/3381)* came into force on 30 December 2005. The legislative objective is to enable occupational pension schemes for qualifying persons to be sponsored by a European employer in other EU member states. Most of the effective dates for the regulations were 23 September 2005, the date by which the IORP Directive had to be complied with, although some regulations came into effect later. This subject is covered in Chapter 9.

The remaining chapters of this book describe a raft of other provisions under the Act. Among other things, a greater simplification of contracting out would also have been beneficial, as had originally been proposed by the DWP, but there has been little headway. It is to be hoped that the matter will be actively addressed in the near future.

The appendices to the book are formed of the most significant regulations and guidance which are likely to be needed on a regular basis by scheme managers, trustees, advisers, employers and members.

In conclusion, it cannot be said that the *Pensions Act 2004* has achieved the simplicity which was envisaged by the DWP in its founding White Paper. Nevertheless, it has certainly increased security for many, and the degree of wider choice which is available under the Act is broadened by the changes under the *Finance Act 2004* and new government initiatives. The cost of the PPF is, perhaps, the main concern. It falls heavily on defined benefits schemes, and the move towards alternative methods of saving for retirement, in particular money purchase provision, seems to be inexorable.

Alec Ure
Pension & Taxation Consultant, Author
Alec Ure & Associates

Gavin Moffatt
Senior Technical Adviser
SBJ Benefit Consultants Ltd

Contents

Contents

4. The Pension Protection Fund

Contents

7. Occupational and personal pension provisions

Contents

Chapter 1
Introduction

The book   1.1

This is the first LexisNexis Butterworths book which has been dedicated entirely to the provisions of the *Pensions Act 2004*. It also covers the significant number of regulations and orders which were enabled to be made, and have been made, by that Act.

The changes which have been brought about by the new legislation, and those which are still developing, are described in detail under the appropriate chapter headings.

One certainty is that further regulations and orders will appear in the future. Indeed, the government already has several matters under active consultation. It is therefore hoped that this book will help scheme managers, trustees, advisers, employers and members to understand the developments to date and to be prepared for the forthcoming changes.

Background to the Pensions Act 2004   1.2

The origins of the *Pensions Act 2004* are described in **CHAPTER 2**. In brief:

- The Act was envisaged by government as a means of providing increased member benefit protection in the wake of market downturns and worrying deficits in pension fund values.

- Several proposals of the December 2002 Green Paper by the Department for Work and Pensions (DWP), *Simplicity, Security and Choice: Working and Saving for Retirement*, were brought into effect by the Act.

- It was estimated by the DWP that there are over 10m members of defined benefits schemes in the United Kingdom, and the Act accordingly impacts heavily on such schemes.

The main purpose of the Pensions Act 2004   1.3

The main intent of the Act is to provide security for members, by introducing new funding requirements for defined benefits schemes, tighter regulation and compliance procedures, and countering pension liberation and the misappropriation and misuse of pension scheme assets. It also introduced the Pension Protection Fund and the Financial Assistance Scheme for the purpose of recompensing many of those members of defined benefits schemes who have suffered loss due to fund deficiencies.

The Act in addition seeks to improve member, employer and trustee awareness through learning programmes on the website of the new Pensions Regulator.

Subjects covered   1.4

The book covers the following areas:

*   the origins of the governing legislation (**CHAPTER 2**);

*   the establishment of the new Pensions Regulator, and a description of its far-reaching powers (**CHAPTER 3**);

*   the formation of a Pension Protection Fund (**CHAPTER 4**);

*   the new scheme-specific statutory funding objective (**CHAPTER 5**);

*   government initiatives on financial planning for retirement (**CHAPTER 6**);

*   the wider occupational and personal pension provisions which apply under the Act (**CHAPTER 7**);

*   the formation of a Financial Assistance Scheme (**CHAPTER 8**);

*   the new rules on 'cross-border activities' for participating schemes (**CHAPTER 9**);

*   a review of the effect of the Act on state pensions (**CHAPTER 10**);

*   further reforms, as appropriate (**CHAPTER 11**).

A short description of the most significant subjects is given under the headings below.

Pensions Regulator   1.5

The new Pensions Regulator has replaced the Occupational Pensions Regulatory Authority (Opra). It has been given considerable powers under the

Pensions Act 2004. These powers are still developing. Its main function is to protect member benefits and to ensure that monies are not misappropriated or misdirected (see **1.3** above). The Regulator can also conduct investigations, or instruct them to be made, and make key decisions on underfunded defined benefits schemes. These decisions include issuing notices, freezing a scheme, removing trustees, repatriation of liberated funds, forcing a wind-up and gathering information. The Regulator publishes guidance on its website, including codes of practice and educational/training material and courses.

Scheme-specific statutory funding objective   1.6

The new scheme-specific funding objective applies to most actuarial valuations of defined benefits schemes from 22 September 2005 (see **CHAPTER 5**). The cost implications can be significant, as it broadly reflects a substantially strengthened funding standard brought in under EU Directive 2003/41/EC of the European Parliament and of the Council of 3 June 2003 on the Activities and Supervision of Institutions for Occupational Retirement Provision (the 'IORP Directive'). The objective replaces the old minimum funding requirement of the *Pensions Act 1995.*

The Pension Protection Fund   1.7

The Pension Protection Fund (PPF) is primarily for the purpose of protecting the benefits of members of defined benefits schemes which have insolvent employers or have no active employers and are in deficit. It mainly applies to schemes of companies which became insolvent after its commencement date of 6 April 2005, but it does not apply to schemes which wound up, or entered into winding up, before that date.

The PPF is funded by a composite levy on schemes, and a significant part of this levy is risk-based. However, certain schemes, including schemes with fewer than 100 members, are exempted from the risk-based levy.

Financial Assistance Scheme   1.8

The Financial Assistance Scheme (FAS) is for the purpose of offering protection for many of those persons who are not covered by the PPF. It applies to persons who suffered loss from their defined benefit schemes when their schemes were wound up, or began winding up, with an insolvent, or non-existent, employer. The FAS applies to the period between 1 January 1997 and 5 April 2005. The FAS is funded out of taxpayer's money, and the bill could be high, as explained in **CHAPTER 8**.

Cross-border activities 1.9

The *Occupational Pension Schemes (Cross-border Activities) Regulations 2005* (*SI 2005/3381*) came into force on 30 December 2005 to enable occupational pension schemes for qualifying persons to be sponsored by a European employer in other EU member states. Most of the effective dates for the regulations were 23 September 2005, the date by which the IORP Directive had to be complied with, although some came into effect later (see **CHAPTER 9**).

Conclusion 1.10

Whereas the *Pensions Act 2004* has replaced some substantial existing legislation, it cannot be said that this has resulted in a true simplification, as was initially signalled. Much of the existing legislation has been replaced by a welter of new legislation. On a positive note, the aim to increase security for many will be welcomed by those persons who have been adversely affected by deficits in their defined benefits schemes. The added protection for hard-earned rights is also welcome, but the complexity of the new system is quite high. Scheme managers, trustees, advisers, employers and members will need to be conversant with the sources of information that apply to them, and to review matters with increasing frequency. The comparative simplicity of regulation of UK money purchase schemes makes the conversion of existing defined benefits schemes, and the establishment of new money purchase schemes, an ever-increasing attraction.

Chapter 2
Origins of the Pensions Act 2004

Introduction 2.1

Of all the measures introduced under the *Pensions Act 1995* specifically relating to occupational pensions, approximately two-thirds have been amended, replaced or repealed by the *Pensions Act 2004*. Perhaps the two most significant areas that needed change were the minimum funding requirement (MFR) and the Occupational Pensions Regulatory Authority (Opra).

The MFR came in for particular criticism in the Myners Review of Institutional Investment due to its effect on trustees' investment decision-making. It was also becoming apparent that scheme wind-ups were leaving members with less than they thought had been protected when their employer became insolvent. Even though a scheme was fully funded on the MFR basis, it might only have enough money to cover about 60% of the benefits. Additionally, the new statutory priority order, which dictated which benefits were secured first, saw some employees with long service lose a large proportion of their benefit while the recently retired fared significantly better.

Opra had been set up as a reactive regulator with powers to intervene in the running of schemes where it had received reports of wrong-doing. The reports soon came in thick and fast since the *Pensions Act 1995* originally required trustees, under threat of penalty, to report any instances of contributions being paid late. Opra was swamped with work even though the majority of these reports did not contain any serious threats to the security of members' benefits. It was also seen that a more proactive regulator would be needed; one that did not have to rely on detailed prescriptive measures before it could act, if there was to be a chance of preventing another Maxwell affair.

The Myners Review of Institutional Investment

Background 2.2

In the 2000 budget the Chancellor expressed concern over factors leading institutional investors to follow 'industry standard investment patterns'. Investors were ignoring venture capital and small and medium-sized enterprises

(SMEs) in favour of quoted equities and gilts. Paul Myners, Chairman of Gartmore Investment Management, was therefore asked to carry out a review of institutional investment in the UK, and in May 2000 he published a short consultation paper inviting comments on the various areas set out for discussion in that paper.

Initial consultation paper   2.3

The original consultation paper noted that there was a large pool of long-term capital in the UK, and raised questions over whether it was invested with a sufficiently long-term view. In particular, Myners questioned whether institutional investors had become too risk averse, and, if that were the case, what factors distorted their investment decisions. Myners was to make his response by the 2001 Budget. However, a consultation issued in September 2000 by the Treasury and the Department of Social Security on MFR reform prompted him, in November 2000, to release an early report on his views of the MFR.

Questions raised   2.4

The May 2000 consultation paper recognised the need for defined benefit schemes to minimise the long-term funding cost for the sponsoring employer and the desire for stable levels of contributions. As a result, defined benefit schemes were more likely to be concerned with not underperforming than with outperforming. The consultation paper also questioned the tendency of defined contribution schemes to focus on fund performance against benchmarks, when they would have been expected to be much more concerned about the risk/benefit relationship and the desire to maximise returns.

Schemes with higher proportions of pensioners tended to match those liabilities against low-risk assets because those liabilities needed to be covered in the short term. Well-funded schemes were less affected by increasing maturity, but increasing longevity and early retirement trends meant that even less well-funded schemes had the potential to invest in higher-risk asset classes. The paper therefore sought views on how investment patterns could be explained by the increasing maturity of pension funds and whether the use of insured annuities would amplify or reduce those effects.

An important question raised was whether trust law provided a suitable framework for taking investment decisions. Pension scheme trustees are not generally experienced investors and rely heavily on advisers. There was not seen to be much incentive for investment consultants to recommend non-standard investment strategies as they were not normally paid by fund results. If they operated in a strongly competitive environment, then they were not likely to propose strategies that differed substantially from those of their competitors.

There was also little incentive for fund managers to outperform, as they would still get paid if they outperformed their target by only a small amount, but could lose the business quickly if they significantly underperformed. As performance is usually measured against a benchmark, appropriate investment strategies tended to be adopted accordingly, and measurement against other pension funds would lead directly to industry-standard strategies. The paper raised many questions about the practices of investment consultants, fund managers' remuneration and incentives, the impact of increasing risk management, concentration in large parts of the fund management industry, and, more importantly, whether the use of short-term return objectives was really appropriate for long-term funds.

Myners noted that scheme members were not sufficiently aware of, or involved in, issues to do with fund performance. The statement of investment principles was not an effective vehicle for stimulating debate about the investment strategy. He therefore asked if the quality of investment decision-making suffers when there is too little public discussion of fund performance. He also questioned the 'reckless conservatism' that can occur in defined contribution schemes, and sought comments about the impact of individual involvement in investment strategy and the range of funds available.

The consultation finally considered the distortion that the MFR could have. When the funding of a defined benefit scheme approached its MFR level there was an incentive to match a liability with an asset whose return matched the discount rate used to discount the liability. This ensured that the value of the asset and the corresponding liability were more likely to move in step. Even without the MFR, asset-liability modelling in pension funds would have a similar effect. Questions were raised around investment decisions and the effects of the MFR, scheme valuation rules, asset-liability modelling and the impact of FRED20 (a proposed new system of accounting which would give far more details on pension scheme performance on an annual basis).

MFR criticism   2.5

Paul Myners was originally due to report on his review of institutional investment for the 2001 budget. However, as noted above, Myners published his views on the MFR in November 2000 shortly after consultation was issued jointly by the Treasury and the Department of Social Security on the subject of MFR reform.

In an open letter addressed jointly to the Chancellor and the Secretary of State for Social Security, Myners concluded that the MFR was flawed and seriously inadequate as a form of protection. Rather than see the MFR reformed, Myners recommended that it should be scrapped altogether. The main criticisms were:

- The MFR distorts investment decision-taking. (In talking to investment managers, Myners commented that he was struck by how often they spoke of 'matching the MFR portfolio'.)

- By preventing investment in an optimal way costs are increased and this is another argument for an employer to close his defined benefit scheme. Regulation such as the MFR is counter-productive if the cost becomes too high; the closure of a defined benefit scheme as a direct result could leave members worse off.

- The MFR records the state of the fund only at one point in time, yet financial and economic conditions change frequently. An historical snapshot would not necessarily provide the same safeguards as a well thought-out policy.

- The MFR does nothing to protect against fraud, despite this being one of the driving factors behind the *Pensions Act 1995*.

- The assumptions of the MFR are determined by legislation and are generally the same on investment return, assets and liabilities for every scheme, with adjustments for maturity. The assumptions should in fact be determined by reference to each scheme, and should differ with maturity, the strength of the employer and the trustees' views on a suitable investment strategy.

- Knowing that their scheme is 100% funded on the MFR basis, trustees could be lead into a spurious sense of security about funding levels. This may weaken their fiduciary responsibility, which should be at the heart of protection for members of defined benefit schemes.

Transparency statements   2.6

While rejecting reform of the MFR, Myners had considered the need for an effective alternative and the criteria it should meet. He had also recognised the need for improved protection against fraud and underfunding and had considered the other options which had been proposed in the government consultation of September 2000 (see **2.9** below). The alternative preferred by Myners took the form of a 'transparency statement' (see below for a specimen transparency statement as proposed by Myners).

Any assessment of funding adequacy turns on the investment assumptions and the method of calculating the scheme liabilities. If the reasonableness and appropriateness of investment assumptions are critical for fund solvency, argued Myners, then the best protection for members is to ensure that these assumptions are as robust and well thought-through as possible. Myners saw greater disclosure as the way forward, opening the investment debate to a wider group of interested parties. A transparency statement designed to meet these disclosures would have the following features:

- It would be produced annually after consultation with the appropriate advisers.

- Certain more detailed information should be available on request from the trustees.

- It should set out in clear and straightforward language:

  - the current value of the assets and in what asset classes they were invested;

  - the assumptions used to determine liabilities;

  - the planned future contributions;

  - the planned asset allocation for the following year or years;

  - the assumed returns and assumed volatilities of those returns for each asset class sufficient to meet the liabilities;

  - the justification by the trustees of the reasonableness of both their asset allocation and the investment returns assumed in the light of the circumstances of the fund and of the sponsor;

  - an explanation of the implications of the volatility of the invest-ment values for possible underfunding, and a justification by the trustees of why this level of volatility is judged to be acceptable.

- It should be merged with the existing statement of investment principles.

- It should be available for public scrutiny.

- It should be distributed to beneficiaries.

- A copy should be lodged with Opra, who will make it publicly available through the Internet.

Myners envisaged that scrutiny of the transparency statement would not just be by beneficiaries, but also by trade unions, the media, trustees' advisers, competitors of trustees' advisers and company shareholders.

If there were any objections to the content of the statement, beneficiaries could raise their concerns with the trustees in the first place. If this proved unsatisfactory, a minimum number of objectors (between 5% and 10% of members) could force trustees to commission an independent report. If the independent report disagreed with the transparency statement and the trustees failed to act on it, Opra could involve itself in the matter with the ultimate sanction of being able to disqualify the trustees. Additionally, Opra would have power on its own initiative to require the scheme to commission an independent report from an appropriate expert on funding and investment policy.

Specimen transparency statement

'ASSETS

Funding Adequacy

1. On current contribution rates, your pension fund needs to make annual investment returns of 3.5% above inflation if it is to meet its likely pattern of pension liabilities without requiring additional funding from the sponsor XYZ Ltd.

2. In practice, your trustees believe it is reasonable to expect your pension fund to make an annual return over the long term of almost 4.5% above inflation on its investments. This reflects the asset allocation of the fund and the trustees' assessment of the returns that can be expected from each asset class. The trustees therefore believe your pension fund is adequately funded.

3. The planned asset allocation of your fund and the relevant returns anticipated are as follows.

Asset class	Allocation	Assumed real return i.e. return in excess of inflation
UK large quoted equities	40%	5.00
UK small cap quoted equities	5%	5.50
UK private equity	5%	6.00
US quoted equities	5%	5.00
Continental equities	10%	5.00
Rest of World equities	5%	6.00
Index-linked gilts	5%	1.75
Conventional gilts	10%	2.00
UK investment grade bonds	5%	3.00
Overseas investment grade bonds	5%	3.00
Real estate	5%	5.00
	100%	4.46

The trustees believe these to be reasonable for the following reasons. [General justification of returns.]

−   There is a case for expecting a higher premium for UK small cap over large cap equities. However, the trustees prefer to assume a premium of only 0.5% because [insert explanation].

–   [Similar for other asset classes.]

The returns are somewhat lower than historical experience in most markets over the last twenty years, as the chart below shows. This is because [explanation].

The exception is bonds, where the trustees believe [ ]. In making these judgements the trustees have been advised by ABC Consultancy Ltd. Historical performance of asset classes over last twenty years: [Insert chart]

SENSITIVITIES

Economic modelling has identified the following as the most likely risks to the fund:

–   Sustained underperformance of UK large quoted equities. A real return of 3% per year for the next 10 years would lead, other things being equal, for liabilities to exceed assets by [ ]%. However, the trustees believe that this would be mitigated by [   ] which would result in improved returns from both domestic bonds and overseas equities, reducing the gap to [ ]%.

[Further discussion of risks].

LIABILITIES

The liabilities of the fund are the money which it has to pay out for your pension and the pensions of other members of the scheme. These will be determined by a number of factors, about which we have made the following assumptions.

Members' contributions:	3% of their pensionable pay
Employer's contributions:	20% of pensionable pay
Earnings growth:	4.5% a year (or approximately 2% above inflation)
Pension increases after retirement:	2.5% a year
Deferred pension increases before retirement:	2.5% a year
[Justification of assumptions].	

Demographic assumptions: mortality of scheme members is assumed to be in line with that of the standard mortality tables PMA92 (for men) and PFA92 (for women) published by the Faculty and Institute of Actuaries, projected as appropriate for the year of birth of the member.

Scheme size: there is no change over time in the number of active members of the scheme.

These assumptions are all the same as used for the last assessment.

The actuary has undertaken an assessment of the level of pension outgo in future years on the basis of the above assumptions, together with more detailed assumptions on matters such as the pension increases before and after retirement on the Guaranteed Minimum Pension element of pensions, the proportion of company employees leaving and retiring from the scheme at each age and the pattern of new entrants to the scheme. On these assumptions, your pension fund needs to make annual investment returns of 3.5% above inflation if it is to meet its likely pattern of pension liabilities without requiring additional funding from the sponsor XYZ Ltd. More detail on the actuarial assessment is available from the Secretary to the Trustees.'

Small schemes 2.7

Myners also considered how small schemes would be accommodated by the transparency statements measure. According to Opra's annual report for 1999/00, 86% of reported problems came from schemes with fund values of less than £10m, and 90% of reported problems came from schemes with 500 members or fewer. Defined benefit schemes accounted for slightly more than half the problems reported. On this basis there was good reason to differentiate between small schemes and large schemes as regards their compliance duties, with the greater risk perceived as coming from small schemes. Myners' proposed transparency statement would have allowed for the strength of the company to be factored into the investment strategy. Given that a large company, which by implication may have a large scheme, is better placed (all other things being equal) to underwrite unexpectedly poor investment returns than a small company, small schemes were arguably more at risk and would need better protection. Myners outlined additional features for small schemes (fewer than 4,000 lives) as follows:

- A statement from the scheme actuary that, having consulted investment experts as appropriate, he felt the investment assumptions were those that a prudent person knowledgeable in investment might reasonably make.

- If the actuary were concerned about the assumptions, he could ask Opra to call for an independent report.

- Opra would be involved automatically if the actuary refused to provide a statement to the above effect.

- Opra should take representations from members about the transparency statement and consider their concerns with particular seriousness.

- Opra's powers of trustee disqualification could still be relied on.

Improved protection against fraud   2.8

The Pensions Compensation Scheme was set up to pay out money where an employer was insolvent and the pension scheme was underfunded following an act of dishonesty or fraud. Under revised proposals in the *Welfare Reform and Pensions Act 1999* the Pensions Compensation Scheme would only restore a defrauded scheme to 100% of its pensioner liabilities and 90% of MFR liabilities for non-pensioner members (or the actual loss if less). Myners proposed that the payout should be increased to something nearer the actual cost of accrued rights for the non-pensioner members. He also advocated a mandatory requirement for the use of independent custodians for scheme assets.

Security for occupational pensions   2.9

The Treasury and the Department of Social Security issued their own 27-page consultation document on the reform of the MFR in September 2000 called *Security for Occupational Pensions* (see **2.13–2.14** below). Among the options mooted for dealing with the MFR problem were:

- A system of prudential supervision by a regulator

- Strengthening the MFR

- Compulsory commercial insurance or compulsory mutual insurance

- A central discontinuance fund

Myners had considered these alternatives but had dismissed them.

A system of active prudential regulation had merit in that the investment strategy would be subjected to external scrutiny. However, he considered that regulators were just as capable of underestimating or overestimating risk, and it would be undesirable to have an external regulator exercise direct power over investment strategy. Myners suggested that such a regulator would tend eventually to a bureaucratic and overcautious approach.

The pensions board of the Faculty and Institute of Actuaries (FIA) had performed a review of the MFR within paramenters requested by the Department of Social Security. Its report was published in September 2000 alongside the Treasury/DSS consultation document *Security for Occupational Pensions*. The Treasury/DSS proposals for changes to strengthen the MFR were dismissed by Myners as they still retained an artificial funding standard and would therefore continue to distort investment decisions.

Myners also ruled out solvency insurance as being expensive and probably impractical. The moral hazard and adverse selection, which could arise from such insurance, could have been overcome, but the system would have been overly complex, not fully protective, and would impose additional cost.

Finally, the idea of a central discontinuance fund was considered and deemed inappropriate. Such a fund should have an underlying guarantee, either from the government or the industry. In the former case taxpayers would effectively be underwriting the pensions in defined benefit schemes. In the latter case the system would not be dissimilar to insurance, except this one would have an extra layer of bureaucracy. Of course, this is the version the government chose in the end. In the face of a number of corporate insolvencies where defined benefit schemes left employees with much less than they thought had been protected, the government announced in June 2003 that it would create the Pension Protection Fund under the control of a statutory body and paid for by a levy on defined benefit pension schemes.

Myners Review March 2001   2.10

In March 2001 Paul Myners published the results of his review into institutional investment launched in May of the previous year. The review ran to 201 pages. The recommendations relating to occupational pension schemes are reproduced below under their relevant headings.

The context for pension scheme investment decision-making

1.   Trustees should assess whether or not the decision-making structures they have in place are effective for the purpose of running the fund. They should question whether their time is divided appropriately between their various responsibilities. They also need to consider whether the trustee board has the right mix of skills and experience and whether the fund's control environment is fit for the purpose.

2.   Trustees should be paid, unless there is a specific reason why this may be unnecessary (eg senior executives of the sponsoring employer).

3.   There should be a legal requirement for trustees to take decisions with the skill and care of someone familiar with the issues concerned. If trustees do not feel they have the necessary skill, they should either take steps to acquire it, or delegate the decision to a person or organisation who does.

4.   The statement of investment principles should be issued to members annually and it should be strengthened so as to provide better quality information.

5.   Pension scheme trustees should set up investment subcommittees.

6. Pension scheme trust deeds should not prohibit the use of particular instruments such as derivatives or prohibit investment in certain asset classes.

7. Trustees and employers should invest more in trustee training.

8. Sponsoring employers should provide sufficient in-house staff to support trustees in their investment responsibilities.

Investment decision-making by trustees

1. Trustees should explicitly set out an overall investment objective which represents their best judgement of what is necessary to meet the scheme's liabilities.

2. Trustees should set objectives for their fund managers that are coherent with the fund's aggregate investment objective.

3. Trustees should set out explicitly what decisions are being taken by whom. Decisions on the investment of the fund should be taken only by those with the skills, information and resources necessary to take them effectively.

Actuaries and investment consultants

1. Contracts for actuarial services and investment advice should be opened to competition separately. Pension funds should be prepared to pay sufficient fees for each service to attract a broad range of potential provider.

2. Trustees should arrange for the formal assessment of their advisers' performance and of any decision-making delegated to them.

3. Trustees should not take investment advice on an asset class from an investment consultant who lacks expertise in that asset class.

3. Fees devoted to asset allocation should properly reflect the contribution it can make to the fund's investment performance.

Fund managers

1. Trustees should consider, in consultation with their investment manager, whether the index benchmarks that they have selected are appropriate; in particular, whether the construction of the index creates incentives to follow sub-optimal investment strategies.

2. Trustees should set limits on divergence from the index which reflect the approximations involved.

3. Trustees should consider whether active or passive management would be more appropriate for each asset class.

4. Where trustees believe that active management has the potential to achieve higher returns, they should set both targets and risk controls which reflect this, allowing sufficient freedom for genuinely active management to occur.

5. Trustees should provide fund managers with clarity about the period over which their performance will be judged – and hold to that under the terms of the contract, unless clearly abnormal circumstances arise.

6. Trustees should incorporate the principle of the US Department of Labor Interpretative Bulletin on activism into fund management mandates, and the principle should be incorporated into UK law in due course.

7. As a matter of good practice, institutional investment management mandates should incorporate a management fee inclusive of any external research, information or transaction services acquired or used by the fund manager, rather than pass these costs on to the client.

Defined contribution schemes: specific issues

1. The National Association of Pension Funds should investigate ways of collecting more comprehensive data on the investment decisions of defined contribution schemes.

2. Investment decisions taken on behalf of defined contribution scheme members should accord with the Myners investment principles (see **2.11**).

3. Where the trustees offer a default investment option, they should ensure that an objective is set for the option, including expected risks and returns.

4. When trustees are selecting other investment options, they should take into account the members' preferences and ensure that they offer a sufficient range of funds to satisfy the risk and return combinations reasonable for most members.

5. Trustees should, as a matter of best practice, consider a full range of investment opportunities, including less liquid and more volatile assets. In particular, investment trusts should be considered as a means of investing in private equity.

6. The government should keep under close review the levels of employer and employee contributions to defined contribution pension schemes, and the implications for retirement incomes.

Pension fund surpluses

1. The tax rate on the withdrawal of surplus should be reduced.

2. The Law Commission should be asked to review whether the objective of maximum clarity over ownership of the surplus can be achieved through legal change.

Minimum funding requirement

1. The MFR should be replaced by a regime based on transparency and disclosure, under which pension funds would report publicly on the current financial state of the fund and on future investment plans.

2. The trustees of each defined benefit pension scheme should be required each year to set out in clear and straightforward language such matters as:

    (*a*)   the current value of scheme assets and in what asset classes they were invested;

    (*b*)   the assumptions used to determine scheme liabilities;

    (*c*)   planned future contributions;

    (*d*)   planned asset allocation for the following year or years;

    (*e*)   the assumed returns and assumed volatilities of those returns for each asset class sufficient to meet the liabilities;

    (*f*)   justification of the reasonableness of both their asset allocation and the investment returns assumed in the light of the circumstances of the fund and of the sponsor;

    (*g*)   an explanation of the implications of the volatility of the investment values for possible underfunding, and a justification of why this level of volatility is judged to be acceptable.

3. The level of compensation provided by the Pensions Compensation Board for non-pensioner members should be increased to cover not just 90% of MFR liabilities but something closer to the cost of securing members' accrued rights (or the amount of the loss, whichever is the lesser).

4. There should be a statutory requirement for funds to have independent custody.

5. The government should continue to take a close interest in the European discussions on pension provision. The government should make the case in Europe that such standardised requirements are flawed and counter-productive, and are not in the best interests of pensioners.

Principles

1. Pension scheme trustees should set out in their Statement of Investment Principles (which should be distributed annually to members) what they are doing to implement each of the Myners Principles (see **2.11** below). Where trustees choose not to meet a given principle, they should explain publicly, and to their members, why not.

2. Trustees should be required to report their compliance with the Myners Principles through legislation if they are not adopted voluntarily.

3. The government should undertake a public assessment of the effectiveness of the principles in bringing about behavioural change after two years.

Local Authority pensions

1. Local authority pension schemes should disclose their compliance or otherwise with the Myners Principles (see **2.11** below).

2. The government should consider to what extent the proposals it has made to replace the MFR should be applicable to local authorities, including the proposal for mandatory independent custody.

3. The prudential limits on particular types of investment, particularly those relating to investment in limited partnerships, should be kept under review by the Department for Environment, Transport and the Regions.

The Myners Principles   2.11

Different principles were set out for defined benefit and defined contribution pension schemes. The following are the original principles proposed in March 2001. However, see below for changes proposed by the government in December 2004.

Defined benefit pension schemes

1. *Effective decision-making*

    Decisions should be taken only by persons or organisations with the skills, information and resources necessary to take them effectively. Where trustees elect to take investment decisions, they must have sufficient expertise to be able to evaluate critically any advice they take.

    Trustees should ensure that they have sufficient in-house staff to support them in their investment responsibilities. Trustees should also be paid, unless there are specific reasons to the contrary.

It is good practice for trustee boards to have an investment subcommittee to provide appropriate focus.

Trustees should assess whether they have the right set of skills, both individually and collectively, and the right structures and processes to carry out their role effectively. They should draw up a forward-looking business plan.

2. *Clear objectives*

Trustees should set out an overall investment objective for the fund that:

- represents their best judgement of what is necessary to meet the fund's liabilities, given their understanding of the contributions likely to be received from employer(s) and employees; and

- takes account of their attitude to risk, specifically their willingness to accept underperformance due to market conditions.

Objectives for the overall fund should not be expressed in terms which have no relationship to the fund's liabilities, such as performance relative to other pension funds, or to a market index.

3. *Focus on asset allocation*

Strategic asset allocation decisions should receive a level of attention (and, where relevant, advisory or management fees) that fully reflect the contribution they can make towards achieving the fund's investment objective. Decision-makers should consider a full range of investment opportunities, not excluding from consideration any major asset class, including private equity.

Asset allocation should reflect the fund's own characteristics, not the average allocation of other funds.

4. *Expert advice*

Contracts for actuarial services and investment advice should be opened to separate competition. The fund should be prepared to pay sufficient fees for each service to attract a broad range of kinds of potential providers.

5. *Explicit mandates*

Trustees should agree with both internal and external investment managers an explicit written mandate covering agreement between trustees and managers on:

- an objective, benchmark(s) and risk parameters that together with all the other mandates are coherent with the fund's aggregate objective and risk tolerances;

- the manager's approach in attempting to achieve the objective; and

- clear timescale(s) of measurement and evaluation, such that the mandate will not be terminated before the expiry of the evaluation timescale other than for clear breach of the conditions of the mandate or because of significant change in the ownership or personnel of the investment manager.

The mandate should not exclude the use of any set of financial instruments, without clear justification in the light of the specific circumstances of the fund.

The mandate should incorporate a management fee inclusive of any external research, information or transaction services acquired or used by the fund manager, rather than these being charged to clients.

6.   *Activism*

The mandate should incorporate the principle of the US Department of Labor Interpretative Bulletin on activism. Managers should have an explicit strategy, elucidating the circumstances in which they will intervene in a company; the approach they will use in doing so; and how they measure the effectiveness of this strategy.

7.   *Appropriate benchmarks*

Trustees should:

- explicitly consider, in consultation with their investment manager(s), whether the index benchmarks they have selected are appropriate; in particular, whether the construction of the index creates incentives to follow sub-optimal investment strategies;

- if setting limits on divergence from an index, ensure that they reflect the approximations involved in index construction and selection;

- consider explicitly for each asset class invested, whether active or passive management would be more appropriate given the efficiency, liquidity and level of transaction costs in the market concerned; and

- where they believe active management has the potential to achieve higher returns, set both targets and risk controls that reflect this, giving managers the freedom to pursue genuinely active strategies.

8.   *Performance measurement*

Trustees should arrange for measurement of the performance of the fund and make formal assessment of their own procedures and decisions as trustees. They should also arrange for a formal assessment of performance and decision-making delegated to advisers and managers.

9.   *Transparency*

A strengthened Statement of Investment Principles should set out:

- who is taking which decisions and why this structure has been selected;

- the fund's investment objective;

- the fund's planned asset allocation strategy, including projected investment returns on each asset class, and how the strategy has been arrived at;

- the mandates given to all advisers and managers; and

- the nature of the fee structures in place for all advisers and managers, and why this set of structures has been selected.

This should also incorporate the transparency statement proposed by the review in its proposals for replacing the MFR.

10. *Regular reporting*

Trustees should publish their Statement of Investment Principles and the results of their monitoring of advisers and managers and send them annually to members of the scheme. The Statement should explain why a fund has decided to depart from any of these principles.

Defined contribution pension schemes

1. *Effective decision-making*

Decisions should be taken only by persons or organisations with the skills, information and resources necessary to take them effectively. Where trustees elect to take investment decisions, they must have sufficient expertise to be able to evaluate critically any advice they take.

Trustees should ensure that they have sufficient in-house staff to support them in their investment responsibilities. Trustees should also be paid, unless there are specific reasons to the contrary.

It is good practice for trustee boards to have an investment subcommittee to provide appropriate focus.

Trustees should assess whether they have the right set of skills, both individually and collectively, and the right structures and processes to carry out their role effectively. They should draw up a forward-looking business plan.

2. *Clear objectives*

In selecting funds to offer as options to scheme members, trustees should:

- consider the investment objectives, expected returns, risks and other relevant characteristics of each fund, so that they can publish their assessments of these characteristics for each selected fund; and

- satisfy themselves that they have taken their members' preferences into account, and that they are offering a wide enough range of options to satisfy the reasonable return and risk combinations appropriate for most members.

3.   *Focus on asset allocation*

Strategic asset allocation decisions (for example for default and lifestyle options) should receive a level of attention (and, where relevant, advisory or management fees) that fully reflect the contribution they can make to achieving investment objectives. Decision-makers should consider a full range of investment opportunities, not excluding from consideration any major asset class, including private equity.

4.   *Choice of default fund*

Where a fund is offering a default option to members through a customised combination of funds, trustees should make sure that an investment objective is set for the option, including expected returns and risks.

5.   *Expert advice*

Contracts for investment advice should be open to competition, and fee rather than commission based. The scheme should be prepared to pay sufficient fees to attract a broad range of kinds of potential providers.

6.   *Explicit mandates*

Trustees should communicate to members, for each fund offered by the scheme:

- the investment objective for the fund, its benchmark(s) and risk parameters; and

- the manager's approach in attempting to achieve the objective.

These should also be discussed with the fund manager concerned, as should a clear timescale(s) of measurement and evaluation, with the understanding that the mandate will not be terminated before the expiry of the evaluation timescale other than for a clear breach of the conditions of the mandate or because of significant change in the ownership or personnel of the investment manager. The management fee should include any external research, information or transaction services acquired or used by the fund manager, rather than these being charged to clients.

7.   *Activism*

The agreement with fund managers should incorporate the principle of the US Department of Labor Interpretative Bulletin on activism. Managers should have an explicit strategy, including the circumstances in which they will intervene in a company; the approach they will use in doing do; and how they measure the effectiveness of this strategy.

8. *Appropriate benchmarks*

Trustees should:

- explicitly consider, in consultation with their investment manager(s), whether the index benchmarks they have selected are appropriate; in particular, whether the construction of the index creates incentives to follow sub-optimal investment strategies;

- if setting limits on divergence from an index, ensure that they reflect the approximations involved in index construction and selection;

- consider explicitly for each asset class invested, whether active or passive management would be more appropriate given the efficiency, liquidity and level of transaction costs in the market concerned; and

- where they believe active management has the potential to achieve higher returns, set both targets and risk controls that reflect this, giving managers the freedom to pursue genuinely active strategies.

9. *Performance measurement*

Trustees should arrange for measurement of the performance of the funds and make formal assessment of their own procedures and decisions as trustees. They should also arrange for a formal assessment of performance and decision-making delegated to advisers and managers.

10. *Transparency*

A strengthened Statement of Investment Principles should set out:

- who is taking which decisions and why this structure has been selected;

- each fund option's investment characteristics;

- the default option's investment characteristics, and why it has been selected;

- the agreements with all advisers and managers; and

- the nature of the fee structures in place for all advisers and managers, and why this set of structures has been selected.

11. *Regular reporting*

Trustees should publish their Statement of Investment Principles and the results of their monitoring of advisers and managers and send them annually to scheme members. The Statement should explain why a fund has decided to depart from any of these principles.

Changes to the Myners Principles

In December 2004 the government proposed to strengthen and amplify the Myners Principles in respect of the areas where progress had lagged. In particular, their revisions were intended to make it clear that:

- The chair of the trustee board should be responsible for ensuring that trustees taking investment decisions are familiar with investment issues and that the board has sufficient trustees for that purpose.

- For schemes with more than 5,000 members, the chair of the trustee board and at least one-third of trustees should be familiar with investment issues (even where investment decisions have been delegated to an investment sub-committee).

- Schemes with more than 5,000 members should have access to in-house investment expertise equivalent at least to one full-time staff member familiar with investment issues.

- As well as contracting separately for investment and actuarial advice (as the Myners Principles required), in relation to investment advice, funds should also contract separately for strategic asset allocation and fund manager selection advice.

- Trustees should provide scheme members with the results of the monitoring of their own performance, and ensure that key information provided to members is also available on a dedicated pension scheme website.

Conclusion 2.12

The Myners Review has had a substantial effect on the way trustees carry out their investment duties. Compliance is voluntary, but research carried out by the DWP at the end of 2003 indicated that pension schemes covering a majority of members in the UK had taken formal decisions on five of the Myners Principles. Compliance was higher among larger schemes (more than 1,000 members) than among smaller schemes, but only 18% of all schemes had taken no action at all on the Myners Principles in the two years since their publication. The three Principles most widely considered were 'asset allocation', 'benchmarks' and 'clear objectives'. Myners had recommended that trustees should include a statement of their compliance with the Principles in their SIP together with an explanation of why they had chosen not to meet any particular principle, and that the SIP should be sent to members automatically each year. This was never legislated for, but the DWP research found that over half of pension schemes did document their approach to the Myners Principles in the SIP, the report and accounts or in a bulletin to members.

The Myners Review was instrumental in the demise of the MFR. At a time when the government was considering simply amending the MFR, it could be said that Myners tipped the balance in favour of it being scrapped altogether. The subsequent proposals for scheme funding and a regime of transparency were overtaken to a large extent when the IORP Directive finally became law. However, the funding regime adopted by the UK to comply with the Directive is still a scheme-specific funding standard.

The Myners Review led directly to the trustee knowledge and understanding requirements of the *Pensions Act 2004*, which built upon the Myners recommendation that trustees should be familiar with the issues.

Another element of the Myners recommendations – that trustees should disclose their compliance – is incorporated in recent consultation from the Pensions Regulator. It proposes that trustees should include a statement in their annual report on the steps they have taken to comply with the knowledge and understanding requirements of the *Pensions Act 2004*.

As part of the knowledge and understanding regime, the Regulator also expects trustees to know the contents of their statement of compliance with the Myners Principles.

Although the Myners Principles are not part of the *Pensions Act 2004*, the Principles and other recommendations in the Myners Review have significantly influenced the formation of pensions policy and legislation.

Security for occupational pensions

Background 2.13

In September 2000 the Treasury published a consultation document entitled *Security for Occupational Pensions*. The consultation sought views on the minimum funding requirement (MFR) and possible alternatives for its replacement. It was accompanied by a report from the pensions board of the Faculty and Institute of Actuaries (FIA) which had been commissioned by the Department of Social Security in March the previous year. The FIA had been asked to put forward proposals for reform and identify wider issues concerning the security and costs of defined benefit schemes. The FIA report had also suggested that the MFR might not be the most appropriate approach to take for the future. The government consultation document acknowledged that the MFR did not in fact provide any guarantee that members' rights would be honoured in full in the event of employer insolvency, and that the MFR could have an adverse influence on the investment decisions reached by scheme trustees. The consultation therefore put forward four main options as alternatives to the MFR.

Proposed alternatives to the MFR

Prudential supervision   2.14

The first option was a system of prudential supervision by a regulator. This would have taken a more proactive form of regulation than Opra was able to accomplish at that time, and so would have required a significant rewrite of Opra's powers and responsibilities. On the plus side, such a system could enable scheme funding to be monitored more regularly, could remove the element of volatility and could take into account important factors such as scheme management and the financial strength of the sponsoring employer. However, the benefits of prudential supervision had to be weighed against the significant additional administrative burden it would bring, and it was thought that such a system would be unlikely to do away with the need for a funding requirement altogether.

Compulsory commercial insurance

The second option was compulsory insurance obtained from the market on a commercial basis. Such insurance would have brought a clear moral hazard in that some employers might neglect their funding obligations, secure in the knowledge that, should the worst happen, the pension liabilities would be covered. Additionally, given the difficulties in assessing the risks involved in such insurance, it was doubtful whether an insurance market could be developed in this area, and if one did develop, whether it would be affordable. There was the danger that the employers most in need of insurance could not afford it.

Compulsory mutual insurance

The third option was compulsory mutual insurance. This would have seen other employers with defined benefit pension schemes having to stand behind the pension liabilities of an insolvent employer, perhaps even a competitor. The premiums would have to reflect the level of underfunding in a pension scheme and the insolvency risk of its sponsoring employer. Even so, there would still have been significant moral hazards, and the consultation recognised that there would probably have to be some sort of funding requirement to accompany such a measure. However, there was another drawback. If the economy took a sustained downturn, this could have led to a large number of scheme failures which would in turn have led to greater claims on other struggling employers at a time when they could afford it least. The government stated it was not prepared to act as ultimate guarantor for such a measure and suggested that some sort of reinsurance market would have to be developed to make the measure workable.

Central discontinuance fund

The fourth option was a central discontinuance fund. In this model, discontinued schemes would be run as one large closed scheme, thereby benefiting from reduced costs due to economies of scale. This also avoided the need to buy expensive annuities to back the liabilities. However, since the only income the fund would have would be the investment returns on the assets it took over, either additional funding would have to be secured or benefits would ultimately have to be scaled back. The government said, once again, that it would not act as guarantor for such a scheme and so any further funding would have to come from those employers who were still solvent and who would be charged a levy from time to time as the need arose.

Decision reached on MFR replacement 2.15

Six months after the consultation was launched, the government finally announced how it was going to proceed. There had been doubts over whether the government would choose to persevere with an amended form of the MFR or whether it would grab the bull by the horns and scrap it altogether. To the relief of all concerned, the government announced it would be abolished as soon as possible, thereby tacitly acknowledging that the MFR had been a complete disaster.

As for its replacement, the government accepted the criticisms which had been made of the alternatives proposed in its September 2000 consultation paper ie prudential supervision, commercial or mutual insurance and a central discontinuance fund. It therefore rejected those ideas and came down in favour of a new long-term scheme-specific funding standard coupled with a strong regime of transparency and disclosure. The new government model built on the framework recommended in the Myners Review, but included further measures to strengthen protection for all defined benefit pension scheme members. The proposals for a new model consisted of the following measures.

A long-term scheme-specific funding standard

Trustees would have to take account of their scheme's own particular circumstances when deciding how the scheme should be funded and how the assets should be invested.

A strong regime of transparency and disclosure

Trustees would have to set down in a funding statement how their scheme's liabilities were expected to change over time and how they proposed to meet those liabilities through the investment of current assets and future contributions. The funding statement would have to be provided automatically to members and made available to the public. It could be scrutinised by unions, shareholders and anyone else with an interest in the sponsoring employer and the funding of its pension liabilities.

A recovery plan

Employers would have to ensure that their pension scheme was adequately funded to meet benefits in full in the long term. However, where a scheme was underfunded, they would have to put in place a recovery plan for returning it to an adequate funding level within three years or such longer period as Opra might allow based on the individual circumstances of the case. The recovery plan would be monitored by Opra, and the trustees and professional advisers would have a whistle-blowing obligation if contributions were not paid in accordance with the plan.

Statutory duty of care on the actuary

The government would legislate so that the scheme actuary would have a statutory duty of care directly towards the scheme members. It was thought this would enhance member protection and clarify the actuary's whistle-blowing duties. Additionally, in protecting members' interests the actuary would need to take account of both the financial strength of the sponsoring employer and the long-term health of the pension scheme.

Voluntary wind-up

Solvent employers would be prevented from walking away from their pension responsibilities. The government would legislate to ensure that solvent employers would be obliged to meet the accrued entitlements of pension scheme members as they fell due.

Pensions Compensation Scheme

Compensation for fraud, paid by the Pensions Compensation Scheme, would be increased to cover the cost of securing members' accrued benefits (or the actual loss if less), rather than just the MFR value.

Priority upon employer insolvency

The government would examine the ranking of pension debts in the priority order of creditors against the assets of an insolvent company with a view to putting them higher in priority.

Resurrection of a central discontinuance fund

2.16

Although the government had rejected the idea of a central discontinuance fund in March 2001, its White Paper of June 2003 resurrected it as an immediate response to continuing scheme failures. It was finally enacted in the form of the Pension Protection Fund (see **CHAPTER 4**). The government had thus managed to introduce both a strengthened funding and transparency regime for the protection of members and a scheme of mutual insurance funded by levies on solvent pension schemes.

The Pickering Report

Background

2.17

In September 2001 the government asked Alan Pickering, former Chairman of the National Association of Pension Funds, to carry out a review of private pension legislation with a view to recommending a package of simplification measures. The review was to identify ways in which it could be made easier for employers to provide good quality pensions, how people could gain easier access to commercial pension products, and how to make it easier for people to accumulate pension benefits. The Pickering Report had three main themes at its heart:

- A proportionate regulatory environment
- A pension is a pension is a pension
- More pension – less prescription

Recommendations

2.18

The Pickering Report was published in July 2002. Its primary recommendation was that there should be a new Pensions Act which would repeal or consolidate all existing private pensions legislation. There were further detailed recommendations as follows.

There should be immediate vesting of all benefits for early leavers i e those who leave an occupational scheme within two years of joining it should not be forced to take a refund of contributions, but should be provided with a deferred pension instead. However, to prevent trustees, and scheme sponsors, suffering the additional cost of administering small pension amounts, trustees should be allowed to transfer pensions of small value (less than £10,000) to a stakeholder or similar pension scheme if the member does not choose to take a transfer within six months of leaving.

Employers should be allowed to make membership of their occupational pension scheme a condition of employment.

Section 67 of the *Pensions Act 1995* (modification of schemes) should be replaced with provisions permitting new benefits to be provided for old on the basis of actuarial equivalence.

There should only be three generic pension products: occupational defined benefit schemes, employer sponsored money purchase schemes and individual pension arrangements.

The contracting-out regime should be simplified by:

- relaxing the reference scheme test from 80^{ths} accrual to 100^{ths} accrual but based on all earnings and only 80% of members need meet the test;

- permitting guaranteed minimum pensions to be converted to reference scheme benefits or protected rights;

- relaxing the timing and form of benefits provided from protected rights;

- removing the requirement to provide a survivor's pension in order to contract out;

- permitting contracted-out rights to be partially commuted for a lump sum provided the pension payable is at least equivalent to an accrual rate of 1%; and

- permitting equivalent pension benefits to be wholly commuted.

Pensions accrued in the future should not have to be indexed in payment. Entitlement to indexation already accrued could be removed as long as benefits of equivalent value are provided.

The internal dispute resolution procedure should be simplified so as to allow trustees to decide whether to have a one or two-stage process.

Multi-employer schemes for non-associated employers should be encouraged.

The winding-up priority order due to come into effect from April 2007 should be brought forward and there should be a new priority to protect those nearing retirement. Provision should also be made to allow defined benefit liabilities to be discharged to a money purchase arrangement rather than a deferred annuity, provided that members do not object.

Disclosure provisions should be consolidated into a single set of requirements based on broad principles rather than prescriptive legislation.

The prescriptive legislative requirements relating to the statement of investment principles (SIP) should be simplified so that legislation simply imposes a requirement to have a SIP, but the detail on content is included in guidance notes, rather than in the legislation.

A 'New Kind of Regulator' should be established, which would be a proactive regulator capable of advising as well as enforcing compliance.

The employer opt-out should be removed from the member-nominated trustee legislation so that all occupational schemes are required to have one-third of the trustee board appointed by scheme members.

Recommendations not adopted   2.19

Not all of the Pickering Report recommendations were adopted. We still do not have one source of statutory requirements for pension schemes, but such a large undertaking was never really going to be feasible, certainly not in the time allotted. Early leavers did not get immediate vesting, but those with at least three months' service now have the option of a transfer value instead of a refund.

Simplification of guaranteed minimum pensions (GMPs) would have benefited many schemes, but there were questions over its practicality in operation and there was probably not enough time to pursue such an option. The government is going to have a second go at GMP simplification under its 2006 White Paper proposals (see **CHAPTER 11**).

Allowing employers to impose compulsory membership of their occupational scheme was not adopted, nor was the proposal to drop future indexation. The government did drop the indexation cap in defined benefit schemes from 5% to 2½% for future service, thereby creating another tranche of escalating benefit; it did not go as far as allowing statutory indexation on past rights to be replaced with an actuarially equivalent benefit, even though non-statutory increases may now be treated in this way. However, the government did finally relent over the issue of statutory indexation on occupational money purchase schemes and agreed to remove it altogether. The requirement to buy an index-linked annuity with occupational money purchase scheme funds was removed after eight years of being in force, thereby bringing them back into line with group personal pensions.

The 2002 Green Paper 'Simplicity, Security and Choice' 2.20

In December 2002 the Department for Work and Pensions (DWP), in conjunction with the Inland Revenue, put forward the government's long awaited proposals for pensions simplification. The main objective of the DWP paper was closing the perceived pension savings gap rather than attempting true simplification of the pensions system. It addressed some issues already covered in past consultation, considered proposals from the Pickering Report, and generally sought views on areas where simplification could be beneficial.

Opra would change from being a reactive regulator and would in future have to take a more proactive, risk-based approach. This would evidently require major legislative change.

The minimum funding requirement (MFR) would be replaced with a scheme-specific funding standard. Extensive consultation had already been carried out on a replacement for the MFR. The Green Paper included the proposal which had previously been set out by the government in its March 2001 response to the consultation paper *Security for Occupational Pensions*. It would require pension scheme trustees to set out their funding approach in a statement of funding principles. The statement of funding principles would contain the strategy for meeting the scheme's liabilities; it would specify how any funding deficit would be corrected; and it would have to be drawn up with the agreement of the sponsoring employer and on the advice of the scheme actuary. If the trustees and the sponsoring employer could not reach agreement, then it was proposed that the trustees would be given power to freeze or wind up the scheme.

Several changes to the contracting-out rules were also proposed for consideration. There was a proposal to reduce the indexation requirement on contracted-out rights so that it only applied to pensions in payment under £30,000 pa, and the reference scheme test might be amended to 1/100th of career-average earnings. It was also proposed to allow contracted-out rights to be partially commuted for cash and to raise the triviality limit to £520 pa.

The abolition altogether of certain contracting-out measures was put forward. These included the possible removal of the requirement to provide survivors' pensions from contracted-out rights. There was a proposal to scrap contracted-out mixed benefit schemes, as it was thought these were seldom used, and the government proposed doing away with safeguarded rights, which were the result of splitting contracted-out rights upon divorce.

The government also announced its intention to hold further consultation on the anti-franking legislation and GMP simplification.

There was a proposal to amend *section 67* of the *Pensions Act 1995* so as to allow changes to accrued rights to be made if the actuarial value of the change were within 5% of the value of the accrued rights.

The removal of the employer opt-out from the requirement to have one-third of member-nominated trustees (MNTs) was once again put forward. Given that the government was very keen on this, it was almost certainly going to find its way into legislation. It was simply a question of deciding what the eventual MNT procedure would look like.

The government announced it would remove prescriptive legislation around disclosure and dispute resolution requirements. This detailed legislation was supposed to be replaced with a few simple requirements, leaving the bulk to be determined by best practice under the watchful eye of a new, proactive Opra.

Finally, there were hints of a measure designed to ensure that solvent employers could not walk away from their pension liabilities. The Green Paper suggested that employers might first have to meet the buy-out cost of accrued pension rights before they could wind up their defined benefit schemes. Although this measure had been mooted in the December 2002 Green Paper and previous consultation documents, it nonetheless hit like a bombshell when it was announced in June 2003, not only because it was going ahead but also because it would, to all intents and purposes, be effective immediately.

The 2003 White Paper 'Action on Occupational Pensions'

Background 2.21

Consultation on the Green Paper closed on 28 March 2003, and the government published its response on 11 June 2003 in a paper entitled *Action on Occupational Pensions*. Whereas the Green Paper proposals were entitled *Simplicity, Security and Choice*, the White Paper contained very little in the way of simplicity or choice, but was heavy on security, especially for defined benefit schemes. The government was not going to consult further and announced its intention to bring the proposed measures into force at various times from June 2003 to summer 2005. The increase in the debt on the employer on scheme wind-up from MFR to full buy-out was to take effect immediately in order to prevent a rush by employers to wind up their pension schemes. Other measures were due to come into effect over the next two years, although some had to be postponed slightly. The measures are described below.

Pension Protection Fund (PPF) 2.22

The government had decided to go ahead with the controversial introduction of an insurance scheme to protect members of underfunded defined benefit schemes whose employer had become insolvent. A similar insurance scheme in the USA had been studied (the Pension Benefit Guaranty Corporation), and, although that scheme was facing increasing financial strains, it was none the less decided to go ahead with a similar scheme in the UK, but with some differences. Crucially, the UK government announced it was not going to stand behind its scheme financially. This meant the insurance burden would have to fall entirely on the defined benefit pension schemes it was supposed to be protecting. Additionally, based on the experience of the US scheme, the government had come up with two ideas to reduce the two major risks it saw as inherent in such an insurance scheme.

The first risk was that the sponsoring employer could fund its scheme to an inappropriately low level, or the scheme trustees could hold investments in an inappropriately high-risk portfolio, secure in the knowledge that should the worst happen there was always a fallback position to protect scheme members. To address this, the government said it would split the premium payable into a flat-rate premium payable by the employer and a risk-based premium payable by the scheme. The risk-based premium would depend on the scheme's funding level and would be higher for poorly-funded schemes. The proposals made no mention of how the levy would be split between the flat and variable rates or how the funding level would be determined.

The second risk was that a company's officers might prefer to wind up their company rather than pay a significantly large debt to the pension scheme. The government proposed to minimise this risk by setting a cap on the salary which would be used for compensation purposes.

The protection fund would pay out 100% of pensions in payment and 90% of pensions for other members based on a capped salary. The government initially said the salary cap would be between £40,000 and £60,000. Later thinking on the PPF changed the cap from a salary cap to a cap on pension benefit, and set it initially at £25,000.

The government reasoned that, as high-earning directors would lose a portion of their pension entitlement if the company pension scheme went into the PPF, the board of directors would have greater incentive to keep their company going rather than wind it up to avoid a debt to the pension scheme. The cap on earnings was also seen as a way of limiting the cost of the PPF.

The PPF in its final form is described in detail in **CHAPTER 4**.

MFR replacement   2.23

Several consultations had already taken place on the preferred replacement for the by now much maligned MFR. The 2003 White Paper reiterated the previous proposals and added only a little more to the debate.

Trustees should draw up a statement of funding principles and obtain actuarial valuations at three-yearly intervals. A schedule of contributions should be put in place after each valuation.

Trustees were to be given the power to freeze or wind up the pension scheme if they could not reach agreement with the sponsoring employer on any funding matter. This obviously gave the trustees a great deal of power and effectively meant they could hold the sponsoring employer to ransom. Although this proposal was subsequently mollified considerably, trustees and employers must still come to an agreement on funding matters. It was also decided that trustees should automatically provide members with key information about the scheme's funding position each year.

Although the government stated in the 2003 White Paper that it would introduce measures to clarify the scheme actuary's duty of care towards scheme members, this was not taken forward.

Before these measures had started to be implemented, however, the IORP Directive had finally become law. The government therefore had to rethink the funding proposals and amend them to be compliant with the Directive. See **CHAPTER 5** for details of the funding regime that was finally enacted.

Debt on the employer   2.24

Due to the weak funding protection offered by the MFR, the government considered this was no longer an appropriate basis for determining the level of an employer's liability to its pension scheme when it winds up. Several cases had been reported at length in the media of where employers had paid their statutory debt to the trustees on scheme wind-up, bringing the funding level of the scheme up to the MFR level: however, many members had been left with significantly lower pensions than they had been led to expect, even though their scheme's employer was still solvent.

The government announced it would legislate so that solvent employers had to meet the full buy-out cost of members' accrued rights if they wanted to wind up their defined benefit schemes. However, the government recognised that the buy-out cost could be so high that it would put the company itself at risk, and in this case it proposed that scheme trustees should be able to compromise the debt and agree a lower amount.

Draft regulations to give effect to this change were laid on 11 June 2003. Once they came into force at a later date, they were to have retrospective effect so as to apply to all schemes which began to wind up on or after 11 June 2003. Schemes which started to wind up before 11 June 2003 were still covered by the MFR basis. The regulations were a hasty measure and, among other things, gave rise to some controversy over their application to multi-employer schemes.

Statutory priority order

2.25

One of the problems with the statutory priority order under the MFR regime had been that pensions in payment had to be secured first together with future pension increases. Members entitled to a deferred pension might therefore only receive a small percentage of their scheme pension. The government announced it would revisit the statutory priority order, and later in the year it published draft regulations to re-order the priority of benefits as follows:

Previous priority order	*Proposed priority order*
1. Benefits derived from AVCs	1. Benefits derived from AVCs
2. Pensions in payment	2. Pensions in payment
3. Deferred pension contracted-out rights and refunds of contributions	3. Fraction of deferred pension based on service-related sliding scale
4. Increases to pensions in payment	4. Deferred pensions not falling within 3 above, and refunds of contributions
5. Increases to deferred pension contracted-out rights	5. Increases to pensions in payment
6. Deferred pension non-contracted-out rights and increases	6. Increases to deferred pensions in 3 above
7. Other benefits provided for in the scheme's winding-up rule	7. Increases to deferred pensions in 4 above
	8. Other benefits provided for in the scheme's winding-up rule

The sliding scale devised to apportion the pension under category 3 of the proposed new order above was to be 2.5% of the deferred pension for each year of service up to a maximum of 40 years. Thus someone with ten years' service would have 25% of their pension fall into a higher category, and 75% in a lower priority category.

The government intended to bring the new regulations into force from early 2004. However, given the complexity of the new priority order and the fact that there would certainly be schemes which did not have enough information to apportion the benefit in accordance with the new order, the regulations were never brought into effect.

The statutory priority order currently in use requires a PPF level of benefits to be secured first (see **7.71**).

Return of surplus 2.26

Return of any surplus to a sponsoring employer was also to be restricted. Funds would only be returned to an employer if the scheme had first been funded to the full buy-out level.

Pensions Compensation Scheme 2.27

The government announced it would legislate so that compensation for defined benefit schemes would no longer be based on the MFR but would reflect the value of the missing assets. Defined contribution schemes were not mentioned.

New kind of regulator 2.28

Following a recommendation in the Pickering Report, the government announced it would revise the legal framework for a new kind of regulator. A new regulator would focus on tackling fraud, bad governance and poor administration. It would encourage best practice, undertake compliance visits and issue codes of practice in place of prescriptive legislation. See **CHAPTER 3** for details of the new Pensions Regulator.

TUPE 2.29

The government had first proposed bringing pensions within the remit of the *Transfer of Undertakings (Protection of Employment) Regulations 1981 (SI 1981/1794)* ('TUPE') in September 2001 when the Department of Trade and Industry issued a consultation document on the subject. Similar proposals appeared in the December 2002 Green Paper and the June 2003 White Paper. The method preferred by the government to achieve an element of protection for ongoing pension rights upon transfer of employment was to require the new employer to match employee contributions up to 6% in a stakeholder pension scheme. The measure was finally incorporated into the *Pensions Act 2004*. See **7.40–7.42** for details.

Consultation of employees 2.30

The government announced it was going to implement its proposal to require employers to consult with their employees before making certain changes to the terms of the pension scheme. **7.43–7.53** contains details of the proposals as finally legislated.

Familiar with the issues   2.31

The government promised legislation requiring pension scheme trustees to be 'familiar with the issues', a phrase taken from the Myners Review on Institutional Investment, and to have relevant knowledge across the full range of their responsibilities. This was subsequently developed into the knowledge and understanding requirements of *sections 247–249* of the *Pensions Act 2004*. See **7.20–7.26** for details.

Immediate vesting   2.32

The government announced it would not give effect to the recommendation in the Pickering Report that all early leavers should be immediately entitled to preserved pension rights. Instead, however, it would adopt a modified version of the recommendation which would see members with more than three months' but less than two years' pensionable service become entitled to either a refund of their own contributions or a transfer value based on employee and employer contributions. See **7.60–7.62** for further details of this provision.

Survivors' pensions   2.33

The government decided not to abolish the requirement for contracted-out schemes to provide a survivor's pension on the death of a member.

Compulsory membership   2.34

The government announced it was not going to proceed with the recommendation that employers should be allowed to make membership of their occupational pension scheme compulsory. However, it did announce that the new regulator could issue a code of practice so that employers could operate an opt-out basis rather than an opt-in basis for joiners ie new employees would be included in the scheme automatically unless they opted out. Employers, of course, already had the means to do this for new hires.

Indexation   2.35

Instead of removing the indexation requirement from occupational pension schemes altogether, as had been recommended, the government said it would drop the cap on annual inflation-proofing from 5% down to 2½% in respect of future service. This would have applied to defined contribution schemes as well as defined benefit schemes. However, the government realised that maintaining the measure for defined contributions schemes would be costly and complex and so later dropped it for such schemes. See **7.75–7.77** for more details.

Scheme modification   2.36

The government announced it would amend the over-restrictive requirements of *section 67* of the *Pensions Act 1995* to allow easier modification of scheme rules. The relaxed provision could be used, subject to the following conditions:

- There is a power in the rules to make the change.

- The change does not involve converting defined benefit rights to defined contribution rights.

- The trustees have given their approval.

- The actuarial value of members' accrued rights at the point of change is maintained.

- Pensions already in payment are not reduced.

- Members are consulted before the change.

See **7.54–7.59** for further details of these new provisions.

Member-nominated trustees (MNTs)   2.37

The government finally signalled the removal of the employer opt-out from the MNT requirements of the *Pensions Act 1995*. It announced it would implement the minimal legislation proposal put forward in the December 2002 Green Paper for schemes to have one-third MNTs. The minimal legislation option provided for the basic outcome, whereby it would be compulsory to have one-third of the trustees elected by the membership, but it would not prescribe the method to be used to achieve this. Responsibility for the method would rest with the trustees under guidance issued by the new regulator. See **7.2–7.13** for details.

AVC facility   2.38

The government announced that the requirement for trustees to offer members the facility to pay additional voluntary contributions would be removed. This was due to coincide with the introduction of the new tax regime which would permit full concurrency among all types of pension arrangement. This measure came into force on 6 April 2006.

Contracting out   2.39

The June 2003 White Paper contained several changes to the contracting-out rules. Probably the most significant was allowing some contracted-out rights to be partly commuted for tax-free cash. The paper touched on other measures as follows:

- Contracted-out mixed benefit schemes would not now be abolished but would remain in their current form.

- Contracted-out rights could be allowed to be paid at the same time as other pension rights.

- The triviality limit would be increased.

- It would be possible to commute equivalent pension benefits (EPBs) without member consent.

- It would be possible to commute contracted-out rights in personal pension schemes on grounds of serious ill-health.

- Safeguarded rights would be abolished.

Simplification of guaranteed minimum pensions (GMPs) was the subject of a separate consultation paper issued previously in February 2003. The consultation paper set out three proposals for simplification:

- Abolition of GMPs altogether.

- Conversion of GMPs to additional scheme benefits on an actuarial equivalence basis.

- Transfer of GMPs back to the state scheme.

The June 2003 White Paper did not cover GMP simplification, but the Department for Work and Pensions announced its intention in October 2003 to allow schemes to convert GMPs to ordinary scheme benefits on the actuarial equivalence basis. Unfortunately, this was never carried through, although it is now back on the agenda in the May 2006 White Paper.

General   2.40

Under a general heading in the 2003 White Paper the government announced its intention to introduce measures, or maintain its commitment, in the following areas.

Disclosure and communication with members

In particular, the government announced it was going to introduce compulsory benefit statements for members of defined benefit pension schemes. This provision was dropped in August 2006.

State pension forecasts

The government announced it would continue its programme of issuing state pension forecasts to cover more people, and has in fact done so with success.

Combined pension forecasts

The government would encourage trustees and employers to provide combined pension forecasts on a voluntary basis but said it would legislate if this did not happen. Reserve powers have been included in the *Pensions Act 2004* to enable the government to do this.

State pension age

The government said it was committed to maintaining state pension age at 65. This was obviously before it received the report from the new Pensions Commission recommending an increase in pension ages.

Public sector retirement age

The government said it would raise the retirement age in public service pension schemes to 65 from 2006. Although this has happened in a few cases for new employees, the government still faces stiff opposition from unions on raising the public sector retirement age.

Internal dispute resolution

This process was to be streamlined to make it easier to use. Although provisions were included in the *Pensions Act 2004* to try to simplify the dispute resolution procedure, they have not been brought into force as it was considered that the legislation as drafted did not deliver the desired simplification after all.

Pensions Ombudsman jurisdiction

This was not extended as had previously been envisaged.

Pension sharing on divorce

Although the government had indicated it would re-examine these provisions, the *Pensions Act 2004* did not contain any measures simplifying this complicated legislation.

The IORP Directive

Background 2.41

At the same time as the UK government was consulting on pensions reform with its December 2002 Green Paper and June 2003 White Paper, the IORP Directive was gradually nearing implementation.

The full title of the Directive is 'Directive 2003/41/EC of the European Parliament and of the Council of 3 June 2003 on the Activities and Supervision of Institutions for Occupational Retirement Provision'. It is also commonly known as the 'Pension Directive'. It took almost twelve years to come to fruition and was a surprise to many in the pensions industry when it did. It had met with stiff opposition from the beginning and its passage had been far from smooth.

It was originally proposed in 1991 but disagreements among the member states meant that it was abandoned in 1994. However, the idea of a single market for pensions was resurrected in 1998 and a new draft Directive was published in October 2000. It once again encountered problems, but, after a series of difficult negotiations, the final agreement was reached in 2002, and it was adopted in May 2003. It was published in the Official Journal of the EU on 23 September 2003. Members states had two years from its publication in the Journal within which to give effect to the Directive. The Department for Work and Pensions carried out a consultation exercise between October and December 2003 and finally started including IORP Directive measures in its forthcoming Pensions Bill.

The purpose of the Directive is threefold. It provides a prudential framework for the protection of members' benefits; it provides schemes with sufficient flexibility to pursue an effective investment strategy; and it permits schemes established in one member state to provide benefits for employees located in another member state.

Applicability 2.42

The Directive applied to funded occupational pension schemes in the UK. This meant that funded unapproved retirement benefit schemes (FURBS) fell within its scope, although the government has used the small-scheme exemption in the Directive to exempt FURBS with fewer than 100 members.

The Directive did not apply to state pension schemes, pay-as-you-go schemes and unfunded schemes. Member states could apply the IORP Directive to insured schemes instead of provisions in the Life Assurance Directive (2002/83/EC), but the UK chose not to do so. Members states were also permitted to exempt statutory schemes and schemes with fewer than 100 members from the IORP measures.

Main provisions 2.43

The Directive consists of 40 preliminary paragraphs and 24 articles. The basic provisions of the Directive that would apply to UK occupational pension schemes are as follows:

- Schemes must be legally separated from their sponsoring employer.

- Schemes must limit their activities to retirement-benefit-related operations and activities arising therefrom.

- Schemes must be registered with the competent supervisory authority ie the Pensions Regulator.

- Schemes must be run by persons of good repute who either have appropriate professional qualifications and experience or employ advisers who do have appropriate professional qualifications and experience.

- Schemes must have properly constituted rules, and scheme members must be informed of those rules.

- Schemes must produce annual reports and accounts.

- There must be a regime for the disclosure of scheme documents and member information.

- Members must receive a statement each year on the financial situation of the scheme and the level of financing of members' accrued rights.

- Schemes must have a statement of investment policy principles, which must be reviewed at least every three years.

- Defined benefit schemes must have annual actuarial valuations, although member states may allow for triennial valuations with annual updates between main valuations.

- Scheme liabilities must be computed and certified by an actuary or other specialist in this field.

- Assets must be invested in accordance with the prudent person principle.

- Assets must be invested predominantly on regulated markets and must be properly diversified.

- There must be restrictions on employer-related investment.

- Schemes must file information and documents with the Regulator.

- The Regulator must ensure that schemes have sound administrative and accounting procedures and adequate internal controls.

- The Regulator may have the power to audit schemes to ensure they comply with good governance.

Cross-border provisions 2.44

The European Court of Justice had decided on a number of previous occasions that restrictions on cross-border pension contributions and/or benefits ran contrary to certain fundamental EU principles, notably the free movement of workers and the freedom to provide services. None the less, it has proven impossible in the past to establish a true pan-European pension scheme. The IORP Directive would now seek to change that.

A key provision of the Directive is that member states must allow employers located in their territory to sponsor occupational pension schemes in other member states. Similarly, schemes authorised in member states must be allowed to accept contributions from employers located in other member states. See **CHAPTER 9** for details of the requirements relating to cross-border operation.

Amendments to the Pensions Act 2.45

Happily, most of the Directive's requirements already reflected elements of the UK pensions system. However, the government has had to make significant changes to its proposed scheme-specific funding standard and introduce new measures to permit cross-border operation. See **CHAPTERS 5** and **9** respectively for further details.

The Pensions Bill 2.46

The original Pensions Bill, which was laid on 10 February 2004, contained 248 clauses and covered the following areas on which the government wanted to legislate:

- Pensions Regulator (80 clauses)

- Pension Protection Fund (97 clauses)

- Scheme funding (13 clauses)

- Financial planning for retirement (5 clauses)

- Occupational and personal pension schemes (24 clauses)

- State pensions (4 clauses)

However, this Bill did not make provision in all the areas in which the government wanted, and had, to legislate. Further, sometimes very important, amendments were made during committee stages. In particular, a great deal of legislation was to be added giving effect to the requirements of the IORP Directive.

By the time the Bill received royal assent on 18 November 2004, it contained a further 78 sections and two new Parts dealing with the Financial Assistance Scheme and cross-border activities within the EU. The two Parts of the Act which saw the greatest expansion were Part 1 (The Pensions Regulator) with an additional 26 sections and Part 5 (Occupational and Personal Pension Schemes) with an additional 23 sections.

During the passage of the Bill it became evident that there were loopholes in the government's provisions to prevent solvent employers escaping the full buy-out debt on winding up a defined benefit pension scheme, which it was backdating to 11 June 2003. There was particularly heated debate over the new 'moral hazard' powers the Regulator was to be given in order to tackle such situations, but finally new sections were introduced which dealt with contribution notices, financial support directions and clearance statements. See **CHAPTER 3** for further information.

The 23 further sections added to Part 5 (Occupational and Personal Pension Schemes) contained the much needed easements to *section 67* of the *Pensions Act 1995* (scheme modification) and other important measures including:

- How to calculate and deal with surplus now that the *Finance Act 2004* had removed the HMRC surplus regulations.

- The requirement for occupational schemes to be set up under trust. (Although the *Finance Act 2004* had removed the HMRC requirement for schemes to be set up under irrevocable trusts, the IORP Directive required legal separation from the sponsor.)

- Consultation of employees by employers before making certain amendments to their pension arrangements.

- The option for early leavers with less than two years' service to take a transfer instead of a refund of contributions.

- The removal of the requirement to provide an additional voluntary contribution facility.

- The priority in which benefits should be secured upon scheme wind-up.

See **CHAPTER 7** for full details of the *Pensions Act 2004* requirements relating to occupational and personal pension schemes.

Chapter 3
The Pensions Regulator

Introduction 3.1

The concept of a new Pensions Regulator to replace the Occupational Pensions Regulatory Authority (Opra) was perceived as a means of enhancing member-protection in pension schemes both by ensuring that proper funding systems are in place and that monies are not misappropriated or misdirected from schemes. The powers of Opra were not considered wide enough to extend to the proposals which were emerging from the various consultative processes on pensions reform, which are described in **CHAPTER 2**, including the December 2002 Green Paper by the Department for Work and Pensions (DWP), *Simplicity, Security and Choice: Working and Saving for Retirement*. That paper stated that the new regulator should focus on 'tackling fraud, bad governance and poor administration' and hold a new role on education and guidance for the future.

Opra was dissolved by the *Pensions Act 2004* and all its assets and liabilities were transferred to the Pensions Regulator. The government statement's was that the new Regulator will 'operate a targeted and proportional regulatory regime, applying greater regulatory scrutiny where it deems members' benefits are most at risk'.

Section 5 of the *Pensions Act 2004* states that the Regulator's duty is to:

- protect the benefits under occupational pension schemes;

- protect the benefits under personal pension schemes;

- reduce the risk of situations arising which may lead to compensation being payable from the Pension Protection Fund;

- promote and improve understanding of the good administration of work-based pension schemes.

Statutory bodies and their sources under the Pensions Act 2004 3.2

The regulatory bodies which relate to the Pensions Regulator under the *Pensions Act 2004* are as follows:

Sections 1–21 and *93–101*	The Pensions Regulator, the Determinations Panel and the transfer of Opra's powers to the Pensions Regulator. The Pensions Regulator's powers and procedures
Sections 102–106	The Pensions Regulator Tribunal
Sections 107–119	The Board of the Pension Protection Fund (PPF)
Sections 209–218	The PPF Ombudsman
Sections 274–276	The Pensions Ombudsman

In addition to the above regulatory bodies, the main provisions which concern the Regulator under the Act are:

Sections 18–21	The Pensions Regulator's powers to counter pension liberation
Sections 22 and *23*	Winding-up orders and freezing orders
Sections 38–42	Moral hazard contribution notices
Sections 43–51	Financial support directions
Sections 52–56	Restoration orders
Sections 59–65	Registration requirements
Sections 120–125	Employer insolvency
Sections 126–181	Pension protection
Sections 182–187	Fraud compensation
Section 226	The recovery plan

Structure of the Pensions Regulator   3.3

The structure of the Pensions Regulator under the *Pensions Act 2004* is as follows:

- A government appointed Chairman.

- A minimum of five other government-appointed members.

- A Chief Executive.

In addition, there is:

- A non-executive committee of members which monitors the activities of the Regulator.

- A Determinations Panel consisting of no fewer than seven members, and a Chairman appointed by a Selection Committee – the remainder being appointed by the Panel Chairman.

Most of the day-to-day functions of the Regulator are delegated to the Determinations Panel.

The DWP's estimate that there were over 10m members of defined benefits schemes in the UK meant that the decisions made during the course of drafting of the Pensions Bill (which later became the *Pensions Act 2004*) placed emphasis on the protection of benefits for such members, and a new pro-active pensions regulator that would have extended powers to act when schemes had insolvent employers, insufficient funds or wound up in similar circumstances. As a result, significant powers have been conferred on the Pensions Regulator, some of which have traditionally been exercised by the courts. Indeed, the extent of the Pensions Regulator's powers are being questioned by some, particularly in the legal profession, as being too extensive.

General powers of the Pensions Regulator   3.4

As stated above, the Pensions Regulator is intended to be flexible in its approach, and to act on major issues such as member protection from fraud and administrative problems, countering pensions liberation and monitoring schemes and their management. In particular, the Regulator has the following powers:

- to issue improvement notices compelling schemes to take or refrain from taking specified action where pension legislation has been contravened;

- to freeze a scheme while it conducts investigations into the scheme's operation;

- to suspend, prohibit and remove trustees;

- to impose a statutory obligation on certain persons involved in a scheme to report suspected breaches of the legislation to itself;

- to take measures to combat pension liberation to ensure that liberated funds are repatriated to a member's pension scheme wherever possible;

- to issue contribution notices and financial support directions;

- to gather information in order to identify and focus on those schemes which are most likely to present a risk to members' benefit security;

- to wind up a scheme if it is in the interests of the members to do so (see **CHAPTER 5** for the funding implications of such a decision).

A complete list of the Regulator's extensive powers can be found in the chart in **APPENDIX 1**.

The Regulator issued a statement in May 2006 entitled *How the Pensions Regulator will Regulate Funding of Defined Benefits*. Scheme funding is dealt with in detail in **CHAPTER 5** of this book. However, it might be useful to provide a list of the main subjects on which the Regulator has given guidance on how it will regulate schemes. The main subjects covered are:

- Its general approach to funding.

- How it will identify schemes to which *Pt 3, Pensions Act 2004,* applies. These matters are explained in greater detail in **CHAPTER 5** concerning the technical provisions of the scheme and recovery plans and periods.

- The actions it will take if a scheme comes to its attention or triggers a need for action.

- Any special circumstances which apply. This concerns employers that are subject to economic regulation, not-for-profit organisations, multi-employer schemes and cross-border schemes. These matters are also addressed in **CHAPTER 5**.

- The position with regard to schemes which are still subject to the minimum funding requirement.

- The use of the Regulator's powers.

- Matters concerning a failure to pay contributions. This area is covered in **CHAPTER 7**.

- A final summary of the Regulator's powers.

The Regulator has also issued his guidance on summary funding statements (see **CHAPTER 5**). The guidance, although short, is a useful reference point and is entitled *Guidance on Some Aspects of Summary Funding Statements*. The matter of contingent assets and their role in scheme funding is also addressed in **CHAPTER 5**. The Regulator's guidance on this matter is entitled *Guidance on the Role of Contingent Assets in Scheme Funding*. **CHAPTER 5** also explains in some detail the timing of scheme funding valuation reports by the actuary. The Regulator's website contains a useful flowchart on this matter entitled *Timings for Scheme Funding Part 3 Actuarial Valuations*.

Compromise agreements 3.5

The Regulator has been involved in various cases since its establishment. One of particular interest involved a compromise agreement with Jacques Vert Plc, and was in the form of an agreement concerning the funding of the Baird Group Pension Scheme (BGPS). This was a defined benefits scheme which was established in 1975. Future accrual ceased on 31 July 2003, and by the date of the agreement only nine members were employed by the Baird Group of companies. The members received fixed annual 5% increases on pensions in payment which clearly had an adverse effect on the scheme's current and future funding position. Jacques Vert Plc acquired Baird and made increased contributions in an endeavour to improve the overall scheme funding position. An agreement was sought for the future, and the terms of that agreement would be of interest to employers who find themselves in a similar position with regard to their defined benefits schemes. The main elements of the agreement were:

- The BGPS would be wound up.

- Jacques Vert Plc would make a one-off contribution in two equal instalments to help fund the deficit.

- Scheme members would have the option of a buy-out or a transfer to the Jacques Vert (2006) Pension Scheme, which was established to replace the BGPS under the sponsorship of Jacques Vert Plc. Jacques Vert Plc would contribute towards the operating costs of the new scheme in the first three years. The new scheme was to be granted a phantom option over 10m shares in Jacques Vert Plc exercisable at a price of 14.75 pence per share in the mid-market price at the date of the compromise agreement between July 2009 and July 2015.

- Future pension increases would be changed to reflect the statutory provisions, although there would be flexibility to increase these should the funding position permit. The expectation was that the scheme would be fully funded on the FRS17 basis at inception.

This was all agreed, and it is a recent and highly significant case. It shows that compromise agreements are achievable in circumstances where the employer would otherwise be financially seriously damaged by restoring full funding (if indeed that were possible). Such an action would cause pension accrual to cease or be reduced and would be no more in the interests of the beneficiaries or members than it would of the employer.

The principal regulations   3.6

The main regulations which apply to the remit of the Pensions Regulator are as follows:

- the *Occupational and Personal Pension Schemes (Pension Liberation) Regulations 2005 (SI 2005/992)*;

- the *Pensions Regulator (Contribution Notices and Restoration Orders) Regulations 2005 (SI 2005/931)*;

- the *Pensions Regulator (Freezing Orders and Consequential Amendments) Regulations 2005 (SI 2005/686)*;

- the *Pensions Regulator (Financial Support Directions etc.) Regulations 2005 (SI 2005/2188)*;

- the *Pensions Regulator (Notifiable Events) Regulations 2005 (SI 2005/900)*;

- the *Pensions Regulator Tribunal (Legal Assistance Scheme) Regulations 2005* (*SI 2005/781*);

- the *Pensions Regulator Tribunal (Legal Assistance Scheme – Costs) Regulations 2005* (*SI 2005/782*);

- the *Pensions Regulator Tribunal Rules 2005* (*SI 2005/690*).

Business plan of the Pensions Regulator   3.7

The Regulator published its business plan on 25 July 2006. The purpose of the plan is to complement the medium-term strategy which had previously been published in April 2006. It states that the Regulator expects to consider, in the year 2006/07: 500–600 clearance/withdrawal applications; 600 reports of notifiable events; 30,000 reports of late payments; and 700 recovery plans. The Regulator also states that its expectation is that it will make approximately 100 active interventions in relation to scheme-specific funding under the new statutory funding objective.

First annual report of the Pensions Regulator, and governance survey   3.8

The Regulator's first annual report, for the financial year 2005/06, was coded PN/06/28 and issued on 31 July 2006. The Regulator's website gives an encouraging assessment of the Regulator's performance of its duties and functions, and the involvement of the pensions industry, to date. An extract is given below:

'During an exceptionally busy year the Regulator has responded to a series of complex issues. Notable achievements include:

- publishing a medium term strategy which establishes the Pensions Regulator's active, risk-based approach to regulation;

- setting up a clearance process for businesses involved in corporate transactions;

- publishing guidance and codes of practice; and

- launching a free online trustee training toolkit.

Under the Pensions Act 2004, the Regulator was also tasked with setting out its approach to ensuring that pension schemes had prudent funding targets and recovery plans in place. Following a consultation exercise a regulatory statement on scheme funding was issued in May 2006.

Via the voluntary clearance process, companies considering corporate transactions where there is an underfunded defined benefit pension scheme can apply to the Regulator for a clearance statement. Guidance on the clearance process was issued in April 2005 and updated during the year. During the 12 months until the end of March 2006, the Regulator had received 330 clearance applications, issued 148 clearance approvals, and refused just two.

Other key facts and figures for the 2005/2006 period include:

- 391 notifiable events reported to the Regulator;

- 54 trustees appointed to the Regulator's trustee register;

- 75 independent trustees appointed by the Rregulator to schemes with a total value of approx 1bn; and

- 43,000 calls received by the Regulator's customer support centre.

Reflecting on performance so far, the Pensions Regulator's chief executive Tony Hobman said:

> "A year of intense transition has given the Regulator a strong platform on which to build for the future. We have consulted extensively with our colleagues in the regulated community on all aspects of our work from scheme funding to codes of practice, actively engaging in dialogue with various industry bodies.
>
> We fully recognise the front line role that trustees play in the protection of members benefit and our interactive e-learning programme will provide them with further practical support. Raising standards of governance, particularly in smaller schemes, remains an important focus for our work in 2006."

Hobman added:

> "We know that much more needs to be done in the coming year but we welcome the prospect of reinforcing a risk-based yet flexible approach to the regulation of occupational pensions."

The Pensions Regulator's chairman David Norgrove concluded:

> "We aim to follow the principles of better regulation, working in a risk-based way. We also want to go with the grain of the markets, because pension deficits will best be tackled through market pressures alongside the work of trustees and managements.

Overall our assessment of progress is: so far so good. The more gloomy predictions by some commentators have not come to pass and progress is being made to tackle issues surrounding work-based pensions." '

The release was accompanied by the following editorial note:

'1.   Reporting notifiable events is a framework designed to reduce the risk of calls on the Pension Protection Fund by acting as an early warning system of possible problems with a pension scheme or an employer.

2.   The trustee register is compiled by the Regulator and lists professional trustees from which it can make professional trustee appointments.

3.   The customer support centre handles queries from the industry about occupational pension schemes. The Regulator's customers include trustees, actuaries, auditors and administrators. The Regulator's website received 782,600 hits in the first year.

4.   The clearance process gives assurance that the transaction does not contravene anti-avoidance legislation and that the regulator will not use its anti-avoidance powers in relation to the transaction once it is completed.

5.   The trustee toolkit is a free, practical and interactive online training programme designed to improve trustees' knowledge and understanding to help them meet statutory requirements. Log on to www.trusteetoolkit.com for more information.

6.   The Pensions Regulator is the regulator of work-based pensions in the UK, with wide ranging and flexible powers under the Pensions Act 2004.

7.   The powers of the Pensions Regulator include the ability to:

   ●   collect more detailed scheme information;

   ●   issue improvement notices and third party notices, enabling the regulator to ensure problems are put right;

   ●   freeze a scheme that is at risk, while the regulator investigates; and

   ●   disqualify trustees who are judged not fit and proper to carry out their duties.

The Pensions Act 2004 also imposes a statutory obligation on "whistleblowers" to report suspected breaches of the legislation to the Regulator.'

Following on from the above, the Regulator published a significant report on governance survey on 5 September 2006 (PN/06/31). An extract from the Regulator's website on the findings of the survey is given below:

'Chief executive Tony Hobman said:

> "We have carried out a lot of work on helping to improve the way pension schemes are run but it is clear from this survey that we must not take our foot off the pedal.

> "While the survey showed that many schemes are well governed it identified areas where we need to maintain our efforts to help schemes and their trustees plug the gaps in important areas of good practice."

Key findings from the survey were that:

- there are clear links between good governance, training and established risk management processes

- larger schemes are better governed than smaller schemes

- although not all big schemes are well-governed in every respect

- scheme trustees considered on the whole that they are performing well, and

- a significant minority of schemes have shortcomings in important areas.

Work already carried out by the Pensions Regulator in this area includes the development of free online learning and the introduction of codes of practice and guidance.

The survey among more than 1200 pension schemes throughout the UK will provide evidence on which the Pensions Regulator can base future work on improving scheme governance.

Editor's notes

1.   Copies of the Governance Survey can be found on the Pensions Regulator website at www.the pensionsregulator.gov.uk. It will be published annually. The survey was carried out on behalf of the regulator by RS Consulting and Critical Research. Representatives from 1235 schemes provided information in short interviews. Chairs, lay trustees and pension managers from 500 of these schemes took part in a full interview. The survey did not include all the schemes for which the Pensions Regulator has regulatory responsibility.

2.   Shortcomings in good practice included:

- 70 per cent of defined benefit schemes have no specific policy to manage conflicts of interest

- 37 per cent of defined benefit schemes do not review sponsoring employers' credit rating

- 20 per cent of all schemes with a main provider of administrative services have no service level agreement with their administrator.

3.   A trustee is required to act in the best interests of the scheme beneficiaries, to act impartially, in line with the trust rules and prudently, responsibly and honestly.

4.   Defined benefit company pensions pay you benefits based on your final salary (or an average of your salary for the last few years of your employment). Typically, the benefits will involve a lump sum and income for life.

5.   The effect of a defined contribution scheme is similar to having a personal pension into which your employer makes contributions. Your benefits depend on what is put into the pension fund and how the investments perform. At retirement you can get a small part of the fund as a lump sum, while the remainder must be used to buy an annuity.

6.   The Pensions Regulator is the regulator of work-based pensions. Our statutory objectives are to protect the benefits of members of work-based pensions; to reduce the risks of situations arising which may lead to calls on the Pension Protection Fund and to promote and improve the understanding of the good administration of work-based pension schemes.'

Codes of practice and sources of related material   3.9

It can be seen that the Pensions Regulator is involved in most aspects of occupational pension schemes. In view of the extent of the involvement of the Regulator, its specific functions in respect of each subject are described separately under the chapters in this book which relate to that subject matter.

The chapters also describe the relevant codes of practice which are issued by the Pensions Regulator on certain matters. The Regulator's website states that the law does not spell out in detail how trustees, employers and others must meet the legal requirements. Instead, one of the Regulator's functions is to issue such codes in order to provide practical guidance. It may be helpful to list the full titles of those, and those which are still in process, together with related material, below.

Codes of practice already in force

Code of Practice 01 – Reporting breaches of the law   **3.10**

This code of practice covers the duty to report significant breaches of the law relating to occupational and personal pension schemes (including stakeholder schemes) to the Pensions Regulator. This is often referred to as 'whistleblowing', and a detailed description of the process and the rules which apply is given in **3.44** below.

This responsibility applies to a wide range of people, including trustees, scheme managers, administrators, professional advisers, custodians of scheme assets, and employers: it also applies to anyone involved in providing advice to trustees or scheme managers.

This code came into force on 6 April 2005.

Code of Practice 02 – Notifiable events   **3.11**

This code of practice covers the duty to notify the Regulator of specified scheme-related events (which trustees/managers must report) and employer-related events (which employers must report). This duty applies to all defined benefit schemes which are eligible for entry to the Pension Protection Fund and to employers that sponsor such schemes. The code came into force on 30 June 2005.

The *Pensions Act 2004* introduced a number of notifiable events for the purpose of giving the Regulator early warning of a possible call on the Pension Protection Fund (see **3.36** below).

The events fall into two groups:

● in respect of pension schemes (scheme-related events); and

● in respect of employers, in relation to their pension schemes (employer-related events).

ANNEX 1 at the end of this chapter gives an example of the different circumstances which can apply, and has been drawn from the code, in shortened form.

Code of Practice 03 – Funding defined benefits   **3.12**

This code of practice assists trustees who must comply with the requirements found in *Pt 3, Pensions Act 2004*, relating to the funding of defined benefits. It also covers duties under the new requirements to disclose information relating to the scheme funding provisions and sets out 'reasonable periods' in relation to the provision of certain information. **CHAPTER 5** describes the scheme funding requirements in detail.

The code came into force on 15 February 2006. The Pensions Regulator subsequently issued a statement on how it will regulate the funding of defined benefits schemes on 4 May 2006. The statement is entitled *How the Pensions Regulator will Regulate the Funding of Defined Benefits*. It followed the completion of a consultation process which had begun in October 2005. The objective was to provide information for trustees, employers and advisors on how the Regulator will regulate funding, and to help trustees and other to make informed decisions in respect of this matter.

The key position is that the Regulator will intervene if it is not satisfied with the prudence of a scheme's funding objective or the appropriateness of its recovery plan. At this early stage it remains to be seen how much information will arrive in the Regulator's office in order to assist it in making informed decisions. The main sources of information are likely to be formal reports under the *Pensions Act 2004,* the submission of recovery plans, scheme returns and specific requests for clearance. The Regulator will also be building up its store of information from general market intelligence. Clearly, many defined benefits schemes are underfunded in view of the market downturns several years ago, and therefore the Regulator needs a trigger mechanism in order to identify those that present the greatest risk. This is a developing field and the Regulator will provide further information in the future. For the time being, the trigger is based on the following assumptions made by the Regulator:

- that there is no requirement to fund schemes to a buy-out level;

- that trustees should take into account scheme-specific factors in determining a funding strategy (eg an employer's covenant and scheme maturity);

- that the accounting standard to determine scheme value which is reflected in company accounts is in accordance with FRS17 or IAS19.

The Regulator is empowered to assess the funding level that is necessary to secure the level of benefits that the Pension Protection Fund (PPF) would provide should the employer become insolvent. It will also assume that legislation translates into UK law the requirement of EU Directive 2003/41/EC on the Activities and Supervision of Institutions for Occupational Retirement Provision (the 'IORP Directive') that schemes should be fully funded against their technical provisions (see **CHAPTER 5**).

The Regulator will compare the technical provisions with a range between two liability values – the PPF liability and the FRS17/IAS19 liability – irrespective of whichever is the higher. This trigger is known as the *technical provisions trigger.*

The Regulator has also announced a *recovery plans trigger*. In doing this it has considered:

- the progressive increase in the maturity of some defined benefits schemes;
- the increase in risk of an employer's business weakening and possibly becoming insolvent;
- the continuing risk to the PPF from underfunded schemes remaining underfunded;
- the effects of longevity in the UK;
- the increase in member awareness;
- the lack of availability of sufficient free cashflows to make good deficits;
- the requirement that recovery plans must set a period over which a shortfall may be met.

The Regulator has identified that a trigger event will occur in, but not exclusively in, the following circumstances:

- a recovery plan exceeds ten years;
- a recovery plan is significantly back-end loaded (meaning higher contributions towards the end);
- inappropriate assumptions are used in the plan.

The Regulator has a raft of powers to consult with trustees in order to make good deficits in defined benefit schemes for the future.

Code of Practice 04 – Early leavers – reasonable periods   **3.13**

This code gives guidelines for trustees in relation to the requirement to notify those who leave occupational pension schemes after three months' and with less than two years' pensionable service, and without vested rights to benefit under the scheme rules, of their rights. The code came into force on 30 May 2006. When a member leaves pensionable service, trustees must, within reasonable periods:

- notify the members of their rights and how they can exercise them; and
- give effect to the members' chosen options.

The code also sets out the Regulator's views as to what constitutes 'reasonable periods' for:

- notifying a member of his rights and telling him how he can exercise those rights;

- the member's response to trustees;

- the trustees to give effect to a member's chosen option; and

- the default process where a member fails to respond to the notification.

The example in **ANNEX 2** at the end of this chapter shows the different circumstances which can apply. It has been drawn from the code, in shortened form.

Code of Practice 05 – Reporting late payment of contributions to occupational money purchase schemes   3.14

This code of practice gives guidelines for trustees of occupational money purchase schemes on reporting late payment of contributions to the Pensions Regulator and to scheme members. The code came into force on 30 May 2006. There is also a *Regulator Briefing No 1 – Reporting Late Payment to Occupational Schemes Money Purchase Schemes up until 6 April 2006* (see **7.69** below).

Trustees will only be required to report late payment of contributions where the late payment is likely to be of material significance to the Regulator. Trustees should use their judgement to assess whether they need to make a report – the code provides practical examples of when trustees should and should not report. See **7.68** for further information.

Code of Practice 06 – Reporting late payment of contributions to personal pension schemes   3.15

This code of practice gives guidelines for managers of personal pensions (including stakeholder schemes), where there is a direct payment arrangement, on reporting late payment of contributions to the Regulator and to employees. The code came into force on 30 May 2006. The code is also relevant to employers in relation to the provision of payment information needed by managers for monitoring purposes. Further details are given in **7.70** below.

Managers will only be required to report late payment of contributions where the late payment is likely to be of material significance to the Regulator. Scheme managers should use their judgement to assess whether they need to make a report – the code provides practical examples of when managers should and should not report. The code is similar to the code for money purchase schemes (Code of Practice 05) (see **7.68** below), with the onus falling on the manager, not the trustees. The important differences are shown in the example in **ANNEX 3**.

Code of Practice 07 – Trustee knowledge and understanding (TKU)   3.16

This code of practice addresses how trustees of occupational schemes will be required to be conversant with their own scheme documents, and to have knowledge and understanding (appropriate to their role as trustee) of trusts and pensions law and of the principles of funding and investment. Further details are given in **3.43** below and **7.20–7.26** below.

This code came into force on 30 May 2006.

The following codes of practice are not yet in force

Dispute resolution – reasonable periods   3.17

Following consultation on the draft regulations and draft code of practice, the DWP has decided not to bring in the new requirement for dispute resolution arrangements. The DWP's reasoning, following consultation, is that the proposed changes would not have simplified the procedures, but made them more arduous. However, *s 50, Pensions Act 2004*, will be revised to make some desirable changes in the future.

Internal controls – Code laid before parliament   3.18

This draft code of practice provides trustees with guidance on their duty to establish and operate adequate internal controls. These controls must be sufficient to ensure that the scheme is administered and managed in accordance with the scheme rules and the relevant legislation. It also provides practical guidelines on developing a risk-management framework, helping trustees to focus on the key risks to their schemes.

The note on the Pensions Regulator's website states that the code is primarily for trustees, but will also be of interest to advisers, employers, service providers and scheme administrators.

Reasonable periods for the purposes of The Occupational Pension Schemes (Disclosure of Information) Regulations 2006 – consultation ended and new regulations abandoned 3.19

This code describes the Regulator's view of 'reasonable periods' within which schemes must provide information. Draft DWP regulations for occupational pension schemes specified what information (for example, member information on joining) must be provided 'within a reasonable period'.

On 14 August 2006 James Purnell, Minister for Pensions Reform, announced that the proposed disclosure regulations due to be brought into force in October 2006 would not now go ahead. One of the proposals in the 2006 pensions White Paper would commit the government to a rolling deregulatory review of pensions. In relation to the decision not to introduce the new disclosure requirements, Purnell said:

> 'We want to take a step back and look again at the broader framework of regulation. That's why we have decided not to go ahead with this package of regulations. It would not be fair to employers to bring in further requirements only for these to be changed as part of our deregulatory review.'

Member-nominated trustees and directors – putting arrangements in place – Code laid before parliament 3.20

This code provides trustees with practical advice and principles on how to comply with legislation on member-nominated trustees and directors. Trustees are required to ensure that arrangements are in place, and implemented, for at least one-third of trustees to be member-nominated; or at least one-third of directors of the trustee company to be member-nominated. The arrangements must include a nomination process, a selection process and other statutory requirements.

The note on the Pensions Regulator's website states that guidance will be published covering timings and transitional issues.

A detailed description of the legislation on member-nominated trustees and directors is given in **7.2–7.13** below.

Modification of subsisting rights – consultation ended and responses being considered   3.21

This code provides trustees with guidance on how they can comply with legislation where changes to scheme rules are being considered. When trustees wish to modify scheme rules where pension scheme members have existing rights, certain conditions need to be met (for example, obtaining the consent of scheme members, or a certificate of actuarial equivalence).

Contribution notices, orders and directions

Effective date of notices and orders   3.22

The *Pensions Act 2004* empowers the Regulator to issue a contribution notice, a restoration order or a deliberate failure to act order. The initial proposal that these notices and orders would be effective from 11 June 2003 was moved to 27 April 2004, being the date on which the government issued its more substantive statement on the proposed moral hazard provisions (see **3.29** below).

The Regulator, and the new Determinations Panel, have published the procedures that they will follow when taking action. The standard procedures are:

- a warning notice will be issued to persons who would be directly affected;

- representations may be made by the recipients;

- representations will be duly considered;

- details will be given of the content of determination notices and warning notices, and the right of appeal.

There are exceptions to the above procedures in the following areas:

- determinations cannot be enforced while a right of appeal exists, or appeal proceedings are in progress, other than in exceptional cases (eg the prohibition/ disqualification of a trustee) – *s 96, Pensions Act 2004*;

- where the Regulator believes there would be an immediate risk to members' interests or scheme assets if it gave a warning notice or allowed time for representations – *ss 97–99, Pensions Act 2004*.

Contribution notice   3.23

A contribution notice may be issued where the employer or someone associated or connected with that employer is party to 'an act or a deliberate failure to act' on or after 27 April 2004.

The notice is triggered by such an act or deliberate failure to act which occurs on or after 27 April 2004, and the purpose of that act is to prevent the recovery of a *s 75, Pensions Act 1995* debt (or otherwise to prevent such a debt becoming due, or to compromise or otherwise settle such a debt or to reduce the amount of such a debt). The act must have occurred within a six-year period prior to the issue of the notice. Such notices cannot be served on insolvency practitioners who are acting in accordance with their duties.

Under a contribution notice, the employer or its associates or connected persons may be required to pay off all or part of the debt and the Regulator has significant powers to determine what is reasonable and who should be served with the notice.

'An act or deliberate failure to act' is one where the main purpose was:

- to prevent the recovery of the whole or part of the debt under *s 75, Pensions Act 1995*;

- otherwise than in good faith, to prevent a *s 75* debt becoming due, compromise or otherwise settle such a debt (however, see **3.4** above concerning compromise agreements) or reduce the amount of such a debt.

The website guidance gives further information on what the Regulator will consider as reasonable cause to issue a contribution notice.

Freezing order   3.24

Freezing orders may be made to prevent the winding up of a scheme commencing, or further benefits accruing, while the Regulator is considering whether it shall wind up the scheme (see **5.23** below). Such an order is only made where it is considered necessary for the purpose of protecting the members' interests.

Financial support direction   3.25

The main criteria which apply to the making of a financial support direction are that the employer is a service company, or the employer is insufficiently resourced (meaning that its resources are less than 50% of the *s 75, Pension Act 1995* scheme deficit and the resources of a connected or associated persons

64

when added to the employer's resources are 50% or more of that deficit). In order to comply with the financial support direction, the person upon whom it is given may set up various arrangements. These arrangements may include:

- making all group companies jointly and severally liable for the company's pension liabilities;

- make a holding company, subject to certain conditions, liable for such liabilities;

- making additional financial resources, subject to certain conditions, available to the scheme.

A direction shall be issued to such one or more persons as the Regulator shall consider appropriate, including an employer or an associate of the employer, or one who would be an associate of the employer if he or she were not an employee of that employer, or a connected person. It is not the intention that individual shareholders or directors shall be liable for any pension deficit. The majority of individuals will be excluded from the scope of financial support directions.

With regard to partnerships, the only persons who may be liable are those associated with an individual employer, such as a sole trader, and associated for a reason other than being an employee of that employer (for example, a spouse).

A direction may not be able to be terminated before the end of the life of the scheme, although the Regulator does have the power to issue a clearance statement. Non-compliance may trigger a contribution notice (see **3.23** above), with similar clearance procedures as for a direction.

A direction may be given by the Regulator in respect of defined benefit schemes (money purchase schemes and certain specified categories of schemes are exempt).

A financial support direction requires financial arrangements to be put in place within the relevant time. The relevant time is likely to be a period of nine months starting with the decision by the Regulator to issue a direction. The guidance gives information on when the Regulator will consider it reasonable to issue a financial support direction. It has powers to enforce the debt unless the scheme is in an assessment period. If it is in an assessment period then the Board of the Pension Protection Fund will enforce it (see **CHAPTER 4**).

Recovery plan   3.26

The Regulator may call for a recovery plan to be put in place where a scheme fails to meet the new scheme-specific statutory funding objective. Such a plan shall specify the period over which steps are taken to remedy deficits. The

Regulator must be sent a copy of the recovery plan by the trustees or scheme managers. Civil penalties will be applied under the *Pensions Act 1995* on any failure to comply.

Restoration order 3.27

Restoration orders may be issued in respect of transactions undervalue, which means significantly less than money for monies-worth, or by way of a gift. The terms of such an order shall be as the Regulator shall think fit, including the return of any assets, property or benefits. These orders do not apply to money purchase schemes.

The criteria that apply are that:

● the action took place on or after 27 April 2004;

● the action was no more than two years prior to the *relevant event.*

The *relevant event* means the employer becoming insolvent or the trustees applying to the Board of the Pension Protection Fund that the employer is unable to continue as a going concern. The relevant event must occur on or after 6 April 2005. *Restoration* means what it says; position must be restored to where it would have been had the transaction not have taken place. There is protection in respect of any property which was a acquired in good faith for proper value.

Failure to comply with a restoration order may lead to the issue of a contribution notice (see **3.23** above). There are special rules for partnerships and limited liability partnerships. Other exempt schemes are listed in the *Pensions Regulator (Contributions, Notices and Restoration Orders) Regulations 2005* (*SI 2005/931*). Such schemes are also listed in the *Pensions Regulator (Financial Support Directions etc) Regulations 2005* (*SI 2005/2188*) which define the meaning of 'insufficiently resourced'. The Regulator may only go back twelve months in order to determine whether a company was insufficiently resourced or was a service company.

If is there is a failure to comply with the order, the individual or person concerned (which may include the Pension Protection Fund, where it has assumed responsibility for the scheme) may be issued with a contribution notice (see **3.23** above).

Disclosure of information to the Financial Reporting Council 3.28

The Regulator is to be given power, under an order, to disclose information to the Financial Reporting Council concerning the size of schemes and the addresses of trustees and managers in order that those schemes may be invoiced.

Moral hazard provisions and clearance statements   3.29

A controversial measure which was introduced by the *Pensions Act 2004*, and which led to lively debate during the passage of the Pensions Bill through the House, was what have become known as the 'moral hazard provisions'. These provisions were clearly going to have a marked impact on corporate reconstructions, and it was maintained that this would stifle UK business. The objective was to empower the Pensions Regulator to intervene where reconstructions and/or mergers could used as a device to off-load deficiencies, thus placing demands on the Pensions Protection Fund and the Financial Assistance Scheme (see **CHAPTERS 4** and **8** respectively).

As a result of the various debates at the time, the provisions of the *Pensions Act 2004* included an ability to obtain a 'green light' clearance system on pension liability issues in advance of deals. This was in response to industry fears that the last remaining employer or principal employer in the scheme could be left 'holding the baby' in respect of any residual liability or deficiency.

The clearance procedure permits potentially affected parties to request the Regulator to confirm in advance whether any of their actions may give rise to such a notice. The procedure is available for legitimate corporate transactions and restructuring.

The main tenets of the hazard provisions are:

* The Regulator can look at acts or failures to act that have occurred not more than six years before its determination to issue a contribution notice in relation to that act or that failure to act.

* The Regulator must recognise situations where pension liabilities may be putting companies and, therefore, employment at serious risk.

* The Regulator needs to consider the purpose of the action, and take into account any adverse effect on the employment.

* The Regulator's clearance procedure on company restructuring, and decisions in relation to clearance, shall be made as soon as reasonably practicable but the Regulator will not be bound by any clearance statement if there is a material change in circumstances, or if the circumstances described in the application are not realised.

In appropriate cases, the Regulator can transfer liabilities from employers to those associated or connected with such persons. The definitions of these terms can be found in *ss 249* and *435, Insolvency Act 1986*. They include directors of other group companies.

Clearance application update   3.30

The Regulator's website contains the following guidance on clearance statements:

> **'Clearance application update**
>
> Companies considering corporate transactions where there is an underfunded defined benefit pension scheme can apply to the regulator for a clearance statement.
>
> This gives assurance that the regulator will not use its anti-avoidance powers in relation to the transaction once it is completed.
>
> The process is voluntary yet has proved popular with industry and over 330 applications have been received in the first year of operation.
>
> There has been some misconception in the press that clearance is a lengthy process. This is not the case, and the regulator is responsive to commercial timescales. Applicants can assist the regulator in meeting such timescales by ensuring that they have:
>
> - complied with our guidance on clearance;
>
> - involved the trustees;
>
> - involved the regulator as early as possible in the process; and
>
> - accompanied their application for clearance with full and accurate disclosure, including financial information relating to the employer covenant where relevant.'

The Regulator publishes an Application for Clearance Form, and this can be found at **APPENDIX 3**.

Corporate transactions and clearance   3.31

It can be seen from **3.4** above that there are circumstances in which the Regulator would be prepared to reach an agreement with the trustees and employer if it is in the best interest of those parties (the trustees representing the beneficiaries' interests) to do so. Such forms of compromise agreement may be a significant consideration when seeking clearance statements from the Regulator. The Regulator has published formal guidance on clearance statements entitled *Clearance Statements: Guidance From the Pensions Regulator* (see **3.32** below). It has also published a Questions and Answers media centre document concerning clearance statements in connection with the moral hazard provisions. This is entitled *Corporate Transactions and Clearance*. A summary of the points raised in this document is given below:

- In order to preserve confidentiality between the employer and the trustee when dealing with the sensitivity of a corporate deal, it is recommended that a confidentiality agreement is signed by each trustee which shall remain in place while the corporate deal is going through.

- It is possible for trustees to seek clearance directly, but this is considered to be uncommon as they are not a person (in normal circumstances) to whom a contribution notice of financial support can be issued. However, trustees should consult the Regulator if they believe that the employer should be seeking clearance but is not doing so.

- If clearance was not sought, a corporate transaction cannot be reversed. The Regulator can issue a contribution notice which will require full payment of the *s 75* debt or a financial support direction for the purpose of guaranteeing the full debt, but it cannot reverse transactions.

- Where money is borrowed on a secured basis for a business venture, it is not a Type A event (see **3.34** below). This is on the understanding that the borrowing is at arms-length. However, if it was a change from unsecured lending to secured, or was used to fund dividends or share buy-backs, it would be such an event.

- A return of capital is not currently notifiable, but it is expected that it will become so. Additionally, any trustee who becomes aware of a material return of capital which may impact on the scheme should immediately enter into discourse with the employer and decide whether to inform the Regulator (if there is a material detriment or known mitigation of the scheme).

- In addition to share buy-backs, the Regulator also considers the payment of equity loans to be a return of capital, and it will look at each transaction on a case-by-case basis.

- The question is raised: 'Where dividend money has been paid out and after some time the company gets into financial difficulties how will it be possible for a financial support direction or contribution notice to recover anything?' The Regulator points out that contribution notices can be issued up to six years after the act, and any associated or connected person may be liable for such a notice. This includes directors or parent companies. A financial support direction can be issued to any company associated or connected to an employer to provide up to the full *s 75* debt.

- Connected or associated parties are generally, in the circumstance of shareholders, the persons who have control of the company. This normally means that over one-third of the shares are under that person's control. This can also extend to overseas employers.

- The Regulator can pass cases to its avoidance team if it considers that the employer is refusing to go for clearance. Trustees who are concerned about a Type A event (see **3.34** below) taking place for which clearance has been sought should contact the Regulator. Material changes after clearance has been given are also reportable.

- Before issuing contribution notices or financial support directions, the Regulator will issue a warning notice. There is an entitlement to respond. It is the Determination Panel which issues notices and directions and there is a right of appeal to the Pensions Regulator Tribunal. There is also a right of appeal to the Court of Appeal from the Tribunal.

- If a company deliberately goes into insolvency in order to avoid pension liabilities, the Regulator will investigate the case. It is not able to publish anything in the public domain at present on this matter.

Clearance statements: Guidance from the Pensions Regulator   3.32

The Regulator's guidance on clearance statements is entitled *Clearance statements: Guidance from the Pensions Regulator*. This guidance states that the underlying aims of the clearance procedure are:

- the protection of jobs, particularly where clearance is needed to prevent the employer becoming insolvent; and

- the continuation of appropriate deal activity involving employers with defined benefits schemes. There is no statutory requirement to seek the clearance, but it will provide certainty for those who may be liable for the imposition of a contribution notice or a financial support decision.

There are no formal rules and regulations which apply to the clearance procedure. The Regulator drew heavily on the City Code of Takeovers and Mergers when determining the guidance principles for this procedure. There is a website for the procedure, for those who have queries, and queries may be made by email to: clearance@thepensions regulator.gov.uk.

The guiding principles of clearance   3.33

The general guiding principles are laid down by the Regulator in its Guidance as follows:

- A pension scheme in deficit should be treated in the same way as any other material unsecured creditor.

- The pensions scheme is a key company stakeholder. Trustees should be given access to information and decision-makers; in return, they should accept confidentiality responsibilities.

- Conflicted trustees should recognise their position and act appropriately. The Regulator encourages the use of independent advice in such circumstances.

- Applications for clearance should contain concise, relevant and accurate information to enable the Regulator to reach a properly informed decision.

- All parties to clearance should act in accordance with issued guidance.

- The Regulator will wish to know of all events having a materially detrimental effect on the ability of pension schemes to meet their liabilities.

- The Regulator's preferred outcome is a properly funded defined benefit pension scheme with a solvent employer.

- The Regulator will deploy its resources in a risk-based manner.

- The Regulator will seek to strike the right balance between reducing the risk to members' benefits and not intervening unnecessarily in the conduct of employers.

- The Regulator will be consistent in its exercise of anti-avoidance powers and the operation of clearance.

Types A, B and C clearance events   3.34

The seeking of clearance notices and financial support directions are described as 'events' in the guidance. Clearance should only be sought for events which are financially detrimental to the pension creditor ('specified events'). The Regulator has considered what the expression 'financially detrimental' means, and it has concluded that it may have various meanings. It observes a distinction between its duty to protect all benefits (ultimately pointing to the *s 75, Pensions Act 1995* basis) and the choice of a sensible deficit figure for operating a risk-based approach to clearance. It is hopeful that the new statutory funding objective which is described in **CHAPTER 5** will in due course become the correct method of calculation.

FRS17 is a high level of test in most circumstances, and indicates a move towards a full funding level. It is also audited and within the company's balance sheet. For the early days, therefore, FRS17 is considered an appropriate measure for seeking clearance. However, FRS17 is only relevant to an ongoing employer. In other circumstances, the *s 75* basis will be appropriate. Where there is no FRS17 calculation, the full *s 75* buy-out level must be used.

In circumstances of insolvency, it is observed that the pension creditor is an unsecured creditor. This does not give him or her a particularly strong claim within the creditor 'pecking order', which is broadly:

1. Creditors with fixed charges

2. Preferential creditors

3. Creditors with floating charges

4.   Unsecured creditors (this is where the pension creditor will normally fit in)

5.   Subordinated creditors

6.   Equity

All events which affect the company will fall into three distinct categories. These are:

TYPE A events. These do not affect the pension creditor. They are specified events which are financially detrimental to the viability of a defined benefit pension scheme to meet its liabilities and for which it may be appropriate to seek clearance.

TYPE B events. These do not affect the pension creditor. The events are not specified events and clearance is not necessary.

TYPE C events. These might affect the pension creditor. They are events which point towards a deterioration in the employer's covenant and which may be outside the control of the employer. Clearance is not available for these events if they do not also fall within Type A.

Additionally, events which breach the law will not be given clearance and should be reported to the Regulator. These fall within Code of Practice 01 (see **3.10** above).

Effect of Type A events

It is important to consider Type A events, and their effect on the pension creditor. There are three main effects.

Change in priority. This is a change in the level of security given to creditors, with the consequence that the pension creditor might receive a reduced dividend on insolvency; for example, the granting or extending of a fixed charge or frozen charge.

Return of capital. This is a reduction in the overall assets of the company that could be used to fund the pensions deficit; for example: dividends; share buy-backs; dividend strips; distribution in species; and demergers.

Change in control of the structure. A change or partial change in the group structure of the employer leading to the reduction of the overall covenant, which could affect the ability of an employer to meet a *s* 75 debt and lead the Regulator to impose a financial support direction. Examples are a change of employer participating in the scheme and a change of parties connected or associated with the employer. A fuller description of the above Type A matters is given in the guidance.

Nature of Type B events

Type B events are described in greater detail in the guidance. In summary, they include:

- mergers and acquisitions;

- fundraising;

- other contractual negotiations such as operating or finance-leased negotiations.

Nature of Type C events

Type C events are also described in greater detail in the guidance. In general, they comprise events which point towards deterioration in the employer's covenant and which may be inside or outside the control of the employer or its directors. Clearances may be sought by various parties from whom a contribution notice or financial support direction may fall. These include the employer and connected or associated persons, and it is expected that these persons will normally have had prior consultation with the trustees.

Trustees must be impartial and without conflicts of interest. This includes taking no part in passing on confidential information obtained from the employer. Paragraphs 108 and 109 of the guidance specifically concern cases which will result in a call upon the Pension Protection Fund for the purposes of assessment by the Fund. The guidance considers matters of equity, which includes straight equity; increased contributions related to a prescribed share of profits; and priority of equity return.

Notices, information requests, inspection visits and seizure of documents 3.35

The Regulator has significant powers which it may exercise in order to enable it to carry out its functions effectively. In particular:

- it can request information from trustees, employers, administrators and anyone else whom it considers to be appropriate;

- it may serve a notice on trustees, employers or administrators to provide a report prepared by a skilled person (*s 71, Pensions Act 2004*);

- it has power to inspect premises connected with a scheme in order to check for compliance, and it may take possession of and copy any document or require its production (there are criminal penalties for non-compliance – *ss 72–77, Pensions Act 2004*);

- it may obtain a warrant from a justice of the peace to enter premises and seize documents (there are criminal penalties for knowingly or recklessly providing the Regulator with false or misleading information – *ss 78–80, Pensions Act 2004*).

- it may issue improvement notices to trustees or employer;

- it may issue third party notices to anyone involved with a pension scheme whose action or inaction is leading to a contravention of pension legislation;

- it may apply to the courts for an injunction against an individual in order to protect funds;

- it can apply to the courts to have scheme assets returned or for assets due;

- it has power to recover unpaid contributions, and may issue a contribution notice and require a schedule of contributions to be drawn up;

- it can authorise a scheme to accept contributions from a specified European employer, issue a ring-fencing notice to a scheme receiving overseas contributions and direct a UK employer with regard to such matters;

- it may make a prohibition order and suspend a trustee, appoint a trustee and vest property on doing either;

- it can impose a civil penalty up to a maximum of £5,000 on individuals and £50,000 in other cases;

- it may make or extend a restraining order in relation to an account with a deposit taker in relation to pension liberation;

- it may make an order permitting payments out of an account that is subject to a restraining order;

- it may make a repatriation order in a case of pension liberation;

- it can freeze a scheme, inhibit or enforce wind-up and issue directions etc;

- it can issue a financial support direction and clearance statement;

- it can demand skilled reports from responsible persons for a scheme;

- it can wind up a scheme;

- it can appoint an independent trustee;

- it can vest or transfer property on a trustee being disqualified;

- it can void a scheme modification by order, and give a modification order for monies to be paid to an employer;

- it has powers of registration and de-registration of schemes;

- it has many other far-reaching powers.

Any information which the Regulator obtains may be disclosed to:

- other statutory authorities;

- individuals holding public office (with a limited right of onward disclosure) including HMRC, the Pensions Ombudsman and the Director of Public Prosecutions.

Disclosures may also be made by the Regulator (or connected third parties) in connection with certain legal proceedings and investigations (*ss 82–88* and *Sch 3, Pensions Act 2004*), with the exception of most correspondence/communications between a lawyer and his or her client (*s 311, Pensions Act 2004*).

Notifiable events   3.36

The duty of employers and trustees to report notifiable events to the Regulator is explained in Code of Practice 02 (see **3.11** above). In particular, if the scheme is likely to qualify for the Pension Protection Fund, the Regulator must be notified.

The main notifiable events for trustees are summarised below:

- decisions which may result in a scheme debt not being met in full;

- two or more changes of scheme auditor/actuary within twelve months;

- transfers in and out with a value which is more than the lesser of 5% of scheme assets and £1.5m;

- granting improved benefits without having first consulted the scheme actuary or without obtaining additional contributions where so recommended by the actuary;

- granting additional benefits which cost more than the lesser of 5% of the scheme assets and £1.5m.

The main notifiable events for employers are summarised below:

- decisions which may result in a scheme debt not being met in full;

- the company ceasing to carry on business in the UK;

- specified offences (under insolvency legislation) in connection with trading at a point when insolvency is imminent;

- breach of a banking covenant;

- a change in the company's credit rating;

- cessation of control of an employer company by a controlling company;

- two or more changes of chief executive/director/partner responsible for finance matters within twelve months.

Anyone who is required to make a report of notifiable events to the Regulator will enjoy statutory protection if such an act would breach any other duty (e g a duty of confidentiality).

Pensions Regulator Tribunal   3.37

Appeals against the Regulator's determinations should be made, within 28 days of the determination date, to the Pensions Regulator Tribunal. The appeal process is available to anyone who receives a notice (or who, in the opinion of the Tribunal, has been directly affected). The Tribunal can summon people to give evidence or to provide required documents which they hold. Fines will be imposed on a failure to attend the Tribunal, or to give evidence without reasonable excuse. Appeals can be made from the Tribunal to the Court of Appeal (or the Court of Session in Scotland) on points of law on leave from the Tribunal or appeal court.

Prohibited persons register   3.38

The Regulator has a duty to maintain a register of persons who are prohibited from acting as trustees by *s 3, Pensions Act 1995.* The contents of that register must not be disclosed or otherwise made available to the members of the public except on receipt of a formal request by a person in accordance with *s 67, Pensions Act 2004.*

Registrable schemes and maintenance of the register   3.39

In addition to the other responsibilities of the Regulator, it must compile and maintain a register of occupational pension schemes and personal schemes which are, or have been, registrable schemes. The registration requirements for occupational pension schemes and personal pension schemes are described in detail in *ss 59–65, Pensions Act 2004.* The duty of the Regulator is to record in the register:

- the registrable information most recently provided to it in respect of a scheme;
- details of the receipt of any of the following:
  - a notice under *s 62(5)* of the Act (this refers to a scheme which is wound up or ceases to be registrable);
  - a copy of a notice under *s 160* of the Act (this refers to a transfer notice);

- any notice, or a copy of any such notice, under any provision in force in Northern Ireland corresponding to a provision mentioned above.

In respect of each scheme which has been a registrable scheme but:

- has been, or is, treated as being wound up; or
- has ceased to be a registrable scheme;

the Regulator must maintain in the register the *registrable information* last provided to it in respect of the scheme.

Registrable information means:

- the name of the scheme;
- the address of the scheme;
- the full names and addresses of each of the trustees or managers of the scheme;
- the status of the scheme in respect of the following matters:
    - whether new members may be admitted;
    - whether further benefits may accrue to, or in respect of members;
    - whether further contributions may be paid;
    - whether any members of the scheme are active members;
    - the categories of benefits under the scheme;
- in the case of an occupational pension scheme:
    - the name and address of each *relevant employer*;
    - any other name by which any relevant employer has been known at any time but not after the *relevant date*;
    - the number of members of the scheme on the later of the last day of the scheme year which ended most recently and the day on which the scheme became a registrable scheme;
- such other information as may be described.

A *relevant employer* is any person who is, or who at any time after April 1975 has been, the employer in relation to the scheme. The *relevant date* in relation to a relevant employer means 6 April 1975, or (if later) the date on which the relevant employer first became the employer in relation to the scheme.

Regulations stipulate when information and extracts from the register, or copies of the register, may be provided to prescribed persons in prescribed circumstances – and for the inspection of such documents by such persons in prescribed circumstances. The Secretary of State, or an authorised person, may make provision with respect to the disclosure of information obtained by virtue of the *Register of Occupational and Personal Pension Schemes Regulations 2005 (SI 2005/597)*. The Secretary of State may also direct the Regulator to submit to him statistical and other reports concerning such information that he shall require and shall publish any report as he shall think appropriate.

The Regulator must be notified by the trustees or managers of the scheme, together with required information, on the establishment of a registrable scheme before the end of the *notification period*.

The initial *notification period* is a period of three months which begins with the date on which a scheme was established or, if later, that date on which it became a registrable scheme. The Regulator must be notified of any changes of any information provided as soon as is practicable, including cessation of registrable scheme status and on scheme wind-up. Civil penalties may be applied under *s 10, Pensions Act 1995*, to any trustee or manager who fails to take reasonable steps to secure compliance.

Scheme return notices   3.40

Among its other duties, the Regulator must issue scheme return notices. A scheme return notice must contain a return date which falls within a period of three years beginning with the date on which the notice was received or, if earlier, the date on which the Regulator first became aware that the scheme was a registrable scheme. For subsequent return notices, the return date must fall after the end of a period of one year beginning with the date on which the information was provided to the Regulator.

The scheme return consists of a number of headed boxes (see **APPENDIX 2** for the content). These boxes contain the following headings:

- About the scheme

- Scheme details

- Scheme trustees, trustee advisors and service providers

- Financial information

- Employer details

- Further information

- Declaration

The form must be signed by the scheme trustee/manager representative.

The trustees or managers must, on or before the return date, provide a scheme return to the Regulator.

The information in the scheme return may also include the following, where appropriate:

- information concerning the Pension Protection Fund levy;

- information concerning the risk assessment for the scheme.

Again, civil penalties may be applied to any trustees or manager who fails to take reasonable steps to secure compliance.

Specific guidance on lump sum death benefits   3.41

The Regulator has published guidance on lump sum death benefits. This guidance has been awaited for a long time, and it did not emerge until summer 2006. It addresses the concerns which were being expressed about how 'death-benefit-only' schemes could continue to operate following the coming into force of *s 255, Pensions Act 2004*. The problem is that the section required registered schemes to limit their activities to operations relating to retirement benefits.

The section stipulates that supplementary benefits such as death and disability benefits must be ancillary to retirement benefits. The Regulator's guidance, on its website, is that if any employee has been offered membership of a pension scheme for pensions benefits (or if an employee will be offered membership of a pension scheme for pension benefits if he or she remains within work long enough – ie a waiting period which is agreed under his or her employment terms), death-benefits-only lump sums may be provided as part of the package of benefits.

(The continuation of existing life assurance cover in any form for retired members would also be acceptable.)

It is not clear how this guidance is intended to be interpreted with regard to 'death-benefit-only' schemes that are linked to retirement benefits which are provided through other registered schemes. See **7.38** for further information.

Trustee register   3.42

The Regulator must compile and maintain a trustee register. At present, the register is made up of professional trustees, from which it can make appointments for a trust scheme under *s 7, Pensions Act 1995*. There may also be circumstances where *ss 22* and *23* appointments are required (the Regulator may make an appointment of an independent trustee under *ss 22* and *23* in the event of insolvency). Appointments are commonly made in respect of trustees on the register, but there is discretion to appoint non-register trustees in appropriate cases.

The Regulator may make an appointment under *s* 7 if it is satisfied that it is necessary to do so in order to secure:

- that the trustees as a whole have, or exercise, the necessary knowledge and skill for the proper administration of the scheme;

- that the number of trustees is sufficient for the proper administration of the scheme; or

- the proper use or application of the assets of the scheme.

Trustees' toolkit and guidance   3.43

The Pensions Regulator's website contains an interactive Trustees' Toolkit. The main purpose of the toolkit is to help trustees to comply with *ss 247–249, Pensions Act 2004*, which require trustees to have knowledge and understanding of the law relating to pensions and trusts and the principles relating to the funding of occupational schemes and the investment of scheme assets.

The duties of trustees also extend to familiarising themselves with the documentation of their schemes and the other documents and practice which govern the policy of those schemes. Trustee training is an important aspect of these new responsibilities, as recommended by the Myners Report.

The toolkit contains links to the following additional tools for trustees:

- a Scope Guidance document for defined benefit schemes;

- a Scope Guidance document for defined contribution schemes;

- an Indicative Syllabus for trustees.

The toolkit delivers learning by use of a variety of techniques such as audio and video snippets, and self-assessment. It allows for a different path for each trustee according to the type of scheme and their own experience. The first three available modules cover trust law and pensions law, and future modules will cover the whole of the Scope Guidance.

A description of the required level of trustee knowledgee and understanding is given in **7.20–7.26** below.

Whistleblowing – breach of material significance 3.44

The duty of certain persons to whistleblow to the Regulator is explained in Code of Practice 02 (see **3.10** above), and a description of the main principles is given below in the form of benchmarks against which such persons can consider breaches that they come across. *Section 70, Pensions Act 2004*, contains the statutory duty to report. The civil penalties which may apply on a failure to report a breach will be incurred under *s 10, Pensions Act 1995*.

The range of persons who carry such responsibility is much wider than under the *Pensions Act 1995*. The Regulator should be notified where a person has 'reasonable cause to believe' that there has been a breach of administrative duty which is likely to be of 'material significance'. The meaning of these terms is important, but somewhat complex, and explanations are given below under appropriate bullet points in this paragraph. The Regulator has provided a RAG (red, amber, green) 'traffic light' system for reporting events, and a decision-tree, on its website. The RAG system is:

- **R**ed: events that the Regulator is interested in.

- **A**mber: events that the Regulator might be interested in.

- **G**reen: events that the Regulator is not interested in.

The legal position 3.45

Under the *Pensions Act 2004,* the duty to report is overriding. The responsible persons are referred to as 'reporters' in the code. The duty is imposed by, or by virtue of, an enactment or rule of law, and it applies to the 'administration' of a scheme where the duty has not been, or is not being, complied with. This is a sweeping law, and it can have a significant effect on existing agreements between parties on a duty to maintain secrecy. However, it does not override 'legal privilege', which means that oral and written communications between a professional legal adviser and their client, or a person representing that client, while obtaining legal advice, do not have to be disclosed. Additionally, employees who whistleblow (for example, if they disagree with their employer's decision not to report) should have protection under the *Employment Rights Act 1996* if they make a report in good faith.

A reporter can also ask the Regulator to protect his or her identity, but it will be of some concern to note that, on practical grounds, this cannot be guaranteed. This could put a potential reporter in a 'catch 22' situation, and he or she may need to seek legal advice in order to protect his or her position.

'Administration' is widely drawn, and extends beyond general record-keeping, dealing with membership movements, calculating benefits and preparing accounts. It includes the consideration of funding in defined benefit schemes, investment policy and investment management, as well as the custody of invested assets and anything which could potentially affect members' benefits or the ability of members and others to access information to which they are entitled.

The decision to report   3.46

The Regulator's guidance states that there are two key judgements required:

- does the reporter have reasonable cause to believe there has been a breach of the law?

- if so, does the reporter believe that the breach is likely to be of material significance to the Pensions Regulator?

The persons with a duty to report, and the timescale for reporting   3.47

The description of the persons to whom a legal duty to report applies is very widely drawn, having been extended in April 2005. Events must be reported 'as soon as is reasonably practicable'. The list of responsible persons ('reporters' in the code) is as follows:

- Trustees and their advisers and service providers (including those carrying out tasks such as administration or fund management). The duty of trustees of trust-based schemes applies to each individually-appointed trustee. In the case of a corporate trustee body with trustee directors, the requirement to report falls on the trustee company. A breach of trust would be a reportable event.

- Managers of schemes not set up under trust. The duty falls on managers of personal pension schemes, including stakeholder schemes. However, the Regulator will only be concerned with breaches where a direct payment arrangement exists.

- Employers sponsoring or participating in work-based occupational pension schemes. The duty falls on participating employers. Where there is more than one employer (ie a multi-employer scheme), the duty to report includes any employer that becomes aware of a breach, whether or not it relates to, or affects, members who are its employees or those of other employers.

- Persons otherwise involved in the administration of a scheme, including any person providing services for trustees or managers that relate to the administration and management of occupational and personal pension schemes, including stakeholder schemes. Such persons include:

- insurance companies and third party administrators who carry out administrative tasks relating to a scheme;

- a participating employer who provides staff to carry out administration tasks in-house (this includes performing payroll and similar functions as well as carrying out or helping with direct administration of the pension scheme); and

- independent financial advisers and consultants who provide services to trustees relating to administration, such as record-keeping or acting as an intermediary receiving and forwarding scheme documents and other materials.

- Professional persons (as defined in *s 47(4)*, *Pensions Act 1995*) who are appointed by the trustees in the role of advisers or service providers. These include scheme actuaries, scheme auditors, legal advisers, fund managers and custodians of scheme assets. If a firm is appointed, the duty to report applies to the firm and it must have appropriate systems in place. Individuals carry a personal duty to report.

- Persons otherwise involved in advising a trustee (or manager of a scheme not established under trust) in relation to the scheme. A duty also falls on other firms (or individuals where the appointments are personal) providing advice to the trustees or managers. Such persons include:

  - independent financial advisers, pensions consultants and investment consultants;

  - actuaries and auditors providing advice to the managers of personal pension schemes;

  - actuaries and auditors engaged to provide advice to the trustees of occupational pension schemes other than would cause them to be classed as professional advisers;

  - reporting accountants appointed to stakeholder schemes; and

  - anyone acting as custodian of the assets of a personal pension scheme.

If a reporter has more than one role in relation to a scheme, he or she must apply his or her wider knowledge in judging whether a matter is likely to be of material significance. Where appropriate, he or she must make a report irrespective of the function he or she was performing when the breach was identified.

There is no requirement to report every breach, and the decision tree on the Regulator's website will help persons determine whether or not to report.

Setting up arrangements, and understanding the meaning of the terminology 3.48

It is important that effective arrangements are put in place by reporters in order to meet their duty to report breaches of the law. These arrangements must not rely on waiting for others to report or expecting others to be responsible for doing so. Persons who may have a duty to report should understand the requirements, and the meaning of 'reasonable cause to believe', 'material significance' and 'as soon as reasonably practicable' (see the following descriptions), visit the Regulator's website frequently and obtain any necessary training. Firms must ensure that their staff are adequately trained to a level commensurate with their roles, and are able to recognise potentially reportable situations.

- *Reasonable cause to believe.* Reasonable cause does not mean having a suspicion that cannot be substantiated. A reporter should normally check with the trustees or manager, or other relevant bodies and parties (except in the case of theft or likely fraud or other serious offence). The Regulator cannot take on a case without reasonable cause having been demonstrated, but it is not necessary for a reporter to gather all the evidence required before the Regulator is able to take legal action. Such judgements can be hard to call, and the potential reporter may need professional assistance in cases of uncertainty.

- *Material significance.* What makes a breach to be of material significance depends on:

  - *The cause of the breach.* If the breach was caused by dishonesty; poor governance (inadequate controls resulting in deficient administration, or slow or inappropriate decision-making practices); incomplete or inaccurate advice; or acting (or failing to act) in deliberate contravention of the law; it is likely to be of material significance. Any other reported and unreported breaches should be taken into consideration, mainly where they were not remedied. Isolated incidents (for example, initial problems with a new system or procedure, or an unusual or unpredictable combination of circumstances) will not normally be of material significance.

  - *The effect of the breach.* A consideration of material significance is the protection of members' benefits (this matter will include appropriate contribution payments; the safety of assets; legitimacy of payments and accuracy of timing of payments; meeting the funding requirements and complying with the scheme's investment policy). The matter of reducing the risk of compensation being payable from the PPF (see **CHAPTER 4**) should also be considered, and the standard of administration and member information provided by a scheme.

  - *The reaction to the breach.* A breach of material significance can generally be negated by prompt and effective action to investigate and correct the breach and its causes, and, where appropriate, to notify any members whose benefits have been affected. If this is not done or put in hand, and the members whose benefits have been affected have not been notified (where appropriate to do so), the breach is likely to be of material significance. The Pensions Regulator's website also states that, even where only a few members are not receiving benefits due to them, the breach is likely to be materially significant unless prompt and robust action is being taken to remedy the situation.

— *The wider implications of the breach.* A breach is likely to be materially significant if it appears that other breaches will emerge in the future because the trustees (or the manager) lack the appropriate knowledge and understanding to fulfil their responsibilities; or that other schemes may be affected (for example, schemes administered by the same organisation where a system failure is to blame). The reporter should consider general risk factors, such as the level of funding (in a defined benefit scheme) or how well run the scheme appears to be. The risk is inevitably higher in a poorly-run and poorly-administered scheme.

- *As soon as reasonably practicable.* Procedures must be in place in order to meet the reporting requirement within an appropriate timescale. Again, there is no definitive guidance on the meaning of this term, other than that it 'depends on the circumstances'. The guidance states that the time taken should reflect the seriousness of the suspected breach. Where there is an immediate risk to scheme assets or the payment of members' benefits, or where there is any indication of dishonesty, reporters need not seek explanations or consider proffered remedies; they should only make such immediate checks as are necessary. Serious potential breaches demand greater urgency.

The reporting arrangements 3.49

A satisfactory reporting procedure (which includes consulting others, where necessary) for evaluating matters to determine whether a breach has occurred and, if it has, whether it is likely to be of material significance to the Regulator, will be required. **ANNEX 2** at the end of this chapter contains the description of what is likely to be considered a satisfactory procedure, although the arrangements are a matter for the reporter in the circumstances of the case. Other than in cases where there is a suspicion of dishonesty or other serious wrongdoing by the trustees or managers, the arrangement is not intended to replace dialogue between trustees or managers and their advisers or service providers.

The Regulator has drawn attention to the fact that duplicate reporting may arise, due to the wide range of potential reporters. It states that such reports carry a cost, which will ultimately be borne by the scheme members or the employer, and that they do not benefit the Regulator. Therefore, once it is aware of a particular breach, it will no longer regard that breach as being of material significance for the purpose of making further reports (unless additional or different information would be made available).

Making a report   3.50

Reports must be submitted in writing, wherever practicable using the standard format available on the Regulator's website (see **ANNEX 4** at the end of this chapter). The report will be acknowledged, and the report (if not previously sent) and the acknowledgement should be sent by the reporter to the trustees or manager. The trustees or manager will be able to copy the original report and its acknowledgement to those other reporters whom they consider may also be likely to come across the breach. It is permitted to make a collective report, for example by trustees, together with one or more of their advisers or other groups. Where there are individual trustees, and a consensus cannot be reached, or if there is insufficient time to agree a collective approach, the Regulator will expect the individuals to report.

A report should be dated and should include, as a minimum, the details contained in **ANNEX 5** at the end of this chapter. It can be sent by post or electronically, including by email or by fax, and urgent reports should be marked as such. Attention should be drawn to matters which are considered particularly serious by the reporter. A written report can be preceded by a telephone call if appropriate. A reporter should ensure that he or she receives an acknowledgement in order to be certain that it has been received. An acknowledgement will be sent within five working days of receipt. There are restrictions on the information that the Regulator may subsequently disclose concerning its investigation, but he or she may request further information.

Reporting to other bodies   3.51

If a duty arises to report to other bodies (for example, in connection with money-laundering or proceeds of crime issues), and that report also falls within the category of reportable events to the Regulator, it is stated on the website that 'it would assist if the report to the Pensions Regulator referred to the other report'. Reporters must be clear as to the relevance of such material and the appropriateness of its divulgence.

Failure to report   3.52

Any failure to report breaches of the law without 'reasonable excuse' is a civil offence. Therefore, a reporter will need to have such a reasonable excuse for not reporting, or for reporting late, any reportable breach. The Pensions

Regulator's website states that the criteria which the Regulator will consider on a failure to report under the code of practice are as follows:

- the legislation, case law, the code of practice and any guidance issued by the Pensions Regulator;

- the role of the reporter in relation to the scheme;

- the training provided to the individual or staff, and the level of knowledge it would be reasonable to expect that individual or those staff to have;

- the procedures put in place to identify and evaluate breaches and whether these procedures had been followed;

- the seriousness of the breach and therefore how important it was to report this matter to the Pensions Regulator without delay;

- any reasons for the delay in reporting;

- any other relevant considerations relating to the case in question.

The Regulator will issue a warning notice to affected parties if it is considering imposing a civil penalty, or exercising one of its functions. The notice will describe the alleged breach and specify the relevant function. It may also, where it considers it appropriate to do so, make a complaint to the reporter's professional or other governing body.

Whereas the above places a great deal of responsibility on reporters, the code does state that such persons are not required to search for breaches, but they must be aware of the relevant circumstances which are applicable to the scheme, such as disclosure rules, transfer value quotations and payments, payment of benefits and receipt of contributions. In particular, all reporters should in particular be alert to any dishonest behaviour.

How the Pensions Regulator will respond to a report 3.53

The Regulator has discretion over whether to take action and, if so, what action to take. Much will depend on the information provided, the nature of the breach and its knowledge of the scheme or arrangement. It can take one or more of a number of actions, including:

- assisting or instructing trustees and others to achieve compliance;

- providing education or guidance;

- appointing trustees to help run the scheme;

- removing trustees from office;

- freezing the scheme;

- imposing special measures where the scheme funding requirements of the *Pensions Act 2004* are not complied with;

- ordering that the scheme's funding position be restored to the level before a breach or other detrimental event occurred; and

- imposing fines where appropriate.

Annex

Annex 1
Notifiable events

Some events only have to be notified by schemes that are funded below the Pension Protection Fund buy-out level or where there has been a report of a materially significant failure by the employer to make a payment in accordance with the schedule of contributions. The code states that, if an event occurs, it must be notified in writing to the Regulator as soon as reasonably practicable. Failure to notify should be reported as a breach of the law likely to be of material significance. Directions by the Regulator give exceptions to the duty to notify. Briefly, fewer events are notifiable if the scheme is funded above the Pension Protection Fund buy-out level, and is adhering to its schedule of contributions.

The notification duty falls on trustees, jointly and severally, in respect of scheme-related events, and on employers in respect of employer-related events. Trustees in particular might prefer to agree a collective approach to notification. If, however, a consensus cannot be reached, or not all the trustees are aware of the event, the Regulator will expect an individual trustee or group of trustees to notify. Employers may wish to channel notifications through one individual such as the company secretary. The duty on employers and trustees to notify overrides any other duty of confidentiality, and any such duty is not breached by notifying. There are also restrictions on the extent to which the Pensions Regulator can in turn pass on confidential information.

Events must be notified in writing as soon as reasonably practicable (dependent on the circumstances. but in all cases this implies urgency). The code states: 'For example, where a trustee is made aware of a notifiable event on a Sunday, the Regulator should be notified on Monday'. Procedures should also be put in place to require those such as administrators working on behalf of trustees and employers to alert trustees and employers quickly to notifiable events.

The minimum information that should be included in a notification is the:

- description of the notifiable event;
- date of the event;
- name of the pension scheme;
- name of the employer; and

- name, position and contact details of the notifier.

The information that would in addition be useful to the Regulator is the:

- address of the pension scheme;
- name and address of the main trustee contact;
- pension scheme registration number;
- name and address of the main employer contact;
- employer's current trading status; and
- name of any controlling company or group to which the employer belongs.

Where contact details are provided, the Regulator will aim to acknowledge notifications within five working days of receipt.

A failure to notify can give rise to civil penalties under *s 10, Pensions Act 1995*. Persons such as the scheme actuary or an independent financial adviser, who are subject to the duty to report breaches of the law to the Regulator and who become aware of a failure by trustees or an employer to notify, should report the failure.

Annex 2
Early leavers – reasonable periods

A member will have a statutory right to take a cash transfer sum or a contribution refund. He has a right to take his benefit either as a cash transfer sum, calculated in the same way as a cash equivalent transfer value, or a refund of his own contributions, if any (less tax and any contributions equivalent premium paid as appropriate). There may be a reduction or increase where permitted/required by legislation (see **CHAPTER 5** in particular). The three-month condition is satisfied if his pensionable service, when aggregated with any previous period of pensionable service under the scheme and any period of employment in linked qualifying service under another scheme, amounts to at least three months.

In a winding-up situation, an active member will be entitled only to a refund of his own contributions. A deferred member, however, will still have the option to take a cash transfer sum, but this may be reduced or increased in accordance with legislation.

The trustees must adequately explain the member's rights in writing, within a reasonable period (normally three months) of a member leaving service. If there is likely to be a delay, the member must be informed. The member must be given a reasonable period (normally three months) within which to reply to the trustees or managers in order to exercise his rights. He can request further time to reply, for example in order to obtain proper financial advice, but the trustees or managers are not obliged to grant an extension. If he sends no reply, he may be provided with a contributions refund under the default procedure, normally one month after the final reply date.

For contracted-out schemes, where there is a possibility of the payment of contributions equivalent premiums to the state, trustees may need to ensure that any affected member is notified within a shorter period in order to ensure that the payment can be made in time (for example, action will need to be taken within six months from the date the member leaves service – which could be exceeded by the aggregate of the notification period, the reply period and the default period).

The member must specify, normally within three months, how the monies are to be used (for example, as a transfer to another occupational or personal pension scheme, or to purchase an annuity, or in any other way that the legislation may prescribe). If he chooses to take a refund, he may require the trustees to pay it directly to him, or at his direction to someone else.

Annex 3
Reporting late payment of contributions to personal pension schemes

Payment information will normally be provided promptly by employers as part of the usual business arrangements between the employer and manager. Exceptionally, where this is not the case, the managers may make a formal request to employers for information to enable them to monitor the payment of contributions. Employers must provide that information within a reasonable period (normally within 30 days of the formal request by the managers).

The reasonable period for managers to report to the Regulator if they have not received payment information from the employer, that they have requested in order to enable them to monitor payments due to the plan (and because of that failure are unable to monitor payments), is within 60 days of the formal request. A report should not be made if the manager expects to receive the information shortly.

Managers may report to employees the non-provision of payment information by employers, but are not required to do so. If managers make a late payment report to the Regulator, they must also report to employees within a reasonable period after the due date, in a similar manner and timescale for money purchase reports.

Annex 4
Extract from the Pension Regulator's website concerning reporting procedures

The Pensions Regulator's website contains the following features of a satisfactory procedure for reporting breaches:

- 'obtaining clarification of the law where it is not clear to the reporter;

- clarifying the facts around the suspected breach where these are not known;

- consideration of the material significance of the breach taking into account its cause, effect, the reaction to it, and its wider implications, including where appropriate dialogue with the trustees or managers;

- a clear process for referral to the appropriate level of seniority at which decisions can be made on whether to report to the Pensions Regulator;

- an established procedure for dealing with difficult cases such as a "Regulator Committee" of experienced persons within the reporter's firm;

- a timeframe for the procedure to take place that is appropriate to the breach and allows the report to be made as soon as reasonably practicable;

- a system to record breaches even if they are not reported to the Pensions Regulator (the principal reason for this is that the record of past breaches may be relevant in deciding whether to report future breaches); and

- a process for identifying promptly any breaches that are so serious they must always be reported.'

Annex 5
Report of material significance

The Pensions Regulator states that a report of material significance should be dated and should include, as a minimum, the following details:

[Extract from the Pension Regulator's website]

- 'name of the scheme;

- description of the breach or breaches;

- any relevant dates;

- name of the employer (in the case of an occupational scheme) or scheme manager (in the case of a personal pension scheme, including stakeholder schemes);

- name, position and contact details of the reporter; and

- role of the reporter in relation to the scheme.

The information that we would expect to see in addition is:

- reason the breach is thought to be of material significance to the Pensions Regulator;

- address of the scheme;

- type of scheme – whether occupational (defined benefit, defined contribution or hybrid) or personal;

- name and contact details of the trustees or scheme manager (if different to the scheme address);

- pension schemes registry number; and

- address of employer.'

Chapter 4
The Pension Protection Fund

Introduction 4.1

Section 107 of the *Pensions Act 2004* announced that a body corporate named 'the Board of the Pension Protection Fund' shall be established. The Pension Protection Fund (PPF) was to be for the purpose of protecting the pension rights of certain persons who are members of underfunded schemes. The PPF has been set up, and is funded by a composite levy. The main provisions for the PPF Board are to be found in *Part 2* of the Act. Most of the provisions of the Act came into force on 5 April 2005. The provisions for the creation of the PPF and the PPF Board had effect from 17 December 2004. The PPF website http://www.pensionprotectionfund.org.uk contains its strategic plan for the year 2006/07.

There is an Ombudsman for the PPF, who deals with reviewable matters, and a Deputy Pensions Ombudsman. The Pensions Regulator can collect information which is relevant to the Board by virtue of *ss 68* and *69* of the Act.

There is also a Financial Assistance Scheme (FAS) (see **CHAPTER 8**) for persons who are not covered by the PPF.

Background 4.2

The government expressed concern about the need to protect the pension rights of members of under-funded schemes in the DWP December 2002 Green Paper *Simplicity, Security and Choice: Working and Saving for Retirement*. The idea of establishing a protection fund evolved, and the June 2003 Paper *Working and Saving for Retirement: Action on Occupational Pensions* introduced the concept of the PPF.

The PPF went live on 6 April 2005. It provides major protection for certain schemes in deficit (effectively final salary schemes, and money purchase schemes in the event of fraud and misappropriation of assets).

The PPF applies to schemes of companies which became insolvent after its commencement date of 6 April 2005, and to schemes of companies which became insolvent before that date provided that the scheme had not yet gone into wind-up. The compensation scheme does not apply if the employer remains solvent, in which circumstance the Pensions Regulator would require a rescue scheme to be put in place (see **CHAPTER 3**).

The establishment of the Fund has given rise to a great deal of ongoing review and some change. The main reviews are listed in **4.24** below, and are referred to at the relevant points in this chapter.

The Board of the PPF   4.3

The PPF Board is made up of the following:

- a chairman;

- a chief executive; and

- at least five other members.

The procedure for the appointment of the ordinary members is laid down in *Pension Protection Fund (Appointment of Ordinary Members) Regulations 2005 (SI 2005/616)*.

The Board has responsibility for managing the PPF and the Fraud Compensation Fund. The PPF operates through its committee, which monitors the Board's activities.

Fraud Compensation Fund   4.4

A scheme may only receive a fraud compensation payment if all the conditions below are met:

- The employer is insolvent, or unable to continue as a going concern.

- No employer has taken over, or is available to take over ('rescue') the scheme.

- The scheme assets have been lost through dishonesty.

- No transfer notice has been issued to the PPF.

Trustees must endeavour to recover any losses, and the PPF must be satisfied that no further money can be recovered before it makes any payments. Compensation shall not exceed the amount of the reduction in the assets, less any amount recovered. The PPF may make interim payments before a final settlement.

This assessment follows the general levy, the PPF levy and the PPF administration levy, where the same principle applies. Schemes which are not covered by the Fraud Compensation Fund include public-service schemes, non-registered schemes, small self-administered schemes, death-benefit-only schemes and schemes with only one member.

Investment and financial accounting by the PPF Board
4.5

The following investment principles apply to the Board's activities:

- Any monies which are invested by the Board must be under the control of at least two appointed fund managers.

- The Board must ensure that it maintains a statement of investment principles. The form and content of the statement is laid down in the *Pension Protection Fund (Statement of Investment Principles) Regulations (SI 2005/675)*.

- Accretions to the fund by way of investment returns and income will remain in the PPF.

- The Board may borrow monies. This facility is limited to £25m by virtue of the *Pension Protection Fund (Limit on Borrowing) Order 2005 (SI 2005/339)*.

In addition to the above, the Board must maintain accounts and obtain actuarial valuations of the PPF. The accounts must be presented to the Secretary of State each year, and include an actuarial valuation of the assets and liabilities of the PPF. The administration costs of the PPF are separate from the funds that are ring-fenced for payment of compensation. They are financed separately by the annual administration levy and should not be included when considering the value of the compensation Fund itself.

The original definition of the appointed actuary for the purpose of carrying out the valuation excluded any actuary who was currently working on a scheme that was in a PPF assessment period, or who was carrying out any valuation that would be used by the scheme in matters relating to the PPF. The response to the consultation which was published in April 2006 (see **4.24** below) stated that this definition was too narrow and could seriously limit the talent pool available to do this work for the Board. It stated:

'Further research with industry professionals and other advisors found that the majority of actuaries would be likely to be involved in PPF relevant work most of the time. Further, the actuarial profession operates a strict code of practice that prohibits actuaries from acting in the manner that motivates this prohibition. It was therefore decided to remove the restrictions and simply require that an actuary be a recognised Fellow of the Institute of Actuaries or Institute of

Actuaries in order to be permitted to sign the valuation'. The Board's statement of investment principles can be accessed at: http://www.pensionprotectionfund.gov.uk/sip05.pdf.

The first annual report and accounts of the PPF, for the financial year 2004/05, is available on the PPF website. It covers the period from 17 December 2004 to 31 March 2005, and mainly concerns the activities of the Board of the PPF on formation issues. The Board set itself both longer-term objectives (five years) and shorter-term (one year) objectives. These are summarised below:

The five-year objectives were:

- to maintain the solvency position of the PPF between predetermined limits;

- for the PPF to play its part in building confidence in pensions;

- to pay the right people the right compensation at the right time;

- to ensure that two-way communications with stakeholders are effective;

- to achieve employee satisfaction levels sufficient to fulfil the PPF's purpose;

- to achieve high levels of stakeholder satisfaction in respect of the organisation's professionalism, policies, processes and helpfulness.

The one-year objectives were:

- to set up and implement effective and robust systems for governance, internal controls and risk management for all aspects of the organisation's operations;

- to establish policies and practices that result in timely decisions enabling eligible pension schemes to be transferred into the PPF, and also timely payments to be made to eligible scheme members;

- to manage investments prudently and effectively to meet liabilities;

- to be in a position during the financial year 2006/07 to implement the risk-based levy (in terms of funding and insolvency);

- to establish and operate strong internal financial and management controls and ensure that the organisation has access to sufficient financing to meet operating and capital expenditure requirements;

- to establish that the organisation has enough staff to meet its needs with the right skills and knowledge and is considered to be a good employer;

- to design and implement the IS/IT strategy which supports the activities of the organisation;

- to operate a strong working partnership with the Pensions Regulator supported by clear documentation detailing the way in which each organisation supports the other;

- to communicate clearly what the PPF does and why, to scheme members, trustees, professional advisers and other stakeholders.

Valuation of scheme assets   4.6

The criteria for making actuarial valuations of schemes for the PPF are contained in the *Pension Protection Fund (Valuation) Regulations 2005 (SI 2005/672)*. The main features are that scheme assets should be based on audited accounts, and liabilities are calculated on a buy-out basis.

Eligible schemes must provide an initial actuarial valuation of the scheme's assets and liabilities, on the *s 179, Pension Act 2004* basis, by a prescribed date. The trustees or managers of eligible schemes must provide actuarial valuations to the Board, or to the Pensions Regulator, at least every three years after the initial actuarial valuation. Schemes must undergo an 'assessment period' (see **4.7** below).

In some circumstances, a payment due to the eligible scheme under a contribution notice, a financial support direction or a restoration order shall be considered to be an asset of the eligible scheme. The regulations provide that where such a payment is considered to be an asset the actuarial valuation shall be adjusted accordingly.

The *Occupational Pension Schemes (Modification of Pension Protection Provisions) Regulations 2005 (SI 2005/705)* explain the actions to be taken where a transfer payment, or other event, reduces part of a scheme's liability.

Eligibility for the PPF: the entry valuation   4.7

The eligibility rules that apply to the PPF and the FAS were uncertain from the outset, particularly with respect to the periods which were covered by the Fund and the Scheme. However, the principal criterion for benefiting from the PPF was clear. The rule was (and remains) that, in order to qualify for the PPF, there has to be an insolvency event and the pension scheme must conduct an entry valuation. The entry valuation needs to demonstrate that the assets of the pension scheme are not adequate to cover PPF liabilities. Where this can be shown to be so, the pension scheme will usually be allowed to enter the PPF. Clearly, there had to be some measure to prevent an abuse of the PPF, and the rule is that any actions taken (or not taken) in order to avoid these debts by employers or directors will be pursued by the Pensions Regulator as a breach of the law and certain transactions could be reversed.

The entry (and levy) valuation bases have to reflect the cost of buying out annuities (and deferred annuities). There are two main differences between the levy and entry valuation bases. These are in respect of mortality and compensation cap increases. The rating of the mortality basis is based on benefit size for the entry valuation, whereas there is no rating, irrespective of benefit size, for the levy valuation. For the entry valuation, the compensation cap at normal pension age is assumed, for non-pensioners, to increase between the assessment date and normal pension age by 1.5% pa more than LPI, whereas for the levy valuation the compensation cap is implicitly assumed (for ease of calculation) to increase in line with deferred compensation increases.

Quotations can obtained from the insurers accepting business at that time, but these can have a disproportionate effect. The PPF bases have been derived by analysis of buy-out quotes and by reference to the principles used by insurers to assess their underlying cost, and the Board of the PPF's intention is to maintain a small margin against the actual underlying bases likely to be used by insurers. This ensures that schemes close to 100% funded on an insured basis would be assessed as having sufficient assets and thus forced to obtain an accurate quotation from the market, with the potential for higher than PPF benefits to be secured for members. The mortality basis was chosen to reflect market practice and is supported by the findings of the most recent Continuous Mortality Investigation reports (CMI Working Papers No 4 and No 9, published on 17 March 2004 and 17 November 2004 respectively). The Board decided a benefit-size rating should be applied for entry valuation purposes and, after considering representations and on the grounds of simplicity, the Board further decided to disregard the requirement to use an age rating for levy valuation purposes.Solvent employers will be required to secure accrued benefits in full by annuity purchase. Other employers within a Group structure may be called on to fund these debts before the PPF takes on the scheme.

The government issued an early statement that the PPF will not be restricted to schemes of companies that became insolvent after its commencement date of 6 April 2005, as long as the pension scheme has not yet gone into wind-up (see **4.21** below), and the FAS was extended to cover schemes which failed before 6 April 2005 in order to provide some level of overall protection for members of schemes for the period from 1997 (see **CHAPTER 8** below).

The *Pension Protection Fund (Entry Rules) Regulations 2005 (SI 2005/590)* and the *Pension Protection Fund (Entry Rules) Amendment Regulations 2005 (SI 2005/2153)* specify the rules which apply to pay the levies and to benefit from the PPF. They determine the criteria which shall apply to establish whether the Board must assume responsibility for the scheme, a 'scheme rescue' has occurred or the scheme should be wound up. A 'scheme rescue' is either:

- where there has been a rescue of the employer's business as a going concern and the employer retains responsibility for the scheme and no one else has entered into an agreement with the PPF Board to compromise a *s 75, Pensions Act 1995* debt; or

- where someone else has assumed responsibility for the employer's liabilities under the scheme.

The main additional criteria which apply to eligibility are:

- Money purchase schemes are ineligible.

- Normally, the employer must be insolvent and a notification must have been sent by the insolvency practitioner (see **4.19** below) stating that a scheme rescue is not possible.

- The scheme assets must be insufficient to secure the liabilities. (Special cases, such as unincorporated charities, may apply to the Board for it to assume responsibility for the scheme if they are in difficulties.)

- The Board must not have issued a withdrawal notice (for example, in cases where it thinks that the scheme can be rescued or insolvency is not inevitable).

- Normally, the scheme must not have been outside the scope of the PPF for three years (or shorter scheme life).

- A transfer to a new scheme with the same employer, which commenced within three years of an assessment period for the new scheme in order to benefit from the PPF, will not be acceptable if the first scheme was not previously eligible.

The main classes of defined benefit schemes which are excluded from the PPF are:

- death-benefit-only schemes;

- single-member schemes;

- public service schemes (for example, civil service and local government);

- schemes under government guarantee, including schemes with guarantees relating to certain employees of privatised utilities;

- non-registered schemes;

- schemes registered outside the UK;

- schemes without a sponsoring employer on or after 6 April 2005 (unless authorised by the Board of the PPF to continue as a closed scheme).

Assessment period
4.8

The assessment period commences when an employer becomes insolvent, and is for the purpose of determining whether the PPF will apply to the scheme. During this period:

- contributions must cease;

- no new members may be admitted;

- no further benefits may accrue;

- transfer payments are restricted;

- a scheme may not begin winding up (see **4.21** below) unless the Board deems it to be consistent with meeting the PPF liabilities;

- any benefits which become payable must be reduced to the PPF level (where there are not sufficient funds to do so, the Board may make a loan);

- if pensionable service ceased at the beginning of the period, no scheme benefits may be paid in the period;

- if a pension sharing order is made on a member's divorce, the pension credit may be transferred into or out of the scheme.

The assessment period ends when the trustees are formally notified that the Board of the PPF is taking over the scheme, or the Board refuses responsibility for the scheme. Additionally, the assessment period ends in the following scenarios:

- the scheme is not being taken over by a new employer but it can pay benefits equal to the compensation that the PPF would otherwise have paid;

- the scheme is taken over by another employer.

At the end of the assessment period, if a valuation shows that the scheme has assets below PPF compensation levels and a scheme rescue is not possible, the Board of the PPF will assume responsibility for the scheme. The property, rights and liabilities transfer to the Board and the trustees or managers are discharged of their responsibilities towards the scheme. The Board is then responsible for providing compensation in accordance with compensation provisions. The scheme must follow the 'priority orders' which state how benefits are to be paid in the event of winding up. Any benefits paid above this level must be recovered.

Directions   4.9

The Board may give directions on investments, legal proceedings and expenses incurred during the assessment period. It may also instruct trustees, manager or employer, or the insolvency practitioner, on matters of spending, legal proceedings and – where the scheme is hybrid – the payment of money purchase benefits. *Hybrid* means a scheme where there is a mix of defined benefit and money purchase benefits.

Employer debt   4.10

Any right to an employer debt payment during the assessment period shall vest in the Board.

Ill-health pension   4.11

Any ill-health pension which was granted within three years before the assessment period, where the member would be entitled to 100% of the compensation under the PPF, may be reviewed. The *Pension Protection Fund (Reviewable Ill Health Pensions) Regulations 2005 (SI 2005/652)* describe the rules that apply.

Fines may be imposed on trustees who do not reach their decision on whether to pay such a pension for an existing application within six months of the commencement of the assessment period.

Transfer to the PPF   4.12

On the identification of a PPF deficit, subject to certain other requirements, responsibility for the scheme must vest in the Board. This is achieved by the issue of a transfer notice to the trustees by the Board, except where a fraud compensation payment is pending, or within the first twelve months of the assessment period.

On the transfer of the assets to the Board:

- the trustees will be discharged from their scheme obligations;
- the scheme will be deemed to have wound up;
- members will receive the available PPF benefits.

The draft Pension Protection Fund (Assumption of Responsibility, Discharge of Liability and Equal Treatment) Regulations 2006 contain the following provisions:

- Power for the Board to change contractual liabilities which transfer to it.
- Power for the Board to deal with the treatment of lump sum death-in-service benefits, where a member dies during the assessment period.
- Power for the Board to determine the rate of interest which shall be payable on overpayments and underpayments.
- Power for the Board to determine how money purchase liabilities can be discharged.

Multi-employer schemes, hybrid schemes and partially-guaranteed schemes   4.13

Special regulations apply to certain schemes:

- The *Pension Protection Fund (Multi-employer Schemes) (Modification) Regulations 2005 (SI 2005/441)*. These regulations state how the PPF applies to multiple-employer schemes, and to schemes which have separate segregated sections.

- The *Pension Protection Fund (Hybrid Schemes) (Modification) Regulations 2005 (SI 2005/449)* state how the PPF applies to hybrid schemes.

- The *Pension Protection Fund (Partially Guaranteed Schemes) (Modification) Regulations 2005 (SI 2005/277)* state how the PPF applies where a public authority has given a guarantee in relation to part of a scheme.

For schemes with non-associated employers, the entry rules for the PPF will depend on whether the scheme is segregated or non-segregated. Non-segregated schemes are where a group of employers pool their pension assets and liabilities, and the risk is shared by all the employers taking part in the scheme. Segregated schemes are schemes that are divided into sections which are effectively treated as separate schemes. Some segregated schemes may have more that one employer in each section.

The PPF will assess each circumstance on its own peculiar structure, and issue notices on winding up in circumstances of insolvency.

Funding the PPF   4.14

The PPF is funded by a composite levy. Payments can be made direct into the PPF bank account, which is detailed on its website: http://www.pensionprotectionfund.org.uk.

The levy comprises an administration levy, an initial levy, a PPF Ombudsman levy and a pension protection levy. The PPF also includes the pension assets of an insolvent employer. The *Pension Protection Fund (Payments to meet Investment Costs) Regulations 2005 (SI 2005/1610)* permit the Board to pay the costs of engaging fund managers and custodians.

The following Press Release (R/09) was published on 11 September 2006:

'Pension Protection Levy Proposals For 2007/08 Published

- Key objective is to provide stability to enable risk based levy regime to bed down

- Changes focus on improvements to practical processes

- 2007/08 levy estimate and changes to the levy scaling factor to be published later this year.

The Board of the Pension Protection Fund has today, Monday, 11 September, published its consultation document setting out proposals for the 2007/08 risk based levy.

The proposals reflect feedback from stakeholders during the 2006/07 levy consultation which called for stability in the second year, and operational experience of implementing the 2006/07 pension protection levy. The Board is therefore recommending limited changes to the way the levy is distributed between eligible schemes.

The proposed changes, which are consistent with the Board's principles of fairness, simplicity and proportionality, focus on the practical processes behind the levy, such as:

- revised standard documentation for contingent assets

- revised section 179 guidance; and

- revised approach to the inclusion of insured liabilities within section 179 valuations.

The document also highlights that the Board is working with D&B to consider whether aspects of the D&B methodology, such as the weighting applied to County Court Judgements, and the application of the methodology to certain types of employers such as large employers and the not-for-profit sector, need to be adjusted for the 2007/08 levy.

Pension Protection Fund Chief Executive, Partha Dasgupta said:

"The Board has been extremely encouraged by the response from industry to the introduction of the risk based levy, and is keen to promote stability to allow the risk based levy regime time to bed down.

"To encourage this stability, and support schemes and their sponsoring employers in implementing risk reduction plans, the Board is proposing limited changes to the way the levy is distributed between eligible schemes, focussing on improvements to practical processes."

The Board will publish its proposed levy estimate for 2007/08 and changes to the levy scaling factor later this year.

Ends.

Notes to editors

1.   Copies of "The 2007/08 Pension Protection Levy Consultation Document" can be found on the Pension Protection Fund's

website at http://www.pensionprotectionfund.org.uk/index/
pension_protection_levy-2/ppl_publications_200708.htm.
Responses to the consultation are requested by 9 October 2007.

2.   For 2007/08 the Board of the Pension Protection Fund
      proposes to make revisions to the way in which the levy is
      calculated. In summary these changes are:

      ●   Revised standard documentation for contingent assets,
           including new standard documentation for a Type C
           contingent asset (letter of credit or bank guarantee) in
           support of a schedule of deficit-reduction contributions;

      ●   Revised section 179 guidance, following earlier consulta-
           tion with the actuarial profession; and

      ●   A revised approach to the inclusion of insured liabilities
           within a section 179 valuation'.

The administration levy   4.15

The administration levy may be used to fund the establishment and ongoing
expenses and certain costs of the Board. The administration levy is set annually
by affirmative instrument. The *Occupational Pension Schemes (Levies) Regulations 2005 (SI 2005/842)* contain a table showing the rates of the administration levy for the financial year ending with 31 March 2006. The rates for
2006/07 are the same as those set for 2005/06, and no levy will be payable in
respect of the Pension Protection Fund Ombudsman for 2006/07.

Regulation 6 states that amount payable for a financial year, in respect of a
scheme with the number of members on the reference day that is specified in
column 1 of the table in *regulation 6(2)* for that year, is:

'(a)   the amount specified for such a scheme in column 2 of the table
        (where M is the number of the scheme's members on the
        reference day); or

(b)   if no amount is so specified or an amount which is greater is
        specified for such a scheme in column 3 of the table, that
        amount'.

Regulation 6(2) states:

'(2)   This is the table for the administration levy for the financial year
        ending with 31st March 2006 –

Column 1	Column 2	Column 3
Number of members on the reference day	Amount of levy calculated by reference to number of members (M)	Minimum amount of levy
2 to 11	–	£24
12 to 99	£2.50 x M	–
100 to 999	£1.80 x M	£250
1,000 to 4,999	£1.40 x M	£1,800
5,000 to 9,999	£1. 06 x M	£7,000
10,000 or more	£0.74 x M	£10,600

(3)   If, in any case where the reference day is determined in accordance with regulation 5(2) (31st March 2005), the number of members of the scheme on that day differs from the number according to the register compiled and maintained under regulations made under section 6 of the 1993 [Pension Schemes] Act, the number according to that register is to be taken as the number on that day for the purposes of these Regulations.

(4)   For schemes that are eligible schemes for only part of the financial year, see regulation 7.

Schemes eligible for only part of the financial year

7(1)   This regulation applies if a scheme that is not an eligible scheme at the beginning of a financial year becomes such a scheme during that year.

(2)   The amount of each of the levies payable in respect of the scheme for that year is such proportion of the full amount so payable as the period beginning with the date on which it becomes such a scheme and ending with the financial year bears to the whole financial year'.

The initial levy   4.16

The initial levy was payable on 6 April 2005. The *Occupational Pension Schemes (Levies) Regulations 2005 (SI 2005/842)* state that the levy was payable at a rate of £15 per member and pensioner, and £5 per deferred member and pension credit member who was not entitled to present payment of a pension as a result of his or her pension credit rights. The regulations have not been subject to any significant changes for the year 2006/07.

The PPF Ombudsman levy   4.17

The PPF Ombudsman levy was not payable in respect of the financial years ending with 31 March 2006 and 31 March 2007.

The pension protection levy and the replacement of the compensation levy   4.18

At least 80% of the pension protection (occupational scheme) levy must be risk-based. Schemes with fewer than 100 members are exempted from the risk-based element of the levy and will effectively pay a flat-rate levy. Schemes are also exempt from paying the risk-based element if they are more than 125% funded on a *s 179, Pensions Act 2004* basis. The remaining 20% comprises the scheme-based levy, which takes into account member numbers, pensionable earnings and scheme liabilities etc.

Guidance is available for anyone that is having to undertake a *section 179* valuation (to determine scheme underfunding) or a *section 143* valuation (relating to the Board of the PPF's obligation to obtain valuation of assets and protected liabilities) of a pension scheme under the *Pensions Act 2004*. This guidance can be found at: http://www.pensionprotectionfund.org.uk/index/other_guidance/valuation_guidance.htm.

The *Pension Protection Fund (Pension Protection Levies Consultation) Regulations 2005 (SI 2005/1440)* came into force on 20 June 2005. If a scheme submitted a PPF valuation prior to 31 March 2006, it will be charged a levy based on risk using the information provided in that valuation.

The earlier draft Pension Protection Levy and Miscellaneous Amendment Regulations are now included in *the Pension Protection Fund (General and Miscellaneous Amendments) Regulations 2006 (SI 2006/580)*. No changes were made to these specific regulations as a result of the consultation described in **4.24** below. The pension protection levy is payable by instalments unless the Board of the PPF agrees there are appropriate exceptional circumstances. The meaning of the 'financial year' for the purpose of the appropriate payment date is given in *s 175(9), Pensions Act 2004*.

It is possible that the Board may be given power to waive the levy in certain circumstances.

If a scheme transfer takes place mid-levy year and a further *s 179* valuation for both schemes is not submitted, information that the PPF will use to calculate the next year's levy for both schemes will be incorrect. It is highly possible that a new *section 179* valuation will not have been completed and so this situation is likely to arise. On becoming aware of the transfer, the PPF will issue a *s 191* notice, under the *Pensions Act 2004,* to allow the PPF to collect the correct information to take the transfer into account when calculating the risk-based levy for the next year. Material transfers of more than 5% of liabilities are notifiable events, which the scheme would be required to bring to the attention of the Pensions Regulator. Where material transfers have taken place prior to 1 April 2006, schemes are encouraged to advise the PPF voluntarily that this has occurred.

In circumstances where an employer operates several defined benefit schemes within the UK, which they merge within a single sectionalised scheme, if the old schemes cease to exist within the financial year they will be charged a full year's levy. The new scheme will be required to pay a proportion of the levy from the time it was established until the end of the financial year. However, it is likely that the Board would use its discretion in such cases to determine the levy to be nil under *s 175(7)*, provided that it is confident that the liabilities had been covered by the levy that was charged to the original schemes.

Risk-based levy 4.19

The risk-based levy has been attracting the greatest comment. In greater detail, the levy involves testing the strength of the employer using market appraisals of employer strength. These appraisals will be based on either credit-rating agencies or credit-scoring agencies. The following information has been obtained from the Board of the PPF.

Employers will be banded in a category, between 1 and 10, and assigned the following 1 year probability of failure:

Insolvency Band	Rating	Prob. (Insolvency)
1	aaa to a–	0.13%
2	bbb+ to bbb–	0.60%
3	bb+ to bb	1.25%
4	bb–	1.70%
5	–	2.35%
6	b+	3.40%
7	–	4.75%
8	b	6.60%
9	b–	9.75%
10	ccc	15.0%

Relative funding: Schemes must carry out the *s 179* valuations on a regular basis, and the scheme funding part of the levy will use the latest PPF valuation as its reference point. Until a PPF valuation is in place, the Board of the PPF will use the latest MFR valuation on an adjusted basis – although this may not allow for the specific detail of each scheme. In order for a PPF valuation to be taken into account for levy purposes, the trustees will need to file the PPF valuation before 31 December in the previous year.

The PPF valuation: The actuary must calculate the value of the PPF liabilities on the PPF basis, and the liabilities are the adjusted scheme liabilities. The PPF valuation basis is likely to use gilt yields as the start point for its assumptions, which is more conservative than say the FRS17 assumptions, which use corporate bonds. The basis also makes use of modern mortality tables and includes an expense allowance for the estimated wind up cost.

The calculation of the levy: The Board of the PPF calculates the amount of money it considers that it would require over the next year. This calculation takes into consideration any surplus or deficit within the PPF, as well as the likely number of new cases it will be required to take on and the estimated degree of underfunding within these schemes.

Estimate of the basic unadjusted risk-based levy: Each scheme then has to estimate the basic unadjusted risk-based levy due to them. The maximum amount which any scheme must pay is 3% of the PPF liabilities, which gives an adjusted premium table below:

Risk based levy per £1m of Pension Protection Fund liability

		Insolvency Risk									
		1	2	3	4	5	6	7	8	9	10
PPF fund- ing level	50%	572	2640	5500	7480	10340	14960	20900	29040	30000	30000
	55%	520	2400	5000	6800	9400	13600	19000	26400	30000	30000
	60%	468	2160	4500	6120	8460	12240	17100	23760	30000	30000
	65%	416	1920	4000	5440	7520	10880	15200	21120	30000	30000
	70%	364	1680	3500	4760	6580	9520	13300	18480	27300	30000
	75%	312	1440	3000	4080	5640	8160	11400	15840	23400	30000
	80%	260	1200	2500	3400	4700	6800	9500	13200	19500	30000
	85%	208	960	2000	2720	3760	5440	7600	10560	15600	24000
	90%	156	720	1500	2040	2820	4080	5700	7920	11700	18000
	95%	104	480	1000	1360	1880	2720	3800	5280	7800	12000
	100%	52	240	500	680	940	1360	1900	2640	3900	6000
	104%	10	48	100	136	188	272	380	528	780	1200
	110%	10	48	100	136	188	272	380	528	780	1200
	115%	10	48	100	136	188	272	380	528	780	1200
	120%	10	48	100	136	188	272	380	528	780	1200

So, a scheme which was 65% funded on the PPF basis, has a bbb– credit rating, and £27million of PPF liabilities, the PPF risk premium levy would be based upon 1920 x 27 = £52,000 (scaled up or down depending upon the assets required by the PPF in that year). However, if the funding ratio were:

- 55%, the levy would be £65,000; or

- 75% the levy would be £39,000.

If the rating were only bb and the funding was 65%, then the premium would be based upon a starting levy of £108,000.

The PPF risk-based levy is still the subject of debate. Nevertheless, the risk based-levy is dependent on the following factors:

- Any scaling up or down of the basic amount.

- The actual PPF liabilities of the pension scheme.

- The actual band assigned due to the credit rating.

- Changes to the above numbers/factors due to changes in the proposals.

- Whether the risk based levy is assigned the 80% value or some other percentage.

At present, it would appear that the nearer a pension scheme is to 104% funded on the PPF basis, the lower the risk based levy will be.

When considering whether or not request an early PPF valuation the following factors may be beneficial in terms of reduced levy:

- if contributions have increased significantly since the previous MFR valuation;

- if the Scheme has a large number of members with high liabilities which would be capped under the PPF.

The PPF assumed the functions of the Pensions Compensation Board for paying compensation to both defined benefit and money purchase schemes in cases of fraud and misappropriation of scheme assets (see **4.4** above). The compensation levy was still in place when the *Pension Act 2004* received royal assent, and was charged for the first year at the maximum rate of £23 per member. For the year 2006/07 the maximum level of £23 continues to apply under the replacement Fraud Compensation Fund.

Level of compensation, and capping   4.20

Compensation is for active and deferred members of underfunded defined benefit schemes whose employers go out of business, where there is no other employer to take over the scheme. The level of compensation for existing pensioners and persons over normal retirement age is 100% of the pension in payment, and 90% for persons below pension age. The maximum amount of compensation which could be paid for the year commencing 1 April 2005 was £27,777.78, so the 90% rate was £25,000 in the first year of retirement for persons retiring at age 65. With effect from 1 April 2006 the maximum amount of compensation payable was increased to £28,944.45.

The maximum amount of pension in payment is linked to:

- increases at 2.5% or the increase in the retail price index (RPI), if less, on post-5 April 1997 service;

- no pension increases on service before that date; and

- a 50% spouse's pension.

For persons under normal retirement age, increases between exit and normal retirement age are made at up to 5% pa. Pension increases are made at 2.5% (or RPI, if less) on post-5 April 1997 service, and there are no pension increases on service before that date.

The following additional circumstances apply:

- Any benefit improvements in the previous three years prior to entry to the PPF will be set aside.

- Ill-health pensions in payment will be paid at 100% irrespective of whether the person is over or under normal retirement age, although the Board of the PPF may revisit cases.

- Survivors' pensions in payment will continue at the 100% level.

Benefits are calculated by reference to:

- the member's age;

- the member's length of pensionable service;

- the scheme accrual rate which applies to the member.

- the member's pensionable earnings under the scheme.

No five-year guarantee lump sum may be paid by the PPF.

The **ANNEX** at the end of this chapter provides an example of compensation levels for a scheme which enters into an assessment period (see **4.19** above) for the year commencing 1 April 2006.

Notifying the Board of an insolvency 4.21

The Board of the PPF, the Pensions Regulator and the trustees must be notified by the administrator or insolvency practitioner on a voluntary basis within 14 days of the insolvency of the employer in the following circumstances:

- an employing company goes into administration;

- an administrative receiver is appointed in respect of an employing company;

- an employing company enters into a creditor's voluntary arrangement, or is wound up.

The Board must formally approve the notice of insolvency for it to be binding. In the event that the insolvency practitioner fails to issue a notice, the Board will do so. The insolvency practitioner must confirm whether there is no prospect of the scheme being taken over by another employer (this will give rise to the issue of a 'scheme failure notice'), or whether the scheme is being taken over by another employer (this will give rise to the issue of a 'withdrawal notice').

If insolvency proceedings are suspended and the insolvency practitioner cannot confirm whether or not the scheme can be taken over by another employer, he or she must confirm this to the PPF, the Pensions Regulator and the scheme's trustees. The PPF must then decide whether to take over the scheme. This depends on how likely it is that insolvency proceedings will start again in the next six months.

Details of the rules and timescales which apply are given in the *Pension Protection Fund* (*Provision of Information*) *Regulations 2005* (*SI 2005/674*) and the *Pension Protection Fund* (*Provision of Information*) (*Amendment*) *Regulations 2006* (*SI 2006/595*). The position for partnerships is described in the *Pension Protection Fund* (*Insolvent Partnerships*) (*Amendment of Insolvency Events*) *Order 2005* (*SI 2005/2893*).

Continuing a scheme as a closed scheme 4.22

There may be cases where there is no available successor-employer, there are sufficient scheme assets to purchase PPF benefits, but a buy-out quotation cannot be obtained from an insurance provider. In this event, the trustees must apply to the Board for permission to continue the scheme as a closed scheme. The Board may require periodic valuations to be obtained for closed schemes. If the assets fall below the PPF liabilities in the future, an application must be made for the Board to assume responsibility for the scheme.

Winding up, and transfer of assets to the PPF
4.23

The *Pensions Act 2004* effectively requires the relevant scheme to wind up and transfer its assets and liabilities to the PPF (see **4.11** above). This also applies to a scheme which, although it would otherwise meet the criteria to be treated as a qualifying scheme, does not have a PPF deficit, but for which a scheme rescue is not possible. The scheme wind-up will be deemed to have begun immediately before the commencement of the assessment period.

If a scheme is required to wind up, the trustees may apply to the Board for reconsideration. The application must be supported by audited accounts and an annuity quote which evidences that the scheme has a PPF deficit.

Appeals/reviews
4.24

The appeal procedure is initially operated by a review system. Applications must be made to the Board in writing. A written application to the Board to review its own determination will trigger a two-stage review procedure. In some cases, a determination may be suspended pending review. The Board also has power to vary or revoke its determination or to make a new one, and the Board may pay compensation in appropriate circumstances.

The PPF Ombudsman and the Deputy PPF Ombudsman are empowered to consider any matter reviewed by the Board, including complaints of maladministration. A dispute may be sent back to the Board with a direction on how to proceed.

Appeals may be made from the PPF Ombudsman to the High Court (or Court of Session in Scotland) on points of law.

The relevant regulations are listed in **4.25** below under their statutory instrument numbers:

SI 2005/600

SI 2005/650

SI 2005/669

SI 2005/824

SI 2005/2023

SI 2005/2024

Codes of practice 4.25

There are no codes of practice on the Pension Regulator's website for the PPF at present.

Significant consultative documents and reviews 4.26

A PPF levy consultation document was published in July 2005, in which the Board of the PPF sought responses to its proposals for the pension protection levy from April 2007, and its modified proposals for the financial year beginning in April 2006.

The document recognised that the new scheme funding requirements were expected to replace the MFR from September 2005, and the Board therefore proposed to use adapted MFR valuations for the 2006/07 financial year only. It also stated that, to promote fairness and the use of best evidence in future years, the Board proposed to ask the government to legislate to require all eligible schemes to provide *s 179, Pensions Act 1995*, valuations by 31 December 2006.

The Board also proposed to scale up the value of the PPF liabilities by 5% to reflect the fact that the Board is exposed to the volatility of scheme deficits during the year following a valuation. The Board further proposed to calculate an underfunding amount for schemes with a funding level greater than 104% that is equal to 1% of the value of PPF liabilities. This would reflect the lower possibility of a claim from these schemes, but take into account that such a claim is not impossible.

The consultation document stated that the Board had taken a wide range of matters into consideration in order to calculate the anticipated cost and impact of the Fund. The following chart, which was provided to the PPF by Opra, is of interest:

'Table 2 – Occupational pension schemes by number of members (in thousands)

Size of scheme by membership	Number of members at 31 March 2004 (in thousands)	As % of total members	Number of members as at 31 March 2003 (in thousands)	As % of total members
2–11	222	1.4%	241	1.5%
12–99	399	2.5%	449	2.8%
100–999	1,813	11.2%	1,862	11.6%
1000–4999	2,508	15.5%	2,488	15.6%
5000–9999	1,436	8.9%	1,390	8.7%

Size of scheme by membership	Number of members at 31 March 2004 (in thousands)	As % of total members	Number of members as at 31 March 2003 (in thousands)	As % of total members
10000+	9,766	60.5%	9,562	59.8%
Totals	16,144	100%	15,992	100%

The main developments since the consultation document are summarised below.

A PPF levy update consultation document was published in October 2005. The document stated that the PPF planned to publish a summary of consultation responses and its detailed final proposals on the pension protection levy. However, the Board had decided to communicate some aspects of its detailed proposals in an update paper to the earlier consultation document.

The main points of significance were:

- Calculations for schemes with multiple participating employers.

- The consideration of special contributions made to the pension scheme since the last formal valuation and modified guidance for completing a *s 179* valuation by 31 March 2006.

- The timetable for providing additional information to the Board.

There were useful annexes to the update paper. Of these, the following are of particular interest:

- A declaration of scheme structure form, with accompanying notes.

- A participating employers form.

- A *s 179* valuation certificate.

- An actuarial certificate of deficit-reduction contributions.

In April 2006 the Pensions Group of the DWP published the government's response to the PPF Regulations concerning the following matters:

- The draft Pension Protection Levy and Miscellaneous Amendment Regulations.

- The fraud compensation levy.

- The draft Levies (Administration & Pension Protection Fund Ombudsman) Compensation Regulations.

- The administration of compensation payments.

- Entry rules amendment.

- The assumption of responsibility, discharge of liabilities and equal treatment.

- Reviewable matters and the review and reconsideration of reviewable matters.

- The valuation of the PPF.

- Provision of information.

The response took into account comments received up until its publication, and included comments received after the consultation ended on 3 January 2006. It drew attention to the regulations which had come into force. The regulations referred to were *SI 2006/558*, *SI 2006/580*, *SI 2006/595*, *SI 2006/597*, *SI 2006/685* and *SI 2006/935*. The regulations are listed in **4.27** below, and named in full. *SI 2006/580* amalgamated five sets of draft regulations that were consulted on in November 2005.

The PPF is clearly going to be the subject of ongoing review. A consultative document entitled *Contributions Equivalent Premiums & Closed Schemes* was issued in July 2006, with a promise of more documents by year end on the following topics:

- Eligible schemes

- Waiver of levy

- Compensation provisions

- Reviewable matters

- Multi-employer schemes

- Miscellaneous technical amendments

Regulations   4.27

A list of the very large number of regulations and orders that have been issued in connection with the PPF is given below:

- the *Dissolution etc. (Pension Protection Fund) Regulations 2006* (*SI 2006/1934*);

- the *Divorce etc. (Pension Protection Fund) Regulations 2006 (SI 2006/1932)*;

- the *Occupational Pension Schemes (Fraud Compensation Levy) Regulations 2006 (SI 2006/558)*;

- the *Occupational Pension Schemes (Levies) Regulations 2005 (SI 2005/842)*;

- the *Occupational Pension Schemes (Levies) (Amendment) Regulations 2006* (*SI 2006/935*);

- the *Pension Protection Fund (Appointment of Ordinary Members) Regulations 2005 (SI 2005/616)*;

- the *Pension Protection Fund (Compensation) Regulations 2005 (SI 2005/670)*;

- the *Pension Protection Fund (Eligible Schemes) Appointed Day Order 2005 (SI 2005/599)*;

- the *Pension Protection Fund (Entry Rules) Regulations 2005 (SI 2005/590)*;

- the *Pension Protection Fund (Entry Rules) Amendment Regulations 2005 (SI 2005/2153)*;

- the *Pension Protection Fund (General and Miscellaneous Amendments) Regulations 2006 (SI 2006/580)*;

- the *Pension Protection Fund (Hybrid Schemes) (Modification) Regulations 2005 (SI 2005/449)*;

- the *Pension Protection Fund (Insolvent Partnerships) (Amendment of Insolvency Events) Order 2005 (SI 2005/2893)*;

- the *Pension Protection Fund (Investigation by PPF Ombudsman of Complaints of Maladministration) Regulations 2005 (SI 2005/2025)*;

- the *Pension Protection Fund (Limit on Borrowing) Order 2005 (SI 2005/339)*;

- the *Pension Protection Fund (Maladministration) Regulations 2005 (SI 2005/650)*;

- the *Occupational Pension Schemes (Modification of Pension Protection Provisions) Regulations 2005 (SI 2005/705)*;

- the *Pension Protection Fund (Multi-employer Schemes) (Modification) Regulations 2005 (SI 2005/441)*;

- the *Pension Protection Fund (Partially Guaranteed Schemes) (Modification) Regulations 2005 (SI 2005/277)*;

- the *Pension Protection Fund (Payments to meet Investment Costs) Regulations 2005 (SI 2005/1610)*;

- the *Pension Protection Fund (Pension Compensation Cap) Order 2006 (SI 2006/347)*;

- the *Pension Protection Fund (Pension Protection Levies Consultation) Regulations 2005 (SI 2005/1440)*;

- the *Pension Protection Fund (Pension Sharing) Regulations 2006 (SI 2006/1690)*;

- the *Pension Protection Fund (PPF Ombudsman) Order 2005 (SI 2005/824)*;

- the *Pension Protection Fund (PPF Ombudsman) Amendment Order 2005 (SI 2005/2023)*;

- the *Pension Protection Fund (Provision of Information) Regulations 2005 (SI 2005/674)*;

- the *Pension Protection Fund (Provision of Information) (Amendment) Regulations 2006 (SI 2006/595)*;

- the *Pension Protection Fund (Reference of Reviewable Matters to the PPF Ombudsman) Regulations 2005 (SI 2005/2024)*;

- the *Pension Protection Fund (Review and Reconsideration of Reviewable Matters) (SI 2005/669)*;

- the *Pension Protection Fund (Reviewable Ill Health Pensions) Regulations 2005 (SI 2005/652)*;

- the *Pension Protection Fund (Reviewable Matters) Regulations 2005 (SI 2005/600)*;

- the *Pension Protection Fund (Reviewable Matters and Review and Reconsideration of Reviewable Matters) (Amendment) Regulations 2006 (SI 2006/685)*;

- the *Pension Protection Fund (Risk-Based Pension Protection Levy) Regulations 2006 (SI 2006/672)*;

- the *Pension Protection Fund (Statement of Investment Principles) Regulations (SI 2005/675)*;

- the *Pension Protection Fund (Tax) Regulations 2006 (SI 2006/575)*;

- the *Pension Protection Fund (Tax) (2005–2006) Regulations 2005 (SI 2005/1907)*;

- the *Pension Protection Fund (Valuation) Regulations 2005 (SI 2005/672)*;

- the *Pension Protection Fund (Valuation of the Assets and Liabilities of the Pension Protection Fund) Regulations 2006 (SI 2006/597)*;

- the *Registered Pension Schemes (Authorised Payments) (Transfers to the Pension Protection Fund) Regulations 2006 (SI 2006/134)*.

NAPF Guide   4.28

The National Association of Pension Funds (NAPF), with the help of industry, produced a guide entitled *The Pension Protection Fund made Simple* in November 2005. This remains a useful reference source, although there have been further developments since its publication. The contents of this publication are shown below.

Contents of the NAPF guide

'Introduction

Summary

Which schemes are covered by the Pension Protection Fund?

How will compensation be paid?

- Members above the scheme's normal pension age or who have retired early because of ill health
- Members who have not retired yet or who are below the scheme's normal pension age
- Indexation
- Revaluation
- Survivor's pensions
- Dependent children
- Reducing compensation payments

How is a scheme taken over by the Pension Protection Fund?

- When an employer becomes insolvent, what needs to be done and who needs to do it?
- What happens if another employer takes over the scheme (known as a scheme rescue)?

What happens next?

- Practical tasks for scheme trustees during the assessment period
- Valuing assets and the protected liabilities
- When will the Pension Protection Fund stop being involved?
- When does the assessment period end?
- What happens when Pension Protection Fund stops being involved with a scheme?

Closed schemes

Schemes with more than one employer (multi-employer schemes)

Reconsideration

Maladministration

How is the Pension Protection Fund paid for?

- Administration and PPF Ombudsman levies
- Pension protection levies

- Investment borrowing and reports

Contacting the Pension Protection Fund

Appendix – Fraud Compensation Fund

Further information'

Conclusion   4.29

There are fears that the cost of the levies will discourage employers from providing final salary/defined benefit pension provision in the future. This is a difficult balancing act for government as the PPF at least offers some comfort to those members who have long lived in expectation of retiring on a reasonable pension in reward for their long years of past service. The cover for such persons is to be welcomed.

Annex

Tables of estimated compensation payable from the PPF

The following tables illustrate the possible compensation that might eventually be expected from the Pension Protection Fund (PPF) for a given level of pension accrued to date if the pension scheme concerned were to enter a PPF assessment period in the 2006/07 PPF year. The tables refer to active and deferred members who were under normal pension age at the assessment date.

They also illustrate the effect of the PPF compensation cap on the amount of eventual compensation payable. The PPF revalues the amount of pension accrued at the PPF assessment date in line with inflation from that date up to normal pension age, subject to a maximum of 5% per annum compound. The compensation cap, however, is increased each year in line with the rise in average earnings. This means that a deferred pension which is greater than the cap at the PPF assessment date will not necessarily have to be restricted at normal pension age, especially if inflation has been higher than 5% over the period. The compensation cap for the 2005/06 year was £27,777,78. The cap for the 2006/07 year is £28,944.45, an increase of 4.2%. The cap is adjusted for pension ages above and below age 65. The adjusted cap at age 60 is currently about 90.5% of the full cap amount. Adjustment factors for other ages above and below 60 can be found on the PPF website at: http://www.pensionprotectionfund.org.uk/compensation_cap_factors_-_september_2006.pdf. The figures in the body of each table show the estimated annual compensation that could be paid from the PPF at normal pension age in respect of an accrued pension shown in the left hand column for someone of current age shown in the top row. This is on the assumption that normal pension age is 65 (tables 1 to 3) or 60 (tables 4 to 6), the pension scheme concerned enters a PPF assessment period in the 2006/07 year and average earnings and inflation are as shown over the period from the assessment date until the member's normal pension age. The figures shown are 90% of the full amount or 90% of the cap as appropriate. Figures falling below the bold line have been affected by the compensation cap and restricted accordingly.

These tables are shown for illustrative purposes only. The amount of compensation actually payable can depend on other factors not considered here.

Table 1

Pension at assessment date	Age at assessment date								
	25	30	35	40	45	50	55	60	65
£5,000	£14,679	£12,662	£10,923	£9,422	£8,128	£7,011	£6,048	£5,217	£4,500
£10,000	£29,358	£25,325	£21,845	£18,844	£16,255	£14,022	£12,095	£10,433	£9,000
£15,000	£44,038	£37,987	£32,768	£28,266	£24,383	£21,033	£18,143	£15,650	£13,500
£20,000	£58,717	£50,650	£43,691	£37,688	£32,510	£28,043	£24,190	£20,867	£18,000
£25,000	£73,396	£63,312	£54,613	£47,110	£40,638	£35,054	£30,238	£26,084	£22,500
£30,000	£88,075	£75,974	£65,536	£56,532	£48,765	£42,065	£36,286	£31,300	£26,050
£35,000	£102,754	£88,637	£76,459	£65,954	£56,893	£49,076	£40,455	£32,463	£26,050
£40,000	£117,433	£101,299	£87,381	£75,376	£62,825	£50,414	£40,455	£32,463	£26,050
£45,000	£132,113	£113,961	£97,566	£78,292	£62,825	£50,414	£40,455	£32,463	£26,050
£50,000	£146,792	£121,584	£97,566	£78,292	£62,825	£50,414	£40,455	£32,463	£26,050
£55,000	£151,516	£121,584	£97,566	£78,292	£62,825	£50,414	£40,455	£32,463	£26,050
£60,000	£151,516	£121,584	£97,566	£78,292	£62,825	£50,414	£40,455	£32,463	£26,050

Assumptions

Normal pension age: 65

Average earnings increases (p.a.c.): 4.50%

Inflation (p.a.c.): 3.00%

Current compensation cap (2006/07): £28,944.45

Pension at assessment date includes scheme revaluation on deferred pension up to the start of the assessment period.

Table 2

Pension at assessment date	Age at assessment date								
	25	30	35	40	45	50	55	60	65
£5,000	£31,680	£24,822	£19,449	£15,239	£11,940	£9,355	£7,330	£5,743	£4,500
£10,000	£63,360	£49,644	£38,897	£30,477	£23,880	£18,710	£14,660	£11,487	£9,000
£15,000	£95,040	£74,466	£58,346	£45,716	£35,820	£28,066	£21,990	£17,230	£13,500
£20,000	£126,720	£99,288	£77,795	£60,954	£47,759	£37,421	£29,320	£22,973	£18,000
£25,000	£158,400	£124,110	£97,244	£76,193	£59,699	£46,776	£36,650	£28,716	£22,500
£30,000	£190,080	£148,932	£116,692	£91,432	£71,639	£56,131	£43,980	£34,460	£26,050
£35,000	£221,760	£173,754	£136,141	£106,670	£83,579	£65,486	£48,899	£35,691	£26,050
£40,000	£253,440	£198,577	£155,590	£121,909	£91,791	£66,996	£48,899	£35,691	£26,050
£45,000	£285,120	£223,399	£172,304	£125,762	£91,791	£66,996	£48,899	£35,691	£26,050
£50,000	£316,799	£236,072	£172,304	£125,762	£91,791	£66,996	£48,899	£35,691	£26,050
£55,000	£323,439	£236,072	£172,304	£125,762	£91,791	£66,996	£48,899	£35,691	£26,050
£60,000	£323,439	£236,072	£172,304	£125,762	£91,791	£66,996	£48,899	£35,691	£26,050

Assumptions

Normal pension age: 65

Average earnings increases (p.a.c.): 6.50%

Inflation (p.a.c.): 5.00%

Current compensation cap (2006/07): £28,944.45

Pension at assessment date includes scheme revaluation on deferred pension up to the start of the assessment period.

Table 3

Pension at assessment date	Age at assessment date								
	25	30	35	40	45	50	55	60	65
£5,000	£31,680	£24,822	£19,449	£15,239	£11,940	£9,355	£7,330	£5,743	£4,500
£10,000	£63,360	£49,644	£38,897	£30,477	£23,880	£18,710	£14,660	£11,487	£9,000
£15,000	£95,040	£74,466	£58,346	£45,716	£35,820	£28,066	£21,990	£17,230	£13,500
£20,000	£126,720	£99,288	£77,795	£60,954	£47,759	£37,421	£29,320	£22,973	£18,000
£25,000	£158,400	£124,110	£97,244	£76,193	£59,699	£46,776	£36,650	£28,716	£22,500
£30,000	£190,080	£148,932	£116,692	£91,432	£71,639	£56,131	£43,980	£34,460	£26,050
£35,000	£221,760	£173,754	£136,141	£106,670	£83,579	£65,486	£51,310	£39,170	£26,050
£40,000	£253,440	£198,577	£155,590	£121,909	£95,519	£74,841	£58,640	£39,170	£26,050
£45,000	£285,120	£223,399	£175,039	£137,147	£107,459	£84,197	£58,899	£39,170	£26,050
£50,000	£316,799	£248,221	£194,487	£152,386	£119,398	£88,563	£58,899	£39,170	£26,050
£55,000	£348,479	£273,043	£213,936	£167,625	£131,338	£88,563	£58,899	£39,170	£26,050
£60,000	£380,159	£297,865	£233,385	£182,863	£133,169	£88,563	£58,899	£39,170	£26,050

Assumptions

Normal pension age: 65

Average earnings increases (p.a.c.): 8.50%

Inflation (p.a.c.): 7.00%

Current compensation cap (2006/07): £28,944.45

Pension at assessment date includes scheme revaluation on deferred pension up to the start of the assessment period.

(Inflation capped at 5% p.a.c.)

125

Table 4

Pension at assessment date	Age at assessment date							
	25	30	35	40	45	50	55	60
£5,000	£12,662	£10,923	£9,422	£8,128	£7,011	£6,048	£5,217	£4,500
£10,000	£25,325	£21,845	£18,844	£16,255	£14,022	£12,095	£10,433	£9,000
£15,000	£37,987	£32,768	£28,266	£24,383	£21,033	£18,143	£15,650	£13,500
£20,000	£50,650	£43,691	£37,688	£32,510	£28,043	£24,190	£20,867	£18,000
£25,000	£63,312	£54,613	£47,110	£40,638	£35,054	£30,238	£26,084	£22,500
£30,000	£75,974	£65,536	£56,532	£48,765	£42,065	£36,286	£29,400	£23,592
£35,000	£88,637	£76,459	£65,954	£56,893	£45,658	£36,638	£29,400	£23,592
£40,000	£101,299	£87,381	£70,905	£56,898	£45,658	£36,638	£29,400	£23,592
£45,000	£110,114	£88,361	£70,905	£56,898	£45,658	£36,638	£29,400	£23,592
£50,000	£110,114	£88,361	£70,905	£56,898	£45,658	£36,638	£29,400	£23,592
£55,000	£110,114	£88,361	£70,905	£56,898	£45,658	£36,638	£29,400	£23,592
£60,000	£110,114	£88,361	£70,905	£56,898	£45,658	£36,638	£29,400	£23,592

Assumptions

Normal pension age: 60

Average earnings increases (p.a.c.): 4.50%

Inflation (p.a.c.): 3.00%

Current compensation cap (2006/07): £26,213.74★

Pension at assessment date includes scheme revaluation on deferred pension up to the start of the assessment period.

★ £28,944.45 x 0.9056568 age 60 cap adjustment factor (adjustment factors are subject to change)

Table 5

Pension at assessment date	Age at assessment date							
	25	30	35	40	45	50	55	60
£5,000	£24,822	£19,449	£15,239	£11,940	£9,355	£7,330	£5,743	£4,500
£10,000	£49,644	£38,897	£30,477	£23,880	£18,710	£14,660	£11,487	£9,000
£15,000	£74,466	£58,346	£45,716	£35,820	£28,066	£21,990	£17,230	£13,500
£20,000	£99,288	£77,795	£60,954	£47,759	£37,421	£29,320	£22,973	£18,000
£25,000	£124,110	£97,244	£76,193	£59,699	£46,776	£36,650	£28,716	£22,500
£30,000	£148,932	£116,692	£91,432	£71,639	£56,131	£43,980	£32,324	£23,592
£35,000	£173,754	£136,141	£106,670	£83,131	£60,676	£44,286	£32,324	£23,592
£40,000	£198,577	£155,590	£113,897	£83,131	£60,676	£44,286	£32,324	£23,592
£45,000	£213,800	£156,049	£113,897	£83,131	£60,676	£44,286	£32,324	£23,592
£50,000	£213,800	£156,049	£113,897	£83,131	£60,676	£44,286	£32,324	£23,592
£55,000	£213,800	£156,049	£113,897	£83,131	£60,676	£44,286	£32,324	£23,592
£60,000	£213,800	£156,049	£113,897	£83,131	£60,676	£44,286	£32,324	£23,592

Assumptions

Normal pension age: 60

Average earnings increases (p.a.c.): 6.50%

Inflation (p.a.c.): 5.00%

Current compensation cap (2006/07): £26,213.74*

Pension at assessment date includes scheme revaluation on deferred pension up to the start of the assessment period.

* £28,944.45 x 0.9056568 age 60 cap adjustment factor (adjustment factors are subject to change).

Table 6

Pension at assessment date	Age at assessment date							
	25	30	35	40	45	50	55	60
£5,000	£24,822	£19,449	£15,239	£11,940	£9,355	£7,330	£5,743	£4,500
£10,000	£49,644	£38,897	£30,477	£23,880	£18,710	£14,660	£11,487	£9,000
£15,000	£74,466	£58,346	£45,716	£35,820	£28,066	£21,990	£17,230	£13,500
£20,000	£99,288	£77,795	£60,954	£47,759	£37,421	£29,320	£22,973	£18,000
£25,000	£124,110	£97,244	£76,193	£59,699	£46,776	£36,650	£28,716	£22,500
£30,000	£148,932	£116,692	£91,432	£71,639	£56,131	£43,980	£34,460	£23,592
£35,000	£173,754	£136,141	£106,670	£83,579	£65,486	£51,310	£35,475	£23,592
£40,000	£198,577	£155,590	£121,909	£95,519	£74,841	£53,342	£35,475	£23,592
£45,000	£223,399	£175,039	£137,147	£107,459	£80,208	£53,342	£35,475	£23,592
£50,000	£248,221	£194,487	£152,386	£119,398	£80,208	£53,342	£35,475	£23,592
£55,000	£273,043	£213,936	£167,625	£120,605	£80,208	£53,342	£35,475	£23,592
£60,000	£297,865	£233,385	£181,349	£120,605	£80,208	£53,342	£35,475	£23,592

Assumptions

Normal pension age: 60

Average earnings increases (p.a.c.): 8.50%

Inflation (p.a.c.): 7.00%

Current compensation cap (2006/07): £26,213.74★

Pension at assessment date includes scheme revaluation on deferred pension up to the start of the assessment period.

★ £28,944.45 x 0.9056568 age 60 cap adjustment factor (adjustment factors are subject to change).

(inflation capped at 5% p.a.c.)

Chapter 5
Scheme funding

Background   5.1

Part 3 of the *Pensions Act 2004* (*ss 221–233*) deals specifically with scheme funding. The concept of a new scheme-specific funding objective, primarily for defined benefits schemes (but including some hybrid schemes with a final salary/defined benefit promise), has been around for many years. The government declared its intent in December 2002 to replace the old minimum funding requirement (MFR) under the *Pensions Act 1995* with a funding approach that would consider the individual circumstances of schemes and also move to an appropriate strategy for meeting those commitments. There had been concerns that there was too much focus on the impact of these short-term market conditions under the existing method (see **CHAPTER 2** for a further discussion of the MFR and the background behind the new funding standard). Among other things, the government has had to take into account the provisions of EU Directive 2003/41/EC on the Activities and Supervision of Institutions for Occupational Retirement Provision (the 'IORP Directive') with regard to the funding of defined benefit schemes.

What has changed?   5.2

The minimum funding requirement is now in the process of being replaced by a new statutory funding objective as envisaged by the *Pensions Act 2004*. The statutory funding objective is described in **5.7** below. As the statutory funding objective was delayed beyond 23 September 2005 (the formal date for compliance with the IORP Directive), the minimum funding requirement transitional period was extended to 6 April 2006 by the *Occupational Pension Schemes (Minimum Funding Requirement and Actuarial Valuations) Amendment Regulations 2004 (SI 2004/3031)*.

While the main purpose of the new statutory funding objective was ostensibly to comply with the IORP Directive, attention was also given to the recommendations in the Myners Report on institutional investment. One of those recommendations, which was first proposed in November 2000, was the replacement of the minimum funding requirement because of the way in which it distorted trustee decision-making. The new objective applies primarily to defined benefit schemes. As it is scheme-specific, there is more flexibility to take into account a scheme's investment policy, the age profile of members, staff turnover and likely future salary increases etc when determining the most appropriate funding strategy for that scheme.

There must be an accompanying statement of funding principles (see **5.10** below) and actuarial valuations at least once every three years, with annual reports in the interim updating the actuarial position (see **5.13** below). The main elements of the new funding requirements may be summarised as follows:

- the new scheme statutory funding objective;

- the statement of funding principles;

- the schedule of contributions;

- actuarial valuations and annual reviews;

- ongoing actuarial valuations and solvency reviews;

- actuarial statements;

- dealing with deficiencies, and the new recovery plan;

- specific powers of the Pensions Regulator.

The main regulations which bring into effect the new statutory funding objective are the *Occupational Pension Schemes (Scheme Funding) Regulations 2005 (SI 2005/3377)* – see **5.13** below. The *Occupational Pension Schemes (Employer Debt) Regulations 2005 (SI 2005/678)* replaced the *Occupational Pension Schemes (Deficiency on Winding Up etc) Regulations 1996 (SI 1996/3128)* where debts arose under *s 75, Pensions Act 1995* in respect of occupational pension schemes (see **5.23** below). The regulations broadly required the liabilities of schemes to be valued on the basis that the trustees or managers will secure benefits at buy-out value. This was in keeping with the spirit of the IORP Directive, but caused considerable concern about the impact such a requirement would have on the future for defined benefit schemes on a cost basis. Consolidating regulation had effect from 2 September 2005, which gave some scope for the situation to be reviewed by the Pensions Regulator (see **5.23** below).

In addition, the Pensions Regulator has published various Codes of Practice on its website: http://www.thepensionsregulator.gov.uk. The main relevant codes of practice are:

Code of Practice 03 – Funding Defined Benefits   5.3

This is the main code which assists trustees in complying with the new requirements, and it also explains their duty to disclose information concerning scheme funding provisions within reasonable periods. The code came into force on 15 February 2006. The key elements of the code are the statement of funding principles, actuarial valuations and reports, schedules of contributions and the recovery plan. It also covers the reporting of late contributions for schemes which have had a valuation carried out under the new funding regime. For more information, see **5.9** below.

Code of Practice 05 – Reporting Payments of Contributions to Occupational Money Purchase Schemes 5.4

This code provides guidelines for trustees of occupational money purchase schemes and reporting the late payment of contributions from 6 April 2006. The report must be made to the Pensions Regulator and the members where the late payment is likely to be of material significance to the Regulator. It places a high degree of responsibility on the trustees in exercising their judgement on whether or not they need to make a report, and provides some practical examples of when trustees should and should not report. Further details are given in **7.68** below.

Code of Practice 06 – Reporting Late Payment of Contributions to Personal Pensions 5.5

This code is similar in effect to Code of Practice 05, and concerns the need for managers to make reports to the Regulator. Further details are given in **7.70** below.

Regulator Briefing No 1 – Reporting Late Payment to Occupational Schemes 5.6

This briefing covers the reporting of late contributions to defined benefit schemes up until the time when a valuation is carried out under the new funding regime. It also covers the reporting of late contributions to occupational money purchase schemes up until 6 April 2006. Further details are given in **7.69** below.

Statutory funding objective 5.7

The scheme-specific statutory funding objective is a primary driver behind the funding changes brought in by the *Pensions Act 2004*. The new statutory funding objective was to be introduced from 23 September 2005 in order to meet the requirements of the IORP Directive. However, matters were delayed and the appointment date under the *Pensions Act 2004* (*Commencement No. 8*)

Order 2005 (SI 2005/3331) was 30 December 2005. This governing legislation applies to actuarial valuations from 22 September 2005. Schemes which started a valuation between 22 September 2005 and 30 December 2005 are allowed 18 months to complete their first valuation under the new regime, as opposed to the usual 15 months.

The statutory funding objective is an objective to have sufficient and appropriate assets to cover a scheme's technical provisions. The term 'technical provisions' has been taken from the IORP Directive. The *Pensions Act 2004* defines it as meaning 'the amount that is required, on an actuarial calculation, to make provision for the scheme's liabilities' (see **5.9** below). The Act requires trustees to obtain the employers' agreement to the method of calculation used in the technical provisions and to report to the Pensions Regulator should they fail to do so. There is also a requirement to obtain actuarial advice and to act prudently, adopting an accrued funding method. Employer consent to the scheme's technical provisions' method of calculation will be satisfied where the rates of contributions payable by the employer are determined by the trustees or managers without the agreement of the employer, and no person other than the trustees or managers is permitted to reduce those rates or to suspend payments of contributions.

Trustees or managers must maintain a schedule of contributions (see **5.12** below) for the scheme and a recovery plan must be put in place; where appropriate (see **5.17** below).

As an aside, the *Occupational Pension Schemes (Regulatory Own Funds) Regulations 2005 (SI 2005/3380)* modify the funding regulations in circumstances where the scheme itself (as opposed to a sponsor such as an employer) underwrites the liability to cover against biometric risk, guarantees an investment performance or guarantees a certain level of performance. These schemes must hold additional assets over the technical provisions (which are referred to in the IORP Directive) 'to absorb discrepancies made between the anticipated and actual expenses and profits of the scheme' . The method of doing this is described in the modifying regulations. According to the response to the government's consultation process on regulatory own funds, there are no such schemes in the UK, but the regulations were laid anyway as a guard against possible cases arising in the future.

Where the statutory funding objective has not been met, there must nevertheless still be a formal statement of funding principles (see **5.10** below) signed by the trustees or managers and the employer.

There are certain exemptions from the new statutory funding objective. In the main, the objective applies to all defined benefits schemes, and for all actuarial valuations which are conducted for such schemes with effective dates on or after 22 September 2005. The exemptions are as follows:

- money purchase schemes;

- schemes established under an enactment and guaranteed by public authority;

- pay-as-you–go schemes;

- schemes which provide pensions for members of the House of Commons etc;

- schemes established in the UK to provide benefits for members in employment outside the UK;

- schemes with fewer than 100 members which are not tax registered;

- schemes with fewer than two members;

- schemes with fewer than twelve members where all members are trustees and unanimous decisions are required, or there is an independent trustee;

- schemes providing insured death benefits only;

- schemes which are under assessment for qualification for the Pension Protection Fund;

- schemes which are in the process of winding up, subject to annual solvency estimates being provided by the actuary;

- the Chatsworth Settlement Estate Pension Scheme.

The application of the funding regulations for multi-employer schemes etc 5.8

For the purpose of the *Occupational Pensions Schemes (Scheme Funding) Regulations 2005 (SI 2005/3377)*:

- In the case of multi-employer schemes, each section of the scheme will be treated as if it were a separate scheme (see also **7.53** below, concerning consultation with the employer).

- If at least one of the sections of the scheme applies to members who are no longer in pensionable service and the scheme provisions have not been amended, it shall still be determined to be a multi-employer scheme. A multi-employer scheme is a scheme with more than one employer with segregated assets and liabilities which fall into separate sections. The sections must have no cross–subsidy between them, and each is treated as a separate scheme for the purpose of the *Pensions Act 2004*.

- There are special provisions for schemes with separate death benefits sections.

- In respect of frozen or paid-up schemes, the regulations apply to the person who was the employer immediately before the occurrence of the event after which the scheme ceased to have any members.

133

- There are special provisions for schemes covering UK and foreign employment, depending on where the main administration of the scheme is situated.

The treatment of multi-employer schemes on winding up and partial winding up is described in **5.23** below.

There are also special provisions where the trustees or managers of the scheme are authorised under *s 288* of the *Pensions Act 2004* to accept contributions from European employers, or are approved under *s 289* of the Act to accept contributions from a particular European employer. However, cross-border schemes in the EU have stringent funding requirements. Such schemes must obtain annual actuarial valuations which are signed by the scheme actuary and delivered to the trustees within twelve months of the valuation's effective date. In addition, shortfalls in the scheme funding must be made good within two years of that date.

Funding defined benefits – general {#funding 5.9}

The key elements of Code of Practice 03 for funding defined benefit schemes are described at **5.3** and **5.8** above. A more detailed analysis of the code's contents is given under the appropriate headings below. In addition:

- Agreement with a sponsoring employer is normally required for a statement of funding principles (see **5.10** below), any recovery plan (see **5.17** below) and a schedule of contributions (see **5.12** below).

- The actuary would generally follow the trustees' instructions. Wherever the term 'trustees' is used; it should be taken to be a reference to trustees or managers.

- For the purpose of the technical provisions (see **5.7** above), benefits include pensions in payment, including those paid to survivors of former members, and benefits accrued by other members which will become payable in the future. From the actuarial viewpoint, market and scheme-specific factors will be relevant, particularly the interest rate which is used to discount the benefit payments (which should be chosen on a prudent basis, taking into account either or both of the yields available on the schemes assets and the market redemption yields on gilts or high-quality corporate bonds). Mortality and other demographic rates should be prudent and be relevant to the types of members in the scheme.

- Trustees of schemes with at least 100 members had to issue an *initial summary funding statement* before 22 September 2006, with an updated statement following in each subsequent year.

- Scheme's *funding statements* are described in **5.10** below. They must contain an explanation of any change in the funding position as this will be the members' principal source of information on funding matters. The Regulator's website contains guidance as to the proper content of such statements.

- Information must also be provided within a reasonable period to the Regulator. The period will also be dependent on the circumstances. Further details of the information contained in the code of practice are given under the specific headings to which they relate below.

Statement of funding principles, and the summary of funding statements

Statement of funding principles   5.10

The production of a written statement of funding principles is the responsibility of the trustees or managers. The statement must set out the policy by which the statutory funding objective is to be met, the methods and assumptions used and the period over which any deficit will be made good. Among other things, the statement should cover the following main points:

- Any scheme-specific funding methods in addition to the statutory funding objective.

- Whether persons other than the employer or members may contribute and the level of such contributions.

- Whether monies may be repaid to the employer out of the scheme and under what circumstances.

- Whether there is discretionary power to provide benefits for members and, if so, to what extent this has been taken into account in the funding objective.

- The trustees' or managers' policy on reducing cash equivalents in respect of deficient scheme funding levels.

- The incidence of obtaining actuarial valuations and whether there will be intermediate valuations sought in any circumstance.

Code of Practice 03 (see **5.3** above) requires the trustees or managers to include in the statement of funding principles any decisions they have taken about the method and timescale for eliminating a deficit. This information must include an explanation of the assumptions that have been used. The statement can be structured in two separate ways, as is the case for a statement of investment principles. To explain, a statement could be produced with retrospective effect in order to document decisions which were made along the way in conducting an actuarial valuation. Alternatively, the decisions that are made can be documented throughout the process which means that the statement would become an audit trial of the valuation process which has been undertaken. This latter approach has similar advantages to that of a statement of investment principles in that it is a document which reflects what has happened rather that just a document which has to be prepared for compliance purposes.

It is possible to combine the statement of funding principles with a statement of investment principles. However, note that the separate requirements for agreement of, and consultation with, the employer still need to be satisfied as they apply to the statement of funding principles and the statement of investment principles respectively.

The summary funding statement must be sent to all members and beneficiaries annually within a reasonable period of receipt of the actuarial valuation or actuarial report by the trustees. The Regulator has suggested that a reasonable period would normally be three months of receipt of such a valuation or report. The first statement had to be issued by 21 September 2006. The main principles to be covered will depend on the circumstances of the scheme, and guidelines are given below:

- the extent to which scheme assets are able to cover the scheme's technical provisions;

- an explanation of the change in the scheme funding position since the last valuation;

- the actuary's explanation of solvency at the last valuation, where this is the first summary funding statement;

- a summary of any recovery plan which is in place;

- whether the scheme has been subject to modification, direction or the imposition of a schedule of contributions by the Regulator as a result of a failure to comply with the *Pensions Act 2004* by the trustees, or the inability of the actuary to provide any certification or material failure of the employer to make payment(s) in accordance with the schedule of contributions;

- a statement as to whether any refund of surplus has been made to the employer during the twelve months prior to preparing the statement (or for subsequent statements during the period since the date of the previous statement) and the amount of any such payment.

See **ANNEX 1** at the back of this chapter for an example of a statement of funding principles, taken from the Pensions Regulator's website.

Summary funding statements   5.11

Scheme trustees must also provide all members and beneficiaries with regular summary funding statements. The initial summary funding statements had to be issued before 22 September 2006, followed by updated statements in each subsequent year prior to a scheme's first valuation under the new regime. The

Regulator's website contains guidance on this matter and clarifies the need for such statements which are issued before a scheme has had its first actuarial valuation under the new statutory funding regime.

Statements must include an explanation of any changes to the scheme's funding position. Clearly, there will be a change from the minimum funding requirement (MFR) basis to the statutory funding objective, but trustees are not required to obtain additional specific actuarial calculations in order to identify whether that change has occurred since the last MFR valuation (except where known changes for some other scheme purpose have taken place). Trustees of hybrid schemes need not issue summary funding statements to members who have solely money purchase benefits.

See **ANNEXES 2** and **3** at the back of this chapter for examples of summary funding statements, which cover the post and pre-new regime, taken from the Pensions Regulator's website.

Schedule of contributions   5.12

Under *s 227, Pensions Act 2004*, the trustees or managers must provide a schedule of contributions to which the statutory funding objective applies. The schedule of contributions must be prepared and agreed (or, for ones already in place, reviewed and revised if necessary) with 15 months of each actuarial valuation, unless a shorter period is directed by the Pensions Regulator due to a failure by the trustees to comply with *Pt 3, Pensions Act 2004*, or a payment failure in respect of an existing schedule of contributions.

If the trustees or managers and the sponsoring employer cannot agree on the amount required to meet the statutory funding objective within a period of 12 of 15 months (as described in **5.7** above) from the date of certification, or such longer period which relates to a recovery plan, the Pensions Regulator has the power of last resort to help to resolve matters. This also applies to a statement of funding principles (see **5.10** above) and a recovery plan (see **5.17** below) as well as to a schedule of contributions. There is no default position; the Regulator must take appropriate action. However, the trustees are expected to endeavour to agree with the employer on modifications to the benefit accrual so that the employer can agree to the documentation. This is for the purpose of ensuring that accrued benefits to date are secure and properly funded. Trustees and the employer must not only consult on the contribution levels but also consider future benefit accrual. Code of Practice 03 (see **5.3** above) provides additional guidance. The main principles are:

- where the trustees have the power to determine a contribution rate, and no other person has the power to reduce or suspend contributions, they must consult the employer but they do not require the employer's agreement;

- where the trustees have power to determine the contribution rate and no other person has the power to reduce or suspend those contributions, but the trustees' power is subject to certain conditions, on meeting those conditions the trustees must consult the employer but they do not require the employer's agreement;

- where the contributions are determined by, or on the advice of, a person other than the trustees or the employer (this is uncommon, but it may, for example, be the actuary) the trustees must obtain the employer's agreement. They must also take into account the other person's recommendation of the method and assumptions used for calculating the technical provisions and the preparation of any recovery plan.

For the record, money purchase schemes continue to operate on a schedule of payments approach.

Trustees and managers must disclose information within reasonable periods (see **5.3** above).

The contents of the schedule of contributions should be as follows:

- An explanation of the rates of employer and employee contributions due, and the dates on which they are due. The separation between employee contributions and member contributions must be made clear, and the employer contributions must be split between the ordinary contributions and the special contributions which are required in order to comply with the recovery plan. The schedule should also cover the treatment of the Pension Protection Fund levy, state whether it is included in the overall employer contribution or is paid in addition and explain the basis of its assessment. The trustees should also be able to monitor the payments being made into the scheme without having to refer to other documents. To enable them to do this, the due payment date of contributions should be clearly stated, and the trustees will need to monitor this under the *Occupational Pension Schemes* (*Scheme Administration*) *Regulations 1996* (*SI 1996/1715*). This means that employee contributions are paid in on the 19th of the month which follows the month in which they were deducted. The schedule of contributions must be signed by the trustees, and must contain a statutory certificate as set out in *Schedule 1* to the *Occupational Pensions Schemes* (*Scheme Funding*) *Regulations 2005* (*SI 2005/3377*). There should also be provision for the employer to sign the schedule.

- An actuarial certification that the scheme is consistent with the statement of funding principles and expects to meet the statutory funding objective throughout the period of the schedule.

- If a recovery plan is in force, then the expectation must be that the statutory funding objective will be met by the time of the end of the recovery plan period.

In the event that the statutory funding objective is not met within the required period, a report must be sent to the Regulator. Similarly, where employer or employee contributions are not made in time, reports are required (see **5.4** and **5.5** above, and **7.67** below).

The PPF levy should be treated as an annual expense item in the schedule. This means that, even where it is included in the sponsoring employer's overall contribution rate, the schedule of contributions should include a note to this effect and indicate the assumed annual amount incorporated for such a purpose.

There should be a robust procedure for monitoring receipt of contributions. See **ANNEX 4** at the back of this chapter for a sample schedule of contributions, taken from the Pensions Regulator's website.

Actuarial valuations and annual reviews   5.13

Actuarial valuations must be completed annually, or every three years if interim reports are received at least annually, concerning the scheme's technical provisions for meeting the statutory funding objective. Interim reports are not required for schemes with fewer than 100 members. Schemes with fewer than 100 members on the effective date of the last actuarial valuation only need to obtain actuarial reports on the anniversary between the valuations if the scheme membership exceeds 100 at anytime during the year. Additionally, the scheme is not required to obtain a summary funding statement (see **5.11** above).

Valuations must be made available to the sponsoring employer within seven days of the trustees receiving them. They must certify that the actuary, in his or her opinion, believes that the scheme has met the required calculation of the technical provisions in accordance with prescribed requirements. Details of the content and timing of the actuary's report, and a specimen actuary's certificate, are contained in the *Occupational Pension Schemes (Scheme Funding) Regulations 2005 (SI 2005/3377)*. Actuarial valuations must be received by the trustees within 15 months of the effective date, and actuarial reports within 12 months of the effective date. They must include a prescribed actuarial certification of the technical provisions.

If the contribution rate which is payable to the scheme by the employer is subject to the consent of the Secretary of State for Defence or some person authorised by him, all valuation reports that the trustees receive must be made available to such a person with seven days of the trustees receiving them.

Actuarial guidance note GN49 (see **APPENDIX 5**) lists matters on which the advice of the actuary should be sought by trustees and managers on scheme funding matters. The guidance note is published by the Institute of Actuaries and the Faculty of Actuaries and is entitled *Occupational Pensions Schemes – Scheme Funding Matters on which Advice of Actuary Must be Obtained*. In summary, the relevant matters are:

- making decisions concerning the statutory funding objective;

- the statement of funding principles;

- any recovery plan;

- the schedule of contributions;

- modifications which affect future accrual, where the sponsoring employer's agreement has not been obtained to any of the above.

Under Code of Practice 03, the trustees and managers are responsible for managing the process of actuarial valuations, and an *action plan* (see **5.14** below) is recommended to ensure actuarial valuations are completed on time. In normal circumstances the required period shall be no longer than 15 months from the effective date of the valuation. Trustees and managers are warned to be alert to circumstances in which they may need further actuarial advice, and be receptive to any further information provided by the actuary that he or she considers relevant in the circumstances.

Action plan 5.14

The main steps that concern the trustees in relation to an action plan and scheme funding include the following:

- discussing the methods and assumptions to be used for the valuation with the scheme actuary;

- preparing the statement of funding principles;

- ensuring that the scheme actuary carries out the valuation within the statutory time limits;

- discussing possible recovery plans firstly with the scheme actuary and then with the employer, and ensuring that the plan is properly documented once it has been agreed;

- setting out their wishes for future contribution levels in a contributions schedule, and getting the agreement to the schedule from the employer;

- considering any appropriate action, which may include modifying future benefits if they are unable to agree with the employer on a contributions schedule;

- submitting all required information to the Pensions Regulator.

There is likely to be a period of settling in under the new statutory funding regime, and the trustees will have to be realistic in the time that they target their objectives. In order to ensure that the timescales may be met, it is of key importance that the scheme administrator has all member data available at the effective date of the valuation. The actuary must be content with the standard of the information that is provided to him if he is to undertake his calculations accurately.

If there are any areas of disagreement between the employer and the trustees which cannot be easily be resolved, it is likely that they will both need to seek separate advice on a professional basis. It has long been undesirable for an actuary to act for both an employer and for the scheme trustees, and this is even more relevant now that a new funding regime has been introduced. Code of Practice 03 discriminates between advice and actuarial and numerical calculation. This is for the purpose of avoiding unnecessary costs incurred by duplication of work. Accordingly, it recognises that an employer make take its own actuarial advice but may use numerical calculations which have been carried out by the scheme actuary, and the general principle that trustees must make information available to the employer about any matter which may be considered relevant to the employer fulfilling its duties under the scheme.

Ongoing valuations and solvency reviews   5.15

The normal procedure to be followed for ongoing valuations under the actuarial process is:

- preparation of data by the administrator and checking by the actuary;

- reconciliation of membership movements between valuations;

- receipt of accounts, which for statutory funding objective purposes means that assets must be audited;

- calculation of assets and liabilities by the actuary;

- analysis of a surplus where this is required by the scheme rules, and reconciliation of results with the previous valuation with a view to explaining how the financial position has changed;

- discussion of preliminary results;

- costing of any benefit improvements;

- preparation of a formal report;

- preparation and agreement of a schedule of contributions.

A solvency valuation must be provided which considers the technical provisions which relate to the financial position of the scheme in order to meet its liabilities. The actuary shall calculate the position in accordance with the actuarial guidance notes and shall issue a solvency certificate. A recovery plan must be put in place by the trustees if the statutory funding objective is not met, as described in **5.17** below.

Actuarial statements for accounts 5.16

The actuary must provide two reports, both on a prescribed basis, for inclusion in the trustee's annual report and accounts:

- a statement concerning prescribed aspects of the latest actuarial valuation; and

- a copy of the latest contribution certificate as required for compliance with the statutory funding objective.

The recovery plan, financial support directions and restitution orders

Recovery plan 5.17

If a scheme fails to meet the new statutory funding objective it must establish a recovery plan which specifies a period over which the deficit will be made good. A copy of the recovery plan must be sent to the Pensions Regulator, and civil penalties may be incurred under *s 10, Pensions Act 1995,* on a failure to comply.

The general rules which apply to the recovery plan are that it must be put in place by the trustees and set out how the statutory funding objective is to be met and over what period. It must be agreed with the employer, and if this cannot be done, this must be reported to the Pensions Regulator. The trustees or managers must also take actuarial advice.

The following considerations must be taken into account upon preparing the plan:

- the scheme assets and liability structure;

- the scheme liquidity requirements;

- the scheme risk profile;

- the business plans of the employer, and the effects that the recovery plan would have on the future viability of the employer;

- how effective the trustees would be in pursuing the employer to make good a deficiency should it determine to wind up the scheme;

- the financial position of the employer and its ongoing commitments;

- a valuation of any contingent securities which the employer has provided, and the nature of the securities, in the event of an enforced wind-up of the scheme;

- the amount and type of any employer-related investments;

- the effect of the assumptions in the recovery plan not being borne out by experience;

- the age profile of the members of the scheme;

- the recommendations of any person who advises on employer contributions, other than the trustees or managers, without the agreement of the employer.

The use of contingent securities might be considered appropriate by the trustees where they are unable to get an additional contribution into the fund by the employer. A description of some types of contingent securities is given below:

- a guarantee which is given by another company within the same employer group;

- a letter of credit which is issued by a third party (this is an arrangement to pay a sum into the scheme should the employer fall insolvent and may typically be obtained from a bank or an insurance company;

- an arrangement to ring-fence securitised assets in a special vehicle in order to pass the assets to the scheme should the employer fall into insolvency;

- an escrow account, being an account where an employer pays funds into a separate account which will pass to a scheme in accordance with certain conditions (or otherwise will return to the employer if not required).

The Regulator's guidance of contingent securities in contained in its guide entitled *Guidance on the Role of Contingent Assets in Scheme Funding.*

The recovery plan must be prepared (or, where appropriate, revised) within the 15-month or the 12-month period that is described in **5.7** above. The trustees must be able to perform an objective assessment as to the financial covenant which is offered by the employer, meaning that the employer's financial position and its willingness to continue to provide scheme benefits will need to be taken into consideration. Most of the financial information would come directly from the employer (and the employer must provide this information if it is necessary in order to assist the trustees in fulfilling their duties). The information must be treated in confidence by the trustees. If they require any specialist support or assistance, the trustees can seek the help of specialist rating agencies, industry regulators or an independent auditor. The main criterion to be followed is that the trustees should do all they can to restore full funding to the scheme on the new basis at the earliest opportunity, taking into account the ability of the employer to meet this target.

See **ANNEX 5** at the end of this chapter for an example of a recovery plan, taken from the Pension Regulator's website.

Financial support direction 5.18

In addition to the recovery plan, the Regulator may issue a financial support direction against connected parties, especially other companies in the same group, if the sponsoring employer has insufficient resources to meet a certain percentage (generally 50%) of the buy-out debt.

Restoration order 5.19

The Regulator may also make a restoration order if a transaction takes place at undervalue or by way of a gift after 11 June 2003. The restoration order will require the return of any assets or property or benefits involved in the transaction.

Transfers 5.20

The *Occupational Pension Schemes (Transfer Values and Miscellaneous Amendments) Regulations 2003 (SI 2003/1727)* enabled the trustees or managers of a scheme which was subject to the minimum funding requirement to make adjustments to the amount of a cash equivalent in certain circumstances. The regulations permitted the trustees or managers of a scheme to make adjustments to the amount of a cash equivalent (other than a guaranteed cash equivalent) before the guarantee date in circumstances where the last valuation showed that the scheme was underfunded by reference to actuarial guidance note GN11 (see **APPENDIX 4**). The trustees or managers could reduce the amount of a cash equivalent by no greater than the amount by which the actuary's report shows the scheme assets as being insufficient to pay the minimum amount of the cash equivalent in respect of all scheme members. The reduction could not be not less than the minimum amount that is required to satisfy the liabilities referred to in *s 73(3), Pension Schemes Act 1993*.

The Pensions Regulator's powers 5.21

The *Pensions Act 2004* confers significant powers on the Pensions Regulator (see **CHAPTER 3**). These powers certainly exceed those which were previously available to the Occupational Pensions Regulatory Authority (Opra). There have been several cases where the Regulator's powers have been challenged by advisors to schemes, and one concern is that they do extend to areas which may have previously been thought relevant only to the courts. The Regulator has stated that it intends to focus on schemes that create the greatest risks to members and will scrutinise schemes with weaker technical provisions and with long recovery plans. Again, there are guidelines on the Regulator's website with regard to these matters. These extend to assisting where a relevant solvency certificate cannot be provided by the actuary, an employer fails to make contributions as required and the trustees and employer are unable to agree to any of the required terms.

The Regulator may modify a scheme for future benefit accrual (but not so as to affect any subsisting rights adversely), direct how the technical provisions should be interpreted and calculated, determine how long a recovery period may be and impose a schedule of contributions.

Statement on the regulation of the funding of defined benefits by the Pensions Regulator 5.22

The Regulator has issued a statement on how it will regulate the funding of defined benefits schemes. The purpose of the statement is to explain that the Regulator will intervene in cases where it considers a scheme's funding objective to be imprudent or a recovery plan to be inappropriate. A summary of the statement is given under **3.11** above.

Winding up, and partial winding up 5.23

The following rules apply to schemes which are in the process of winding up.

Preferential order. The preferential order of beneficiaries on winding up was amended by substituting *s 73, Pensions Act 1995,* with *s 270, Pensions Act 2004.* The change, among other things, takes into consideration the Pension Protection Fund, so that liabilities do not generally exceed the corresponding liability of the Fund. Therefore, it is not possible for the winding-up rule of the receiving scheme to be amended so as to accord a greater priority to benefits represented by transfer credits granted by the trustees of the receiving scheme than would be the case without any such amendment.

Winding-up regulations: The following regulations apply to the winding up of defined benefits schemes:

- The *Occupational Pension Schemes* (*Winding Up and Deficiency on Winding Up etc*) (*Amendment*) *Regulations 2004* (*SI 2004/403*) described the method of calculation of liabilities under *s 75, Pensions Act 1995,* for any scheme which began to wind up before 11 June 2003 in circumstances where the sponsoring employer was not insolvent. They also provided a new method of calculating liabilities when a scheme begins to wind up on or after 11 June 2003 in circumstances where the sponsoring employer is not insolvent. In the latter circumstance, a scheme's liabilities are to be calculated on a basis which assumes that any accrued rights to a pension or other benefit under the scheme for members with more than two years of pensionable service, as well as any entitlement to the payment of a pension that has arisen under the scheme (including any increase in a pension), will be discharged by the purchase of annuities.

- The *Occupational Pension Schemes* (*Winding Up, Deficiency on Winding Up and Transfer Values*) (*Amendment*) *Regulations 2005* (*SI 2005/72*), which came into force on 15 February 2005, described the changes in the calculation of liabilities where winding up commences, and the date of calculation falls, on or after 15 February 2005 for the purposes of *s 75* of the *Pensions Act 1995*. They required the trustees to inform members who requested a transfer payment that their cash equivalent may be affected by the wind-up and that the member should consider taking independent financial advice. The regulations made amendments to the *Occupational Pension Schemes* (*Winding Up*) *Regulations 1996* (*SI 1996/3126*), the *Occupational Pension Schemes* (*Deficiency on Winding Up etc*) *Regulations 1996* (*SI 1996/3128*) and the *Occupational Pension Schemes* (*Transfer Values*) *Regulations 1996* (*SI 1996/1847*). The regulations required a scheme's liabilities to be calculated and valued on a basis which assumes that any accrued rights to a pension or other benefit under the scheme for members with more than two years of pensionable service, as well as any entitlement to the payment of a pension that has arisen under the scheme (including any increase in a pension), will be discharged by the purchase of annuities.

- The *Occupational Pensions Schemes* (*Employer Debt etc*) *Regulations 2005* (*SI 2005/678*) mainly concern the winding up of multiple employer schemes. They do not apply in the case of schemes that began to wind up before 6 April 2005 (unless a debt arose under *s 75* before that date). The regulations make provision for the valuation of assets and liabilities for the purposes of *s 75* and provide for all liabilities in respect of pensions and other benefits to be valued on the basis that the trustees or managers will provide for them by buying annuities. The costs of winding up the scheme are included among its liabilities, and the regulations explain how these rules apply to multi-employer schemes. In addition, the regulations update the preceding legislation in respect of sectionalised schemes. They also enable trustees or managers to modify schemes by resolution for the purpose of apportioning *section 75* debts.

- The *Occupational Pension Schemes* (*Winding up etc.*) *Regulations 2005* (*SI 2005/706*) came into force on 6 April 2005 (except where otherwise stated), largely in respect of schemes which begin to wind up from that date. They prescribe when trustees or managers of schemes are required to adjust entitlements to discretionary awards and to survivors' benefits when schemes are winding up. They also:

    - make provision where, after the winding-up begins, someone becomes entitled to payment of benefits in respect of the member;

    - provide for the calculation of the value or amount of scheme assets and liabilities of cash equivalents and pension credits and the trustees' discharge;

- modify the provisions where the liabilities of a scheme are discharged during an assessment period (concerning an insolvency event occurring in relation to a scheme's employer and ending with either the Board of the Pension Protection Fund assuming responsibility for the scheme or ceasing to be involved with it);

- provide for treating as separate schemes: sections of multi-employer schemes; the guaranteed and unguaranteed parts of partially government-guaranteed schemes; and sections of schemes that only apply to members in employment inside or, as the case may be, outside the UK;

- revise pension compensation from 6 April 2006 by reference to the Pension Protection Fund.

- The *Occupational Pension Schemes (Winding Up) (Modification for Multi-employer Schemes and Miscellaneous Amendments) Regulations 2005 (SI 2005/2159)* modify the *Pensions Act 1995* for schemes with more than one employer, or with more than one employer at any time since 6 April 2005, whose rules do not provide for the partial winding-up of the scheme if it is being wound up. They apply where an insolvency event has occurred in relation to one of the persons who is an employer in relation to an occupational pension scheme since 6 April 2005, and where the trustees or managers of the scheme have determined in the last three months that it is probable that the scheme will enter an assessment period in the next twelve months (that is, a period when the Board of the Pension Protection Fund determines whether to assume responsibility for the scheme for the purposes of pension protection).

  The normal obligation of trustees or managers to reduce the benefits that they pay out in respect of a member during the winding-up period, so that members do not receive more than they should according to the priority rules, is modified by the regulations. Trustees may, if they wish, pay in full the level of benefits that would be payable if the Board were to assume responsibility for the scheme.

- The *Occupational Pensions Schemes (Employer Debt etc) Regulations 2005 (SI 2005/2224)* consolidated the minimum funding basis for calculating debt from 2 September 2005 as the full buy-out cost of securing benefits with annuities, unless an alternative arrangement has been agreed by the trustees or managers and approved by the Regulator. Primarily, the regulations cover the circumstance of a withdrawing employer under an approved withdrawal arrangement with the Regulator (see **7.72**) and an employer that has ceased to have employees.

Transitional provisions   5.24

It is stated in **5.7** above that the trustees must comply with the new funding regime for a valuation which has an effective date on or after 22 September

2005. Valuations normally will take place after the last MFR valuation but may be required earlier if the scheme actuary is unable to sign the schedule of contributions. Actuarial reports and actuarial valuations will not be required until the first triennial valuation. The trustees are also required to provide all members and beneficiaries with the summary funding statement before 22 September 2006 and annually thereafter, whether or not they have carried out a valuation on the new funding basis. Until they have carried out such a valuation they must summarise the MFR position and the extent to which the assets of the scheme are adequate to meet its liabilities as at its last MFR valuation, and provide an explanation of the change of the funding position since then, and an estimate of the solvency of the scheme. This requirement is waived if the scheme has fewer than 100 members during the twelve-month period ending on 31 August in the relevant year.

Conclusion   5.25

The changes which are described in this chapter are fundamental. They use as their starting point a replacement of the minimum funding requirement in the wake of poor investment returns by pension schemes in recent years due to market depression. In keeping with the requirements of the *Pensions Act 2004*, guidance is given both on the compulsory basis (ie by statute) and by means of practical advice (such as the Pensions Regulator's codes of practice). The amount of information available on the Pension Regulator's website is improving in content and value. However, it is clear that defined benefit schemes are hardest hit in view of the pension promises made under the nature of such pension arrangements. Combined with the effect of the new Pension Protection Fund (see **CHAPTER 4**) and the increasing regulatory environment, the inexorable move to money purchase schemes and other forms of retirement saving in the future is being accelerated.

Annex

Annex I

Document I – Example of Statement of Funding Principles
ABC Pension Scheme

'Status

This statement was prepared by the trustees on [*date*] for the purposes of the actuarial valuation as at [*the effective date of the valuation*] after obtaining the advice of [*name*], the actuary to the scheme.

The statutory funding objective

This statement sets out the trustees' policy for securing that the statutory funding objective[1] is met.

Funding objectives in addition to the statutory funding objective

[NB There is no requirement to have additional objectives]

The trustees and the employers have the objective in addition to the statutory funding objective of having sufficient assets by [date] to cover [x%] of the cost of securing discontinuance benefits with an insurance company. However, future contributions will always be set at least at the level required to satisfy the statutory funding objective.

The technical provisions

Method:

The actuarial method to be used in the calculation of the technical provisions is the [*name of method*] Method.

Assumptions:

Sufficient detail should be given on each assumption, using an appendix if necessary, to allow a different actuary to carry out a valuation without further information and obtain the same valuation result.

Where:

- a table has been specified, example rates should be shown;

- a link to a market index is adopted, the actual rate applicable at the effective date should be clearly identified;

- specific figures (such as percentage rates) or standard tables are specified, the principle underlying the choice should be stated.

Discount interest rate (or equivalently the expected return on assets): *[A variety of approaches will be acceptable. There may be a number of different assumptions needed, perhaps rates pre and post retirement or for different slices of benefit. Approaches could use different rates according to the term of the liabilities.]*

Pension increases: *[One or more increase rates may be specified, for example differing before and after expected retirement date, differing by term of liability or for different slices of benefit.]*

Pay increases: *[One or more pay increase rates may be specified, for example with or without the addition of a promotional scale or for different time periods.]*

Mortality: *[One or more standard tables may be specified, with or without adjustment. Allowance for expected future improvements in longevity should be adequately specified and example rates shown.]*

New entrants: *[A formula can be used or rates may be illustrated.]*

Leaving service: *[A formula can be used or rates may be illustrated.]*

Retirement: *[A formula can be used or rates may be illustrated for normal, early, late and ill-health retirements.]*

Age difference of dependants: *[A formula can be used or rates may be illustrated.]*

Percentage with dependants' benefits at death: *[A formula can be used or rates may be illustrated.]*

Expenses: *[The treatment of administrative and other expenses should be described, including the extent to which (if at all) they are capitalised, or paid by the employer. They may be expressed as a percentage of pensionable pay or as monetary amounts. The provision made for Pension Protection Fund levies should be stated.]*

Policy on discretionary increases and funding strategy

Pensions in excess of Guaranteed Minimum Pensions earned by service before [*date*], may be increased from time to time once in payment at the discretion of ABC (Northern) Ltd and ABC (Southern) Ltd. These increases are to be taken into account for the purpose of calculating technical provisions at the rate of the increase in the index of retail prices limited to [p%] in any one year.

Period within which and manner in which a failure to meet the statutory funding objective is to be rectified

The trustees and the employers have agreed that any funding shortfalls identified at an actuarial valuation should be eliminated as quickly as the employers can reasonably afford by the payment of additional contributions increasing over the recovery period on an annual basis by no more than the annual increase in the retail prices index. In determining the actual recovery period at any particular valuation the trustees' principles are to take into account the following factors:

- the size of the funding shortfall;

- the business plans of the employers;

- the trustees' assessment of the financial covenant of the employers (and in making this assessment the trustees will make use of appropriate credit assessment providers); and

- any contingent security offered by the employers or ABC Holdings Ltd.

The trustees normally expect the recovery period to be no longer than [a] years for funding shortfalls up to [q%] of technical provisions and no longer than [b] years for shortfalls above that percentage.

The assumptions to be used in these calculations will be those set out above for calculating the technical provisions.

Arrangements by a person other than the employer or a scheme member to contribute to the scheme

ABC Holdings Ltd, the parent company of ABC (Northern) Ltd and ABC (Southern) Ltd, has given an undertaking that if either of ABC (Northern) Ltd or ABC (Southern) Ltd become insolvent within the next [n] years, it will meet any shortfall in respect of technical provisions at that time not available from the proceeds of the insolvency.

Policy on reduction of cash equivalent transfer values (CETVs)

The trustees will ask the actuary to advise them at each valuation of the extent to which assets are sufficient to provide CETVs for all non pensioners without adversely affecting the security of the benefits of other members and beneficiaries. Where coverage is less than [k %] of benefits in excess of the first priority slice (broadly those benefits which would be provided were the scheme to be admitted to the Pension Protection Fund), the trustees will reduce CETVs as permitted under legislation, after obtaining actuarial advice as to the appropriate extent.

If at any other time, after obtaining advice from the actuary, the trustees are of the opinion that the payment of CETVs at a previously agreed level may adversely affect the security of the benefits of other members and beneficiaries, the trustees will commission a report from the actuary and will use the above criterion to decide whether, and to what extent, CETVs should be reduced.

Payments to the employer

If the scheme is not being wound up and the assets of the scheme exceed the estimate by the actuary of the cost of buying out the benefits of all beneficiaries from an insurance company, including the expenses of doing so, the employer may request a payment of the excess,[*under clause [c] of the Trust Deed dated [date]*]. If the actuary certifies that the requirements of the Pensions Act 2004 have been met and certifies the maximum amount that may be paid, the trustees will consider whether a payment would be in the interest of the members, and if so, the trustees will give notice to the members of the proposal.

Frequency of valuations and circumstances for extra valuations

The scheme's first actuarial valuation under Part 3^2 is being carried out as at the effective date of [*date*] and subsequent valuations will in normal circumstances be carried out every three years thereafter. An actuarial report on developments affecting the scheme's funding level will be obtained as at each intermediate anniversary of that date.

The trustees may call for a full actuarial valuation instead of an actuarial report when, after considering the actuary's advice, they are of the opinion that events have made it unsafe to continue to rely on the results of the previous valuation as the basis for future contributions. However, the trustees will consult the employers before doing so.

This statement has been agreed by the employers:

Signed on behalf of ABC (Northern) Ltd

Name:

Position: [*Director/Company Secretary*]

Date:

Signed on behalf of ABC (Southern) Ltd

Name

Position: [*Director/Company Secretary*]

Date:

This statement was agreed by the trustees at their meeting on [*date*]:

Signed on behalf of the trustees of the ABC Pension Scheme

Name:

Position: Trustee

Date:

[*Optional*] This statement has been agreed by the trustees after obtaining actuarial advice from me:

Signed

Name:

Position: Actuary to the ABC Pension Scheme

Date:

Appendix to the Statement of Funding Principles

Illustrative death rates

Mortality prior to retirement: probability of death within one year

	Effective date	*Effective date*	*20 years after effective date*	*20 years after effective date*
Age x	Male death rate q_x	Female death rate q_x	Male death rate q_x	Female death rate q_x
20				
25				
30				
35				
40				
45				
50				
55				
60				

	Effective date	*Effective date*	*20 years after effective date*	*20 years after effective date*
Age x	Male death rate q_x	Female death rate q_x	Male death rate q_x	Female death rate q_x
65				

* Mortality in retirement (normal health): probability of death within one year

	Effective date	*Effective date*	*20 years after effective date*	*20 years after effective date*
Age x	Male death rate q_x	Female death rate q_x	Male death rate q_x	Female death rate q_x
60				
65				
70				
75				
80				
85				
90				
95				
100				
105'				

[1]   The statutory funding objective is defined in section 222 of the Pensions Act 2004. Every scheme must have sufficient and appropriate assets to cover its technical provisions.

[2]   Part 3 of the Pensions Act 2004 covering scheme funding.

Annex 2

Document 4a – Example of Summary Funding Statement (after first scheme funding valuation under the Pensions Act 2004)

'XYZ Trustees

Address

Telephone number, etc

Dear Mr Smith

XYZ PENSION SCHEME: SUMMARY FUNDING STATE-MENT FOR PERIOD ENDING *[effective date of latest actuarial valuation or actuarial report if later]*

As a person entitled to benefits from the scheme we are writing to give you an update of the scheme's funding position. The trustees look after the scheme. We will send you a statement like this each year to let you have updated information about the funding of the scheme.

The latest scheme funding valuation

The latest valuation of the pension scheme showed that on *[effective date of valuation]* the funding position was as follows:

Assets	£[x]
Amount needed to provide benefits (technical provisions)	£[y]
Shortfall/excess	£[z]
Funding level	[k%]

As a result, XYZ has agreed to pay additional contributions of [£q] p a for [n] years which are expected to eliminate the shortfall. There is no change in the rate of active members' contributions.

The estimated amount needed to ensure that all members' benefits could be paid in full if the scheme had started winding up (full solvency) was [£s]. Inclusion of this information does not imply that XYZ is thinking of winding-up the scheme.

More up-to-date information

The latest report by the actuary showed that on *[effective date of the latest report obtained subsequent to the valuation (if applicable)]* the funding of the scheme was progressing as anticipated and the funding level was estimated to be *[j%]* with a *[shortfall/excess]* of [£w].

Change in funding position since the previous statement[3]

The position has got *[better/worse]* since the previous statement. *[List here the principal factors contributing to the change in the funding position based on the latest actuarial report or valuation.]* ➡

155

Payment to XYZ[4]

There has not been any payment to XYZ out of scheme funds since the last statement was issued. [*If a payment to the employer has been made, details must be provided here.*]

Important: If you are thinking of leaving the scheme for any reason, you should consult a professional advisor, such as an independent financial advisor, before taking any action.

How the scheme operates

How is my pension paid for?

XYZ pays contributions to the pension scheme so that the scheme can pay pensions to scheme members when they retire. Active members also pay contributions to the scheme, and these are deducted from gross [*pay/salary/wages*].

The money to pay for members' pensions is held in a common fund. It is not held in separate funds for each individual.

How is the amount the scheme needs worked out?

The trustees have a funding plan (the *Statement of Funding Principles*) agreed with XYZ which aims to make sure there is enough money in the scheme to pay for pensions now and in the future. The amount of money which XYZ pays into the pension scheme may go up or down following regular funding checks by our actuary (called actuarial valuations).

The importance of XYZ's support

The trustees' objective is to have enough money in the scheme to pay pensions now and in the future. However, success of the plan relies on XYZ continuing to support the scheme because:

- XYZ will be paying the future expenses of running the scheme on an annual basis;

- the funding level can fluctuate, and when there is a funding shortfall, XYZ will usually need to put in more money; and

- the target funding level may turn out not to be enough so that XYZ will need to put in more money.

What would happen if the scheme started to wind up?

If the scheme winds up, you might not get the full amount of pension you have built up even if the scheme is fully funded under our plan.

However, whilst the scheme remains ongoing, even though funding may temporarily be below target, benefits will continue to be paid in full.

If the scheme were to start to wind up, XYZ is required to pay enough into the scheme to enable the members' benefits to be completely secured with an insurance company. It may be, however, that XYZ would not be able to pay this full amount. If XYZ became insolvent, the *Pension Protection Fund* might be able to take over the scheme and pay compensation to members.

Further information and guidance is available on the Pension Protection Fund's website at www.pensionprotectionfund.org.uk. Or you can write to the Pension Protection Fund at Knollys House, 17 Addiscombe Road, Croydon, Surrey, CR0 6SR.

Why does the funding plan not call for full solvency at all times?

The full solvency position assumes that benefits will be secured by buying insurance policies. Insurers are obliged to take a very cautious view of the future and need to make a profit. The cost of securing pensions in this way also incorporates the future expenses involved in administration. By contrast, our funding plan assumes that XYZ will continue in business and support the plan.

What is the scheme invested in?

The trustees' policy is to invest in a broad range of assets subject to asset class limits as follows:

Government securities	[*range %*]
Company shares	[*range %*]
Corporate bonds	[*range %*]
Commercial property	[*range %*]
Cash/other	[*range %*]

Where can I get more information?

If you have any other questions, or would like any more information, please contact us. A list of more detailed documents which provide further information is attached. If you want us to send you any of these documents please let us know.

Please help us to keep in touch with you by telling us if you change address. A form for this purpose is enclosed.

Yours sincerely

XYZ Trustees

Additional documents available on request

The Statement of Funding Principles. This sets out the scheme's funding plan.

The Recovery Plan. This explains how the funding shortfall is being made up.

The Statement of Investment Principles. This explains how the trustees invest the money paid into the scheme.

The *Schedule of Contributions.* This shows how much money is being paid into the scheme.

The *Annual Report and Accounts of the XYZ Pension Scheme,* which shows the scheme's income and expenditure in the year up to [*date*].

The full report on the *Actuarial Valuation* following the actuary's check of the scheme's situation as at [*date*].

The shorter *Actuarial Report* following the actuary's review of the scheme's situation as at [*date*].

The XYZ Pension Scheme Information Booklet (you should have been given a copy when you joined the scheme, but we can let you have another copy).

An Annual Benefit Statement – If you are not getting a pension from the scheme (and have not received a benefit statement in the previous 12 months), you can ask for a statement that provides an illustration of your likely pension.'

---

[3] In the case of the summary funding statement following the scheme's first actuarial valuation under section 224 of the Pensions Act 2004, the change in the funding position is in relation to the last actuarial valuation under regulation 30 of the MFR regulations or (if there was no such valuation) under the rules of the scheme.

[4] In the case of a scheme's first summary funding statement, details provided of payments made to the employer must relate to the previous 12 months.

Annex 3

Document 4b – Example of Summary Funding Statement (before first scheme funding valuation under the Pensions Act 2004)

'*XYZ Trustees*

Address

Telephone number, etc

Dear Mr Smith

XYZ PENSION SCHEME: SUMMARY FUNDING STATE-MENT FOR PERIOD ENDING [*effective date of latest actuarial valuation*]

As a person entitled to benefits from the scheme we are writing to give you an update of the scheme's funding position. The trustees look after the scheme. We will send you a statement like this each year to let you have updated information about the funding of the scheme. From [*date*] the statement will be based on an actuarial valuation carried out under the new scheme funding requirements.

The last ongoing funding valuation

The most recent funding valuation[5] of the pension scheme showed that on [*effective date of valuation*] the funding position was as follows:

Assets	[£x]
Amount needed to provide benefits	[£y]
Shortfall/excess	[£z]
Funding level	[k%]

As a result, XYZ is paying additional contributions of [£q] pa to eliminate the shortfall. There is no change in the rate of active members' contributions.

The estimated amount needed to ensure that all members' benefits could have been paid in full if the scheme had started winding up (full solvency) was [£s]. Inclusion of this information does not imply that XYZ is thinking of winding-up the scheme. [*This only needs to be included where there has been such an estimate.*]

Change in funding position

The position has got [*better/worse*] since the previous funding valuation. [*List here the principal factors contributing to the change in the funding position based on information available to the trustees.*]

Payment to XYZ[6]

There has not been any payment to XYZ out of scheme funds in the previous twelve months. [*If a payment to the employer has been made, details must be provided here.*]

Important: If you are thinking of leaving the scheme for any reason, you should consult a professional advisor, such as an independent financial advisor, before taking any action.

How the scheme operates

How is my pension paid for?

XYZ pays contributions to the pension scheme so that the scheme can pay pensions to scheme members when they retire. Active members also pay contributions to the scheme, and these are deducted from gross [*pay/salary/wages*].

The money to pay for members' pensions is held in a common fund. It is not held in separate funds for each individual.

How is the amount the scheme needs worked out?

The trustees obtain regular valuations of the benefits earned by members. Using this information, the trustees come to an agreement with XYZ on future contributions. [*Or other suitable text appropriate to the scheme's practice before implementation of Part 3 of the Pensions Act 2004.*]

The importance of XYZ's support

The trustees' objective is to have enough money in the scheme to pay pensions now and in the future. However, success of the plan relies on XYZ continuing to support the scheme because:

- XYZ will be paying the future expenses of running the scheme on an annual basis;

- the funding level can fluctuate, and when there is a funding shortfall, XYZ will usually need to put in more money; and

- the target funding level may turn out not to be enough so that XYZ will need to put in more money.

What would happen if the scheme started to wind up?

If the scheme winds up, you might not get the full amount of pension you have built up even if the scheme is fully funded under our plan. However, whilst the scheme remains ongoing, even though funding may temporarily be below target, benefits will continue to be paid in full.

If the scheme were to start to wind up, XYZ is required to pay enough into the scheme to enable the members' benefits to be completely secured with an insurance company. It may be, however, that XYZ would not be able to pay this full amount. If XYZ became insolvent, the *Pension Protection Fund* might be able to take over the scheme and pay compensation to members.

Further information and guidance is available on the Pension Protection Fund's website at www.pensionprotectionfund.org.uk. Or you can write to the Pension Protection Fund at Knollys House, 17 Addiscombe Road, Croydon, Surrey, CR0 6SR.

Why does the funding plan not call for full solvency at all times?

The full solvency position assumes that benefits will be secured by buying insurance policies. Insurers are obliged to take a very cautious view of the future and need to make a profit. The cost of securing pensions in this way also incorporates the future expenses involved in administration. By contrast, our funding plan assumes that XYZ will continue in business and support the plan.

What is the scheme invested in?

The trustees' policy is to invest in a broad range of assets subject to asset class limits as follows:

Government securities	[*range %*]
Company shares	[*range %*]
Corporate bonds	[*range %*]
Commercial property	[*range %*]
Cash/other	[*range %*]

Where can I get more information?

If you have any other questions, or would like any more information, please contact us. A list of more detailed documents which provide further information is attached. If you want us to send you any of these documents please let us know.

Please help us to keep in touch with you by telling us if you change address. A form for this purpose is enclosed.

Yours sincerely

XYZ Trustees

Additional documents available on request

The Statement of Investment Principles. This explains how the trustees invest the money paid into the scheme.

The *Schedule of Contributions*. This shows how much money is being paid into the scheme.

The *Annual Report and Accounts of the XYZ Pension Scheme*, which shows the scheme's income and expenditure in the year up to [*date*].

The full report on the *Actuarial Valuation* following the actuary's check of the scheme's situation as at [*date*].

The XYZ Pension Scheme Information Booklet (you should have been given a copy when you joined the scheme, but we can let you have another copy).

An Annual Benefit Statement – If you are not getting a pension from the scheme (and have not received a benefit statement in the previous 12 months) you can ask for a statement that provides an illustration of your likely pension.'

---

5   This must be the last valuation under regulation 30 of the MFR regulations; but if there was no such valuation it must be the last valuation under the rules of the scheme.

6   In the case of a scheme's first summary funding statement, details provided of payments made to the employer must relate to the previous 12 months.

Annex 4

Document 3 – Example of Schedule of Contributions
GHI Pension Scheme

'Status

This schedule of contributions has been prepared by the trustees, after obtaining the advice of [*name*], the actuary to the scheme.

Contributions to be paid towards the scheme from [*date*] to [*date*]

By active members:

Category A Members	[*x % of pensionable pay*]
Category B Members	[*y % of pensionable pay*]

To be deducted from [*pay/salary/wages*] by the employers and paid towards the scheme on or before the [*date not later than the nineteenth*] of the calendar month following deduction.

By GHI (*Eastern*) Ltd and GHI (*Western*) Ltd.

In respect of future accrual of benefits, the provision of death-in-service lump sum benefits and the expenses of administering the scheme each will pay the following:

In respect of Category A Members: [*a% of pensionable pay (of which s% is in respect of death-in-service lump sum benefits and t% in respect of administrative expenses)*]

In respect of Category B Members: [*b% of pensionable pay (of which u% is in respect of death-in-service lump sum benefits and v% in respect of administrative expenses)*]

To be paid towards the scheme on or before the [m^{th}] of the calendar month following that to which the payment relates.

In respect of the shortfall in funding in accordance with the recovery plan dated [*date*]:

GHI (Eastern) Ltd will pay [*f%*] of monthly pensionable pay for each active member

GHI (Western) Ltd will pay [*g%*] of monthly pensionable pay for each active member

To be paid towards the scheme on or before the [n^{th}] of the calendar month following that to which the payment relates.

Expenses: [*Treatment of any expenses not covered above to be explained here.*]

In respect of the risk-based element of the Pension Protection Fund levy the employers will pay a monthly amount calculated as [*1/nth*] of the levy for [*n*] successive months following the month of receipt of the levy invoice by the trustees each year.

In respect of augmentations granted, GHI (Eastern) will pay [*£z*] on or before [*date*].

Pensionable pay

Category A members

Basic salary.

Category B members

Basic salary plus bonus payments.

Signed on behalf of GHI (Eastern) Ltd

Name:

Position: [*Director/Company Secretary*]

Date:

Signed on behalf of GHI (Western) Ltd.

Name:

Position: [*Director/Company Secretary*]

Date:

Signed on behalf of the trustees of the GHI Pension Scheme

Name:

Position: Trustee

Date:

[*Optional*] This schedule of contributions, dated [*date*] has been agreed by the trustees of the GHI Pension Scheme after obtaining actuarial advice from me.

Signed

Name:

Position: Actuary to the GHI Pension Scheme

Date:

Note: The actuary's certification is an integral part of the schedule and should be incorporated within a single document.

Form of actuary's certification of schedule of contributions

Name of scheme: GHI Pension Scheme

Adequacy of rates of contributions

1. I hereby certify that, in my opinion, the rates of contributions shown in this schedule of contributions are such that—

   the statutory funding objective could have been expected on [*effective date of valuation on which the schedule is based*] to be met by the end of the period specified in the recovery plan.

Adherence to statement of funding principles

2. I hereby certify that, in my opinion, this schedule of contributions is consistent with the Statement of Funding Principles dated [*date*].

The certification of the adequacy of the rates of contributions for the purpose of securing that the statutory funding objective can be expected to be met is not a certification of their adequacy for the purpose of securing the scheme's liabilities by the purchase of annuities, if the scheme were wound up.

Signature: Date:

Name: Qualification:

Address: Name of employer
                                              (if applicable):

Note: One of the prescribed forms of wording must be used in the Certificate as set out in Schedule 1 and paragraphs 6 and 12 of Schedule 2 to The Occupational Pension Schemes (Scheme Funding) Regulations 2005 (SI 2005/3377).'

Annex 5

Document 2 – Example of Recovery Plan DEF Pension Scheme

'Status

This recovery plan has been prepared by the trustees on [*date*] after obtaining the advice of [*name*], the actuary to the scheme.

The actuarial valuation of the scheme as at [*effective date of the valuation*] revealed a funding shortfall (technical provisions minus value of assets) of [£*x*].

Steps to be taken to ensure that the statutory funding objective[7] is met

To eliminate this funding shortfall, the trustees and the employers have agreed that additional contributions will be paid to the scheme by DEF (Holdings) Ltd and DEF (Contractors) Ltd as follows:

DEF (Holdings) Ltd   [£*y per annum*]

DEF (Contractors) Ltd   [£*z per annum*]

payable in equal monthly instalments for a period of [*n*] years, increasing annually on [*dd/mm*] in line with increases in the index of national average earnings (as published by the Office for National Statistics) over the year ending two months earlier, from [*date*] to [*date*] inclusive.

Period in which the statutory funding objective should be met

The funding shortfall is expected to be eliminated in [*n*] years, which is by [*date*]. This expectation is based on the following assumptions:

- technical provisions calculated according to the method and assumptions set out in the statement of funding principles dated [*date*];

- the return on existing assets and the return on new contributions during the period as set out in the statement of funding principles dated [*date*] for the calculation of technical provisions and applicable to that period.

Progress towards meeting the Statutory Funding Objective

It is expected that 50% of the above additional contributions will be paid in [*m*] years, which is by [*date*].

This Recovery Plan was agreed by the trustees at their meeting on [*date*]:

Signed on behalf of the trustees of the DEF Pension Scheme

Name:

Position: Trustee

Date:

This Recovery Plan has been agreed by the employers:

Signed on behalf of DEF (Holdings) Ltd

Name:

Position: [*Director/Company Secretary*]

Date:

Signed on behalf of DEF (Contractors) Ltd

Name:

Position: [*Director/Company Secretary*]

Date:

[*Optional*] This Recovery Plan has been agreed by the trustees of the DEF Pension Scheme after obtaining actuarial advice from me:'

Signed

Name:

Position: Actuary to the DEF Pension Scheme

Date:

<hr>

[7] The statutory funding objective is defined in section 222 of the Pensions Act 2004. Every scheme must have sufficient and appropriate assets to cover its technical provisions.

Chapter 6
Financial planning for retirement

Introduction

The increased longevity of the population in the UK, and the ever-increasing number of people over state pension age, has caused the government to become concerned that many people are not saving enough for a comfortable retirement. The situation has been exacerbated by the comparatively low level of state benefits which are available in the UK compared with other western European countries.

The balance between state and private provision

It appears that the avowed intention of government, following the introduction of stakeholder pension schemes, to shift the retirement provision ratio from 60% state/40% private to 40% state/60% private, is not happening. Many pensioners may therefore find themselves poorly off in retirement and having to rely on means-tested benefits.

Financial studies and government initiatives

A study commissioned by the Association of British Insurers, *The Future Regulation of UK Savings and Investment – Targeting the Savings Gap*, had estimated there was an annual 'savings gap' of £27bn between the amount being saved and the amount that needed to be saved for a comfortable retirement. The government therefore aimed to increase the planning and forecasting tools which are available to individuals to help them make better plans for their retirement.

Financial planning measures alone would not overcome the existing barriers that discourage people from saving more, but the Pensions Green Paper of

2002 saw the provision of appropriate financial planning advice and information as a key element of the solution. Even though the government now proposes, in its 2006 Pensions White Paper (see **CHAPTER 11**), to introduce soft compulsion for non-pensioned workers (and compulsory contributions from employers), there would still appear to be a need for a wider range of planning and forecasting tools to be available, perhaps even more so if the pensions landscape becomes more cluttered and complex than it already is.

Enabling legislation for government   6.4

Part 4 of the *Pensions Act 2004*, provides the government with the powers needed to introduce retirement planning measures. In particular, it will enable the government to collect a volume of information about individuals' savings and finances and use it in individual-specific retirement planners, including web-based facilities. It also contains a power to make the provision of combined pension forecasts compulsory, and a power to compel employers to provide information and advice in the workplace. None of these provisions has yet been brought into force.

Promoting and facilitating retirement planning   6.5

The Green and White Papers preceding the *Pensions Act 2004* both referred to proposals for developing:

> 'a web-based retirement planner which will for the first time give people the opportunity to look at all their pension information together. The planner will allow people to view their total projected pension income from both state and private sources against their expectations for retirement, calculate any savings shortfall and consider options to address it.'

Sections 234–236, and *Sch 10, Pensions Act 2004*, give the government the power it needs to achieve this.

Section 234 authorises the DWP to take action for the purpose of promoting or facilitating financial planning for retirement. The action it may take includes the provision of facilities to enable an individual, or someone authorised by him or her, to:

- estimate the financial resources that the individual is likely to need in his or her retirement;

- estimate the financial resources that are likely to be available to the individual after his or her retirement (from pensions and other sources);

- ascertain what action might be taken with a view to increasing the financial resources available to the individual after retirement.

Providing information to the DWP 6.6

Anyone may supply information to the DWP to enable it to provide the facilities described in **6.5** above. This includes the trustees of occupational pension schemes and HM Revenue & Customs. The information which is supplied must:

- be relevant for determining the pensions and other benefits that may become payable to or in respect of the individual;

- relate to the financial resources of, or available to, an individual; or

- relate to action taken in connection with providing or promoting savings facilities for individuals.

A few safeguards are provided which would prevent the further disclosure of information except in cases where it was already authorised, where the individual consents, or where it is to be used in criminal proceedings under the *Pension Schemes Act 1993*, the *Pensions Act 1995*, the *Pensions Act 2004* or any corresponding Northern Ireland provision.

Combined pension forecasts 6.7

The government has been issuing state pension forecasts for many years, but in 2001, under provisions of the *Child Support, Pensions and Social Security Act 2000*, it started issuing state pension information (to those scheme sponsors who requested it) for inclusion in benefit statements that combined scheme projections with state pension forecasts.

Responses to consultation on the 2002 Green Paper indicated that one of the key elements in making an informed choice is the provision of personalised information, particularly a projection of the likely pension income someone will derive from their occupational, private and state pensions. The government therefore went on to announce in its June 2003 White Paper that, if voluntary persuasion failed, it would legislate to require employers to provide combined pension forecasts:

> 'Currently, pension schemes are not required to provide state pension information, but many do so on a voluntary basis. Feedback from the consultation exercise suggests a high level of support for the provision of combined pension forecasts, particularly from those who are already providing them.

There are concerns that some businesses may not have the resources to deliver combined pension forecasts. While we acknowledge that some organisations have a number of questions and concerns over the practicalities of the proposal, the government remains convinced that combined pension forecasts have the potential to be a key motivator in encouraging people to engage in financial planning.

Therefore, we wish to extend this service across the pensions industry, in the first instance by encouraging voluntary participation through concerted and targeted marketing activity. However, if the voluntary approach does not achieve the desired coverage, we will reconsider the question of whether there should be a statutory requirement on pension schemes and employers to provide this service. We will legislate to allow us to require pension schemes to issue combined pension forecasts on a regular basis if we believe it to be necessary in the future.'

The power to require pension scheme trustees to provide combined pension forecasts is included in *s 237, Pensions Act 2004*. It enables the government to lay regulations at any time to require trustees to provide the following information to members of the scheme:

- State pension information comprising of:
    - the member's date of birth and the age at which, and date on which, he or she attains pensionable age;
    - the amount of any entitlement to basic or additional state retirement pension which has already accrued to the member;
    - a projection of the amount of basic or additional state retirement pension to which the member is likely to become entitled (or to which he or she might become entitled in particular circumstances); and
    - a projection of the amount of any lump sum to which the member is likely to become entitled (or to which he or she might become entitled in particular circumstances).

- Occupational pension scheme information:
    - relating to the pension and other benefits likely to accrue to the member, or capable of being secured by him or her, under the pension scheme; and
    - of a description to be specified in the relevant regulations.

The June 2003 White Paper also announced that defined benefit pension schemes, like their defined contribution counterparts, would be required to issue annual benefit statements to their members. Regulations to give effect to this and other disclosure measures were laid in draft and consulted on in 2005. They were due to come into force in April 2006 but were postponed until

October 2006 and have finally been shelved. A key element of the pensions White Paper of May 2006 was a review of regulation in order to ease the burden on employers and make it easier for them to run workplace pension schemes.

Due to this impending overhaul of unnecessary pension scheme regulation under the 2006 White Paper, it has been deemed, somewhat ironically, inappropriate to implement the disclosure measures proposed in the previous pensions White Paper a mere three years earlier.

Requirement on employers to provide information to employees 6.8

In the week before the Pensions Bill was published, the government issued a further paper in the *Simplicity, Security and Choice* series. In this paper the government announced it would 'take powers in the forthcoming Pensions Bill to require all employers who do not actively support their employees' pension saving to give them access to a decent standard of pension information in the workplace.' Such powers are now contained in *s 238, Pensions Act 2004.*

Section 238, Pensions Act 2004, permits the government to lay regulations at any time requiring employers to take action for the purpose of enabling employees to obtain information and advice about pensions and saving for retirement. *Section 238* is very widely drawn, and it allows government a great deal of latitude in deciding what to impose on employers, whether or not they already actively support their employees' pension saving.

In particular, regulations may:

- prescribe the information to be provided;

- determine the form and manner in which it is to be provided;

- specify the period within which it is to be provided;

- apply to employers of a prescribed description and employees of a prescribed description;

- make different provision for different descriptions of employers and employees;

- make provision as to the action to be taken by employers (including the frequency, time and place at which such action is to be taken);

- make provision as to the description of information and advice in relation to which requirements apply;

- make provision about the description of persons authorised to provide information and advice; and

- require employers to provide the Pensions Regulator with information about the action they have taken to comply with these requirements.

Conclusion

The powers that are described in **6.8** above must be questioned. The government has held back over the introduction of further disclosure requirements. Indeed, the draft Occupational Pensions Schemes (Disclosure of Information) Regulations 2006, which were to have effect from October 2006, have been withdrawn. The government's view is that it would have been unfair to employers to bring in regulations in advance of its deregulatory review. Therefore, the *s 238* powers must be seen to run counter to the stated aim of reducing the regulatory burden on scheme sponsors.

Although the Pickering Report was in favour of raising awareness about pensions and educating employees about the importance of pension provision, a detailed set of regulations under the *Pensions Act 2004* would surely be contrary to the principles of simplification espoused by that report.

Chapter 7

Occupational and personal pension provisions

Introduction 7.1

Part 5 of the *Pensions Act 2004* concerns itself with miscellaneous provisions relating to occupational and personal pension schemes. When the Pickering Report was published in July 2002, one of its hopes was that a new Pensions Act would repeal and consolidate all DWP private pension legislation. There was obviously not enough time within the legislative schedule for such a substantial undertaking. The majority of the recommendations in the Pickering Report that were accepted are contained in this Part of the Act, which either adds to or amends legislation already in force. Also included in this Part are measures necessary to give effect to some provisions of Directive 2003/41/EC on the Activities and Supervision of Institutions for Occupational Retirement Provision (the 'IORP Directive') and some changes to fit with the new pensions tax regime brought into force on 6 April 2006.

Member-nominated trustees

Background 7.2

Whether a requirement for member-nominated trustees (MNTs) is a good thing or not has been argued about ever since it was first proposed. However, commentators are almost universally agreed that the original MNT legislation was overly complex, unclear and confusing. This point was made by Opra in its first annual report:

> 'It is apparent that the member-nominated trustee and director (MNT and MND) provisions are not widely understood, and that the terminology introduced under the Pensions Act [1995] is frequently misapplied. We believe that there may be many cases where MNTs are claimed to be appointed but where actually the opt-out procedures have been followed. Generally, it seems from our compliance monitoring work that little weight is given to the difference between

MNTs appointed in accordance with the requirements of the Pensions Act [1995] and the involvement of members at any other level.'

The Labour government has been keen to remove the employer opt-out from the MNT provisions. The *Child Support, Pensions and Social Security Act 2000* contained measures to remove the opt-out and put in place two alternative nomination and selection arrangements. These measures were due to come into force in late 2001 but were put on hold pending the outcome of the Pickering Report on simplification and flexibility. Interim legislation had to be introduced to extend the first opt-out period from six years to ten years (or to four years in the case of new opt-outs).

The Pickering Report recommended that all trust-based occupational schemes (apart from centralised or industry-wide schemes) have a minimum of one-third MNTs and that the employer opt-out be removed. However, it also proposed that there should be no legislative prescription on how this aim was to be achieved. The *Pensions Act 2004* therefore contains some elementary overriding requirements for MNTs, which are supplemented by a code of practice issued by the Pensions Regulator.

Repeal of previous legislation   7.3

The MNT provisions in both the *Pensions Act 1995* and the *Child Support, Pensions and Social Security Act 2000* have now been repealed, and the following MNT provisions of the *Pensions Act 2004* came into force on 6 April 2006. However, the *Occupational Pension Schemes (Member-nominated Trustees and Directors) Regulations 2006 (SI 2006/714)* permit existing alternative arrangements to run until their expiry date under the previous legislation or until 31 October 2007 if earlier.

Requirements for MNT arrangements   7.4

The *Pensions Act 2004* requires the trustees of an occupational trust-based pension scheme to secure that arrangements are in place which provide for at least one-third of trustees to be member-nominated trustees, and that those arrangements are implemented. The arrangements must be put in place within a reasonable period from when the requirement first applies. In its draft code of practice the Pensions Regulator indicates that six months would be a reasonable period, although this may vary depending on the size, structure or circumstances of the scheme. In any event, the Regulator would not expect trustees to take longer than six months. For schemes with an opt-out from the previous MNT legislation, the expiry date of that opt-out will be known, and so trustees should be able to commence putting MNT arrangements in place well before then.

Prospective MNTs must be nominated through a process in which all the active members of the scheme and all the pensioners of the scheme are eligible to participate. Alternatively, prospective MNTs may be nominated by organisations that adequately represent the active members and pensioners of the scheme. Once nominated, prospective MNTs must then be selected through a process which involves some or all of the members of the scheme. Note that this does not have to be a ballot of all the members, but may involve some other selective process as long as scheme members are represented in the selection arrangements.

The actual nomination and selection of MNTs must take place within a reasonable period from when the requirement applies under the MNT arrangements that the trustees have put in place. Once again, the Regulator considers that six months is a reasonable period for the actual nomination and selection process, but that this may vary depending on the size, structure and circumstances of the scheme.

An employer may require any person, who is not a member of the scheme, to have its approval before being eligible to be nominated for selection. The MNT arrangements may provide that where the number of nominations is less than or equal to the number of vacancies, the nominees are deemed to be selected. Where any MNT vacancy is not filled because insufficient nominations were received, the nomination and selection process must be repeated at reasonable intervals. The Regulator considers a period of no more than three years to be a reasonable interval, but if there were a significant change in the membership before then, trustees should consider an earlier re-run of the nomination and selection process. If deferred pensioners were excluded from the nomination and selection process first time round, trustees could consider including them in a re-run.

Other than the above, trustees are free to design their MNT arrangements as they see fit, but should obviously have regard to the Regulator's code of practice. Note that neither the Act nor the code of practice sets out a minimum or maximum term of office for MNTs. Nor does either provide for circumstances where active members leave service or MNTs resign. These scenarios are deliberately omitted so as to permit trustees a greater degree of flexibility in the design of their arrangements.

Restriction and removal   7.5

Nothing in the MNT arrangements or in the provisions of the scheme may exclude MNTs from exercising any of the functions exercisable by other trustees simply by virtue of the fact that they are MNTs.

The MNT arrangements must provide that an MNT may only be removed from office with the agreement of all the other trustees. The exception to this is where scheme rules provide that trustees may be removed by a vote of the scheme membership.

However, MNTs may presumably also be removed when they have come to the end of any term of office or possibly also when an active member leaves pensionable service, and such matters should be covered in the MNT arrangements that trustees put in place.

Member-nominated directors   7.6

Similar requirements apply to the nomination and selection of directors of corporate trustees as they apply to individual trustees.

If a corporate trustee is trustee of more than one occupational scheme, then the schemes are treated as if they were a single scheme and the members of each scheme are treated as if they were members of a single scheme. However, in such a case a corporate trustee may elect that some or all of the schemes are not to be treated as a single scheme.

Exemptions   7.7

The following schemes are exempt from the MNT legislation.

- Schemes where every member is a trustee of the scheme and there is no other trustee.

- Schemes with fewer than two members.

- Schemes to which *section 22* of the *Pensions Act 1995* applies (independent trustees).

- Occupational pension schemes which are not registered pension schemes under *section 150* of the *Finance Act 2004*.

- Schemes with fewer than twelve members where all the members are trustees and either decisions are reached unanimously or there is an independent trustee.

- Certain centralised schemes with at least two non-associated employers.

- Paid-up insured schemes where the insurer has agreed to pay beneficiaries directly.

- Old code schemes formerly approved under *section 208* of the *Income and Corporation Taxes Act 1970*.

- Schemes of a type covered by *section 615* of the *Income and Corporation Taxes Act 1988*.

- Parliamentary pension schemes.

- Schemes modified under the *Coal Industry Act 1994*.

- Schemes where all the trustees (or directors of the trustee company) are independent within the meaning of *section 23* of the *Pensions Act 1995*.

- Stakeholder pension schemes.

- Schemes with fewer than twelve members where all the benefits are secured under an insurance or annuity contract.

- Schemes which are independent of the employer by virtue of the employer's dissolution or liquidation before 6 April 2005.

- Schemes where the trustee is a body governed by church legislation.

In addition to the above, the following two types of scheme are exempt from the requirement to have member-nominated director arrangements where the trustee is a corporate trustee:

- Schemes where the company is the sole trustee and also the only employer in relation to the scheme, but only if the members of the scheme are either current or former directors of the company and the scheme covers at least one-third of the current directors.

- Schemes with a sole trustee where all the benefits are secured through insurance or annuity contracts, some or all of which are with an insurer who is connected with the trustee but not with the employer.

Scheme rules requiring more than one-third MNTs   7.8

MNT arrangements may provide for more than one-third of the trustees to be MNTs, but only where the employer gives its approval. However, where scheme rules already provide for more than one-third of the trustees to be MNTs, the MNT arrangements, which the trustees are required to put in place, must provide at least for that higher proportion.

Schemes with only deferred pensioners   7.9

Where a scheme has no active members or pensioners, the trustees must determine which deferred pensioners are eligible to participate, and ensure that the nomination process covers those deferred pensioners. Some or all of the deferred pensioners must be involved in the selection process. This provision of the MNT legislation allows trustees to cater for the situation where a scheme may be closed to further accrual of benefits and to distinguish between those deferred pensioners who have left service and those who are still employees.

Penalties 7.10

If the required MNT arrangements are not in place, or if they are not being implemented, fines may be levied on trustees who have failed to take all reasonable steps to secure compliance. Individual trustees can be fined up to £5,000 and corporate trustees can be fined up to £50,000.

Code of practice 7.11

The Regulator is required to issue a code of practice on MNT arrangements and has now laid its draft before Parliament. The code will not come into force until it has been laid before Parliament for 40 sitting days (excluding recesses). The code was laid on 13 July 2006 and, if no representations are made within those 40 days, the code will be brought into force.

The draft code follows a principles-based approach and identifies three core principles which trustees should follow in drawing up their MNT arrangements; proportionality, fairness and transparency. The draft code, as laid before Parliament, can be found on the Regulator's website at http://www.thepensionregulator.co.uk/pdf/codeMntMndAgreed.pdf, and is essential reading for trustees.

Increase in MNT proportion 7.12

In its response to the pensions Green Paper of 2002, the TUC argued for the proportion of MNTs to be increased from one-third to one-half. This argument was not accepted in the initial Pensions Bill, but in September 2004, five days after he was appointed Secretary of State for Work and Pensions, Alan Johnson announced a late amendment to the Bill to be included at the report stage in the Lords. The amendment, now part of the *Pensions Act 2004*, gives the government the power to increase the MNT proportion to one-half at any time. At the time of the amendment the government indicated it might use this power by around 2009 if the proportion of MNTs was not voluntarily moved to one-half by then. 2009 was thought an appropriate date because the government wanted the one-third MNT provision to settle down before introducing further upheaval.

MNT legislation, first introduced in the wake of the Maxwell scandal, unfortunately sometimes gives rise to a perception that MNTs have a partisan role, whereas in fact *all* trustees are under an obligation to act impartially regardless of the origins of their appointment.

Periodic review   7.13

The Regulator expects trustees to review their MNT arrangements every three to five years to establish whether they remain appropriate for the scheme. Trustees should also consider an earlier review if there is a significant change in the scheme's membership or circumstances. If, after reviewing their arrangements, trustees decide they are still appropriate, no further action would be required until the next review.

Investment and borrowing

Background   7.14

New investment regulations, were brought in under the *Pensions Act 2004* predominantly to comply with the IORP Directive. The *Occupational Pension Schemes (Investment) Regulations 2005 (SI 2005/3378)* were laid on 9 December 2005 and came into force on 30 December 2005. The main areas covered by the regulations are the preparation of a statement of investment principles, investments by trustees, borrowing and employer-related investments.

Statement of investment principles (SIP)   7.15

The main change from the pre-*Pensions Act 2004* position is that SIPs must now be reviewed at least every three years. SIPs must also be reviewed immediately if there is any significant change in investment policy. In preparing or revising their SIP, trustees must still consult the employer and obtain and consider the written advice of a pension investment professional. The SIP itself must be in writing and must cover the following matters:

- the trustees' policy for securing compliance with the requirements of *section 36* of the *Pensions Act 1995* (choosing investments);

- the trustees' policy in relation to:

    - the kinds of investments to be held;

    - the balance between different kinds of investments;

    - risks, including the ways in which risks are to be measured and managed;

    - the expected return on investments;

    - the realisation of investments; and

    - the extent (if at all) to which social, environmental or ethical considerations are taken into account in the selection, retention and realisation of investments;

- the trustees' policy in relation to the exercise of rights (including voting rights) attaching to the investments.

Investment by trustees 7.16

Trustees must exercise their powers of investment in accordance with the following provisions of the investment regulations.

The scheme's assets must be invested in the best interests of the members, and where there is a potential conflict of interest, the assets must be invested in the sole interests of the members.

The powers of investment must be exercised in a manner calculated to ensure the security, quality, liquidity and profitability of the portfolio as a whole.

Assets held to cover the scheme's technical provisions under the new statutory funding objective (see **CHAPTER 5**) must also be invested in a manner appropriate to the nature and duration of the expected future retirement benefits payable under the scheme.

The assets of the scheme must consist predominantly of investments traded on regulated markets. Investment in assets which are not admitted to trading on such markets must in any event be kept to a prudent level. An investment in a collective investment scheme is treated as an investment on a regulated market if the underlying investments are traded on regulated markets. Investment in insurance policies is also treated as if it were an investment on a regulated market.

The assets of the scheme must be properly diversified in such a way as to avoid excessive reliance on any particular asset and so as to avoid accumulations of risk in the portfolio as a whole. Investments in assets issued by the same issuer or by issuers belonging to the same group must not expose the scheme to excessive risk concentration. Investment in insurance policies would not contravene the diversification requirement.

Investment in derivative instruments may be made only in so far as they contribute to a reduction of risks or facilitate efficient portfolio management (including the reduction of cost or the generation of additional capital or income with an acceptable level of risk). Any such investment must be made and managed so as to avoid excessive risk exposure to a single counterparty and to other derivative operations.

Note that the above provisions apply equally to any fund manager to whom the trustees have delegated investment discretion under *section 34* of the *Pensions Act 1995*.

Borrowing   7.17

Trustees must not borrow money, or act as guarantor for another person, where the borrowing, or guarantee, is liable to be repaid or satisfied out of the assets of the scheme. However, this does not preclude borrowing made solely for the purpose of providing liquidity for the scheme, on the condition that it is only on a temporary basis.

Employer-related investments   7.18

As applied pre-*Pensions Act 2004*, there are general restrictions on employer-related investments, the main one being that investment in the sponsoring employer is limited to 5% of a scheme's assets. This restriction does not apply to a scheme with fewer than twelve members where all the members are trustees and either decisions must be unanimous or there is an independent trustee.

Exemptions   7.19

Schemes with fewer than 100 members are not required to have a SIP. Schemes established by an enactment and guaranteed by a public authority also need no SIP.

Schemes with fewer than 100 members are exempt from the provisions relating to investment by trustees (see **7.16** above), although the assets of the scheme must still be diversified as far as is appropriate for the scheme's circumstances. Schemes with less than 100 members are also exempt from the borrowing restriction.

Wholly insured schemes must obtain a SIP, but it may be a simplified SIP which only covers the reasons for the scheme being a wholly insured scheme.

Trustee knowledge and understanding

Background   7.20

The requirement under the *Pensions Act 2004* for trustees to have knowledge and understanding of various pensions issues derives predominantly from a recommendation in the Myners Review of Institutional Investment in the UK, published in March 2001:

> 'The level of expertise of pension fund trustees is clearly key to the effectiveness of investment decision-making. The trust structure places them at the heart of pension fund decision-making, yet there is no

legal requirement for them to develop the skills they need to carry out their investment duties. They are only expected to show the skill and prudence of an "ordinary man of business".

The review therefore proposes that there should be a legal requirement that, where trustees are taking a decision, they should be able to take it with the skill and prudence of someone familiar with the issues concerned, as in the US. If trustees do not feel that they possess such a level of skill and care, then they should either take steps to acquire it, or delegate the decision to a person or organisation who they believe does.'

According to the Regulatory Impact Assessment on the Pensions Bill, consultations had revealed that practitioners thought it was 'inappropriate to limit coverage to investment, since trustees require expertise across the full range of their responsibilities (including, for example, funding requirements)'.

Consequently, the scope was expanded to encompass the trustee knowledge and understanding requirements which are currently contained in *sections 247–249* of the *Pensions Act 2004.*

General requirement   7.21

Trustees of occupational pension schemes have always had to be familiar with their scheme's trust deed and rules in order to fulfil their fiduciary duties. There was also a large amount of pensions-related legislation that had to be followed to ensure the lawful running of the scheme. However, the *Pensions Act 2004* now imposes a statutory requirement on pension scheme trustees to be conversant with scheme documents and to have knowledge and understanding of general pension matters. Specifically, a trustee of an occupational pension scheme must:

(*a*)   be conversant with:

- the trust deed and rules of the scheme;

- the scheme's statement of investment principles;

- the scheme's statement of funding principles (if applicable); and

- any other document recording policy for the time being adopted by the trustees relating to the administration of the scheme generally;

(*b*)   have knowledge and understanding of:

- the law relating to pensions and trusts;

- the principles relating to the funding of occupational pension schemes;

- the principles relating to investment of the assets of occupational pension schemes; and

- any other prescribed matters (to date no other matters have been prescribed).

The degree of knowledge and understanding required should be appropriate for the purposes of enabling an individual properly to exercise his or her functions as a trustee of the scheme in question, especially where investment discretions have been delegated to him or her or where he or she is a member of any trustee sub-committee.

Directors of corporate trustees 7.22

Similar requirements apply to any individual exercising the functions of a corporate trustee in relation to an occupational pension scheme.

Code of practice 7.23

The Pensions Regulator has now published its code of practice on trustee knowledge and understanding. In addition to the code, the Regulator has produced two scope documents, one for defined benefit schemes with a money purchase section, and one for pure money purchase schemes. All of these documents can be found on the Regulator's website at http://www.thepensionregulator.co.uk/codesAndGuidance/codes/inForce/index.aspx, and are essential reading for trustees.

Conversance with scheme documents 7.24

Being conversant with scheme documents is taken to mean having a working knowledge of those documents so that trustees are able to use them effectively when they are required to do so in the course of carrying out their duties as a trustee of a scheme. Trustees should be familiar with the following particular aspects of their scheme documentation:

Trust deed and rules (including amending deeds)

- The duties, powers and discretions of trustees.

- The balance of power between employer and trustees (including when it is appropriate to exercise various trustee powers, especially where a scheme or employer is under threat or a scheme is in wind-up).

- Classes of members in the scheme (including eligibility for membership).

- Benefits offered (including the circumstances under which they are payable and how the payments are made).

Statement of investment principles

- Responsibilities for investment decisions (including why this structure has been selected and, if appropriate, the terms of reference of the investment sub-committee).

- The investment objectives (including the reasons for them (defined benefit schemes) and/or the reasons for the range of funds offered (money purchase schemes or sections)).

- The asset allocation strategy (including how the strategy has been arrived at) (defined benefit schemes only).

- Investment mandates (including an understanding of the nature of the contract between the trustees and their advisers).

- Fee structures (including why these structures have been selected) (defined benefit schemes only).

- Charges (only money purchase schemes or sections).

- The type of investments undertaken (defined benefit schemes only).

- Socially responsible investment and corporate governance.

Statement of funding principles (SFP) (defined benefit schemes only)

- Responsibilities for preparing the SFP.

- The scheme's statutory funding objective.

- Contents of the SFP.

- Review of the SFP (including changes to the status of the scheme).

Other relevant scheme documents

- Scheme booklet, announcements and other member communications.

- Actuarial valuation and advice (especially the key elements of the most recent actuarial valuation and subsequent advice).

- Minutes of meetings (including their importance and policy decisions recorded in them).

- Annual report and accounts.

- Any significant insurance policy.

- Any significant agreement or contract (including those with delegated authorities or professional advisers).

- Any trustee-approved procedures (including dispute resolution, appointment of trustees and appointment of a chairperson).

- Statement of compliance with the Myners' Principles (where appropriate).

- Terms of reference of any sub-committee (where relevant).

- Memorandum and Articles of a corporate trustee (where applicable).

- The scheme business plan (including a skills audit (where applicable) and/or training plan).

- Trustees should be aware of where all original documents are kept and of the arrangements for their custody, safekeeping and access.

Knowledge and understanding of pension matters 7.25

While trustees are not expected to become pension lawyers, they should at least have a basic understanding of trust law and essential pension legislation. Similarly, they are not expected to become investment or actuarial specialists, but they need to understand the basic principles relating to the funding of occupational schemes and the investment of scheme assets. The Pensions Regulator would expect trustees to be familiar with the following aspects (reproduced from the Scope Guidance).

The law relating to trusts

- The definition and nature of a pension trust (including the separation between the scheme and the employer).

- Fiduciary duties (including the obligation to act prudently, taking into account the needs of all beneficiaries).

- Conflicts of interest (especially the range of situations which may give rise to conflicts and how those conflicts may be managed).

- Professional advice and decision making (especially the need for obtaining professional advice (where appropriate) in reaching decisions).

- The role of advisers and suppliers to the scheme (including (as appropriate) actuaries, benefits consultants, financial advisers, fund managers, lawyers and statutory independent trustees).

- The particular role and use of advisers where a scheme or employer is under threat or a scheme is in wind-up.

- Fitness and properness to act as trustees (including the need for regular attendance at meetings).

- Taking office (especially personal duties and responsibilities).

- Ceasing to hold office (especially personal liability for past decisions).

- Investing funds (especially the trustees' responsibility to act prudently).

- Operating the scheme in accordance with the trust deed, rules and subsequent amendments (including the power to delegate functions while retaining responsibility).

- The role of the auditors (including internal and external auditors).

- Protections offered to trustees.

- The importance of sound administration arrangements (including risks, controls and contingency planning).

The law relating to pensions

- Key provisions of the *Pensions Act 2004*.

- Key remaining provisions of the *Pensions Act 1995*.

- The Pensions Regulator, codes of practice and guidance.

- Internal disputes resolution procedure.

- The role of the Pensions Advisory Service.

- The role of the Pensions Ombudsman.

- Pensions-related legislation (including the impact of other key provisions on the running of pension schemes).

- The tax privileges and requirements for occupational pension schemes.

- The interface between occupational schemes and state pensions provision.

- The particular powers of the Regulator in the event of disagreement between the trustees and the employer.

Investment principles

- Capital markets (including, in broad terms, the effect of economic cycles).

- The major asset classes and their characteristics.

- The implications of overseas investment (including foreign exchange risk).

- The existence of specialised asset classes, instruments and techniques.

- Risk v reward (especially the nature of risk and the risk/reward profile of each asset class).

- Valuation of assets (e g actuarial valuations and company balance sheets) · (defined benefit schemes only).

- With-profits arrangements and how they work (as appropriate).

Funding (defined benefit schemes)

- How the funding for occupational defined benefit schemes works.

- The nature of the employer/trustee relationship and the effect of pension liabilities on the sponsoring employers.

- The nature and strength of the employer covenant and its ability and willingness to meet the costs of members' benefits (especially an awareness of the employer's business and its risk exposure).

- How liabilities are valued.

- Funding targets (including how funding targets are set in relation to the underlying value of the liabilities).

- Potential risks to the scheme (including those arising from financial instability of the sponsoring employer or corporate restructuring).

- The impact of trustee powers (including the financial and reputational impact of exercising discretions).

- Transfers and bulk transfers in and out of schemes.

- Additional pension funding by employees.

Contributions (defined benefit schemes)

- The assumptions underlying the contribution calculations (including the process of setting contributions, the relationship between contributions and the scheme's liabilities, and the effect of the assumptions on valuations of the fund).

- The nature and status of professional advice.

- Funding deficits (including the requirements placed on trustees where there is an actual or potential funding deficit and disagreement between them and the employer on the rate of contributions required to correct it).

Strategic asset allocation (defined benefit schemes)

- How to fund particular future benefits (especially through selecting an appropriate mix of asset classes).

- The process of strategic asset allocation.

- Reviewing asset allocation decisions (especially where there is a change in status or maturity of the scheme).

Funding (money purchase arrangements)

- How the funding for occupational money purchase pension arrangements works (including expenses of the scheme, especially in the event of a wind-up).

- The risks borne by members.

- The implications of contracting out.

Investment choices (money purchase arrangements)

- Investment strategy and member investment choices.

- Administration procedures specific to money purchase arrangements (including the responsibilities of trustees in relation to effective administration and the risks to members' benefits).

Fund management (defined benefit and money purchase arrangements)

- The statement of investment principles (SIP) (especially the investment considerations necessary to meet the provisions of the SIP).

- Measuring performance, including the use of indices.

- The ownership of assets (especially the implications for trustees in relation to corporate governance).

- The structure of investment portfolios.

- The selection of fund managers (including how the process is managed).

- Continuing review of investment arrangements.

Exceptions

The requirements to be conversant with scheme documents and to have knowledge and understanding do not apply in the case of a scheme with fewer than twelve members where all the members are trustees (or trustee directors) and either decisions must be made unanimously or there is an independent trustee.

New trustees have a six-month period of grace before being expected to be compliant. (This exception does not apply to independent trustees meeting the definition in *section 23(1)* of the *Pensions Act 1995*, nor to any trustee who was appointed because of his or her knowledge of investments, funding, trust law or pension legislation.)

Internal controls

Background

Although Article 14(1) of the IORP Directive contained a requirement for occupational pension schemes to have appropriate internal controls, no provision was made for this in the drafting of the Pensions Bill, not even when other clauses were being added at committee and report stages. However, just over a year after the Bill received royal assent, the *European Communities Act 1972* was used to amend it so as to include provision for internal controls. The *Occupational Pension Schemes (Internal Controls) Regulations 2005 (SI 2005/3379)* were laid on 9 December 2005, came into force on 30 December 2005 and added one more section (*section 249A*) to the *Pensions Act 2004*.

Internal controls

Section 249A requires the trustees or managers of an occupational pension scheme to establish and operate internal controls that are adequate for the purpose of securing that the scheme is administered and managed in accordance with its rules and in accordance with the requirements of the law.

Internal controls are:

- arrangements and procedures to be followed in the administration and management of the scheme;

- systems and arrangements for monitoring that administration and management; and

- arrangements and procedures to be followed for the safe custody and security of the assets of the scheme.

Exceptions 7.29

The internal controls provisions do not apply to any scheme established under an Act of Parliament and which is guaranteed by a public authority. Nor do they apply to pay-as-you-go schemes or parliamentary pension schemes for members of the House of the Commons etc.

Code of practice 7.30

The Pensions Regulator is obliged to issue a code of practice on internal controls. The draft code was laid before Parliament on 19 July 2006. A copy of the draft is available on the Regulator's website at: http://www.thepensionregulator.co.uk/pdf/codeInternalControlsConsultation.pdf.

The code recommends that trustees should carry out a risk-based review of their scheme. They should first determine the various functions and activities carried out in the running of the scheme and then identify the key risks associated with those functions and activities. Trustees should consider maintaining a risk register to track significant funding, operational, financial, regulatory and compliance risks. Once identified, risks need to be managed and resolved. By way of example, the code lists some key risks that trustees may face and suggests a possible risk control for each:

Risk	*Possible types of control (where appropriate)*
Risk that existing controls are not operating effectively.	Periodic control reviews with changes made on a timely basis.
Risk of fraud (misappropriation of assets and fraudulent financial reporting).	Segregation of duties; frequent reconciliation procedures for cash and investment balances.
Corporate risk (risk of deterioration in strength of employer covenant and ongoing funding).	Monitor financial performance and corporate risk (e.g. inability of employer to fund scheme); procedures in place to detect corporate transactions in the public domain and assess impact on the scheme.
Funding/investment risk (inappropriate investment strategies).	Reconciliation procedures; review of investment strategies; independent peer review of funding advice.
Compliance/regulatory risk (failure to comply with scheme rules and legislation).	Compliance audits; stewardship and compliance reports from third parties.

Non-compliance or maladministration by administration team or third party advisers, eg outsourced administrators (poor record keeping).	Peer review of key controls by administration team; authorisation procedures; periodic meetings between trustees and provider (when required); service-level agreement reviews; performance appraisal of providers; internal quality review procedures by third party administrators (ie independent control reviews – 'Assurance Reports').
Computer system and database failures.	System recovery plans; data back-up procedures; password controls.
Poor scheme management (ineffective stewardship by those with delegated responsibility).	Regular trustee meetings; decisions taken within the formal structure of trustee meetings; minutes prepared for all meetings; sub-committees; manage conflicts of interest.

Trustees should review their governance procedures against the Regulator's code of practice. Trustees' core governance objectives should include:

- safeguarding the assets of the scheme;

- maintaining suitable funding levels (defined benefit schemes);

- ensuring members receive the benefits to which they are entitled; and

- ensuring the scheme operates within the law and in accordance with the scheme's trust deed and rules.

Under the heading of 'safeguarding assets' trustees should have regard to:

- investment and banking signing limits and procedures;

- the use of custodian services;

- cashflow/account reconciliation (and frequency thereof); and

- the monitoring of payments due to the scheme.

Under the heading of 'maintenance of funding levels' trustees should:

- monitor actuarial valuations against the statutory funding objective;

- receive regular actuarial reports; and

- manage the deficit/monitor performance against the recovery plan.

Under the heading of 'payment of benefits' trustees should consider obtaining:

- administration reports (statements that benefits have been applied in accordance with the rules of the scheme and within set service-level agreements); and

- periodic audits to verify benefit calculations in sampled cases.

Under the heading of 'compliance' trustees should, among other things, take account of the following:

- trustee knowledge and understanding requirements;

- escalating breaches of the law/whistleblowing;

- notifiable events (defined benefit schemes);

- conflicts of interest (identification and management);

- general trustee duties;

- adherence to a *Pensions Act 2004* checklist;

- adherence to accounting-for-tax and other procedures under the *Finance Act 2004*; and

- adherence to scheme rules and practice.

Surplus

Background 7.31

Prior to 6 April 2006 an approved occupational pension scheme was not permitted to hold a surplus calculated on a statutory basis under HMRC surplus regulations. One of the permitted methods of disposing of the surplus was to make a repayment to the sponsoring employer. Before a repayment could be made, the requirements of *section 37, Pensions Act 1995* (payment of surplus to employer) had to be satisfied. From 6 April 2006 HMRC no longer imposes any funding or surplus rules and the *Pensions Act 2004* substitutes a new section for *section 37* of the *Pensions Act 1995*. The requirements of *section 37* apply where a scheme is not being wound up. A different section (*section 76, Pensions Act 1995*) applies in cases where a scheme is being wound up. The new requirements for a return of surplus are set out at **7.33** below.

Exercise of power 7.32

If the power to return surplus to a sponsoring employer rests with any person other than the trustees of the scheme, it cannot be exercised by that person, but may instead be exercised by the trustees. If any restrictions applied to the person who had the power to return surplus, those restrictions would apply equally to the trustees as far as possible.

Conditions for return of surplus   7.33

Before trustees are able to make a repayment of surplus, they must ensure certain conditions are met.

The trustees must have obtained a written valuation of the scheme's assets and liabilities prepared and signed by the scheme's actuary. The value of the assets is the value shown in the audited accounts at the valuation date less any liabilities not related to members' benefits. The value of the liabilities is the actuary's estimate of the winding up costs plus the cost of purchasing annuities on terms consistent with those available in the market. Trustees may either commission a valuation for the specific purpose of returning surplus or use the scheme's last valuation prepared under the statutory funding objective.

There must be a certificate in force that states the maximum amount of the payment that may be made to the employer. Where a valuation has been prepared specifically for the purpose of returning surplus, the certificate is valid for 12 months from the effective date of the valuation. Where a valuation prepared under the statutory funding objective is used, the certificate is valid for 15 months from the effective date of the valuation. Trustees must ensure any amount repaid does not exceed the maximum specified in the certificate.

Before making any repayment, trustees must be satisfied that it is in members' interests that the power to return surplus is exercised in the manner proposed. This would seem to be a particularly difficult requirement to meet. If schemes are ever returned to a position of surplus in the future, this requirement would lead to some difficult conversations among trustees and between trustees and the sponsoring employer.

Additionally, the scheme must not be subject to a freezing order (see **3.24**), and where the employer previously exercised the power to return surplus, the power can only be exercised now at the employer's request or with its consent.

Notice to members (scheme not winding up)   7.34

Where a scheme is not being wound up, the trustees must notify the members of the scheme in writing that they have decided to make a repayment, and they must specify the proposed amount. The notice must show the date of the proposed payment. This date must be before the expiry date of the valuation certificate and at least three months from the date on which the notice is sent to members. Members may request a copy of the valuation certificate within one month of the notice, and trustees have one month to supply it. After trustees have made the repayment of surplus, they must notify the Pensions Regulator of that fact within one week of the payment date.

Notice to members (scheme winding up) 7.35

Where a scheme is being wound up, the trustees must take all reasonable steps to ensure that each member is sent a two-part notice of the proposal to return surplus.

The first part must contain an estimate of assets remaining after liabilities have been fully discharged, and the persons to whom, and proportions in which, the excess is to be distributed. Members must be given at least two months in which to make representations to the trustees or employer and told that part two will be sent if the repayment is to go ahead.

Part two must be given after the expiry date for representations, but at least three months before the repayment is made. It must show the amount of excess assets, and members must be advised that they may make representations to the Pensions Regulator by a date which is at least three months from the date on which part two is sent. Where that date has passed, trustees, or the employer, must obtain written confirmation from the Regulator that it has not received any representations, and the repayment may then go ahead.

Multi-employer schemes 7.36

Each section of a sectionalised multi-employer scheme is treated as if it were a scheme in its own right.

Trust requirement 7.37

The IORP Directive requires an occupational pension scheme to be legally separated from its sponsoring employer. It also requires those who run an occupational scheme to follow a prudent person rule. Fortunately, private sector funded occupational schemes are almost invariably established under irrevocable trusts which meet these requirements of the Directive. However, the requirement for occupational schemes to be set up under trust was a feature of the tax regime prior to 6 April 2006. From 6 April 2006 it is no longer necessary to establish a scheme under trust to secure tax privileges.

Section 252 of the *Pensions Act 2004* therefore re-introduces the legislative requirement for occupational schemes to be set up under trust. Any occupational pension scheme that has its main administration in the UK must be established under irrevocable trusts. If it is not, then the trustees or managers of the scheme must secure that no funding payment is accepted.

The following schemes are exempt from the trust requirement:

- a public service pension scheme;

- an occupational scheme with fewer than two members;

- an occupational scheme which has fewer than 100 members but is not a registered pension scheme under the terms of the *Finance Act 2004*.

Activities of occupational pension schemes
7.38

Section 255 of the *Pensions Act 2004* has created something of a controversy in its application to occupational schemes which have a life-assurance-only category of membership. This section of the Act is designed to give effect to Article 7 of the IORP Directive. Article 7 reads, 'Each Member State shall require institutions [ie pension schemes] located within its territory to limit their activities to retirement-benefit related operations and activities arising therefrom.' According to Article 6(d) of the Directive, retirement benefits are:

> 'benefits paid by reference to reaching, or the expectation of reaching, retirement or, where they are supplementary to those benefits and provided on an ancillary basis, in the form of payments on death, disability, or cessation of employment or in the form of support payments or services in case of sickness, indigence or death. In order to facilitate financial security in retirement, these benefits usually take the form of payments for life. They may, however, also be payments made for a temporary period or as a lump sum.'

These definitions were incorporated practically verbatim into *section 255*, but the problem arises because it would seem that the provision of life assurance is not a retirement-benefit-related activity if that is the only benefit provided for a member under the scheme. *Section 255* requires trustees to secure that the activities of the scheme are limited to retirement benefit activities, and, if they fail to take all reasonable steps to do so, they may be liable to a fine of up to £5,000 (for individual trustees) or up to £50,000 (for corporate trustees).

In what circumstances a life-assurance-only benefit is 'supplementary to a retirement benefit and provided on an ancillary basis' has been the subject of much discussion, and, in February 2006, the Department for Work and Pensions published its views on the matter.

Where an employee is in a waiting period before becoming eligible to join the scheme for retirement benefits, life assurance may be provided without contravening *section 255*. Where an employee opts not to join the scheme, or later opts out, but is still covered by the scheme's life assurance provisions, this too should be in order.

However, there would seem to be a problem where life assurance is provided for an employee and he or she either has not been or will not have a chance to become a member for retirement benefits. The Department for Work and

Pensions considered whether, in these circumstances, it would be acceptable for an occupational scheme to provide life-assurance-only benefit if the employee covered was in another pension scheme relating to the same employment eg a group personal pension or stakeholder pension scheme. Its considered view was as follows:

'Where there is a link between the provision of death-in-service benefits and the provision of retirement benefits provided by a third party, it is thought that it might be possible to argue that the supplementary test in Article 6(d) would be satisfied. The Department considers that this possibility would require an identifiable and concrete link between the provision of the two benefits, so that the two benefits are part of an overall arrangement provided by an employer in the employment relationship. The ancillary test would also have to be satisfied, and the mere fact that both benefits are available would not be sufficient to satisfy the test. This is, of course, no more than a view of the Department and it is for occupational pension schemes and their advisers to consider the merits of this possibility in relation to their own arrangements.'

As failure to comply could result in a hefty fine, the opinion of the Pensions Regulator was also sought. The Regulator concurred with the views of the DWP, and in regards to the provision of life assurance under an occupational scheme and retirement benefits under a group personal pension scheme it said:

'If a [occupational] pension scheme is closed to new members for pension benefits, or is closed for the future accrual of pension benefits but new members are provided with lump sum death benefits under this scheme, and with pension benefits under another scheme of the same employer, it is possible that this may not infringe the terms of section 255 of the Act.

This would be so, provided that there is a sufficient concrete and identifiable link through the employer between the provision of the lump sum death benefits under the one scheme, and the pension benefits under the other scheme.

Such a link would need to be stronger than the simple fact that the two schemes were set up and run by the same employer.'

It therefore appears that the life assurance and retirement benefit need to be interlinked under the two schemes in order to escape contravention of *section 255*, perhaps by way of one being conditional on the other. This would seem to be another matter for trustees' legal advisers. Of course, if the only benefits that a scheme provides are life assurance benefits, then there is no contravention as this would not fall to be defined as an occupational pension scheme. Therefore one answer for employers who find themselves in this situation is to set up a separate group life assurance scheme.

However, if any trustee is concerned about the possibility of being fined for a breach of *section 255*, they should note the Regulator's last word on the subject: 'If the regulator is notified of any breach of *section 255*, we will take a proportionate and risk-based approach to this, based on the risks to members' benefits caused by the breach concerned.'

Indemnification for fines 7.39

One of the first things a prudent person does upon becoming a pension scheme trustee is to check the indemnity clause in the scheme's trust deed to see how he or she is covered if something goes wrong. Almost invariably, pension trust deeds will include a clause which indemnifies the trustees of the scheme against any liabilities they may incur while acting as a trustee, just so long as those liabilities do not arise from a breach of trust knowingly and intentionally committed by the trustee. Trustees may be indemnified by the sponsoring employer, by a policy of insurance taken out for that purpose, out of the assets of the scheme, or by a combination of these depending on the circumstances.

Where trustees are indemnified out of the assets of the scheme, the *Pensions Act 1995* contained provisions to ensure that scheme trustees should not be reimbursed out of the scheme for any fine imposed following conviction of an offence or for any penalty levied under the *Pensions Act 1995* or the *Pension Schemes Act 1993*. The *Pensions Act 2004* replaced those provisions with new ones which are almost identical. The major difference between the two is that personal pension schemes are now covered whereas only trust schemes were covered previously. The new provisions are as follows.

No amount may be paid out of the assets of an occupational or personal pension scheme for the purpose of reimbursing any trustee or manager of the scheme in respect of a fine imposed for an offence of which he or she is convicted or a penalty imposed under *section 10* of the *Pensions Act 1995* or *section 168* of the *Pension Schemes Act 1993*.

Where a policy of insurance is taken out to cover scheme trustees or managers against fines and penalties, the premiums must not be paid out of scheme assets.

In the event that any amount is actually paid out of scheme assets to reimburse trustees or managers for fines or penalties, then those trustees or managers who failed to take all reasonable steps to prevent it will themselves be subject to penalty under *section 10* of the *Pensions Act 1995*.

If a trustee or scheme manager knows, or has reasonable grounds to believe, that he or she has been reimbursed out of scheme assets for a fine or penalty, he or she must take all reasonable steps to reverse the position and ensure that he or she is not reimbursed from the scheme. Failure to do so is an offence punishable on summary conviction by a fine not exceeding the statutory maximum, or, on conviction on indictment, by a prison term of up to two years and/or a fine.

Use of scheme assets to pay for trustees' criminal behaviour is obviously taken very seriously under the *Pensions Act 2004*. However, it is still in order for an employer to reimburse trustees for fines or penalties, just so long as the money does not come out of scheme funds. Given the number of pitfalls that trustees may come across in the ever more regulated area of pensions, it is possible that they may become subject to a fine at some point. Trustees have therefore started to take a greater interest in their schemes' indemnity provisions to ensure that, where they cannot be indemnified out of scheme assets, they will at least be protected by the sponsoring employer.

Pension protection on transfer under TUPE

Background 7.40

European legislation protecting the continuing employment rights of workers under a transfer of undertakings does not, generally speaking, extend to pension rights. However, early retirement conditions have been held to transfer in certain circumstances, and where an employer is contractually bound to pay contributions to a personal pension, those contractual rights would also transfer. Under both the *Transfer of Undertakings (Protection of Employment) Regulations 1981 (SI 1981/1794)* ('TUPE') and the subsequent *Transfer of Undertakings (Protection of Employment) Regulations 2006 (SI 2006/246)* which replaced them, rights relating to old age, invalidity and survivors' benefits are excluded from protection on transfer, reflecting the provisions of the European legislation. Rights already accrued are safeguarded, but there is no obligation for a new employer to offer ongoing pension benefits on the same terms. To try and address this lack of protection, the government included provisions in the *Pensions Act 2004* which would require a new employer to offer pension benefits to workers who transferred under TUPE. These provisions came into force on 6 April 2005.

Protection conditions 7.41

For pension protection to apply, the transfer of employment must have been protected under TUPE, and the employees concerned must either be active members of an occupational pension scheme immediately before the transfer or be eligible to become members of the occupational scheme (or be in a waiting period) immediately before the transfer. The new employer must offer an occupational pension scheme or a stakeholder pension scheme, as described below, and the pension protection terms must be written into the employment contracts of the transferred workers. Note that this does not mean that the trustees or managers of any scheme set up under the new employment have to accept a transfer of rights from the previous scheme, but employees must be eligible to accrue future rights. Note also, however, that a transferred employee and the new employer may come to an agreement whereby the pension protection conditions are not to apply.

Form of protection   7.42

A new employer must offer either an occupational or stakeholder pension scheme that meets the following requirements.

If an occupational scheme is offered, then:

- if it is a money purchase scheme, the employer must match employee contributions up to at least 6% of basic pay in each pay period (contracted-out rebates are to be ignored for this purpose);

- if it is not a money purchase scheme, then *one* of the following conditions must be met:

    (*a*)   the scheme must satisfy the contracting-out reference scheme test;

    (*b*)   members are entitled to benefits the value of which equals or exceeds 6% of pensionable pay for each year of employment together with the amount of members' own contributions, and members are not required to contribute at a rate of more than 6% of pensionable pay (the definition of pensionable pay must be the same for both benefits and contributions);

    (*c*)   the employer must match employee contributions up to at least 6% of basic pay in each pay period (contracted-out rebates are to be ignored for this purpose).

If a stakeholder scheme is offered, then the employer must match employee contributions up to at least 6% of basic pay in each pay period.

It is difficult to legislate for a form of protection that is both of value as a protection and not an undue burden on competitive business. Undoubtedly some employees will still be worse off after a transfer eg where a defined benefit scheme is replaced with a money purchase scheme, but some employees may be better off eg where a previous money purchase occupational scheme only provided matching up to a rate less than 6%. Contractual contributions an employer makes to the personal pensions of employees are unaffected by the *Pensions Act 2004*; if 3% contractual contributions were required before the TUPE transfer, 3% would continue to apply afterwards. Similarly, if 10% contractual contributions were due before the transfer, 10% could be required after transfer.

Consultation by employers

Background 7.43

There has never really been a specific piece of legislation requiring employers to consult generally about changes they were about to make to their pension scheme. Of course, employers had to consult independent trade unions about certain contracting-out matters; the designation of a stakeholder scheme required employee consultation; and pensions may have been included in collective bargaining arrangements in the past. But *sections 259–261* of the *Pensions Act 2004* for the first time involve scheme members in the amendment process where an important change to benefits is concerned. Note that this does not mean member consent is required before a change is made, but the parties involved must work together in a spirit of co-operation.

Application 7.44

The *Occupational and Personal Pension Schemes (Consultation by Employers and Miscellaneous Amendment) Regulations 2006 (SI 2006/349)* were laid under *sections 259–261, Pensions Act 2004* and provide the meat of the pension consultation legislation. They came into force on 6 April 2006. The regulations apply to any employer that proposes to make any amendment covered by the consultation regulations. Where the amendment power lies with the trustees, they must notify the employer of their proposal to make any amendment covered by the consultation regulations. The trustees must not make that change until they are satisfied that the employer has carried out the necessary consultation.

If there has been a failure to follow the consultation requirements, this will not of itself invalidate the amendment. However, the Pensions Regulator may require information from employers and trustees about action taken by them for the purpose of complying with the pension consultation regulations, and this in turn may have further consequences.

Changes to occupational pension schemes 7.45

None of the changes specified in the list below may be made by either the employer or the trustees unless the employer has first carried out the required consultation:

- to increase the normal pension age specified in the scheme rules;

- to prevent new members, or new members of a particular description, from being admitted to the scheme;

- to prevent the future accrual of benefits under the scheme;

- to remove the liability to make employer contributions towards the scheme;

- to introduce member contributions in any circumstances in which no such contributions were previously payable;

- to make any increase in member contributions;

- to make any reduction in the amount of employer contributions towards money purchase benefits;

- to convert to money purchase benefits some or all of the benefits that may be provided under the scheme;

- to change, in whole or in part, the basis for determining the rate of future accrual under a defined benefit scheme;

- to modify the scheme under *section 229(2)* of the *Pensions Act 2004* (matters requiring agreement of the employer) so as to reduce the rate of future accrual under a defined benefit scheme;

- to make any other reduction in the rate of future accrual under a defined benefit scheme.

Changes to personal pension schemes 7.46

Where employer contributions are made to a personal pension under direct payment arrangements, the employer may not make any of the three changes listed below without first carrying out the required consultation:

- to stop making employer contributions towards the scheme in respect of any members;

- to reduce the amount of employer contributions towards the scheme;

- to make any increase in contributions required of any member of the scheme.

Provision of information 7.47

Where a proposed change is covered by the pension consultation regulations, an employer must provide information about the proposed change to those employees who appear to be affected and to any recognised trade unions, to any representatives appointed in accordance with the *Information and Consultation of Employees Regulations 2004 (SI 2004/3426)*, to representatives appointed under any pre-existing agreement, or to representatives elected under the pension consultation regulations. The information to be provided must:

- be in writing;

- be provided before the start of the consultation;

- describe the change and state what effects it would have, or would be likely to have, on the scheme and its members;

- be accompanied by any relevant background information;

- indicate the timescale for the introduction of the proposed changes; and

- be given in such a way and contain sufficient information so as to enable, in particular, representatives of affected members to consider, conduct a study of, and give their views to the employer on, the impact of the change.

Persons to be consulted   7.48

If affected employees are already represented by a recognised trade union, by representatives appointed in accordance with the *Information and Consultation of Employees Regulations 2004* (*SI 2004/3426*) or by representatives appointed under any pre-existing agreement, then those representatives must be consulted by the employer. If there are no such representatives, an employer may arrange an election specifically for representatives for the purpose of consulting on pension scheme changes covered by the regulations. Elections must meet the following requirements:

- the employer must make such arrangements as are reasonably practical to ensure that the election is fair;

- the employer must determine the number of representatives to be elected so that there are sufficient representatives to represent the interests of active and prospective members;

- the employer must determine whether active and prospective members should be represented together or by separate representatives;

- the employer must determine the term of office for representatives;

- the candidates for election must be active or prospective members of the scheme on the date of the election;

- no active or prospective member may unreasonably be excluded from standing for election;

- all active or prospective members on the date of the election are entitled to vote for member representatives;

- voters may vote for as many candidates as there are representatives to be elected;

- voting must be conducted in secret, as far as possible, and votes must be counted accurately;

- where members' interests are no longer represented because an elected representative has ceased to act as such, the members must elect another representative;

- the employer must review the number of representatives from to time to ensure there are still sufficient representatives to represent the interests of active and prospective members.

Where the interests of any affected members are not represented by elected representatives, or by any trade union etc, then the employer must consult directly with each affected member.

Consultation

Employers need to ensure that, as far as possible, the consultation covers all affected members. Both the employer and any person consulted are under a duty to work in a spirit of co-operation, taking into account the interests of both sides.

At the start of consultation an employer must specify an end date for the consultation or an end date for the submission of written comments. The consultation period must not be less than 60 days.

After the end of the period allowed for the consultation, the person who proposed the change must consider the responses (if any) received in the course of consultation before making his or her decision as to whether or not to make a change. If no responses are received before the end of the consultation period, the consultation process is regarded as complete.

Exceptions

The regulations contain several exceptions. The following are exempt from the pension consultation provisions:

- employers with fewer than:
  - (a) 150 employees from 6 April 2006 to 5 April 2007;
  - (b) 100 employees from 6 April 2007 to 5 April 2008; and
  - (c) 50 employees from 6 April 2008 onwards;
- public service pension schemes;
- single-life schemes;
- employer-financed retirement benefits schemes;
- occupational pension schemes which are not registered for UK tax relief and which have their main administration outside the EU member states;
- schemes with fewer than twelve members where all the members are trustees and either decisions must be made by the trustees unanimously or there is an independent trustee;

- employers in relation to a personal pension scheme where there is no employer contribution due to the scheme;

- changes made for the purpose of complying with a statutory provision;

- changes necessary to comply with a determination made by the Pensions Regulator;

- changes which have no lasting effect on a person's rights to be admitted to a scheme or on the benefits that may be provided under it;

- regulated modifications under the subsisting rights provisions (*sections 67–67I* of the *Pensions Act 2004*);

- changes made after 5 April 2006 but where affected members were notified before 6 April 2006 of the proposal to make the change.

The Pensions Regulator may waive or relax any of the pension consultation requirements if it is satisfied that it is necessary to do so in order to protect the interests of the generality of the members of the scheme.

Subsisting rights provisions 7.51

The pension consultation regulations do not apply where the proposed amendment is a regulated modification under the new subsisting rights provisions (see **7.54–7.59** below). Member consent is required where the change is a protected modification. Where the change is a detrimental modification using the actuarial equivalence provisions, member consultation would be required in accordance with the subsisting rights regulations. Before a detrimental modification is made, trustees must have taken all reasonable steps to:

- give affected members information in writing adequate to explain the nature of the modification and its effect on them;

- notify affected members in writing that they may make representations to the trustees about the modification;

- afford affected members a reasonable opportunity to make such representations; and

- notify affected members in writing that the actuarial equivalence requirements apply in their case in respect of the modification.

Note that, although failure to consult properly under the pension consultation regulations will not invalidate any scheme change, a failure to follow the subsisting rights provisions properly will result in those changes being voidable by the Pensions Regulator.

ICE regulations   7.52

The *Information and Consultation of Employees Regulations 2004 (SI 2004/3426)* ('ICE') give employees in larger firms the right to be informed and consulted about the business they work for. The regulations implement EU Directive 2002/14/EC establishing a general framework for informing and consulting employees in the European Community. They are based on a framework agreed with the CBI and the TUC, and came into force on 6 April 2005.

If an employer has already established consultation arrangements under the ICE regulations, it is possible that they may cover pension matters. Guidance from the Department of Trade and Industry, published in January 2006, considers that, where information about changes in contractual relations has to be provided under ICE, this would cover changes to an occupational pension scheme, but only where there was a contractual right to participate in the scheme. However, any existing ICE provisions concerning consultation about pension matters may be disapplied where they are now covered by the pension consultation regulations. If any pension changes are proposed which are not specifically covered by the pension consultation regulations, it may be necessary to ascertain whether they are covered by any existing consultation arrangements under ICE.

Multi-employer schemes   7.53

The *Occupational Pension Schemes (Consultation by Employers) (Modification for Multi-employer Schemes) Regulations 2006 (SI 2006/16)* were laid on 12 January 2006 and came into force on 2 February 2006. They modify the consultation provisions of *sections 259* and *261, Pensions Act 2004*, as regards occupational pension schemes. Essentially, where the occupational scheme is a multi-employer scheme, any reference to trustees or managers in *sections 259* or *261* is to be treated as if it includes reference to any other person who has the power under scheme rules to make a decision in relation to the scheme.

Modification of subsisting rights

Background   7.54

Amendment powers in pension scheme trust deeds must be used for changes compatible with promoting the purposes of the scheme. This protects the beneficiaries against improper rule amendments and generally safeguards members' accrued rights. *Section 67* of the *Pensions Act 1995* was introduced to put this protection on a statutory footing, but it has been widely criticised for being too restrictive. If any modification would, or might, have affected any member's accrued rights then the trustees had to agree to the modification and had to obtain a certificate from the scheme actuary confirming that the modification would not adversely have affected any member in respect of their entitlements or accrued rights without their consent. Alternatively, member consent could be sought. The Pickering Report recognised the difficulties this imposed when trying to make sensible restructurings of a scheme's provisions:

> 'It is practically impossible to assess in all possible cases whether a particular restructuring would adversely affect accrued rights, and there is no clear definition of "modification" or of "entitlements". (There is a definition of "accrued rights", but it raises as many questions as it addresses.)
>
> If a relatively cautious interpretation of Section 67 is adopted, many wholly proper amendments, which are justifiable in terms of members' interests and are essential to enable a scheme to adapt to changing circumstances, simply cannot be made.
>
> A less cautious interpretation of Section 67, by contrast, runs the risk of perfectly reasonable amendments being made which turn out, many years later, to have been invalid. A scheme finding itself in this position would then have to go through the process of unravelling years of benefit payments, with the funding consequences and implications for members' expectations that this would entail.
>
> As a result, defined benefit schemes faced with unsustainable costs are increasingly left only with the drastic option of closing down the scheme altogether or switching to a defined contribution arrangement (often with reduced employer contributions). This was not the intention of the legislation.'

The Pickering Report recommended that the scheme actuary should provide a certificate of actuarial equivalence rather than having to certify that members' accrued rights would not be adversely affected. If the value of benefits before the amendment was the same as the value of overall benefits after the amendment, then the change could go ahead. The *Pensions Act 2004* contains provisions to give effect to this. It replaces *section 67* of the *Pensions Act 1995* with ten new sections (*section 67–67I*) known as the subsisting rights provisions. Originally targeted for 6 April 2005, these provisions did not actually come into force until 6 April 2006.

The subsisting rights provisions   7.55

The subsisting rights provisions apply to any 'regulated modification'. A modification is a regulated modification if it is a 'protected modification' or a 'detrimental modification'. The main distinction between these two for practical purposes is that a protected modification requires member consent whereas a detrimental modification may be made under the actuarial equivalence test.

A protected modification is one which would, or might, have the effect of reducing a pension already in payment or substituting money purchase benefits for rights already accrued on a non-money purchase basis. A detrimental modification is simply one which would, or might, adversely affect accrued rights.

Before a regulated modification can be made, the trustees of the scheme must have given their approval to the amendment. Trustees must not give their approval unless, in the case of a protected modification, members have given their consent to the change, or, in the case of a detrimental modification, either the actuarial equivalence conditions are met or members have given their consent. Additionally, trustees must notify each affected member that they have approved the amendment, but where the actuarial equivalence conditions are met, the legislation only requires them to take reasonable steps to notify the affected members.

If any regulated modification is not made in accordance with the subsisting rights provisions, the Pensions Regulator has the power to make void any such modification or any part of such a modification.

The consent requirements   7.56

The consent requirements apply where a protected modification is proposed or a detrimental modification is proposed which is not being dealt with under actuarial equivalence provisions.

The consent requirements are met if:

- the trustees give each affected member enough written information to explain the nature of the amendment and its effect on him or her;

- the trustees have notified him or her in writing that he or she may make representations to the trustees about the proposed amendment;

- the trustees have afforded him or her a reasonable opportunity to make representations;

- the trustees have notified him or her in writing that the consent requirements apply;

- the member has consented in writing to the amendment; and

- the modification takes effect within a reasonable period after the member has consented.

The actuarial equivalence requirements   7.57

To meet the actuarial equivalence requirements trustees must take all reasonable steps to:

- give each affected member enough written information to explain the nature of the modification and its effect on him or her;

- notify each affected member that he or she may make representations to them about the modification;

- afford each affected member a reasonable opportunity to make representations; and

- notify each affected member that the actuarial equivalence requirements apply in his or her case.

Trustees must secure that, immediately after the modification takes effect, the actuarial value of any member's accrued rights is equal to or greater than the actuarial value of accrued rights immediately before the modification, and they must obtain a written statement from the scheme actuary to that effect.

In determining whether actuarial value has been maintained, the scheme actuary must:

- adopt methods and make assumptions which are consistent with those used by trustees for calculating cash equivalent transfer values;

- ensure trustees have been notified of those methods and assumptions;

- ignore any reduction in cash equivalent transfer values due to scheme underfunding;

- exclude any rights which have been surrendered, commuted or forfeited, or are discretionary or money purchase rights; and

- follow guidance note GN51 issued by the Faculty and Institute of Actuaries (see **APPENDIX 6**).

If there are any matters which would not prevent the actuarial equivalence of accrued rights being maintained, but which might be relevant to the trustees' decision to approve a modification, the actuary must draw those matters to the attention of the trustees as soon as possible.

Exemptions   7.58

There are several exemptions to the subsisting rights provisions. For the most part, these are contained in the *Occupational Pension Schemes (Modification of Schemes) Regulations 2006 (SI 2006/759)*.

Schemes which are not registered pension schemes, or which only have one member, are exempt from the subsisting rights provisions. Additionally, the subsisting rights provisions do not apply to any of the following:

- pension debits created as a result of a pension sharing order following a divorce;

- any modification of a scheme which provides for accrued rights to be assigned, commuted, surrendered or charged, or have a lien or set-off exercised in respect of them, provided that such a modification is not prohibited by *section 91* of the *Pensions Act 1995* (inalienability of occupational pension) or any other law;

- any modification which provides for accrued rights to be forfeited, provided that such a modification is not prohibited under *section 92* of the *Pensions Act 1995* (forfeiture) or any other law;

- any modification required for the revaluation of guaranteed minimum pensions in respect of early leavers;

- any modification which provides for a protected rights annuity to be purchased on a single-life basis providing the member has given his or her consent;

- any modification which provides for the transfer of accrued rights either with a member's consent or without consent in accordance with the *Occupational Pension Schemes (Preservation of Benefit) Regulations 1991 (SI 1991/167)*;

- any modification which ensures that any payment made by the scheme, relating to rights which accrued on or after 6 April 2006, is not an unauthorised member payment in terms of the *Finance Act 2004*;

- any modification which ensures that the trustees can pay any tax they owe HMRC in respect of short service refund lump sums, special lump sum death benefits or benefits in excess of a member's lifetime allowance;

- any modification to incorporate the effect of the *Registered Pension Schemes (Modification of the Rules of Existing Schemes) Regulations 2006 (SI 2006/364)* into scheme rules;

- any modification to treat a surviving civil partner in the same way as a widow or widower.

Code of practice   7.59

The Pensions Regulator is obliged to issue a code of practice on the modification of subsisting rights. A draft code was issued for consultation in July 2005, and the consultation closed on 30 September 2005. However, the final regulations relating to scheme modification were not laid until 16 March 2006, so the draft code of practice may need to be revisited. At the time of writing the code of practice remains in draft. The draft code can be found on the Regulator's website at: http://www.thepensionregulator.co.uk/pdf/codeModificationConsultation.pdf.

Early leavers

Background 7.60

The Pickering Report recommended immediate vesting for all members of occupational pension schemes ie early leavers should not receive a refund of their contributions if they leave with less than two years' service but should instead receive the full value of a deferred pension. This recommendation was made in recognition of the fact that it was difficult for people with broken work histories to build up worthwhile retirement provision. However, to ease the burden on scheme trustees who would have had to administer a large number of small benefits, and to spare the scheme sponsor the cost of this, it was recommended that trustees should be allowed to transfer small value benefits (worth less than, say, £10,000) out of the scheme to a safe harbour pension savings vehicle. This would be done without members' consent, but members would at least have received the value of a deferred pension as opposed to just a refund of contributions.

Although the recommendation was not incorporated exactly into the *Pensions Act 2004*, the government did at least implement the principle of the recommendation. From 6 April 2006, members who leave pensionable service with at least three months' but less than two years' pensionable service have the option of taking a transfer value to another pension arrangement instead of having to take a refund of contributions. Schemes may still force early leavers with less than three months' pensionable service to take a refund.

To give effect to this seemingly simple measure, the *Pensions Act 2004* had to insert an additional nine sections into the *Pension Schemes Act 1993* (*sections 101AA–101AI*). These were necessary to ensure that the transfer value is treated in the same way as a normal cash equivalent transfer value and to provide the necessary statutory discharges for trustees when they pay either the transfer value or the refund of contributions.

The new provisions are overriding. However, they do not apply to schemes which already confer a right to a full deferred pension for early leavers with less than two years' service.

Transfer option 7.61

Where an occupational scheme member has at least three months' but less than two years' pensionable service at the date of leaving, he or she acquires a right to either a cash transfer sum or a contribution refund as he or she may elect.

The cash transfer sum is calculated on the basis of the full deferred pension he or she would have notionally been entitled to. For example, if the accrual rate is $\frac{1}{60}$ths and a member leaves with $1\frac{1}{2}$ years' pensionable service, the transfer value is based on a notional deferred pension equal to $\frac{1}{60}$ x 1½ x final pensionable salary. Note that if the trustees reduce transfer values generally because the scheme is underfunded, they may also reduce the cash transfer sums offered to early leavers covered by these provisions.

The contribution refund must include interest if the scheme would have awarded interest otherwise. Where the scheme is a money purchase scheme and normally refunds only the investment value of the member's contributions, the contribution refund should reflect the investment value. Contribution refunds may also be reduced to account for tax, and any amount required to buy the member back into the additional state pension.

Within a reasonable period after his or her date of leaving, the trustees must write to the member to explain his or her right to a transfer or a refund and how he or she may exercise that right. The trustees' letter must cover the following matters:

- It must show the amount of the cash transfer sum and must describe the ways in which it can be used.

- If the cash transfer sum has been reduced, it must give the reason together with details of the reduction.

- It must show the amount of the contribution refund together with reductions in respect of tax, and the member's share of the premium to reinstate him or her into the state scheme.

- It must describe how taking a transfer or a refund would affect any other rights he or she may have under the scheme.

- It must specify the last day by which the member may exercise his or her right to a transfer value.

- It must inform the member that if he or she fails to exercise his or her right to a transfer value by the time indicated, the trustees will be entitled to pay him or her only a contribution refund.

If a member misses the deadline indicated in the trustees' letter for the exercise of his or her right to a transfer value, he or she may still apply for it at a later date. Although the trustees are not bound to pay the transfer if the deadline has been missed, they may allow the member another chance to take the transfer.

Code of practice 7.62

These provisions of the Act contain reference to 'reasonable periods' within which trustees must do certain things. The Pensions Regulator is obliged to issue a code of practice on what would be reasonable for these timescales. The Regulator laid its code of practice on 14 March 2006, and the code came into effect in May 2006.

Trustees should inform early leavers covered by these provisions of their rights as soon as possible after the date of leaving, but in any event within three months of leaving. It would be reasonable for trustees to allow three months from the date of their letter for a response from the member concerned, and trustees should action the transfer or refund within three months of the member's request.

Short service benefit 7.63

The *Pensions Act 2004* introduced a change to the payable age for short service benefit. Where an occupational pension scheme has a normal pension age of less than 60, the rules must provide that a deferred member's preserved pension (short service benefit) must be paid no later than age 60. Occupational schemes with retirement ages less than 60 will usually cover those in hazardous occupations such as the police and firemen. However, in line with moves to extend working lives and attempts to raise public sector retirement ages, the government altered the latest payable age for short service benefit from 60 to 65. From 6 April 2005, schemes may adopt a rule which provides that a deferred member's preserved pension must be paid no later than age 65. If a scheme's normal pension age is greater than 65, preserved pensions may still be deferred until that later age. Although the change took effect from 6 April 2005, scheme rules would have to be amended to take advantage of it, and any change should therefore be confined to future service benefits.

Paternity and adoption leave 7.64

Schedule 5 of the *Social Security Act 1989* contains provisions protecting the pension rights of those on maternity leave. *Section 265* of the *Pensions Act 2004* inserts two new paragraphs into *Schedule 5* so as to bring the pension rights of those on paternity or adoption leave under the same protection. The measure came into force on 6 April 2005.

During any period of paternity or adoption leave when an employee receives contractual or statutory paternity or adoption pay, he or she must be treated no less favourably than if he or she were working normally. Although an employer must maintain the accrual of any defined benefit pension while the employee is absent, the employee only need contribute on the remuneration he or she actually receives. The position is not so clear when it comes to money purchase pension schemes, and there is still some argument over the extent to which employers may be required to make good any contribution shortfalls. Unfortunately, the government did not take this as an opportunity to clarify the uncertainties.

Inalienability 7.65

Prior to the *Pensions Act 2004*, there was some uncertainty, due to the inalienability provisions, over whether trustees could recover from existing benefits any money they had paid to beneficiaries by mistake.

Section 266 of the *Pensions Act 2004* now amends the inalienability provisions of the *Pensions Act 1995* so as to permit, specifically, the reduction of a member's pension entitlement or right under an occupational pension scheme for the purpose of discharging some monetary obligation due from the member to the scheme arising out of a payment made in error in respect of the pension. If trustees do this, they must provide the member concerned with a certificate showing the amount of the reduction and its effect on his or her benefits under the scheme. If, however, the member disputes the amount of the reduction, the trustees must not reduce his or her benefits until they receive an appropriate court order.

Voluntary contributions 7.66

Prior to 6 April 2006 the pensions tax regime prevented members of approved occupational pension schemes from contributing to other types of pension arrangement except in certain limited circumstances. These restrictive tax provisions were swept away on 6 April 2006, and from that date onwards members are free to contribute to any additional pension arrangement. Consequently, there is no longer any need for trustees of occupational schemes to be required to offer members the facility to pay additional voluntary contributions (AVCs). The Pickering Report recommended that the AVC requirement should remain until full concurrency was achieved under the new tax regime, and at that time trustees and employers should be free to decide what, if any, additional savings vehicle is offered.

Section 267 of the *Pensions Act 2004* removed the AVC requirement from the *Pension Schemes Act 1993* with effect from 6 April 2006, thereby giving effect to the Pickering Report recommendation. Occupational scheme sponsors are now free to decide whether their scheme should continue to offer an AVC arrangement or whether they limit member contributions to those required under the rules of the scheme. Whatever happens, however, trustees will still have to look after, and apply, any AVC funds already accrued.

Contribution monitoring

Background 7.67

When the *Pensions Act 1995* came into force on 6 April 1997, trustees of occupational pension schemes had to ensure that a schedule was in place showing the due dates by which employers had to pay over contributions to the pension scheme. If any contribution was not paid over by the due date, trustees had to report the matter to Opra. Consequently, Opra was inundated with reports from trustees. Similar measures were introduced where employers paid contributions to employees' personal pensions. Trustees, insurers and employers were not the only ones who found the reporting system burdensome. Opra, too, was straining under the weight of reports being made, a great many of which were not actually serious breaches. What had seemed like a good idea at the time was obviously proving to be a cumbersome piece of legislation. Furthermore, it created the danger that a serious breach might be overlooked if it was buried under a number of trivial reports. In the years since 1997 the legislation has been toned down, and, following further amendments in the *Pensions Act 2004*, it has now become a more risk-orientated measure, bolstered by codes of practice and guidance from the Pensions Regulator.

Occupational money purchase pension schemes 7.68

Trustees of money purchase occupational schemes must still draw up a payment schedule of the contributions due and monitor the receipt of contributions against the due dates. However, they only need to make a report to the Regulator if they have reasonable cause to believe that a late payment is likely to be of *material significance* to the Regulator in the exercise of its functions. Where they do make a report, it must be made within a reasonable timescale.

According to the Regulator's code of practice, the following are likely to be of material significance and should be reported:

- where contributions remain unpaid 90 days after the due date (unless it is a one-off or infrequent administration error, which is discovered after the 90 days, and which is corrected when found or is thereafter corrected as soon as practicable);

- where there is a late payment involving possible dishonesty or a misuse of assets or contributions (eg contributions being used to alleviate employer cashflow problems);

- where the failure to pay contributions carries a criminal penalty (eg the employer is knowingly concerned in the fraudulent evasion of the obligation to pay member contributions);

- where the trustees become aware that the employer does not have adequate procedures or systems in place to ensure the correct and timely payment of contributions due and appears not to be taking adequate steps to remedy the situation;

- where there is no early prospect of outstanding contributions being paid; for example, because of the financial circumstances of the employer.

If the late payment falls into one of the following circumstances, the Regulator would not normally want to be informed, even if contributions remain unpaid 90 days after the due date:

- where there are infrequent late payments and the overdue contributions have now been paid, or arrangements are being put in place for the prompt payment of the overdue amount (eg an administrative failing which is now being rectified);

- where there is a late payment and there are four or fewer active members in the scheme (unless the late payment is a result of dishonesty or would carry a criminal penalty);

- where there are short periods of lateness of contributions resulting from, for example, members leaving, new members joining, or changes in salary not being notified to trustees;

- where a claim has been submitted to the Redundancy Payments Service of the Department of Trade and Industry for the outstanding contributions.

Although these are examples, trustees will need to exercise their judgement in any particular situation with regard to whether a breach, or combination of breaches, is likely to be of material significance.

Where trustees do decide to report a breach, the Regulator considers that trustees should reasonably report it in writing within ten working days of identifying the breach. However, shorter timescales will apply in the case of more serious breaches, and in extreme cases trustees should report immediately by telephone.

If trustees make a report to the Pensions Regulator, they must also report the matter to those members who are affected by the late payment. The Regulator considers such a report should be made as soon as reasonably practicable and in any event within 30 days. If trustees do not need to report to the Regulator, they are not required to report to members.

The Regulator's code of practice on reporting late payment of contributions to occupational money purchase schemes can be found on the Regulator's website at http://www.thepensionregulator.co.uk/pdf/codeLpmpsFinal.pdf, and is essential reading for trustees. The new measures came into effect on 6 April 2006.

Occupational defined benefit schemes   7.69

Where the trustees of a defined benefit scheme have carried out their first valuation under the new statutory funding objective, they should carry out contribution monitoring on the basis set out in the Regulator's code of practice on funding defined benefits. Where trustees have not yet carried out their first valuation under the statutory funding objective, they should continue to monitor contributions on the pre–*Pensions Act 2004* basis, as set out in the Regulator's Briefing No. 1 *Contributions – Reporting Late Payment to Occupational Pension Schemes*. Defined benefit schemes will therefore gradually all become subject to the new, less prescriptive contribution monitoring requirements over the period up to December 2009, depending on when their next scheme valuation is due.

Valuation already carried out under new funding regime

Where trustees have completed their first valuation on the new scheme funding basis, the prescriptive timescales surrounding the reporting of late contributions is replaced with the more general responsibility of trustees to ensure that contributions are actually paid as agreed in the schedule of contributions, and, where they have serious concerns about the payment of contributions, to make a report to the Pensions Regulator. The following extract is taken from the Regulator's code of practice on funding defined benefits:

> 'Trustees should ensure there is a robust procedure in place for monitoring the receipt of contributions. To do so they will usually need the relevant pensionable payrolls of all of the participating employers in the scheme. They may wish to obtain independent verification from the employer's auditor that the payroll is relevant, complete and correct, or make other checks to verify it.
>
> Trustees need to investigate any apparent employer failure to adhere to the schedule of contributions. Where a contribution failure is identified, trustees should normally discuss it with the employer as soon as practicable with a view to finding out the cause of the failure, rectifying any underpayment and taking steps to avoid a recurrence in the future. The more serious the contribution failure appears, the more urgent the investigation should be. Following the trustees' investigation they may be required to make a report to the Pensions Regulator.'

In deciding whether or not to make a report to the Regulator, trustees must consider whether the late or non-payment of a contribution due under the schedule of contributions is likely to be materially significant to the Regulator in the exercise of its functions. The following situations are likely to be of material significance to the Regulator:

- the employer appears to be involved in the fraudulent evasion of the obligation to pay members' pension deductions;

- there is reasonable cause to believe a form of dishonesty is involved other than the fraudulent evasion of the obligation to pay members' pension deductions;

- there is an immediate risk to members' benefits such as pensions in payment normally met by the employer's contribution;

- contributions remain unpaid 90 calendar days after the due date (unless it is a one-off or infrequent administrative error, which is discovered after the 90 days, and which is already corrected when found or is thereafter corrected as soon as is reasonably practicable);

- the employer appears not to have adequate procedures or systems in place to ensure the normal, correct and timely payment of contributions and appears not to be taking adequate steps to remedy the situation;

- the trustees conclude, after discussions with the employer, that there is no early prospect of contribution underpayments being corrected (eg because of the financial circumstances of the employer).

The following situations are unlikely to be of material significance to the Regulator:

- contribution failures in schemes where all the members of the scheme are directors of the employing company or family members of the directors;

- the contribution failures stem from administrative lapses which are corrected as soon as reasonably practicable and where reasonable steps are being taken to avoid recurrence;

- a claim has been submitted to the Redundancy Payments Service of the Department of Trade and Industry for the outstanding contributions.

If trustees decide they should report a contribution failure to the Regulator, they must do so within a reasonable period. This should be within ten working days of identifying the breach. However, shorter timescales would apply in the case of more serious breaches, and in extreme cases trustees should make a report immediately by telephone.

Where trustees have reported a contribution failure to the Pensions Regulator, they should also report it to scheme members. This should be done within a reasonable period. The Regulator's code of practice on funding defined benefits considers that one month is a reasonable period. The code can be found on the Regulator's website at: http://www.thepensionregulator.co.uk/pdf/codeFundingFinal.pdf.

Valuation not yet carried out under new funding regime

Until the first valuation is carried out on the new funding basis, trustees should adhere to the existing measures in place requiring them to report late contributions to the Reguator and to members within statutory timescales. Trustees must receive employee and employer contributions by the due date specified in the schedule of contributions. The due date for employee contributions to be received must be no later than the 19th of the month following the month in which they were deducted from employees' pay.

The Regulator would only expect trustees to make a report if contributions remain outstanding 90 days after their due date. However, if late payment is symptomatic of a more serious or more widespread problem (e g administrative failings or using contributions to alleviate cashflow problems), trustees should make an earlier report to the Regulator. The Regulator would not expect to be informed of:

- isolated late payments of contributions, where the matter has been put right and action has been taken to prevent late payment occurring again;

- a temporary failure to pay the correct contributions when due, where the contributions were paid promptly when the failure was found, and the administrative error has been, or is being, corrected in an effective and timely way;

- short periods of lateness of small amounts of contributions resulting from, for example, changes in pensionable pay, or new members joining the scheme, where the contributions have subsequently been corrected;

- late payment where a scheme has no more than two members.

Trustees must still comply with the requirement to notify members when contributions are paid 60 days or more after the due date. They must inform members of this fact within 90 days of the due date.

Personal pension schemes 7.70

Similar requirements apply to the trustees or managers of personal pension schemes as apply to the trustees of occupational money purchase schemes, but only where direct payment arrangements exist. Direct payment arrangements are arrangements under which contributions fall to be paid to the scheme by an employer either on its own account (but in respect of employees) or on behalf of employees out of deductions from their earnings.

The overly prescriptive requirement to put in place, and maintain, a record of payments due has now fallen away. However, personal pension providers must still monitor the payment of contributions under the direct payment arrangements, and they may request an employer to provide them with sufficient information to enable them to do this. The Regulator would expect employers to provide the information promptly and in any event within 30 days of it being requested. If the required information is not supplied, a provider should report this fact to the Regulator before the end of 60 days from the date on which the information was requested. Providers may also notify members of this fact, but are not obliged to do so.

Providers are under an obligation to make a report to the Pensions Regulator if they have reasonable cause to believe that a late payment of contributions is likely to be of material significance to the Regulator in the exercise of its functions. According to the Regulator's code of practice, the following are likely to be materially significant:

- where contributions remain unpaid 90 days after the due date (unless it is a one-off or infrequent administration error, which is discovered after the 90 days, and which is corrected when found or is thereafter corrected as soon as practicable);

- where there is a late payment involving possible dishonesty or a misuse of assets or contributions (eg contributions are used to alleviate an employer's cashflow problems);

- where there is a failure to pay contributions which carries a criminal penalty (eg the employer is knowingly concerned in the fraudulent evasion of the obligation to pay employee contributions);

- where the provider becomes aware that the employer does not have adequate procedures or systems in place to ensure the correct and timely payment of contributions due and appears not to be taking adequate steps to remedy the situation;

- where there is no early prospect of outstanding contributions being paid (eg because of the financial circumstances of the employer).

The Pensions Regulator would not normally want to be informed if the late payment falls into one of the following categories, even if contributions remain unpaid 90 days after the due date:

- where there are infrequent late payments and the overdue contributions have now been paid, or arrangements are being put in place for the prompt payment of the overdue amount (eg an administrative failing which is now being rectified);

- where there are four or fewer employees with a direct payment arrangement with the same employer and same provider (unless the late payment is a result of dishonesty or would carry a criminal penalty);

- where there are short periods of lateness of contributions resulting from, for example, employees leaving, new employees joining, or changes in salary not being notified to the provider;

- where a claim has been submitted to the Redundancy Payments Service of the Department of Trade and Industry for the outstanding contributions.

Where a provider needs to report a breach to the Regulator, the report should be made within ten working days of the breach being identified. However, shorter timescales will apply in the case of more serious breaches, and in extreme cases providers should report immediately by telephone.

Where a late payment report is made to the Pensions Regulator, providers must also inform those members who are affected by the late payment. The Regulator considers such a report should be made as soon as reasonably practicable and in any event within 30 days. If providers do not need to report to the Regulator, they are not required to report to members.

The Regulator's code of practice on reporting late payment of contributions to personal pensions can be found on the Regulator's website at: http://www.thepensionregulator.co.uk/pdf/codeLpppFinal.pdf. The new measures came into effect on 6 April 2006.

Winding-up priority

7.71

Section 73 of the *Pensions Act 1995* must be the most heavily amended and modified section of the Act. It introduced an overriding statutory priority governing the order in which the benefits of scheme members should be secured when a defined benefit scheme winds up. With the introduction of the Pension Protection Fund (PPF) on 6 April 2005, *section 73* once again needed to be amended, this time to ensure that the first call on scheme assets on wind-up was to secure an equivalent PPF level of benefits (see **CHAPTER 4**). The assets of the scheme must be applied to provide benefits in the following order:

(*a*) benefits provided from insurance policies which cover pensions already in payment and were taken out before 6 April 1997 (but only if those policies cannot be surrendered or if the surrender value is less than the liability secured);

(*b*) liability for pensions or other benefits to the extent that the amount of the liability does not exceed the corresponding level of compensation that would have been provided by the PPF (other than a liability in (*a*) above).

(*c*) liability for pensions or other benefits derived from the payment of voluntary contributions by any member (other than already covered under (*a*) or (*b*) above).

(*d*)   any other liability in respect of pensions or other benefits.

Any money purchase benefits (including money purchase additional voluntary contributions (AVCs)) fall outside this priority order and must be secured separately. This means that while money purchase AVCs are still safe, AVCs paid in exchange for added years might be lost depending on the circumstances.

The amount of the scheme's assets to be used to secure benefits in each category above must be equal to the actuary's estimate of the cost of buying annuities (including expenses) in order to meet the liabilities in those categories. Where the amounts of liabilities mentioned in a category above cannot be met in full by the assets remaining after previous categories have been satisfied, the liabilities in that category must be satisfied in the same proportions.

Any members who would have been entitled to the option of a refund of contributions or a transfer value (because their pensionable service was between three months and two years when the scheme started to wind up) are only entitled to a refund.

Debt on the employer   7.72

On 11 June 2003 the government announced that solvent employers would have to meet the full buy-out cost of benefits where schemes start to wind up after that date. Subsequent legislation extended the buy-out debt to insolvent employers and employers exiting a multi-employer scheme. The *Pensions Act 2004* adds further to the debt-on-the-employer legislation.

Where a defined benefit scheme has started to wind up but the employer has undergone an insolvency event before the trustees have called in any debt due, a debt is to be treated as due immediately before the date of the insolvency event. The *Pensions Act 2004* also introduces the concept of a withdrawal arrangement. Instead of an employer becoming subject to a buy-out debt upon exit from a multi-employer scheme, it may be possible for it to enter into a withdrawal arrangement. Under a withdrawal arrangement, an exiting employer may be permitted to discharge itself if:

- it pays a debt calculated on the basis of the minimum funding requirement (MFR) or on the new scheme-specific funding basis as appropriate;

- another party (usually another employer in the scheme) guarantees to pay the difference between the debt paid and the buy-out debt if the scheme subsequently goes into wind-up; and

- it is more likely that the debt will be met under the withdrawal arrangement.

There are several conditions which a withdrawal arrangement must meet. These are covered in guidance from the Pensions Regulator as follows:

- The arrangement must consist of an agreement to which the trustees and the exiting employer are parties. Where the exiting employer is not the guarantor, the guarantor must also be a party.

- The parties to the agreement must agree that the law of England and Wales applies to the agreement (or the law of Northern Ireland where applicable). (Where the scheme and/or the employer is based in Scotland, the parties may need to obtain legal advice as the law of England and Wales must apply to the agreement.)

- The exiting employer must agree to pay at least the amount of any debt, calculated on either the MFR or scheme-specific funding basis, as appropriate, by a specified date.

- The agreement must require the guarantor to pay the debt outstanding if:

  - the scheme commences wind-up;

  - there is no employer in the scheme that has not suffered an insolvency event; or

  - the Pensions Regulator calls in the debt.

- Where there are two or more guarantors the agreement must provide whether they are joint and severally liable, and also whether the amount is a fixed amount or whether it is the amount required to cover the liabilities for which the exiting employer would have been liable.

- The agreement must provide for the amount due from the exiting employer and the guarantors to be paid to the trustees unless the PPF has assumed responsibility for the scheme, in which case it should be paid to the PPF.

- The agreement must provide for all the costs reasonably incurred by the trustees in connection with making the agreement and obtaining and implementing the Pensions Regulator's approval of the withdrawal arrangements, to be borne by a party to the agreement other than the trustees.

- The agreement must provide that it will continue to remain in force until:

  - the wind-up of the scheme is completed;

  - the Pensions Regulator issues a direction stipulating that the agreement is no longer required; or

  - the agreement is replaced by another agreement forming part of an approved withdrawal arrangement.

Dispute resolution   7.73

Occupational pension schemes were first required to have an internal disputes resolution procedure under *section 50* of the *Pensions Act 1995*. It prescribed a cumbersome two-stage process and set down exact timescales by which certain actions had to happen. The Pickering Report recommended that the prescriptive requirements be removed; trustees should be free to decide whether they needed a one-stage or two-stage process, the complainant should ultimately have access to the trustees as part of the process, and there should be only one, final deadline by which decisions had to be reached.

Accordingly, the *Pensions Act 2004* was to replace *section 50*, plus associated regulations, with three new sections and a code of practice. However, the new *section 50* would seem to have required all disputes to be settled by the trustees, arguably meaning that disputes could not be settled at the first stage of a two-stage process, unless of course the trustees were involved at the first stage (thereby defeating the point of a two-stage process).

After some consideration, the Department for Work and Pensions announced, in January 2006, that the new disputes resolution legislation would not after all have the desired effect of simplifying the process or giving trustees greater flexibility, and could in fact place additional burdens on trustees. Consequently, no commencement order for the new dispute resolution legislation has been made, and the old provisions continue to apply. Simplification of the process will probably be attempted again when the opportunity next presents itself.

Pensions Ombudsman   7.74

Certain provisions in the *Child Support, Pensions and Social Security Act 2000* could have extended the powers and jurisdiction of the Pensions Ombudsman, but they were never brought into force pending the outcome of the Pickering Report on simplification, and part of that legislation has now been repealed by the *Pensions Act 2004*.

However, to ease the ever increasing workload on the Ombudsman's office, *section 274* of the *Pensions Act 2004* allows a Deputy Pensions Ombudsmen to be appointed, and one has in fact now been appointed.

The Ombudsman concerns himself primarily with rectifying acts of maladministration by those who are involved in the administration of pension schemes. As there have been a number of arguments over what exactly constitutes an adminstrator in various scenarios, *section 275* of the *Pensions Act 2004* introduces a new definition: 'A person or body of persons is concerned with the administration of an occupational or personal pension scheme where the person or body is responsible for carrying out an act of administration concerned with the scheme.'

Therefore, someone who carries out a single, one-off act of administration would fall within the Ombudsman's remit.

These measures came into effect on 6 April 2005.

Indexation and revaluation

Background   7.75

Although the compulsory indexation of occupational pensions had been considered under previous social security legislation, it was never implemented, and it was not until the sweeping changes of the *Pensions Act 1995* that such a measure finally came into force. The *Pensions Act 1995* introduced the requirement for occupational pensions to increase, once they came into payment, in line with the increase in the Retail Prices Index each year, subject to a maximum of 5%. This requirement only applied to service accrued from 6 April 1997 in a defined benefit scheme, and to the annuity purchased with regular contributions paid after 6 April 1997 to a money purchase scheme. Paradoxically, this requirement did not apply to any additional voluntary contributions a member may have paid into an occupational scheme. Nor did it apply to personal pensions (apart from protected rights), meaning that members of an employer's group personal pension were not constrained in the way their counterparts in an occupational money purchase scheme were. Protected rights in personal and occupational schemes had to be indexed before 6 April 1997, but whereas indexation was capped at 3% pre-1997, the cap was raised to 5% for post-1997 funds, which complicated the annuity purchase process. Guaranteed minimum pensions accrued between 1988 and 1997 still had to be increased in line with RPI up to 3%.

The Pickering Report recommended the complete removal of the compulsory indexation requirement from both occupational schemes and the protected rights elements of personal pensions; pensions already in payment would not be affected, there would be no compulsory indexation for future service and rights already accrued in defined benefit schemes should be altered, where desired, on an actuarial equivalence basis. These proposals were not adopted in their entirety, but at least the inequalities of treatment between money purchase occupational and personal pension schemes were addressed.

Money purchase schemes   7.76

The requirement to index any pension derived from post-1997 contributions was dropped for any pension not yet in payment. While the government was initially reluctant to remove the indexation requirement from protected rights funds, it finally did so after further consultation. This extended to protected rights in personal pensions as well as those in occupational schemes. These changes took effect on 6 April 2005 and apply retrospectively for any pension not in payment on that date; there is no longer any need to separate funds into different tranches according to the date on which contributions were paid.

Defined benefit schemes 7.77

As far as defined benefit schemes are concerned, the only change was lowering the indexation cap from 5% to 2½% for future service from 6 April 2005. The Pickering Report had recommended that compulsory indexation on accrued rights could be removed as long as it was converted to another benefit on an actuarially equivalent basis. Although conversion of accrued rights is no longer prohibited by the new modification provisions of the *Pensions Act 2004*, it does not, unfortunately, permit the conversion of statutory pension increases. Additionally, simplification of guaranteed minimum pensions fell into the 'too difficult' box, so defined benefit schemes are still subject to a compulsory indexation requirement as follows:

Tranche of pension	*Increase in payment*
Guaranteed minimum pension accrued between 6 April 1988 and 5 April 1997	In line with RPI up to 3%
Pension in respect of service between 6 April 1997 and 5 April 2005	In line with RPI up to 5%
Pension in respect of service from 6 April 2005 onwards	In line with RPI up to 2½%

These statutory requirements override any scheme increase rule that does not provide at least this much of an increase. They do not, however, automatically reduce any scheme provision requiring a higher increase.

Revaluation 7.78

Orders made under the *Pension Schemes Act 1993* require occupational pension schemes to increase deferred pensions by the rise in the Retail Prices Index between the date of leaving and normal retirement age subject to a maximum increase of 5% pa. The application of these orders depends on when a member actually left pensionable service.

The *Pensions Act 2004* makes a minor administrative change so as to exempt an occupational pension scheme from the statutory revaluation requirements if it maintains the value of deferred benefits by reference to the rise in the Retail Prices Index.

Contracting out

Background 7.79

The Pickering Report identified contracting-out requirements as being overly complex and administratively burdensome. The Report contained a range of recommendations to make it easier for schemes to administer contracted-out rights, including the removal of restrictions on payable age and commutation for cash.

Protected rights 7.80

Protected rights have finally been brought into line with other money purchase rights and are now partially commutable for cash (up to 25% of the protected rights fund) and no longer have to be paid from age 60. Protected rights may be paid at the same time as other rights are payable ie age 50 up to 2010 and age 55 thereafter.

Guaranteed minimum pensions 7.81

The Pickering Report recognised that the existing guaranteed minimum pension (GMP) legislation placed a heavy administrative burden on some schemes and made it difficult for people to understand their overall pension rights. One of the more radical recommendations of the Report advocated that schemes should be allowed to replace their GMPs with benefits of equivalent actuarial value. GMP simplification was the subject of a further consultation paper, but in the end it appears it was too tough a nut to crack, certainly within the timescale allowed.

However, the *Pensions Act 2004* does contain a provision permitting GMPs to be commuted for cash. GMPs may still not be partially commuted for cash upon retirement, but this measure did allow regulations to be made permitting the commutation of a member's GMP in circumstances of serious ill-health. Those regulations were laid on 23 May 2006 and came into force on 14 June 2006. From that date, a lump sum may be paid in total commutation of a member's GMP on the grounds of serious ill-health as long as it also qualifies as a serious ill-health lump sum under the provisions of the *Finance Act 2004*. However, any GMP in respect of a widow, widower or surviving civil partner must continue to be provided, so the survivor's element should not figure in the commuted amount payable to the member.

There was also a minor amendment to the definition of 'working life' in the calculation of GMPs so as to maintain the provision that working life runs to age 65 for a man and to age 60 for a woman. (Despite the equalisation of state pension ages for men and women from 2010, the payable age for GMPs will still be 65 for men and 60 for women.)

Reference scheme test 7.82

The Pickering Report recommended the introduction of a new reference scheme test, one which only had to provide an accrual of ⅟₁₀₀th for each year of pensionable service for 80% of members. It would have removed the upper earnings limit from the definition of qualifying earnings but would also have removed the requirement for a survivor's pension. The recommendation was not adopted.

Safeguarded rights 7.83

Safeguarded rights are created when some or all of a member's contracted-out benefits are transferred to an ex-spouse as part of a pension sharing order following divorce. Regulations and procedures concerning safeguarded rights are complicated and even today there are still uncertainties over how they should be treated in certain circumstances. Although the Pickering Report recommended the abolition of safeguarded rights, this opportunity was not taken, and the *Pensions Act 2004* is silent on the matter.

Stakeholder pension schemes 7.84

A stakeholder pension scheme must fulfil several conditions if it is to operate as a stakeholder scheme. One of those conditions is that the scheme must accept transfer payments from other pension schemes. There was originally no requirement for stakeholder schemes to obtain a contracting-out certificate, so it was not clear whether they had to accept a transfer of contracted-out rights. However, it was generally accepted that a stakeholder scheme must accept contracted-out rights, and where it does not already hold a contracting-out certificate, it should obtain one in order to accept such rights.

The *Pensions Act 2004* removes any doubt over this matter by requiring stakeholder schemes to be covered by a contracting-out certificate. If the scheme is an occupational scheme, it needs to be specified in the contracting-out certificate relating to the categories of employment it covers. If the scheme is a personal pension, it needs to be an appropriate personal pension as defined in the *Pension Schemes Act 1993*. This change came into force on 6 April 2006.

Chapter 8
The Financial Assistance Scheme

Introduction 8.1

The *Pensions Act 2004* established the Financial Assistance Scheme (FAS) for the purpose of offering protection for many of those persons who are not covered by the Pension Protection Fund (PPF). The FAS applies to persons who suffered loss from their defined benefit (traditionally referred to as final salary) schemes when their schemes were wound up with an insolvent, or non-existent, employer. The PPF is described in detail in **CHAPTER 4**. The operation and administration of the FAS is through the national FAS Operational Unit (FAS OU). The FAS OU is based in York.

The government's statement during the drawing up of the Pensions Bill 2004, which became the *Pensions Act 2004*, was as follows:

'Solvent employers have a duty to support their schemes and provide the benefits that members were expecting. So, it is right that the FAS focuses on insolvent employers. Nevertheless, issues concerning the definition of "employer solvency" remain under active consideration'.

Initial consultation 8.2

During the year 2004 the DWP sent out questionnaires to trustees of schemes which were wound up between 1997, the date when the deficiency provisions of the *Pensions Act 1995* came into effect, and 14 May 2004, the date on which the FAS was formulated. Trustees of schemes which could be eligible for help were reminded to provide the department with the relevant information by 10 December 2004. They were informed that: 'It is important that all scheme trustees and actuaries who think their schemes might be eligible respond as quickly as possible.'

Formal consultation on the structure of the FAS, the final details of who will be eligible and the level of assistance to be provided, began in spring 2005. The process involved stakeholders such as pension scheme members, trustees, trade unions and key business representatives. Trustees who had not already submitted information to the government concerning the FAS had six months from 1 September 2005 to apply. By 1 September 2005 several schemes had already provided data to the government and were being contacted directly by the FAS OU. The schemes were given the opportunity to check and confirm that the details that had been recorded were correct.

The Minister of State for Pensions Reform stated on 1 September 2005 that the government had already made a lot of progress in collating all the necessary information. He urged trustees to provide further information, as it was an essential formal step towards being in the position to decide whether a pension scheme is eligible for the FAS. Although there was regular reference to scheme trustees during consultation periods, a call for information was aimed equally at scheme administrators. Scheme members were urged to contact their own trustees or administrators for further information rather than the FSA OU directly.

The FAS OU has the roll of contacting all eligible members of Qualifying schemes (see **8.5** below), and telling them of the level of benefit that they are entitled to receive and may expect to receive. The contact telephone number for the FAS OU for trustees and administrators is 0845 6019941. Form FSA A1 could be obtained on that number and it had a return date of 28 February 2006. In order to cater for schemes which had already wound up, and had no remaining trustees, it was acceptable for individuals to complete the notification form on behalf of their scheme.

Where individual members required information, this was available on the FAS website, which is: http://www.dwp.gov.uk/FAS. The website contains details of all the schemes which have completed the notification process and which are qualifying pension schemes. If members are concerned that their scheme does not appear on the website, they should contact their scheme trustees or administrators.

The FAS, which was formed by virtue of the *Pensions Act 2004*, came into effect on 19 November 2005.

Administering the FAS   8.3

The government has been reviewing the administration of the FAS, and details of the review were published on 6 June 2006. The review was entitled *Review of the Administration of the Financial Assistance Scheme to Parliament*. The announcement was made by the Minister of State for Pensions Reform, and the review was presented to the FAS. The main subject matter covered by the review was as follows:

- Consideration was given as to the best means of providing sound administration and management for the FAS. The main driver was to ensure that all people who are eligible for the FAS would receive their payments as promptly as possible.

- The review considered how to ensure that the most cost-effective operation of the FAS could be achieved, and looked at a wide range of options in order to seek an appropriate method.

- One aspect that the review did not look at was stated to be the rationale for the scheme – the way in which the scheme is funded or designed or any related legislative issues.

The Minister of State for Pensions Reform announced to Parliament the outcome of the review on 24 July 2006. Some key findings were published, and these are summarised below:

(*a*) It will be necessary to devise a different skill set and a revised approach to gathering data on scheme members if the ambition of expediting payment of benefit to members is to be achieved efficiently.

(*b*) The skills referred to, and sought after, in point (*a*) above already exist in the private sector in the UK and in the Pensions Protection Fund. Nevertheless, it was not considered appropriate to outsource in order to obtain such skills. Accordingly, further options will be considered in order to be able to inject the required skills into the operations of the FAS in the shortest time feasible.

(*c*) It was observed that the length that a winding-up process can take (and there is no doubt that there have been some very lengthy winding-up processes in past years), combined with the competing trustee priorities which often arise, are significant constraints to the making of more FAS payments.

(*d*) It has been decided that a detailed work analysis is essential. The analysis will critically review job roles, examine process timings and establish optimum staffing levels for the FAS OU.

Finally, it was determined that the long-term governance of the FAS is best placed within The Pension Service.

Funding the FAS   8.4

Unlike the PPF (see **4.14–4.19** above), the FAS is not funded by levies. It was to receive £400m from public funds over 20 years, and could receive further funding if required. Additionally, it was not to be reviewed for three years. However, in the White Paper on pensions reform published on 25 May 2006, entitled *Security in Retirement: Towards a New Pensions System*, the government proposed to extend its total commitment to approximately £2.3bn. This would call for a very significant commitment of public funds, as the original intent to obtain support for the FAS from industry has been abandoned.

The above development is reflected in draft regulations entitled the Financial Assistance Scheme (Miscellaneous Amendments) Regulations 2006. These regulations are under public consultation (see **8.16** below), and the government hopes that they will come into force before the end of 2006, subject to parliamentary approval. They are available on the DWP website and the FAS website.

The end date for the consultation on the White Paper was 11 September 2006, and for the draft regulations was 17 September 2006.

Member qualification   8.5

The FAS is intended to compensate members of schemes who lost accrued rights when their schemes wound up before 6 April 2005. The eligible categories are:

- members of an underfunded scheme;

- members who have ceased to be active members but have lost benefits due to a scheme deficiency.

The specific eligibility conditions for members are listed below.

- Members of schemes that commenced winding up before 1 January 1997 are not eligible.

- Members of other schemes which started to wind up right through to the introduction of the PPF on 5 April 2005 are potentially eligible. The original intent was for the FAS to be restricted to schemes which failed before 14 May 2004 – see **8.2** above for the significance of this date – but there has been a change of heart by government.

- Persons who were within 15 years of retirement on 14 May 2004 (previously this was limited to within three years of scheme pension age on 14 May 2004) may be eligible. This was proposed in the White Paper on pensions reform (see **8.4** above).

Scheme qualification   8.6

At present there are two stages of qualification for schemes: 'notification' and 'qualification'.

Notification **8.7**

Basic information about the scheme name and that of any employer under the scheme may be given to the FAS by trustees and members. The notification period began on 1 September 2005 and ended on 28 February 2006. However, whereas the general notification period ended on 28 February 2006, the scheme manager, may at his or discretion, accept notification of the details of any particular scheme after that date.

The notification process calls for information to be provided in different circumstances, these circumstances are described below.

Schemes that have been wound up

The information requirements are:

- the name of the scheme;
- the scheme's pension scheme registration number;
- the current name and address of an employer in relation to the scheme;
- the name and address of at least one trustee of the scheme.

Any of the following can supply this information:

- a member of the scheme or his or her appointed representative;
- a surviving spouse or civil partner of a member who has died;
- a trustee or professional advisor associated with the scheme.

Schemes that have already completed winding up

The information required is:

- the name of the scheme;
- the current name and address of an employer in relation to the scheme.

Any of the following can supply this information:

- a former member of the scheme or his or her appointed representative;
- a surviving spouse or civil partner of a former member of the scheme who has died;
- a former trustee or manager of the scheme;

- a former professional adviser to the scheme or any insurance company that is making payments to former members.

Qualification   8.8

Qualifying schemes are schemes which have met the notification conditions and:

- are not money purchase schemes, or schemes of a prescribed description;
- began winding up between 1 January 1997 and 5 April 2005 (the winding up may be complete).

The employer must normally have become insolvent in the UK by 28 February 2006 for the FAS to apply. However, the Secretary of State may accept a later date according to the individual case of a scheme. Although the period covered by the FAS is for schemes which wound up between 1 January 1997 and 5 April 2005, there is scope to extend the notification period for any scheme, and this also extends the period in which an insolvency event can occur. In other words, it may be possible for some schemes which would not otherwise qualify for the FAS or for the PPF to become qualifying schemes for the FAS.

The Minister of State for Pensions Reform has confirmed in a ministerial statement that the government may be prepared to provide help for members who have lost part or all of their occupational pensions even if they would not otherwise have been deemed to have qualified under either the FAS or the PPF. However, the government will be setting a definitive cut-off date for insolvency events before the end of 2006. Up until that time, the scheme manager will be able to consider requests for an extension to the notification period for the various pension schemes that are undergoing a qualified insolvency event after 28 February 2006. The ministerial statement was laid in the House of Commons on 16 February 2006.

Member information concerning qualifying
pension schemes   8.9

It is important that all schemes that have successfully qualified for the FAS are displayed on the Qualifying Pension Schemes list, and that information is provided on the eligibility of future members for payment and on the level of payments that may be expected.

In order to determine the eligibility of the individual scheme members for payments, it is necessary to consider such members under two scenarios. These scenarios are described under the headings below.

Members of a qualifying scheme that is currently winding up 8.10

It is not possible determine the amount of financial assistance which may be due for eligible members until the winding-up process has been completed. It is possible that this process may take many years. Accordingly, members are advised that they may be able to obtain initial payments from the scheme manager (see **8.13** below). Such initial payments shall be made at the same rate until the winding-up process has been completed and it is possible to determine the final levels of assistance which are available. However, before initial payments can be considered, an application must be made to the trustees or scheme manager on behalf of the members. Such members must be, or shortly will be, aged 65. It is only after this application is received that the scheme manager has the discretion to award initial payments. If the scheme manager does agree to make such payments, the trustees must supply data on the members with regard to their age – whereupon the levels of assistance payable can be calculated and the initial payments can commence. The reasoning behind the 60% maximum ceiling on initial payments, rather than applying 80% of expected core pensions rights, is stated to be that the final annuity rate which will be available to a member will not be secured until the completion of the winding-up process.

Members are advised that the scheme to which they belong has not requested initial payment if it has successfully qualified, is currently winding up and does not appear on the FAS List. The FAS list is in the form of a table. The last column illustrates that a decision has been made to make initial payments to eligible members of individual schemes. It is acknowledged that there may not be any eligible members when making this decision.

Members are further advised that they are able to check to see whether a request for a review of their pension scheme has been made. This can be achieved by visiting the 'Notifying and Qualifying Pension Scheme' pages on the website. If the FAS has received a request it will be highlighted by the addition of the letter '**R**' at the end of the scheme name. If the letter '**A**' appears next to the scheme name, this indicates that the PPF Ombudsman has received an appeal on the review decision.

Members of a scheme that has completed winding up 8.11

If a wound-up scheme has qualified for the FAS, the trustees or administrators must provide the scheme manager with information on all members. Once he or she has received this information, the scheme manager can determine which members fall within the eligible category and calculate the final levels of assistance which are payable. On achieving this, the assistance payments may begin (see **8.12** below for the levels of payments which may be made).

The website contains a list of schemes that have already qualified for the FAS or have completed their wind-up and provided the required relevant data in respect of their members. The last column of the table on the website shows that a decision to make payments to eligible members of individual schemes has been made. Again, it is acknowledged that there may not be any eligible members within a scheme who are entitled to receive payment.

The level of compensation which may be paid   8.12

Under the 2006 White Paper (see **8.4** above), pensions will be topped up to the following percentage levels:

- 80% of core pension for those within seven years of scheme pension age;

- 65% of core pension for those within eight to eleven years of scheme pension age; and

- 50% of core pension for the rest.

Benefits may include a top-up pension, a cash lump sum or the purchase of an annuity at age 65.

The FAS applies only to those persons who will receive at least £10 a week, or equivalent, and it has a maximum ceiling of £12,000 p a. Otherwise, no 'means-testing' is applied to members.

Surviving spouses and civil partners of qualifying members who died after the commencement of scheme wind-up may benefit from a lower rate payment.

Date of payment   8.13

FAS payments will normally begin on attainment of age 65. Survivors and qualifying members who are terminally ill may receive earlier payment. Normally it will not be possible to determine the level of annual payments until wind-up is complete. However, the FAS may exercise its discretion, on application by the trustees, to make an earlier initial payment for qualifying members who have attained age 65 before the wind-up is complete. The level of such an initial payment may be up to 60% of the expected core pension. Initial payments can also be made to survivors.

How many people will be affected?   8.14

Following the publication of the 2006 White Paper (see **8.5** above), the government estimates that approximately 40,000 people may be helped by the FAS.

Regulations and draft regulations 8.15

The main sets of regulations which apply to the FAS are:

- the *Financial Assistance Scheme Regulations 2005 (SI 2005/1986)*;

- the *Financial Assistance Scheme (Internal Review) Regulations 2005 (SI 2005/1994)*;

- the *Financial Assistance Scheme (Provision of Information and Administration of Payments) Regulations 2005 (SI 2005/2189)*;

- the *Financial Assistance Scheme (Appeals) Regulations 2005 (SI 2005/3273)*;

- the *Financial Assistance Scheme (Modification and Miscellaneous Amendments) Regulations 2005 (SI 2005/3256)*.

In brief summary:

- The *Financial Assistance Scheme Regulations 2005 (SI 2005/1986)* came into effect on 1 September 2005, which was the date on which the FAS opened. They established the FAS and prescribed the rules which apply.

- *SI 2005/1994* and *SI 2005/3273* established arrangements for internal reviews and appeals to the external PPF Ombudsman or a Deputy PPF Ombudsman with effect from 20 July 2005 and 29 November 2005 respectively.

- The *Financial Assistance Scheme (Modification and Miscellaneous Amendments) Regulations 2005 (SI 2005/3256)* brought in ancillary changes to regulations governing appeals in relation to the FAS, and amended *SI 2005/1994* and *SI 2005/2189*, on 24 November 2005.

- The draft Financial Assistance Scheme (Miscellaneous Amendments) Regulations 2006 (see **8.5** above) would amend *SI 2005/1986*, *SI 2005/1994* and *SI 2005/3273*.

The latest developments 8.16

The latest developments concerning the FAS were described in the consultative document to the draft regulations entitled the Financial Assistance Scheme (Miscellaneous Amendments) Regulations 2006 and the draft regulations themselves (see **8.5** above). The regulations will extend to Northern Ireland. The consultative document was issued by the Pensions Group part of the DWP on 24 July 2006. The main proposals are:

- to extend FAS cover to persons who are within 15 years of retirement on 14 May 2004 (see **8.2** above);

- to introduce 'Group 1–3' members, for the different levels of payment which are described in **8.12** above;

- to provide for FAS qualification where, in a multi-employer scheme, only the principal employer (or a section, in the case of a sectionalised scheme) becomes insolvent – together with associated changes and clarifications;

- to extend the date by which an insolvency event must occur (see **8.8** above) to 31 December 2006 – although the notification period may be extended by the scheme manager, who (exceptionally) may also consider an employer whose assets are less than its liabilities even if no insolvency event has occurred;

- for a scheme manager to accept an overseas insolvency event of equal circumstance to a UK event;

- to accept a member as a qualifying member even if he or she died before 1 September 2005, when *SI 2005/1986* came into effect (see **8.15** above);

- to provide for initial payments as described in **8.13** above, together with a raft of associated rules;

- to provide for annuity calculations on an even basis, whether or not commutation has taken place;

- to align the understanding and meaning of 'crystallisation date' and 'winding up date'. This is an issue which has long been a thorn in the side of those who have to determine scheme liabilities under the *Pensions Act 1995*;

- to remove similar difficulties and anomalies under the *Pensions Act 1995* which relate to the 'certification' date under that Act, and to provide flexibility to use annuity rates at the date that they are known and apply. Annual and initial payments will be based on normal retirement dates rather than certification dates;

- to provide notional annuity rates dependent on age and market adjustment factors, approximating closely to non-indexed linked pensions at normal retirement date;

- to define what is meant by a 'qualifying survivor';

- to codify the calculation of entitlements and revaluation methods;

- to further revise *SI 2005/1994*, as amended by *SI 2005/3256*, and related regulations, in a tidying-up exercise;

- to revise the appeals process in order to accommodate the main changes above which affect it.

Code of practice   8.17

There is no code of practice from the Pensions Regulator on the FAS at present. The main advice and guidance is on the DWP and FAS websites.

Conclusion   8.18

There is no doubt that the extent of the coverage of the FAS has increased greatly since its original conception by government. This has also caused an immense increase in potential cost. In effect, the UK taxpayer will be paying for the scheme and it remains to be seen how much of a burden this will place on taxation. Nevertheless, there is widespread concern about the loss to pensions rights under defined benefits schemes, and to date there appears to have been no major move to overturn this legislation.

Chapter 9
Cross-border activities

Introduction 9.1

Sections 287–295 of the *Pensions Act 2004* are intended to largely comply with Article 20 of Directive 2003/41/EC on the Activities and Supervision of Institutions for Occupational Retirement Provision (the 'IORP Directive'). Compliance with the Directive was further strengthened with the making of the *Occupational Pension Schemes (Cross-border Activities) Regulations 2005 (SI 2005/3381)*. These regulations came into force on 30 December 2005.

The legislative objective is to enable occupational pension schemes for qualifying persons to be sponsored by a European employer in other EU member states. This, from a UK perspective, means that provisions have been brought into force for occupational pension schemes which have their main administration in the UK but which operate cross-border in another member state. Most of the effective dates for the regulations were 23 September 2005, the date by which the Directive had to be complied with, although some came into effect later as explained below.

The regulations also assist the Pensions Regulator in carrying out its functions under *Pt 7, Pensions Act 2004*.

Background – the consultative process 9.2

The consultation process on the regulations began on 4 August 2005 and ended on 30 September 2005. The government stated that it had decided to enter into limited consultation in order to strike the appropriate balance between compliance with the IORP Directive, protection for those persons who were contributing to another scheme in an EU state, and regulating matters in an appropriate manner. Because of the technical nature of the subject, it was considered inappropriate to put it through a Cabinet Office Code of Practice procedure. Instead, it was referred to the Pensions Regulator and specialist industry representatives.

During the consultation process, there were concerns about:

- how the regulations would impact on existing schemes (schemes based in the UK with members based in the UK and the Republic of Ireland); and

- the requirement for schemes to be fully funded at all times.

The main issues concerned the meanings of 'European employer'; 'home' and 'host' member states and 'seconded worker'. Discussion was also invited on the Anglo-Irish arrangement and the ring-fencing of assets.

The government's response to the consultation was published in November 2005 by the DWP. It covered the above points and the functions of the Pensions Regulator in relation to cross-border activities.

A list of the main issues which were agreed is given in **9.3** below.

The main rules which were agreed   9.3

The following main rules were agreed:

- the regulations allow existing schemes three years from the date of directly coming into force to reach full funding;

- in the case of any secondment which started before regulations came into force, the arrangements for secondment may be allowed to run for the duration of that secondment before the requirements take effect;

- secondments which began after that date are allowed a limited period (which could be up to five years) before the requirements take effect;

- the right to approach the UK Pensions Ombudsman was extended to European members of UK-based schemes;

- any disputes involving schemes in other EU member states shall be dealt with within those other member states' jurisdictions;

- institutions that operate on a 'pay as you go' basis are not subject to the IORP Directive.

The funding requirement is that schemes must provide annual valuations and make up any deficit within 24 months of a deficient valuation shortfall. This requirement is under *s 222, Pensions Act 2004*. It means that a scheme which operates cross-border within the EU is subject to more stringent scheme funding requirements than a UK-only scheme. Each valuation must be signed by the actuary and be received by the trustees within one year of its effective date. A schedule of contributions covering a two-year period must be prepared or, if one is already in place, reviewed and if necessary revised within twelve months of the valuation's effective date.

The new rules were effective from 30 December 2005, and apply to pre-23 September 2005 arrangements and post-23 September 2005 arrangements (see **9.8** below) in the manner shown in the table at **9.17** below.

Monitoring by the Pensions Regulator   9.4

The Pensions Regulator will monitor the compliance of pensions institutions in other member states with the relevant legal requirements, and shall notify the competent authority of the home state if it becomes aware of any contravention of those requirements.

To whom do the cross-border regulations apply?   9.5

The cross-border regulations apply to *European members* and *European survivors*.

A *European member* is a person whose contractual place of work is in an EU member state (other than the UK) who is subject to the social and labour laws of that state and in respect of whom contributions are made to the scheme by his or her employer.

A *European survivor* is a survivor of a European member who is currently or prospectively entitled to benefits under the scheme. In order to understand the effect of the regulations it is *also* necessary to know the meaning of the terms *European employer* and *qualified person*. These terms have the following meanings:

- A *European employer* is a person who either employs qualifying persons, or is a qualifying person, and contributes to the scheme in respect of either.

- A *qualifying person* is a person who is governed by the social and labour law of the non-UK state (this does not include secondees) by virtue of his or her employment or self-employment. Qualifying persons therefore include self-employed persons, and such persons are separately defined in the regulations.

Avoiding cross-border status   9.6

It can be seen from **9.3** above that employers will need to be alert to the cost-implications of becoming a cross-border scheme unintentionally. Advisers, trustees and managers will need to advise employers at an early stage of the triggers to such a status, and before any contributions are received from overseas employers. Employers will also be best advised to review their employment policy, in particular with regard to secondments. The latter point is of importance for employers that operate overseas branches of their UK company, should such branches fall to be considered as employers for the purposes of the Directive.

The result of a failure to register a cross-border scheme can be costly in fines (see **9.15** below).

What is meant by the 'social and labour laws' of another state? 9.7

Social and labour laws are the national laws applicable to the fields of employment and occupational pension schemes. To provide a cross-border scheme for European members and/or European survivors whose contractual workplace is in another state, those persons shall be subject to such laws of that state (the home member state) in respect of whom contributions are made to the scheme by their employers. A home member state may be asked by the host member state of which such a person is a member to ring-fence assets and liabilities attributable to the home member state's activities in the host member state.

The Budapest Protocol gives a full explanation of how this and the passporting procedures under the Directive operate. The Protocol is entitled *The Provisions Relating to the Collaboration of the Relevant Competent Authorities of the Member States of the European Union in Particular in the Application of the Directive 2003/41/EC of the European Parliament and of the Council of 3rd June 2003 on the Activities and Supervision of Institutions for Occupational Retirement Provision (IORPs) Operating Cross-Border.* The Protocol has been agreed by pension supervisors within the EU and the EEA. The main purpose is to ensure that any attaching entitlements, rights or restrictions which the state is able to impose on its citizens on secondment or working overseas in another state shall be complied with. In practical terms, this means that the persons joining other member states' schemes or retaining membership of other such schemes must seek proper advice in their local jurisdiction of employment with regard to any terms which apply to ongoing pension provision and investment of assets.

Funding cross-border schemes 9.8

Under the terms of the IORP Directive, stringent funding requirements apply. Cross-border schemes must be fully funded at all times, meaning that the ability in the UK to restore funding over a period (see **CHAPTER 5** and **9.3** above) is not available. This rule extends to the entire scheme. In the UK full actuarial valuations would otherwise only need to be conducted every three years in most circumstances.

There are transitional provisions for schemes which did not operate cross-border before the required in-force date of the Directive (23 September 2005), but such schemes must still demonstrate that they meet the fully-funded requirement when they apply to be treated as a cross-border scheme (see **9.11** below). Under the transitional provisions, schemes which operated on a cross-border basis before 23 September 2005, and which have applied to continue to be treated as such, have until the 22 September 2008 to demonstrate full funding. Additionally, new schemes with no current members that wish to apply must be fully funded within two years of application.

How does all this work in practice? 9.9

The question as to whether or not a scheme is to be regarded as a cross-border scheme is of primary importance. It is possible for UK schemes with members seconded to work in other member states to escape being treated as cross-border schemes subject to certain rules. Completion of the authorisation and approval forms is essential for qualifying schemes. These key forms are reproduced in the **ANNEX** at the end of this chapter. Full guidance is still awaited on how cross-border schemes work in practice, but the Pensions Regulator's website states that secondments will be exempt from the cross-border requirements where:

- the employee was working in the UK for the same employer immediately before he or she was seconded overseas;

- the employee's employment was for a limited period only;

- when the secondment started, the employee was expected to return to work with the same employer in the UK or to retire from employment at the end of the secondment.

In this connection, secondments which are for five years or less will be exempted if the conditions are met. Nevertheless, it is still not entirely certain what is meant by 'limited period'. It is certainly implied that a limited period must mean that secondment will end on a pre-determined date or when a certain event takes place, and the Pensions Regulator's website gives the guidance set out at **9.10** below on this matter.

Who are 'seconded employees'? 9.10

'If employees are sent by a UK employer to work overseas for a period in another EU member state, and at the end of that period intend to return to resume work for that employer in the UK or intend to retire, then:

- if they were sent to the other EU member state before 30 December 2005, for a limited period which had not expired by that date; or

- if they were sent to the other EU member state on or after 30 December 2005 for a limited period; and

- they are still working under the control of the UK employer; and

- they intend at the end of that period either to return to the UK to work for the same employer, or to retire,

then they are counted as "seconded employees".

Postings overseas that conform to these characteristics may be regarded as secondments; other cases which do not have these characteristics (if, for example, no limited period was expressed, or there was no expectation of return to the UK or retirement at the end of the limited period) should not be regarded as secondments.

If employees are working in another EU state but are not seconded, it does not automatically follow that they are subject to that state's social and labour law. Whether that is the case will depend on the sorts of considerations set out above.

The main characteristic of a limited period is that it will end on a specified date, although it is also possible for a period to be "limited" if it ends when a specific event, such as the completion of a project, takes place. If employees work abroad for an indefinite period, or for their entire career, that would not be a secondment.

If a member of a scheme is seconded overseas and, at the end of that secondment is seconded again, either to the same or to another EU member state, this should be looked at as a "fresh start" rather than a single secondment. Provided that each such secondment maintains the characteristics of a secondment, this should be acceptable to the trustees.

If the question of extending a secondment arises, the trustees should be sure that the secondment is really for a limited period, and that the total period of secondment is not such that it would cause them to consider that the secondment was really a permanent posting.

It is up to the trustees of a scheme to determine whether any members of the scheme who work in EU member states other than the UK are seconded employees.

The fact that an employer has seconded employees in its pension scheme does not mean that the scheme is operating as a cross-border scheme. If the only employees working overseas are seconded employees then the scheme will not be operating as a cross-border scheme and the rest of this guidance does not apply.

UK employers should make sure that they are aware of all employees who are posted to other EU member states, and should be sure whether they are "seconded employees". If employees working in another state are not seconded employees, it does not automatically follow that they are subject to that other state's social and labour law'.

Applying to the Pensions Regulator for authorisation and approval 9.11

A scheme cannot operate as a cross-border scheme in the UK, or receive contributions from another member state, until it has been authorised and approved by the Pensions Regulator. It is also the Regulator's duty to notify the scheme of the social and labour laws which apply under the host member state (see **9.7** above). Accordingly, scheme trustees and managers must apply for authorisation and approval before they begin to operate as a cross-border scheme. They have the responsibility of ensuring that, to the extent that the scheme relates to members in another member state, it is operated in accordance with the social and labour laws of that state.

The main powers and duties of the Regulator cover the following matters:

- The trustees or managers of the UK scheme must apply to the Regulator for authorisation to operate as a cross-border scheme and for approval in relation to a particular European employer. They must provide information concerning their intent to accept contributions and details of the host member state and other prescribed information. Within three months of the receipt of such notice of intention the Regulator must, if it is satisfied with the information, notify the competent authority of the host member state of its receipt and contents. The Regulator must notify the applicant whether or not they are approved.

- The appropriate period before contributions are received must have expired (generally, two months from the date on which the Regulator notified the trustees or managers of its approval).

- The Regulator will forward as soon as practically possible to such persons any information which it receives from the competent authority of the host member state.

- The trustees or managers must ensure that the scheme is operated in a way consistent with the requirements of the social and labour laws of the host member state.

- The Regulator may determine upon direction whether or not the trustees or managers shall ring-fence some or all of the scheme assets.

- The Regulator is responsible for monitoring the compliance of a European pensions institution in respect of any contributions made by a UK employer. It must notify that authority of any relevant legal requirements within two months of receipt of a notice from the competent authorities of the host member state.

- The Regulator has power to prohibit any payment if it thinks it appropriate to do so.

The Regulator is bound to comply with any request from the competent authority of the member state to prohibit the disposal of UK assets of an EU pensions institution that has its main administration in that member state.

Guidance, forms and the timescales which apply   9.12

The Regulator publishes guidance and application forms on its website. Forms are provided to accommodate a two-stage registration process, and registration will only need to take place once. Existing schemes had to make an application to the Regulator by 30 March 2006. The forms are:

- The authorisation form (application must be made before or at the same time as for approval).

- The approval form.

The forms must be signed by the trustees or scheme managers and sent to: The Pensions Regulator, Napier House, Trafalgar Place, Brighton, BN1 4DW. The main application requirements are contained in the tables at the end of this chapter.

Ring-fencing of assets   9.13

Ring-fenced assets and liabilities shall be determined in accordance with the statutory funding objective (*Pt 3, Pensions Act 2004*). The Regulator may issue a ring-fencing notice where it has reasonable grounds for believing that a person has or intends to misuse or misappropriate the assets, or there is a material threat to the members' interests. The notice may direct the trustees/managers to notify the Regulator within three months of a date of issue of the details and assets of the liability attributable to each European employer.

The scheme should be divided into two or more sections for the purpose of ensuring that any contributions payable by the relevant European employer are allocated to the appropriate section, and that a specified part of the portion of the assets is attributable to that section and cannot be used for any other purpose.

What is the position with regard to contributions for deferred pensioners and pensioners? 9.14

The general rules if a deferred pensioner or pensioner is in a scheme which receives contributions are as follows:

- Where such a person is still employed by the same employer, they are not members for cross-border purposes provided that:

  (i) they held such status by 29 March 2006, or, if the trustees or manager had made a full or outlined application for authorisation and approval by that date, by 29 June 2006;

  (ii) there must be no link between contributions being paid and current salaries (ie contributions to meet shortfalls in the funding of deferred pension rights are permitted, but those deferred rights should not be revalued in line with a member's salary increases);

  (iii) no contributions are made for future accrual of benefits.

  Any contributions which have to be made to satisfy a *s 75, Pensions Act 1995* debt, statutory revaluation or revaluation under scheme rules, will not cause such members to be treated as cross-border members.

- If liabilities for any such members are met in full (by transferring to another arrangement to which the employer does not contribute or by buying out benefits) they would not count as members for cross-border purposes.

It should be noted that there is still some lack of certainty about the guidelines, and further developments are awaited.

Compliance and penalties 9.15

Trustees and managers need to be aware that failure to comply with many of the requirements of the *Pensions Act 2004* and the regulations thereunder can lead to penalties being incurred under *s 10, Pensions Act 1995,* not exceeding:

(a) £5,000 in the case of an individual and £50,000 in any other case; or

(b) such lower amount as may be prescribed in the case of an individual or in any other case.

Withdrawing an application 9.16

It is possible to withdraw an application to be treated as a cross-border scheme. If the trustees of a scheme find that an application for authorisation or approval is no longer needed, they can advise the Regulator in writing of the circumstance and apply for the application to be withdrawn. This action may be precipitated (for example) because:

- the potential cross-border members have retired from the scheme and the employment;

- the potential cross-border members have left employment, and taken a transfer value representing all their benefits to another arrangement.

The Regulator must be notified before authorisation or approval has been granted. It will then confirm that the request has been withdrawn and that the scheme has not been authorised or approved to operate as a cross-border scheme, as appropriate.

Schemes which had applied in full or in outline for authorisation or approval by 29 March 2006 as pre-existing schemes (that is, schemes which were already operating as cross-border schemes at 23 September 2005 – see the table at **9.17** below), that wished to withdraw their applications, had to do so by 29 June 2006.

In a case where authorisation or approval has been granted to a scheme, but is no longer required because:

- there are no benefits remaining in the scheme in respect of any member or deferred member who is or was a cross-border member; and

- there are no benefits remaining to be paid to the survivor of such a member;

the trustees can apply to the Regulator to have the authorisation and approval revoked. The application can be made by letter, giving details of the scheme and setting out the circumstances. The Regulator will consider the circumstances of the request and, if it is satisfied that there are no cross-border benefits remaining which require protection, will confirm the revocation.

The main application requirements 9.17

NOTE: The requirements of the main regulations in relation to applications for approval and authorisation are summarised below. They prescribed the manner and form in which occupational pension schemes that currently carry out cross-border activity had to apply to the Regulator for authorisation and approval to carry out such activity, and specified that such applications had to be made by 29 March 2006. The regulations were amended by the *Occupational Pension Schemes (Cross-border Activities) (Amendment) Regulations 2006 (SI 2006/925)* to the following effect so that, provided that they did make such applications by that date, such schemes could submit some of the information required to be included as part of such an application after that date, provided that the remaining information was submitted by 15 May 2006. In addition, it should be noted that the minimum funding objective is being replaced by the statutory funding objective (see **5.2** above).

'Applications for Authorisation

1. Applications for general authorisation to accept contributions from European employers by established schemes not carrying on cross-border activity.

Where a scheme is a new scheme, or a pre 23 September 2005 scheme, the information required is:

Money purchase scheme:

(*a*)   the pension scheme registration number;

(*b*)   a statement by the trustees/managers that they have provided the registrable information to the Regulator;

(*c*)   a statement by such persons that the scheme complies with the requirements of a UK based scheme to be a trust with effective rules

(*d*)   a statement by such persons that any statutory disclosure of information to members, investment principles and chosen investment requirements have been complied with;

(*e*)   a statement by such persons that any requirements for the trustees to have knowledge and understanding are enforced;

(*f*)   the most recent payment schedule.

A scheme which is not a money purchase scheme:

(i)   a statement by the trustees/managers that the scheme complies with the statutory minimum funding objective, the requirements in respect of actuarial valuations and reports, actuarial certification, and schedules of contributions;

(ii)   a copy of the most recent statement of funding principles;

(iii)   the latest actuarial valuation

2. Applications for general authorisation in respect of schemes which are carrying on cross-border activity

This applies to a scheme which is a pre 23 September 2005 scheme and the trustees/managers apply within 3 months beginning on the commencement date for authorisation. The information required is:

Money purchase scheme:

The information described in 1(*a*) to (*f*) above

A scheme which is not a money purchase scheme:

The information which is described in 1(*a*) to (*e*) above, together with the most recent minimum funding valuation for the scheme.

3. Applications for general authorisation in respect of new schemes

Where a scheme is a new scheme at the date of authorisation, the information required is:

Money purchase scheme:

The information described in 1(*a*) to (*f*) above

A scheme which is not a money purchase scheme:

The information which is described in 1(*a*) to (*e*) above

4. When may the Regulator revoke general authorisation?

The main matters which may cause a revocation of authorisation by the Regulator are:

- the scheme has no European members who have any accrued European rights; and

- there are not, in relation to the scheme, any survivors of such a member who have any accrued European rights

The Regulator may also revoke his decision where there is an unacceptable degree of seriousness, frequency and persistence by the trustees or managers to operate the scheme in the required manner, or for the scheme to comply with the prescribed requirements.

Applications for approval

5. Applications for approval in relation to a particular European employer for established schemes which are not carrying on cross–border activity

Other than for new schemes at the date of application, or pre 23 September 2005 schemes, or segregated multi-employer schemes where the notice of intention stated that contributions payable by the specified employer will be allocated to a new section, the information required is:

Money purchase scheme:

(*a*)   where the approval application is made on a different day to the authorisation application, and it is not clear to the Regulator that there has been no material change in information since the application for authorisation, the information in respect of which there has been any material change;

(*b*)   where the trustees/managers have been authorised, the date on which authorisation was granted;

(*c*)   where such persons are already accepting contributions from a European employer, the name and address of that employer and the host member state of that employer;

(*d*)   a copy of the scheme rules;

(*e*)   the most recent payments schedule;

(*f*)   the names of any other member states where the scheme has members who are qualifying persons;

(*g*)   where the scheme was established, or is intending to establish, a branch in the host member state, contact details including the persons authorised to represent the scheme in that branch;

(*h*)   the contact details of the host member state;

(*i*)   a description of the type of scheme involved;

(*j*)   the conditions to be met before benefits are payable;

(*k*)   the types and rates of contributions payable in respect of qualifying persons;

(*l*)   a description of any guarantees and additional coverage;

(*m*)   a description of excluded persons from membership;

(*n*)   whether the assets or liabilities or both of the scheme which corresponds to the activities carried out in the host member state will be ring-fenced.

A scheme which is not a money purchase scheme:

The information described in 5(*a*) to (*d*) and (*f*) to (*n*) above together with, where the application is not made the same day as the authorisation application and the Regulator is not satisfied that there has not been any material change to the information provided, the information in respect of which there has been any material change, together with the most recent schedule of contributions.

6. Applications for approval in respect of established schemes which are carrying on cross-border activity

Where the scheme is a pre 23 September 2005 scheme and the trustees/managers make an application for approval within 3 months from the commencement date, the information required is:

A money purchase scheme:

The information which is described in 5(*a*) to (*n*) above

Where the scheme is not a money purchase scheme:

The information which is described in 5(*a*) to (*d*) and (*f*) to (*n*) above, together with the most recent minimum funding valuation.

7. Applications for approval in respect of new schemes and new sections of segregated multi-employer schemes

The rules apply to a scheme which is a new scheme on the date an application or where the scheme is a segregated multi-employer scheme and the trustees/managers have stated on the notice of intention that any contributions to the scheme by a European employer specified in that notice will be allocated to a new section. The information to be provided is:

The information which is described in 5(*a*) to (*d*) and (*f*) to (*n*) above, and a signed statement by the trustees/managers showing the rates of contributions payable by or on behalf of the active members and the dates on or before which such contributions are to be paid.

8. Revocation of approval by the Regulator

The Regulator may revoke any approval in relation to a particular European employer where the scheme does not have any European members with European accrued rights or there are not in relation to the scheme any survivors of such a member who has such rights.'

Annex

Authorisation application form

Authorisation application form

Cross-border pension schemes

The Pensions Regulator

For more information in completing this form please see the guidance notes on our website: www.thepensionsregulator.gov.uk

The trustees of a pension scheme must apply for authorisation and approval before a scheme can start to operate cross border. Use this form to apply for authorisation.

Please note: schemes which apply for authorisation must comply with the full funding requirements – the Pensions Regulator cannot authorise schemes which do not meet these requirements.

1. Scheme information

1.1	Scheme name:	
1.2	Scheme address:	
		Postcode:
1.3	Principal employer's name:	
1.4	Principal employer's postcode:	
1.5	The Pensions Regulator's registration number, if known: *(new schemes will need to register before making this application)*	
1.6	Has the scheme been established under trust?	Yes No
1.7	How many trustees are appointed to the scheme?	

1. **Scheme information** *(continued)*

Please provide names and addresses of all trustees. For additional trustees, see Appendix 1.

Name	Address
	Postcode:
	Postcode:
	Postcode:
	Postcode:

1.8 Trustee, advisers and service providers:
(please tick each box, as applicable, and state name of company / individual)

	Tick box	Name
Insurance company:		
Scheme auditor:		
Scheme actuary:		

2. Application basis

Please tick **one** option:

- Are you applying as an established scheme which is not accepting contributions from a European employer at date of application?

- Are you applying as an established scheme which is accepting contributions from a European employer at date of application?

  If ticked yes, have you been accepting contributions before the 23 September 2005

  Yes / No (delete as applicable)

- Are you applying as a new scheme?

  If a new scheme, please give the date the PR1 form was sent:

3. Contact information

For queries relating to this application.

3.1 Name:

3.2 Address:

Postcode:

3.3 Telephone number:

3.4 Fax number:

3.5 Email address:

4. Additional information

Documentation that you must submit with this application is listed below. Please select the correct scheme type and use the corresponding tick boxes to indicate which documents you have included with this application form.

The Pensions Regulator has the right to request additional information, where necessary, whilst processing this application.

4.1 Defined contribution (money purchase) schemes

- A copy of the most recent payment schedule.

4.   **Additional information** *(continued)*

4.2   **Defined benefit (including final salary and salary related) schemes**

If you are making an application as an established scheme not accepting contributions from a European employer at date of application as specified in section 2, please provide:

- A copy of the most recent statement of funding principles for the scheme.

- A copy of the actuarial valuation for the scheme (the effective date of which is within the period of 12 months ending on the date of application).

If you are making an application as an established scheme which is accepting contributions from a European employer at date of application, please provide:

- A copy of the most recent minimum funding valuation for the scheme.

5.   **Declaration**

I / We declare that the scheme is compliant with the following regulatory requirements.

That all registrable information has been supplied:

the scheme complies with the requirements of section 252(2) and (3) (UK-based scheme to be trust with effective rules);

the scheme is complying with section 113 of the 1993 Act (a) disclosure information to members of schemes, etc;

section 35 of the 1995 Act (b) a statement of investment principles (SIP) exists and being complied with; and

section 36 of the 1995 Act (c) requirement for knowledge and understanding: individual trustees, and section 248 (e) requirement for knowledge and understanding: corporate trustees are in force on the date on which the application is made, any requirements made by or under those sections have been complied with; or

where section 247 and section 248 are not in force on the day on which the application is made, any requirements made by or under those sections, or in any instrument made under either or both those sections, will be complied with once those sections are in force.

If you are making an application as an established scheme which is not accepting contributions from a European employer at date of application:

I / We confirm that:

that the scheme meets the statutory funding objective;

that the scheme complies with the requirements of section 222; and

any requirement imposed by or under section 224 (actuarial valuations and reports), section 225 (certification of technical provisions) and section 227 (schedule of contributions), have been complied with.

5. **Declaration** *(continued)*

If you are making an application as a new scheme:

I / We confirm that the scheme will meet its statutory funding objective by the expiry of the period two years beginning on the date on which the application was made.

I/We hereby apply for authorisation of the retirement benefits scheme named in Section 1 of this form under section 288 of the Pensions Act 2004 and the Occupational Pension Schemes (Cross-border Activities) Regulations 2005, (Regulation 4/5/6).

I / We also declare that to the best of my / our knowledge and belief, the information given in this application and contained in the supporting documentation is correct and complete.

Signatories

This form must be signed by the trustee(s) or scheme manager(s).

For additional signatories see Appendix 1.

Signed	Print name	Date *(of application)*	Role
			Trustee / Scheme manager *
			Trustee / Scheme manager *
			Trustee / Scheme manager *
			Trustee / Scheme manager *

* delete as applicable

6. Submission

Please note that the information provided in this form will be used by the Pensions Regulator in exercising its functions under section 288(2) of the Pensions Act 2004 (general authorisation to accept contributions from European employers). It is a criminal offence knowingly or recklessly to provide the regulator with false or misleading information.

Please ensure that all relevant sections are complete and that you have provided all the requested additional documentation. Incomplete applications will be rejected or delayed until all required information has been supplied.

Until you have been notified in writing that your application has been successfully processed, you are not authorised to operate on a cross-border basis.

Please send the completed application form together with all relevant supporting documentation to:

The Pensions Regulator
Napier House
Trafalgar Place
Brighton
BN1 4DW

If you have any queries about this application please call our customer support team on
0870 606 3636.

Alternatively you can email this document to

customersupport@thepensionsregulator.gov.uk

Please note that sending information by email is not secure and is done so at your own risk.

Additional names and addresses of all trustees (see section 1.7 above)

Please photocopy as many times as required.

Name	Address
	Postcode:
	Postcode:
	Postcode:
	Postcode:

Additional signatories (see section 5 above)

Please photocopy as many times as required.

Signatories

This form must be signed by the trustee(s) or scheme manager(s).

Signed	Print name	Date *(of application)*	Role
			Trustee / Scheme manager *
			Trustee / Scheme manager *
			Trustee / Scheme manager *
			Trustee / Scheme manager *

* delete as applicable

Approval application form – notice of intention

Approval application form – notice of intention
Cross-border pension schemes

The Pensions Regulator

For more information in completing this form please see the guidance notes on our website: www.thepensionsregulator.gov.uk

Please note: you will need to apply for authorisation before or at the same time as applying for approval. Schemes which apply for approval must comply with the full funding requirements – the Pensions Regulator cannot approve schemes which do not meet these requirements.

If there have been any material changes since applying for authorisation please provide details of these changes with this application.

Part 1

Home member state regulation – required information

Scheme information

1.1	Scheme name:	
1.2	Scheme address:	
		Postcode:
1.3	Principal employer's name:	
1.4	Principal employer's postcode:	

1.5	Has the scheme been established under trust? *(if no, please provide information about what type of scheme this is)*	Yes	No
1.6	The Pensions Regulator's registration number: *(new schemes will need to register before making this application)*		

Scheme information *(continued)*

			Yes, enclosed		No

1.7 Date scheme authorised to operate cross–border activity:

1.8 Are you applying for authorisation at the same time? *(your application for authorisation will be processed first)*

If no, the date when authorisation was granted.

1.9 Are you already accepting contributions from a European employer? — Yes / No

1.10 Are you a segregated multi-employer scheme? (or will you become one if this application is successful) — Yes / No

If yes, are you applying for approval for a new section(s) of your segregated multi-employer scheme? — Yes / No

1.11 Please provide the names and addresses of European employer(s) or new section(s) of a segregated multi-employer scheme you wish to apply to accept contributions from (if more than one, approval will be given on an employer by employer basis). Please provide additional names and addresses at Appendix 1, if required.

Separate Parts 2 and 3 will need to be completed for each employer stated.

Employer *(or new section(s) of a segregated multi-employer scheme)*	Address *(main operating address in the host state)*	Please state name of host member state(s): *(if more than one, list all)*
	Postcode:	
	Postcode:	
	Postcode:	
	Postcode:	

Cross-border activities

Scheme information *(continued)*

1.12 **Application basis**

Please tick **one** option:

- Are you applying as an established scheme which is not accepting contributions from a European employer at date of application?

- Are you applying as an established scheme which is accepting contributions from a European employer at date of application?

  If ticked yes, have you been accepting contributions before the 23 September 2005

  Yes / No (delete as applicable)

- Are you applying as a new scheme?

  If a new scheme, please provide the date the PR1 form was sent:

Certification

1.13 For all schemes, please provide:

- A copy of the scheme rules.

  Enclosed

1.14 **For defined benefit schemes**

Where application is being made as an established scheme which is not accepting contributions from a European employer or as a new scheme, please also provide:

- A copy of the most recent schedule of contributions.
  (new schemes – see Note 1 below)

  Enclosed

Where application is being made as an established scheme which is accepting contributions from a European employer, please also provide:

- A copy of the most recent minimum funding valuation for the scheme
  (unless submitting this form with an authorisation application only one copy of the valuation is required)

  Enclosed

1.15 **For defined contribution schemes**

Where application is being made as an established scheme or new scheme, please also provide:

- A copy of the most recent payment schedule.
  (unless submitting this form with an authorisation application only one copy of the valuation is required) (new schemes – see Note 1 below)

  Enclosed

Please note: The Pensions Regulator has the right to request additional information, where necessary, whilst processing this application.

Note 1:
Where there is currently no schedule of contributions or payment schedule in place, please provide a statement outlining the rates of contributions payable to the scheme on behalf of each employer within this application and the active members of the scheme. Please also state the dates on or before such contributions are to be paid. The statement must be signed by the trustees or scheme managers.

Contact information

For queries relating to this application.

1.16   Name:

1.17   Address:

Post code:

1.18   Telephone number:

1.19   Fax number:

1.20   Email address:

Part 2

List of the main characteristics regarding the Institution for Occupational Retirement Provision (IORP), i.e. the pension scheme, offered by IORP in the host member state.

This list specifies the minimum level of information that the Pensions Regulator has to provide to the host member state. For further information please see the CEIOPS website: www.ceiops.org

To be supplied by the trustees / scheme managers in English and also in the language of the relevant host member state. **Please complete Part 2 for each employer or new section of a segregated multi-employer scheme listed at 1.11 above.**

General information about IORP

2.1	IORP name (eg scheme)	
2.2	IORP full address	
		Country:
		Postcode:
	IORP contact details	
2.3	Name:	
2.4	Address: *(if different from 2.2)*	
		Country:
		Postcode:
2.5	Telephone number:	
2.6	Fax number:	
2.7	Email address: *(if applicable)*	
2.8	IORP identification code number: *(eg The Pensions Regulator's registration number)*	
2.9	Legal status of IORP	UK Trust Based

General information about IORP *(continued)*

2.10 Please list **all** member states in
which IORP (scheme) is currently
operating:

269

Cross-border activities

Part 3

Information to be provided by the Pensions Regulator to the host member state regarding the pension scheme to be operated for the sponsoring undertaking

To be supplied by the trustees / scheme managers in English and also in the language of the relevant host member state. **Please complete Part 3 for each employer or new section of a segregated multi-employer scheme listed at 1.11 above.**

Authorised representative of IORP in the host member state (if any)

3.1	Legal status	
3.2	Full address:	Town: Country: Postcode:
3.3	Contact name:	
3.4	Contact's telephone number: *(including international dialing code)*	
3.5	Contact's fax number: *(including international dialing code)*	
3.6	Contact's email address: *(if applicable)*	
3.7	Identification code number: *(if any)*	

Sponsoring undertaking (eg name of sponsoring employer of IORP)

3.8	Name in full:	
3.9	Full address:	Town: Country: Postcode:
3.10	Contact name and title: *(eg company secretary)*	
3.11	Contact's telephone number: *(including international dialling code)*	
3.12	Contact's fax number: *(including international dialling code)*	

Sponsoring undertaking (eg name of sponsoring employer of IORP) *(continued)*

3.13 Contact's email address:
(if applicable)

Description of the pension scheme

Membership

3.14 Describe the categories of the sponsoring undertaking's employees that can be members of the pension scheme:
(if there are any restrictions)

What type of scheme is offered to the sponsoring undertaking? *(describe the scheme)*

3.15 Defined contributions only:

Are there investment options and how many are there?

3.16 Defined benefit:
(final salary / salary related)

3.17 Hybrid:
(separate defined contribution and defined benefit sections)

Benefits offered and conditions for payment of benefits

3.18 Describe the types of benefit offered:
(eg retirement pension, lump sums, widow's and orphans pensions, dependant's pensions, disability annuities, death in service cover etc)

3.19 Describe the conditions for payment of benefits:
(eg age, contribution)

271

Description of the pension scheme *(continued)*

3.20 Describe any guarantees offered (eg investment performance, a given level of benefits etc) and who provides additional coverage:	Description:	Provided by:
3.21 Describe the additional coverage offered (eg long-term care, additional biometric risks etc) and who provides additional coverage:	Description:	Provided by:

Who is responsible for the payment of benefits?

3.22 The IORP (pension scheme) itself: ☐ Yes ☐ No

3.23 Another company:
(eg insurance company) ☐ Yes ☐ No

If yes, please state company name in full:

Contributions

3.24 Describe the types of contributions paid by the sponsoring undertaking (employer) and by the members:	Employers:	Members:

Assets and liabilities

3.25 Will the assets and liabilities attributable to the IORP in the host member state be ring-fenced as permitted by the directive? ☐ Yes ☐ No

Part 4

Declaration

Where authorisation has already been granted:

I / We declare that where some or all of the information supplied in the application and by means of certification and / or documentation at authorisation has changed, we have enclosed documentation of these changes within this application.

Where I / we have not indicated changes to the information, I / we declare that the information supplied in the application and by means of certification and / or authorisation has not changed.

If a segregated multi-employer scheme:

I / We declare that any contributions payable to the scheme by the European employer specified in this 'Notice of Intention' will be allocated to a new section, that section.

I / We hereby apply for approval of the retirement benefits scheme named in Part 1 of this form under section 289 of the Pensions Act 2004 and the Occupational Pension Schemes (Cross-border Activities) Regulations 2005 (Regulation 9/10/11).

I / We also declare that to the best of my / our knowledge and belief, the information given in this application and contained in the supporting documentation is correct and complete.

Signatories

This form must be signed by the trustee(s) or scheme manager(s).

For additional signatories see Appendix 1.

Signed	Print name	Date (of application)	Role
			Trustee / Scheme manager *
			Trustee / Scheme manager *
			Trustee / Scheme manager *
			Trustee / Scheme manager *

* delete as applicable

Submission

Please note that the information provided in this form will be used by the Pensions Regulator in exercising its functions under section 289(2) of the Pensions Act 2004 (approval to accept contributions from European employers). It is a criminal offence knowingly or recklessly to provide the regulator with false or misleading information.

Please ensure that all relevant sections are complete and that you have provided all the requested additional documentation. Incomplete applications will be rejected or delayed until all required information has been supplied.

Until you have been notified in writing that your application has been successfully processed, you are not approved in relation to a particular European employer or a new section of a segregated multi-employer pension scheme to operate on a cross-border basis.

Please send the completed application form together with all relevant supporting documentation to:

> **The Pensions Regulator**
> **Napier House**
> **Trafalgar Place**
> **Brighton**
> **BN1 4DW**

If you have any queries relating to this application please call our customer support team on **0870 606 3636**.

Alternatively you can email this document to

> **customersupport@thepensionsregulator.gov.uk**

Please note that sending information by email is not secure and is done so at your own risk.

Additional names and addresses of all employers (see section 1.11 above)
Please photocopy as many times as required.

Employer (or new section(s) of a segregated multi-employer scheme)	Address (main operating address in the host state)	Please state name of host member state(s): (if more than one, list all)
	Postcode:	
	Postcode:	
	Postcode:	
	Postcode:	

Additional signatories (see Part 4 above)
Please photocopy as many times as required.

Signatories

This form must be signed by the trustee(s) or scheme manager(s).

Signed	Print name	Date*(of application)*	Role
			Trustee / Scheme manager *
			Trustee / Scheme manager *
			Trustee / Scheme manager *
			Trustee / Scheme manager *

* delete as applicable

Chapter 10
State pensions

Introduction

Part 8 of the *Pensions Act 2004* deals with changes to state pensions. The most significant of these changes is to permit deferred state pension to be taken as a lump sum, albeit in a taxable form, as part of wider measures to promote flexible retirement practices and encourage older people to continue working. (Note, however, that more radical measures are proposed under the government's 2006 pensions White Paper; these are covered later in **CHAPTER 11**.)

Increases for deferred state pensions

Prior to 6 April 2005, where entitlement to state pension was deferred past state pension age, an increment of $\frac{1}{7}\%$ was added for each week of deferment (up to a maximum of five years' deferment). A provision in the *Pensions Act 1995* would have amended the *Social Security Contributions and Benefits Act 1992* so as to increase the increment from $\frac{1}{7}\%$ to $\frac{1}{5}\%$ with effect from 6 April 2010.

However, in its Pensions Green Paper of December 2002 the government declared its intention to promote employment among older people in order to reduce the strain on retirement savings, avoid the retirement cliff edge and re-introduce the skills of older workers into the economy. One of the measures it would use to further this aim was to make the deferment of state pension more attractive.

Consequently, *s 297, Pensions Act 2004*, has brought the *Pensions Act 1995* amendment forwards so that periods of deferment after 6 April 2005 now attract the higher increment of $\frac{1}{5}\%$ for each week of deferment (10.4% pa). State pension must be deferred for at least five weeks in order to qualify for increments and all elements of state pension must be deferred ie it would not be permitted to draw basic state pension while deferring additional state pension (except in some limited circumstances). However, the five-year limit on deferment has now been removed meaning that increments can be earned for as long as someone decides to put off drawing their state pension. The following table (taken from DWP leaflet SPD2) illustrates the effect of this.

Amount of state pension		Number of years' deferment	Extra state pension earned		Cumulative amount of extra state pension after it has been paid for :		
pw	pa		pw	pa	5 years	10 years	15 years
£100	£5,200	1	£10.40	£540	£2,700	£5,410	£8,110
		2	£20.80	£1,080	£5,410	£10,820	£16,220
		3	£31.20	£1,620	£8,110	£16,220	£24,340
		4	£41.60	£2,160	£10,820	£21,630	£32,450
		5	£52.00	£2,700	£13,520	£27,040	£40,560

Note that guaranteed minimum pensions paid by contracted-out occupational pension schemes still only attract the ½% increment despite the increase in the corresponding state benefit.

Deferred pension increases taken as lump sum 10.3

Section 297 of the *Pensions Act 2004* also introduced the more radical measure of allowing people to take any deferred state pension as a lump sum. It was hoped this would provide an even greater incentive to defer retirement beyond state pension age.

Where state pension has been deferred for at least twelve months, the person, on claiming his or her entitlement to it, can elect to receive either an increased pension or a lump sum. Where no election is made, the person is treated as electing to take the lump sum. Interest must be added to the pension foregone at a rate which is 2% higher than the Bank of England base rate, or at such higher rate as may be prescribed. The calculation of the lump sum is based on a weekly roll-up and is arrived at through the following prescribed formula:

$$(A + P) \times \sqrt[52]{(1 + R/100)}$$

where:

P is the amount of category A or category B retirement pension to which the person would have been entitled for that week if it had not been deferred;

A is the lump sum amount arrived at for the previous week of deferment (or nil if this is the first week in the calculation);

R is the percentage rate 2% higher than Bank of England base rate (or such higher rate as is prescribed).

Note that any change in the Bank of England base rate is not to be treated as taking effect until the next week of state pension deferment has started. If the government wants to prescribe an interest rate higher than 2% above base rate, it must have regard to the national economic situation and any other matters considered relevant.

The following table illustrates the lump sum that could be payable if a state pension of £100 per week is deferred and the interest rate remains at a constant 6.75% throughout the period of deferment:

Weekly state pension	Number of years' deferment	Lump sum payment
£100	1	£ 5,380
	2	£11,120
	3	£17,240
	4	£23,790
	5	£30,770

The figures shown above are before deduction for income tax. Any deferred pension taken as lump sum will be paid by the government less income tax due, but the income tax rate that applies will only be the rate that would have applied otherwise. If receipt of the lump sum payment would take a person's earnings into the 40% tax bracket, say, only 22% tax would continue to be applicable on the lump sum. Similarly, anyone in the 10% tax bracket would not automatically be thrown into the 22% bracket.

Additionally, if a person starts to draw his or her state pension and elects to take the deferred instalments as a lump sum, he or she may elect to receive the lump sum in a later tax year. This means that if a person knows that they will be in a lower tax bracket in the following tax year, they can save the difference in the tax rates.

Receiving deferred entitlement to state pension as a lump sum in this way would not affect entitlements to pension credit, housing benefit, council tax benefit or the age-related income tax allowance.

Similar provisions were introduced for additional state pension which has been shared in consequence of a court order dealing with divorce.

Disclosure of state pension information   10.4

Section 298 of the *Pensions Act 2004* makes two amendments to the provisions of the *Child Support, Pensions and Social Security Act 2000* that govern the disclosure of state pension information.

There is a range of people who can apply to the DWP for disclosure of state pension information. Such people are normally the trustees or managers of occupational or personal pension schemes or a sponsoring employer, that want to provide combined pension forecasts for their members or employees. If any other parties provide services to the trustees, managers or sponsoring employer that involve giving advice or forecasts where state pension information may be relevant, they too may now apply for and receive state pension information as long as they have been authorised in writing by the trustees, managers or sponsoring employer, as appropriate.

This measure would also help smooth the way if the provision of combined pension forecasts becomes compulsory in the future.

The second change made by *s 298* of the *Pensions Act 2004* amends the list of items to be disclosed by the DWP as part of state pension information. This list now includes a projection of the amount of any lump sum to which an individual is likely to become entitled, or to which he or she might become entitled in particular circumstances.

Other amendments 10.5

Part 8 of the Pensions Act 2004 contains two other amendments, one relating to further provisions arising out of the termination of the reciprocal agreement on state pensions with Australia in February 2001, and one relating to which category B retirement pension will apply where there are two such pension entitlements.

Conclusion 10.6

The move to increase people's awareness of state pension information is to be welcomed. However, it remains to be seen whether the facility to defer state pensions, and to take a taxable lump sum, will be seen as attractive. It is likely that the cultural habit of taking state pension as soon as it becomes available will be difficult to change.

Chapter 11
Further reforms

Introduction

11.1

The last six years have been witness to significant upheaval in the field of pensions, both private and state, and pensions issues now feature regularly in the broadsheet newspapers. Among other things, we have seen the introduction of stakeholder pensions, state pension credit, high-profile corporate insolvencies with significant loss of pension rights, pension sharing on divorce, the Equitable Life affair, a European pensions Directive, the state second pension, the demise of the minimum funding requirement, a whole new pensions tax regime, FRS17, age discrimination, the decline of defined benefit pension schemes and numerous debates, reports, consultations and initiatives. These are in addition to the measures contained in the *Pensions Act 2004*, and there are further reforms still to come. This final chapter looks at a few of those possible reforms, by far the greatest of which is promised by the 2006 pensions White Paper.

2006 White Paper

Introduction

11.2

The White Paper on state and private pension reform was published on 25 May 2006. It is entitled *Security in Retirement: Towards a New Pensions System*. The White Paper takes into consideration many matters which have been raised by industry representatives, commissions and trades unions.

The Work and Pensions Secretary, John Hutton, stated that the government's first priority was to make it easier for people to save for their retirement, and that it has addressed this with the introduction of new personal accounts for all workers. These will be provided under a state-run national pension savings scheme or a similar model or models which have been proposed by the pensions industry representatives who have been involved in the consultations to date.

The government has given specific consideration to the recommendations which were made by Lord Adair Turner's Pensions Commission in its Second Report, dated 30 November 2005, and the Final Report on the National

Pensions Debate which concluded at the end of March 2006 and involved over 1,000 members of the public in simultaneous, satellite-linked events spanning six locations. Its response to the Pensions Commission's National Pension Savings Scheme (NPSS), as a model for a state-run national pension savings scheme, has been favourable. However, it has not agreed with all the proposals which were contained in the Second Report.

The White Paper outlines a proposed savings and benefit infrastructure for the next 40 years in the face of an aging population. The steady decline in defined benefit schemes and a reduction in levels of employer support for private pension provision in recent years, in particular for defined benefit schemes, have accelerated the need for action. The main objectives of the Paper are:

- a state pension which is linked to earnings;
- compulsory employer contributions; and
- a fairer system for women.

The proposals have been positively received by the majority of employer and employee groups and pensions advisers. In particular:

(i)   The National Association of Pension Funds (NAPF) has stated that it fully supports the proposals to extend the basic state pension (BSP) to a wider category of recipients, to index-link BSP to earnings (in place of the link with inflation over the past 20 years) and to enrol automatically people who do not have adequate private pension provision into a national scheme.

(ii) The Pensions Commission has welcomed the commitment to increased state pension provision, the provision of a better deal for women and automatic enrolment into low-cost personal pension accounts with an employer contribution.

(iii) The TUC General Secretary has welcomed the proposals as 'progressive'.

Events leading up to the White Paper

Awareness of the need for action   11.3

There has been a great deal of ongoing debate on the impact of the increased life expectancy of UK citizens on the ability of the state to provide sustainable pensions at an acceptable level for all in the long-term future. This has been accompanied by an awareness that the real value of state pension provision in the UK is inadequate compared with the levels which are provided by many neighbouring member states in the EU. Furthermore, the real value of state pensions has been steadily declining since the abandonment of the earnings-link for a link with inflation 20 years ago.

Assessment of the position for recent retirers   **11.4**

The government states that current pensioners are now better off than ever before, and that the past private provision of generous defined benefit schemes has been a significant contributor to this situation. In addition to the introduction of the state earnings-related pension scheme (SERPS) in 1978, and the doubling of value of housing wealth as a percentage of GDP since 1980 (with home ownership among recently retired people approaching 80%), the White Paper also draws attention to the significant changes to encourage pension provision and to protect beneficiaries' interests which have taken place since 1997. These include:

- the introduction in April 2001 of low-cost stakeholder schemes for all, including the self-employed and non-employed;

- the pension credit system, which has provided for those most in need pending a longer-term solution to the pensions problem;

- the impact of tax simplification under the *Finance* Act *2004*, with increased levels of tax-relievable contributions and tax-free funds and the widening of membership rules and transferability of pension rights;

- the establishment of the Pension Protection Fund and the Financial Assistance Scheme under the *Pensions Act 2004*;

- the introduction of a Pensions Regulator, in place of Opra, with increased powers to protect beneficiaries' interests.

The call to action   **11.5**

Nevertheless, the decline in the real value of state provision and the effect of greater longevity must be addressed for the future. The actuarial profession has supported the view that state pensions must increase and the earnings-link be restored in tandem with a rise in state pension age (SPA). However, it is strongly opposed to any increase in the current level of National Insurance contributions. The main recent developments were:

1. The First and Second Reports of the Pensions Commission, which was commissioned by the government to be led by Lord Adair Turner. The Second Report was published on 30 November 2005.

2. A DWP News Release, in September 2005 ('Speech to Trades Union Congress Adair Turner'), in which Lord Turner stated the main issues and expressed the view that to introduce compulsory contributions by employers would cause them to cut back wages.

3. The provision of a National Pension Savings Scheme ('NPSS') model by the Pension Commission, and its support for a two-tier system, in contrast to the NAPF's support for a Citizen's Pension.

4.   The government's general acceptance of the key points made by the
     Pensions Commission.

Informing people of their current entitlements and expectations   **11.6**

The White Paper draws specific attention to the matter of pensioner-awareness.
The following initiatives since 2002 were identified:

- The Informed Choice programme, which endeavoured to raise public
  awareness and understanding of retirement provision, and to promote
  individual responsibility for retirement planning. A range of pension
  forecasts were introduced in order to give individuals an understanding
  of the income they are likely to receive in retirement, based on their
  National Insurance contributions or credits. They were supplemented by
  leaflets that set out options for improving their position – such as
  working longer and deferring receipt of their pensions or making
  additional contributions.

- DWP Combined Pension Forecasts, which provide information on state
  pension provision and a forecast of an individual's current private
  pension. Over 6.3m forecasts have been produced.

- DWP Individual Pension Forecasts, which are tailored to an individual's
  personal and employment status and current employment status. Over
  7m forecasts have been produced.

- DWP Real-Time Pension Forecasts, whereby individuals can contact the
  DWP electronically to obtain an online Individual Pension Forecast.
  Over 107,000 requests have been received.

- DWP Automatic State Pension Forecasts, which are unsolicited forecasts
  sent by the DWP to all working-age people who have not received any
  other type of forecast in the previous twelve months. Over 12m forecasts
  have been issued.

Changing current state provision   **11.7**

In addition to the need to reform state pension provision for all in the future,
the White Paper has focused strongly on the government's ongoing commitment to reducing remaining inequalities in the pension and benefit system,
particularly for women and carers. It makes reference to the DWP's publication
Women and Pensions: The Evidence, which considers in detail the disadvantages
women have faced in building pension provision. There is also consideration of
the DWP's *Family Resources Survey,* which shows that there are around 3.6m

carers below state pension age (SPA) caring for adults in the UK. Around 390,000 carers are not accruing BSP rights and 120,000 of them are caring for 20 hours or more a week.

The proposed changes to current state provision take into consideration these matters, and better provision for all. They are described under the relevant headings below.

Earnings indexation and contracting out   11.8

The White Paper states that:

'people's expectations for their incomes in retirement are largely based on their earnings and standard of living during working age. If the state system is to serve as a foundation for their retirement planning, it must retain its level relative to these expectations. This will help to address the problem of undersaving by enabling people to predict with confidence what they are likely to receive from the state when they retire, and therefore what they will need to save in addition to meet their expectations'.

In accordance with the above:

- Index-linking on an average-earnings basis (which was in place for a brief period in the 1970s) is to be restored in the next government, with a target date of 2012 (or the end of the parliament at the latest) and subject to an affordability test and the fiscal position. The date will be confirmed at the beginning of the next parliament.

  Note: promising restoration of the earnings link subject to an affordability test has been criticised by some observers as a get-out clause for the government. However, this was refuted by James Purnell, Minister for Pensions Reform, when he addressed a conference for pension scheme trustees organised by the TUC two weeks after the publication of the White Paper. According to Purnell, restoration of the earnings link is 'a firm pledge, guaranteed by the end of the next Parliament', which is likely to be 2015.

- Contracting out for defined contribution schemes, both occupational and personal/stakeholder, is to be abolished at the same time that index-linking commences. The government has already removed several restrictions applying to contracted-out rights in such schemes, notably the requirement to buy an index-linked annuity, the minimum payable age of 60 and the prohibition on commutation for cash. In September 2006 the government issued a consultation on further proposals which would see the remaining restrictions on contracted-out rights from such schemes abolished, notably the investment restrictions, the requirement to purchase an annuity on unisex rates and the requirement to provide a survivor's pension if the member was married. These measures would bring the treatment of contracted-out rights in defined contribution schemes into line with the treatment of other pension rights in such schemes, so that there would no longer be any distinction between the two.

- The defined contribution contracted-out rebate will end at the same time as the BSP is uprated in line with earnings.

- Schemes will be permitted to convert GMP rights into ordinary scheme benefits by offering the actuarial equivalent of the entitlements in exchange for the extra rights.

Pensions credit   11.9

The government will continue uprating the 'guarantee credit' element of pensions credit over the long term. The starting point for the 'savings credit' element, for those aged over 65, will be raised as state second pension (S2P) matures. From 2008 the lower threshold of earnings credit will be uprated by earnings, and from 2015 the maximum savings credit will be frozen in real terms.

Qualifying for the state pension and tackling inequalities   11.10

The following proposals were made concerning the number of years which are required in order to build up a state pension:

- The qualifying period for a full basic state pension will be cut to 30 years, compared to 44 years (for males) or 39 years (for females) at present. This is primarily to provide for persons who have interrupted work records (e g women, and carers for children as well as severely disabled people who cannot qualify for a full state pension). The government states that 85% of males currently qualify for such a pension, compared with 30% of females.

- Home Responsibilities Protection (HRP) will be converted into a positive weekly credit for the BSP, and there will be an alignment of the rules for when the credit is available between the BSP and the S2P so that those caring for children aged under twelve years of age are eligible.

- There will be an alignment of credits for foster carers across the BSP and the S2P, a move from a system of annual credits in S2P to weekly credits, enabling people to combine credited and paid contributions in order to accrue a year of entitlement to S2P, and a new Carer's Credit in the BSP and S2P for those undertaking care for the sick and severely disabled for 20 hours or more a week.

- The minimum contribution conditions in the BSP will be abolished as will the Labour Market Attachment Test in the S2P, to ensure that every year of contributions or credits counts.

- The measures above would apply to people reaching SPA on or after 6 April 2010.

- The proposals will facilitate the abolition of adult dependency increases which, as announced in *A New Deal for Welfare: Empowering People to Work*, were not to be carried forward into the Employment and Support Allowance, and the abolition of National Insurance 'autocredits' awarded to those between 60 and 65, in line with the equalisation of women's SPA.

- The Pensions Commission's call for qualification on a residency-test basis has been rejected, and the Commission has acknowledged this decision. The government again refers to its publication *A New Deal for Welfare* which reaffirmed its view that 'the system of welfare should be based on the recognition that with rights come responsibilities'. It states that it is right for people to receive state pension in return for making economic or social contributions during their working lives. It does not think it is 'fair to recognise people for state pension purposes purely on the basis of residence while others are contributing to society through working and caring'. The government also details a number of practical and operational concerns with a residence test.

- It is expected that, by 2010, 70% of females will qualify for a full pension and that by 2025 over 90% of people will qualify for the full amount.

Raising the state pension age   **11.11**

It has been clear for some time that SPA would have to be raised in order to deal with an aging population. The Pensions Commission recommended raising SPA to age 68, and the White Paper proposes that this should be done in stages, as follows:

- between 2024 and 2026, from age 65 to 66;

- between 2034 and 2036, to age 67; and

- between 2044 and 2046, to age 68.

Persons who retire early will need to make provision for the extra years before they receive their state pension, perhaps through the NPSS or an employer's scheme.

State second pension (S2P)   **11.12**

The earnings-related S2P benefit, which is paid on top of the basic state pension (BSP), is to be changed. The intent is to cap the upper earnings limit so that, as average earnings rise, the same flat-rate payment will eventually apply to all. Accruals will gradually start to become flat rate at the same time as the government starts to uprate the BSP by earnings. The expected date by which S2P will become flat rate is 2030.

The Pensions Commission had called for an extension of S2P to the self-employed on a voluntary, age-related contribution basis. However, the government considers that self-employment is too unpredictable and often temporary, and it does not support this recommendation.

There have been calls to allow contracted-out pension schemes to 'buy back' their members' rights in the S2P in order to simplify their administration. The government accordingly undertook a preliminary investigation of both the legal and the financial feasibility of creating a facility for more broad-based buy-backs. This investigation suggested that buy-backs would be feasible in principle, but very complex in practice, and it has therefore been decided not to include a provision for buy-backs in the new pension reform.

The government's impact assessment   **11.13**

The government has pointed out that the effect of the changes depends on the age of the person concerned, due to the phasing-in of the various provisions. In particular:

- As the link between earnings and the state pension is set to be restored in 2012, the pensions which are being paid to existing pensioners will continue to rise in line with inflation, rather than earnings, for at least the next six years.

- Persons aged below 47 will be affected by the introduction of a higher retirement age, although the changes will only affect the state pension.

- If an employee's employer does not make contributions into any scheme on his or her behalf, he or she could receive a boost to their pension savings under the new proposals.

A state-run national pension savings scheme   **11.14**

There will be consultation on whether to establish a state-run NPSS, as recommended and structured by the Pensions Commission, or one of a range of other schemes which have been suggested by the pensions industry. The Pensions Commission considers that the NPSS should be established as a non-departmental public body with the administration, servicing and fund management functions outsourced to private contractors. This view is reflected in the White Paper. The alternative products which have been considered are:

- The NAPF's proposed model of Supertrusts, which builds on existing multi-employer occupational schemes. It envisages between 10 and 20 Supertrusts, which would each be overseen by a board of governors who would outsource operations and determine investment strategy.

- The Association of British Insurers' (ABI) concept of Partnership Pensions, built on the existing stakeholder platform, where collections were paid directly from employers to pension providers through the BACS system of collection. The ABI has proposed a Retirement Income Commission to oversee the system and ensure that it works for individuals. The initial choice of providers should be with employers, with individual member choice, if wished.

- The Investment Managers Association's (IMA) option based largely on the Pensions Commission's proposals, but focusing on how some of the processes, such as governance and fund management, could work in practice.

The government did not feel that Supertrusts or Partnership Pensions contained all of the features needed for personal accounts. However, it has used features of all of the proposals to refine and improve the models which are outlined in the White Paper. It is also considering whether Supertrusts could work alongside personal accounts to offer more choice in pension provision. The main government proposals for a state-run national pension savings scheme are described below.

Automatic enrolment for employees   **11.15**

The following proposed details should apply to membership:

- There will be automatic enrolment in the new state-run national pension savings scheme, with the chance for employees to opt out. Enrolment will be for employees aged 22 or older (the age at which the adult rate for the national minimum wage is payable) and on starting a new job from 2012.

- Employees will be automatically enrolled on changing employer, and then every three years, should they initially choose to opt out and continue to work for the same employer; and employees earning below the lower threshold will be automatically enrolled when their earnings exceed that level.

Alternative employer-provision schemes/opting out   11.16

Employees may join an employer's scheme as an alternative, if it meets certain minimum standards. In such an arrangement, employer contributions will not be compulsory.

Annuities, lump sums and accessing pension savings   11.17

The proposal is for a broadly level playing field with the rules that apply to *Finance Act 2004* registered schemes. However, the White Paper proposals did not specifically mention any facility for 25% to be paid as tax-free cash. Pension would have to be drawn by age 75 at the latest, usually by purchasing an annuity. Income drawdown was discussed, but the drawdown facility was found to be only really viable for those with large pension pots or sufficient other assets to bear investment risk. Nevertheless, the government's thinking is open to other new products that might be suitable for the mid-market. It has, however, rejected the idea of only requiring funds up to a certain limit to be annuitised.

Employee and employer contributions   11.18

If employees do not opt out, they must contribute 4% of any earnings between approximately £5,000 and £33,000 pa. The contribution will be matched with 3% from their employer, phased in over at least three years, and 1% from the state.

The rates of contributions will be laid down in primary legislation. This is to try to provide some reassurance to employers that the rate of their compulsory contributions cannot be altered without parliamentary approval.

In order to ease the burden for small businesses, the government has stated that it will consult on a package of measures to provide them with transitional support.

The contributions will be paid into the member's 'personal account' (see **11.20** below). A simple, low-cost payment collection system is proposed. Account scheme functions will be centralised in order to allocate a default pension provider or pension fund for those individuals who do not make an active choice, and to ensure that individuals can continue to contribute to a single personal account as their circumstances change.

Investment choice   **11.19**

The scheme will provide each personal account with a wide range of appropriate investment choices. Investment funds will be run by professional and independent fund managers, and a range of investment options will be offered, including socially responsible investment.

Personal accounts

General description   **11.20**

The scheme will take the form of individual personal accounts for all workers on a defined contributions basis. The government anticipates that up to 10m people will be covered, and that their pension funds could be worth up to around 25% more at their retirement date because of lower charges under the scheme compared with other retirement provision. It is intended that government involvement in delivery will be minimised. The government is committed to developing a full employer communications and education package to support the introduction and implementation of personal accounts.

Administration of personal accounts

The government wishes to consult further on the method of administration of personal accounts. It has outlined two possible approaches:

1. The Pensions Commission's approach, which envisages competition for contracts. Essentially, accounts would be provided by a single organisation and the day-to-day running of the scheme would be outsourced to a number of pension administrators.

2. An alternative approach, which involves competition through branded providers. This would build on existing pension provision, and a number of pension providers would offer personal accounts. Unlike the ABI model, there would be a centralised function to collect and reconcile contributions, allocate default providers and collate information. People would be able to choose their preferred provider, or they would be allocated one.

It is felt that individual choice is important, but that it could increase costs. The government will conduct further analysis in order to strike the best balance between value for money for the taxpayer and value for money for the saver.

Costs

Personal accounts are to be low cost. The Pensions Commission suggested an annual management charge (AMC) of 0.3% in the long run. The government feels that this may be achievable, depending on scheme design, and it will invite views on this later in 2006. Overall, it is confident that it can deliver a system that radically reduces charges, and which will be self-financing. Initially, charges will need to reflect the choice of delivery mechanism, funds under management, contract specification and financing arrangements.

Although AMCs are normally expressed as a percentage of funds under management, it is usually deducted from individual accounts monthly. However, the government will consider other charging structures as well.

Portability   **11.21**

Personal accounts will be portable between employers, and between periods of employment, self-employment and periods of economic activity. It is stated that portable and flexible accounts will fit in with modern life and the greater likelihood of people moving between jobs. Contributions will continue when individuals move between participating employers, which will offer a far simpler product that the multiple schemes and arrangements that many people have accumulated in the modern climate of frequent job change.

Regulation and governance   **11.22**

The government states as follows:

> 'A range of enforcement powers will also be needed to enable regulatory authorities to respond to the minority of employers who persistently fail to comply with their obligations. We are giving careful consideration to the precise nature of the regulatory approach.'

It is clear that this regulation will, to some degree, fall on the Pensions Regulator. However, given that there are a reported 70,000 employers who have not even designated a stakeholder pension scheme when required to do so, this could be a very large policing exercise.

The new regime will also need to be transparent, sustainable and create consumer confidence. Personal accounts would be managed independently from government, including decisions on the range of fund choices and the structure of the default fund. The government will be seeking advice from the financial sector, existing regulatory organisations and those with similar experience in other countries. There will need to be an overriding duty of care to scheme members, assurances that their accounts are being administered efficiently and information for individuals about their investment choices.

The self-employed and non-working 11.23

The self-employed and non-working may join the scheme on a voluntary opt-in basis. The government has still to determine how the contribution system will work for the self-employed and will report back later in 2006. There are approximately 3m working-age self-employed people in the UK, and less than half have a personal pension.

Those people who are not in current work, including those with caring responsibilities, may also contribute to the new personal accounts. They will receive £28 from the government for every £100 they contribute, up to a maximum of £3,600 of total contributions a year, in line with the current registered scheme legislation under the *Finance Act 2004*.

Other categories of persons – young and old 11.24

- Persons who are over SPA and young employees may join the scheme.

- Those who are over SPA who are in employment will be entitled to opt in and receive an employer contribution. Those people who are still in employment with a personal account when they reach SPA will remain within it unless they choose to opt out. People over 74 will not be able to remain in the scheme as the scheme must secure an income by the age of 75.

- People aged between 16 and 21 will be able to join the scheme on an opt-in basis and have access to an employer contribution.

Financial Assistance Scheme (FAS) 11.25

The White Paper confirms additional support for the FAS, which is extended to include eligible people who were within 15 years of their scheme pension age on or before 14 May 2004. The benefits will be tapered so that:

- 80% of benefits will be paid to those persons within seven years of scheme pension age;

- 65% of benefits will be paid to those within eight to eleven years of scheme pension age; and

- 50% of benefits will be paid to those within twelve to fifteen years of scheme pension age.

See **CHAPTER 8** for further details.

Monitoring the pensions system   11.26

The TUC has stated that it intends to lobby the government for a 'Pensions Commission to continue to monitor the pensions system and make periodic recommendations to government'. The DWP minister has restated that there will be no standing commission. However, there will be 'periodic reviews' of the progress to 'ensure direction of travel remains the right one.'

On another front, the White Paper states that the Social Exclusion Unit has promised a review to consider the establishment of an office for ageing and older people, and the government committed in *Opportunity Age* to explore the scope for an observatory on ageing that would improve the evidence base available to policymakers. The Social Exclusion Unit review will be complete later in 2006, and options exist regarding how any institutional changes would take effect.

The consultative process on the White Paper   11.27

The consultative process on the White Paper ended on 11 September 2006. An electronic version of the White Paper is available at http://www.dwp.gov.uk/pensionsreform. The White Paper proposals for reform were formulated after an extensive programme of Government consultation with key stakeholders and the National Pensions Debate, a process which involved 10,000 members of the public in the debate either face-to-face or via the DWP website. A list of organisations consulted is available on the DWP website alongside the White Paper.

The reform proposals are accompanied by regulatory impact assessments and technical appendices, also to be found at the above website address.

The government's view on the Pensions Commission's performance, and the setting up of future commissions   11.28

The Pensions Commission recommended the creation of a government advisory body to provide an independent and trusted voice that would spell out 'the unavoidable trade-offs'. The government has stated that it recognises the value of the Commission's recommendations and that it will 'periodically commission reviews drawing on a range of independent expert advice in the light of emerging evidence on demographic change'.

While these important matters do need to be kept under review, there is some concern in the industry that acting through formal commissions can delay process and add to the taxpayers' cost.

The promised government publication on a new state-run national pension savings scheme   11.29

The government has pledged to issue a document towards the end of 2006 setting out the approach that it intends to take on the new scheme and the operation of personal accounts. This will include:

- the administration of personal accounts;

- the structure and type of investments;

- the process of taking a pension;

- the exemption process for qualifying workplace schemes;

- linking the contributions band to earnings growth;

- transitional issues on implementing the new scheme; and

- further detail on the information supporting personal accounts, with a detailed update on progress achieved in its *Informed Choice* programme and the timing of future activity.

Pensions law rewrite, and review of pension regulation and regulatory bodies

Pensions law rewrite   11.30

The government has undertaken to start a project to establish whether there would be value for business in a substantive rewrite of pensions law. A single legislative source for pensions regulation had in fact been one of the recommendations in the Pickering Report four years earlier. In the wake of a deluge of regulations and orders made under the *Pensions Act 2004* and the *Finance Act 2004*, this may cause some alarm in the industry and among those who sponsor occupational schemes. However, if it does anything to simplify the sourcing of new legislation and its meaning, this could be a positive move.

The project will draw on the experience of the recent Tax Law Rewrite Project, which the government considers to be a success. The rewrites do, however, have their detractors, as the sourcing of subject matter is not always straightforward and is sometimes quite diversely laid out. The tax treatment of 'earnings' in the *Income Tax (Earnings and Pensions) Act 2003* is an example of the latter point.

It is intended to involve a mixed team of public and private sector lawyers and other professionals, and to run a pilot which would focus on one or more sets of regulations which have an impact on business, to test whether the approach is likely to produce worthwhile dividends in terms of simplicity and, ultimately, savings for schemes and employers.

Review of organisations and current regulation   11.31

The government has undertaken to bring forward its proposals in autumn 2006 for a review of those organisations which were established through the *Pensions Act 2004* to ensure they are configured in the most effective way in order to achieve the Act's long-term objectives. The main organisations are the Pensions Regulator, the Pension Protection Fund and the Financial Assistance Scheme.

The White Paper also promises a rolling deregulatory review of pensions regulation in light of the *Pensions Act 2004,* and a review of some of the requirements of the *Pensions Act 1995.* These reviews may cover some or all of the following:

- mandatory indexation of pensions in payment;
- member-nominated trustees;
- administrative and internal control requirements;
- restrictions on changes to accrued rights (*section 67, Pensions Act 1995*);
- payments to employers where surplus funds exist;
- deemed buy-back; and
- internal dispute resolution.

The government's detailed summary of the objectives of the White Paper

General observation on the summary   11.32

The White Paper comments at length on the need for people to work longer in an ageing society. The issue that many people in the UK already work much longer hours than their European counterparts is not addressed, as it does not overcome the financial problem of pension provision for people in their long retirement years. Nevertheless, the more demanding a person's working life, the less fit that person is likely to be for working into old age. It is important, therefore, to look at the opportunities for part-time work or lighter work in old age. The main government comments on the White Paper are summarised below.

Working longer   **11.33**

The introductory statement on working longer is as follows:

> 'We must enable and encourage people to work longer. Higher employment will sustain national wealth, while longer working provides a greater opportunity for people to build provision for their retirement through private saving. Over 1 million people are currently working after SPA, but there is a need to encourage more people to do so.'

The following measures are proposed:

- enabling greater flexibility to allow people to choose a phased approach to retirement;
- providing improved communications and information in support of longer working; and
- working in partnership with employers to encourage them to retain older workers, and to offer them greater flexibility around retirement.

The key elements of government policy will endeavour to aid the sustainability and affordability of the pensions system, by targeting an employment rate equivalent to 80% of the working-age population.

Current employment data   **11.34**

It is stated as follows:

- There has been a significant increase in the employment rate of 50 to 69-year-olds, which has risen by 6.1 percentage points from 48.7% in 1997 to 54.8% in 2005.
- The employment rate for people aged 50 to the current state pension age (70.7%) is still lower than for the overall working population (75%), and considerably lower than for the 25–49 age group (over 80%).

Achieving an 80% employment rate   **11.35**

The main objectives are to:

- reduce by 1m the number of people on incapacity benefits;
- help 300,000 more lone parents into work; and
- increase the number of older workers by 1m.

Reaching 80% is expected to lead to a significant increase in GDP, perhaps by as much as 2.7 percentage points by 2050.

Age discrimination   11.36

The White Paper comments as follows:

> 'In October this year, new legislation will come into force, which, for the first time, will give people the right to challenge age discrimination in the workforce. We will also be introducing a default retirement age of 65, below which employers will not be able to force people to retire on the grounds of age (unless it can be objectively justified). The default retirement age will be carefully monitored and after five years, in 2011, we will undertake a formal, evidence-based review. The default retirement age will be abolished if this review concludes that it is no longer appropriate. Of course, employers can operate without a retirement age and many are already realising the benefits of doing so.'

Helping older workers   11.37

The government's recent publication, *A New Deal for Welfare: Empowering People to Work*, proposed a series of measures to boost support for older people returning to work, and to improve the information available about options for work and retirement. The government describes the following measures as moving towards implementation:

- 'Aligning its additional employment support for long-term unemployed older people with that of younger age groups by requiring people aged 50 to 59 to take up the additional jobseeking support available through New Deal 25 plus. Phased national roll-out will commence from April 2007.

- Requiring unemployed older people to participate in New Deal 50 plus activities after six months claiming benefits, including attending work-focused interviews and developing action plans. It is planning towards piloting this measure.

- Improving back-to-work support for Jobseeker's Allowance claimants and their dependent partners who are over 50. This is already required for couples claiming Jobseeker's Allowance who were born after 1957, and keeps both partners in contact with the work-focused help and support available through Jobcentre Plus. This will happen from April 2007.

- Piloting face-to-face guidance sessions tailored to help people approaching or over 50 and in work to understand the options available to them for work, training and retirement, and to support them in planning for later life. The pilots are due to begin in 2007'.

Looking ahead: a long-term approach   11.38

The government has proposed a two-pronged long-term approach that:

(*a*)   effectively supports people who are sick, disabled or unemployed in returning to work, with greater focus on those in their late 50s and over 60s as SPA is equalised; and

(*b*)   supports people in work for longer (potentially for a year or two more).

The measures are outlined in *A New Deal for Welfare: Empowering People to Work.*

Working with employers   11.39

The government states that:

> 'There are still many employers that operate policies and practices that are potentially discriminatory – indeed, one-fifth of employers say that some jobs in their establishment are more suitable for some age groups than others, with a tendency to favour workers between 25 and 49 years of age. Building on our current employer engagement programmes, we will work in partnership with employers to better support longer working.'

The public sector as an employer   11.40

Government departments are committed to improving working practices to support older workers and to ensure best practices. The government will identify the best practice that already exists, and the DWP has already taken the decision to operate without a compulsory retirement age for its staff. This decision is based on the evidence of successfully operating with a retirement age of 65, with a right for employees to request working longer, for the past two years.

Conclusion   11.41

Means-testing has never been a popular or desirable form of providing reasonable living standards, and the Pensions Commission had suggested that the number of pensioners seeking means-tested top-ups could reach almost

70% by 2050. Additionally, the current level of UK state provision is widely thought to be less than satisfactory and it is clear that a practical solution must be put forward in order to improve pensioner care in the longer term. This has presented the government with a considerable challenge, given the financial implications and the ever-increasing life expectancy of UK citizens. To some extent, the phasing-in of the proposed new scheme has been spread out over a longer period than some would have hoped. Nevertheless, the White Paper has been favourably received. There have been few detractors to the proposals, which include a proposed target date for raising SPA to age 68 over the next 40 years.

The promised revisions to the contracting-out rules are most welcome, if not as broad as had been hoped, and the government has assured a rolling deregulatory review of pensions regulation to investigate further ways to lighten the regulatory burden on business. This review will feed into the DWP's simplification plan, which will be published towards the end of 2006. It is to be hoped that this, and the other proposals which are contained in the White Paper, will become a reality. As much will depend on the next parliament, it would seem appropriate to seek an all-party agreement on the introduction of the new state-run national pension savings scheme at the earliest opportunity.

Transfer values

Background 11.42

Transfer values were first given a statutory footing when preservation came into being in the mid-1970s. As an alternative to preserving a benefit within the scheme, trustees could transfer the value of the accrued pension to another arrangement with the consent of the member. In the mid-1980s members acquired the statutory right to compel trustees to pay a transfer value to another arrangement chosen by the member. The statutory basis for calculating the transfer value of a defined benefit pension is now contained in the *Pension Schemes Act 1993* and the *Occupational Pension Schemes (Transfer Value) Regulations 1996 (SI 1996/1847)*. However, this legislation defers to the actuarial profession by requiring that transfer values are calculated and verified by adopting methods and making assumptions that are certified by an actuary as being consistent with guidance note GN11 (see **APPENDIX 4**) issued by the Faculty and Institute of Actuaries (FIA).

GN11 is generally read to mean that the transfer value must fairly reflect the deferred benefit to which a member is entitled under the scheme and which would be given up on transfer. Transfer values could thus be calculated based on market rates of return on equities, bonds or any other asset class deemed appropriate in the circumstances. There could be a wide variation in results depending not just on the asset class chosen but also on the assumed rate of return used to discount future pension payments.

Proposed GN11 revision   **11.43**

There has been debate within the actuarial profession for some time over the appropriate basis for calculating transfer values. Typically, however, a transfer value would be calculated on a 'scheme asset' basis which allows the cost of the liability to be discounted by an assumed rate of return on equities. A lower discount would be applied if the liability were valued at a 'market cost' using a discount rate more akin to bonds, thereby increasing the transfer payment.

The pensions board of the FIA decided to review GN11 in 2003. Consultation was carried out in 2004 and a revised version of GN11 was issued in draft for further comment in May 2005. The main points of the revised GN11 draft were:

- It used a more prescriptive method, using discount rates derived from bonds.

- The risk of default should be assessed and factored in. If scheme benefits were considered secure, the transfer value would be higher.

- In assessing default risk the actuary should take instructions from the trustees on the risk posed by the strength of the sponsoring employer, and could apply different risk factors to different tranches of benefit e g benefits equal to PPF compensation levels would be more secure than other benefits.

- If the trustees do not instruct the actuary to take the default risk of the employer into account, he or she must use a discount rate equal to the yield on government bonds (but subject to an upper limit determined by the yield on any bonds issued by the sponsoring company).

A crucial element of the argument for moving to a 'market cost' basis such as this was the fact that the government now required solvent employers to buy out their pension liabilities in full when winding up their scheme. Furthermore, even if a scheme were to wind up with an insolvent employer, members could be reasonably assured that they would get something like the PPF level of benefits as a minimum. Since members' benefits were now more secure, arguably they should receive higher transfer values.

This argument produced strong objections from actuaries and sponsoring employers. They claimed the new transfer values would be too high and they would not fairly represent the cost to the scheme.

The conclusion of the consultation was that there was no consensus on what the transfer value basis should be. Indeed, there were fundamental differences of opinion. Therefore, since there appeared to be some agreement that determining a fair transfer value should take account of wider social policy issues, it was thought to be a more appropriate matter for the government to resolve.

DWP consultation   11.44

The DWP therefore considered the matter and published its consultation on the approach to the calculation of transfer values in June 2006. It stated that a new policy on transfer values should have three possible objectives:

- to be broadly fair to the transferring member;

- to avoid weakening the scheme's funding position and avoid the likelihood of the sponsor having to make extra contributions in the future;

- to be broadly neutral in its impact on the existing level of unreduced transfer values.

The consultation put forward three possible approaches to the calculation of transfer values, as follows.

Using prescribed assumptions

Regulations would set out the assumptions and the extent of any actuarial discretion allowed. For example, regulations could define the mortality tables to be used, expected revaluation rates and a discount rate linked to AA corporate bonds or a rate reflecting a degree of equity outperformance.

Using a scheme-specific basis

Trustees would be able to calculate transfer values by reference to assumptions and values that reflected the funding position of their scheme. One such approach mooted was to follow the principles governing FRS17, which require assumptions underlying a valuation to be 'mutually compatible and lead to the best estimate of the future cash flows that will arise under the scheme liabilities'. Such an approach would result in transfer values based on the trustees' best estimate, on actuarial advice, of the cost to the scheme of providing the deferred pension.

Using a value to the member basis

This was essentially the same as the revised GN11 method put forward by the Pensions Board of the FIA. Discount rates would reflect the risk that benefits might not be paid, therefore taking account of employer strength and the PPF.

In each case above the transfer value could be cut back if the scheme was underfunded.

The consultation closed on 11 August 2006. The DWP will consider the responses and issue new legislation for further consultation and implementation by April 2007.

EU Portability Directive

Background 11.45

If a worker's pension rights are significantly reduced when he or she moves jobs, this could be seen as tantamount to restricting that person's free movement within the labour market. In October 2005 the European Commission therefore proposed a Directive to improve the portability of occupational pension rights in the EU. This draft Directive has four key elements:

- the acquisition of pension rights;
- the preservation of dormant rights;
- transfers; and
- information.

The intention of the draft Directive is:

- to allow workers who start a new job to join a pension scheme which provides them with vested pension rights within a reasonable time;
- to give such workers the choice of having their pension rights preserved or taking their rights with them as a transfer when leaving a job;
- to ensure that schemes make sufficient information available to workers to allow them to make an informed decision about how moving jobs would affect their pension rights.

Provisions 11.46

The draft Directive reflects what is for the most part already provided for in the UK. Should the draft Directive become law, there should not be too many difficulties in achieving compliance. The main provisions of the draft Directive are as follows:

- Pension rights must be preserved after no more than two years.
- If a worker leaves employment without preserved pension rights, his or her contributions must be refunded or transferred to another scheme.
- If there is a waiting period to join the scheme, this can not be more than one year, or if later, the period up to the minimum age required for the acquisition of pension rights.

- Where a scheme operates a minimum age for the acquisition of pension rights, this cannot be more than age 21.

- Preserved rights must be adjusted fairly so that early leavers are not penalised.

- Early leavers must be able to obtain a transfer of their pension rights within 18 months of leaving.

- Actuarial and interest–rate assumptions used in calculating transfer values must not penalise early leavers.

- Transferred rights must be granted immediate preservation in the receiving scheme.

- Where administrative costs are deducted from a transfer value, they must not be disproportionate to the length of time the member has been in the scheme.

- Within a reasonable period of requesting it, members must be provided with information as to:

  - the conditions governing the acquisition of pension rights and how those rights are treated on leaving employment;

  - the pension benefits envisaged when employment is terminated;

  - the conditions governing preserved pension rights; and

  - the conditions governing the transfer of acquired rights.

- Member states may make more favourable provisions for the treatment of pension rights than are contained in the draft Directive.

Note that the Directive is currently in draft form, but if it does become law it will probably have to be implemented by July 2008.

Possible issues   11.47

The DWP issued a consultation on the draft Directive in January 2006. A few areas had been highlighted during this consultation which might cause problems. The DWP published its response to the consultation in July 2006 addressing the problem areas.

It had been thought that schemes with an entry age of more than 21 might have to reduce it to 21. However, the DWP confirmed that this was not the case and schemes may continue to set a minimum entry age greater than 21.

Occupational schemes might have been required to accept transfers from other schemes. The DWP said it had received reassurances that this was not intended to be the case.

Given that the terms on which a transfer value is calculated must not penalise the member, any reduction due to a scheme being underfunded could fall foul of the Directive. The DWP has therefore requested an exemption for underfunded schemes.

The Pensions Regulator: Regulatory functions

Regulatory functions

Pensions Act 2004

Legislative reference PA95	Legislative reference PA04	Power	Who can exercise the power? (DP = Determinations Panel)			Which procedure is used?	
			Regulator	Delegable to DP?	DP	Standard procedure	Special procedure
	s13	Issue improvement notices to trustees or employers with directions attached to anyone with a fiduciary or contractual duty to a scheme to do something to enable those to whom the notice is directed to comply.	Y	Y	Y		N
	s14	Issue third party notices to anyone involved with a pension scheme whose action or inaction is leading to a contravention of pensions legislation.	Y	Y	Y		N
s13 replaced by s15 of the Act	s15	Apply to the courts to grant an injunction against an individual to prevent misuse or misappropriation of scheme funds in both occupational and personal pension schemes.	Y	N	N		N/A
s14 replaced by s16 of the Act	s16	Apply to the courts to have returned to a scheme any assets or assets due.	Y	N	N		N/A
	s17	Power to recover unpaid contributions using such powers as trustee or managers have to recover contributions.	Y	N	N/A		N

Appendix 1

Legislative reference PA95	Legislative reference PA04	Power	Who can exercise the power? (DP = Determinations Panel)			Which procedure is used?	
			Regulator	Delegable to DP?	DP	Standard procedure	Special procedure
	s20	To make or extend a restraining order in relation to an account with a deposit taker – pensions liberation.	N		Y		Y
	s20(10)	Make an order permitting payments out of an account that is subject to a restraining order.	N		Y		Y
	s21	To make a repatriation order – pensions liberation.	N		Y		Y
	s23	Freeze a scheme to: prevent contributions being due and liabilities accruing; or prevent members moving in the priority order and transfers being made in or out. Inhibit wind-up. Issue directions re benefits etc.	N		Y		Y
	S25(3)	Extend the period of a freezing order.	N		Y		Y
	S26	Order validating action in contravention of a freezing order.	N		Y		Y
	s30	To give directions when freezing order ceases to have effect.	N		Y		Y
	S31(3)	An order directing the notification of members in respect of a freezing order.	N		Y		Y
	s36(3)(4)	Maintain a register of independent trustees.	N	N	N/A		
	s38	Issue a contribution notice where there is avoidance of employer debt.	N		Y		N

Legislative reference PA95	Legislative reference PA04	Power	Who can exercise the power? (DP = Determinations Panel)			Which procedure is used?	
			Regulator	Delegable to DP?	DP	Standard procedure	Special procedure
	S41(4)	Issue a direction to trustees to not pursue s75 debt.	N		Y		
	S41(7) – (12)	To issue a revised contribution notice.	N		Y		N
	s42	The issue of a clearance statement in relation to a s38 contribution notice.	Y	Y	Y		N
	s43	To issue a financial support direction.	N		Y		N
	s46	The issue of a clearance statement in relation to a financial support direction.	Y	Y	Y		N
	s47	Contribution notice where non-compliance with financial support direction.	N		Y		N
	s50(4)	Issue a direction to the trustees or managers not to take any further steps to recover the debt due to them under s75 of PA 1995 pending the recovery of all or part of the debt due to them by virtue of a contribution notice.	N		Y		N
	s50(9)	To issue a revised contribution notice.	N		Y		N
	s52-54	Restoration order where transactions at an undervalue.	N		Y		N
	s55	Contribution notice where failure to comply with restoration order.	N		Y		N
	s64	Require trustees to provide information about schemes on the scheme return.	Y		N/A		
	s71	Issue a notice to the trustees, employer or anyone involved in the administration of the scheme to provide a skilled persons report.	N		Y		N

309

Appendix 1

Legislative reference PA95	Legislative reference PA04	Power	Who can exercise the power? (DP = Determinations Panel)			Which procedure is used?	
			Regulator	Delegable to DP?	DP	Standard procedure	Special procedure
s98	s72	Demand information and documents from occupational and personal pension schemes.	Y		N/A		
s99 (inspection)	s73-76	Inspect premises and retain documents found (including those on computer).	Y		N/A		
	s76(8)	Make a direction extending the retention period for documents taken into possession under s75.	N		Y	Y	N
s100	s78(2)(a)	Obtain warrant to search premises and seize documents.	Y		N/A	Y	
	s78(10)	Make a direction extending the retention period for documents taken into possession.			Y		N
s103 replaced by s89 of PA2004	s89	Make public, with absolute privilege, a report of any investigation and its outcome.	Y	Y	Y		N
	s99	Review those determinations made under the special procedure.	N		Y		N
	s101	To vary or revoke any determination, orders, notices or directions made, issued or given by the Pensions Regulator.	N	Y	Y	Y	N
	S154(8)	Order directing person to take steps in relation to the winding up of a scheme which has entered assessment period and has been found to have sufficient assets to meet protected liabilities.	Y	Y	Y	Y	N

Legislative reference PA95	Legislative reference PA04	Power	Who can exercise the power? (DP = Determinations Panel)			Which procedure is used?	
			Regulator	Delegable to DP?	DP	Standard procedure	Special procedure
	S219(4)	Order directing person to take steps in relation to the winding up of a scheme backdating the winding up.	Y	Y	Y	Y	N
	s231(2)(a)	Modifying future accruals.	N		Y		Y
	s231(2)(b)	Give directions in relation to: the manner in which technical provisions are calculated; or the period within which any shortfall re statutory funding objective has to be met.	N		Y		Y
	s231(2)(c)	Impose a schedule of contributions.	N		Y		Y
	S288	Authorising an occupational pension scheme to accept contributions from European employers.	Y	Y	N	Y	N
	S288	Authorising an occupational pension scheme to accept contributions from specified European employer.	Y	Y	N	Y	N
	s292	To issue a ring fencing notice to trustees or managers of a scheme that receives contributions from a European employer.	N		Y		
	S293	Direct a UK employer contributing to EU pension institution: to take or refrain from taking such steps as are specified in the notice in order to remedy the failure by the institution, or to cease to make further contributions to the institution.	N		Y	Y	

Appendix 1

Legislative reference PA95	Legislative reference PA04	Power	Who can exercise the power? (DP = Determinations Panel)			Which procedure is used?	
			Regulator	Delegable to DP?	DP	Standard procedure	Special procedure
s3(1)	amended by s33(1)	Power to make a prohibition order under section 3 of PA 1995.	N		Y	Y	Y
s3(3)	amended by s33(3)	Power to revoke a prohibition order under section 3 of PA 1995.	N		Y	Y	Y
s4(1)	amended by s34	Power to suspend a trustee under section 4 of PA 1995.	N		Y	Y	Y
S4(2)	amended by s34	Power to extend period of suspension.	N		Y	Y	N
s4(5)	amended by s34	Power to revoke suspension of a trustee under section 4 of PA 1995.	N		Y	Y	Y
s7, s8 (exclusive powers)	amended by s35	Appoint a trustee to schemes with exclusive powers if required. Order the employer or scheme to pay fees and expenses.	7(3)(B) appts only	Y	7(3)(A) and (C)	Y	Y
S9		Power to vest or transfer property as consequence of appointing or removing a trustee.	N		Y	Y	Y
s10		Apply a civil penalty (maximum £5,000 fine in the case of individuals, maximum £50,000 in any other case).	N		Y		N
s11	s22	Wind up a scheme.	N		Y	Y	Y
s15		Issue directions to anyone with a fiduciary or contractual duty to a scheme (similar to current wind-up directions).	N		Y		N

312

Legislative reference PA95	Legislative reference PA04	Power	Who can exercise the power? (DP = Determinations Panel)			Which procedure is used?	
			Regulator	Delegable to DP?	DP	Standard procedure	Special procedure
s23(1)	s36	Appoint an independent trustee: during an assessment period for PPF; when the scheme is authorised to continue as a closed scheme; or when sponsoring employer becomes insolvent.	Y	Y	Y	Y	Y
s29(5)		Waive a disqualification in relation to one scheme, class of schemes or all schemes.	N		Y	Y	Y
S30(2)		Power to vest or transfer property as consequence of a trustee being disqualified under s29.	N		Y	Y	Y
s60 and MFR regs		Allow extension to time period for making up serious shortfall on individual schemes. Can also give a general extension to all schemes in exceptional circumstances.	N		Y		N
S67G(2)	added by s262	The power to make an order voiding any modification of, or grant of rights under, an occupational pension scheme to any extent.	N		Y		Y
S67H(2)	added by s262	The power to make an order prohibiting, or specifying steps to be taken in relation to, the exercise of a power to modify an occupational pension scheme.	N		Y		Y
s69		Grant an order to enable scheme rules to be modified for the return of surplus to the employer.	N		Y		N
s71A		Modify scheme rules to allow wind-up.	N	Y	Y		N
s72B		Directions regarding schemes and wind-up.	Y	Y	Y	Y	N

Welfare Reform and Pensions Act 1999

Legislative reference WRPA 99	Legislative reference Bill	Power	Regulator	Delegable to DP?	DP	Standard immediate effect	Special procedure
s2		Register a stakeholder scheme.	Y	N	N		N
s2(3)(B)		Deregister a stakeholder scheme.	N		Y		N
s33(4)		Extend time to discharge pension credit liability.	N		Y		N
S99 (4) psa		Extension of period in which trustees or managers have to carry out certain duties.	N		Y	Y	N
S101J		Time for compliance with transfer notice.	N		Y	Y	N

314

Appendix 2

Scheme return information

Scheme return

What questions are in the form?

The following questions appear in the latest version of the scheme return form.

1.   About the scheme

- Scheme name and address

- Registration and approval details

- Date scheme established

- Date scheme became registrable

- HMRC approval number

- Pension Schemes Registry number

- Type of scheme

- Scheme description

2.   Scheme details

- Scheme status and relevant date (if applicable)

- Scheme year end date

- Breakdown of scheme membership before 1 April 2005

- Breakdown of scheme membership before 1 April 2006 (if available)

- If there are now fewer than two members in the whole scheme, please confirm the date when this happened

- Average age of scheme members

3.   Scheme trustees, trustee advisers and service providers

- Scheme trustees

- Is the scheme written under trust?

- Category of trustee

- Insurance company's details

- Scheme auditor's details

- Scheme actuary's details

- In the last year, has there been any change in the day-to-day administration of the scheme that has meant scheme records have been transferred to another party?

- How many firms provide third-party administration to the scheme?

- Scheme administrator's details

4. Financial information

- Fund value of scheme

- What is the market value of the scheme assets?

- What percentage of the market value of scheme assets relates to employer-related investments?

- Information from the last minimum funding requirement (MFR) valuation

- Information on the latest scheme funding valuation (if any) under *Part 3* of the *Pensions Act 2004*

- Have you obtained a scheme funding valuation for this scheme?

- Effective date of this valuation

- Information from the latest PPF Section 179 valuation

- Information from the latest estimate of the coverage on a buyout basis

- FRS17 liabilities

- What value has been placed on this scheme's accrued defined benefit liabilities for the purposes of inclusion in the sponsoring employer's latest published accounts?

- Scheme indexation

- Scheme asset investment policy

5. Employer details

- Principal employer details

- Other employers

- How many employers participate in the scheme in addition to the employer mentioned above?

- Employer with the most defined benefit members

- Details of the employer with the most defined benefit members

- How many defined benefit members does this employer have in the scheme?
- What is the employer's current trading status?
  - Actively trading
  - Dormant
  - Liquidated or dissolved
  - In administration
  - In receivership
  - In liquidation, including voluntary liquidation
- Type of organisation
  - Private limited company
  - Public limited company
  - Limited liability partnership
  - Partnership
  - Sole trader
  - Registered charity
  - College or educational institution
- Are there any additional employers for this scheme?

6. Further information
   - Further information

7. Declaration
   - Scheme trustee/manager representative's declaration
   - Contact details if we have questions about this scheme return

This information was taken from the Pensions Regulator's website on 2 October 2006.

Appendix 3

Application for clearance

Application for Clearance

The Pensions Regulator

Part 1: Application details

1	Name of applicant:	
2	Address of applicant:	
3	Applicant's relationship to the scheme:	
4	If this form is being completed by someone other than the applicant, please give details including address:	
5	What is the event giving rise to the request for clearance?	
6	What effect does this event have on the pension scheme? NB: Where the event has no impact on the scheme there is generally no need to apply for clearance, and any application will be treated as low priority.	

---

7 For which of the following would you like the regulator to issue a statement?

In the Pensions Regulator's opinion …

☐ the applicant would not be, for the purposes of subsection (3)(a) of section 38 of Pensions Act 2004, a party to an act or a deliberate failure to act falling within subsection (5)(a) of that section.

☐ it would not be reasonable to impose any liability on the applicant under a contribution notice issued under s 38.

☐ it would not be reasonable to impose the requirements of a financial support direction, in relation to the scheme, on the applicant.

8	On what basis do you believe these statements to be true? In particular, if you do not believe it would be reasonable for the Pensions Regulator to impose liability, please detail why not:	
9	What are the timescales for carrying out this event including any critical deadlines?	
10	What discussions have been held between the employer and the trustees in relation to the event or situation and its impact on the pension scheme? *If there has been no contact please confirm permission for the Pensions Regulator to approach trustees or if refused, reasons for that refusal.*	
11	Please provide names and contact details of any parties holding security over the employer, and consent to enable the Pensions Regulator to approach them:	
12	Please provide names and contact details of any key advisers with whom the applicant believes it would be useful for the Pensions Regulator to discuss the application:	

Page 2 of 7

13	I confirm that the contents of this application and the information provided with it are true to the best of my knowledge and belief.
	Signed by (applicant):
	Dated:
14	I am being represented by the person detailed in section 4 above. I confirm I am content for them to represent me.
	Signed by (applicant):
	Dated:
15	Address for correspondence:

16	Please provide us with the following documents:

Where the information asked for is not relevant or available please tell us why.

a) ☐ Family tree showing the group structure to which any employer relating to the pension scheme belongs including company registration numbers

b) ☐ Proposed board minute regarding the event / situation described in the application

c) ☐ Relevant correspondence with key stakeholders regarding the event / situation

d) ☐ Any resolutions required in relation to the event / situation

e) ☐ Any other relevant board minutes

f) ☐ Executive summaries of any independent reviews or reports relating to the event or the employer's viability

Where relevant:

g) ☐ Table showing comparison of position of all creditors pre- and post-event

h) ☐ Statutory accounts

i) ☐ Financial forecasts / management accounts

j) ☐ Details of debt that ranks above the pension scheme

k) ☐ Up-to-date valuation of significant assets

Please provide any other documents relating to the application.

NB: Please ensure that documents are relevant. Receiving a large amount of irrelevant information means that it will take us longer to make a decision on clearance.

Appendix 3

Part 2: Scheme information

Scheme name:			
PSR number:			
Type of scheme:	☐ DB ☐ DC ☐ Hybrid	Scheme status:	☐ Open ☐ Paid-up ☐ Frozen ☐ Winding-up
Principal employer:			
All participating employers: *Please include any employers who have ceased to participate since 27 April 2004.*			
Number of members:	Total		
	Pensioners		
	Deferred		
	Active		
Where there are no active members, how many deferred members are employed by employers related to the scheme?			
Size of fund:		Date of valuation:	

Deficit:	On s 75 buy-out	
	FRS17	
	On-going	
	PPF	

Payments specified on schedule of contributions:		When is the schedule of contributions due to be re-negotiated?	

Please provide name and contact details of all scheme trustees:

Do trustees have any conflicts of interest and how are these dealt with?

What is the trustee's view of the application?

Please provide:

☐ any independent reports that the trustees have commissioned in respect of the event or situation described in this application

☐ a copy of the winding-up power from the scheme deed and rules

☐ a copy of the power to set contributions from the scheme deed and rules

Page 6 of 7

Appendix 3

All documents and correspondence should be clearly labelled and addressed as follows:

Clearance Department
The Pensions Regulator
Napier House
Trafalgar Place
Brighton
BN1 4DW

To be opened by the Addressee Only

Page 7 of 7

Appendix 4

Actuarial Guidance Note GN11

GN11: Retirement Benefit Schemes - Transfer Values

Classification
Practice Standard

**MEMBERS ARE REMINDED THAT THEY MUST ALWAYS COMPLY
WITH THE PROFESSIONAL CONDUCT STANDARDS (PCS) AND THAT
GUIDANCE NOTES IMPOSE ADDITIONAL REQUIREMENTS UNDER
SPECIFIC CIRCUMSTANCES**

Application
Any actuary responsible for the calculation of cash equivalents under the Regulations,
other individual transfer values from all types of retirement benefit schemes and the
assessment of benefits in such schemes in respect of incoming transfer payments and
pension credits.

This Guidance Note may be used for purposes of the UK Listing Authority Rules, the
Companies Act 1985 (see Appendix 4) and the Proceeds of Crime Act (Recovery from
Pension Schemes) Regulations 2003.

Legislation or Authority
Pension Schemes Act 1993. (c.48).

Pensions Act 1995. (c.26).

Matrimonial Causes Act 1973. (c.18).

Family Law (Scotland) Act 1985. (c.37).

Welfare Reform and Pensions Act 1999. (c.30).

Financial Services Authority (the UK Listing Authority). *The listing rules* (as
updated).

Companies Act 1985 (c6).

Proceeds of Crime Act 2002 (C29).

Regulations set out in Appendices 1 (the 'Principal Regulations'), 2, 3 and 4.

Northern Ireland has its own body of law relating to pensions and to family law. In
relation to Northern Ireland, references to the Great Britain legislation contained in
this Guidance Note should be read as including references to the corresponding
Northern Ireland legislation. The Northern Ireland Regulations corresponding to the
Great Britain Regulations are included in Appendices 1, 2 and 3. Appendix 5 shows
the Northern Ireland legislation corresponding to the Great Britain Acts mentioned in
this Guidance Note.

Author
Pensions Board

Appendix 4

Status
Approved under Due Process (Technical Amendment)

Version	*Effective from*
1.0	01.12.85
2.0	01.11.87
3.0	01.07.88
4.0	01.03.90
5.0	01.05.91
5.1	31.03.93
6.0	01.07.94
7.0	06.04.97
7.1	01.03.98
7.2	01.04.98
8.0	01.12.00
8.1	06.04.01
9.0	04.08.03
9.1	01.03.04
9.2	30.12.05

1 Introduction

1.1　These guidelines apply to the basis of calculation of cash equivalents under the Regulations (including the treatment of pension debits and credits under pension sharing legislation, for the recovery of the proceeds of crime from pension schemes and to the assessment of benefits in retirement benefit schemes in respect of incoming transfer payments). The guidelines also apply under the listing rules to the calculation of directors' remuneration.

1.2　The guidelines relate to United Kingdom requirements and conditions.

1.3　The guidelines also apply to other individual transfer values from retirement benefit schemes where no cash equivalent, within the provisions of the Pension Schemes Act 1993, arises and in those cases reference in this Guidance Note to the Regulations should be ignored and references to "cash equivalent" should be read as references to "transfer value".

1.4　This Guidance Note is not intended to inhibit trustees from paying transfer values greater than cash equivalents.

1.5　The guidelines also apply to the calculation of pension costs for the purpose of disclosure in the annual report and accounts of companies in respect of directors of certain UK companies. In such cases it may be necessary to calculate the value of accrued benefits in circumstances in which no entitlement to a transfer value exists. In such cases, the valuation must be consistent with the calculation of transfer values for the scheme concerned subject to paragraph 3.2 below; or (where no transfer values are payable from the scheme) for other schemes of the same employer. If benefits are payable from an overseas scheme, the calculation should be consistent with this Guidance Note, taking account of economic conditions in the country concerned.

1.6 The guidelines also apply to the calculation and verification of the value of benefits under a pension scheme for the purposes of divorce proceedings as specified in Regulations (Appendix 3). The calculation of cash equivalents for the purposes of this paragraph must be consistent with the calculation of cash equivalents for the purpose of paying transfer values where an actuarial basis exists for such calculations in the scheme concerned. References to 'deferred pensioners' and 'pensioners' should be taken as including 'pension credit members' and 'pension credit benefit members' respectively, as defined in Section 124(1) of the Pensions Act 1995 and Regulation 2 of the Occupational Pension Schemes (Minimum Funding Requirement and Actuarial Valuations) Regulations 1996 (SI 1996/1536). References to 'members' should be taken as including 'pension credit members' and 'pension credit benefit members'.

2 Purposes of the Guidelines

2.1 The purposes of the guidelines are

(a) to ensure that members of retirement benefit schemes exercising a right to a cash equivalent can be assured that it fairly reflects the benefits otherwise available (subject to the requirements of Section 4 below),

(b) to ensure that incoming transfers are dealt with consistently with outgoing cash equivalents,

(c) to facilitate consistency in the calculation of pension costs in respect of directors in companies' accounts, and

(d) to ensure that pension debits and credits are calculated in accordance with the pension sharing legislation.

3 Basis of Calculation

3.1 It is a fundamental requirement, stemming from the legislation, that a cash equivalent should represent the actuarial value of the corresponding accrued benefits. Such actuarial value should represent the expected cost within the scheme of providing such benefits and should be assessed having regard to market rates of return on equities, gilts or other assets as appropriate.

3.2 Where a cash equivalent is to be calculated in respect of a member who has reached pension age, but whose benefits are not yet in payment, the benefit entitlement to be valued must be that which would apply if payment were to commence immediately. In such cases, and in respect of pensioners, market rates of return may be based on a different asset class from that used for deferred pensioners if the actuary considers that to be appropriate.

3.3 Where a deferred pensioner has a right to exercise an option on terms which are specified in the scheme documentation and are financially disadvantageous to the scheme, account must be taken of the likely cost of such an option on the basis of the assumed probability of deferred pensioners generally exercising the option.

3.4 Guaranteed or statutory increases, both in deferment and after retirement, must be valued as part of the accrued benefit.

3.5   The actuary has to bear in mind that Regulation 8(2) of the Principal
       Regulations requires that the discretionary grant of additional benefits must be
       taken into account in certain circumstances unless the trustees direct otherwise.
       The actuary must therefore establish with the trustees the extent to which they
       consider it appropriate to make an addition for future discretionary increases to
       the accrued benefit or for any other benefits granted on a discretionary basis
       when calculating its value for transfer.

3.6   In calculating benefits in respect of pension credits or transfer values received
       by a retirement benefit scheme the actuary must use methods and assumptions
       which are reasonable and consistent with the methods and assumptions
       (including any allowance for future discretionary benefits) normally used for
       outgoing cash equivalents from that scheme. Appropriate adjustment would be
       required to take account of expected salary increases in cases where 'added
       years' are to be credited. In cases where the trustees, in accordance with
       paragraph 3.5, have given a general direction to the actuary that discretionary
       benefits should *not* be taken into account, then the same principles must be
       applied to the calculation of the benefits in respect of incoming transfer values
       and pension credits.

3.7   In the case of both incoming transfers and outgoing cash equivalents, allowance
       for expenses may be made where appropriate, e.g. to reflect administrative costs
       incurred, the saving in cost of paying pensions and any relevant costs of sale or
       purchase of investments.

3.8   A separate value should be quoted of the part of the cash equivalent which
       represents safeguarded rights or benefits in respect of service after 5 April 1997
       (other than those relating to voluntary contributions or to the part of a transfer
       credit relating to a transfer from a personal pension which does not derive from
       protected rights). Where the payment is to an Appropriate Personal Pension
       Scheme or to a Contracted-out Money Purchase Scheme, separate values should
       be quoted of the part which represents Guaranteed Minimum Pensions (GMPs)
       under the transferring scheme. These values must be calculated consistently
       with the calculation of the total cash equivalents, in particular with a consistent
       assumption as to the expected annual statutory increases in the GMPs.

4   Departures from the Foregoing Basis of Calculation

4.1   Where an age-related payment by the HM Revenue and Customs is outstanding,
       the cash equivalent must first be calculated on the basis of the benefits to which
       the member would have been entitled had the payment already been made. The
       cash equivalent must then be reduced by the amount of the age-related payment,
       where this is payable to the receiving scheme rather than to the transferring
       scheme.

4.2   The report referred to in regulation 8(4) of the Principal Regulations may be
       provided in conjunction with a valuation in accordance with Section 224 of the
       Pensions Act 2004 or at such other time as the trustees or managers may direct.
       The actuary must consider whether to discuss with the trustees or managers, in
       advance of producing the report, any of the matters in paragraphs 4.2.3, 4.2.4
       and 4.2.5 below. When a report is provided other than in conjunction with a
       formal valuation, it need not be based on audited accounts or on full

membership data. If cash equivalents are reduced following provision of a report, a new report must be provided as at the same effective date as, and at the same time as, the next valuation in accordance with Section 224.

4.2.1 This report must make clear that its scope is limited to the reduction permitted by Regulation 8(4) of the Principal Regulations.

4.2.2 The report must set out the results of a comparison of the sum of the full cash equivalents of all members with the market value of the assets of the scheme or, exceptionally, such higher amount as the actuary considers more appropriate, less an allowance for the expenses of winding-up.

4.2.3 The allowance for the expenses of winding-up shall be such amount as the actuary considers appropriate.

4.2.4 The cash equivalents for members already in receipt of pension or over normal pension age must be the same as the cash equivalents of such members that would apply for the purposes of divorce proceedings (see paragraph 1.6). If a basis for such calculations has not been specified, the cash equivalents must be determined in a manner consistent with what the actuary would regard as appropriate if such a divorce case were to arise, having regard to the circumstances of the scheme.

4.2.5 The actuary must consider to what extent and in what way the liabilities in the report should be subdivided into some or all of the elements receiving different orders of priority on a winding-up.

4.2.6 The report must provide a comparison, for each of the separate classes of liability decided upon under 4.2.5 above, of the relevant assets with the relevant liabilities. For this purpose, the "relevant liabilities" for a given class is the sum for all members of the cash equivalent values falling into that class of the chosen priority order. The "relevant assets" for that class is the value of the scheme assets, less the allowance specified in 4.2.3 and less the total of the "relevant liabilities" for all classes with greater priority under the chosen priority order.

4.3 If the immediate payment of a full cash equivalent or a cash equivalent reduced as a consequence of a report under 4.2 would reduce the security for the benefits of other members, the actuary should advise the trustees as to any reduced cash equivalent which would be appropriate having regard to the provisions of Regulation 8(4) and 8(4A) of the Principal Regulations. The actuary should also advise them that the member's interests might be better served by deferring the taking of a cash equivalent until a later date. Where no reduction is applied, the actuary should draw the implications of this to the trustees' attention. Where the cash equivalent resulting from the maximum reduction permitted under the Principal Regulations or the actual reduction proposed by the trustees would reduce the security for the remaining members, the actuary should draw the implications of this to the trustees' attention.

4.4 In cases where an outgoing cash equivalent is under consideration in respect of a member, in respect of whom a transfer value has previously been received, special care may be needed in the choice of the method of calculation -

particularly where 'added years' have been credited - to ensure that the outgoing cash equivalent is, subject to paragraphs 4.2 and 4.3, both equitable in relation to, and consistent with, the transfer value received. Except as described in paragraphs 4.2 and 4.3, the cash equivalent must not be less than the value of the alternative accrued benefits.

4.5 Special considerations apply in cases where the circumstances of a previous transfer had been such that the assets transferred bore no direct relationship to the leaving service benefits under the previous scheme. Where such cases give rise to an entitlement to the member for a cash equivalent under Chapter IV of Part IV of the Pension Schemes Act 1993, then, for the purpose of paragraph 4.4, the cash equivalent must take account of the preserved benefit which would otherwise have been available had the member actually left service at the previous transfer date.

4.6 However, in cases where the former preserved benefit and/or the cash equivalent were augmented in connection with a full or partial dissolution of the former scheme (either in circumstances where the trustees were obliged to augment benefits in terms of the documents governing the scheme or alternatively at the discretion of the trustees or employer with the objective of enhancing the cash equivalents which would otherwise have been available for the purpose of buying out individual annuity contracts), then, for the purpose of paragraph 4.4, comparison must be made with such higher values.

4.7 If in the actuary's opinion an incoming transfer value would be insufficient to provide minimum statutory benefits (e.g. a Guaranteed Minimum Pension), the actuary should advise the trustees accordingly.

4.8 Regulation 8(8) of the Principal Regulations requires cash equivalents to be reduced in certain circumstances to less than those which would otherwise apply under this guidance. Such circumstances would include some 'Transfer Club' arrangements.

5 'Partial' Cash Equivalents

5.1 Partial cash equivalents can occur when a transfer is made from a contracted-out a contracted-in scheme leaving the liability for GMP and post-5 April 1997 Contracted-out Salary Related rights behind. In that circumstance, the whole cash equivalent must be calculated in the normal way and an amount deducted which is calculated consistently in respect of the retained liability.

6 Money Purchase Schemes and Personal Pension Schemes

6.1 Generally the above principles apply to transfers arising out of money purchase schemes and personal pension schemes where the cash equivalents depend on making estimates of the value of benefits. Where all or part of the member's benefits depend directly on the proceeds of an earmarked investment, the corresponding cash equivalents will be the realisable value of that investment, e.g. the amount of a building society deposit or the cash value of a policy of insurance earmarked for the member. Similarly, if all or part of an incoming transfer value is to be applied to an earmarked investment, the benefit to be granted will depend on the proceeds of the investment.

6.2   In respect of personal pension schemes and other money purchase schemes these guidelines do not apply where cash equivalents depend on rights which do not fall to be valued in a manner which involves making estimates of the value of benefits, since the relevant Regulations make specific rules regarding the calculation of such cash equivalents.

7 Presentation

7.1   It is not necessary for each cash equivalent to be authorised separately by the actuary. The actuary may supply tables, instructions, computer files or computer programs, for use by the trustees and administrators, for calculating the amount of any cash equivalent payable and the pensionable service or other benefits to be credited for an incoming payment or pension credit. The actuary should specify the circumstances (e.g. changes in investment conditions or cases involving previous receipt of a transfer value) in which adjustments should be made.

7.2   The actuary is required to certify to the trustees that the method and assumptions adopted for the calculation of a cash equivalent are consistent with the legislation. A specimen certificate for this purpose is provided in Appendix A. This should be amended as necessary to make it appropriate for the scheme concerned.

Appendix 4

Appendix A

To the Trustees of the [   ] Pension Scheme:

I certify that the methods and assumptions underlying the calculation of cash
equivalents under the [   ] Pension Scheme as specified in
the tables and instructions dated [   ] are consistent with:

  (i) the requirements of Chapter IV of Part IV and Chapter II of Part IVA of the
      Pension Schemes Act 1993;

  (ii) *Retirement Benefit Schemes - Transfer values (GN11)* issued by the
      Institute of Actuaries and the Faculty of Actuaries; and

  (iii) the methods currently adopted and assumptions currently made in
      calculating the benefits to which entitlement arises under the Rules of the
      Scheme for a person who is acquiring transfer credits under those Rules

[I also certify that the methods and assumptions underlying the calculation of the rights
conferred within the scheme on a person entitled to a pension credit are consistent
with:

  (i) *Retirement Benefit Schemes – Transfer values (GN11)* issued by the
      Institute of Actuaries and the Faculty of Actuaries; and

  (ii) the methods currently adopted and assumptions currently made when
      transfers of other pension rights are received by the Scheme.]

Signed: ....Date: ....

Fellow of the Institute of Actuaries or
Fellow of the Faculty of Actuaries

Appendix 1: Principal Regulations *	GB Reference	NI Reference
The Occupational Pension Schemes (Transfer Values) Regulations 1996 as amended	SI 1996/1847	SR 1996 No 619

Appendix 2: Other Pensions Regulations *

	GB Reference	NI Reference
The Occupational Pension Schemes (Contracted-Out Protected Rights Premiums) Regulations 1987 as amended	SI 1987/1103	SR 1987 No 281
The Personal Pension Schemes (Personal Pension Protected Rights Premiums) Regulations 1987 as amended	SI 1987/1111	SR 1987 No 289
The Personal Pension Schemes (Transfer Values) Regulations 1987 as amended	SI 1987/1112	SR 1987 No 290
The Protected Rights (Transfer Payment) Regulations 1996 as amended	SI 1996/1461	SR 1996 No 509
The Contracting-out (Transfer and Transfer Payment) Regulations 1996 as amended	SI 1996/1462	SR 1996 No 618
The Occupational Pension Schemes (Minimum Funding Requirement and Actuarial Valuations) Regulations 1996 as amended	SI 1996/1536	SR 1996 No 570
The Personal and Occupational Pension Schemes (Protected Rights) Regulations 1996 as amended	SI 1996/1537	SR 1997 No 56
The Occupational Pension Schemes (Disclosure of Information) Regulations 1996 as amended	SI 1996/1655	SR 1997 No 98

* The title of the Northern Ireland Regulations are identical to those for Great Britain save for the insertion of '(Northern Ireland)' after the word 'Regulations' and in some instances where the year may be different this will be indicated by the NI Reference.

Appendix 3: Family Law Regulations*	GB Reference	NI Reference
The Divorce etc (Pensions) Regulations 1996 as amended	SI 1996/1676	SR 1996 No 296
The Divorce etc (Pensions) (Scotland) Regulations 1996 as amended	SI 1996/1901 (S.153)	
The Pensions on Divorce etc (Provision of Information) Regulations 2000 as amended	SI 2000 No 1048	SR 2000/142
The Pension Sharing (Valuation) Regulations 2000 as amended	SI 2000 No 1052	SR 2000/144
The Pension Sharing (Implementation and Discharge of Liability) Regulations 2000 as amended	SI 2000 No 1053	SR 2000/145
The Pension Sharing (Pension Credit Benefit) Regulations 2000 as amended	SI 2000 No 1054	SR 2000/146

* The title of the Northern Ireland Regulations are identical to those for Great Britain save for the insertion of '(Northern Ireland)' after the word 'Regulations' and in some instances where the year may be different this will be indicated by the NI Reference.

Appendix 4: UK Listing Authority Rules and DTI and Home Office Regulations

Financial Services Authority (the UK Listing Authority). *The listing rules* (as updated).

The Directors' Remuneration Report Regulations 2002.**	S.I. 2002 No 1986
The Proceeds of Crime Act (Recovery from Pension Schemes) Regulations 2003	S.I. 2003 No 291

** At the time of publishing this Guidance Note, the Regulations refer to GN11 Version 8.1.

Appendix 5: Northern Ireland Legislation Corresponding to Great Britain Acts

GB Provision	NI Provision
Pension Schemes Act 1993 (c.48)	Pension Schemes (Northern Ireland) Act 1993 (c.49)
Pensions Act 1995 (c.26)	Pensions (Northern Ireland) Order 1995 (SI 1995/3213 (NI 22))
Matrimonial Causes Act 1973 (c.18)	Matrimonial Causes (Northern Ireland) Order 1978 (SI 1978/1045 (NI 15))
Welfare Reform and Pensions Act 1999 (c. 30)	Welfare Reform and Pensions (Northern Ireland) Order 1999 (SI 1999/3147 NI 11))
Section (of Act)	Article (of Order) or Section (of Act)
Companies Act 1985	Companies (Northern Ireland) Order 1986 (SI1986/1032 NI6)

Actuarial Guidance Note GN49

GN49 : Occupational Pension Schemes – Scheme funding matters on which advice of actuary must be obtained

Classification
Practice Standard

MEMBERS ARE REMINDED THAT THEY MUST ALWAYS COMPLY WITH THE PROFESSIONAL CONDUCT STANDARDS (PCS) AND THAT GUIDANCE NOTES IMPOSE ADDITIONAL REQUIREMENTS UNDER SPECIFIC CIRCUMSTANCES

Purpose
This Guidance Note contains specific guidance to an actuary in relation to his or her role of giving advice to the *trustees* under Section 230(1) of the Pensions Act 2004 ("the Act") and is issued pursuant to Regulation 15 of the Occupational Pension Schemes (Scheme Funding) Regulations 2005.

Definitions
For the purpose of the Guidance Note:

Reference	Definition
Trustees	The trustees or managers of an occupational pension scheme to which Part 3 of the Pensions Act 2004 applies.
Regulator	The Pensions Regulator established by Section 1 of the Pensions Act 2004
Relevant advice	Advice given to the *trustees* under Section 230(1) of the Pensions Act 2004.
Code of Practice	The code of practice on funding defined benefits produced by the *Regulator* dated December 2005.

Application
An actuary to an occupational pension scheme appointed under Section 47(1)(b) of the Pensions Act 1995 or, where the scheme is exempt from the requirement to appoint an actuary, the actuary authorised by the *trustees* of the occupational pension scheme as provided for in Schedule 2 to the Regulations mentioned below.

Legislation or Authority
Pensions Act 2004, Section 230.

The Occupational Pension Schemes (Scheme Funding) Regulations 2005, SI 2005/3377, ("the Regulations").

The Pensions Regulator's Code of Practice – 'Funding defined benefits' dated December 2005.

Northern Ireland has its own body of law relating to pensions and, in relation to Northern Ireland, references to Great Britain legislation contained in this guidance note should be read as including references to the corresponding Northern Ireland legislation. The Northern Ireland legislations corresponding to the Great Britain legislation mentioned in this Guidance Note are included in Appendix A. Except as indicated in the table there is no difference in the numbering of the provisions mentioned in this guidance note.

This Guidance Note has been approved by the Secretary of State in accordance with Regulation 15 of the Regulations and the Department for Social Development in Northern Ireland in accordance with Regulation 15 of the Occupational Pension Schemes (Scheme Funding) Regulations (Northern Ireland) 2005, SR 2005 No 568.

Author
Pensions Board

Status
Approved under Due Process

Version	*Effective from*
1.0	30.12.05

1 Introduction

1.1 This Guidance Note contains specific guidance to an actuary in relation to his or her role of giving advice to the *trustees* under Section 230(1) of the Pensions Act 2004 ("the Act").

2 Advising Trustees

2.1 Under Section 230(1) of the Act the *trustees* must obtain the advice of the actuary before doing any of the following:

  (a) making any decision as to the methods and assumptions to be used in calculating the scheme's technical provisions (section 222(4) of the Act);
  (b) preparing or revising the statement of funding principles (section 223 of the Act);
  (c) preparing or revising a recovery plan (section 226 of the Act);
  (d) preparing or revising the schedule of contributions (section 227 of the Act); and,
  (e) modifying the scheme as regards the future accrual of benefits under section 229(2) of the Act.

2.2 In giving *relevant advice* the actuary must have regard to the *Code of Practice* and any other relevant guidance on funding defined benefits issued by the *Regulator.*

2.3 In advising the *trustees* under 2.1(a) or 2.1(c) above, the actuary must bring to the attention of the *trustees* those matters in the lists in paragraphs 75, 79, or 102 of the *Code of Practice* respectively on which he or she has not given advice.

2.4 The actuary's obligation in advising on 2.1(e) above is limited to the implications (of modifying benefits for the future) for the statement of funding principles, the recovery plan, and the schedule of contributions.

2.5 The actuary must confirm in writing all *relevant advice* that is given orally so the *trustees* have proof of their compliance with their duties under section 230(1) of the Act.

3 Information required prior to giving advice

3.1 The actuary must bring to the attention of the *trustees* that, prior to obtaining his or her advice, they must provide sufficient and up to date information concerning the scheme and the employer(s).

3.2 If, in the opinion of the actuary, insufficient information has been provided, the actuary must (having first taken reasonable steps to obtain the missing information) make it clear to the *trustees* where and to what extent he or she has felt it appropriate to make assumptions with regard to the missing information and the effect on the advice given. The advice may have to be limited in scope if insufficient information has been provided. It must be made clear to the *trustees* that the actuary will only be able to accept responsibility for the advice based on the information that has been provided, the nature of which must be summarised.

3.3 If the actuary believes that the *trustees* are not complying with their obligation to provide adequate information, the actuary must consider what other actions it would be appropriate to take. Depending on the circumstances, appropriate actions might include making a report to the *Regulator* under Section 70 of the Act or resigning his or her appointment.

Appendix A: Northern Ireland Legislation

GB Provision	NI Provision
Pensions Act 1995 (c. 26)	Pensions (Northern Ireland) Order 1995, SI 1995/3213 (NI 22)
Section 47	Article 47
Pensions Act 2004 (c. 35)	Pensions (Northern Ireland) Order 2005, SI 2005/255 (NI 1)
Section 222	Article 201
Section 223	Article 202
Section 226	Article 205
Section 227	Article 206
Section 229	Article 208
Section 230	Article 209
Occupational Pension Schemes (Scheme Funding) Regulations 2005, SI 2005/3377.	Occupational Pension Schemes (Scheme Funding) Regulations (Northern Ireland) 2005, SR 2005 No 568.

Appendix 6

Actuarial Guidance Note GN51

GN51: Retirement Benefit Schemes – Modification of Subsisting Rights Without Consent

Classification
Practice Standard

MEMBERS ARE REMINDED THAT THEY MUST ALWAYS COMPLY WITH THE PROFESSIONAL CONDUCT STANDARDS (PCS), AND THAT GUIDANCE NOTES IMPOSE ADDITIONAL REQUIREMENTS UNDER SPECIFIC CIRCUMSTANCES

Definitions
For the purposes of this Guidance Note:

Reference	Definition
Act	The Pensions Act 1995
actuarial equivalence statement	As defined in Section 67C (7) of the Pensions Act 1995
actuarial equivalence statement requirement	As defined in Section 67C (6) of the Pensions Act 1995
actuarial value of subsisting rights	The value of a member's *subsisting rights* calculated in accordance with regulation 5 of the *Subsisting Rights Regulations*
actuarial value requirement	As defined in Section 67C (5) of the Pensions Act 1995
detrimental modification	As defined in Section 67 A (4) of the Pensions Act 1995
protected modification	As defined in Section 67A (3) of the Pensions Act 1995
regulated modification	As defined in section 67A (2) of the Pensions Act 1995
subsisting rights	As defined in Section 67A (6) of the Pensions Act 1995
Subsisting Rights Regulations	The Occupational Pension Schemes (Modification of Schemes) Regulations 2006. SI 2006/759

| *trustees* | The trustees or, for schemes not established under trust, the managers as defined in Section 318(1) of the Pensions Act 2004 |

Purpose and Application

The purpose of this guidance is to advise actuaries of the information that they must give to *trustees* in order to alert the *trustees* to the need to consider wider issues in relation to a detrimental modification which is to be effected without member consent.

The circumstances when this information will be required are:-

- when providing advice to trustees regarding the satisfaction of the *actuarial value requirement*, or
- when responsible for issuing an *actuarial equivalence statement*.

Legislation or Authority

Pensions Act 1995. (c26).

The Occupational Pension Schemes (Modification of Schemes) Regulations 2006. SI 2006/759.

Northern Ireland has its own body of law relating to pensions and, in relation to Northern Ireland, references to Great Britain legislation contained in this Guidance Note should be read as including references to the corresponding Northern Ireland legislation. The Northern Ireland regulations corresponding to the Great Britain regulations are included in Appendix A.

Author

Pensions Board

Status

Approved under Due Process

Version	Effective from
1.0	06.04.06
1.1	06.11.06

1 Introduction

1.1 The rules of a pension scheme may provide for members' *subsisting rights* to be modified without their consent. Where a *regulated modification* is taking place it must comply with Section 67 to Section 67I of the *Act* and its accompanying regulations. The Pensions Regulator has indicated that it will issue additional Guidance on these Regulations. The actuary must have regard to any such Guidance.

1.2 Section 67C of the *Act* requires that *trustees* wishing to approve a *detrimental modification*, which is not a *protected modification*, without member consent fulfil both the *actuarial value requirement* and the *actuarial equivalence statement requirement*.

1.3 The *actuarial value requirement* requires *trustees*, before the modification is made, to take such steps as are necessary to ensure that the *actuarial value of subsisting rights* will be maintained.

1.4 The *actuarial equivalence statement requirement* requires that an *actuarial equivalence statement*, certifying that the *actuarial value of subsisting rights* has been maintained, must be obtained from an actuary

1.5 There may be matters connected with the *detrimental modification* which do not prevent the *actuarial value requirement* being satisfied but which the *trustees* should consider before deciding whether or not to approve the modification. This guidance advises actuaries of the information that must be given when providing advice to the *trustees* in relation to the *actuarial value requirement* in order to alert them to the need to consider these wider issues. Where the *trustees* have not taken actuarial advice in relation to the *actuarial value requirement*, this requirement applies to the actuary issuing the *actuarial equivalence statement*.

2 Information that must be given to the *trustees* by an actuary providing advice in relation to the *actuarial value requirement*

2.1 There is no requirement for *trustees* to seek actuarial advice when fulfilling the *actuarial value requirement*. Where *trustees* do seek advice from an actuary, that actuary will need to consider whether the *actuarial value of subsisting rights* will be maintained.

2.2 There may be some matters connected with the *detrimental modification* which do not prevent the *actuarial value requirement* from being satisfied but which, in the actuary's opinion, might be relevant to the *trustees'* decision to approve the modification. Such matters could include:
- the adverse modification of a benefit or option which is not included in the definition of *subsisting rights*,
- the adverse modification of an element of *subsisting rights* which is not included within the *actuarial value of subsisting rights*,
- changes which, in the opinion of the actuary, alter *subsisting rights* in a way or ways which could be material for any members with particular characteristics, or
- funding or solvency issues such as the effect on an individual's asset coverage of benefits on a scheme wind up.

2.3 The actuary must draw to the attention of the *trustees* any matters which fall under paragraph 2.2 above. In providing this information, the actuary is not expected to carry out any investigations into the potential effect on individual members (or their survivors) of the matters referred to. However, when providing the information, the actuary must advise the *trustees* whether any such investigations should, in his or her opinion, be carried out before they approve the *detrimental modification*.

2.4   The information referred to in paragraph 2.3 above must be provided as soon as is practicable but no later than when the actuary gives the *trustees* his or her advice as to whether the *actuarial value of subsisting rights* will be maintained.

2.5   The actuary must ensure that the *trustees* are aware of the need to take legal advice before approving the *detrimental modification*.

2.6   If the actuary believes that the *trustees* are wrongfully refusing to consider properly the matters advised to them in accordance with paragraphs 2.3 and 2.5 above, the actuary must consider what actions it would be appropriate to take. Depending on the circumstances, appropriate actions might include making a report to the Pensions Regulator under Section 70 of the Pensions Act 2004 and/or resigning his or her appointment.

3   Requirement for the actuary providing the *actuarial equivalence statement*

3.1   An actuary asked to provide an *actuarial equivalence statement* must, before he or she issues the statement, seek to satisfy himself or herself whether or not the *trustees* received advice from an actuary in relation to the *actuarial value requirement*.

3.2   If the actuary is unable to satisfy himself or herself that the advice referred to in paragraph 3.1 has been given, then the actuary must comply with paragraphs 2.3 and 2.5 above.

3.3   The information referred to in paragraphs 2.3 and 2.5 must be provided to the *trustees* in sufficient time for the *trustees* to be able to consider it before they receive the *actuarial equivalence statement*.

3.4   If the actuary believes that the *trustees* are wrongfully refusing to consider properly the matters advised to them in accordance with paragraphs 2.3 and 2.5 above, the actuary must consider whether or not he or she should refuse to provide an *actuarial equivalence statement* and/or what other actions it would be appropriate to take. Depending on the circumstances, appropriate actions might include making a report to the Pensions Regulator under Section 70 of the Pensions Act 2004 and/or resigning his or her appointment.

Appendix A: Regulations*

	GB Reference	NI Reference
The Occupational Pension Schemes (Modification of Schemes) Regulations 2006	SI 2006/759	SR 2006 149

* The titles of the Northern Ireland Regulations are identical to those for Great Britain
save for the insertion of '(Northern Ireland)' after the word 'Regulations'.

The Transfer of Employment (Pension Protection) Regulations 2005

SI 2005 No 649

Transfer of Employment (Pension Protection) Regulations 2005

Made 10th March 2005

Laid before Parliament 16th March 2005

Coming into force 6th April 2005

I Citation, commencement, application and interpretation

(1) These Regulations may be cited as the Transfer of Employment (Pension Protection) Regulations 2005 and shall come into force on 6th April 2005.

(2) These Regulations apply in the case of a person ("the employee") in relation to whom section 257 of the Act (conditions for pension protection) applies, that is to say a person who, in the circumstances described in subsection (1) of that section, ceases to be employed by the transferor of an undertaking or part of an undertaking and becomes employed by the transferee.

(3) In these Regulations "the Act" means the Pensions Act 2004.

> **NOTES**
> **Initial Commencement**
> *Specified date*
> Specified date: 6 April 2005: see para (1) above.

2 Requirements concerning a transferee's pension scheme

(1) In a case where these Regulations apply, and the transferee is the employer in relation to a pension scheme which is not a money purchase scheme, that scheme complies with section 258(2)(c)(ii) of the Act (alternative standard for a scheme which is not a money purchase scheme) if it provides either—

(a) for members to be entitled to benefits the value of which equals or exceeds 6 per cent of pensionable pay for each year of employment together with the total amount of any contributions made by them, and, where members are required to make contributions to the scheme, for them to contribute at a rate which does not exceed 6 per cent of their pensionable pay; or

(b) for the transferee to make relevant contributions to the scheme on behalf of each employee of his who is an active member of it.

(2) In this regulation—

"pensionable pay" means that part of the remuneration payable to a member of a scheme by reference to which the amount of contributions and benefits are determined under the rules of the scheme.

> **NOTES**
> **Initial Commencement**
> *Specified date*
> Specified date: 6 April 2005: see reg 1(1).

3 Requirements concerning a transferee's pension contributions

(1) In a case where these Regulations apply, the transferee's pension contributions are relevant contributions for the purposes of section 258(2)(b) of the Act in the case of a money purchase scheme, section 258(3) to (5) of the Act in the case of a stakeholder pension scheme, and regulation 2(1)(b) above in the case of a scheme which is not a money purchase scheme, if—

(a)   the contributions are made in respect of each period for which the employee is paid remuneration, provided that the employee also contributes to the scheme in respect of that period, and

(b)   the amount contributed in respect of each such period is—

     (i)   in a case where the employee's contribution in respect of that period is less than 6 per cent of the remuneration paid to him, an amount at least equal to the amount of the employee's contribution;

     (ii)   in a case where the employee's contribution in respect of that period equals or exceeds 6 per cent of the remuneration paid to him, an amount at least equal to 6 per cent of that remuneration.

(2) In calculating the amount of an employee's remuneration for the purposes of paragraph (1)—

(a)   only payments made in respect of basic pay shall be taken into account, and bonus, commission, overtime and similar payments shall be disregarded, and

(b)   no account shall be taken of any deductions which are made in respect of tax, national insurance or pension contributions.

(3) In calculating the amount of a transferee's pension contributions for the purposes of paragraph (1) in the case of a scheme which is contracted-out by virtue of section 9 of the Pension Schemes Act 1993, minimum payments within the meaning of that Act shall be disregarded.

NOTES

Initial Commencement

Specified date

Specified date: 6 April 2005: see reg 1(1).

Appendix 8

The Pension Protection Fund (Provision of Information) Regulations 2005

SI 2005 No 674

Pension Protection Fund (Provision of Information) Regulations 2005

Made 11th March 2005

Laid before Parliament 16th March 2005

Coming into force 6th April 2005

I Citation and commencement

These Regulations may be cited as the Pension Protection Fund (Provision of Information) Regulations 2005 and shall come into force on 6th April 2005.

> **NOTES**
> **Initial Commencement**
> *Specified date*
> Specified date: 6 April 2005: see above.

2 Interpretation

(1) In these Regulations—

"the Act" means the Pensions Act 2004 (any reference to a numbered section being to the section so numbered in that Act);

["the 1995 Act" means the Pensions Act 1995;]

"appointed representative" means a person—

    (a)   whose name, address and appointment by the member or beneficiary for the purposes of—

        (i)   providing information to the Board; or

        (ii)   receiving information from the Board,

under regulation 3 or 5 have been notified to the Board in a document signed by the member or beneficiary in question or by his legal representative; and

    (b)   whose appointment has been consented to by the Board;

["the assessment date" means the date on which the assessment period in relation to the scheme or section, or (where there has been more than one such assessment period) the last one, began;]

"assessment period" shall be construed in accordance with section 132 (assessment periods);

"beneficiary" in relation to an eligible scheme means any person, other than a member of that scheme, who is entitled to compensation in accordance with the pension compensation provisions;

["compensation payments" means one or more payments under section 83 of the 1995 Act;

"the Compensation Regulations" means the Occupational Pension Schemes (Pensions Compensation Provisions) Regulations 1997;]

"eligible scheme" shall be construed in accordance with section 126 (eligible schemes);

["fraud compensation payments" means one or more payments under section 182(1) of the Act;

"the Fraud Compensation Regulations" means the Occupational Pension Schemes (Fraud Compensation Payments and Miscellaneous Amendments) Regulations 2005;]

"insolvency practitioner" shall be construed in accordance with section 121 (insolvency event, insolvency date and insolvency practitioner);

"multi-employer scheme" shall be construed in accordance with section 307(4);

["non-segregated scheme" means a multi-employer scheme which is not a segregated scheme;]

"normal pension age" in relation to any pension or lump sum in respect of which compensation is payable shall be construed in accordance with paragraph 34 of Schedule 7 to the Act (pension compensation provisions);

["the Pensions Compensation Board" means the Board established under section 78 of the 1995 Act;]

"pension compensation provisions" shall be construed in accordance with section 162 (the pension compensation provisions);

"personal representative" means the executor, original or by representation, or administrator for the time being of a deceased person;

["recovery of value" shall be construed in accordance with section 184(3) of the Act or, as the case may be, in accordance with section 81(3)(f) of the 1995 Act;]

"review decision" shall be construed in accordance with section 207(1)(a) (review and reconsideration by the Board of reviewable matters); …

["segregated scheme" means a multi-employer scheme which is divided into two or more sections where—

    (a)   any contributions payable to the scheme by an employer in relation to the scheme or by a member are allocated to that employer's or that member's section; and

    (b)   a specified proportion of the assets of the scheme is attributable to each section of the scheme and cannot be used for the purposes of any other section;]

"transfer notice" shall be construed in accordance with section 160 (transfer notice).

[(2) In these Regulations, "employer", in relation to—

(a)   an occupational pension scheme which is not a multi-employer scheme; or

(b)   a single-employer section of a segregated scheme,

which has no active members, includes the person who was the employer of persons in the description of employment to which the scheme or section relates immediately before the time at which the scheme or section ceased to have any active members in relation to it.]

[(3) In these Regulations, "employer", in relation to a non-segregated scheme or a multi-employer section of a segregated scheme—

(a)   in an assessment period, includes any person who before the assessment date has ceased to be the employer of persons in the description of employment to which the scheme or section relates unless condition A, B, C or D is satisfied where—

    (i)   condition A is that a debt under section 75 of the Pensions Act 1995 became due from that employer and the full amount of the debt has been paid before the assessment date;

    (ii)   condition B is that—

        (aa)   such a debt became due;

        (bb)   a legally enforceable agreement has been entered into the effect of which is to reduce the amount which may be recovered in respect of the debt; and

        (cc)   the reduced amount has been paid in full before the assessment date;

    (iii)   condition C is that such a debt became due but before the assessment date it is excluded from the value of the assets of the scheme or section because it is unlikely to be recovered without disproportionate costs or within a reasonable time;

    (iv)   condition D is that at the time at which any such person ceased to be the employer of persons in the description of employment to which the scheme or section relates the value of the assets of the scheme or section was such that no such debt was treated as becoming due;

(b)   in any other case, includes any person who has ceased to be the employer of persons in the description of employment to which the scheme or section relates unless condition A, B, C or D is satisfied where—

    (i)   condition A is that a debt under section 75 of the Pensions Act 1995 became due from that employer and the full amount of the debt has been paid;

(ii)   condition B is that—

    (aa)   such a debt became due;

    (bb)   a legally enforceable agreement has been entered into the effect of which is to reduce the amount which may be recovered in respect of the debt; and

    (cc)   the reduced amount has been paid in full;

(iii)   condition C is that such a debt became due but it is excluded from the value of the assets of the scheme or section because it is unlikely to be recovered without disproportionate costs or within a reasonable time;

(iv)   condition D is that at the time at which any such person ceased to be the employer of persons in the description of employment to which the scheme or section relates the value of the assets of the scheme or section was such that no such debt was treated as becoming due.]

NOTES

Initial Commencement

Specified date

Specified date: 6 April 2005: see reg 1.

Amendment

Para (1): definition "the 1995 Act" inserted by SI 2005/2184, reg 23(1), (2).

Date in force: 1 September 2005: see SI 2005/2184, reg 1(1).

Para (1): definition "the assessment date" inserted by SI 2005/2113, reg 4(1), (2)(d).

Date in force: 19 August 2005: see SI 2005/2113, reg 1(1).

Para (1): definitions "compensation payments" and "the Compensation Regulations" inserted by SI 2005/2184, reg 23(1), (2).

Date in force: 1 September 2005: see SI 2005/2184, reg 1(1).

Para (1): definitions "fraud compensation payments" and "the Fraud Compensation Regulations" inserted by SI 2005/2184, reg 23(1), (2).

Date in force: 1 September 2005: see SI 2005/2184, reg 1(1).

Para (1): definition "non-segregated scheme" inserted by SI 2005/2113, reg 7(1), (2)(b).

Date in force: 19 August 2005: see SI 2005/2113, reg 1(1).

Para (1): definition "the Pensions Compensation Board" inserted by SI 2005/2184, reg 23(1), (2).

Date in force: 1 September 2005: see SI 2005/2184, reg 1(1).

Para (1): definition "recovery of value" inserted by SI 2005/2184, reg 23(1), (2).

Date in force: 1 September 2005: see SI 2005/2184, reg 1(1).

Para (1): in definition "review decision" word omitted revoked by SI 2005/2113, reg 12(1), (2).

Date in force: 19 August 2005: see SI 2005/2113, reg 1(1).

Para (1): definition "segregated scheme" inserted by SI 2005/2113, reg 8(1), (2)(b).

Date in force: 19 August 2005: see SI 2005/2113, reg 1(1).

Para (2): substituted by SI 2005/2113, reg 5(4).

Date in force: 19 August 2005: see SI 2005/2113, reg 1(1).

Para (3): substituted by SI 2005/2113, reg 6(4).

Date in force: 19 August 2005: see SI 2005/2113, reg 1(1).

3   Information to be provided by the Board

(1) In this regulation—

"insolvency event" shall be construed in accordance with section 121;

"qualifying insolvency event" shall be construed in accordance with section 127 (duty to assume responsibility for schemes following insolvency event); and

"segregated scheme" means a multi-employer scheme which is divided into two or more sections where—

    (a)   any contributions payable to the scheme by an employer in relation to the scheme or by a member are allocated to that employer's or that member's section; and

    (b)   a specified proportion of the assets of the scheme is attributable to each section of the scheme and cannot be used for the purposes of any other section.

(2) Where the Board receives a notice under section 120(2) (duty to notify insolvency events in respect of employers) from an insolvency practitioner that an insolvency event has occurred in relation to an employer, and—

(a)   the scheme to which the notice relates is an eligible scheme; or

(b)   in the case of a multi-employer scheme which is a segregated scheme, the section to which the notice relates is an eligible section,

it shall, [within the period specified in paragraph (12)], provide that insolvency practitioner, the Regulator, and the trustees or managers of that scheme or section with the information described in paragraph (3).

[(2A) This paragraph applies where the Board receives a notice under section 120(2) from an insolvency practitioner that an insolvency event has occurred in relation to an employer, and—

(a)   the scheme to which the notice relates is not an eligible scheme; or

(b)   the section of the segregated scheme to which the notice relates is not an eligible section.

(2B) Where paragraph (2A) applies the Board shall within the period specified in paragraph (12) inform—

(a)   the Regulator;

(b)   the trustees or managers of that scheme or section of a segregated scheme; and

(c)   that insolvency practitioner,

that the scheme is not an eligible scheme or, as the case may be, the section is not an eligible section.]

(3) The information to be provided under paragraph (2) is—

(a)   where the insolvency event is not a qualifying insolvency event, that the insolvency event is not such an insolvency event; or

(b)   where the insolvency event is a qualifying insolvency event, that the insolvency event is such an insolvency event and the date on which the assessment period began.

(4) Where the Board—

(a)   receives, during the assessment period, an application for a loan from the trustees or managers of a scheme under section 139(2) (loans to pay scheme benefits); and

(b)   decides whether or not it will make a loan to those trustees or managers,

it shall within the period of 14 days beginning with the day on which it made its decision notify those trustees or managers of its decision, of the amount that it considers appropriate to lend and of the terms on which it will make the loan.

(5) Where a person is authorised by the Board for the purposes of these Regulations as mentioned in section 190(1)(b)(ii) (information to be provided to the Board etc) in relation to a scheme, the Board shall, within 14 days of making that authorisation, notify the identity of the person so authorised to—

(a)   the trustees or managers of that scheme;

(b)   the employer in respect of that scheme; and

(c)   the insolvency practitioner in relation to that employer.

(6) Where the Board has given the trustees or managers of a scheme a transfer notice, the information to be provided by the Board to members and beneficiaries of that scheme shall be determined in accordance with the provisions of Schedule 1.

[(7) Where an application for fraud compensation payments has been made by a person prescribed by regulation 5 (applications) of the Fraud Compensation Regulations ("the applicant") the information to be provided by the Board to the applicant and the trustees or managers of the scheme shall be determined in accordance with the provisions of Schedule 1A.

(8) Where the Board is exercising the functions of the Pensions Compensation Board and an application for compensation payments has been made by a person prescribed by regulation 4 (applications) of the Compensation Regulations ("the applicant") the information to be provided by the Board to the applicant and the trustees or managers of the scheme shall be determined in accordance with the provisions of Schedule 1A.]

[(9) Where the Board receives—

(a)   an application under section 129(1) (applications and notifications for the purposes of section 128) from the trustees or managers; or

(b)   a notice under section 129(4) from the Regulator,

it shall provide the information specified in paragraph (10) to the persons specified in paragraph (11) within the period specified in paragraph (12).

(10) The information to be provided under paragraph (9) is—

(a)   where the scheme is not an eligible scheme, that the scheme is not such a scheme;

(b)   where the scheme is an eligible scheme, that the scheme is such a scheme and the date on which the assessment period began;

(c) where the section of the segregated scheme to which the application or, as the case may be, the notice relates is not an eligible section, that the section of the segregated scheme is not such a section; or

(d) where the section of the segregated scheme to which the application or, as the case may be, the notice relates is an eligible section, that the section of the segregated scheme is such a section and the date on which the assessment period began.

(11) The persons specified in this paragraph are—

(a) the Regulator;

(b) the trustees or managers of that scheme or section of a segregated scheme;

(c) the employer who is the employer in relation to that scheme or section of a segregated scheme; and

(d) the insolvency practitioner in relation to that employer.

(12) The Board shall provide the information specified in paragraph (3) or (10) within the period of 28 days beginning with—

(a) the date it receives the notice under section 120(2);

(b) the date it receives the application under section 129(1);

(c) the date it receives the notice under section 129(4);

(d) where the Board requires the—

    (i) Regulator,

    (ii) insolvency practitioner, or

    (iii) trustees or managers,

    to produce a document or provide information in connection with a notice given under section 120(2) or 129(4) or, as the case may be, an application under section 129(1), the date on which the document is produced to, or the information received by, either the Board or a person authorised by the Board for the purposes of section 191(2)(b) (notices requiring provision of information); or

(e) where a person is required to produce a document or provide information in connection with a notice given under section 191(1), the date on which the document is produced to, or the information received by, either the Board or a person authorised by the Board for the purposes of section 191(2)(b).

(13) This regulation does not impose any duty on the Board to provide any information to the trustees or managers of a scheme where the address of the trustees or managers has not been provided by the person who referred the notice or application to the Board.]

NOTES

Initial Commencement

Specified date

Specified date: 6 April 2005: see reg 1.

Amendment

Para (2): words "within the period specified in paragraph (12)" in square brackets substituted by SI 2006/595, reg 2(1), (2).

Date in force: 6 April 2006: see SI 2006/595, reg 1(1).

Paras (2A), (2B): inserted by SI 2006/595, reg 2(1), (3).

Date in force: 6 April 2006: see SI 2006/595, reg 1(1).

Paras (7), (8): inserted by SI 2005/2184, reg 23(1), (3).

Date in force: 1 September 2005: see SI 2005/2184, reg 1(1).

Paras (9)–(13): inserted by SI 2006/595, reg 2(1), (4).

Date in force: 6 April 2006: see SI 2006/595, reg 1(1).

4 Information to be provided by trustees or managers

(1) This regulation applies where there is an assessment period in relation to an eligible scheme.

(2) The information to be provided to—

(a) the Board; and

(b) members of that scheme,

by the trustees or managers of that scheme shall be determined in accordance with the provisions of Schedule 2.

[4A   Information to be provided to the Board]

[(1) This paragraph applies where an application for a fraud compensation payment has been made by a person prescribed by regulation 5 of the Fraud Compensation Regulations in respect of an occupational pension scheme and the trustees or managers of that scheme have reasonable grounds for believing that they have obtained a recovery of value.

(2) This paragraph applies where an application for a compensation payment has been made by a person prescribed by regulation 4 of the Compensation Regulations in respect of an occupational pension scheme and the trustees of that scheme have reasonable grounds for believing that they have obtained a recovery of value.

(3) Where paragraphs (1) or (2) apply, the trustees or managers shall within the period of 14 days beginning with the day on which they have reasonable grounds for believing that they have obtained a recovery of value notify the Board of—

(a)   the amount of the recovery of value; and

(b)   the grounds on which they have considered it reasonable to believe that they have obtained a recovery of value.]

5   Information to be provided by members and beneficiaries and their personal representatives

(1) This regulation applies where the Board has given the trustees or managers of a scheme a transfer notice.

(2) The information to be provided to the Board by members and beneficiaries of that scheme shall be determined in accordance with the provisions of Schedule 3.

(3) Where a member or a beneficiary dies, his personal representative shall, within the period of 28 days beginning with the day of the death, notify the Board of the death and provide the death certificate to the Board.

6   Method of providing information

(1) Where, under these Regulations, any information is to be provided to any person that information shall be provided in writing.

(2) Where—

(a)   under these Regulations any information is to be provided—

    (i)   to the Board by any member or beneficiary; or

    (ii)   by the Board to any member or beneficiary; and

(b)   there is an appointed representative in relation to that member or beneficiary,

that information shall be provided by or to his appointed representative.

(3) Any document sent, or notification given, by the Board to any member or beneficiary under regulation 3(6) shall include—

(a)   the name of the scheme to which it relates or other information sufficient to identify the subject matter of the document or notification;

(b)   the address and telephone number of the Board;

(c)   the name in legible characters of the sender of the document or giver of the notification; and

(d)   the date on which it was sent or given.

(4) Any notification given by the Board to any person under regulation 3(2), (4) or (5) shall include—

(a)   the name of the person to whom it is given;

(b)   the name of the scheme to which the notification relates;

(c)   the pension scheme registration number which is allocated to that scheme in the register;

(d)   the address and telephone number of the Board;

(e)   the name in legible characters of the giver of the notification; and

(f)   the date on which it was given.

(5) Any document sent, or notification given, by any trustees or managers to the Board under regulation 4(2) shall include—

(a)   the names of the trustees or managers sending the document or giving the notification;

(b)   the name of the scheme to which the document or notification relates; and

(c)   the pension scheme registration number which is allocated to that scheme in the register.

(6) Any document sent, or notification given, to the Board by any member under regulation 5(2), or by the personal representative of a deceased member under regulation 5(3), shall include, in relation to that member—

(a)   the name, address, date of birth and national insurance number of that member;

(b)   the name of the employer in relation to the scheme in which that member's pension rights accrued; and

(c)   the address or location of a place of business of that employer.

(7) Any document sent, or notification given, to the Board by any beneficiary under regulation 5(2), or by the personal representative of a deceased beneficiary under regulation 5(3), shall include, in relation to the member from whom that beneficiary has accrued pension rights, the information described in sub-paragraphs (a), (b) and (c) of paragraph (6) and the name, address, date of birth and national insurance number of that beneficiary.

NOTES

Initial Commencement

Specified date

Specified date: 6 April 2005: see reg 1.

SCHEDULE 1
Information to be Provided by the Board

Regulation 3

1   (1) In this Schedule—

"interested person" shall be construed in accordance with regulations made under section 207(2); and

"reviewable matter" shall be construed in accordance with section 206 (meaning of "reviewable matters").

(2) Information to be provided by the Board to members and beneficiaries shall be determined in accordance with the provisions of the table of information to be provided by the Board set out below—

Table of information to be provided by the Board

Description of persons to whom information is to be provided	Description of information to be provided	Period during which or time at which information is to be provided
All members and beneficiaries.	Notification that the Board has assumed responsibility for the scheme, or any part thereof, together with the date on which the Board assumed that responsibility.	The period of two months beginning on the day on which the Board gave the transfer notice to the trustees or managers.

Appendix 8

Description of persons to whom information is to be provided	Description of information to be provided	Period during which or time at which information is to be provided
All members and beneficiaries.	The identity of any person authorised by the Board for the purposes of these Regulations as mentioned in section 190(1)(b)(ii) in relation to the scheme in respect of which the member or beneficiary is receiving or may receive compensation.	Where the Board so authorised a person before it gave the transfer notice, the period of two months beginning on the day on which it gave such notice; or, where the Board so authorises a person after it gave that notice, the period of two months beginning on the day on which that person was so authorised.
Any member who makes a request in writing to the Board for it to provide a forecast of his compensation entitlement.	A forecast, determined in accordance with the pension compensation provisions, of the compensation to be paid to him in relation to that scheme.	The period of 28 days beginning on the day when the Board receives the request.
Any member who will attain normal pension age on his next birthday.	**1** A forecast, determined in accordance with the pension compensation provisions, of the compensation to be paid to him in relation to that scheme. **2** Details of any options to commute which may be exercised by him in relation to that scheme in accordance with paragraph 24 of Schedule 7 to the Act (commutation of periodic compensation) and forecasts, determined in accordance with the pension compensation provisions, of— (a) the lump sum to be paid to him under any such option; and (b) the reduced level of annual compensation payments which he would receive if he exercised any such option.	The period of six months beginning 12 months before the day on which he will attain normal pension age.
Any member who makes a request in writing to the Board for it to provide—(i) information about any options to commute which may be exercised by him in relation to that scheme in accordance with paragraph 24 of Schedule 7 to the Act; or—(ii) a forecast of the lump sum payable to him on the exercise of any such option.	Details of any options to commute available to him, and forecasts, determined in accordance with the pension compensation provisions, of— (a) the lump sum to be paid to him under any such option; and (b) the reduced level of annual compensation payments which he would receive if he exercised any such option.	The period of 28 days beginning on the day on which the Board receives the request.

Description of persons to whom information is to be provided	Description of information to be provided	Period during which or time at which information is to be provided
Any member who makes a request in writing to the Board for it to provide information about any entitlement he may have to early payment of compensation under paragraph 25 of Schedule 7 to the Act (early payment of compensation).	Details of any entitlement he may have to early payment of compensation and a forecast, determined in accordance with the pension compensation provisions, of the periodic compensation and of any lump sum payment payable to him under paragraph 25.	The period of 28 days beginning on the day on which the Board receives the request.
Any member who becomes entitled to compensation under the pension compensation provisions and any beneficiary of such a member where that beneficiary becomes entitled to such compensation.	1 A copy of the determination by the Board of the entitlement to compensation of the member or beneficiary in question. 2 Details of any options to commute which may be exercised by him in relation to that scheme in accordance with paragraph 24 of Schedule 7 to the Act and forecasts, determined in accordance with the pension compensation provisions, of— (a) the lump sum to be paid to him under any such option; and (b) the reduced level of annual compensation payments which he would receive if he exercised any such option.	The period of 28 days beginning on the day on which— (a) the Board gave the transfer notice to the trustees or managers; or (b) the member or beneficiary became entitled to compensation; whichever is the later.
All members and beneficiaries.	Details of any variation in the amounts of payments of compensation payable under that scheme where the variation will result from the operation of paragraph 27, 28, 29 or 30 of Schedule 7 to the Act, and the date when the variation will become effective ("the operative date").	Not less than 28 days before the operative date.
Any member or beneficiary who is an interested person in relation to a particular reviewable matter.	A statement describing how an application may be made to the Board for the review of that reviewable matter, how it will be considered and the Board's powers on making a review decision.	The period of 28 days beginning on the day on which the Board knew or ought to have known that that reviewable matter had occurred.
Any member who is a [party to matrimonial or civil partnership proceedings or who is contemplating such proceedings] and who makes a request in writing to the Board for information about his compensation entitlement.	A statement, determined in accordance with the pension compensation provisions, of the compensation to be paid to him in relation to that scheme.	The period of three months beginning on the day on which the Board receives the request, or by the date the Board complies with any court order to provide such information, whichever is the sooner.

NOTES

Initial Commencement

Specified date

Specified date: 6 April 2005: see reg 1.

Amendment

Para 1: in sub-para (2) in the Table in column 1 words from "party to matrimonial" to "contemplating such proceedings" in square brackets substituted by SI 2006/595, reg 3.

Date in force: 6 April 2006: see SI 2006/595, reg 1(1).

[SCHEDULE 1A
Further Information to be Provided by the Board]

NOTES

Amendment

Inserted by SI 2005/2184, reg 23(1), (5), Sch 3.

Date in force: 1 September 2005: see SI 2005/2184, reg 1(1).

[Regulation 3(7) and (8)]

NOTES

Amendment

Inserted by SI 2005/2184, reg 23(1), (5), Sch 3.

Date in force: 1 September 2005: see SI 2005/2184, reg 1(1).

[In this Schedule the "applicant" shall be construed in accordance with regulation 3(7) or (8), as appropriate.

Description of persons to whom information is to be provided	Description of information the Board must provide	Period during which the Board must provide information
Trustees or Managers and applicant.	Notification of the settlement date determined by the Board under section 184(2).	The period of 14 days beginning on the day on which the Board determined the settlement date.
Trustees or Managers and applicant.	Notification of the Board's determination that a payment received is to be treated as a payment in respect of any act or omission constituting a prescribed offence under section 182(1).	The period of 14 days beginning on the day on which the Board made that determination.
Trustees or Managers and applicant.	Notification of the Board's determination of the terms and conditions on which an interim payment will be made under section 186.	The period of 14 days beginning on the day on which the Board determined to make the payment.
Trustees or Managers and applicant.	Notification of the Board's determination to recover so much of the interim payment as it considers appropriate.	The period of 14 days beginning on the day on which the Board determined to seek the recovery.
Trustees or Managers and applicant.	Notification of the Board's determination of the terms and conditions on which a fraud compensation payment will be made under section 182(1).	The period of 14 days beginning on the day on which the Board determined to make the payment.
Trustees or Managers and applicant.	Notification of the Board's determination under section 186(3) to recover any interim payments made and of the amount it considers appropriate to recover.	The period of 14 days beginning with the day on which the Board made that determination.
Trustees or Managers and applicant.	Notification of the settlement date under section 81(3)(d) of the 1995 Act determined by the Board.	The period of 14 days beginning on the day on which the Board determined the settlement date.

Trustees or Managers and applicant.	Notification by the Board that a payment received is to be treated as a payment in respect of any act or omission constituting a prescribed offence under section 81(1)(c) of the 1995 Act.	The period of 14 days beginning on the day on which the Board made that determination.
Trustees or Managers and applicant.	Notification of the Board's determination of the terms and conditions on which a payment in anticipation will be made under section 84 of the 1995 Act.	The period of 14 days beginning on the day on which the Board determined to make the payment.
Trustees or Managers and applicant.	Notification of the Board's determination to recover so much of the payment in anticipation made under section 84 of the 1995 Act as it thinks appropriate.	The period of 14 days beginning on the day on which the Board determined to seek the recovery.
Trustees or Managers and applicant.	Notification of the Board's determination of the terms and conditions on which a compensation payment will be made under section 83 of the 1995 Act.	The period of 14 days beginning on the day on which the Board determined to make the payment.]

NOTES

Amendment

Inserted by SI 2005/2184, reg 23(1), (5), Sch 3.

Date in force: 1 September 2005: see SI 2005/2184, reg 1(1).

SCHEDULE 2
Information to be Provided by Trustees or Managers

Regulation 4

1 (1) In this Schedule—

…

"hybrid scheme" shall be construed in accordance with section 307(4);

"notification date" means the day on which the Board notifies the trustees or managers of the scheme [in accordance with regulation 3(3)(b), (10)(b) or (d)] of the date on which the assessment period began;

"partially guaranteed scheme" shall be construed in accordance with section 307(3);

"relevant contract of insurance" shall be construed in accordance with section 161(8) (effect of Board assuming responsibility for a scheme);

"reviewable ill health pension" shall be construed in accordance with section 140 (reviewable ill health pensions);

"valuation" means a valuation, or further valuation, which has been—

    (a)   obtained by the Board in respect of the scheme under—

        (i)   section 143 (Board's obligation to obtain valuation of assets and protected liabilities); or

        (ii)   regulation 43 or 59 of the Pension Protection Fund (Multi-employer Schemes) (Modification) Regulations 2005; and

    (b)   approved by the Board under section 144(2) (approval of valuation);

"valuation summary" means, in relation to each member of the scheme, a summary of the valuation which contains—

    (a)   a summary of the overall assets and liabilities of the scheme;

    (b)   details of how that member's entitlement to compensation would be calculated if the Board assumed responsibility for the scheme;

    (c)   details of any information the Board holds on that member's pensionable service and accrued rights;

(d)   where there is a pension in payment to that member at the assessment date, the annual amount of that pension; and

(e)   a statement describing how an application may be made to the Board for the review of the Board's decision to approve the valuation under section 144(2), how it will be considered and the Board's powers on making a review decision; and

"withdrawal notice" means a notice issued under section 122(2)(b) (insolvency practitioner's duty to issue notices confirming status of scheme) or section 130(3) (Board's duty where application or notification received under section 129).

(2) Information to be provided to the Board and members by trustees or managers shall be determined in accordance with the table of information to be provided by trustees or managers set out below—

Table of information to be provided by trustees or managers

Description of persons to whom information is to be provided	Description of information to be provided	Period during which information is to be provided
The Board.	In respect of each member of that scheme entitled to a reviewable ill health pension— (a) his name; (b) a description of his position as an employee in relation to the employer in relation to that scheme; (c) the annual amount of his reviewable ill health pension; and (d) the date on which the award of that pension was made; [(e) if applicable, the date he left the employment of the employer in relation to that scheme; and (f) a statement containing a brief description of his illness or injury].	The period of 28 days beginning on the notification date.
[The Board.	The number of ill health pensions awarded each year for the previous six years immediately before the assessment date.	The period of 28 days beginning on the notification date.]
The Board.	**1** Details of any legal proceedings by or against any of the trustees or managers of the scheme in their capacity as trustees or managers which are pending immediately before, or in existence on, the assessment date. **2** Details of any relevant contract of insurance which is in being on the assessment date.	The period of 28 days beginning on the notification date.
The Board.	The identity of the maker of any further contributions towards the scheme paid under section 133 (admission of new members, payment of contributions etc), together with the amount of any such contributions.	The period of 14 days beginning on the last day of the month in which the contribution was paid.

358

Description of persons to whom information is to be provided	Description of information to be provided	Period during which information is to be provided
The Board.	Details of any significant changes— (a) in the investment of the scheme's assets; or (b) in the level of expenditure incurred by the scheme.	The period of 14 days beginning on the day the change took place.
The Board.	Details of any change in the address or telephone number of the trustees or managers.	Before the expiry of the period of five days beginning on the day the change took place.
The Board.	The identity of those individuals within the trustees' or managers' organisation who will have responsibility for providing information to the Board.	The period of 28 days beginning on the notification date.
The Board.	Any change in the identity of— (a) the individuals who have been notified to the Board as having responsibility for providing information to the Board; and (b) the insolvency practitioner.	The period of 14 days beginning on the day the change took place.
All members.	Notification that there is an assessment period in relation to the scheme, together with a description of the effect this will have on the rights and obligations of members of that scheme.	The period of 28 days beginning on the notification date.
All members.	An explanation of the provisions of Chapter 3 of Part 2 (pension protection) of the Act in so far as they will operate during the assessment period in relation to— (a) benefits payable under the scheme; and (b) contributions towards the scheme; together with an explanation of how, when a withdrawal notice becomes binding, contributions may become payable by or on behalf of the member.	The period of 28 days beginning on the notification date.
Where the scheme is not a hybrid scheme, a multi-employer scheme or a partially guaranteed scheme, all members.	A copy of the valuation summary.	The period of 28 days beginning on the day on which the trustees or managers receive a copy of the valuation approved under section 144(2).
Where the scheme is a hybrid scheme, all members other than those who receive only money purchase benefits.	A copy of the valuation summary	The period of 28 days beginning on the day on which the trustees or managers receive a copy of the valuation approved under section 144(2).

Description of persons to whom information is to be provided	Description of information to be provided	Period during which information is to be provided
Where the scheme is a multi-employer scheme, all members who are in the section of the scheme to which the valuation relates.	A copy of the valuation summary.	The period of 28 days beginning on the day on which the trustees or managers receive a copy of the valuation, or further valuation, approved under section 144(2).
Where the scheme is a partially guaranteed scheme, all members who are in the unsecured part of the scheme.	A copy of the valuation summary.	The period of 28 days beginning on the day on which the trustees or managers receive a copy of the valuation, or further valuation, approved under section 144(2).
Where the trustees or managers of a scheme make an application in respect of the scheme in accordance with section 151 (application for reconsideration), all members.	Notification of the application under section 151.	The period of 28 days beginning on the day the trustees or managers make that application.

NOTES

Initial Commencement

Specified date

Specified date: 6 April 2005: see reg 1.

Amendment

Para 1: in sub-para (1) definition "assessment date" (omitted) revoked by SI 2005/2113, reg 12(1), (3).

Date in force: 19 August 2005: see SI 2005/2113, reg 1(1).

Para 1: in sub-para (1) in definition "notification date" words "in accordance with regulation 3(3)(b), (10)(b) or (d)" in square brackets substituted by SI 2006/595, reg 4(1), (2).

Date in force: 6 April 2006: see SI 2006/595, reg 1(1).

Para 1: in sub-para (2) in the Table in column 2 row 1 paras (e), (f) inserted by SI 2006/595, reg 4(1), (3).

Date in force: 6 April 2006: see SI 2006/595, reg 1(1).

Para 1: in sub-para (2) in the Table in column 2 row 2 inserted by SI 2006/595, reg 4(1), (4).

Date in force: 6 April 2006: see SI 2006/595, reg 1(1).

SCHEDULE 3
Information to be Provided by Members and Beneficiaries

Regulation 5

1 Information to be provided by members and beneficiaries to the Board shall be determined in accordance with the provisions of the table of information to be provided by members and beneficiaries set out below—

Table of information to be provided by members and beneficiaries

Description of persons by whom information is to be provided	Description of information to be provided	Period during which or time at which information is to be provided
Any member or beneficiary whose address is changed.	Details of any changes in the address of that member or beneficiary.	The period of eight weeks beginning four weeks before the day on which the change will take place.
Any member whose marriage ends in divorce [or whose civil partnership is dissolved].	Notification of the [divorce or dissolution of the civil partnership and a copy of the decree of divorce or dissolution of civil partnership].	The period of 28 days beginning on the day on which the decree became absolute [or the civil partnership was dissolved].

Description of persons by whom information is to be provided	Description of information to be provided	Period during which or time at which information is to be provided
Any member whose circumstances change in a way which— (a) is not otherwise notifiable to the Board under regulation 5; and (b) he has reasonable cause to believe may affect his present or future entitlement or the future entitlement of any person who may become entitled in respect of him.	Details of the change in his circumstances.	The period of three months beginning on the day on which the change took place.
Any member or beneficiary who wishes to make any change to the means by which compensation payments are made to him.	Details of the proposed change and the date on which it is to take effect ("the operative date").	At least 28 days before the operative date.
Where the member or beneficiary terminates the appointment of his appointed representative, or where there is any change in the address of an appointed representative, the member or beneficiary who appointed that appointed representative.	Notification of the termination or of the change in the address of the appointed representative, and the date on which the termination or change became effective.	The period of 28 days beginning on the day on which the termination or change became effective.

NOTES

Initial Commencement

Specified date

Specified date: 6 April 2005: see reg 1.

Amendment

Para 1: in the Table in row 2 in column 1 words "or whose civil partnership is dissolved" in square brackets inserted by SI 2006/595, reg 5(1), (2)(a).

Date in force: 6 April 2006: see SI 2006/595, reg 1(1).

Para 1: in the Table in row 2 in column 2 words from "divorce or dissolution" to "of civil partnership" in square brackets substituted by SI 2006/595, reg 5(1), (2)(b).

Date in force: 6 April 2006: see SI 2006/595, reg 1(1).

Para 1: in the Table in row 2 in column 3 words "or the civil partnership was dissolved" in square brackets inserted by SI 2006/595, reg 5(1), (2)(c).

Date in force: 6 April 2006: see SI 2006/595, reg 1(1).

The Occupational Pension Schemes (Employer Debt) Regulations 2005

SI 2005 No 678

Occupational Pension Schemes (Employer Debt) Regulations 2005

Made 11th March 2005

Laid before Parliament 16th March 2005

Coming into force 6th April 2005

Preliminary

1   Citation, commencement, application and extent

(1) These Regulations may be cited as the Occupational Pension Schemes (Employer Debt) Regulations 2005.

(2) These Regulations come into force on 6th April 2005.

(3) These Regulations do not apply to—

(a)   any scheme other than a money purchase scheme if a debt to the trustees or managers of the scheme has been treated as arising under section 75(1) of the 1995 Act before that date;

(b)   any scheme which immediately before that date was regarded by virtue of regulation 2 of the Occupational Pension Schemes (Winding Up) Regulations 1996 as having begun to be wound up before that date for the purposes of those Regulations; or

(c)   any scheme which according to the rules in section 124(3A) to (3E) of the 1995 Act began to wind up before that date.

(4) These Regulations extend to England and Wales and Scotland.

NOTES

Initial Commencement

Specified date

Specified date: 6 April 2005: see para (2) above.

2   Interpretation

(1) In these Regulations—

"the 1993 Act" means the Pension Schemes Act 1993;

"the 1995 Act" means the Pensions Act 1995;

"the 2004 Act" means the Pensions Act 2004;

"the 1996 Regulations" means the Occupational Pension Schemes (Deficiency on Winding Up etc) Regulations 1996;

"the actuary" means the actuary appointed for the scheme in pursuance of subsection (1)(b) of section 47 of the 1995 Act or, in the case of a scheme to which that provision does not apply by virtue of regulations made under subsection (5) of that section, an actuary otherwise authorised by the trustees or managers to provide such valuations or certifications as may be required under these Regulations;

"the applicable time" means the time as at which the value of the assets of a scheme and the amount of its liabilities are to be determined, calculated and verified for the purposes of section 75 of the 1995 Act;

"employer" has the same meaning as in section 75 of the 1995 Act (but see paragraph (2) and regulations 9 and 13);

"employment-cessation event" has the meaning given in regulation 6(4);

"the MFR Regulations" means the Occupational Pension Schemes (Minimum Funding Requirement and Actuarial Valuations) Regulations 1996;

"money purchase scheme" means an occupational pension scheme under which all the benefits that may be provided other than death benefits are money purchase benefits;

"multi-employer scheme" means a scheme in relation to which there is more than one employer (including, except in regulation 8, any section of a scheme treated under that regulation as a scheme if there is more than one employer in relation to that section);

"the tax condition", in relation to a scheme, means—

    (a)   that the scheme has been approved by the Commissioners of the Board of Inland Revenue for the purposes of section 590 or 591 of the Taxes Act at any time before 6th April 2006; or

    (b)   that the scheme is registered under section 153 of the Finance Act 2004;

"the Taxes Act" means the Income and Corporation Taxes Act 1988;

["withdrawal arrangement" and "approved withdrawal arrangement" are to be read in accordance with paragraph 1(1) of Schedule 1A to these Regulations].

(2) In these Regulations "scheme" must be read in appropriate cases in accordance with the modifications of section 75 of the 1995 Act made by regulation 8, 14 or 15, as the case may be; and "employer" and "member" must be read accordingly.

(3) References in these Regulations to the guidance in GN19 are to the guidelines on winding up and scheme asset deficiency (GN19), prepared and published by the Institute of Actuaries and the Faculty of Actuaries and approved for the purposes of these Regulations by the Secretary of State, with such revisions as have been so approved at the applicable time.

(4) References in these Regulations to the guidance in GN 27 are to the guidelines on minimum funding requirement (GN 27), prepared and published by the Institute of Actuaries and the Faculty of Actuaries and approved for the purposes of the MFR Regulations by the Secretary of State, with such revisions as have been so approved at the applicable time.

(5) Subject to the previous provisions of this regulation, expressions used in these Regulations have the same meaning as in Part 1 of the 1995 Act (see section 124).

NOTES

Initial Commencement

Specified date

Specified date: 6 April 2005: see reg 1(2).

Amendment

Para (1): definition "withdrawal arrangement" and "approved withdrawal arrangement" inserted by SI 2005/2224, reg 2(1).

Date in force: 2 September 2005 (except in relation to an employment-cessation event occuring before that date): see SI 2005/2224, reg 1(2), (3).

3   Disapplication of the 1996 Regulations

The 1996 Regulations do not apply in any case where these Regulations apply (and accordingly they only apply to a scheme as respects which regulation 1(3)(a), (b) or (c) applies).

NOTES

Initial Commencement

Specified date

Specified date: 6 April 2005: see reg 1(2).

4   Schemes to which section 75 of the 1995 Act does not apply

(1) Section 75 of the 1995 Act does not apply to any scheme which is—

(a)   a public service pension scheme under the provisions of which there is no requirement for assets related to the intended rate or amount of benefit under the scheme to be set aside in advance (disregarding requirements relating to additional voluntary contributions);

(b)   a scheme which is made under section 7 of the Superannuation Act 1972 (superannuation of persons employed in local government etc) and provides pensions to local government employees;

(c)   a scheme which is made under section 2 of the Parliamentary and Other Pensions Act 1987 (power to provide for pensions for Members of the House of Commons etc);

(d)   a scheme in respect of which a relevant public authority, as defined in section 307(4) of the 2004 Act, has given a guarantee or made any other arrangements for the purposes of securing that the assets of the scheme are sufficient to meet its liabilities;

(e)   a scheme which does not meet the tax condition;

(f)   a scheme which—

    (i)   has been categorised by the Commissioners of the Board of Inland Revenue for the purposes of its approval as a centralised scheme for non-associated employers;

    (ii)   which is not contracted-out; and

    (iii)   under the provisions of which the only benefits that may be provided on or after retirement (other than money purchase benefits derived from the payment of voluntary contributions by any person) are lump sum benefits which are not calculated by reference to a member's salary;

[(g)   a scheme—

    (i)   which has such a superannuation fund as is mentioned in section 615(6) of the Taxes Act (exemption from tax in respect of certain pensions); and

    (ii)   in relation to which the trustees or managers are not—

        (aa)   authorised under section 288 of the 2004 Act (general authorisation to accept contributions from European employer); or

        (bb)   approved under section 289 of the 2004 Act (approval in relation to particular European employer) in relation to a European employer);]

(h)   a scheme with fewer than two members;

(i)   a scheme with fewer than twelve members where all the members are trustees of the scheme and either—

    (i)   the rules of the scheme provide that all decisions are made only by the trustees who are members of the scheme by unanimous agreement; or

    (ii)   the scheme has a trustee who is independent in relation to the scheme for the purposes of section 23 of the 1995 Act (power to appoint independent trustees) (see subsection (3) of that section) and is registered in the register maintained by the Authority in accordance with regulations made under subsection (4) of that section;

(j)   a scheme with fewer than twelve members where all the members are directors of a company which is the sole trustee of the scheme and either—

    (i)   the rules of the scheme provide that all decisions are made only by the members of the scheme by unanimous agreement, or

    (ii)   one of the directors of the company is independent in relation to the scheme for the purposes of section 23 of the 1995 Act and is registered in the register maintained by the Authority in accordance with regulations made under subsection (4) of that section;

(k)   the Chatsworth Settlement Estate Pension Scheme; or

(l)   …

(2) Before 6th April 2006 paragraph (1)(e) applies with the addition at the end of the words "and is not a relevant statutory scheme providing relevant benefits"; and for the purposes of that paragraph "relevant statutory scheme" and "relevant benefits" have the same meaning as in Chapter 1 of Part 14 of the Taxes Act (see sections 611A and 612(1) of that Act).

NOTES

Initial Commencement

Specified date

Specified date: 6 April 2005: see reg 1(2).

Amendment

Para (1): sub-para (g) substituted by SI 2006/467, reg 6.

Date in force: 30 March 2006: see SI 2006/467, reg 1(2).

Para (1): sub-para (l) revoked by SI 2005/2224, reg 4(1).

Date in force: 2 September 2005: see SI 2005/2224, reg 1(2).

Valuations

5   Calculation of the value of scheme liabilities and assets: defined benefit schemes

(1) The liabilities and assets of a scheme which are to be taken into account for the purposes of section 75(2) and (4) of the 1995 Act and their amount or value must be determined, calculated and verified by the actuary as at the applicable time—

(a)   in the case of liabilities in respect of pensions or other benefits, on the assumption that the liabilities will be discharged by the purchase of annuities of the kind described in section 74(3)(c) of the 1995 Act (discharge of liabilities: annuity purchase);

(b)   subject to sub-paragraph (a), on the general assumptions specified in regulation 3(2)(a) to (c) and (3) of the MFR Regulations (determination, valuation and verification of assets and liabilities: general);

(c)   subject to sub-paragraph (a) and paragraphs (2), (3), [(3A),] (5) and (6), in accordance with regulations 4 to 8 of the MFR Regulations (determination and valuation of assets and liabilities);

(d)   subject to sub-paragraph (e), so far as the guidance given in GN 27 applies as respects regulations 3(2)(a) to (c) and (3) and 4 to 8 of the MFR Regulations or as respects sub-paragraph (a) and paragraphs (2) and (3) of this regulation, in accordance with that guidance; and

(e)   in accordance with the guidance given in GN 19 so far as that guidance applies for the purposes of these Regulations.

(2) For the purposes of paragraph (1)(a) the actuary must estimate the cost of purchasing the annuities.

(3) The liabilities of a scheme which are to be taken into account under paragraph (1) include all expenses (except the cost of the annuities referred to in paragraph (1)(a)) which, in the opinion of the trustees or managers of the scheme, are likely to be incurred in connection with the winding up of the scheme.

[(3A) If the modification specified in regulation 7(3) has applied in the case of an employment-cessation event that occurred in relation to an employer before the applicable time—

(a)   the liabilities of the scheme that are attributable to employment with that employer, and

(b)   the debts treated as due under section 75(4) of the 1995 Act in accordance with that modification,

are not to be taken into account under paragraph (1).]

(4) Where in these Regulations (or in the MFR Regulations as applied by this regulation) there is a reference to the value of any asset or the amount of any liability being calculated or verified in accordance with the opinion of the actuary or as he thinks appropriate, he must comply with any relevant provision in the guidance given in GN 27 or, as the case may be, GN 19 in making that calculation or verification.

(5) The value of the assets and the amount of the liabilities of a scheme which are to be taken into account for the purposes of section 75(2) and (4) of the 1995 Act must be certified by the actuary in the form set out in Schedule 1 to these Regulations, but if the scheme is being wound up on the date as at which the valuation is made, the actuary must modify the note at the end of the certificate by omitting the words from "if the scheme" onwards.

(6) For the purposes of this regulation—

(a)   references in regulations 3(2), 4, 5, 7 and 8 of the MFR Regulations to the relevant date are to be taken as references to the applicable time;

(b)   regulations 4(1), 7(1) and 8(2) of the MFR Regulations have effect with the substitution for the words "the minimum funding requirement is met" of the words "the value of the assets of the scheme is less than the amount of the liabilities of the scheme";

(c)   regulation 6(1)(b) of the MFR Regulations has effect with the addition at the end of the words " (and any amount treated as a debt due to the trustees or managers of the scheme under section 75(2) or (4) by virtue of the valuation in question)".

(7) In its application for the purposes of this regulation in a case where the applicable time falls after the scheme has begun to be wound up, regulation 6(1) of the MFR Regulations has effect with the addition after sub-paragraph (c) of the words—

"; and for the purposes of sub-paragraph (a), regulation 5(1)(a) of the Occupational Pension Schemes (Investment) Regulations 1996 (exclusion of employer-related investments over 5 per cent of current market value) shall be disregarded.".

(8) This regulation has effect subject to regulation 7 (multi-employer schemes: [employment-cessation events and withdrawal arrangements]).

Multi-employer schemes

6   Multi-employer schemes: general

(1) In its application to a multi-employer scheme, section 75 of the 1995 Act has effect in relation to each employer as if—

(a)   the reference in section 75(2)(a) to a time which falls before any relevant event in relation to the employer which occurs while the scheme is being wound up were a reference to a time which falls before relevant events have occurred in relation to all the employers;

(b)   the reference in section 75(2) to an amount equal to the difference being treated as a debt due from the employer were a reference to an amount equal to that employer's share of the difference being treated as a debt due from that employer;

(c)   the references in section 75(3)(a)(i) and (b) to no relevant event of the kind there mentioned occurring in relation to the employer were references to no event of that kind occurring in relation to all the employers;

(d)   the reference in section 75(4)(a) to a relevant event ("the current event") occurring in relation to the employer were a reference to a relevant event or an employment-cessation event occurring only in relation to that employer;

(e)   the reference in section 75(4) to an amount equal to the difference being treated as a debt due from the employer were—

(i)   in a case where the difference is ascertained immediately before a relevant event occurs in relation to the employer, a reference to an amount equal to the employer's share of the difference being treated as a debt due from the employer; and

(ii)   in a case where the difference is ascertained immediately before an employment cessation event occurs in relation to the employer, a reference to an amount equal to the sum of the cessation expenses attributable to the employer and the employer's share of the difference being treated as a debt due from the employer; and

(f)   section 75(4)(d) and (e) were omitted.

(2) For the purposes of paragraph (1), an employer's share of the difference is—

(a)   such proportion of the total difference as, in the opinion of the actuary after consultation with the trustees or managers, the amount of the scheme's liabilities attributable to employment with that employer bears to the total amount of the scheme's liabilities attributable to employment with the employers; or

(b)   if the scheme provides for the total amount of that debt to be otherwise apportioned amongst the employers, the amount due from that employer under that provision.

(3) For the purposes of paragraph (2)—

(a)   the total amount of the scheme's liabilities which are attributable to employment with the employers; and

(b)   the amount of the liabilities attributable to employment with any one employer, are such amounts as are determined, calculated and verified by the actuary in accordance with the guidance given in GN 19; and a determination under this paragraph must be certified by the actuary as being in accordance with that guidance.

(4) For the purposes of these Regulations an employment-cessation event occurs in relation to an employer if he ceases to be an employer employing persons in the description of employment to which the scheme relates at a time when at least one other person continues to employ such persons.

(5) For the purposes of paragraph (1), the cessation expenses attributable to an employer are all expenses which, in the opinion of the trustees or managers of the scheme, are likely to be incurred in connection with the employment-cessation event occurring in relation to the employer.

NOTES
Initial Commencement
Specified date
Specified date: 6 April 2005: see reg 1(2).

[7   Multi-employer schemes: employment-cessation events and withdrawal arrangements]

[(1) This regulation applies where—

(a)   section 75 of the 1995 Act applies to a trust scheme with the modifications referred to in regulation 6 (multi-employer schemes: general); and

(b)   as a result of the occurrence of an employment-cessation event in relation to an employer, a debt ("the cessation debt") calculated on the basis of assets and liabilities valued in accordance with regulation 5 is treated as due from the employer ("the cessation employer") under section 75(4) of that Act.

(2) If the cessation employer notifies the Authority in writing that he proposes to enter into a withdrawal arrangement—

(a)   the Authority may issue a direction that the cessation debt is to be unenforceable for such period as the Authority may specify in the direction, and where such a direction has been issued the debt is unenforceable for that period; and

(b)   the Authority may issue a direction that if an approved withdrawal arrangement has come into force within that period, section 75 of the 1995 Act is to apply in the case of the employment-cessation event with the modification specified in paragraph (3) instead of the modification referred to in regulation 6(1)(e)(ii), and where such a direction has been issued and such an arrangement has so come into force, that modification so applies.

(3) The modification is that section 75 of the 1995 Act has effect as if the reference in section 75(4) to an amount equal to the difference being treated as a debt due from the employer were a reference to—

(a)   amount A being treated as a debt due from the employer; and

(b)   unless and until the Authority issue a direction that it is not to be so treated, amount B being treated as a debt due from the guarantors at the guarantee time for which (if there is more than one guarantor) they are jointly or, if the approved withdrawal arrangement so provides, jointly and severally liable,

where amount A is calculated in accordance with regulation 7A and amount B is calculated in accordance with regulation 7B.

(4) In this regulation—

"the guarantee time" means the earliest time when an event specified in paragraph 1(3) of Schedule 1A to these Regulations occurs; and

"the guarantors" means such one or more of the parties to the approved withdrawal arrangement as are specified in the arrangement as the persons who are the guarantors for the purposes of this regulation.

(5) The Authority may issue a direction extending the period mentioned in paragraph (2)(a) by such further period as they may specify (so that the debt is unenforceable for the extended period).

(6) The Authority may only issue a direction under paragraph (3)(b)—

(a)   before the guarantee time, and

(b)   if the Authority consider that the approved withdrawal arrangement is no longer required.

(7) Schedule 1A to these Regulations applies for the purpose of making further provision in cases where this regulation applies; and in that Schedule and regulations 7A and 7B "the cessation employer" has the same meaning as in this regulation.]

NOTES
Amendment
Substituted, together with regs 7A, 7B for this reg as originally enacted, by SI 2005/2224, reg 2(3).

Appendix 9

Date in force: 2 September 2005 (except in relation to an employment-cessation event occuring before that date): see SI 2005/2224, reg 1(2), (3).

[7A   Calculation of amounts due from cessation employer by virtue of regulation 7]

[(1) For the purposes of regulation 7(3), amount A depends on whether or not a debt (a "scheme funding basis debt") would have been treated as due from the cessation employer under section 75(4) of the 1995 Act if—

(a)   regulation 5 had applied with the modifications specified in paragraph (4); and

(b)   section 75(4) had applied in accordance with regulation 6(1)(d) and (e) but subject to the modifications of regulation 6 specified in paragraph (5) (instead of in accordance with the modification specified in regulation 7(3)).

(2) If a debt would have been so treated, amount A is the sum of the scheme funding basis debt and the cessation expenses attributable to the employer.

(3) If a debt would not have been so treated, amount A is equal to the amount of the cessation expenses attributable to the employer.

(4) The modifications of regulation 5 are that—

(a)   paragraphs (1)(a) and (2) and the references to those provisions in paragraph (1)(b), (c) and (d) (by virtue of which liabilities for pensions and other benefits are to be valued on the assumption that they will be discharged by the purchase of annuities) are omitted;

(b)   paragraph (3) and the references to that paragraph in paragraph (1)(c) and (d) (by virtue of which winding up expenses are to be taken into account) are omitted; and

(c)   in paragraph (5) for the words "for the purposes of section 75(2) and (4) of the 1995 Act" there are substituted the words "for the purposes of section 75(2) of the 1995 Act and for the purposes of section 75(4) of the 1995 Act where no approved withdrawal arrangement has been entered into by the employer".

(5) The modifications of regulation 6 are that—

(a)   for paragraph (ii) of paragraph (1)(e) there is substituted—

"(ii)   in a case where the difference is ascertained immediately before an employment-cessation event occurs in relation to the employer, a reference to an amount equal to the employer's share of the difference, less the relevant transferred liabilities deduction, being treated as a debt due from the employer;";

(b)   after paragraph (5) there is added—

"(6) In this regulation "the relevant transferred liabilities deduction" means the amount of any relevant transferred liabilities, less the value of the corresponding assets.

(7) For the purposes of paragraph (6)—

(a)   "corresponding assets", in relation to relevant transferred liabilities, means the assets transferred from the scheme in connection with the transfer from the scheme of those liabilities; and

(b)   the value of the corresponding assets is to be determined—

(i)   in the case of corresponding assets that are assets of the scheme at the applicable time, as at that time; and

(ii)   in the case of corresponding assets that are not assets of the scheme at that time, as at the date of the transfer of the assets.

(8) For the purposes of paragraph (6)—

(a)   "relevant transferred liabilities" means liabilities in respect of members—

(i)   which are transferred from the scheme in circumstances where the conditions set out in paragraphs (2)(a) or (b) and (3) of regulation 12 of the Occupational Pension Schemes (Preservation of Benefit) Regulations 1991 (transfer without consent) are met;

(ii)   which are so transferred during the period beginning with the applicable time and ending with the date on which the approved withdrawal arrangement is approved ("the relevant period");

(iii)   the transfer of which reduces the amount of the scheme's liabilities attributable to employment with the employer in relation to whom the employment-cessation event has occurred; and

(iv)   in connection with the transfer of which there is a transfer of corresponding assets during the relevant period; and

(b)   the amount of the relevant transferred liabilities is to be calculated in accordance with regulation 5 as modified by regulation 7A(4).".

(6) The value of the assets and the amount of the liabilities of a scheme which are to be taken into account for the purposes of determining whether a scheme funding basis debt would have been treated as due as mentioned in paragraph (1) must be certified by the actuary in the form set out in Schedule 1B to these Regulations, but—

(a)   if the actuary is of the opinion that the value of the assets of the scheme was not less than the amount of the liabilities of the scheme—

        (i)   substituting in the first sentence of the comparison of value of scheme assets with amount of scheme liabilities for the words "was less" the words "was not less"; and

        (ii)   omitting the last sentence of that comparison; and

(b)   if the scheme is being wound up on the date as at which the valuation is made, omitting from the Note the words from "if the scheme" onwards.

(7) In this regulation "the cessation expenses attributable to the employer" has the meaning given by regulation 6(5).]

NOTES

Amendment

Substituted, together with regs 7, 7B for reg 7 as originally enacted, by SI 2005/2224, reg 2(3).

Date in force: 2 September 2005 (except in relation to an employment-cessation event occurring before that date): see SI 2005/2224, reg 1(2), (3).

[7B   Calculation of amounts due from guarantors by virtue of regulation 7]

[(1) For the purposes of regulation 7(3), amount B depends on whether the approved withdrawal arrangement provides for amount B to be the amount provided for under paragraph (2).

(2) If the approved withdrawal arrangement so provides, amount B is equal to the amount (if any) that would be the amount of the debt due from the cessation employer under section 75(4) of the 1995 Act if—

(a)   the employment-cessation event had occurred at the guarantee time;

(b)   the cessation employer had not entered into an approved withdrawal arrangement; and

(c)   there were no cessation expenses attributable to the employer.

(3) If the approved withdrawal arrangement does not provide for amount B to be the amount provided for under paragraph (2), amount B is equal to the amount that would be the amount treated as due from the cessation employer under section 75(4) of the 1995 Act if the cessation employer had not entered into an approved withdrawal arrangement, less the sum of—

(a)   the amount that is amount A for the purposes of regulation 7(3);

(b)   if the amount that the approved withdrawal arrangement provides for the cessation employer to pay exceeds that amount, an amount equal to the excess; and

(c)   the relevant transferred liabilities deduction.

(4) The value of the assets and the amount of the liabilities of a scheme which are to be taken into account for the purposes of determining the amount (if any) that would be the amount of the debt due from the cessation employer under section 75(4) of the 1995 Act in the case mentioned in paragraph (2) must be certified by the actuary in the form set out in Schedule 1 to these Regulations, but—

(a)   substituting for the reference to regulation 5 a reference to paragraph (2) of this regulation;

(b)   if the actuary is of the opinion that the value of the assets of the scheme was not less than the amount of the liabilities of the scheme—

        (i)   substituting in the first sentence of the comparison of value of scheme assets with amount of scheme liabilities for the words "was less" the words "was not less"; and

        (ii)   omitting the last sentence of that comparison; and

(c)   if the scheme is being wound up on the date as at which the valuation is made, omitting from the Note the words from "if the scheme" onwards.

(5) In this regulation—

"the cessation expenses attributable to the employer" has the meaning given by regulation 6(5); and "the relevant transferred liabilities deduction" has the meaning given by regulation 6(6), as inserted by the modification of regulation 6 made by regulation 7A(5)(b), except that for the purposes of this regulation the amount of the relevant transferred liabilities is to be calculated in accordance with regulation 5 without the modifications made by regulation 7A(4).]

NOTES

Amendment

Substituted, together with regs 7, 7B for reg 7 as originally enacted, by SI 2005/2224, reg 2(3).

Date in force: 2 September 2005 (except in relation to an employment-cessation event occurring before that date): see SI 2005/2224, reg 1(2), (3).

8 Multi-employer schemes: sectionalised schemes

(1) In its application to a multi-employer scheme—

(a)   which is divided into two or more sections; and

(b)   the provisions of which are such that the sections meet conditions A and B,

section 75 of the 1995 Act and the provisions of these Regulations (apart from this regulation) apply as if each section of the scheme were a separate scheme.

(2) Condition A is that contributions payable to the scheme by an employer, or by a member in employment under that employer, are allocated to that employer's section (or, if more than one section applies to that employer, to the section which is appropriate in respect of the employment in question).

(3) Condition B is that a specified part or proportion of the assets of the scheme is attributable to each section and cannot be used for the purposes of any other section.

(4) In their application to a scheme—

(a)   which has been such a scheme as is mentioned in paragraph (1);

(b)   which is divided into two or more sections, one or more of which apply only to members who are not in pensionable service under the section;

(c)   the provisions of which have not been amended so as to prevent conditions A and B being met in relation to two or more sections; and

(d)   in relation to one or more sections of which those conditions have ceased to be met at any time by reason only of there being no members in pensionable service under the section and no contributions which are to be allocated to it,

section 75 of the 1995 Act and the provisions of these Regulations (apart from this paragraph) apply as if any section in relation to which those conditions have ceased to be met were a separate scheme.

(5) For the purposes of paragraphs (1) to (4), any provisions of the scheme by virtue of which contributions or transfers of assets may be made to make provision for death benefits are disregarded.

(6) But if paragraph (1) or (4) applies and, by virtue of any provisions of the scheme, contributions or transfers of assets to make such provision are made to a section ("the death benefits section") the assets of which may only be applied for the provision of death benefits, the death benefits section is also to be treated as a separate scheme.

(7) For the purpose of this regulation, any provisions of the scheme by virtue of which assets attributable to one section may on the winding up of the scheme or a section be used for the purposes of another section are disregarded.

NOTES

Initial Commencement

Specified date

Specified date: 6 April 2005: see reg 1(2).

Former employers

9 Former employers

(1) In the application of section 75 of the 1995 Act and these Regulations to a scheme which has no active members, references to employers include every person who employed persons in the description of employment to which the scheme relates immediately before the occurrence of the event after which the scheme ceased to have any active members.

(2) In the application of section 75 of the 1995 Act and these Regulations to a scheme, references to employers include—

(a)   any pre-April 1997 participator (see paragraph (7)); and

(b)   any person who has ceased on or after 6th April 1997 and before the applicable time to be a person employing persons in the description of employment to which the scheme relates, unless—

    (i)   when he so ceased the scheme was not being wound up and continued to have active members; and

    (ii)   [condition A, B, BB], C or D is met.

(3) Condition A is that no debt was treated as becoming due from him under section 75(2) or (4) of the 1995 Act (or, if he so ceased before 6th April 2005, under section 75(1) of that Act) by virtue of his so ceasing.

(4) Condition B is that such a debt was treated as becoming due from him and has been paid before the applicable time.

[(4A) Condition BB is that such a debt was treated as becoming due from him, the modification in regulation 7(3) applied, and the amount treated as becoming due from him under regulation 7(3)(a) has been paid before the applicable time.]

(5) Condition C is that such a debt was treated as becoming due from him and has not been so paid solely because he was not notified of the debt, and of the amount of it, sufficiently in advance of the applicable time for it to be paid before that time.

(6) Condition D is that such a debt was treated as becoming due from him but at the applicable time it is excluded from the value of the assets of the scheme because it is unlikely to be recovered without disproportionate cost or within a reasonable time.

(7) In this regulation "pre-April 1997 participator" means a person who immediately before 6th April 2005 was regarded as an employer for the purposes of the 1996 Regulations by virtue of regulation 6 of those Regulations (ceasing to participate: transitional provision).

NOTES

Initial Commencement

Specified date

Specified date: 6 April 2005: see reg 1(2).

Amendment

Para (2): in sub-para (b)(ii) words "condition A, B, BB" in square brackets substituted by SI 2005/2224, reg 2(4)(a).

Date in force: 2 September 2005: see SI 2005/2224, reg 1(2).

Para (4A): inserted by SI 2005/2224, reg 2(4)(b).

Date in force: 2 September 2005: see SI 2005/2224, reg 1(2).

Money purchase schemes

10   Money purchase schemes: fraud and levy deficiencies etc

(1) Notwithstanding subsection (1)(a) of section 75 of the 1995 Act, that section applies to money purchase schemes as if—

(a)   subsection (2)—

    (i)   provided that if the levy deficit condition is met the levy deficit is to be treated as a debt due from the employer to the trustees or managers of the scheme; and

    (ii)   was not subject to subsection (3) of that section;

(b)   subsection (4) provided that where the criminal reduction conditions are met the criminal deficit is to be treated as a debt due from the employer to the trustees or managers of the scheme; and

(c)   subsections (4A) to (4C) and (6) were omitted.

(2) The levy deficit condition is that an amount payable by way of general levy [or fraud compensation levy] in respect of any money purchase scheme exceeds the value of the unallocated assets of the scheme either—

(a)   at the time when the amount first becomes payable to the Secretary of State; or

(b)   at a later time designated by the trustees or managers of the scheme for the purposes of this paragraph.

(3) The criminal reduction conditions are that—

(a)   a reduction in the aggregate value of the allocated assets of the scheme occurs;

(b)   the reduction is attributable to an act or omission which—

    (i)   constitutes an offence prescribed for the purposes of section 81(1)(c) of the 1995 Act; or

    (ii)   in the case of an act or omission which occurred outside England and Wales or Scotland, would constitute such an offence if it occurred in England and Wales or in Scotland; and

(c)   immediately after the act or omission or, if that time cannot be determined, at the earliest time when the auditor of the scheme knows that the reduction has occurred, the amount of that reduction exceeds the value of the unallocated assets of the scheme.

(4) [In this regulation]—

"allocated assets", in relation to a scheme, means assets which have been specifically allocated for the provision of benefits to or in respect of members (whether generally or individually) or for the payment of the scheme's expenses (and "unallocated" is to be read accordingly);

"the criminal deficit" means the amount of the excess mentioned in paragraph (3)(c);

["the fraud compensation levy" means the levy imposed in accordance with section 189 of the 2004 Act;]

"the levy deficit" means the amount of the excess mentioned in paragraph (2);

"the general levy" means the levy imposed under section 175 of the 1993 Act by regulation 3(1) or (2) of the Occupational and Personal Pension Schemes (General Levy) Regulations 2005.

NOTES

Initial Commencement

Specified date

Specified date: 6 April 2005: see reg 1(2).

Amendment

Para (2): words "or fraud compensation levy" in square brackets inserted by SI 2006/558, reg 12(a).

Date in force: 1 April 2006: see SI 2006/558, reg 1.

Para (4): words "In this regulation" in square brackets substituted by SI 2006/558, reg 12(b)(i).

Date in force: 1 April 2006: see SI 2006/558, reg 1.

Para (4): definition "the fraud compensation levy" inserted by SI 2006/558, reg 12(b)(ii).

Date in force: 1 April 2006: see SI 2006/558, reg 1.

11   Money purchase schemes: valuations etc

(1) For the purposes of section 75 of the 1995 Act as applied by regulation 10, this regulation applies instead of regulation 5 and 7.

(2) In the case of a scheme other than an ear-marked scheme—

(a)   the value at any time of the unallocated assets of the scheme is to be taken to be the value of those assets as certified in a statement by the scheme's auditor; and

(b)   the amount of the criminal reduction in the aggregate value of the allocated assets of the scheme at any time is to be calculated by subtracting the actual aggregate value of those assets at that time from the notional aggregate value of those assets.

(3) The notional aggregate value mentioned in paragraph (2)(b) is to be taken to be the sum of the values of the assets—

(a)   as stated in the audited accounts which most immediately precede the relevant act or omission; or

(b)   if there are none, as certified in a statement by the scheme's auditor,

adjusted appropriately to take account of any alteration in their values (other than any alteration attributable to that act or omission) between the date as at which those accounts are prepared or, as the case may be, as at which that statement is given and the time in question.

(4) The actual aggregate value mentioned in paragraph (2)(b) is to be calculated in the same manner as it was calculated for the purposes of the accounts mentioned in paragraph (3)(a) or, as the case may be, the statement mentioned in paragraph (3)(b).

(5) In the case of an ear-marked scheme—

(a)   the value at any time of the unallocated assets of the scheme; and

(b)   the amount of the criminal reduction in the aggregate value of the allocated assets of the scheme,

are the amounts certified in a statement by the relevant insurer.

(6) In this regulation—

"ear-marked scheme" means a scheme under which all the benefits are secured by one or more policies of insurance or annuity contracts, being policies or contracts specifically allocated to the provision of benefits for individual members or any other person who has a right to benefits under the scheme; and

"the relevant insurer", in relation to such a scheme, is the insurer with whom the insurance contract or annuity contract is made.

NOTES

Initial Commencement

Specified date

Specified date: 6 April 2005: see reg 1(2).

12   Multi-employer money purchase schemes

(1) In its application to a money purchase scheme that is a multi-employer scheme regulation 10 applies with the substitution for paragraph (1) of the following paragraphs—

"(1) Notwithstanding subsection (1)(a) of section 75 of the 1995 Act, that section applies to money purchase schemes as if—

(a)   subsection (2)—

      (i)   provided that if the levy deficit condition is met each employer's share of the levy deficit is to be treated as a debt due from that employer to the trustees or managers of the scheme; and

      (ii)   was not subject to subsection (3) of that section;

(b)   subsection (4) provided that where the criminal reduction conditions are met each employer's share of the criminal deficit is to be treated as a debt due from the employer to the trustees or managers of the scheme; and

(c)   subsections (4A) to (4C) and (6) were omitted.

(1A) For the purposes of paragraph (1), an employer's share of the levy deficit or the criminal deficit is—

(a)   such proportion of that total deficit as, in the opinion of [the trustees or managers], the amount of the scheme's liabilities attributable to employment with that employer bears to the total amount of the scheme's liabilities attributable to employment with the employers; or

(b)   if the scheme provides for the total amount of that debt to be otherwise apportioned amongst the employers, the amount due from that employer under that provision.

(1B) For the purposes of paragraph (1A)—

(a)   the total amount of the scheme's liabilities which are attributable to employment with the employers; and

(b)   the amount of the liabilities attributable to employment with any one employer,

are such amounts as are determined, calculated and verified by the actuary in accordance with the guidance given in GN 19; and a determination under this paragraph must be certified by the actuary as being in accordance with that guidance.".

(2) Regulation 6 does not apply to a money purchase scheme that is a multi-employer scheme.

NOTES

Initial Commencement

Specified date

Specified date: 6 April 2005: see reg 1(2).

Amendment

Para (1A): in sub-para (a) words "the trustees or managers" in square brackets substituted by virtue of SI 2005/2224, reg 4(2).

Date in force: 2 September 2005 (except where the applicable time is before that date): see reg 2(1) hereof and SI 2005/2224, reg 1(2), (4).

13   Former employers of money purchase schemes

Regulation 9 does not apply to a money purchase scheme, but in the application of section 75 of the 1995 Act and these Regulations to such a scheme which has no active members references to employers include every person who employed persons in the description of employment to which the scheme relates immediately before the occurrence of the event after which the scheme ceased to have any active members.

NOTES

Initial Commencement

Specified date

Specified date: 6 April 2005: see reg 1(2).

Other schemes treated as more than one scheme

14   Schemes covering United Kingdom and foreign employment

(1) Paragraph (2) applies where a scheme which applies to members in employment in the United Kingdom and members in employment outside the United Kingdom is divided into two or more sections and the provisions of the scheme are such that—

(a)   different sections of the scheme apply to members in employment in the United Kingdom and to members in employment outside the United Kingdom ("the United Kingdom section" and "the foreign section");

(b)   contributions payable to the scheme in respect of a member are allocated to the section applying to that member's employment;

(c)   a specified part or proportion of the assets of the scheme is attributable to each section and cannot be used for the purposes of any other section; and

(d)   the United Kingdom section meets the tax condition and the foreign section does not do so.

(2) If this paragraph applies—

(a)   section 75 of the 1995 Act and these Regulations (apart from this regulation) apply as if each section of the scheme were a separate scheme; and

(b)   the reference to the scheme in the form set out in Schedule 1 may be modified appropriately.

(3) Paragraph (4) applies where—

(a)   a scheme applies to members in employment in the United Kingdom and members in employment outside the United Kingdom;

(b)   paragraph (2) does not apply to the scheme; and

(c)   part of the scheme meets paragraph (b) of the tax condition by virtue of that part having been treated as a separate scheme under section 611(3) of the Taxes Act that is treated as becoming a registered pension scheme under paragraph 1(1) of Schedule 36 to the Finance Act 2004 by virtue of paragraph 1(2) of that Schedule.

(4) If this paragraph applies—

(a)   section 75 of the 1995 Act and these Regulations (apart from this regulation) apply as if the approved and unapproved parts of the scheme were separate schemes; and

(b)   the reference to the scheme in the form set out in Schedule 1 may be modified appropriately.

(5) Paragraph (6) applies where—

(a)   a scheme has been such a scheme as is mentioned in paragraph (1) or (3),

(b)   the scheme is divided into two or more sections, some or all of which apply only to members who are not in pensionable service under the section;

(c)   the provisions of the scheme have not been amended so as to prevent the conditions in paragraph (1) or, as the case may be, paragraph (3) being met in relation to two or more sections; and

(d)   in relation to one or more sections of the scheme those conditions have ceased to be met at any time by reason only of there being no members in pensionable service under the section and, in the case of paragraph (1), no contributions which are to be allocated to it.

(6) If this paragraph applies—

(a)   section 75 of the 1995 Act and these Regulations (apart from this regulation) apply as if any section in relation to which those conditions have ceased to be met were a separate scheme; and

(b)   the reference to the scheme in the form set out in Schedule 1 may be modified appropriately.

(7) Before 6th April 2006 paragraph (3) applies with the substitution for sub-paragraph (c) of the following paragraph—

"(c)   part of the scheme meets paragraph (a) of the tax condition by virtue of section 611(3) of the Taxes Act."

NOTES

Initial Commencement

Specified date

Specified date: 6 April 2005: see reg 1(2).

15   Schemes with partial government guarantee

(1) This regulation applies if a relevant public authority has—

(a)   given a guarantee in relation to any part of a scheme, any benefits payable under the scheme or any member of the scheme; or

(b)   made any other arrangements for the purposes of securing that the assets of the scheme are sufficient to meet any part of its liabilities.

(2) Where this regulation applies—

(a)   section 75 of the 1995 Act and these Regulations (apart from this regulation) apply as if the guaranteed part of the scheme and the other part of the scheme were separate schemes; and

(b)   the reference to the scheme in the form set out in Schedule 1 may be modified appropriately.

(3) In this regulation—

"the guaranteed part of the scheme" means the part of the scheme—

 (a)   in relation to which the guarantee has been given;

 (b)   which relates to benefits payable under the scheme in relation to which the guarantee has been given; or

 (c)   which relates to benefits payable under the scheme in relation to the liabilities for which those other arrangements have been made; and

"relevant public authority" has the meaning given in section 307(4) of the 2004 Act.

NOTES

Initial Commencement

Specified date

Specified date: 6 April 2005: see reg 1(2).

Supplementary

16   Modification of schemes: apportionment of section 75 debts

(1) This regulation applies for the purposes of section 68(2)(e) of the 1995 (power of trustees to modify schemes by resolution for prescribed purposes).

(2) In the case of a trust scheme (whether or not a money purchase scheme) which apart from this regulation could not be modified for the purpose of making provision for the total amount of a debt due under section 75(2) or (4) of the 1995 Act to be apportioned amongst the employers in different proportions from those which would otherwise apply by virtue of regulation 6(2)(a) or, as the case may be, regulation 10(1A) (as it has effect by virtue of regulation 12), for the purposes of section 68(2)(e), such a modification of the scheme is a modification for a prescribed purpose.

NOTES

Initial Commencement

Specified date

Specified date: 6 April 2005: see reg 1(2).

17   Disregard of staying of voluntary winding up of employer for purposes of section 75 of the 1995 Act

(1) This regulation applies for the purposes of section 75(6D)(i) of the 1995 Act (by virtue of which where a members' voluntary winding up of an employer is stayed section 75 of the 1995 Act has effect as if the resolution for the winding up had never been passed and any debt which arose under that section by virtue of the passing of the resolution had never arisen, except where the winding up is stayed in prescribed circumstances).

(2) The circumstances that are prescribed are where the stay is granted for a limited period.

NOTES

Initial Commencement

Specified date

Specified date: 6 April 2005: see reg 1(2).

18   Consequential amendments

The Regulations specified in Schedule 2 are amended as specified in that Schedule.

NOTES
Initial Commencement
Specified date
Specified date: 6 April 2005: see reg 1(2).

SCHEDULE 1
Form of Actuary's Certificate

Regulation 5

Actuarial Certificate Given for the Purposes of Regulation 5 of the Occupational Pension Schemes (Employer Debt) Regulations 2005

Name of scheme

Date as at which valuation is made

1 Comparison of value of scheme assets with amount of scheme liabilities

In my opinion, at the above date the value of the assets of the scheme was less than the amount of the liabilities of the scheme.

The value of the assets of the scheme was

The amount of the liabilities was

The amount of the difference was

2 Valuation principles

The scheme's assets and liabilities are valued in accordance with section 75(5) of the Pensions Act 1995, the Occupational Pension Schemes (Employer Debt) Regulations 2005 and the guidelines on winding up and scheme asset deficiency (GN19) and on minimum funding requirement (GN27) prepared and published by the Institute of Actuaries and the Faculty of Actuaries (so far as those guidelines are applicable).

Signature Date

Name Qualification

Address Name of employer (if applicable)

Note:

The valuation of the amount of the liabilities of the scheme may not reflect the actual cost of securing those liabilities by the purchase of annuities if the scheme were to have been wound up on the date as at which the valuation is made.

NOTES
Initial Commencement
Specified date
Specified date: 6 April 2005: see reg 1(2).
See Further
See further, in relation to the continued application of the reference "minimum funding requirement" to a scheme on or after 6 April 2007, notwithstanding the repeal of that definition by the Pensions Act 2004, s 320, Sch 13, Pt I and SI 2006/2272, arts 2, 3.

[SCHEDULE 1A
Multi-employer Schemes: Employer-cessation Events and Approved Withdrawal Arrangements]

NOTES
Amendment
Inserted by SI 2005/2224, reg 2(5), Schedule.
Date in force: 2 September 2005 (except in relation to an employment-cessation event occuring before that date): see SI 2005/2224, reg 1(2), (3).

[Withdrawal arrangements

1   (1) For the purposes of these Regulations—

(a)   a withdrawal arrangement is an arrangement that meets the conditions specified in sub-paragraph (2), and

(b)   a withdrawal arrangement is approved if the details—

    (i)   of the arrangement, and

    (ii)   if the arrangement is amended, of any amendments of the arrangement,

    are approved by the Authority.

(2) The conditions are that—

(a)   the arrangement consists of an agreement to which the trustees of the scheme and the cessation employer are parties;

(b)   the agreement is enforceable under the law of England and Wales, and the parties to the agreement have agreed that—

    (i)   that law applies to the agreement; and

    (ii)   they are subject to the jurisdiction of the court in England and Wales as respects the agreement;

(c)   the agreement provides that at or before a time specified in the agreement the cessation employer will pay an amount equal to or greater than the amount that is amount A for the purposes of regulation 7(3)(a);

(d)   the agreement—

    (i)   provides that if an event specified in sub-paragraph (3) occurs whilst the agreement is in force the parties to the agreement who are specified in the agreement as the persons who are the guarantors for the purposes of regulation 7 (the "guarantors") (who may be or include the cessation employer) will pay an amount equal to the amount that is amount B for the purposes of regulation 7(3)(b) (but without prejudice to their powers to make a payment on account of that amount at any earlier time);

    (ii)   if there are two or more guarantors, provides whether or not the guarantors are to be jointly and severally liable for that amount for those purposes; and

    (iii) provides whether or not that amount is to be the amount provided for under regulation 7B(2);

(e)   the agreement provides that an amount payable under paragraph (c) or (d) is payable—

    (i)   to the trustees of the scheme; or

    (ii)   if the Board of the Pension Protection Fund has assumed responsibility for the scheme in accordance with Chapter 3 of Part 2 of the 2004 Act (pension protection), to the Board on behalf of the trustees of the scheme;

(f)   the agreement provides that one or more of the parties to the agreement other than the trustees of the scheme are to bear any expenses incurred by the parties in connection with—

    (i)   the making of the agreement; or

    (ii)   the making of any calculations by the actuary for the purposes of the agreement;

(g)   the agreement will continue in force until—

    (i)   the winding up of the scheme is completed;

    (ii)   the Authority issue a notice to the parties to the agreement stating that the Authority consider that the agreement is no longer required; or

    (iii) the agreement is replaced by another agreement that is approved by the Authority as an approved withdrawal arrangement,

    whichever occurs first.

(3) The events are that—

(a)   the scheme begins to be wound up;

(b)   an event occurs as a result of which there is no person who is an employer in relation to the scheme for the purposes of these Regulations in relation to whom a relevant event has not occurred for the purposes of section 75 of the 1995 Act (see section 75(6A) of that Act);

(c)   the Authority issue a notice to the parties to the agreement stating that they consider that the amount referred to in sub-paragraph (2)(d)(i) should be paid.

(4) The Authority may not issue such a notice at any time unless the Authority consider that it is reasonable for the guarantors to be required to pay that amount at that time.

(5) In forming an opinion for the purposes of sub-paragraph (4), the Authority must have regard to such matters as the Authority consider relevant including—

(a)   whether the guarantors have taken reasonable steps to comply with the approved withdrawal arrangement;

(b)   whether the guarantors have complied with their obligations under paragraph 5; and

(c)   the guarantors' financial circumstances.

Approval of withdrawal arrangements

2   (1) Approval by the Authority of an agreement as a withdrawal arrangement is to be given in a notice issued by the Authority.

(2) Such an approval may be given subject to such conditions as the Authority consider appropriate.

(3) The Authority may not approve an agreement as a withdrawal arrangement unless they are satisfied that—

(a)   the agreement meets the conditions in paragraph 1(2); and

(b)   the guarantors have or will have such resources that the debt becoming due under section 75 of the 1995 Act is more likely to be met if the agreement is approved.

3   (1) Nothing in this Schedule prevents the Authority from approving as a withdrawal arrangement an agreement that will take effect only if an employment-cessation event occurs in relation to an employer.

(2) And in the case of such an approval, references in paragraphs 1 and 2 to that event and debt must be read accordingly.

(3) But, subject to that, references in these Regulations to an approved withdrawal arrangement only include references to an arrangement approved under this paragraph if the agreement has taken effect.

4   (1) Paragraphs 1, 2 and 5 of this Schedule apply to any arrangement replacing an approved withdrawal arrangement as they applied to the replaced arrangement.

(2) No directions may be issued under regulation 7(2) as a result of a notification about an arrangement that is to replace another arrangement if—

(a)   directions have been issued under that regulation as a result of a notification about the replaced arrangement; and

(b)   the replaced arrangement is an approved withdrawal arrangement that has come into force.

(3) But if an approved withdrawal arrangement replaces another such arrangement—

(a)   any directions issued under regulation 7(2) as a result of a notification about the replaced arrangement continue to apply, and

(b)   after the replacing arrangement comes into force the references to the approved withdrawal arrangement in regulations 7(3)(b), (4) and (6) and 7B(1) to (3) and in regulation 6(6)(b), as inserted by regulation 7A(5)(b), are to be taken as references to the replacing arrangement.

(4) Once sub-paragraph (2) has applied to an arrangement ("the second arrangement") that is to replace another arrangement—

(a)   no further directions may be issued under regulation 7(2) as a result of a notification about any arrangement that is to replace the second arrangement or any subsequent replacing arrangement;

(b)   sub-paragraph (3)(a) continues to apply to any directions about the arrangement replaced by the second arrangement notwithstanding the replacement of the second arrangement, or any subsequent replacement, by an approved withdrawal arrangement; and

(c)   if such a replacement of the second arrangement or subsequent replacement occurs, references in sub-paragraph (3)(b) to the replacing arrangement are references to the latest replacing arrangement.

Notifiable events

5   (1) Where an approved withdrawal arrangement is in force in relation to a scheme, each relevant person must give notice to the Authority if such an event as is mentioned in sub-paragraph (3) occurs in relation to that person.

(2) For the purposes of this paragraph each of the guarantors is a relevant person.

(3) The following are the events referred to in sub-paragraph (1)—

(a) any decision by the relevant person to take action which will, or is intended to, result in a debt which is or may become due—

   (i) to the trustees of the scheme, or

   (ii) if the Board of the Pension Protection Fund has assumed responsibility for the scheme in accordance with Chapter 3 of Part 2 of the 2004 Act, to the Board,

   not being paid in full;

(b) a decision by the relevant person to cease to carry on business (including any trade or profession) in the United Kingdom or, if the relevant person ceases to carry on such business without taking such a decision, his doing so;

(c) where applicable, receipt by the relevant person of advice that the person is trading wrongfully within the meaning of section 214 of the Insolvency Act 1986 (wrongful trading), or circumstances occurring in which a director or former director of the company knows that there is no reasonable prospect that the company will avoid going into insolvent liquidation within the meaning of that section, and for this purpose section 214(4) of that Act applies;

(d) any breach by the relevant person of a covenant in an agreement between the relevant person and a bank or other institution providing banking services, other than where the bank or other institution agrees with the relevant person not to enforce the covenant;

(e) any change in the relevant person's credit rating, or the relevant person ceasing to have a credit rating;

(f) where the relevant person is a company, a decision by a controlling company to relinquish control of the relevant person or, if the controlling company relinquishes such control without taking such a decision, its doing so;

(g) two or more changes in the holders of any key relevant person posts within a period of 12 months;

(h) where the relevant person is a company or partnership, the conviction of an individual, in any jurisdiction, for an offence involving dishonesty, if the offence was committed while the individual was a director or partner of the relevant person;

(i) an insolvency event occurring in relation to the relevant person for the purposes of Part 2 of the 2004 Act (see section 121 of that Act: insolvency event, insolvency date and insolvency practitioner).

(4) A notice under sub-paragraph (1) must be given in writing as soon as reasonably practicable after the relevant person becomes aware of the event.

(5) No duty to which a relevant person is subject is to be regarded as contravened merely because of any information or opinion contained in a notice under this paragraph.

(6) But sub-paragraph (5) does not require any person to disclose protected items within the meaning of section 311 of the 2004 Act (protected items).

(7) Section 10 of the 1995 Act (civil penalties) applies to any relevant person who without reasonable excuse fails to comply with an obligation imposed on him under this paragraph.

(8) In this paragraph—

"control" has the meaning given in section 435(10) of the Insolvency Act 1986 (meaning of "associate" – meaning of "control") and "controlling company" is to be read accordingly;

"director" has the meaning given in section 741(1) of the Companies Act 1985 (meaning of "director" and "shadow director");

"key relevant person posts" means the Chief Executive and any director or partner responsible in whole or in part for the financial affairs of the relevant person.]

NOTES

Amendment

Inserted by SI 2005/2224, reg 2(5), Schedule.

Date in force: 2 September 2005 (except in relation to an employment-cessation event occuring before that date): see SI 2005/2224, reg 1(2), (3).

[SCHEDULE 1B
Form of Actuary's Certificate: Scheme Funding Basis Debts in Approved Withdrawal Arrangement Cases]

NOTES

Amendment

Inserted by SI 2005/2224, reg 2(5), Schedule.

Date in force: 2 September 2005 (except in relation to an employment-cessation event occuring before that date): see SI 2005/2224, reg 1(2), (3).

[Actuarial Certificate Given for the Purposes of Regulation 7A(6) of the Occupational Pension Schemes (Employer Debt) Regulations 2005

Name of scheme

1 Comparison of value of scheme assets with amount of scheme liabilities

In my opinion, at the above date the value of the assets of the scheme was less than the amount of the liabilities of the scheme.

The value of the assets of the scheme was

The amount of the liabilities was

The amount of the difference was

2 The scheme's assets and liabilities are valued in accordance with regulation 5 of the Occupational Pension Schemes (Employer Debt) Regulations 2005, subject to the modifications specified in regulation 7A(4) of those Regulations, and the guidelines on winding up and scheme asset deficiency (GN19) and on minimum funding requirement (GN27) prepared and published by the Institute of Actuaries and the Faculty of Actuaries (so far as those guidelines are applicable)

Signature	Date
Name	Qualification
Address	Name of employer (if applicable)
Note:	

The valuation of the amount of the liabilities of the scheme may not reflect the actual cost of securing those liabilities by the purchase of annuities if the scheme were to have been wound up on the date as at which the valuation is made.]

NOTES

Amendment

Inserted by SI 2005/2224, reg 2(5), Schedule.

Date in force: 2 September 2005 (except in relation to an employment-cessation event occuring before that date): see SI 2005/2224, reg 1(2), (3).

See Further

See further, in relation to the continued application of the reference "minimum funding requirement" to a scheme on or after 6 April 2007, notwithstanding the repeal of that definition by the Pensions Act 2004, s 320, Sch 13, Pt I and SI 2006/2272, arts 2, 3.

SCHEDULE 2
Consequential Amendments

Regulation 18

...

1 ...

The Occupational Pension Schemes (Winding Up) Regulations 1996

2 In regulation 10(2) of [the Occupational Pension Schemes (Winding Up) Regulations 1996] for "relevant insolvency event" and "subsection (4) of section 75 (definition of relevant insolvency events)" substitute "relevant event" and "subsection (6A) of section 75 (definition of relevant events)" respectively.

...

3   ...

NOTES

Initial Commencement

Specified date

Specified date: 6 April 2005: see reg 1(2).

Amendment

Para 1: revoked by SI 2005/3377, reg 21, Sch 5.

Date in force: 30 December 2005: see SI 2005/3377, reg 1; for transitional and savings provisions see reg 20(2), Sch 4 thereto.

Para 2: words "the Occupational Pension Schemes (Winding Up) Regulations 1996" in square brackets substituted by SI 2005/2224, reg 4(3).

Date in force: 2 September 2005: see SI 2005/2224, reg 1(2).

Para 3: revoked by SI 2005/3378, reg 18, Schedule.

Date in force: 30 December 2005: see SI 2005/3378, reg 1(1).

The Occupational Pension Schemes (Levies) Regulations 2005

SI 2005 No 842

Occupational Pension Schemes (Levies) Regulations 2005

Made 17th March 2005

Coming into force 1st April 2005

Whereas a draft of this instrument was laid before Parliament in accordance with section 316(2)(a), (c) and (g) of the Pensions Act 2004 and approved by resolution of each House of Parliament;

The Secretary of State for Work and Pensions, in exercise of the powers conferred upon him by sections 117(1), (3) and (7)(a), 126(1)(b), 174(1), (2), 181(5), (8)(a), 189(11)(a), 209(7) and (8), 315(2), (4) and (5) and 318(1) of the Pensions Act 2004 and of all other powers enabling him in that behalf, having consulted the Board, and with the approval of the Treasury, by this instrument, which is made before the end of the period of six months beginning with the coming into force of the provisions of that Act by virtue of which it is made, hereby makes the following Regulations:

PART I
PRELIMINARY

1   Citation, commencement and extent

(1)   These Regulations may be cited as the Occupational Pension Schemes (Levies) Regulations 2005.

(2)   These Regulations come into force on 1st April 2005.

(3)   These Regulations extend to England and Wales and Scotland.

> **NOTES**
> **Initial Commencement**
> *Specified date*
> Specified date: 1 April 2005: see para (2) above.

2   Interpretation

In these Regulations——

"the 1993 Act" means the Pension Schemes Act 1993;

"the 1995 Act" means the Pensions Act 1995;

"the 2004 Act" means the Pensions Act 2004;

"active member", in relation to a scheme, has the meaning given by section 318 of the 2004 Act (but subject to regulation 10(7));

"the administration levy" means the levy imposed under section 117 of the 2004 Act by regulation 4(1);

"deferred member" has the meaning given by section 124(1) of the 1995 Act (but subject to regulation 10(7));

"eligible scheme" has the meaning given by section 126 of the 2004 Act (but subject to regulations 15 to 18);

"financial year" means a period of 12 months ending with 31st March;

"the initial levy" means the levy imposed under section 174 of the 2004 Act by regulation 9;

"the initial period" means the period provided for by regulation 8;

"life member", in relation to a scheme, means a person who is an active member but whose service under the scheme is only pensionable service by virtue of qualifying him for death benefits;

"member", in relation to a scheme, has the meaning given by section 318 of the 2004 Act (but subject to regulations 5(6) and 11(4));

"the PPF Ombudsman levy" means the levy imposed under section 209(7) of the 2004 Act by regulation 4(2);

"pension credit member" has the meaning given by section 124(1) of the 1995 Act;

"pension credit rights" has the meaning given by section 124(1) of the 1995 Act;

"pension protection levy" means a levy imposed in accordance with section 175 of the 2004 Act;

"pensionable service" has the meaning given by section 124(1) of the 1995 Act;

"pensioner member" has the meaning given by section 124(1) of the 1995 Act;

"registrable scheme" has the meaning given by section 59(2) of the 2004 Act and regulations made under that section;

"scheme year", in relation to a scheme, means—

    (a)   a year specified for the purpose of the scheme in any document comprising the scheme or, if none, a period of 12 months beginning on 1st April or on such other date as the trustees or managers select; or

    (b)   such other period (if any) exceeding 6 months but not exceeding 18 months as is selected by the trustees or managers—

        (i)   in connection with the commencement or termination of the scheme; or

        (ii)   in connection with a variation of the date on which the year or period referred to in paragraph (a) is to begin.

NOTES

Initial Commencement

Specified date

Specified date: 1 April 2005: see reg 1(2).

PART 2
ADMINISTRATION AND PPF OMBUDSMAN LEVIES

3   Meaning of "the levies" in Part 2

In this Part "the levies" means the administration levy and the PPF Ombudsman levy.

NOTES

Initial Commencement

Specified date

Specified date: 1 April 2005: see reg 1(2).

4   Liability for the levies

(1) The trustees or managers of each eligible scheme are liable to pay a levy ("the administration levy") to the Secretary of State in respect of the scheme for the purpose of meeting—

(a)   expenditure of the Secretary of State relating to the establishment of the Board;

(b)   any expenditure of the Secretary of State under section 116 of the 2004 Act.

(2) The trustees or managers of each eligible scheme are liable to pay a levy ("the PPF Ombudsman levy") to the Secretary of State in respect of the scheme for the purpose of meeting expenditure of the Secretary of State under section 209(6) of the 2004 Act.

(3) Subject to paragraph (4), the levies are payable in respect of each financial year.

(4) The PPF Ombudsman levy is not payable in respect of the financial [years] ending with 31st March 2006 [and 31st March 2007].

(5) The levies in respect of a financial year are payable on the first day of that year, unless paragraph (6) applies.

(6) If a scheme is not an eligible scheme on that day but becomes such a scheme during the financial year, the levies are payable on the day after that on which that year ends.

NOTES
Initial Commencement
Specified date
Specified date: 1 April 2005: see reg 1(2).
Amendment
Para (4): word "years" in square brackets substituted by SI 2006/935, reg 2(1), (2)(a).
Date in force: 1 April 2006: see SI 2006/935, reg 1(1).
Para (4): words "and 31st March 2007" in square brackets inserted by SI 2006/935, reg 2(1), (2)(b).
Date in force: 1 April 2006: see SI 2006/935, reg 1(1).

5   The reference day

(1) The amount of each of the levies payable for a financial year ("the levy year") in respect of a scheme is calculated by reference to the number of the scheme's members on the reference day.

(2) In the case of a scheme established on or before 31st March 2005, for the levy [year] beginning on 1st April 2005 ..., the reference day is 31st March 2005.

(3) In the case of a scheme established on or after 1st April 2005, for the levy [year] beginning on 1st April 2005 ..., the reference day is the date on which the scheme becomes a registrable scheme.

(4) For a levy year beginning on or after [1st April 2006] the general rule is that the reference day for a scheme is the last day of the scheme year which ended before the beginning of the previous levy year.

(5) But if the scheme was established too late to have such a scheme year, the reference day is the date on which the scheme becomes a registrable scheme.

(6) In this regulation and regulation 6 "member", in relation to a scheme, does not include a life member of the scheme, unless he—

(a)   is a pensioner or pension credit member of the scheme, or

(b)   would be a deferred member if he were not an active member.

NOTES
Initial Commencement
Specified date
Specified date: 1 April 2005: see reg 1(2).
Amendment
Para (2): word "year" in square brackets substituted by SI 2006/935, reg 2(1), (3)(a)(i).
Date in force: 1 April 2006: see SI 2006/935, reg 1(1).
Para (2): words omitted revoked by SI 2006/935, reg 2(1), (3)(a)(ii).
Date in force: 1 April 2006: see SI 2006/935, reg 1(1).
Para (3): word "year" in square brackets substituted by SI 2006/935, reg 2(1), (3)(a)(i).
Date in force: 1 April 2006: see SI 2006/935, reg 1(1).
Para (3): words omitted revoked by SI 2006/935, reg 2(1), (3)(a)(ii).
Date in force: 1 April 2006: see SI 2006/935, reg 1(1).
Para (4): words "1st April 2006" in square brackets substituted by SI 2006/935, reg 2(1), (3)(b).
Date in force: 1 April 2006: see SI 2006/935, reg 1(1).

6   The amount payable

(1) In the case of the administration levy, the amount payable for a financial year in respect of a scheme with the number of members on the reference day that is specified in column 1 of the table for that levy for that year is—

(a)   the amount specified for such a scheme in column 2 of the table (where M is the number of the scheme's members on the reference day); or

(b)   if no amount is so specified or an amount which is greater is specified for such a scheme in column 3 of the table, that amount.

(2) This is the table for the administration levy for the financial [years] ending with 31st March 2006 [and 31st March 2007]—

Column 1	Column 2	Column 3
Number of members on the reference day	*Amount of levy calculated by reference to number of members (M)*	*Minimum amount of levy*
2 to 11		£24
12 to 99	£2.50 x M	
100 to 999	£1.80 x M	£250
1,000 to 4,999	£1.40 x M	£1,800
5,000 to 9,999	£1.06 x M	£7,000
10,000 or more	£0.74 x M	£10,600

(3) If, in any case where the reference day is determined in accordance with regulation 5(2) (31st March 2005), the number of members of the scheme on that day differs from the number according to the register compiled and maintained under regulations made under section 6 of the 1993 Act, the number according to that register is to be taken as the number on that day for the purposes of these Regulations.

(4) For schemes that are eligible schemes for only part of the financial year, see regulation 7.

NOTES

Initial Commencement

Specified date

Specified date: 1 April 2005: see reg 1(2).

Amendment

Para (2): word "years" in square brackets substituted by SI 2006/935, reg 2(1), (4)(a).

Date in force: 1 April 2006: see SI 2006/935, reg 1(1).

Para (2): words "and 31st March 2007" in square brackets inserted by SI 2006/935, reg 2(1), (4)(b).

Date in force: 1 April 2006: see SI 2006/935, reg 1(1).

7 Schemes eligible for only part of the financial year

(1) This regulation applies if a scheme that is not an eligible scheme at the beginning of a financial year becomes such a scheme during that year.

(2) The amount of each of the levies payable in respect of the scheme for that year is such proportion of the full amount so payable as the period beginning with the date on which it becomes such a scheme and ending with the financial year bears to the whole financial year.

NOTES

Initial Commencement

Specified date

Specified date: 1 April 2005: see reg 1(2).

PART 3
THE INITIAL LEVY

8 The initial period

For the purposes of section 174(1) of the 2004 Act the period for which the initial levy is imposed begins with 6th April 2005; and accordingly the initial period begins with that date and ends with 31st March 2006.

NOTES

Initial Commencement

Specified date

Specified date: 1 April 2005: see reg 1(2).

9 Liability for the initial levy

(1) The trustees or managers of each eligible scheme are liable to pay the initial levy to the Board in respect of the scheme for the initial period.

(2) The initial levy is payable on 6th April 2005.

(3) Paragraph (2) is subject to paragraphs (4) to (7).

(4) If the amount of the initial levy in respect of a scheme is not notified under section 181(3)(c) of the 2004 Act to the person liable to pay it before the day on which it would (apart from this paragraph) be payable, the levy is payable within the period of 28 days beginning with the date on which the notification is given or, if earlier, on 31st March 2006.

(5) If, on an application to the Board by trustees or managers who are liable to pay the initial levy to the Board in respect of a scheme, the Board considers that it is appropriate to do so in view of any exceptional circumstances that apply in relation to the scheme, it may agree to accept payment of the initial levy by instalments and, if it does so—

(a)   the first instalment is payable as mentioned in paragraph (2) or, as the case may be, paragraph (4); and

(b)   any subsequent instalment is payable at such later time or times during the initial period as are notified under section 181(3)(c) of the 2004 Act to the person liable to pay the levy.

(6) If the Board requires the Regulator to discharge its functions under section 181(3)(c) on the Board's behalf, the reference to the Board in paragraph (5) is to be taken as a reference to the Regulator.

(7) If—

(a)   on 6th April 2005 a scheme is not an eligible scheme; but

(b)   it becomes such a scheme during the initial period,

then, subject to paragraphs (4) and (5), the initial levy in respect of the scheme is payable on 31st March 2006.

> **NOTES**
> **Initial Commencement**
> *Specified date*
> Specified date: 1 April 2005: see reg 1(2).

10   The amount of the initial levy

(1) The amount of the initial levy payable in respect of a scheme is calculated by reference to the number of persons appearing to the Board or, if the Board requires the Regulator to discharge its functions under section 181(3)(b) on the Board's behalf, to the Regulator, to fall within paragraphs (3), (4) and (5) on the reference day.

(2) In paragraph (1) "the reference day" means—

(a)   in the case of a scheme that was established on or before 31st March 2005, that day; and

(b)   otherwise, the date on which the scheme becomes a registrable scheme.

(3) For each active member of the scheme, £15 is payable.

(4) For—

(a)   each pensioner member of the scheme;

(b)   each pension credit member who by reason of rights under the scheme attributable (directly or indirectly) to a pension credit is entitled to the present payment of pension; and

(c)   each other person who is entitled to the present payment of pension by reason of rights under the scheme in respect of a deceased member,

£15 is payable.

(5) For—

(a)   each deferred member of the scheme; and

(b)   each pension credit member who is not entitled to present payment of a pension as a result of his pension credit rights,

£5 is payable.

(6) If a person falls within more than one paragraph in this regulation or within more than one sub-paragraph in a paragraph, a separate amount is payable under this regulation in respect of that person as a result of his falling within each of those paragraphs or, as the case may be, sub-paragraphs.

(7) For the purposes of this regulation, a person is not regarded as an active member of a scheme if he is a life member of the scheme; and such a person is not excluded from being a deferred member by reason only of being an active member.

> **NOTES**
> **Initial Commencement**
> *Specified date*
> Specified date: 1 April 2005: see reg 1(2).

11   Supplementary provisions relating to the calculation of the initial levy

(1) If, in the case of a scheme that was established on or before 31st March 2005, the Board is unable on or before 6th April 2005 to determine the number of persons falling within paragraphs (3) to (5) of regulation 10 on the reference day (as defined in regulation 10(2)(a)), it is to be assumed for the purposes of regulation 10 that on that day—

(a)   all the members of the scheme were active members; and

(b)   there were no persons falling within paragraph (4)(c) of that regulation.

(2) If the Board requires the Regulator to discharge its functions under section 181(3)(b) on the Board's behalf, the reference in paragraph (1) to the Board includes a reference to the Regulator.

(3) In the case of a scheme that was established on or after 1st April 2005, it is to be assumed for the purposes of regulation 10 that on the reference day—

(a)   all the members of the scheme were active members; and

(b)   there were no persons falling within paragraph (4)(c) of that regulation.

(4) If by virtue of paragraph (7) of that regulation a person is not regarded as either an active or deferred member of the scheme for the purposes of that regulation, he is not regarded as a member of it for the purposes of paragraph (1)(a) or (3)(a) of this regulation.

(5) Nothing in paragraph (1) or (3) prevents a determination of the amount of the initial levy payable in respect of a scheme that is made on the basis of the assumption mentioned in that paragraph from being reviewed by virtue of Chapter 6 of Part 2 of the Act of 2004 (reviews, appeals and maladministration) on the ground that the assumption is in fact incorrect.

NOTES

Initial Commencement

Specified date

Specified date: 1 April 2005: see reg 1(2).

12   Schemes eligible for only part of the levy period

(1) This regulation applies where a scheme is an eligible scheme for only part of the period in respect of which the initial levy is payable.

(2) Section 181(5) of the 2004 Act (by virtue of which only a proportionate part of the levy is payable by such schemes) does not apply if the scheme ceases to be an eligible scheme during the period in question (and so the full amount of the initial levy is payable).

NOTES

Initial Commencement

Specified date

Specified date: 1 April 2005: see reg 1(2).

PART 4
GENERAL

13   Meaning of "the levies" in Part 4

(1) In this Part "the levies" means the administration levy, [the pension protection levy,] the PPF Ombudsman levy and the initial levy.

(2) But that is subject to regulation 14(3) [or, as the case may be, 15(7)].

NOTES

Initial Commencement

Specified date

Specified date: 1 April 2005: see reg 1(2).

Amendment

Para (1): words "the pension protection levy," in square brackets inserted by SI 2006/935, reg 2(1), (5)(a).

Date in force: 1 April 2006: see SI 2006/935, reg 1(1).

Para (2): words "or, as the case may be, 15(7)" in square brackets inserted by SI 2006/935, reg 2(1), (5)(b).

Date in force: 1 April 2006: see SI 2006/935, reg 1(1).

14 Attribution of payments in respect of levies

(1) This regulation applies where—

(a)   a payment is made in respect of a levy; and

(b)   it is not apparent to which of two or more of the levies the payment relates.

(2) The amount paid is to be apportioned between those two or more levies in the same proportions as the amounts outstanding in respect of each of them at the date the payment is made bear to the total amount outstanding in respect of both or, as the case may be, all of them at that date.

(3) In this regulation "the levies" includes ... any fraud compensation levy imposed by regulations under section 189 of the 2004 Act.

> **NOTES**
> **Initial Commencement**
> *Specified date*
> Specified date: 1 April 2005: see reg 1(2).
> **Amendment**
> Para (3): words omitted revoked by SI 2006/935, reg 2(1), (6).
> Date in force: 1 April 2006: see SI 2006/935, reg 1(1).

15 Multi-employer schemes

(1) If a scheme in relation to which there is more than one employer is divided into two or more sections and the provisions of the scheme are such that they meet conditions A and B, the provisions of these Regulations (apart from this regulation) apply as if each section of the scheme were a separate scheme.

(2) Condition A is that contributions payable to the scheme by an employer, or by a member in employment under that employer, are allocated to the section that applies to that employer or, if more than one section applies to the employer, to the section which is appropriate in respect of the employment in question.

(3) Condition B is that a specified part or proportion of the assets of the scheme is attributable to each section and cannot be used for the purposes of any other section.

(4) For the purposes of paragraph (1), any provisions of the scheme by virtue of which contributions or transfers of assets may be made to make provision for death benefits are disregarded.

(5) But if paragraph (1) applies and, by virtue of any provisions of the scheme, contributions or transfers of assets to make provision for death benefits are made to a section ("the death benefits section") the assets of which may only be applied for the provision of death benefits, the death benefits section is also to be treated as a separate scheme.

(6) For the purpose of this regulation, any provisions of the scheme by virtue of which assets attributable to one section may on the winding up of the scheme or a section be used for the purposes of another section are disregarded.

[(7) This regulation does not apply to any pension protection levy.]

> **NOTES**
> **Initial Commencement**
> *Specified date*
> Specified date: 1 April 2005: see reg 1(2).
> **Amendment**
> Para (7): inserted by SI 2006/935, reg 2(1), (7).
> Date in force: 1 April 2006: see SI 2006/935, reg 1(1).

16 Partially guaranteed schemes

(1) This regulation applies if a relevant public authority has—

(a)   given a guarantee in relation to any part of a scheme, any benefits payable under the scheme or any member of the scheme; or

(b)   made any other arrangements for the purposes of securing that the assets of the scheme are sufficient to meet any part of its liabilities.

(2) The provisions of these Regulations (apart from this regulation) apply as if the scheme did not include any part of the scheme—

(a)   in relation to which the guarantee has been given;

(b)   which relates to benefits payable under the scheme in relation to which the guarantee has been given; or

(c)   which relates to benefits payable under the scheme in relation to the liabilities for which those other arrangements have been made.

(3) In this regulation "relevant public authority" has the meaning given in section 307(4) of the 2004 Act.

> **NOTES**
> **Initial Commencement**
> *Specified date*
> Specified date: 1 April 2005: see reg 1(2).

17   Hybrid schemes

The provisions of these Regulations (apart from this regulation) apply in the case of any scheme that is a hybrid scheme (as defined in section 307(4) of the 2004 Act) as if the scheme did not include any part of the scheme relating to money purchase benefits.

> **NOTES**
> **Initial Commencement**
> *Specified date*
> Specified date: 1 April 2005: see reg 1(2).

18   Avoidance of double liability: schemes in Northern Ireland

(1) This regulation applies if, apart from paragraph (2), any of the levies would be payable in respect of a scheme in respect of which a corresponding Northern Ireland levy is imposed.

(2) The scheme is only an eligible scheme for the purposes of the levy in question if the address of the scheme is in Great Britain.

(3) For this purpose the address of the scheme is the place in the United Kingdom at which the management of the scheme is conducted or, if there is more than one such place, the principal such place.

(4) For the purposes of paragraph (1), a levy is a corresponding Northern Ireland levy—

(a)   in the case of the administration levy, if it is imposed under any equivalent provision to regulation 4(1);

(b)   in the case of the PPF Ombudsman levy, if it is imposed under any equivalent provision to regulation 4(2)[;]

(c)   in the case of the initial levy, if it is imposed under any equivalent provision to regulation 9[; and

(d)   in the case of the pension protection levy, if it is imposed under any equivalent provision to section 175 of the 2004 Act].

> **NOTES**
> **Initial Commencement**
> *Specified date*
> Specified date: 1 April 2005: see reg 1(2).
> **Amendment**
> Para (4): in sub-para (b) semicolon in square brackets substituted by SI 2006/935, reg 2(1), (8)(a).
> Date in force: 1 April 2006: see SI 2006/935, reg 1(1).
> Para (4): sub-para (d) and word "; and" immediately preceding it inserted by SI 2006/935, reg 2(1), (8)(b).
> Date in force: 1 April 2006: see SI 2006/935, reg 1(1).

Appendix 11

The Occupational and Personal Pension Schemes (Pension Liberation) Regulations 2005

SI 2005 No 992

Occupational and Personal Pension Schemes (Pension Liberation) Regulations 2005

Made 30th March 2005

Laid before Parliament 6th April 2005

Coming into force 27th April 2005

1   Citation, commencement and interpretation

(1) These Regulations may be cited as the Occupational and Personal Pension Schemes (Pension Liberation) Regulations 2005 and shall come into force on 27th April 2005.

(2) In these Regulations—

"the 1993 Act" means the Pension Schemes Act 1993; and

"the 2004 Act" means the Pensions Act 2004.

(3) In these Regulations, unless otherwise specified, any reference to a numbered section is a reference to the section bearing that number in the 1993 Act.

> NOTES
>
> **Initial Commencement**
>
> *Specified date*
>
> Specified date: 27 April 2005: see para (1) above.

2   Modification of references to "transfer" in the 1993 Act

(1) In their application to cases where an order is made under section 19(6) or 21(2)(b) of the 2004 Act (pension liberation: court's power to order restitution and restraining orders), the provisions referred to in this regulation and in regulation 3 shall have effect with the modifications there specified.

(2) The reference to "a transfer payment" in the relevant provisions shall be modified so as to have effect as though that reference included a reference to—

(a)   property or money transferred by virtue of an order made by a court under section 19(4) of the 2004 Act and applied in accordance with directions contained in an order made by virtue of section 19(6) of that Act; or

(b)   money paid by virtue of an order made by the Regulator under section 21(2)(a) of the 2004 Act and applied in accordance with directions contained in an order made by virtue of section 21(2)(b) of that Act.

(3) The "relevant provisions" referred to in paragraph (2) are sections 10, 68A and 71 (protected rights and money purchase benefits; safeguarded rights; basic principle as to short service benefit), and any regulations made under any of those sections.

(4) Paragraph (6) shall cease to have effect when paragraph 31 of Schedule 12 to the 2004 Act (consequential amendment to the 1993 Act) comes into force.

(5) Paragraph (7) shall have effect from the coming into force of paragraph 31 of Schedule 12 to the 2004 Act.

(6) In relation to the reference to "transfer credits" in sections 56, 73 and 75 (provisions supplementary to section 55; form of short service benefit and its alternatives; credits), and any regulations made under any of those sections, the definition of "transfer credits" in section 181(1) shall be modified so as to apply as if there were added at the end—

"or by reference to a transfer or payment made by virtue of an order under section 19(4) or 21(2)(a) of the Pensions Act 2004 (c 35) which the trustees or managers have been directed to apply, pro rata, as though it were a transfer of his accrued rights from another scheme;".

(7) In relation to the reference to "transfer credits" in sections 56, 73 and 75, and any regulations made under any of those sections, the definition of "transfer credits" in section 181(1) shall be modified so as to apply as if there were added at the end—

"or

(c)   a transfer or payment made by virtue of an order under section 19(4) or 21(2)(a) of the Pensions Act 2004 (c 35) which the trustees or managers have been directed to apply, pro rata, as though it were a transfer of his accrued rights from another scheme;".

(8) The references in subsections (1)(a)(i) and (b) and (3) of section 179 (linked qualifying service), and any regulations made under that section, to a transfer of rights accrued under one scheme to a second scheme shall be modified so as to have effect as if they included a transfer or payment made by virtue of an order under section 19(4) or 21(2)(a) of the 2004 Act which the trustees or managers of the second scheme have been directed to apply, pro rata, as though it were a transfer of accrued rights from the first scheme.

(9) From the coming into force of paragraph 30 of Schedule 12 to the 2004 Act (consequential amendment to the 1993 Act), the modification of section 179, and any regulations made under that section, made in paragraph (8) above shall also apply to references in subsection (1)(a)(i) and (iii) and (b) of that section, and in any such regulations, to a transfer payment made in respect of accrued rights to the second scheme or to the trustees or managers of that scheme, and to a cash equivalent or cash transfer sum paid in respect of the member to the trustees or managers of the second scheme.

NOTES

Initial Commencement

Specified date

Specified date: 27 April 2005: see reg 1(1).

3   Modification of statutory discharges in the 1993 Act

(1) Section 99(1) (trustees' duties after exercise of option-discharge) shall be modified so as to have effect as if there were inserted after paragraph (b)—

"and

(c)   the trustees or managers of the scheme have taken all reasonable steps to ensure that, where the member requires them to use the cash equivalent in one of the ways specified in section 95(2)(a) or (b) or, as the case may be, section 95(3)(a) or (b) (ways of taking right to cash equivalent), the occupational pension scheme or, as the case may be, the personal pension scheme to which the payment is to be made is a scheme whose trustees or managers are acting in good faith in relation to the scheme,".

(2) Section 101M (effect of transfer on trustees' duties) shall be modified so as to have effect as if the reference to compliance with a transfer notice included a duty to take all reasonable steps to ensure that where such compliance involved making a payment to an eligible scheme as defined in section 101F(6) (power to give transfer notice – meaning of "eligible scheme"), that scheme is a scheme whose trustees or managers are acting in good faith in relation to the scheme.

(3) From the coming into force of section 264 of the 2004 Act (early leavers: cash transfer sums and contribution refunds), section 101AG(3) (duties of trustees or managers following exercise of right) shall be modified so as to have effect as if after the words "carry out that requirement" there were inserted the words "and have taken all reasonable steps to ensure that where the member has opted for one of the permitted ways of using the cash transfer sum set out in section 101AE(2)(a) or (b) (permitted ways of using cash transfer sum), that scheme to whose trustees or managers the payment is made is a scheme whose trustees or managers are acting in good faith in relation to the scheme".

NOTES

Initial Commencement

Specified date

Specified date: 27 April 2005: see reg 1(1).

The Financial Assistance Scheme Regulations 2005

SI 2005 No 1986

Financial Assistance Scheme Regulations 2005

Made 19th July 2005

Coming into force in accordance with regulation 1

PART I
GENERAL

I   Citation, commencement and extent

(1) These Regulations may be cited as the Financial Assistance Scheme Regulations 2005 and shall come into force—

(a)   for the purposes of this regulation, regulation 4 and paragraphs 4, 5, 15 and 16 of Schedule 1 in so far as they relate to regulation 4, for the purpose only of the making of regulations, on the day after the day on which these Regulations are made;

(b)   in so far as these Regulations apply in relation to civil partnerships, on 5th December 2005; and

(c)   for all other purposes, on 1st September 2005.

(2) These Regulations extend to Northern Ireland.

>   **NOTES**
>   **Initial Commencement**
>   *Specified date*
>   Specified date (for certain purposes): 1 September 2005: see reg 1(1)(c).
>   Specified date (for remaining purposes): 5 December 2005: see reg 1(1)(b).

2   Interpretation

(1) In these Regulations—

"the Act" means the Pensions Act 2004 and references to a numbered section are, unless the context otherwise requires, to a section of the Act;

"the Northern Ireland Order" means the Pensions (Northern Ireland) Order 2005 and references to a numbered Article are, unless the context otherwise requires, to an Article of that Order;

"the 1993 Act" means the Pension Schemes Act 1993;

"the 1995 Act" means the Pensions Act 1995;

"the FSMA" means the Financial Services and Markets Act 2000;

"the ICTA" means the Income and Corporation Taxes Act 1988;

"the Commissioners of HMRC" means the Commissioners of Her Majesty's Revenue and Customs;

"annual payment" means the amount payable to a beneficiary in respect of each year determined in accordance with regulation 17 and Schedule 2;

"beneficiary" means a qualifying member or, after his death, his survivor;

"initial payment" means a payment made to a beneficiary in accordance with regulation 18;

"multi-employer scheme" and "relevant public authority" have the meanings given in section 307(4) or, as the case may be, Article 280(4);

"notification period" shall be construed in accordance with regulation 14(5)(b);

"qualifying member" shall be construed in accordance with regulation 15;

"qualifying pension scheme" shall be construed in accordance with regulation 9;

"scheme manager" shall be construed in accordance with regulation 5;

"survivor" means, in relation to a member [or former member] of a qualifying pension scheme who has died—

    (a)   the member's widow or widower; or

    (b)   the member's surviving civil partner,

but shall not include a person who comes within paragraph (a) or (b) but who is regarded as a qualifying member by virtue of regulation 15(5);

"tax approved scheme" means a scheme which is approved or was formerly approved under section 590 (conditions for approval of retirement benefit schemes) or 591 (discretionary approval) of the ICTA or in respect of which an application for such approval has been duly made but has not been determined;

"trustees or managers" shall be construed in accordance with the definition in section 124(1) of the 1995 Act,

and other expressions have the meaning given to them in the Act or, as the case may be, in the Northern Ireland Order.

(2) References in these Regulations to provisions of the 1993 Act, the 1995 Act, the Welfare Reform and Pensions Act 1999 and to the Social Security Contributions and Benefits Act 1992 include references to the provisions in force in Northern Ireland corresponding to those provisions.

(3) In these Regulations, "insurance company" means—

(a)   a person who has permission under Part 4 of the FSMA to effect or carry out contracts of long-term insurance; or

(b)   an EEA firm of the kind mentioned in paragraph 5(d) of Schedule 3 to that Act (certain direct insurance undertakings) which has permission under paragraph 15 of that Schedule (as a result of qualifying for authorisation under paragraph 12 of that Schedule) to effect or carry out contracts of long-term insurance,

and in this paragraph, "contracts of long-term insurance" means contracts which fall within Part 2 of Schedule 1 to the Financial Services and Markets Act 2000 (Regulated Activities) Order 2001.

(4) Paragraph (3) shall be read with—

(a)   section 22 of the FSMA (regulated activities);

(b)   any relevant order under that section; and

(c)   Schedule 2 to that Act.

(5) In these Regulations, "normal retirement age" means, subject to paragraph (6), in relation to a member of an occupational pension scheme, the age specified in the rules of that scheme at which that member will normally retire.

(6) Where the normal retirement age—

(a)   determined in accordance with paragraph (5) is more than 65, that age shall be 65;

(b)   cannot be determined in accordance with paragraph (5) from the rules of the qualifying pension scheme, that age shall be such age as the scheme manager shall determine having regard to the rules of that scheme and to such other information as he considers relevant.

(7) [Subject to paragraph (8), in these Regulations,] "appointed representative" means—

(a)   a person whose name, address and appointment by a beneficiary or by a person who believes himself to be a beneficiary ("[possible] beneficiary") for the purposes of—

    (i)   notifying the scheme manager of the details prescribed in regulation 14(1) and (3); or

    (ii)   receiving payments made under these Regulations,

have been notified to the scheme manager in a document signed by the beneficiary or [possible] beneficiary in question or by his legal representative and whose appointment has been consented to by the scheme manager; or

(b)   where a beneficiary or a [possible] beneficiary—

    (i)   dies; or

(ii)   is otherwise incapable of acting for himself,

and there is no person appointed under sub-paragraph (a) in respect of that beneficiary or [possible] beneficiary, a person who has been appointed by the scheme manager to act as the beneficiary's or the [possible] beneficiary's representative for the purposes of these Regulations.

[(8) If a beneficiary or a possible beneficiary appoints a person under sub-paragraph (a) of paragraph (7), and then—

(a)   dies, or

(b)   becomes otherwise incapable of acting for himself,

the person appointed under sub-paragraph (a) of that paragraph is deemed to have been appointed under sub-paragraph (b) of that paragraph.

(9) For the purposes of these Regulations, a person is "terminally ill" at any time if at that time he suffers from a progressive disease and his death, in consequence of that disease, can reasonably be expected within six months.]

NOTES

Initial Commencement

Specified date

Specified date (for certain purposes): 1 September 2005: see reg 1(1)(c).

Specified date (for remaining purposes): 5 December 2005: see reg 1(1)(b).

Amendment

Para (1): in definition "survivor" words "or former member" in square brackets inserted by SI 2005/3256, reg 4(1), (2)(a).

Date in force: 24 November 2005: see SI 2005/3256, reg 1(1).

Para (7): words "Subject to paragraph (8), in these Regulations," in square brackets substituted by SI 2005/3256, reg 4(1), (2)(b)(i).

Date in force: 24 November 2005: see SI 2005/3256, reg 1(1).

Para (7): in sub-para (a) word "possible" in square brackets in both places it occurs substituted by SI 2005/3256, reg 4(1), (2)(b)(ii).

Date in force: 24 November 2005: see SI 2005/3256, reg 1(1).

Para (7): in sub-para (b) word "possible" in square brackets in each place it occurs substituted by SI 2005/3256, reg 4(1), (2)(b)(ii).

Date in force: 24 November 2005: see SI 2005/3256, reg 1(1).

Paras (8), (9): inserted by SI 2005/3256, reg 4(1), (2)(c).

Date in force: 24 November 2005: see SI 2005/3256, reg 1(1).

3   Commencement of winding up

(1) For the purposes of these Regulations, the time when an occupational pension scheme begins to be wound up shall be determined in accordance with this regulation.

(2) Subject to paragraphs (3) to (6), where the rules of the scheme require or permit the scheme to be wound up and the scheme is wound up under those rules, the scheme begins to be wound up—

(a)   either—

(i)   at such time as the rules provide that it does so; or

(ii)   if the rules make no provision as to that time, at such time as the trustees or managers determine that the scheme shall begin to be wound up; or

(b)   as soon as there are no members who are in pensionable service under the scheme,

whichever is the later.

(3) Where the rules of the scheme require or permit the scheme to be wound up but the trustees or managers determine in pursuance of section 38 of the 1995 Act or otherwise that the scheme is not to be wound up for the time being, then for the purposes of paragraph (2), in so far as any provision made by the rules of the scheme as to the time when it begins to be wound up is inconsistent with the trustees' or managers' determination, that provision shall be disregarded.

(4) Where under the rules of the scheme, any person other than the trustees or managers may determine that the scheme is to be wound up, or is not to be wound up for the time being, then the references in paragraphs (2)(a)(ii) and (3) to the trustees' or managers' determination shall be taken, in a case where the winding up begins or is deferred by virtue of that other person's determination, as a reference to his determination.

(5) Paragraph (4) applies where such power is vested in the trustees or managers jointly with another person, or in some but not all of the trustees, as it applies where such a power is vested only in a person other than the trustees or managers.

(6) Where—

(a)   the scheme manager is satisfied that the scheme began to wind up during the period prescribed in regulation 9(1)(b); but

(b)   the exact date on which the scheme began to wind up cannot be determined,

the scheme begins to be wound up on such date, within that period, as the scheme manager determines.

(7) Where—

(a)   a scheme is wound up in pursuance—

    (i)   of an order by the Determinations Panel on behalf of the Regulator under section 11 of the 1995 Act (see section 9); or

    (ii)   of an order of a court; and

(b)   the order makes provision as to the time at which the scheme is to begin to be wound up,

the scheme begins to be wound up at the time specified in the order or, if none is so specified, the date on which the order takes effect.

NOTES
Initial Commencement
Specified date
Specified date (for certain purposes): 1 September 2005: see reg 1(1)(c).
Specified date (for remaining purposes): 5 December 2005: see reg 1(1)(b).

4   Application of Parts 1 and 2 of the Act

(1) The provisions of Parts 1 and 2 of the Act specified in paragraph (2) apply for the purposes of these Regulations with the modifications prescribed in Schedule 1.

(2) The specified provisions are—

(a)   section 68 (power for the Regulator to collect information relevant to the Board of the Pension Protection Fund);

(b)   section 85 (power to enable the Regulator to disclose restricted information to the Board);

(c)   section 168 (administration of compensation payable by the Board);

(d)   sections 190 to 204 (except section 202) (information gathering powers of the Board and provisions relating to disclosure of information by the Board); and

(e)   Schedule 8 (permitted disclosures by the Board to facilitate exercise of functions).

(3) Subject to paragraph (5), the provisions of Parts 1 and 2 of the Act which are applied by paragraph (1), shall apply to Northern Ireland for the purposes of these Regulations, with the prescribed modifications, as if those provisions extended to Northern Ireland.

(4) Section 88(4) shall also apply to Northern Ireland for the purposes of these Regulations as if that provision extended to Northern Ireland.

(5) Sections 197 to 201 and 203 shall apply to Northern Ireland only in so far as they relate to disclosure or provision of information—

(a)   by or to the scheme manager;

(b)   by any person who receives information directly or indirectly from the scheme manager;

(c)   by any person for the purpose of enabling or assisting the scheme manager to exercise his functions; and

(d)   by trustees or managers of occupational pension schemes in respect of matters relating to these Regulations.

(6) In so far as this regulation extends provisions to Northern Ireland—

(a)   a person may not be required under or by virtue of those provisions to produce, disclose or permit the inspection of protected items within the meaning given in section 311(2) to (4); and

(b)   if a person claims a lien on a document, its production under any provision made by, or by virtue of, those provisions, does not affect the lien.

NOTES

Initial Commencement

Specified date

Specified date (for the purpose of making regulations): 20 July 2005: see reg 1(1)(a).

Specified date (for certain purposes): 1 September 2005: see reg 1(1)(c).

Specified date (for remaining purposes): 5 December 2005: see reg 1(1)(b).

PART 2
ESTABLISHMENT OF THE FINANCIAL ASSISTANCE SCHEME

5 Scheme manager

(1) The financial assistance scheme established by these Regulations shall be managed by the Secretary of State.

(2) References in these Regulations—

(a)   to the scheme manager are to the Secretary of State acting in his capacity as manager of the financial assistance scheme;

(b)   to the Secretary of State are to the Secretary of State acting other than in that capacity.

NOTES

Initial Commencement

Specified date

Specified date (for certain purposes): 1 September 2005: see reg 1(1)(c).

Specified date (for remaining purposes): 5 December 2005: see reg 1(1)(b).

6 Funding

(1) Any payments which are required to be made in accordance with these Regulations shall be paid out of a fund which is held, managed and applied by the scheme manager ("the fund").

(2) The Secretary of State shall pay amounts into the fund out of monies provided by Parliament.

(3) The Secretary of State may pay other amounts into the fund where he—

(a)   is notified in writing that a person wishes to pay an amount into the fund;

(b)   is of the opinion that that amount can be paid into the fund; and

(c)   receives that amount.

NOTES

Initial Commencement

Specified date

Specified date (for certain purposes): 1 September 2005: see reg 1(1)(c).

Specified date (for remaining purposes): 5 December 2005: see reg 1(1)(b).

7 Annual reports

(1) The Secretary of State must prepare a report on the financial assistance scheme for each financial year.

(2) Each report must deal with the operation of the financial assistance scheme in the financial year for which it is prepared and in particular—

(a)   the number of persons who have received payments under these Regulations; and

(b)   the total amount of those payments.

(3) The Secretary of State must lay before each House of Parliament a copy of every report prepared by him under this regulation.

(4) In this regulation, "financial year" means—

(a)   the period beginning on 1st September 2005 and ending on 31st March 2006; and

(b)   each successive period of 12 months.

NOTES

Initial Commencement

Specified date

Specified date (for certain purposes): 1 September 2005: see reg 1(1)(c).

Specified date (for remaining purposes): 5 December 2005: see reg 1(1)(b).

8 Delegation

The scheme manager may make arrangements for any of his functions conferred by, or by virtue of, these Regulations to be exercised, in accordance with those arrangements, by a person on his behalf.

NOTES

Initial Commencement

Specified date

Specified date (for certain purposes): 1 September 2005: see reg 1(1)(c).

Specified date (for remaining purposes): 5 December 2005: see reg 1(1)(b).

PART 3
QUALIFYING PENSION SCHEMES

9 Qualifying pension schemes

(1) An occupational pension scheme shall be a qualifying pension scheme for the purposes of these Regulations where—

(a) immediately before the time when the scheme began to wind up, it was neither a money purchase scheme nor a scheme of a description prescribed in regulation 10;

(b) the scheme began to wind up during the period beginning on 1st January 1997 and ending on 5th April 2005;

(c) the employer in relation to that scheme satisfies the condition in regulation 11 or in relation to a multi-employer scheme, the condition in regulation 12 is satisfied; and

(d) the details prescribed in regulation 14 have been notified to the scheme manager by a person, in the form and manner and before the date prescribed in that regulation.

(2) The following shall be treated as separate schemes for the purposes of these Regulations—

(a) in relation to an occupational pension scheme which is not a tax approved scheme but contains one or more sections which, by virtue of section 611(3) of the ICTA (definition of "retirement benefits scheme"), are treated by the Commissioners of HMRC as a tax approved scheme, those sections which are so treated;

(b) sections of sectionalised multi-employer schemes as defined for the purposes of regulation 12,

and references in these Regulations to schemes shall be construed accordingly.

NOTES

Initial Commencement

Specified date

Specified date (for certain purposes): 1 September 2005: see reg 1(1)(c).

Specified date (for remaining purposes): 5 December 2005: see reg 1(1)(b).

10 Other schemes which are not qualifying pension schemes

The following are descriptions of schemes for the purposes of regulation 9(1)(a)—

(a) a public service pension scheme under the provisions of which there is no requirement for assets related to the intended rate or amount of benefit under the scheme to be set aside in advance (disregarding requirements relating to additional voluntary contributions);

(b) a scheme which is made under section 7 of the Superannuation Act 1972 or under Article 9 of the Superannuation (Northern Ireland) Order 1972 (superannuation of persons employed in local government service etc) and provides pensions to persons employed in local government service;

(c) a scheme which is made under section 2 of the Parliamentary and Other Pensions Act 1987 (power to provide for pensions for Members of the House of Commons etc);

(d)   a scheme which is established under section 48 of the Northern Ireland Act 1998 (pensions of members), or which was established under Part 2 of the Ministerial Salaries and Members' Pensions Act (Northern Ireland) 1965 or Article 3 of the Assembly Pensions (Northern Ireland) Order 1976;

(e)   a scheme in respect of which a relevant public authority has given a guarantee or made any other arrangements for the purposes of securing that the assets of the scheme are sufficient to meet its liabilities;

(f)   a scheme which provides relevant benefits within the meaning of section 612(1) of the ICTA but which is neither a tax approved scheme nor a relevant statutory scheme within the meaning of section 611A of that Act (definition of "relevant statutory scheme");

(g)   a scheme—

      (i)   which has been categorised before 18th April 2005, by the Commissioners of Inland Revenue, and on or after that date, by the Commissioners of HMRC, for the purposes of its approval as a centralised scheme for non-associated employers;

      (ii)   which is not contracted-out in accordance with section 9 of the 1993 Act; and

      (iii)   under the provisions of which the only benefits that may be provided on or after retirement (other than money purchase benefits derived from the payment of voluntary contributions by any person) are lump sum benefits which are not calculated by reference to a member's salary;

(h)   a scheme—

      (i)   the only benefits provided by which (other than money purchase benefits) are death benefits; and

      (ii)   under the provisions of which no member has accrued rights (other than rights to money purchase benefits);

(i)   a scheme with such a superannuation fund as is mentioned in section 615(6) of the ICTA (exemption from tax in respect of certain pensions);

(j)   a scheme which does not have its main place of administration registered in the United Kingdom;

(k)   a scheme with fewer than two members;

(l)   a scheme which is a small self-administered scheme for the purposes of the Retirement Benefits Schemes (Restriction on Discretion to Approve) (Small Self-administered Schemes) Regulations 1991 as in force on the day on which this regulation comes into force.

NOTES

Initial Commencement

Specified date

Specified date (for certain purposes): 1 September 2005: see reg 1(1)(c).

Specified date (for remaining purposes): 5 December 2005: see reg 1(1)(b).

11   Condition to be satisfied by employer

(1) The condition to be satisfied by the employer for the purposes of regulation 9(1)(c), where the scheme is not a multi-employer scheme, is that an insolvency event has occurred in relation to the employer on or before the last day of the notification period.

(2) The reference to the employer in paragraph (1)—

(a)   includes every person who employed persons in the description or category of employment to which the scheme relates or related immediately before the time when the scheme began to wind up; or

(b)   where the scheme had no active members immediately before the time it began to wind up, includes every person who employed persons in the description or category of employment to which the scheme relates or related immediately before the time at which the scheme ceased to have any active members.

NOTES

Initial Commencement

Specified date

Specified date (for certain purposes): 1 September 2005: see reg 1(1)(c).

Specified date (for remaining purposes): 5 December 2005: see reg 1(1)(b).

12 Condition to be satisfied: multi-employer schemes

(1) In relation to a section of a sectionalised multi-employer scheme, the condition to be satisfied for the purposes of regulation 9(1)(c) is that an insolvency event has occurred on or before the last day of the notification period—

(a)   in relation to the employer in that section;

(b)   where there is more than one employer in that section, in relation to the principal employer in that section; or

(c)   where there is more than one employer in that section and there is no principal employer in that section, in relation to all the employers participating in that section.

(2) In relation to a multi-employer scheme which is not a sectionalised multi-employer scheme, the condition to be satisfied for the purposes of regulation 9(1)(c) is that an insolvency event has occurred on or before the last day of the notification period—

(a)   in relation to the principal employer; or

(b)   where there is no principal employer, in relation to all the employers participating in the scheme.

(3) The references to the employer in paragraph (1) are—

(a)   to the person who employed persons in the description or category of employment to which the section of the scheme relates or related immediately before the time when the scheme began to wind up; or

(b)   where the scheme had no active members immediately before the time it began to wind up, to the person who was the employer of persons in the description or category of employment to which the section of the scheme relates or related immediately before the time when the scheme ceased to have any active members in relation to that section.

(4) The references to the employer in paragraph (2) are—

(a)   to the person who employed persons in the description or category of employment to which the scheme relates or related immediately before the time when the scheme began to wind up; or

(b)   where the scheme had no active members immediately before the time it began to wind up, to the person who was the employer of persons in the description or category of employment to which the scheme relates or related immediately before the time when the scheme ceased to have any active members in relation to it.

(5) The references to the principal employer in paragraphs (1)(b) and (c) and (2) are to the employer who was the principal employer immediately before the time when the scheme began to wind up.

(6) In this regulation—

"principal employer" means the employer who—

(a)   is the principal employer for the purposes of the scheme, or of a section of a sectionalised multi-employer scheme, in accordance with the rules of the occupational pension scheme; or

(b)   has power to act on behalf of all the employers in the scheme, or in a section of a sectionalised multi-employer scheme, in relation to the rules of that scheme;

"sectionalised multi-employer scheme" means a multi-employer scheme which is divided into two or more sections and the provisions of the scheme are such that—

(a)   different sections of the scheme apply or applied to different employers or groups of employers (whether or not more than one section applies or applied to any particular employer or groups including any particular employer);

(b)   any contributions payable or paid to the scheme by an employer, or by a member in employment under that employer, are allocated to that employer's section (or if more than one section applies or applied to the employer, to the section which is, or was, appropriate in respect of the employment in question); and

(c)   a specified part or proportion of the assets of the scheme is, or was, attributable to each section of the scheme and cannot or could not be used for the purpose of any other section of the scheme.

NOTES

Initial Commencement

Specified date

Specified date (for certain purposes): 1 September 2005: see reg 1(1)(c).

Specified date (for remaining purposes): 5 December 2005: see reg 1(1)(b).

13   Insolvency events

(1) "Insolvency event" shall, for the purposes of regulations 11 and 12, be interpreted in accordance with—

(a)   section 121(2) to (4) (other than subsection (3)(f) of that section); or

(b)   Article 105(2) to (4) and (12) (other than paragraph (3)(f) of that Article),

and the following provisions of this regulation.

(2) Where the employer in relation to an occupational pension scheme is a person specified in paragraph (3), an insolvency event shall be treated as having occurred in relation to that employer for the purposes of regulations 11 and 12 where the scheme manager is satisfied that—

(a)   that employer was unlikely to continue as a going concern; and

(b)   that situation applied to that employer on or before the last day of the notification period.

(3) The persons specified in this paragraph are—

(a)   a public body—

      (i)   in relation to which it is not possible for an insolvency event within the meaning of section 121 or Article 105 to occur; and

      (ii)   which is not the employer in relation to an occupational pension scheme in respect of which a relevant public authority has either—

          (aa)   given a guarantee in relation to any part of the scheme, any benefits payable under the scheme or any member of the scheme; or

          (bb)   made any other arrangements for the purposes of securing that the assets of the scheme are sufficient to meet any part of its liabilities;

(b)   a charity (as construed in accordance with the Charities Act 1993 or the Charities Act (Northern Ireland) 1964) which is not a company or other body corporate; or

(c)   a trade union within the meaning given in section 1 of the Trade Union and Labour Relations (Consolidation) Act 1992 or in Article 3(1) of the Industrial Relations (Northern Ireland) Order 1992 in relation to which it is not possible for an insolvency event within the meaning of section 121 or Article 105 to occur.

(4) An insolvency event also occurs for the purposes of regulations 11 and 12 where any of the following events occur on or before the last day of the notification period—

(a)   in relation to a company—

      (i)   where an administration order is made—

          (aa)   by the court in relation to the company under, or by virtue of any enactment which applies, Part 2 of the 1986 Act (administration orders) (with or without modification); or

          (bb)   by the High Court in relation to the company under, or by virtue of any statutory provision which applies, Part 3 of the Insolvency (Northern Ireland) Order (administration orders) (with or without modification);

      (ii)   where a resolution is passed for a voluntary winding up of the company with a declaration of solvency under section 89 of the 1986 Act or under Article 75 of the Insolvency (Northern Ireland) Order; or

      (iii)   where notice is published in the Gazette that the company has been struck off the register pursuant to section 652 or 652A of the Companies Act 1985 or Article 603 or 603A of the Companies (Northern Ireland) Order 1986;

(b)   in relation to a relevant body, where—

      (i)   any of the events referred to—

          (aa)   in section 121(3) occurs in relation to that body by virtue of the application (with or without modification) of any provision of the 1986 Act or by or under any other enactment; or

          (bb)   in Article 105(3) (insolvency events) occurs in relation to that body by virtue of the application (with or without modification) of any provision of the Insolvency (Northern Ireland) Order or by or under any other statutory provision; or

      (ii)   an administration order is made by the court in respect of the relevant body by virtue of any enactment which applies Part 2 of the 1986 Act or Part 3 of the Insolvency (Northern Ireland) Order (with or without modification);

(c) in relation to a limited liability partnership, where notice has been published in the Gazette that the partnership has been struck off the register pursuant to section 652 or 652A of the Companies Act 1985 or Article 603 or 603A of the Companies (Northern Ireland) Order 1986;

(d) in relation to a building society, where there is dissolution by consent of the members under section 87 of the Building Societies Act 1986 (dissolution by consent);

(e) in relation to a friendly society, where there is dissolution by consent of the members under section 20 of the Friendly Societies Act 1992 (dissolution by consent); and

(f) in relation to an industrial and provident society, where there is dissolution by consent of the members under section 58 of the Industrial and Provident Societies Act 1965 or section 67 of the Industrial and Provident Societies Act (Northern Ireland) 1969 (instrument of dissolution).

(5) In this regulation, a reference to Part 2 of the 1986 Act (administration orders) shall, in so far as it relates to a company or society listed in section 249(1) of the Enterprise Act 2002 (special administration regimes), have effect as if it referred to Part 2 of the 1986 Act as it had effect immediately before the coming into force of section 248 of the Enterprise Act 2002 (replacement of Part 2 of the 1986 Act).

(6) In this regulation—

"the 1986 Act" means the Insolvency Act 1986;

"the Insolvency (Northern Ireland) Order" means the Insolvency (Northern Ireland) Order 1989;

"administration order" means an order whereby the management of the company or relevant body, as the case may be, is placed in the hands of a person appointed by the court or, in Northern Ireland, by the High Court;

"the Gazette" means, in respect of companies or limited liability partnerships registered—

(a) in England and Wales, the London Gazette;

(b) in Scotland, the Edinburgh Gazette; or

(c) in Northern Ireland, the Belfast Gazette;

"public body" means a government department or any non-departmental public body established by—

(a) in relation to Great Britain, an Act of Parliament or by a statutory instrument made under an Act of Parliament to perform functions conferred on it under, or by virtue of, that Act or instrument or any other Act or instrument;

(b) in relation to Northern Ireland, a statutory provision to perform functions conferred on it under that statutory provision or any other such statutory provision;

"relevant body" means—

(a) a credit union within the meaning given in section 31(1) of the Credit Unions Act 1979 or Article 2(2) of the Credit Unions (Northern Ireland) Order 1985 (interpretation);

(b) a limited liability partnership within the meaning given in section 57(6) or Article 53(6) (partnerships and limited liability partnerships);

(c) a building society within the meaning given in section 119 of the Building Societies Act 1986 (interpretation);

(d) a person who has permission to act under Part 4 of the FSMA (permission to carry out regulated activities);

(e) the society of Lloyd's and Lloyd's members who have permission under Part 19 of the FSMA (Lloyd's);

(f) a friendly society within the meaning given in the Friendly Societies Act 1992; or

(g) a society which is registered as an industrial and provident society under the Industrial and Provident Societies Act 1965 or under the Industrial and Provident Societies Act (Northern Ireland) 1969;

"statutory provision" has the meaning given in section 1(f) of the Interpretation Act (Northern Ireland) 1954.

NOTES

Initial Commencement

Specified date

Specified date (for certain purposes): 1 September 2005: see reg 1(1)(c).

Specified date (for remaining purposes): 5 December 2005: see reg 1(1)(b).

14 Notification of details

(1) Where an occupational pension scheme is winding up, the prescribed details for the purposes of regulation 9(1)(d) are—

(a)   the name of the scheme;

(b)   the pension scheme registration number which is allocated to that scheme in the register;

(c)   the name (and if there has been a change of name, the previous name) and address of any employer of earners in employment to which the scheme relates or has related;

(d)   the name and address of at least one trustee of the scheme.

(2) The persons who may supply the details in paragraph (1) are—

(a)   any trustee of the scheme including a trustee appointed by the Regulator under section 7 or 23(1) of the 1995 Act;

(b)   a member of the scheme or his appointed representative;

(c)   a surviving spouse or civil partner of a member of the scheme who has died; or

(d)   any professional adviser in relation to the scheme.

(3) Where an occupational pension scheme has wound up, the prescribed details for the purposes of regulation 9(1)(d) are—

(a)   the name of the scheme; and

(b)   the name (and if there has been a change of name, the previous name) and address of any employer of earners in employment to which the scheme related.

(4) The persons who may supply the details in paragraph (3) are—

(a)   a former trustee or manager of the scheme;

(b)   a former member of the scheme or his appointed representative;

(c)   a surviving spouse or civil partner of a former member of the scheme who has died;

(d)   any former professional adviser in relation to the scheme; or

(e)   any insurance company which is paying annuities to former members of that scheme.

(5) The details in paragraphs (1) and (3) must—

(a)   be notified in writing; and

(b)   have been notified to the scheme manager—

  (i)   no earlier than 1st September 2005; but

  (ii)   by no later than 28th February 2006 or by no later than such later date by which the scheme manager has indicated that he may accept notification of those details in the case of any particular scheme.

NOTES

Initial Commencement

Specified date

Specified date (for certain purposes): 1 September 2005: see reg 1(1)(c).

Specified date (for remaining purposes): 5 December 2005: see reg 1(1)(b).

PART 4
QUALIFYING MEMBERS

15 Qualifying members

(1) A member or a former member of a qualifying pension scheme is a qualifying member of that scheme for the purposes of these Regulations where—

(a)   he is a member of the scheme in respect of whom that scheme's pension liabilities are unlikely to be satisfied in full because the scheme has insufficient assets; or

(b)   he had ceased to be a member of the scheme and in respect of whom that scheme's pension liabilities were not satisfied in full, at the time he ceased to be a member, because the scheme had insufficient assets,

and the conditions in paragraphs (2) to (4) are satisfied in relation to that member or former member.

(2) The condition in this paragraph is that the member or former member must have an accrued right to a benefit under the scheme.

(3) The condition in this paragraph is that the member or former member—

(a)   was a member of the qualifying pension scheme immediately before the scheme began to wind up; or

(b)   was not a member of the scheme at that time but became a pension credit member of the scheme on or after the day on which the scheme began to wind up.

(4) The condition in this paragraph is that the member or former member—

(a)   had attained his normal retirement age for the scheme of which he is or was a member as at 14th May 2004;

(b)   had not attained that age as at that date but would attain that age on or before 14th May 2007; or

(c)   had died before attaining that age but would have attained that age on or before 14th May 2007.

(5) A person who is not a member or a former member of a qualifying pension scheme is to be regarded as a qualifying member of such a scheme for the purposes of these Regulations where—

(a)   he was entitled to a present payment from a qualifying pension scheme immediately before the scheme began to wind up;

(b)   that payment was attributable to the pensionable service of a former member of that scheme who has died;

(c)   the scheme's pension liabilities in respect of that person are unlikely to be satisfied in full because the scheme has insufficient assets; and

(d)   that person, as at 14th May 2004—

(i)   had attained the normal retirement age for the member of that scheme in respect of whose pensionable service the payment from that scheme was attributable; or

(ii)   had not attained that age but would attain that age on or before 14th May 2007.

NOTES

Initial Commencement

Specified date

Specified date (for certain purposes): 1 September 2005: see reg 1(1)(c).

Specified date (for remaining purposes): 5 December 2005: see reg 1(1)(b).

16   Insufficient assets

(1) A scheme has or had insufficient assets for the purposes of regulation 15 if—

(a)   in relation to a scheme which is winding up, at any time during the period beginning immediately before the scheme began to wind up and ending immediately before the liabilities of the scheme were discharged; or

(b)   in relation to a scheme which has wound up, immediately before the liabilities of the scheme were discharged,

the assets of the scheme are, or were, insufficient to satisfy in full the liabilities of the scheme.

(2) The liabilities of the scheme which are to be taken into account for the purposes of paragraph (1) are the liabilities of the scheme estimated by reference to the scheme rules but disregarding—

(a)   any provision of the scheme rules which limits the amount of its liabilities by reference to the amount of its assets; and

(b)   any liabilities in respect of money purchase benefits.

(3) The amount or value of the liabilities referred to in paragraph (2) must be estimated on the assumption that the liabilities will be, or have been, discharged by the purchase of annuities of the kind described in section 74(3)(c) of the 1995 Act (discharge of liabilities: annuity purchase).

(4) The liabilities of the scheme which are to be taken into account under paragraph (2) include all expenses (except the cost of the annuities referred to in paragraph (3)) which—

(a)   in the opinion of the trustees or managers of the scheme, are likely to be incurred in connection with the winding up of the scheme; or

(b)   in the case of a wound up scheme, were so incurred.

Appendix 12

NOTES
Initial Commencement
Specified date
Specified date (for certain purposes): 1 September 2005: see reg 1(1)(c).
Specified date (for remaining purposes): 5 December 2005: see reg 1(1)(b).

PART 5
ANNUAL AND INITIAL PAYMENTS

17   Annual payments

(1) Schedule 2 makes provision for the determination of the amount of annual payments to be paid to, or in respect of, qualifying members of qualifying pension schemes including provision for—

(a)   a cap to be imposed on such amounts; and

(b)   an amount to be paid only where an amount determined under that Schedule is equal to, or exceeds, a specified amount.

(2) Except where paragraph (3) applies, a qualifying member of a qualifying pension scheme shall be entitled to an annual payment determined in accordance with Schedule 2 from—

(a)   14th May 2004; or

(b)   the day on which the qualifying member attains the age of 65,

whichever is the later.

(3) Where the scheme manager is satisfied that a qualifying member is terminally ill …, that member shall be entitled to an annual payment determined in accordance with Schedule 2 from the day on which the scheme manager is first notified that that member may be terminally ill.

(4) A survivor of a qualifying member of a qualifying pension scheme shall be entitled to an annual payment determined in accordance with Schedule 2 from—

(a)   14th May 2004; or

(b)   the day after the day on which that qualifying member died,

whichever is the later.

(5) The year in respect of which the annual payment is to be made shall be the year starting on the day on which a monthly instalment of the annual payment or, as the case may be, an initial payment, is first payable to a beneficiary by virtue of regulation 19 and in respect of subsequent years, on each anniversary of that day.

[(5A) In determining the amount of annual payment that is payable to, or in respect of, a beneficiary for any previous year or years ("arrears payable"), the total of all monthly instalments of an initial payment that have been made to, or in respect of, the beneficiary for any previous year or years is to be deducted from the amount of arrears payable to that beneficiary.

(5B) From the day after the day on which a beneficiary dies, any further monthly instalments of an annual payment that would have been payable to that beneficiary, in respect of that year, cease to be payable.]

(6) [Subject to paragraph (5B), annual] payments which are payable to a beneficiary under this Part shall continue for life.

[(7) Paragraphs 7 and 8 of Schedule 2 provide for the circumstances in which an annual payment is not payable under this Part.]

NOTES
Initial Commencement
Specified date
Specified date (for certain purposes): 1 September 2005: see reg 1(1)(c).
Specified date (for remaining purposes): 5 December 2005: see reg 1(1)(b).
Amendment
Para (3): words omitted revoked by SI 2005/3256, reg 4(1), (3)(a).
Date in force: 24 November 2005: see SI 2005/3256, reg 1(1).
Paras (5A), (5B): inserted by SI 2005/3256, reg 4(1), (3)(b).
Date in force: 24 November 2005: see SI 2005/3256, reg 1(1).
Para (6): words "Subject to paragraph (5B), annual" in square brackets substituted by SI 2005/3256, reg 4(1), (3)(c).
Date in force: 24 November 2005: see SI 2005/3256, reg 1(1).
Para (7): inserted by SI 2005/3256, reg 4(1), (3)(d).
Date in force: 24 November 2005: see SI 2005/3256, reg 1(1).

[18   Initial payments]

[(1) This regulation applies where a qualifying pension scheme is winding up and—

(a)   a qualifying member of that scheme—

    (i)   has attained the age of 64; or

    (ii)   has not attained that age, but the scheme manager—

        (aa)   has been notified that a qualifying member is terminally ill; and

        (bb)   is satisfied as to that fact; or

(b)   a qualifying member of that scheme has died and leaves a survivor.

(2) The trustees or managers of the scheme may make a written request to the scheme manager for a payment ("an initial payment") to be made to, or in respect of, a qualifying member or his survivor—

(a)   in anticipation of an annual payment being payable under this Part to the qualifying member or his survivor; and

(b)   before any monthly instalment of that annual payment is made.

(3) If a request for an initial payment is made in respect of a qualifying member who dies before any monthly instalment of an annual payment has been made to that qualifying member, the trustees or managers may make a further request that an initial payment be made in respect of any survivor of that qualifying member.

(4) On receipt of a request for an initial payment, the scheme manager may, in his discretion, make an initial payment—

(a)   to the qualifying member in respect of whom the request was made, with effect from whichever is the later of—

    (i)   14th May 2004; or

    (ii)   the day on which—

        (aa)   the qualifying member attains the age of 65, or

        (bb)   the scheme manager is first notified that the qualifying member is terminally ill,

    whichever is the earlier; or

(b)   if the qualifying member has died, to a survivor of that qualifying member with effect from whichever is the later of—

    (i)   14th May 2004; or

    (ii)   the day after the day on which that qualifying member died.

(5) In exercising his discretion under paragraph (4), the scheme manager may only have regard to—

(a)   the amount, if any, of any interim pension that was in payment, is in payment, or is proposed to be paid, from the qualifying pension scheme—

    (i)   to a qualifying member up until his death; or

    (ii)   after his death, to his survivor; and

(b)   any circumstances relating to the scheme which, in the opinion of the scheme manager, are relevant to determining whether an initial payment should be made.

(6) Schedule 2 makes provision for the determination of the amount of initial payments.

(7) If the scheme manager determines that an initial payment may be made under paragraph (4), the initial payment is payable—

(a)   to a qualifying member from the relevant day mentioned in that paragraph until the day on which that qualifying member—

    (i)   would have been paid, or is paid, the first monthly instalment of an annual payment in accordance with regulation 19, if an annual payment were payable, or is payable, to him under this Part; or

    (ii)   dies,

    whichever is the earlier; and

(b)   in respect of a qualifying member who has died, to a survivor of that qualifying member from the day after the day on which that qualifying member died until the day on which his survivor—

(i)   would have been paid, or is paid, the first monthly instalment of an annual payment in accordance with regulation 19, if an annual payment were payable, or is payable, to him under this Part; or

(ii)   dies,

whichever is the earlier.

(8) From the day after the day on which a beneficiary dies, any further monthly instalments of an initial payment that would have been payable to that beneficiary in respect of that year cease to be payable.

(9) The scheme manager may, at any time before the amount of the annual payment is determined, redetermine the amount of any initial payment paid under paragraph (4) if he is satisfied that the amount being paid by way of initial payment, as determined in accordance with Schedule 2, may be incorrect.

(10) In this regulation, "interim pension" has the meaning given by paragraph 2 of Schedule 2.]

NOTES
Amendment

Substituted by SI 2005/3256, reg 4(1), (4).

Date in force: 24 November 2005: see SI 2005/3256, reg 1(1).

PART 6
ADMINISTRATION OF PAYMENTS

19   Time and manner of payment: general provisions

(1) The scheme manager shall pay the annual payment or an initial payment to the beneficiary or to his appointed representative, in equal monthly instalments on the day of each month specified by the scheme manager for the making of such payments.

(2) For the purposes of paragraph (1), where the amount of a monthly instalment would, but for this paragraph, include a fraction of a penny, that fraction shall be disregarded if it is less than half a penny and shall otherwise be treated as a penny.

(3) The scheme manager shall start to pay the monthly instalments payable to a beneficiary on the first day specified in paragraph (1) which is as soon as reasonably practicable after the day on which—

(a)   the beneficiary becomes entitled to an annual payment under regulation 17(2) to (4); or

(b)   the scheme manager determines that an initial payment may be made under regulation [18(4)].

(4) Monthly instalments shall be paid by means of direct credit transfer or by such other means as appear to the scheme manager to be appropriate in the circumstances of any particular case.

NOTES
Initial Commencement

Specified date

Specified date (for certain purposes): 1 September 2005: see reg 1(1)(c).

Specified date (for remaining purposes): 5 December 2005: see reg 1(1)(b).

Amendment

Para (3): in sub-para (b) reference to "18(4)" in square brackets substituted by SI 2005/3256, reg 4(1), (5).

Date in force: 24 November 2005: see SI 2005/3256, reg 1(1).

20   Direct credit transfer

(1) Subject to paragraphs (3) and (4), monthly instalments under regulation 19 may, by an arrangement between the scheme manager and the beneficiary or his appointed representative, be paid by way of direct credit transfer into a bank or other account—

(a)   in the name of the beneficiary, his appointed representative or any other person with the consent of the beneficiary; or

(b)   in the joint names of the beneficiary and any other person or the appointed representative and any other person.

(2) Monthly instalments shall be paid in accordance with paragraph (1) within seven days of the day on which each instalment is payable under regulation 19(1).

(3) The scheme manager may make a particular payment by direct credit transfer otherwise than in accordance with paragraph (1) if it appears to him to be appropriate to do so for the purpose of paying any arrears.

(4) The arrangements under this regulation may be terminated—

(a)   by the beneficiary or his appointed representative, by notice in writing delivered or sent to the scheme manager; or

(b)   by the scheme manager if the arrangement seems to him to be no longer appropriate to the circumstances of the particular case.

(5) A direct credit transfer into the account of an appointed representative or of any person to whom an amount is paid with the consent of the beneficiary, shall be a good discharge to the scheme manager for any sum paid under these Regulations.

NOTES
Initial Commencement

Specified date

Specified date (for certain purposes): 1 September 2005: see reg 1(1)(c).

Specified date (for remaining purposes): 5 December 2005: see reg 1(1)(b).

SCHEDULE I
Modification of Certain Provisions of Parts I and 2 of the Act

Regulation 4(1)

1   In section 68 (power for the Regulator to collect information relevant to the Board of the Pension Protection Fund), for "the Board of the Pension Protection Fund", substitute "the scheme manager of the financial assistance scheme which are conferred on him by regulations made under, or by virtue of, section 286".

2   In section 85 (disclosure by the Regulator for facilitating the exercise of functions by the Board)—

(a)   for "Section 82 does not preclude" substitute "Neither section 82 nor Article 77 of the Pensions (Northern Ireland) Order 2005 precludes";

(b)   for the words "the Board of the Pension Protection Fund to exercise its functions", substitute "the scheme manager of the financial assistance scheme to exercise functions conferred on him by regulations made under or by virtue of section 286, and Part 2 of the Pensions (Northern Ireland) Order 2005 shall be read accordingly".

3   In section 88(4) (disclosure of tax information by the Regulator), after "subsection (3)" insert "or as mentioned in Article 83(3) of the Pensions (Northern Ireland) Order 2005".

4   In section 168 (administration of compensation payable by the Board)—

(a)   in subsection (1), for "this Chapter" substitute "the financial assistance scheme established by regulations under section 286";

(b)   for subsection (2), substitute—

"(2) Regulations under subsection (1) may, in particular, make provision—

(a)   for the recovery of amounts paid by the scheme manager of the financial assistance scheme in excess of entitlement;

(b)   specifying the circumstances in which payments from the financial assistance scheme can be suspended.";
and

(c)   omit subsection (3).

5   In section 190 (information to be provided to the Board etc)—

(a)   in subsection (1), for paragraphs (a) and (b), substitute—

"(a)   to the scheme manager, or

(b)   to a person—

(i)   with whom the scheme manager has made arrangements for any of his functions to be exercised on his behalf, and

(ii)   who is authorised by the scheme manager for the purposes of the regulations,"; and

(b)   in subsection (2), for "of entitlement to compensation under Chapter 3 of this Part" substitute "that a person is entitled to a payment from the financial assistance scheme".

6   In section 191 (notices requiring provision of information to the Board)—

(a)   in subsection (1)(b), for "the Board's" substitute "the scheme manager's";

(b)   in subsections (2) and (3), for "the Board", in each place, substitute "the scheme manager"; and

(c)   in subsection (3)—

    (i)   omit "and" at the end of paragraph (d);

    (ii)   after paragraph (d), insert—

"(da)   in the case of a wound up scheme, any insurance company (within the meaning in the Financial Assistance Scheme Regulations 2005) which is paying annuities to former members of the scheme, and"; and

    (iii)   in paragraph (e), for "the Board's" substitute "the scheme manager's".

7   In section 192 (entry of premises to enable performance of functions by the Board)—

(a)   for "the Board", in each place, substitute "the scheme manager";

(b)   in subsection (1)(f), for "the Board's" substitute "the scheme manager's"; and

(c)   in subsection (6), for "The Board" substitute "The scheme manager".

8   In section 194 (warrants to enforce entry of premises and obtaining of documents by, or on behalf, of the Board)—

(a)   for "the Board", in each place, substitute "the scheme manager";

(b)   omit in both places ", or any corresponding provision in force in Northern Ireland";

(c)   in subsection (1), after "information on oath" insert "or, in Northern Ireland, on complaint on oath";

(d)   in subsection (1)(b), for "the Board's" substitute "the scheme manager's";

(e)   in subsection (2)(a), after "the information" insert "or complaint"; and

(f)   in subsection (6), for "The Board" substitute "The scheme manager".

9   In section 195(1)(b) (offence of providing false or misleading information to the Board), for the words from "by the Board" to the end of that paragraph substitute "by the scheme manager for the purposes of exercising his functions.".

10   In section 196 (use of information by the Board)—

(a)   for "the Board", in each place, substitute "the scheme manager"; and

(b)   for "its functions", in each place, substitute "his functions".

11   In section 197 (restricted information)—

(a)   in subsections (1) and (3), after "the Board", in each place, insert "or the scheme manager";

(b)   in subsection (4), after "its functions" insert "or by the scheme manager in the exercise of his functions";

(c)   in subsection (6)(a), after "that section" insert " (disregarding any modifications of that section made by the Financial Assistance Scheme Regulations 2005)"; and

(d)   after subsection (6), insert—

"(6A) Information which—

(a)   is obtained under section 191 by a person authorised under subsection (2)(b) of that section, but

(b)   if obtained by the scheme manager, would be restricted information,

is treated for the purposes of subsections (1) and (3) and sections 198 to 201 and 203 as restricted information which the person has received from the scheme manager.".

12   In section 198 (disclosure by the Board of restricted information for facilitating exercise of functions by the Board)—

(a)   at the end of subsection (1), add "or the scheme manager to exercise his functions";

(b)   in subsection (2)—

(i)   after "its functions", insert "or the scheme manager properly to exercise any of his functions"; and

(ii)   after "the Board", in the second place, insert "or, as the case may be, the scheme manager"; and

(c)   in subsection (3)—

(i)   after "the Board", in both places, insert "or, as the case may be, the scheme manager"; and

(ii)   for "he" substitute "that person".

13   In section 200(1) (disclosure by the Board of restricted information for facilitating the exercise of functions by other supervisory authorities)—

(a)   after "the Board", in the first place, insert "or the scheme manager"; and

(b)   after "the Board", in the second place, insert "or, as the case may be, the scheme manager".

14   In section 201 (other permitted disclosures of restricted information by the Board)—

(a)   in subsection (1)—

(i)   after "the Board", in the first place, insert "or the scheme manager";

(ii)   after "the Board", in the second place, insert "or, as the case may be, the scheme manager";

(b)   in subsection (2), after "the Board", in both places, insert "or the scheme manager";

(c)   in subsection (2)(d), for "it has a right" substitute "the Board or the scheme manager has a right";

(d)   in subsection (8), for "with the consent of the Board" substitute—

"—

(a)   in a case where the disclosure under that subsection was made by the Board, with the consent of the Board, and

(b)   in a case where the disclosure under that subsection was made by the scheme manager, with his consent";

(e)   for subsection (9)(a), substitute—

"(a)   in a case where the disclosure under that subsection was made by the Board, with the consent of the Board,

(aa)   in a case where the disclosure under that subsection was made by the scheme manager, with his consent, and"; and

(f)   in subsection (10)—

(i)   after "its" insert "or his";

(ii)   after "the Board" insert "or, as the case may be, the scheme manager"; and

(iii)   after "it" insert "or him".

15   In section 203 (provision of information to members of schemes etc by the Board)—

(a)   in subsection (1), after "the Board" insert "or the scheme manager";

(b)   in subsections (3)(c), (5)(b) and (c) and (6)(c), after "the Board", in each place, insert "or, as the case may be, the scheme manager";

(c)   after "the Board's", in each place, insert "or the scheme manager's";

(d)   omit "or" at the end of subsection (1)(b)(ii) and insert after that sub-paragraph—

"(iia)   relating to any determination made in relation to the financial assistance scheme, or";

(e)   in subsection (2), after "Chapter 3" insert "or, as the case may be, to a payment from the financial assistance scheme";

(f)   in subsection (4)—

(i)   in paragraph (a), after "who is" insert "or was";

(ii)   in paragraph (b), after "member" insert "or former member"; and

(g)   after subsection (6)(a)(iv), insert—

"(v)   in the case of a wound up scheme, any insurance company (within the meaning in the Financial Assistance Scheme Regulations 2005) which is paying annuities to former members of the scheme,".

16   In section 204 (interpretation of sections 190 to 203)—

(a)   after subsection (2), insert—

"(2A) The "scheme manager" is the person who manages the financial assistance scheme.

(2B) The "financial assistance scheme" is the scheme established by regulations under section 286."; and

(b)   after subsection (3), add—

"(4) Where the scheme manager has functions in relation to a scheme which is wound up, any reference to a trustee, manager, professional adviser or employer in relation to the scheme is to be read as reference to a person who held that position in relation to the scheme before it wound up.".

NOTES

Initial Commencement

Specified date

Paras 1–3, 6–14: Specified date (for certain purposes): 1 September 2005: see reg 1(1)(c).

Paras 1–3, 6–14: Specified date (for remaining purposes): 5 December 2005: see reg 1(1)(b).

Paras 4, 5, 15, 16: Specified date (for the purpose of making regulations): 20 July 2005: see reg 1(1)(a).

Paras 4, 5, 15, 16: Specified date (for certain purposes): 1 September 2005: see reg 1(1)(c).

Paras 4, 5, 15, 16: Specified date (for remaining purposes): 5 December 2005: see reg 1(1)(b).

SCHEDULE 2
Determination of Annual and Initial Payments

Regulations 17 and 18(5)

Introductory

1   (1) This Schedule applies for the purposes of determining the amount of an annual payment or of an initial payment payable to or in respect of qualifying members of qualifying pension schemes.

(2) In this Schedule—

["appropriate person" has the meaning given by regulation 2(1) of the FAS Information and Payments Regulations (interpretation);]

["the certification date" means the date for which the relevant information provided in relation to a qualifying member, or a survivor of a qualifying member, is correct;]

["the FAS Information and Payments Regulations" means the Financial Assistance Scheme (Provision of Information and Administration of Payments) Regulations 2005;]

"guaranteed minimum pension" has the meaning given in section 8(2) of the 1993 Act;

["relevant information" means any information—

(a)   that is described in any of paragraphs (j) to (l) of the fourth item of the table in paragraph 1(2) of Schedule 1 to the FAS Information and Payments Regulations (information to be provided by appropriate persons);

(b)   that is to be provided by an appropriate person to the scheme manager in accordance with regulation 3(3)(a) of those Regulations; and

(c)   from which the amount of the actual pension or interim pension of a qualifying member, or of a survivor of a qualifying member, may be derived;]

"scheme rules" means the rules of the qualifying pension scheme.

(3) Paragraphs 2 to 5 are subject to paragraphs 6 to 9.

Actual pension

2   (1) In this Schedule, "actual pension" means, subject to sub-paragraph (3), the annual rate of annuity [which has been,] or could have been, purchased for the beneficiary as at the certification date with the assets available to discharge the liability of the scheme to him after that liability has, or had been, determined.

(2) The liability of the scheme to the beneficiary shall be determined for the purposes of sub-paragraph (1)—

(a)   in accordance with section 73 of the 1995 Act; or

(b)   where that section does not apply, in accordance with the scheme rules.

(3) The annual rate of annuity which can be purchased for the beneficiary for the purposes of sub-paragraph (1) with the assets referred to in that sub-paragraph, shall be determined—

[(a)   where the beneficiary was an active or a deferred member of the qualifying pension scheme immediately before that scheme began to wind up, on the basis that the sum which will be, or has been, used to discharge the liability of the scheme to him will only be, or has only been, used to purchase an annuity when the qualifying member attains, or attained, his normal retirement age;]

(b)   where the beneficiary is a survivor of a member of that scheme, having regard to the annual rate of annuity which will come into payment to him immediately on the purchase of the annuity from the assets of the scheme;

(c)   on the basis that benefits payable to survivors and increases in the annual rate of annuity in payment are no more generous than provided in relation to pensions under the scheme rules; and

(d)   on the basis that there has been no commutation of benefits deriving from the scheme.

(4) Where the scheme manager is satisfied that it is not possible for him to determine the annual rate of annuity for the purposes of sub-paragraph (1) having regard to the information available to him, he shall determine the annual rate of annuity on the basis of the sum which would discharge the liability of the scheme to the beneficiary and to such other matters as he considers relevant.

Qualifying members receiving pensions from the qualifying pension scheme

3   (1) This paragraph applies where immediately before a qualifying pension scheme began to wind up, a qualifying member was entitled to present payment of a pension under the scheme rules.

(2) The annual payment payable to a qualifying member to whom this paragraph applies shall be—

(expected pension x 0.8)-actual pension

(3) In this paragraph, "expected pension" means the annual rate of the pension which would have been in payment to the qualifying member in respect of rights accrued in a qualifying pension scheme as at the certification date if the scheme had not started to wind up.

4   Active and deferred members

(1) This paragraph applies in respect of a qualifying member of a qualifying pension scheme who immediately before a qualifying pension scheme began to wind up, was an active member or a deferred member of that scheme.

(2) The annual payment payable to a qualifying member to whom this paragraph applies shall be—

(expected pension x 0.8)-actual pension.

(3) In sub-paragraph (2), "expected pension" means, subject to sub-paragraph (4), the aggregate of—

(a)   the annual rate of the pension to which the qualifying member would have been entitled in accordance with the scheme rules had he attained his normal retirement age when the pensionable service relating to the pension ended;

(b)   the revaluation amount for the first revaluation period (see sub-paragraphs (5) and (6)); and

(c)   the revaluation amount for the second revaluation period (see sub-paragraphs (7) to (11)).

(4) In any case where the scheme manager is satisfied, having regard to the information available to him, that it is not possible for him to identify any one of the elements in sub-paragraph (3), he may determine how the annual payment is to be calculated having regard to such matters as he considers relevant.

(5) The first revaluation period is the period beginning on the day on which the qualifying member's pensionable service ended and ending on the day before the day on which the scheme began to wind up.

(6) The revaluation amount for the first revaluation period is the amount by which the annual rate of the pension under sub-paragraph (3)(a) would fall to be revalued—

(a)   in relation to any guaranteed minimum pension, in accordance with section 16 of the 1993 Act, having regard to the relevant scheme rules; and

(b)   in relation to the remainder of the pension, in accordance with Chapter 2 of Part 4 of the 1993 Act.

(7) The second revaluation period is the period beginning on the day on which the scheme began to wind up and ending on the certification date.

(8) The revaluation amount for the second revaluation period is, subject to sub-paragraph (12)—

(a)   where that period is less than one month, nil; or

(b)   in any other case, the revaluation percentage of the aggregate of the annual rate of the pension under sub-paragraph (3)(a) and the revaluation amount for the first revaluation period under sub-paragraph (6).

(9) In sub-paragraph (8), "the revaluation percentage" means the lesser of—

(a)   the percentage increase in the general level of prices in Great Britain during the second revaluation period determined in accordance with sub-paragraph (7); and

(b)   the maximum revaluation rate.

(10) The method for determining the percentage increase in the general level of prices in Great Britain during the second revaluation period is—

$$(100 \times (A / B)) - 100$$

where—

A is the level of the retail prices index for the month which falls two months before the month in which the certification date falls;

B is the level of the retail prices index for the month two months before the month during which the relevant qualifying pension scheme began to wind up.

(11) In sub-paragraph (9)(b), "the maximum revaluation rate" in relation to the second revaluation period is—

(a)   if that period is a period of 12 months, 5%; or

(b)   in any other case, the percentage that would be the percentage mentioned in sub-paragraph (9)(a) had the general level of prices in Great Britain increased at the rate of 5% compound per annum during that period.

(12) In determining the revaluation amount for the second revaluation period in accordance with sub-paragraphs (8) to (11), no revaluation shall be made in respect of any benefits which are not subject to revaluation under the scheme rules.

Survivors of qualifying members

5   (1) This paragraph applies where, immediately before a qualifying pension scheme began to wind up, a qualifying member—

(a)   was entitled to present payment of a pension under the scheme rules and that pension was attributable—

      (i)   to the member's pensionable service; or

      (ii)   (directly or indirectly) to a pension credit to which the member became entitled under section 29(1)(b) of the Welfare Reform and Pensions Act 1999; or

(b)   was an active member or a deferred member of that scheme,

and that member dies on or after the day on which the scheme began to wind up.

(2) The annual payment payable to the survivor of a qualifying member to whom this paragraph applies shall be determined in accordance with sub-paragraph (3) or (6).

(3) Where the qualifying member dies on or before the certification date, the annual payment payable to his survivor shall be—

$$\frac{expected\ pension \times 0.8}{2} - actual\ pension$$

(4) In sub-paragraph (3), "expected pension" shall, subject to sub-paragraph (5), be determined—

(a)   where the qualifying member was entitled to present payment of a pension under the scheme rules immediately before his death, in accordance with paragraph 3(3); or

(b)   where the qualifying member was an active member or a deferred member of a qualifying pension scheme immediately before his death, in accordance with paragraph 4(3).

(5) In any case where the scheme manager is satisfied that it is not possible for him to identify either or both elements of the formula in sub-paragraph (3), he may determine how the annual payment is to be calculated having regard to the scheme rules and such other matters as he considers relevant.

(6) Where the qualifying member dies after the certification date, the annual payment payable to his survivor shall be—

(a)   one-half of the annual payment which was payable to that member in accordance with paragraph 3 or 4 immediately before his death; or

(b)   where the annual payment was not payable to that member immediately before his death, one-half of the annual payment which would have been payable to him in accordance with [paragraph 3 or 4 if—

   (i)   he had attained the age of 65 before his death; or

   (ii)   he had not attained that age, but the scheme manager, after being notified that the qualifying member was terminally ill, was satisfied as to that fact].

Exclusion of certain benefits

6   (1) No account shall be taken of the benefits specified in sub-paragraph (2) when determining, for the purposes of this Schedule—

(a)   the assets available to be used to discharge a liability of a qualifying pension scheme;

(b)   the liabilities of such a scheme; and

(c)   the annual rate of pension from such a scheme.

(2) The specified benefits are—

(a)   money purchase benefits;

(b)   benefits derived from the payment of voluntary contributions where, on the winding up of the scheme, the assets of the scheme have first been applied to satisfy liabilities in respect of those benefits; and

(c)   any guaranteed minimum pension where an accrued rights premium or a pensioner's right's premium was paid in respect of the qualifying member.

(3) In sub-paragraph (2)(c), "accrued rights premium" and "pensioner's right's premium" respectively have the meaning given in section 55(6)(a) and (b) of the 1993 Act as in force before 6th April 1997.

Cap on expected pension and actual pension

7   (1) Where the amount of a qualifying member's expected pension determined in accordance with the previous provisions of this Schedule multiplied by 0.8, exceeds £12,000, the amount of the annual payment payable to, or in respect of, that member under paragraphs 3 to 5 shall be determined on the basis that the product of that calculation was £12,000.

(2) Where the amount of a qualifying member's actual pension determined in accordance with paragraph 2 exceeds—

(a)   the amount of a qualifying member's expected pension determined in accordance with the previous provisions of this Schedule multiplied by 0.8; or

(b)   £12,000,

no annual payment shall be payable to, or in respect of, that member.

De minimis rule

8   Where the amount of an annual payment determined in accordance with the previous provisions of this Schedule would, but for this paragraph—

(a)   in the case of paragraphs 3 and 4, be less than £520;

(b)   in the case of paragraph 5, be less than £260,

the amount of that payment shall be nil.

Revaluation

9   (1) The amount of the annual payment shall be determined in accordance with the preceding paragraphs of this Schedule on the basis of the circumstances applying as at the certification date.

(2) Where there is a period of one month or more between the certification date and the date on which the annual payment is first payable to the beneficiary in accordance with regulation 17, the annual payment shall be increased by the appropriate revaluation percentage of that amount.

(3) In sub-paragraph (2), "the appropriate revaluation percentage" means the lesser of—

(a)   the percentage increase in the general level of prices in Great Britain during the second revaluation period determined in accordance with paragraph 4(7); and

(b)   the maximum revaluation rate.

(4) The method for determining the percentage increase in the general level of prices in Great Britain during that period is—

$(100 \times (A / B)) -100$

where—

A is the level of the retail prices index for the month which falls two months before [the month] in which the annual payment is first payable to the beneficiary under regulation 17;

B is the level of the retail prices index for the month two months before the month in which the certification date falls.

(5) In sub-paragraph (3)(b), "the maximum revaluation rate" in relation to that period is—

(a)   if that period is a period of 12 months, 5%; and

(b)   in any other case, the percentage that would be the percentage mentioned in sub-paragraph (3)(a) had the general level of prices in Great Britain increased at the rate of 5% compound per annum during that period.

Initial payments

10   The preceding provisions of this Schedule shall apply for the purposes of determining the amount of an initial payment with the following modifications—

[(a)   for paragraph 2, substitute—

"Interim pension

2   In this Schedule, "interim pension" means the annual rate of pension that was in payment, is in payment, or is proposed to be paid, to a qualifying member, or to a survivor of that qualifying member, from the assets of the qualifying pension scheme of which that qualifying member is, or was, a member—

(a)   on or after the time when the scheme began to wind up; but

(b)   before the day on which the scheme's liabilities in respect of the qualifying member are, or were, discharged.";]

(b)   for "actual pension", in each place, substitute "interim pension";

(c)   for "0.8", in each place, substitute "0.6";

[(d)   for "annual payment", in each place that it occurs (except in paragraph 1(1)), substitute "initial payment"; and

(e)   in paragraph 5—

(i)   for sub-paragraph (3) substitute—

"(3) The initial payment payable to a survivor of a qualifying member shall be—

(expected pension $\times 0.6 / 2$—interim pension payable to that survivor."; and

(ii)   omit sub-paragraphs (2) and (6)].

Rounding

11   Where the amount of an annual payment or an initial payment determined in accordance with this Schedule results in a fraction of a penny, that fraction shall be treated as a penny.

NOTES

Initial Commencement

Specified date

Specified date (for certain purposes): 1 September 2005: see reg 1(1)(c).

Specified date (for remaining purposes): 5 December 2005: see reg 1(1)(b).

Amendment

Para 1: in sub-para (2) definition "appropriate person" inserted by SI 2005/3256, reg 4(1), (6)(a)(ii).

Date in force: 24 November 2005: see SI 2005/3256, reg 1(1).

Para 1: in sub-para (2) definition "the certification date" substituted by SI 2005/3256, reg 4(1), (6)(a)(i).

Date in force: 24 November 2005: see SI 2005/3256, reg 1(1).

Para 1: in sub-para (2) definition "the FAS Information and Payments Regulations" inserted by SI 2005/3256, reg 4(1), (6)(a)(ii).

Date in force: 24 November 2005: see SI 2005/3256, reg 1(1).

Para 1: in sub-para (2) definition "relevant information" inserted by SI 2005/3256, reg 4(1), (6)(a)(ii).

Date in force: 24 November 2005: see SI 2005/3256, reg 1(1).

Para 2: in sub-para (1) words "which has been," in square brackets substituted by SI 2005/3256, reg 4(1), (6)(b)(i).

Date in force: 24 November 2005: see SI 2005/3256, reg 1(1).

Para 2: sub-para (3)(a) substituted by SI 2005/3256, reg 4(1), (6)(b)(ii).

Date in force: 24 November 2005: see SI 2005/3256, reg 1(1).

Para 5: in sub-para (6)(b) words from "paragraph 3 or" to "to that fact" in square brackets substituted by SI 2005/3256, reg 4(1), (6)(c).

Date in force: 24 November 2005: see SI 2005/3256, reg 1(1).

Para 9: in sub-para (4) in definition of "A" words "the month" in square brackets inserted by SI 2005/3256, reg 4(1), (6)(d).

Date in force: 24 November 2005: see SI 2005/3256, reg 1(1).

Para 10: sub-para (a) substituted by SI 2005/3256, reg 4(1), (6)(e)(i).

Date in force: 24 November 2005: see SI 2005/3256, reg 1(1).

Para 10: sub-paras (d), (e) inserted by SI 2005/3256, reg 4(1), (6)(e)(ii).

Date in force: 24 November 2005: see SI 2005/3256, reg 1(1).

The Financial Assistance Scheme (Provision of Information and Administration of Payments) Regulations 2005

SI 2005 No 2189

Financial Assistance Scheme (Provision of Information and Administration of Payments) Regulations 2005

Made 4th August 2005

Laid before Parliament 11th August 2005

Coming into force in accordance with regulation 1(1)

1   Citation, commencement and extent

(1) These Regulations may be cited as the Financial Assistance Scheme (Provision of Information and Administration of Payments) Regulations 2005 and shall come into force—

(a)   in so far as these Regulations apply in relation to civil partnerships, on 5th December 2005; and

(b)   for all other purposes, on 1st September 2005.

(2) These Regulations extend to Northern Ireland.

> **NOTES**
> **Initial Commencement**
> *Specified date*
> Specified date (for certain purposes): 1 September 2005: see para (1)(b) above.
> Specified date (for remaining purposes): 5 December 2005: see para (1)(a) above.

2   Interpretation

(1) In these Regulations—

"the FAS Regulations" means the Financial Assistance Scheme Regulations 2005;

"appointed representative" means a person—

(a)   whose name, address and appointment by a beneficiary or potential beneficiary, for the purposes of providing information to the scheme manager under regulation 4, has been notified to the scheme manager in a document signed by the beneficiary or potential beneficiary in question or by his legal representative; and

(b)   whose appointment has been consented to by the scheme manager;

"appropriate person" means, in relation to an occupational pension scheme—

(a)   a trustee or manager of the scheme or, where the scheme has fully wound up, a former trustee or manager of that scheme;

(b)   a professional adviser in relation to the scheme or, where the scheme has fully wound up, a former professional adviser in relation to that scheme;

(c)   in relation to a scheme which has fully wound up, any insurance company which is paying annuities to former members of that scheme; and

    (d)   any other person appearing to the scheme manager to be a person who holds, or is likely to hold, information relevant to—

        (i)   whether an occupational pension scheme is a qualifying pension scheme; or

        (ii)   a qualifying member's entitlement to an annual payment under the FAS Regulations and the amount of such a payment;

"beneficiary" means a qualifying member or, after his death, his survivor;

"member" includes—

    (a)   a person who was entitled to a present payment from a qualifying pension scheme immediately before the scheme began to wind up where—

        (i)   that payment was attributable to the pensionable service of a former member of that scheme who has died; and

        (ii)   the scheme's pension liabilities in respect of that person are unlikely to be satisfied in full because the scheme has insufficient assets;

    (b)   a person who is entitled to, but not in receipt of, a present payment from a qualifying pension scheme where that payment would have been attributable to the pensionable service of a former member of that scheme who died on or after the day on which the scheme began to wind up; and

    (c)   a person who became a pension credit member of the scheme on or after the day on which the scheme began to wind up,

and for the purposes of this definition, the day on which the scheme began to wind up shall be determined in accordance with regulation 3 of the FAS Regulations;

"normal retirement age" means, in relation to a member of an occupational pension scheme, the age specified in the rules of that scheme at which that member will normally retire;

"personal representative" means the executor, original or by representation, or administrator for the time being of a deceased person;

["potential beneficiary" means any person—

    (a)   in respect of whom the information determined in accordance with the fourth item of the table in paragraph 1(2) of Schedule 1 is to be provided to the scheme manager in accordance with regulation 3(3)(a); but

    (b)   who has not yet been determined to be a beneficiary;]

"qualifying member" shall be construed in accordance with regulation 15 of the FAS Regulations;

"qualifying pension scheme" shall be construed in accordance with regulation 9 of the FAS Regulations;

"scheme manager" shall be construed in accordance with regulation 5 of the FAS Regulations;

"survivor" means, in relation to a member [or former member] of a qualifying pension scheme who has died—

    (a)   the member's [or former member's] widow or widower; or

    (b)   the member's [or former member's] surviving civil partner,

but shall not include a person who comes within paragraph (a) or (b) but who is regarded as a qualifying member by virtue of regulation 15(5) of the FAS Regulations,

and other expressions have the meaning given to them in the Pensions Act 2004 or, as the case may be, in the Pensions (Northern Ireland) Order 2005.

(2) For the purposes of the definition of "appropriate person" in paragraph (1), "insurance company" means—

(a)   a person who has permission under Part 4 of the Financial Services and Markets Act 2000 to effect or carry out contracts of long-term insurance; or

(b)   an EEA firm of the kind mentioned in paragraph 5(d) of Schedule 3 to that Act (certain direct insurance undertakings) which has permission under paragraph 15 of that Schedule (as a result of qualifying for authorisation under paragraph 12 of that Schedule) to effect or carry out contracts of long-term insurance,

and in this paragraph, "contracts of long-term insurance" means contracts which fall within Part 2 of Schedule 1 to the Financial Services and Markets Act 2000 (Regulated Activities) Order 2001.

(3) Paragraph (2) shall be read with—

(a)   section 22 of Financial Services and Markets Act 2000 (regulated activities);

(b)   any relevant order under that section; and

(c)   Schedule 2 to that Act.

NOTES

Initial Commencement

Specified date

Specified date (for certain purposes): 1 September 2005: see reg 1(1)(b).

Specified date (for remaining purposes): 5 December 2005: see reg 1(1)(a).

Amendment

Para (1): definition "potential beneficiary" substituted by SI 2005/3256, reg 6(1), (2)(a).

Date in force: 24 November 2005: see SI 2005/3256, reg 1(1).

Para (1): in definition "survivor" words "or former member" in square brackets inserted by SI 2005/3256, reg 6(1), (2)(b)(i).

Date in force: 24 November 2005: see SI 2005/3256, reg 1(1).

Para (1): in definition "survivor" words "or former member's" in square brackets in both places they occur inserted by SI 2005/3256, reg 6(1), (2)(b)(ii).

Date in force: 24 November 2005: see SI 2005/3256, reg 1(1).

3   Information to be provided by, and to, appropriate persons

(1) Where the scheme manager has been notified in accordance with regulation 14 of the FAS Regulations that an occupational pension scheme may be a qualifying pension scheme, an appropriate person shall provide such information to the scheme manager as is necessary for him to determine whether the scheme is a qualifying pension scheme for the purposes of Part 3 of the FAS Regulations, within the period of 6 months beginning on the day on which the scheme manager requests that information or within such longer period as the scheme manager may determine.

(2) Where the scheme manager has determined whether or not an occupational pension scheme is a qualifying pension scheme, he shall, no later than 14 days after making that determination—

(a)   notify the relevant appropriate person relating to that scheme, in writing, of that determination; and

(b)   where the determination is that the scheme is not a qualifying pension scheme, notify that person in writing of the reasons for that determination.

(3) Where the scheme manager has determined that an occupational pension scheme is a qualifying pension scheme, the information to be provided to—

(a)   the scheme manager; [or]

[(b)   all potential beneficiaries,]

by an appropriate person shall be determined in accordance with the provisions of Schedule 1.

NOTES

Initial Commencement

Specified date

Specified date (for certain purposes): 1 September 2005: see reg 1(1)(b).

Specified date (for remaining purposes): 5 December 2005: see reg 1(1)(a).

Amendment

Para (3): in sub-para (a) word "or" in square brackets substituted by SI 2005/3256, reg 6(1), (3)(a).

Date in force: 24 November 2005: see SI 2005/3256, reg 1(1).

Para (3): sub-para (b) substituted by SI 2005/3256, reg 6(1), (3)(b).

Date in force: 24 November 2005: see SI 2005/3256, reg 1(1).

4   Information to be provided by beneficiaries and potential beneficiaries and their personal representatives

(1) The information to be provided to the scheme manager by beneficiaries and potential beneficiaries shall be determined in accordance with the provisions of Schedule 2.

(2) Where a beneficiary or a potential beneficiary dies, his personal representative shall, within the period of 28 days beginning with the date of the death, notify the scheme manager of the death and provide a copy of the death certificate to the scheme manager.

NOTES

Initial Commencement

Specified date

Specified date (for certain purposes): 1 September 2005: see reg 1(1)(b).

Specified date (for remaining purposes): 5 December 2005: see reg 1(1)(a).

5   Method of providing information

(1) Where, under these Regulations, any information is to be provided to any person, that information shall be provided in writing.

(2) Where, under these Regulations—

(a)   any information is to be provided to the scheme manager by any beneficiary or potential beneficiary; and

(b)   there is an appointed representative in relation to that beneficiary or potential beneficiary,

that information shall be provided by or to his appointed representative.

(3) Any document sent, or notification given, by an appropriate person to the scheme manager under regulation 3(1) or (3) and Schedule 1 shall include—

(a)   the names of the persons sending the document or giving the notification;

(b)   the name of the scheme to which the document or notification relates; and

(c)   the pension scheme registration number which is allocated to that scheme in the register.

(4) Any document sent, or notification given, to the scheme manager by any beneficiary or potential beneficiary under regulation 4(1) and Schedule 2, or by the personal representative of a such a person under regulation 4(2), shall include, in relation to that person—

(a)   the name, address, date of birth and national insurance number of that person;

(b)   where the beneficiary or potential beneficiary concerned is, or purports to be, a survivor, the name and date of birth of the qualifying member from whom that person has accrued pension rights;

(c)   the name of the employer in relation to the scheme in which that qualifying member's pension rights accrued; and

(d)   the address or location of a place of business of that employer.

NOTES

Initial Commencement

Specified date

Specified date (for certain purposes): 1 September 2005: see reg 1(1)(b).

Specified date (for remaining purposes): 5 December 2005: see reg 1(1)(a).

6   Insufficient or unsuitable information

(1) Where the scheme manager—

(a)   has not been provided with the information or evidence required to be provided to him under regulation 3(1) or (3) or 4(1) or Schedule 1 or 2 within the period allowed for in that regulation or those Schedules;

(b)   is of the opinion that he has insufficient information or evidence; or

(c)   has been provided with such information or evidence but in an inappropriate form or manner,

he may, at any time after the expiry of the relevant period prescribed in that regulation or those Schedules, refuse to make a determination in relation to the matters in respect of which that information and evidence was, or was to have been, provided and shall notify the person who provided, or was to have provided, the information and evidence in writing accordingly.

(2) The scheme manager shall only be bound to make a determination in relation to the matters specified in paragraph (1) once he receives the information or evidence or receives it in an appropriate form or manner.

NOTES

Initial Commencement

Specified date

Specified date (for certain purposes): 1 September 2005: see reg 1(1)(b).

Specified date (for remaining purposes): 5 December 2005: see reg 1(1)(a).

7   Recovery of overpayments

(1) The scheme manager shall be entitled to recover the amount of any payment made in excess of the beneficiary's entitlement under Part 5 of the FAS Regulations where it has been determined that an amount has been so paid.

(2) An amount recoverable under paragraph (1) is recoverable from—

(a)   the beneficiary;

(b)   his appointed representative for the purposes of the FAS Regulations; or

(c)   the beneficiary's estate.

(3) An amount recoverable under paragraph (1) may, without prejudice to any other method of recovery, be recovered by abating future payments made under Part 5 of the FAS Regulations.

NOTES

Initial Commencement

Specified date

Specified date (for certain purposes): 1 September 2005: see reg 1(1)(b).

Specified date (for remaining purposes): 5 December 2005: see reg 1(1)(a).

8   Suspension of payments

(1) Payment of monthly instalments under regulation 19 of the FAS Regulations may be suspended, in whole or in part, where the scheme manager is of the opinion that a beneficiary may not be entitled to receive payments under those Regulations.

(2) The suspension in paragraph (1) shall continue until such time as the scheme manager is satisfied as to the beneficiary's entitlement to a payment under those Regulations.

NOTES

Initial Commencement

Specified date

Specified date (for certain purposes): 1 September 2005: see reg 1(1)(b).

Specified date (for remaining purposes): 5 December 2005: see reg 1(1)(a).

SCHEDULE I
Information to be Provided by Appropriate Persons

Regulation 3(3)

I   (1) In this Schedule, "notification date" means the day on which the scheme manager notifies the appropriate person that he has determined that a scheme is a qualifying pension scheme.

(2) Information to be provided to the scheme manager [or all potential beneficiaries] by appropriate persons shall be determined in accordance with the table of information set out below—

Table of information to be provided by appropriate persons		
Description of persons to whom information is to be provided	*Description of information to be provided*	*Period during which information is to be provided*
The scheme manager.	The identity of those individuals within the appropriate person's organisation who will have responsibility for providing information to the scheme manager.	The period of 28 days beginning on the notification date.
The scheme manager.	Details of any change in the address or telephone number— (a) in relation to a qualifying pension scheme which is winding up, of the trustees or managers of the scheme; (b) in relation to a qualifying pension scheme which has wound up, of the appropriate person who has responsibility for providing information to the scheme manager.	The period of 5 days beginning on the day on which the change took place.

The scheme manager.	Any change in the identity of the individuals who have been notified to the scheme manager as having responsibility for providing information to the scheme manager.	The period of 14 days beginning on the day on which the change took place.
The scheme manager.	In relation to each member or former member[, or any survivor of a member or former member,] of a qualifying pension scheme to whom, or in respect of whom, a payment might be made under the FAS Regulations— (a) his full name; (b) his date of birth; (c) his address and telephone number; (d) his national insurance number; (e) where that member [or former member] has died, the date of his death; (f) his marital or civil partnership status; (g) such evidence as is necessary to prove that [the member or former member is, or was,] a member of that scheme; (h) his normal retirement age; (i) information necessary to determine the amount of pension to which he would have been entitled from the scheme if the scheme's' liabilities to the member [or former member] had been satisfied in full; (j) where applicable, the annual rate of annuity which can be purchased for him with the assets available to be used to discharge the liability of the scheme to him, after the liabilities of the scheme have been determined in accordance with section 73 of the Pensions Act 1995 or Article 73 of the Pensions (Northern Ireland) Order 1995 (preferential liabilities on winding up) or, where that section or Article does not apply, the rules of that scheme;	The period of 6 months beginning on the day on which the scheme manager requested the information or during such longer period as the scheme manager may determine for the provision of that information.

	(k) the sum which is available to be used to discharge the liability of the scheme to [him] when the scheme is fully wound up; and (l) where the information referred to in paragraphs (i) to (k) cannot be provided or where that information might be inappropriate or inaccurate in a particular case, such other information from which the amount of his actual pension, expected pension and interim pension for the purposes of Schedule 2 to the FAS Regulations may be derived.	
[All potential beneficiaries].	In relation to a qualifying pension scheme which is winding up, notification that the scheme manager has determined that the scheme is, or is not, a qualifying pension scheme.	The period of 28 days beginning on the notification date.

NOTES

Initial Commencement

Specified date

Specified date (for certain purposes): 1 September 2005: see reg 1(1)(b).

Specified date (for remaining purposes): 5 December 2005: see reg 1(1)(a).

Amendment

Para 1: in sub-para (2) words "or all potential beneficiaries" in square brackets substituted by SI 2005/3256, reg 6(1), (4)(a).

Date in force: 24 November 2005: see SI 2005/3256, reg 1(1).

Para 1: Table: in item 4 in column 2 words ", or any survivor of a member or former member," in square brackets inserted by SI 2005/3256, reg 6(1), (4)(b)(i).

Date in force: 24 November 2005: see SI 2005/3256, reg 1(1).

Para 1: Table: in item 4 in column 2 in sub-para (e) words "or former member" in square brackets inserted by SI 2005/3256, reg 6(1), (4)(b)(ii).

Date in force: 24 November 2005: see SI 2005/3256, reg 1(1).

Para 1: Table: in item 4 in column 2 in sub-para (g) words "the member or former member is, or was," in square brackets substituted by SI 2005/3256, reg 6(1), (4)(b)(iii).

Date in force: 24 November 2005: see SI 2005/3256, reg 1(1).

Para 1: Table: in item 4 in column 2 in sub-para (i) words "or former member" in square brackets inserted by SI 2005/3256, reg 6(1), (4)(b)(ii).

Date in force: 24 November 2005: see SI 2005/3256, reg 1(1).

Para 1: Table: in item 4 in column 2 in sub-para (k) word "him" in square brackets substituted by SI 2005/3256, reg 6(1), (4)(b)(iv).

Date in force: 24 November 2005: see SI 2005/3256, reg 1(1).

Para 1: Table: in item 5 in column 1 words "All potential beneficiaries" in square brackets substituted by SI 2005/3256, reg 6(1), (4)(c).

Date in force: 24 November 2005: see SI 2005/3256, reg 1(1).

SCHEDULE 2
Information to be Provided by Beneficiaries and Potential Beneficiaries

Regulation 4(1)

I   Information to be provided by beneficiaries and potential beneficiaries to the scheme manager shall be determined in accordance with the table of information set out below—

Table of information to be provided by beneficiaries and potential beneficiaries		
Description of persons by whom information is to be provided	*Description of information to be provided*	*Period during which information is to be provided*
Any potential beneficiary relating to a qualifying pension scheme which has fully wound up.	In relation to that potential beneficiary— (a) such evidence as is necessary to prove that he was either a qualifying member of that scheme or the survivor of such a member; (b) his name, address, date of birth and national insurance number; (c) information from which [his] actual pension, expected pension and interim pension for the purposes of Schedule 2 to the FAS Regulations may be derived.	The period of 6 months beginning on the day on which the scheme manager requested the information or during such longer period as the scheme manager may determine for the provision of that information.
Any beneficiary whose address is changed.	Details of any change in the address of that beneficiary.	(a) Except where paragraph (b) applies, the period of 8 weeks beginning four weeks before the day on which the change will take place; (b) Where the beneficiary was not aware of the change at the beginning of the period referred to in paragraph (a), the period of 8 weeks beginning on the day on which he became aware of the change.
Any qualifying member whose marriage ends in divorce.	Notification of the divorce and a copy of the decree of divorce.	The period of 28 days beginning on the day on which the decree became absolute.
Any qualifying member who has married or remarried.	Notification of the marriage and a copy of the marriage certificate.	The period of 28 days beginning on the day of the marriage or remarriage.
Any qualifying member who enters into a civil partnership.	Notification of the civil partnership and a copy of the civil partnership certificate.	The period of 28 days beginning on the day on which the civil partnership was entered into.
Any qualifying member whose civil partnership is dissolved.	Notification of the dissolution of the civil partnership and a copy of the dissolution certificate.	The period of 28 days beginning on the day of the dissolution.

Where the beneficiary or potential beneficiary terminates the appointment of his appointed representative, or where there is any change in the address of an appointed representative, the beneficiary or potential beneficiary who appointed that appointed representative.	Notification of the termination or of the change in the address of the appointed representative and the date on which the termination or change became effective.	The period of 28 days beginning on the day on which the termination or change became effective.

NOTES

Initial Commencement

Specified date

Specified date (for certain purposes): 1 September 2005: see reg 1(1)(b).

Specified date (for remaining purposes): 5 December 2005: see reg 1(1)(a).

Amendment

Para 1: Table: in item 1 in sub-para (c) word "his" in square brackets substituted by SI 2005/3256, reg 6(1), (5).

Date in force: 24 November 2005: see SI 2005/3256, reg 1(1).

The Occupational Pension Schemes (Employer Debt etc) (Amendment) Regulations 2005

SI 2005 No 2224

Occupational Pension Schemes (Employer Debt etc) (Amendment) Regulations 2005

Made 9th August 2005

Laid before Parliament 12th August 2005

Coming into force 2nd September 2005

I Citation, commencement and interpretation

(1) These Regulations may be cited as the Occupational Pension Schemes (Employer Debt etc) (Amendment) Regulations 2005.

(2) These Regulations come into force on 2nd September 2005.

(3) Regulation 2(1), (2)(c), (3) and (5) does not apply if the employment-cessation event occurs before that date.

(4) Regulation 4(2) does not apply if the applicable time is before that date.

(5) In these Regulations—

"the 2004 Act" means the Pensions Act 2004;

"the 2005 Regulations" means the Occupational Pension Schemes (Employer Debt) Regulations 2005;

"the applicable time" has the meaning given in regulation 2(1) of the 2005 Regulations (interpretation);

"employment-cessation event" has the meaning given in regulation 6(4) of the 2005 Regulations (multi-employer schemes: general).

> NOTES
>
> **Initial Commencement**
>
> **Specified date**
>
> Specified date: 2 September 2005: see see para (2) above.

2 Multi-employer schemes: employment-cessation events and withdrawal arrangements etc

(1) At the end of regulation 2(1) of the 2005 Regulations (interpretation) add—

""withdrawal arrangement" and "approved withdrawal arrangement" are to be read in accordance with paragraph 1(1) of Schedule 1A to these Regulations.".

(2) In regulation 5 of the 2005 Regulations (calculation of the value of scheme liabilities and assets: defined benefit schemes)—

(a) in paragraph (1)(c) after "paragraphs (2), (3)," insert "(3A),";

(b) after paragraph (3) insert—

"(3A) If the modification specified in regulation 7(3) has applied in the case of an employment-cessation event that occurred in relation to an employer before the applicable time—

(a) the liabilities of the scheme that are attributable to employment with that employer, and

(b) the debts treated as due under section 75(4) of the 1995 Act in accordance with that modification,

425

are not to be taken into account under paragraph (1).";

(c)   in paragraph (8) for "valuations for employment cessation events" substitute "employment-cessation events and withdrawal arrangements".

(3) For regulation 7 of the 2005 Regulations (multi-employer schemes: valuations for employment cessation events) substitute—

"7   Multi-employer schemes: employment-cessation events and withdrawal arrangements

(1) This regulation applies where—

(a)   section 75 of the 1995 Act applies to a trust scheme with the modifications referred to in regulation 6 (multi-employer schemes: general); and

(b)   as a result of the occurrence of an employment-cessation event in relation to an employer, a debt ("the cessation debt") calculated on the basis of assets and liabilities valued in accordance with regulation 5 is treated as due from the employer ("the cessation employer") under section 75(4) of that Act.

(2) If the cessation employer notifies the Authority in writing that he proposes to enter into a withdrawal arrangement—

(a)   the Authority may issue a direction that the cessation debt is to be unenforceable for such period as the Authority may specify in the direction, and where such a direction has been issued the debt is unenforceable for that period; and

(b)   the Authority may issue a direction that if an approved withdrawal arrangement has come into force within that period, section 75 of the 1995 Act is to apply in the case of the employment-cessation event with the modification specified in paragraph (3) instead of the modification referred to in regulation 6(1)(e)(ii), and where such a direction has been issued and such an arrangement has so come into force, that modification so applies.

(3) The modification is that section 75 of the 1995 Act has effect as if the reference in section 75(4) to an amount equal to the difference being treated as a debt due from the employer were a reference to—

(a)   amount A being treated as a debt due from the employer; and

(b)   unless and until the Authority issue a direction that it is not to be so treated, amount B being treated as a debt due from the guarantors at the guarantee time for which (if there is more than one guarantor) they are jointly or, if the approved withdrawal arrangement so provides, jointly and severally liable,

where amount A is calculated in accordance with regulation 7A and amount B is calculated in accordance with regulation 7B.

(4) In this regulation—

"the guarantee time" means the earliest time when an event specified in paragraph 1(3) of Schedule 1A to these Regulations occurs; and

"the guarantors" means such one or more of the parties to the approved withdrawal arrangement as are specified in the arrangement as the persons who are the guarantors for the purposes of this regulation.

(5) The Authority may issue a direction extending the period mentioned in paragraph (2)(a) by such further period as they may specify (so that the debt is unenforceable for the extended period).

(6) The Authority may only issue a direction under paragraph (3)(b)—

(a)   before the guarantee time, and

(b)   if the Authority consider that the approved withdrawal arrangement is no longer required.

(7) Schedule 1A to these Regulations applies for the purpose of making further provision in cases where this regulation applies; and in that Schedule and regulations 7A and 7B "the cessation employer" has the same meaning as in this regulation.

7A   Calculation of amounts due from cessation employer by virtue of regulation 7

(1) For the purposes of regulation 7(3), amount A depends on whether or not a debt (a "scheme funding basis debt") would have been treated as due from the cessation employer under section 75(4) of the 1995 Act if—

(a)   regulation 5 had applied with the modifications specified in paragraph (4); and

(b)   section 75(4) had applied in accordance with regulation 6(1)(d) and (e) but subject to the modifications of regulation 6 specified in paragraph (5) (instead of in accordance with the modification specified in regulation 7(3)).

(2) If a debt would have been so treated, amount A is the sum of the scheme funding basis debt and the cessation expenses attributable to the employer.

(3) If a debt would not have been so treated, amount A is equal to the amount of the cessation expenses attributable to the employer.

(4) The modifications of regulation 5 are that—

(a)   paragraphs (1)(a) and (2) and the references to those provisions in paragraph (1)(b), (c) and (d) (by virtue of which liabilities for pensions and other benefits are to be valued on the assumption that they will be discharged by the purchase of annuities) are omitted;

(b)   paragraph (3) and the references to that paragraph in paragraph (1)(c) and (d) (by virtue of which winding up expenses are to be taken into account) are omitted; and

(c)   in paragraph (5) for the words "for the purposes of section 75(2) and (4) of the 1995 Act" there are substituted the words "for the purposes of section 75(2) of the 1995 Act and for the purposes of section 75(4) of the 1995 Act where no approved withdrawal arrangement has been entered into by the employer".

(5) The modifications of regulation 6 are that—

(a)   for paragraph (ii) of paragraph (1)(e) there is substituted—

     "(ii)   in a case where the difference is ascertained immediately before an employment-cessation event occurs in relation to the employer, a reference to an amount equal to the employer's share of the difference, less the relevant transferred liabilities deduction, being treated as a debt due from the employer;";

(b)   after paragraph (5) there is added—

"(6) In this regulation "the relevant transferred liabilities deduction" means the amount of any relevant transferred liabilities, less the value of the corresponding assets.

(7) For the purposes of paragraph (6)—

(a)   "corresponding assets", in relation to relevant transferred liabilities, means the assets transferred from the scheme in connection with the transfer from the scheme of those liabilities; and

(b)   the value of the corresponding assets is to be determined—

     (i)   in the case of corresponding assets that are assets of the scheme at the applicable time, as at that time; and

     (ii)   in the case of corresponding assets that are not assets of the scheme at that time, as at the date of the transfer of the assets.

(8) For the purposes of paragraph (6)—

(a)   "relevant transferred liabilities" means liabilities in respect of members—

     (i)   which are transferred from the scheme in circumstances where the conditions set out in paragraphs (2)(a) or (b) and (3) of regulation 12 of the Occupational Pension Schemes (Preservation of Benefit) Regulations 1991 (transfer without consent) are met;

     (ii)   which are so transferred during the period beginning with the applicable time and ending with the date on which the approved withdrawal arrangement is approved ("the relevant period");

     (iii)   the transfer of which reduces the amount of the scheme's liabilities attributable to employment with the employer in relation to whom the employment-cessation event has occurred; and

     (iv)   in connection with the transfer of which there is a transfer of corresponding assets during the relevant period; and

(b)   the amount of the relevant transferred liabilities is to be calculated in accordance with regulation 5 as modified by regulation 7A(4).".

(6) The value of the assets and the amount of the liabilities of a scheme which are to be taken into account for the purposes of determining whether a scheme funding basis debt would have been treated as due as mentioned in paragraph (1) must be certified by the actuary in the form set out in Schedule 1B to these Regulations, but—

(a)   if the actuary is of the opinion that the value of the assets of the scheme was not less than the amount of the liabilities of the scheme—

     (i)   substituting in the first sentence of the comparison of value of scheme assets with amount of scheme liabilities for the words "was less" the words "was not less"; and

     (ii)   omitting the last sentence of that comparison; and

(b)   if the scheme is being wound up on the date as at which the valuation is made, omitting from the Note the words from "if the scheme" onwards.

(7) In this regulation "the cessation expenses attributable to the employer" has the meaning given by regulation 6(5).

7B   Calculation of amounts due from guarantors by virtue of regulation 7

(1) For the purposes of regulation 7(3), amount B depends on whether the approved withdrawal arrangement provides for amount B to be the amount provided for under paragraph (2).

(2) If the approved withdrawal arrangement so provides, amount B is equal to the amount (if any) that would be the amount of the debt due from the cessation employer under section 75(4) of the 1995 Act if—

(a)   the employment-cessation event had occurred at the guarantee time;

(b)   the cessation employer had not entered into an approved withdrawal arrangement; and

(c)   there were no cessation expenses attributable to the employer.

(3) If the approved withdrawal arrangement does not provide for amount B to be the amount provided for under paragraph (2), amount B is equal to the amount that would be the amount treated as due from the cessation employer under section 75(4) of the 1995 Act if the cessation employer had not entered into an approved withdrawal arrangement, less the sum of—

(a)   the amount that is amount A for the purposes of regulation 7(3);

(b)   if the amount that the approved withdrawal arrangement provides for the cessation employer to pay exceeds that amount, an amount equal to the excess; and

(c)   the relevant transferred liabilities deduction.

(4) The value of the assets and the amount of the liabilities of a scheme which are to be taken into account for the purposes of determining the amount (if any) that would be the amount of the debt due from the cessation employer under section 75(4) of the 1995 Act in the case mentioned in paragraph (2) must be certified by the actuary in the form set out in Schedule 1 to these Regulations, but—

(a)   substituting for the reference to regulation 5 a reference to paragraph (2) of this regulation;

(b)   if the actuary is of the opinion that the value of the assets of the scheme was not less than the amount of the liabilities of the scheme—

(i)   substituting in the first sentence of the comparison of value of scheme assets with amount of scheme liabilities for the words "was less" the words "was not less"; and

(ii)   omitting the last sentence of that comparison; and

(c)   if the scheme is being wound up on the date as at which the valuation is made, omitting from the Note the words from "if the scheme" onwards.

(5) In this regulation—

"the cessation expenses attributable to the employer" has the meaning given by regulation 6(5); and

"the relevant transferred liabilities deduction" has the meaning given by regulation 6(6), as inserted by the modification of regulation 6 made by regulation 7A(5)(b), except that for the purposes of this regulation the amount of the relevant transferred liabilities is to be calculated in accordance with regulation 5 without the modifications made by regulation 7A(4).".

(4) In regulation 9 of the 2005 Regulations (former employers)—

(a)   in paragraph (2)(b)(ii) for "condition A, B" substitute "condition A, B, BB";

(b)   after paragraph (4) insert—

"(4A) Condition BB is that such a debt was treated as becoming due from him, the modification in regulation 7(3) applied, and the amount treated as becoming due from him under regulation 7(3)(a) has been paid before the applicable time.".

(5) The Schedules set out in the Schedule to these Regulations are inserted after Schedule 1 to the 2005 Regulations.

NOTES

Initial Commencement

Specified date

Specified date: 2 September 2005: see reg 1(2).

3   The Pensions Regulator's functions under the 2005 Regulations

(1) The following functions under the 2005 Regulations are regulatory functions for the purposes of Part 1 of the 2004 Act—

(a)   the power to issue directions under regulation 7;

(b)   the power to issue a notice under paragraph 1(3)(c) of Schedule 1A; and

(c)   the power to issue a notice under paragraph 2 of Schedule 1A.

(2) The Pensions Regulator may, if it thinks fit, delegate the functions specified in paragraph (1) to the Determinations Panel established under section 9 of the 2004 Act (the Determinations Panel).

NOTES
Initial Commencement
Specified date
Specified date: 2 September 2005: see reg 1(2).

4   Minor amendments of the 2005 Regulations

(1) In regulation 4(1) of the 2005 Regulations (schemes to which section 75 of the 1995 Act does not apply) omit sub-paragraph (l) (the scheme established by the Salvation Army Act 1963).

(2) In regulation 10 of the 2005 Regulations (money purchase schemes: fraud and levy deficiencies etc), as it applies by virtue of regulation 12 of those Regulations (multi-employer money purchase schemes), in paragraph (1A)(a) (under which, unless the scheme makes contrary provision, an employer's share of the levy deficit or the criminal deficit is such proportion of the total deficit as, in the opinion of the actuary, the amount of the scheme's liabilities attributable to employment with that employer bears to the total amount of the scheme's liabilities attributable to employment with the employers) for "the actuary" substitute "the trustees or managers".

(3) In paragraph 2 of Schedule 2 to the 2005 Regulations (consequential amendment of the Occupational Pension Schemes (Winding Up) Regulations 1996) for "the Occupational Pension Schemes Winding Up Regulations 1996" substitute "the Occupational Pension Schemes (Winding Up) Regulations 1996".

NOTES
Initial Commencement
Specified date
Specified date: 2 September 2005: see reg 1(2).

5   Consequential amendments of the Pensions Regulator (Financial Support Directions etc) Regulations 2005

In regulation 15(2) of the Pensions Regulator (Financial Support Directions etc) Regulations 2005 (former employers)—

(a)   for "condition A, B" substitute "condition A, AA, B"; and

(b)   after sub-paragraph (a) insert—

"(aa)   condition AA is that—

(i)   such a debt became due;

(ii)   the modification in regulation 7(3) of the Occupational Pension Schemes (Employer Debt) Regulations 2005 (multi-employer schemes: employment-cessation events and withdrawal arrangements) applied, and

(iii)   the amount treated as becoming due from him under regulation 7(3)(a) of those Regulations has been paid;".

NOTES
Initial Commencement
Specified date
Specified date: 2 September 2005: see reg 1(2).

6   ...

...

7   Amendment of the Pension Protection Fund (Entry Rules) Regulations 2005

In regulation 16(1)(a)(ii) of the Pension Protection Fund (Entry Rules) Regulations 2005 (restrictions on winding up, discharge of liabilities etc) for "section 94(1)(a)" substitute "section 94(1)(aa)".

SCHEDULE
Schedules Inserted in the 2005 Regulations

Regulation 2(5)

"SCHEDULE 1A
Multi-employer Schemes: Employer-cessation Events and Approved Withdrawal Arrangements

Withdrawal arrangements

1   (1) For the purposes of these Regulations—

(a)   a withdrawal arrangement is an arrangement that meets the conditions specified in sub-paragraph (2), and

(b)   a withdrawal arrangement is approved if the details—

    (i)   of the arrangement, and

    (ii)   if the arrangement is amended, of any amendments of the arrangement,

are approved by the Authority.

(2) The conditions are that—

(a)   the arrangement consists of an agreement to which the trustees of the scheme and the cessation employer are parties;

(b)   the agreement is enforceable under the law of England and Wales, and the parties to the agreement have agreed that—

    (i)   that law applies to the agreement; and

    (ii)   they are subject to the jurisdiction of the court in England and Wales as respects the agreement;

(c)   the agreement provides that at or before a time specified in the agreement the cessation employer will pay an amount equal to or greater than the amount that is amount A for the purposes of regulation 7(3)(a);

(d)   the agreement—

    (i)   provides that if an event specified in sub-paragraph (3) occurs whilst the agreement is in force the parties to the agreement who are specified in the agreement as the persons who are the guarantors for the purposes of regulation 7 (the "guarantors") (who may be or include the cessation employer) will pay an amount equal to the amount that is amount B for the purposes of regulation 7(3)(b) (but without prejudice to their powers to make a payment on account of that amount at any earlier time);

    (ii)   if there are two or more guarantors, provides whether or not the guarantors are to be jointly and severally liable for that amount for those purposes; and

    (iii)   provides whether or not that amount is to be the amount provided for under regulation 7B(2);

(e)   the agreement provides that an amount payable under paragraph (c) or (d) is payable— .

    (i)   to the trustees of the scheme; or

    (ii)   if the Board of the Pension Protection Fund has assumed responsibility for the scheme in accordance with Chapter 3 of Part 2 of the 2004 Act (pension protection), to the Board on behalf of the trustees of the scheme;

(f)   the agreement provides that one or more of the parties to the agreement other than the trustees of the scheme are to bear any expenses incurred by the parties in connection with—

    (i)   the making of the agreement; or

    (ii)   the making of any calculations by the actuary for the purposes of the agreement;

(g)   the agreement will continue in force until—

    (i)   the winding up of the scheme is completed;

    (ii)   the Authority issue a notice to the parties to the agreement stating that the Authority consider that the agreement is no longer required; or

    (iii)   the agreement is replaced by another agreement that is approved by the Authority as an approved withdrawal arrangement,

whichever occurs first.

(3) The events are that—

(a)   the scheme begins to be wound up;

(b)   an event occurs as a result of which there is no person who is an employer in relation to the scheme for the purposes of these Regulations in relation to whom a relevant event has not occurred for the purposes of section 75 of the 1995 Act (see section 75(6A) of that Act);

(c)   the Authority issue a notice to the parties to the agreement stating that they consider that the amount referred to in sub-paragraph (2)(d)(i) should be paid.

(4) The Authority may not issue such a notice at any time unless the Authority consider that it is reasonable for the guarantors to be required to pay that amount at that time.

(5) In forming an opinion for the purposes of sub-paragraph (4), the Authority must have regard to such matters as the Authority consider relevant including—

(a)   whether the guarantors have taken reasonable steps to comply with the approved withdrawal arrangement;

(b)   whether the guarantors have complied with their obligations under paragraph 5; and

(c)   the guarantors' financial circumstances.

Approval of withdrawal arrangements

2   (1) Approval by the Authority of an agreement as a withdrawal arrangement is to be given in a notice issued by the Authority.

(2) Such an approval may be given subject to such conditions as the Authority consider appropriate.

(3) The Authority may not approve an agreement as a withdrawal arrangement unless they are satisfied that—

(a)   the agreement meets the conditions in paragraph 1(2); and

(b)   the guarantors have or will have such resources that the debt becoming due under section 75 of the 1995 Act is more likely to be met if the agreement is approved.

3   (1) Nothing in this Schedule prevents the Authority from approving as a withdrawal arrangement an agreement that will take effect only if an employment-cessation event occurs in relation to an employer.

(2) And in the case of such an approval, references in paragraphs 1 and 2 to that event and debt must be read accordingly.

(3) But, subject to that, references in these Regulations to an approved withdrawal arrangement only include references to an arrangement approved under this paragraph if the agreement has taken effect.

4   (1) Paragraphs 1, 2 and 5 of this Schedule apply to any arrangement replacing an approved withdrawal arrangement as they applied to the replaced arrangement.

(2) No directions may be issued under regulation 7(2) as a result of a notification about an arrangement that is to replace another arrangement if—

(a) directions have been issued under that regulation as a result of a notification about the replaced arrangement; and

(b) the replaced arrangement is an approved withdrawal arrangement that has come into force.

(3) But if an approved withdrawal arrangement replaces another such arrangement—

(a) any directions issued under regulation 7(2) as a result of a notification about the replaced arrangement continue to apply, and

(b) after the replacing arrangement comes into force the references to the approved withdrawal arrangement in regulations 7(3)(b), (4) and (6) and 7B(1) to (3) and in regulation 6(6)(b), as inserted by regulation 7A(5)(b), are to be taken as references to the replacing arrangement.

(4) Once sub-paragraph (2) has applied to an arrangement ("the second arrangement") that is to replace another arrangement—

(a) no further directions may be issued under regulation 7(2) as a result of a notification about any arrangement that is to replace the second arrangement or any subsequent replacing arrangement;

(b) sub-paragraph (3)(a) continues to apply to any directions about the arrangement replaced by the second arrangement notwithstanding the replacement of the second arrangement, or any subsequent replacement, by an approved withdrawal arrangement; and

(c) if such a replacement of the second arrangement or subsequent replacement occurs, references in sub-paragraph (3)(b) to the replacing arrangement are references to the latest replacing arrangement.

Notifiable events

5 (1) Where an approved withdrawal arrangement is in force in relation to a scheme, each relevant person must give notice to the Authority if such an event as is mentioned in sub-paragraph (3) occurs in relation to that person.

(2) For the purposes of this paragraph each of the guarantors is a relevant person.

(3) The following are the events referred to in sub-paragraph (1)—

(a) any decision by the relevant person to take action which will, or is intended to, result in a debt which is or may become due—

    (i) to the trustees of the scheme, or

    (ii) if the Board of the Pension Protection Fund has assumed responsibility for the scheme in accordance with Chapter 3 of Part 2 of the 2004 Act, to the Board,

not being paid in full;

(b) a decision by the relevant person to cease to carry on business (including any trade or profession) in the United Kingdom or, if the relevant person ceases to carry on such business without taking such a decision, his doing so;

(c) where applicable, receipt by the relevant person of advice that the person is trading wrongfully within the meaning of section 214 of the Insolvency Act 1986 (wrongful trading), or circumstances occurring in which a director or former director of the company knows that there is no reasonable prospect that the company will avoid going into insolvent liquidation within the meaning of that section, and for this purpose section 214(4) of that Act applies;

(d) any breach by the relevant person of a covenant in an agreement between the relevant person and a bank or other institution providing banking services, other than where the bank or other institution agrees with the relevant person not to enforce the covenant;

(e) any change in the relevant person's credit rating, or the relevant person ceasing to have a credit rating;

(f) where the relevant person is a company, a decision by a controlling company to relinquish control of the relevant person or, if the controlling company relinquishes such control without taking such a decision, its doing so;

(g) two or more changes in the holders of any key relevant person posts within a period of 12 months;

(h) where the relevant person is a company or partnership, the conviction of an individual, in any jurisdiction, for an offence involving dishonesty, if the offence was committed while the individual was a director or partner of the relevant person;

(i) an insolvency event occurring in relation to the relevant person for the purposes of Part 2 of the 2004 Act (see section 121 of that Act: insolvency event, insolvency date and insolvency practitioner).

(4) A notice under sub-paragraph (1) must be given in writing as soon as reasonably practicable after the relevant person becomes aware of the event.

(5) No duty to which a relevant person is subject is to be regarded as contravened merely because of any information or opinion contained in a notice under this paragraph.

(6) But sub-paragraph (5) does not require any person to disclose protected items within the meaning of section 311 of the 2004 Act (protected items).

(7) Section 10 of the 1995 Act (civil penalties) applies to any relevant person who without reasonable excuse fails to comply with an obligation imposed on him under this paragraph.

(8) In this paragraph—

"control" has the meaning given in section 435(10) of the Insolvency Act 1986 (meaning of "associate" – meaning of "control") and "controlling company" is to be read accordingly;

"director" has the meaning given in section 741(1) of the Companies Act 1985 (meaning of "director" and "shadow director");

"key relevant person posts" means the Chief Executive and any director or partner responsible in whole or in part for the financial affairs of the relevant person.

SCHEDULE 1B
Form of Actuary's Certificate: Scheme Funding Basis Debts in Approved Withdrawal Arrangement Cases

ACTUARIAL CERTIFICATE GIVEN FOR THE PURPOSES OF REGULATION 7A(6) OF THE OCCUPATIONAL PENSION SCHEMES (EMPLOYER DEBT) REGULATIONS 2005

Name of scheme

1   Comparison of value of scheme assets with amount of scheme liabilities

In my opinion, at the above date the value of the assets of the scheme was less than the amount of the liabilities of the scheme.

The value of the assets of the scheme was

The amount of the liabilities was

The amount of the difference was

2   The scheme's assets and liabilities are valued in accordance with regulation 5 of the Occupational Pension Schemes (Employer Debt) Regulations 2005, subject to the modifications specified in regulation 7A(4) of those Regulations, and the guidelines on winding up and scheme asset deficiency (GN19) and on minimum funding requirement (GN27) prepared and published by the Institute of Actuaries and the Faculty of Actuaries (so far as those guidelines are applicable).

Signature   Date
Name   Qualification
Address   Name of employer (if applicable)
Note:

The valuation of the amount of the liabilities of the scheme may not reflect the actual cost of securing those liabilities by the purchase of annuities if the scheme were to have been wound up on the date as at which the valuation is made."

NOTES
Initial Commencement
Specified date
Specified date: 2 September 2005: see reg 1(2).

The Occupational Pension Schemes (Scheme Funding) Regulations 2005

SI 2005 No 3377

Occupational Pension Schemes (Scheme Funding) Regulations 2005

Made 8th December 2005

Laid before Parliament 9th December 2005

Coming into force 30th December 2005

I Citation and commencement

These Regulations may be cited as the Occupational Pension Schemes (Scheme Funding) Regulations 2005 and shall come into force on 30th December 2005.

> **NOTES**
> **Initial Commencement**
> *Specified date*
> Specified date: 30 December 2005: see above.

2 Interpretation

(1) In these Regulations—

"the 1993 Act" means the Pension Schemes Act 1993;

"the 1995 Act" means the Pensions Act 1995;

"the 2004 Act" means the Pensions Act 2004;

"the actuary", in relation to a scheme, means the actuary appointed under section 47(1)(b) of the 1995 Act (professional advisers) in relation to that scheme;

"the commencement date" means 30th December 2005;

"insurance policy" means an insurance policy which is a contract on human life or a contract of annuity on human life, but excluding a contract which is linked to investment funds;

"pension credit rights" has the meaning given by section 124(1) of the 1995 Act;

"the relevant accounts", for the purposes of identifying and valuing the assets of a scheme, are audited accounts for the scheme—

    (a)   which comply with the requirements imposed under section 41 of the 1995 Act (provision of documents for members), and

    (b)   which are prepared in respect of a period ending with the effective date of the valuation.

(2) In these Regulations "scheme" must be read in appropriate cases in accordance with the modifications of Part 3 of the 2004 Act made by paragraphs 1, 4, 5 and 7 of Schedule 2 (multi-employer sectionalised schemes, partly foreign schemes and schemes with a partial public authority guarantee), and "employer" and "member" must be construed accordingly.

> **NOTES**
> **Initial Commencement**
> *Specified date*
> Specified date: 30 December 2005: see reg 1.

3 Determination of assets and liabilities

(1) The assets of a scheme to be taken into account for the purposes of Part 3 of the 2004 Act are the assets attributed to the scheme in the relevant accounts, excluding—

(a) any resources invested (or treated as invested by or under section 40 of the 1995 Act) in contravention of section 40(1) of the 1995 Act (employer-related investments);

(b) any amounts treated as a debt due to the trustees or managers under section 75(2) or (4) of the 1995 Act (deficiencies in the assets) or section 228(3) of the 2004 Act (amounts due in accordance with a schedule of contributions) which are unlikely to be recovered without disproportionate cost or within a reasonable time, and

(c) where it appears to the actuary that the circumstances are such that it is appropriate to exclude them, any rights under an insurance policy.

(2) The liabilities of a scheme to be taken into account for the purposes of Part 3 of the 2004 Act are any liabilities—

(a) in relation to a member of the scheme by virtue of—

(i) any right that has accrued to or in respect of him to future benefits under the scheme rules, or

(ii) any entitlement to the present payment of a pension or other benefit which he has under the scheme rules, and

(b) in relation to the survivor of a member of the scheme, by virtue of any entitlement to benefits, or right to future benefits which he has under the scheme rules in respect of the member.

(3) For the purposes of paragraph (2)—

"right" includes a pension credit right, and

"the survivor" of a member is a person who—

(a) is the widow, widower or surviving civil partner of the member, or

(b) has survived the member and has any entitlement to benefit, or right to future benefits, under the scheme in respect of the member.

(4) Where rights under an insurance policy are excluded under paragraph (1)(c), the liabilities secured by the policy shall be disregarded for the purposes of paragraph (2).

(5) Where arrangements are being made by the scheme for the transfer to or from it of accrued rights and any pension credit rights, until such time as the trustees or managers of the scheme to which the transfer is being made ("the receiving scheme") have received assets of the full amount agreed by them as consideration for the transfer, it shall be assumed—

(a) that the rights have not been transferred, and

(b) that any assets transferred in respect of the transfer of those rights are assets of the scheme making the transfer and not of the receiving scheme.

NOTES

Initial Commencement

Specified date

Specified date: 30 December 2005: see reg 1.

4 Valuation of assets and determination of the amount of liabilities

(1) Subject to paragraph (2), the value to be given to the assets of a scheme for the purposes of Part 3 of the 2004 Act is the value given to those assets in the relevant accounts, less the amount of the external liabilities.

(2) The value to be given to any rights under an insurance policy taken into account under regulation 3(1) is the value the actuary considers appropriate in the circumstances of the case.

(3) In paragraph (1), "the external liabilities" of a scheme are such liabilities of the scheme (other than liabilities within regulation 3(2)) as are shown in the net assets statement in the relevant accounts, and their amount shall be taken to be the amount shown in that statement in respect of them.

(4) The assets of the scheme shall be valued, and the amount of the liabilities determined, by reference to the same date.

NOTES

Initial Commencement

Specified date

Specified date: 30 December 2005: see reg 1.

5 Calculation of technical provisions

(1) Subject to paragraphs (2) and (3), it is for the trustees or managers of a scheme to determine which method and assumptions are to be used in calculating the scheme's technical provisions.

(2) The method used in calculating a scheme's technical provisions must be an accrued benefits funding method.

(3) In determining which accrued benefits funding method and which assumptions are to be used, the trustees or managers must—

(a)   follow the principles set out in paragraph (4), and

(b)   in the case of a scheme under which the rates of contributions payable by the employer are determined—

   (i)   by or in accordance with the advice of a person other than the trustees or managers, and

   (ii)   without the employer's agreement,

   take account of the recommendations of that person.

(4) The principles to be followed under paragraph (3) are—

(a)   the economic and actuarial assumptions must be chosen prudently, taking account, if applicable, of an appropriate margin for adverse deviation;

(b)   the rates of interest used to discount future payments of benefits must be chosen prudently, taking into account either or both—

   (i)   the yield on assets held by the scheme to fund future benefits and the anticipated future investment returns, and

   (ii)   the market redemption yields on government or other high-quality bonds;

(c)   the mortality tables used and the demographic assumptions made must be based on prudent principles, having regard to the main characteristics of the members as a group and expected changes in the risks to the scheme, and

(d)   any change from the method or assumptions used on the last occasion on which the scheme's technical provisions were calculated must be justified by a change of legal, demographic or economic circumstances.

NOTES
Initial Commencement
Specified date
Specified date: 30 December 2005: see reg 1.

6 Statement of funding principles

(1) A statement under section 223 of the 2004 Act must include the following matters, in addition to those specified in that section—

(a)   any funding objectives provided for in the rules of the scheme, or which the trustees or managers have adopted, in addition to the statutory funding objective;

(b)   whether there are arrangements for a person other than the employer or a member of the scheme to contribute to the funds held by the scheme, and, if there are such arrangements, the circumstances in which they apply;

(c)   whether there is a power to make payments to the employer out of funds held for the purposes of the scheme and, if there is such a power, the circumstances in which it may be exercised;

(d)   whether there are discretionary powers to provide or increase benefits for, or in respect of, all or any of the members and, if there are such powers, the extent to which they are taken into account in the funding of the scheme;

(e)   the policy of the trustees or managers regarding the reduction of the cash equivalent of benefits which have accrued to or in respect of members on account of the state of the funding of the scheme, and

(f)   the intervals at which the trustees or managers will obtain actuarial valuations in accordance with section 224(1)(a) of the 2004 Act, and the circumstances in which and occasions on which they will, or will consider whether to, obtain actuarial valuations in addition to those obtained at such intervals.

(2) The first statement under section 223 of the 2004 Act in respect of a scheme must be prepared by the trustees or managers within 15 months after the effective date of the first actuarial valuation obtained by them under section 224 of that Act.

(3) A statement under section 223 must be reviewed, and if necessary revised—

(a)   within 15 months after the effective date of each subsequent actuarial valuation, and

(b)   within a reasonable period after any occasion on which the Regulator has exercised any of the powers conferred by section 231(2) of the 2004 Act in relation to the scheme.

(4) A statement under section 223 must specify the date on which it was prepared, or, if it has been revised, the date on which it was last revised.

NOTES

Initial Commencement

Specified date

Specified date: 30 December 2005: see reg 1.

See Further

See further, in relation to the application with modifications of this provision to an occupational pension scheme that is subject to the regulatory own funds requirement: the Occupational Pension Schemes (Regulatory Own Funds) Regulations 2005, SI 2005/3380, reg 5(2)(a).

7   Actuarial valuations and reports

(1) In addition to the regular valuations provided for in section 224(1)(a) of the 2004 Act, the trustees or managers of a scheme must obtain an actuarial valuation where the Regulator has given directions under section 231(2)(b)(i) of that Act as to the manner in which the scheme's technical provisions are to be calculated.

(2) Where the trustees or managers have obtained an actuarial valuation or an actuarial report, they must ensure that it is received by them—

(a)   in the case of a valuation under section 224(1)(a), within 15 months after its effective date;

(b)   in the case of a valuation where the Regulator has given directions under section 231(2)(b)(i)—

        (i)   within three months after the date of the directions if the effective date of the valuation is before the date of the directions, and

        (ii)   within six months after the effective date of the valuation if that date is the same as or later than the date of the directions;

(c)   in the case of a report, within 12 months after its effective date.

(3) Where the assets taken into account in an actuarial valuation include rights under an insurance policy, the valuation must state the reason why the value given to such rights is considered appropriate in the circumstances of the case.

(4) An actuarial valuation must include—

(a)   the actuary's certification of the calculation of the technical provisions, in the relevant form set out in Schedule 1, and

(b)   the actuary's estimate of the solvency of the scheme.

(5) An actuarial report must include an assessment by the actuary of changes in the value of the scheme's assets since the last actuarial valuation was prepared.

(6) In paragraph (4), "the actuary's estimate of the solvency of the scheme" means—

(a)   except in the case referred to in sub-paragraph (b), an estimate by the actuary of whether, on the effective date of a valuation, the value of assets of the scheme to be taken into account under paragraph (1) of regulation 3 exceeded or fell short of the sum of—

        (i)   the cost of purchasing annuities, of the type described in section 74(3)(c) of the 1995 Act (discharge of liabilities by purchase of annuities satisfying prescribed requirements) and on terms consistent with those in the available market, which would be sufficient to satisfy the liabilities taken into account under paragraph (2) of regulation 3, and

        (ii)   the other expenses which, in the opinion of the actuary, would be likely to be incurred in connection with a winding up of the scheme,

        and the amount of the excess or, as the case may be, the shortfall;

(b)   where the actuary considers that it is not practicable to make an estimate in accordance with sub-paragraph (a), an estimate of the solvency of the scheme on the effective date of the valuation made in such manner as the actuary considers appropriate in the circumstances of the case.

(7) Where the actuary's estimate of solvency is made under paragraph (6)(b), the valuation must include a brief account of the principles adopted in making the estimate.

NOTES

Initial Commencement

Specified date

Specified date: 30 December 2005: see reg 1.

See Further

See further, in relation to the application with modifications of this provision to an occupational pension scheme that is subject to the regulatory own funds requirement: the Occupational Pension Schemes (Regulatory Own Funds) Regulations 2005, SI 2005/3380, reg 5(2)(a), (b).

8 Recovery plan

(1) Where section 226(1) of the 2004 Act applies, and the trustees or managers of a scheme are required, following an actuarial valuation, either to prepare a recovery plan or to review and if necessary revise an existing recovery plan, they must do so—

(a)   in the case of the first actuarial valuation obtained by them under section 224 of the Act and each subsequent valuation under section 224(1)(a), within 15 months after the effective date of the valuation;

(b)   in the case of a valuation under section 224(1)(b) and regulation 7(1), within whichever period is applicable under regulation 7(2)(b).

(2) In preparing or revising a recovery plan, the trustees or managers must take account of the following matters—

(a)   the asset and liability structure of the scheme;

(b)   its risk profile;

(c)   its liquidity requirements;

(d)   the age profile of the members, and

(e)   in the case of a scheme under which the rates of contributions payable by the employer are determined—

    (i)   by or in accordance with the advice of a person other than the trustees or managers, and

    (ii)   without the agreement of the employer,

the recommendations of that person.

(3) A recovery plan must be reviewed, and if necessary revised, where the Regulator has given directions under section 231(2)(b)(ii) of the 2004 Act as to the period within which, and manner in which, a failure to meet the statutory funding objective is to be remedied.

(4) Where paragraph (3) applies, the review and any necessary revision must be completed within a reasonable period after the date of the Regulator's directions.

(5) A recovery plan may be reviewed, and if necessary revised, where the trustees or managers consider that there are reasons that may justify a variation to it.

(6) A recovery plan must specify the date on which it was prepared, or, if it has been revised, the date on which it was last revised.

(7) A copy of any recovery plan sent to the Regulator by the trustees or managers of a scheme must be accompanied—

(a)   in a case where the plan has been prepared or revised following an actuarial valuation, by a summary of the information contained in the valuation, and

(b)   in a case where the plan has been revised in the circumstances described in paragraph (5), by an explanation of the reasons for the revision.

(8) ...

NOTES

Initial Commencement

Specified date

Specified date: 30 December 2005: see reg 1.

Amendment

Para (8): revoked by SI 2006/1733, reg 5(1), (2).

Date in force: 24 July 2006: see SI 2006/1733, reg 1.

See Further

See further, in relation to the disapplication of this provision in relation to an occupational pension scheme that is subject to the regulatory own funds requirement: the Occupational Pension Schemes (Regulatory Own Funds) Regulations 2005, SI 2005/3380, reg 5(2)(b).

9 Schedule of contributions

(1) A schedule of contributions for a scheme must be prepared within 15 months after the effective date of the first actuarial valuation following the establishment of the scheme.

(2) Where a schedule of contributions has been prepared, it must be reviewed, and if necessary revised—

(a) within 15 months after the effective date of each subsequent actuarial valuation under section 224(1)(a) of the 2004 Act;

(b) within whichever period is applicable under regulation 7(2)(b) after any valuation under section 224(1)(b) and regulation 7(1), and

(c) within a reasonable period after any revision of a recovery plan under regulation 8(3) or (5).

NOTES

Initial Commencement

Specified date

Specified date: 30 December 2005: see reg 1.

See Further

See further, in relation to the application with modifications of this provision to an occupational pension scheme that is subject to the regulatory own funds requirement: the Occupational Pension Schemes (Regulatory Own Funds) Regulations 2005, SI 2005/3380, reg 5(2)(a).

10 Content and certification of schedules of contributions

(1) A schedule of contributions must show the rates and due dates of all contributions (other than voluntary contributions) payable towards the scheme by or on behalf of the employer and the active members during the relevant period.

(2) In this regulation, "the relevant period" means the period of five years after the date on which the schedule is certified, or, in a case where—

(a) a recovery plan is in force, and

(b) the period set out in the recovery plan as the period within which the statutory funding objective is to be met is longer than five years after the date on which the schedule is certified,

that longer period.

(3) The schedule must show separately—

(a) the rates and due dates of contributions payable by or on behalf of active members of the scheme;

(b) the rates and due dates of the contributions payable by or on behalf of the employer, and

(c) if separate contributions to satisfy liabilities other than those referred to in regulation 3(2) which are likely to fall due for payment by the trustees or managers during the relevant period are made to the scheme, the rates and due dates of those contributions.

(4) Where additional contributions are required in order to give effect to a recovery plan, the rates and dates of those contributions must be shown separately from the rates and dates of contributions otherwise payable.

(5) The schedule must be signed by the trustees or managers of the scheme, and make provision for signature by the employer in order to signify his agreement to the matters included in it.

(6) The schedule must incorporate the actuary's certification, in the relevant form set out in Schedule 1.

NOTES

Initial Commencement

Specified date

Specified date: 30 December 2005: see reg 1.

See Further

See further, in relation to the application with modifications of this provision to an occupational pension scheme that is subject to the regulatory own funds requirement: the Occupational Pension Schemes (Regulatory Own Funds) Regulations 2005, SI 2005/3380, reg 5(2)(c).

11 Records

(1) The trustees or managers of a scheme to which Part 3 of the 2004 Act applies must keep records of all contributions made to the scheme by any person, showing separately—

(a)   the aggregate amounts of contributions paid by or on behalf of active members of the scheme (whether by deductions from their earnings or otherwise) and the dates on which they are paid, distinguishing voluntary contributions from other contributions, and showing the amounts of voluntary contributions paid by each member, and

(b)   the aggregate amounts of contributions paid by or on behalf of each person who is an employer in relation to the scheme and the dates on which they are paid.

(2) The trustees or managers must also keep records of any action taken by them to recover—

(a)   the amount of any contributions which are not paid on the date on which they are due, and

(b)   the amount of any debt which has arisen under section 75(2) or (4) of the 1995 Act (deficiencies in the assets).

NOTES
Initial Commencement
Specified date
Specified date: 30 December 2005: see reg 1.

12   Failure to make payments

The trustees or managers of a scheme are not required to give notice, under section 228(2) of the 2004 Act (requirement to notify Regulator of failure likely to be of material significance), of a failure to make a payment in accordance with the schedule of contributions where they have given the Regulator notice of the failure under—

(a)   section 49(9)(b) of the 1995 Act (failure to remit deductions from members' earnings), or

(b)   section 30(7)(c) of the 2004 Act (failure to pay employer's contributions in accordance with Regulator's order).

NOTES
Initial Commencement
Specified date
Specified date: 30 December 2005: see reg 1.

13   Period for obtaining employer's agreement

Where, following an actuarial valuation, the trustees or managers of a scheme are required under section 229(1) of the 2004 Act to obtain the agreement of the employer to any of the matters mentioned in paragraphs (a) to (d) of that provision, they must do so within 15 months after the effective date of the valuation.

NOTES
Initial Commencement
Specified date
Specified date: 30 December 2005: see reg 1.

See Further
See further, in relation to the application with modifications of this provision to an occupational pension scheme that is subject to the regulatory own funds requirement: the Occupational Pension Schemes (Regulatory Own Funds) Regulations 2005, SI 2005/3380, reg 5(2)(a).

14   Powers of the Regulator

(1) In exercising any of the powers conferred by section 231 of the 2004 Act in the case of a scheme of the kind referred to in regulations 5(3)(b) and 8(2)(e), the Regulator must take into account any relevant recommendations made to the trustees or managers under those regulations.

(2) In exercising the power in section 231(2)(b)(i) to give directions as to the manner in which a scheme's technical provisions are to be calculated, the Regulator must include a direction specifying the effective date by reference to which assets are valued and the amount of liabilities is determined.

NOTES
Initial Commencement
Specified date
Specified date: 30 December 2005: see reg 1.

15 Guidance relating to actuarial advice

When advising the trustees or managers of a scheme on any of the matters specified in section 230(1) of the 2004 Act, the actuary shall have regard to the guidance note "Occupational Pension Schemes – scheme funding matters on which advice of actuary must be obtained" (GN49) prepared and published by the Institute of Actuaries and the Faculty of Actuaries and approved for the purposes of these Regulations by the Secretary of State, with such revisions as have been so approved.

NOTES

Initial Commencement

Specified date

Specified date: 30 December 2005: see reg 1.

16 Modification of shared cost schemes

(1) The trustees of a shared cost scheme to which Part 3 of the 2004 Act applies may by resolution modify the scheme with a view to making such provision that, where any additional contributions are required to give effect to a recovery plan, those contributions are payable by the employer and the members in the appropriate proportions, unless the employer and the trustees or managers agree—

(a)   that the additional contributions should be payable by the employer alone, or

(b)   that he should pay a greater proportion than would otherwise fall to be paid by him.

(2) In paragraph (1)—

"shared cost scheme" means a scheme under the provisions of which—

(a)   the level of benefits expected to be provided is defined;

(b)   contributions are payable by the employer and the active members in specified proportions, and

(c)   if—

(i)   it appears to the trustees or managers, or

(ii)   an actuarial valuation shows,

that otherwise the assets of the scheme will (or are likely to) fall short of its technical provisions, the rates of contributions payable by both the active members and the employer may be increased in specified proportions, and

"the appropriate proportions" means those specified proportions.

(3) For the purposes of paragraph (2) there shall be disregarded—

(a)   voluntary contributions by members and any associated contributions by the employer, and

(b)   any temporary suspension of the liability to make contributions, or alteration in the proportions in which the contributions are payable, under any provision of the scheme allowing such a suspension or alteration in any circumstances.

NOTES

Initial Commencement

Specified date

Specified date: 30 December 2005: see reg 1.

17 Exemptions—general

(1) Part 3 of the 2004 Act does not apply to—

(a)   a scheme which—

(i)   is established by or under an enactment (including a local Act), and

(ii)   is guaranteed by a public authority;

(b)   a pay-as-you-go scheme;

(c)   a scheme which is made under section 2 of the Parliamentary and other Pensions Act 1987 (power to provide for pensions for Members of the House of Commons etc);

(d)   a scheme which is treated as such by virtue of paragraph 4 or 5 of Schedule 2 to these Regulations and—

(i)   in the cases described in paragraphs 4(2) and 5(2)(a) of that Schedule, applies to members in employment outside the member States, and

       (ii)   in the cases described in paragraphs 4(3) and 5(2)(b) of that Schedule, applies to members in employment outside the United Kingdom;

(e)   a scheme which—

       (i)   provides relevant benefits;

       (ii)   is neither a relevant statutory scheme nor a tax approved scheme, or, from 6th April 2006, is not a tax registered scheme, and

       (iii)   has fewer than 100 members;

(f)   a section 615(6) scheme which has fewer than 100 members;

(g)   a scheme which has fewer than two members;

(h)   a scheme which has fewer than 12 members, where all the members are trustees of the scheme and either—

       (i)   the provisions of the scheme provide that all decisions which fall to be made by the trustees are made by the unanimous agreement of the trustees who are members of the scheme, or

       (ii)   the scheme has a trustee who is an independent trustee in relation to the scheme for the purposes of section 23 of the 1995 Act (power to appoint independent trustees) and is registered in the register maintained by the Authority in accordance with regulations made under subsection (4) of that section;

(i)   a scheme which has fewer than 12 members, where a company is a trustee of the scheme and all the members of the scheme are directors of the company and either—

       (i)   the provisions of the scheme provide that any decision made by the company in its capacity as trustee is made only by the unanimous agreement of the directors who are members of the scheme, or

       (ii)   one of the directors is a trustee who is independent in relation to the scheme for the purposes of section 23 of the 1995 Act and is registered in the register maintained by the Authority in accordance with regulations made under subsection (4) of that section;

(j)   a scheme under which the only benefits provided for (other than money purchase benefits) are death benefits, if the death benefits are secured by insurance policies or annuity contracts;

(k)   a scheme which is the subject of a scheme failure notice under section 122 or 130 of the 2004 Act;

(l)   [subject to paragraph (1A) and regulation 18], a scheme which is being wound up, or

(m)   the Chatsworth Settlement Estate Pension Scheme.

[(1A) Section 231A of the 2004 Act applies to a scheme where—

(a)   a recovery plan has been prepared under section 226 of the 2004 Act, and

(b)   the scheme begins to wind up during the recovery period.]

(2) In paragraph (1)—

"enactment" includes an enactment comprised in, or in an instrument under, an Act of the Scottish Parliament;

"pay-as-you-go scheme" means an occupational pension scheme under which there is no requirement for assets to be set aside in advance for the purpose of providing benefits under the scheme (disregarding any requirements relating to additional voluntary contributions);

"public authority" means—

       (a)   a Minister of the Crown (within the meaning of the Ministers of the Crown Act 1975);

       (b)   a government department (including any body or authority exercising statutory functions on behalf of the Crown);

       (c)   the Scottish Ministers;

       (d)   the National Assembly for Wales, or

       (e)   a local authority;

"relevant benefits" has the meaning given in section 612(1) of the Income and Corporation Taxes Act 1988 (interpretation) or, from 6th April 2006, section 393B of the Income Tax (Earnings and Pensions) Act 2003 (relevant benefits);

"relevant statutory scheme" has the meaning given in section 611A(1) of the Income and Corporation Taxes Act 1988 (definition of relevant statutory scheme);

"section 615(6) scheme" means a scheme with such a superannuation fund as is mentioned in section 615(6) of the Income and Corporation Taxes Act 1988 (funds for the provision of benefits in respect of employment outside the United Kingdom);

"a tax approved scheme" means a scheme which is approved or was formerly approved under section 590 or 591 of the Income and Corporation Taxes Act 1988 (approval of retirement benefit schemes) or in respect of which an application for such approval has been duly made but has not been determined;

"a tax registered scheme" means a scheme which is, or is treated as, registered under Chapter 2 of Part 4 of the Finance Act 2004 (registration of pension schemes).

[(2A) In paragraph (1A) "recovery period" means the period specified in the scheme's recovery plan in accordance with section 226(2)(b) of the 2004 Act.]

(3) In paragraph (2), "local authority" means—

(a)   in relation to England, a county council, a district council, a London borough council, the Greater London Authority, the Common Council of the City of London in its capacity as a local authority or the Council of the Isles of Scilly;

(b)   in relation to Wales, a county council or county borough council;

(c)   in relation to Scotland, a council constituted under section 2 of the Local Government etc (Scotland) Act 1994 (constitution of councils);

(d)   an administering authority as defined in Schedule 1 to the Local Government Pension Scheme Regulations 1997.

(4) Where Part 3 of the 2004 Act ceases to apply to a scheme to which it previously applied, because the scheme satisfies any of the criteria for exemption in paragraph (1), that does not affect any rights or obligations arising before Part 3 ceased to apply.

NOTES

Initial Commencement

Specified date

Specified date: 30 December 2005: see reg 1.

Amendment

Para (1): in sub-para (l) words "subject to paragraph (1A) and regulation 18" in square brackets substituted by SI 2006/1733, reg 5(1), (3)(a).

Date in force: 24 July 2006: see SI 2006/1733, reg 1.

Para (1A): inserted by SI 2006/1733, reg 5(1), (3)(b).

Date in force: 24 July 2006: see SI 2006/1733, reg 1.

Para (2A): inserted by SI 2006/1733, reg 5(1), (4).

Date in force: 24 July 2006: see SI 2006/1733, reg 1.

See Further

See further, in relation to the disapplication of this provision in relation to an occupational pension scheme that is subject to the regulatory own funds requirement: the Occupational Pension Schemes (Regulatory Own Funds) Regulations 2005, SI 2005/3380, reg 5(2)(d).

18   Exemption connected with winding up

(1) Where the winding up of a scheme begins on or after the commencement date, the exemption provided for in regulation 17(1)(l) is subject to the condition set out in paragraph (2).

(2) The condition referred to in paragraph (1) is that the trustees or managers of the scheme ensure that they receive, before the end of each scheme year following the scheme year in which the winding up of the scheme begins, the actuary's estimate of the solvency of the scheme as at the end of the preceding scheme year.

(3) In paragraph (2)—

"the actuary's estimate of the solvency of the scheme" means—

(a)   except in the case referred to in sub-paragraph (b), an estimate by the actuary of whether, at the end of the relevant scheme year, the value of assets of the scheme to be taken into account under paragraph (1) of regulation 3 exceeded or fell short of the sum of—

(i)   the cost of purchasing annuities, of the type described in section 74(3)(c) of the 1995 Act and on terms consistent with those in the available market, which would be sufficient to satisfy the liabilities to be taken into account under paragraph (2) of regulation 3, and

(ii)   the other expenses which, in the opinion of the actuary, would be likely to be incurred in connection with the winding up of the scheme, and the amount of the excess or, as the case may be, the shortfall;

(b) where the actuary considers that it is not practicable to make an estimate in accordance with sub-paragraph (a), an estimate of the solvency of the scheme at the end of the relevant scheme year made in such manner as the actuary considers appropriate in the circumstances of the case;

"scheme year" means—

(a) either—

(i) a year specified for the purposes of the scheme rules in any document which contains those rules, or

(ii) if no such year is specified, the period of 12 months commencing on 1st April or on such date as the trustees or managers select, or

(b) such other period (if any) exceeding six months but not exceeding 18 months as is selected by the trustees or managers in connection with—

(i) the commencement or termination of the scheme, or

(ii) a variation of the date on which the year or period referred to in paragraph (a) is to commence.

NOTES

Initial Commencement

Specified date

Specified date: 30 December 2005: see reg 1.

See Further

See further, in relation to the disapplication of this provision in relation to an occupational pension scheme that is subject to the regulatory own funds requirement: the Occupational Pension Schemes (Regulatory Own Funds) Regulations 2005, SI 2005/3380, reg 5(2)(d).

19   Modification of provisions of the 2004 Act

Schedule 2 has effect for the purpose of modifying Part 3 of the 2004 Act and these Regulations as they apply in the circumstances specified there.

NOTES

Initial Commencement

Specified date

Specified date: 30 December 2005: see reg 1.

20   Supplementary and consequential provisions, transitional provisions and savings

(1) Schedule 3 has effect for the purpose of making supplementary provisions and consequential amendments connected with the commencement of Part 3 of the 2004 Act and Part IV of the Pensions (Northern Ireland) Order 2005 and the coming into force of these Regulations.

(2) Schedule 4 has effect for the purpose of making transitional modifications of the 2004 Act and these Regulations, and saving the effect of repealed provisions of the 1995 Act and provisions revoked by these Regulations.

NOTES

Initial Commencement

Specified date

Specified date: 30 December 2005: see reg 1.

21   Revocations

The enactments mentioned in Schedule 5 are revoked to the extent specified, subject to the savings in Schedule 4.

NOTES

Initial Commencement

Specified date

Specified date: 30 December 2005: see reg 1.

SCHEDULE I
Actuary's Certificates

Regulations 7(4)(a) and 10(6)

Form of actuary's certification of the calculation of technical provisions

Name of scheme

Calculation of technical provisions

I certify that, in my opinion, the calculation of the scheme's technical provisions as at [*insert effective date of valuation on which the calculation is based*] is made in accordance with regulations under section 222 of the Pensions Act 2004. The calculation uses a method and assumptions determined by the [trustees] [managers] [*delete whichever does not apply*] of the scheme and set out in the Statement of Funding Principles dated [dd/mm/yyyy].

Signature: Date:

Name: Qualification:

Address: Name of employer (if applicable):

Form of actuary's certification of schedule of contributions

Name of scheme

Adequacy of rates of contributions

1 I certify that, in my opinion, the rates of contributions shown in this schedule of contributions are such that—

the statutory funding objective can be expected to be met by the end of the period specified in the recovery plan dated [*dd/mm/yyyy*](a).

the statutory funding objective can be expected to continue to be met for the period for which the schedule is to be in force(b).

[*delete whichever alternative does not apply*]

Adherence to statement of funding principles

2 I hereby certify that, in my opinion, this schedule of contributions is consistent with the Statement of Funding Principles dated [*dd/mm/yyyy*].

The certification of the adequacy of the rates of contributions for the purpose of securing that the statutory funding objective can be expected to be met is not a certification of their adequacy for the purpose of securing the scheme's liabilities by the purchase of annuities, if the scheme were to be wound up.

Signature: Date:

Name: Qualification:

Address: Name of employer (if applicable)

(a) This applies where the statutory funding objective was not met on the effective date of the last actuarial valuation.

(b) This applies where the statutory funding objective was met on the effective date of the last actuarial valuation.

NOTES

Initial Commencement

Specified date

Specified date: 30 December 2005: see reg 1.

SCHEDULE 2
Modifications of the Act and Regulations

Regulation 19

Multi-employer schemes

I   (1) Where—

(a)   a scheme in relation to which there is more than one employer is divided into two or more sections, and

(b)   the provisions of the scheme are such that they meet conditions A and B,

Part 3 of the 2004 Act and these Regulations shall apply as if each section of the scheme were a separate scheme.

(2) Condition A is that contributions payable to the scheme by an employer, or by a member in employment under that employer, are allocated to that employer's section (or, if more than one section applies to the employer, to the section which is appropriate in respect of the employment in question).

(3) Condition B is that a specified part or proportion of the assets of the scheme is attributable to each section and cannot be used for the purposes of any other section.

(4) In their application to a scheme—

(a)   which has been such a scheme as is mentioned in sub-paragraph (1);

(b)   which is divided into two or more sections, at least one of which applies only to members who are not in pensionable service under the section;

(c)   the provisions of which have not been amended so as to prevent conditions A and B being met in relation to two or more sections, and

(d)   in relation to one or more sections of which those conditions have ceased to be met at any time by reason only of there being no members in pensionable service under the section and no contributions which are to be allocated to it,

Part 3 of the 2004 Act and these Regulations apply as if the section in relation to which those conditions have ceased to be satisfied were a separate scheme.

(5) For the purposes of sub-paragraphs (1) to (4), any provisions of the scheme by virtue of which contributions or transfers of assets may be made to make provision for death benefits are disregarded.

(6) But if sub-paragraph (1) or (4) applies and, by virtue of any provisions of the scheme, contributions or transfers of assets to make provision for death benefits are made to a section ("the death benefits section") the assets of which may only be applied for the provision of death benefits, the death benefits section is also to be treated as if it were a seperate scheme for the purpose of Part 3 of the 2004 Act and these Regulations.

(7) For the purpose of this paragraph, any provisions of a scheme by virtue of which assets attributable to one section may on the winding up of the scheme or a section be used for the purposes of another section are disregarded.

(8) In their application in a case of the kind described in sub-paragraph (1) or (4), the forms set out in Schedule 1 are modified as follows—

(a)   after "*Name of scheme*", there is inserted "*and name of section*", and

(b)   for "scheme" and "scheme's", wherever else they occur, there is substituted "section" and "section's".

2   In the application of section 229 of the 2004 Act to a scheme in relation to which there is more than one employer, references to the employer have effect as if they were references to a person nominated by the employers, or by the rules of the scheme, to act as the employers' representative for the purposes of the section or, if no such nomination is made—

(a)   for the purposes of agreement to any of the matters mentioned in subsection (1) of that section, to all of the employers other than any employer who has waived his rights under that sub-section, and

(b)   for the purposes of agreement to a modification of the scheme under subsection (2) of that section, to all of the employers.

Frozen or paid-up schemes

3   In the application of Part 3 of the 2004 Act and these Regulations to a scheme which has no active members, references to the employer have effect as if they were references to the person who was the employer immediately before the occurrence of the event after which the scheme ceased to have any such members.

Schemes covering United Kingdom and foreign employment

4   (1) This paragraph applies in the cases described in sub-paragraphs (2) and (3).

(2) The first case referred to in sub-paragraph (1) is where a scheme—

(a)   has its main administration in the United Kingdom;

(b)   applies to members in employment in the member States and members in employment outside the member States;

(c)   is divided into two or more sections, and

(d)   makes provision whereby—

    (i)   different sections of the scheme apply to members in employment in the member States and to members in employment outside the member States;

    (ii)   contributions payable to the scheme in respect of a member are allocated to the section applying to that member's employment, and

(iii)   a specified part or proportion of the assets of the scheme is attributable to each section and cannot be used for the purposes of any other section.

(3) The second case referred to in sub-paragraph (1) is where a scheme—

(a)   has its main administration outside the member States;

(b)   applies to members in employment in the United Kingdom and members in employment outside the United Kingdom;

(c)   is divided into two or more sections, and

(d)   makes provision whereby—

(i)   different sections of the scheme apply to members in employment in the United Kingdom and to members in employment outside the United Kingdom;

(ii)   contributions payable to the scheme in respect of a member are allocated to the section applying to that member's employment, and

(iii)   a specified part or proportion of the assets of the scheme is attributable to each section and cannot be used for the purposes of any other section.

(4) Where this paragraph applies, Part 3 of the 2004 Act and these Regulations shall apply as if each section of the scheme were a separate scheme.

5   (1) This paragraph applies in the case described in sub-paragraph (2).

(2) The case referred to in sub-paragraph (1) is where a scheme either—

(a)   satisfies the criteria in sub-paragraphs (a) and (b) of paragraph 4(2), but is not divided into sections in the manner described in sub-paragraphs (c) and (d) of that paragraph, or

(b)   satisfies the criteria in sub-paragraphs (a) and (b) of paragraph 4(3), but is not divided into sections in the manner described in sub-paragraphs (c) and (d) of that paragraph,

and part of the scheme is or was treated as a separate scheme under section 611(3) of the Income and Corporation Taxes Act 1988.

(3) Where this paragraph applies, Part 3 of the 2004 Act and these Regulations shall apply as if the separated parts of the scheme were separate schemes.

Schemes undertaking cross-border activities

6   (1) This paragraph applies where the trustees or managers of a scheme are authorised under section 288 of the 2004 Act to accept contributions from European employers or approved under section 289 of that Act to accept contributions from a particular European employer.

(2) Where this paragraph applies, and subject to sub-paragraphs (3) and (4), Part 3 of the 2004 Act and these Regulations shall apply as if they were subject to the following modifications—

(a)   in section 224 of the Act—

(i)   in subsection (1)(a), the words from "or," to the end of the subsection are omitted;

(ii)   paragraphs (c) and (d) of subsection (2) are omitted;

(iii)   the word "and" at the end of paragraph (a) of subsection (3) and paragraph (b) of that subsection are omitted;

(iv)   the words "or report" in subsections (4), (6) and (7) and the words "or reports" in subsection (5) are omitted;

(b)   in section 226—

(i)   in subsection (1), for the words from "within the prescribed time" to the end of the subsection there is substituted—

"(a)   send a summary of the valuation to the Regulator within a reasonable period, and

(b)   take such steps as are necessary to ensure that the statutory funding objective is met within two years after that date.", and

(ii)   subsections (2) to (6) are omitted;

(c)   in section 227, for the words "by the end of the period specified in the recovery plan" in subsection (6)(b)(i) there is substituted "within two years after that date";

(d)   in section 231, the words from "with respect to" in paragraph (d) of subsection (1) to the end of that paragraph are omitted;

(e)   in regulations 6(2) and (3)(a), 7(2)(a), 9(1) and (2)(a) and 13 of these Regulations, for "15 months" there is substituted "12 months";

(f)   in regulation 7(2), the words "or an actuarial report" are omitted;

(g)   regulations 7(2)(c) and (5), 8, 9(2)(c) and 17(1)(a) and (e) to (i) are omitted;

(h)   in regulation 10—

      (i)   in paragraph (2), for "five years", where those words first appear, there is substituted "two years", and the words from "or, in a case where" to the end of that paragraph are omitted;

      (ii)   in paragraph (4), for "give effect to a recovery plan", there is substituted "comply with section 226", and

(i)   in Schedule 1, in the first of the alternative statements in the form of certification of the adequacy of the rates of contributions, for "by the end of the period specified in the recovery plan dated [*dd/mm/yyyy*]" there is substituted "within two years after the effective date of the last actuarial valuation".

(3) In the case of a pre-23rd September 2005 scheme—

(a)   section 226 of the 2004 Act applies as if it were subject to the following modifications in place of the modifications in sub-paragraph (2)(b)—

      (i)   for the words from "they must, within the prescribed time" in subsection (1) to the end of that subsection there is substituted—

"they must—

      (a)   send a summary of the valuation to the Regulator within a reasonable period, and

      (b)   take such steps as are necessary to ensure that the statutory funding objective is met—

            (i)   if the valuation is the first valuation the trustees or managers have obtained under section 224, by 22nd September 2008, and

            (ii)   in any other case, within two years after that date.", and

      (ii)   subsections (2) to (6) are omitted;

(b)   these Regulations apply as if, in addition to the modifications in sub-paragraph (2)(e) to (i), paragraph 2(a)(i) of Schedule 4 is modified so that, after "this Schedule" there is inserted "and, without prejudice to any of those requirements, by reference to an effective date which is no later than 22nd September 2006".

(4) In sub-paragraph (3), "pre-23rd September 2005 scheme" has the meaning given by article 3 of the Pensions Act 2004 (Commencement No 8) Order 2005.

Schemes with a partial guarantee by a public authority

7   Where such a guarantee has been given as is mentioned in regulation 17(1)(a)(ii) in respect of only part of a scheme, Part 3 of the 2004 Act and these Regulations shall apply as if that part and the other part of the scheme were separate schemes.

Schemes relating to certain defence contractors

8   (1) This paragraph applies in the case of a scheme under which variations to the rate of contributions payable towards the scheme by the employer are subject, either in particular cases or generally, to the consent of—

(a)   the Secretary of State for Defence;

(b)   a person duly authorised by him, or

(c)   a company of which the Secretary of State for Defence or a nominee of his is a shareholder, or a subsidiary (within the meaning of section 736 of the Companies Act 1985) of such a company.

(2) Where this paragraph applies, sections 224(7) and 229 of the 2004 Act shall apply as if references to the employer were both to the employer and the Secretary of State for Defence or, in a case where the consent of a company is required, both to the employer and that company.

Schemes under which the rates of contributions are determined by the trustees or managers or by the actuary

9   (1) In the case of a scheme under which—

(a)   the rates of contributions payable by the employer are determined by the trustees or managers without the agreement of the employer, and

(b)   no person other than the trustees or managers is permitted to reduce those rates or to suspend payment of contributions,

section 229 of the 2004 Act and regulation 13 shall apply as if they were subject to the modifications set out in sub-paragraphs (2) and (3), and the reference to section 229 in paragraph 8(2) above shall be read as a reference to that section as modified by sub-paragraph (2).

(2) The modifications of section 229 of the 2004 Act are as follows—

(a)   in the heading, for "**agreement of the employer**" there is substituted "**consultation or agreement**";

(b)   in subsection (1), for "obtain the agreement of the employer to" there is substituted "consult the employer regarding";

(c)   in subsection (2), for the words before " (if the employer agrees)" there is substituted "After consulting the employer regarding any such matter, the trustees or managers may";

(d)   subsection (5) is omitted, and

(e)   in subsection (6), for " (1), (4) or (5)" there is substituted " (1) or (4)".

(3) The modifications of regulation 13 are as follows—

(a)   in the heading, for "**obtaining employer's agreement**" there is substituted "**consulting employer**", and

(b)   in the text, for "obtain the agreement of the employer to" there is substituted "consult the employer regarding".

(4) Where the power of the trustees or managers to determine the rates of contributions payable by the employer without the employer's agreement is subject to conditions, the modifications provided for in sub-paragraphs (2) and (3) have effect only in circumstances where the conditions are satisfied.

(5) In the case of a scheme under which the rates of contributions payable by the employer are determined by the actuary without the agreement of the employer, section 227(6) of the 2004 Act shall apply as if it required that, in addition to the matters specified there, the actuary's certificate must state that the rates shown in the schedule of contributions are not lower than the rates he would have provided for if he, rather than the trustees or managers of the scheme, had the responsibility of preparing or revising the schedule, the statement of funding principles and any recovery plan.

(6) In the case to which sub-paragraph (5) applies, regulation 10(6) and Schedule 1 apply as if the form of certification of the adequacy of the rates of contributions shown in the schedule of contributions included an additional statement that—

"I also certify that the rates of contributions shown in this schedule are not lower than I would have provided for had I had responsibility for preparing or revising the schedule, the statement of funding principles and any recovery plan".

(7) Where the power of the actuary to determine the rates of contributions payable by the employer without the employer's agreement is subject to conditions, the modifications provided for in sub-paragraphs (5) and (6) have effect only in circumstances where the conditions are satisfied.

(8) In the case of a scheme to which paragraph 8 applies, the references to the employer's agreement in sub-paragraphs (4), (5) and (7) of this paragraph shall be read as if the extended meaning of "employer" given by paragraph 8(2) applied.

Schemes which are not required to appoint an actuary

10   Where a scheme is exempt from the application of section 47(1)(b) of the 1995 Act (requirement to appoint a scheme actuary) by virtue of regulations made under subsection (5) of that section, Part 3 of the 2004 Act and these Regulations shall apply as if references to the actuary were to an actuary authorised by the trustees or managers to provide such valuations and certifications as may be required under that Part and these Regulations.

Schemes with fewer than 100 members

11 (1) This paragraph applies in the case of a scheme which—

(a) had fewer than 100 members on the effective date of its last actuarial valuation;

(b) is not exempted from the application of Part 3 of the 2004 Act by regulation 17(1), and

(c) is not a scheme in relation to which the application of that Part of the Act is modified by paragraph 6 of this Schedule.

(2) Where this paragraph applies—

(a) section 224(1)(a) of the 2004 Act shall apply as if it required the trustees or managers of the scheme to obtain an actuarial valuation the effective date of which is not more than three years after that of the last such valuation, and an actuarial report for any intervening year at any time in which the scheme had 100 or more members, and

(b) section 224(3) of that Act shall apply as if—

(i) all but paragraph (b) were omitted, and

(ii) that paragraph required that the effective date of any actuarial report must be an anniversary of the effective date of the last actuarial valuation.

Schemes subject to a change of circumstances affecting the certification of the schedule of contributions

12 (1) In circumstances where the actuary considers that, because of the possibility of significant changes in the value of the assets of the scheme or in the scheme's technical provisions since the effective date of the last actuarial valuation, he is unable to certify the schedule of contributions in the terms set out in paragraph (b) of section 227(6) of the 2004 Act, that paragraph applies as if it provided for a statement that the rates shown in that schedule are such that—

(a) where the statutory funding objective was not met on the effective date of the last actuarial valuation, the statutory funding objective could have been expected on that date to be met by the end of the period specified in the recovery plan, or

(b) where the statutory funding objective was met on the effective date of the last actuarial valuation, the statutory funding objective could have been expected on that date to continue to be met for the period for which the schedule is to be in force.

(2) In circumstances where the statutory funding objective was met on the effective date of the last actuarial valuation but the actuary considers that, having regard to—

(a) the rates of contributions payable towards the scheme since that date, or

(b) the rates of contributions payable since that date taken together with the possibility of significant changes in the value of the assets of the scheme or in the scheme's technical provisions,

he is unable to certify the schedule of contributions in the terms set out in paragraph (b)(ii) of section 227(6) of the 2004 Act, that paragraph applies as if it provided for a statement that the rates shown in that schedule are such that the statutory funding objective could have been expected on that date to be met by the end of the period for which the schedule is to be in force.

(3) In the case to which sub-paragraph (1) applies, regulation 10(6) and Schedule 1 apply as if the alternative statements in the form of certification of the adequacy of the rates of contributions shown in the schedule of contributions were as follows—

""the statutory funding objective could have been expected on [*effective date of valuationon which the schedule is based*] to be met by the end of the period specified in the recovery plan.

the statutory funding objective could have been expected on [*effective date of valuationon which the schedule is based*] to continue to be met for the period for which the schedule is to be in force.".

(4) In the case to which sub-paragraph (2) applies, regulation 10(6) and Schedule 1 apply as if the alternative statements in the form of certification of the adequacy of the rates of contributions shown in the schedule of contributions were replaced by the following statement—

""the statutory funding objective could have been expected on [*effective date of valuationon which the schedule is based*] to be met by the end of the period for which the schedule is to be in force.".

(5) Where paragraph 6 of this Schedule applies, sub-paragraphs (1) and (3) of this paragraph, apply as if the references to the period specified in the recovery plan were to the period of two years from the effective date of the last actuarial valuation.

NOTES
Initial Commencement
Specified date
Specified date: 30 December 2005: see reg 1.

SCHEDULE 3
Supplementary and Consequential Provisions

Regulation 20(1)

Occupational Pension Schemes (Contracting-out) Regulations 1996

1 (1) The Occupational Pension Schemes (Contracting-out) Regulations 1996 are amended as follows.

(2) In regulation 1(2) (interpretation)—

(a) after the definition of "the 1995 Act" insert—

""the 2004 Act" means the Pensions Act 2004;";

(b) omit the definition of "minimum funding requirement".

(3) In regulation 6(2) (information to be confirmed by an employer in writing), for sub-paragraph (g) substitute—

"(g) in the case of a scheme to which Part 3 of the 2004 Act (scheme funding) applies, that the requirements of sections 224, 225, 226 (if applicable) and 227 of that Act and any regulations under those provisions are complied with.".

(4) In regulation 18 (requirement as to the resources of a salary-related contracted-out scheme)—

(a) in paragraph (1), for the words from "the amount of the resources of the scheme must be" to the end substitute "either the resources of the scheme must be sufficient to enable the scheme to meet the statutory funding objective provided for in section 222(1) of the 2004 Act, or the actuary to the scheme must have certified under section 227(6)(b)(i) of that Act that in his opinion the rates shown in the schedule of contributions are such that the statutory funding objective can be expected to be met by the end of the period specified in the recovery plan.";

(b) in paragraph (2), for "section 56 of the 1995 Act" substitute "Part 3 of the 2004 Act";

(c) after paragraph (2) add the following paragraph—

"(3) In a case where the trustees of a scheme are authorised under section 288 of the 2004 Act to accept contributions from European employers or approved under section 289 of that Act to accept contributions from a particular European employer, paragraph (1) has effect with the substitution for the words "by the end of the period specified in the recovery plan" of "within two years after the date of the last actuarial valuation under section 224 of the 2004 Act".".

(5) In regulation 49(4)(a)(i) (determination of cash equivalent of rights under a scheme which is not a money purchase scheme)—

(a) . for "section 56 of the 1995 Act applies (minimum funding requirement)" substitute "Part 3 of the 2004 Act applies (scheme funding)";

(b) for "subsection (1) of that section" substitute "section 222(1) of that Act".

(6) In regulation 72 (transitional requirements as to sufficiency of resources of salary-related schemes)—

(a) in paragraph (1A), for "section 58 of the 1995 Act" substitute "section 227 of the 2004 Act";

(b) in paragraph (3), for "section 56(3) of the 1995 Act (minimum funding requirement)" substitute "section 222(3) of the 2004 Act (statutory funding objective)";

(c) in paragraph (6), for "section 56 of the 1995 Act" substitute "Part 3 of the 2004 Act".

(7) The amendments in this paragraph have effect subject to paragraph 17 of Schedule 4.

Occupational Pension Schemes (Disclosure of Information) Regulations 1996

2 (1) Subject to paragraph 3, the Occupational Pension Schemes (Disclosure of Information) Regulations 1996 ("the Disclosure Regulations") are amended as follows.

(2) In regulation 1(2) (interpretation)—

(a) after the definition of "the 1995 Act" insert—

""the 2004 Act" means the Pensions Act 2004;";

(b)   after the definition of "public service pension scheme" insert—

""the Regulator" means the Pensions Regulator established under section 1 of the 2004 Act;".

(3) In regulation 5 (information to be made available to individuals)—

(a)   in paragraph (1), for "paragraphs (2) to (12)" substitute "paragraphs (2) to (12ZA)";

(b)   after paragraph (12) insert the following paragraph—

"(12ZA) Where the trustees of a scheme to which Part 3 of the 2004 Act applies have obtained an actuarial valuation or report under section 224 of that Act, they shall furnish the information mentioned in paragraphs 17 to 22 of Schedule 2, in the form of a summary funding statement, as of course to all members and beneficiaries (except excluded persons), within a reasonable period after the date by which they are required by that section to ensure that the valuation or report is received by them.";

(c)   after paragraph (12AA) insert the following paragraph—

"(12AB) If a scheme has been modified by the Regulator under section 231(2)(a) of the 2004 Act (modifications as regards the future accrual of benefits), the trustees must inform all active members of the fact within one month of the modification taking effect.";

(d)   in paragraph (12A) (sectionalised multi-employer schemes)—

   (i)   for "Schedule 5 to the Occupational Pension Schemes (Minimum Funding Requirement and Actuarial Valuations) Regulations 1996" substitute "Schedule 2 to the Occupational Pension Schemes (Scheme Funding) Regulations 2005";

   (ii)   for "section 56 of the 1995 Act" substitute "Part 3 of the 2004 Act", and

   (iii)   for "section 56 does not apply" substitute "Part 3 does not apply".

(4) In regulation 6(1)(c) (annual report to contain actuary's certificate)—

(a)   for "section 56 of the 1995 Act" substitute "Part 3 of the 2004 Act", and

(b)   before "that Act" insert "section 227 of".

(5) For the heading to regulation 7, substitute "**Availability of other documents**".

(6) For sub-paragraphs (a) to (c) in regulation 7(1), substitute the following sub-paragraphs—

"(a)   the statement of funding principles where required under section 223 of the 2004 Act;

(b)   where Part 3 of the 2004 Act applies to the scheme, the last actuarial valuation under section 224 of that Act received by the trustees, or, if an actuarial report under that section was received by them more recently than the last actuarial valuation, both that valuation and any report received subsequently;

(c)   any recovery plan prepared under section 226 of the 2004 Act which is currently in force;

   (ca)   the payment schedule where required under section 87 of the 1995 Act or schedule of contributions where required under section 227 of the 2004 Act, and".

(7) In Schedule 2 (information to be made available to individuals), after paragraph 16 add—

17 A summary, based on the last actuarial valuation under section 224 of the 2004 Act received by the trustees and any actuarial report received subsequently, of the extent to which the assets of the scheme are adequate to cover its technical provisions.

18   An explanation of any change in the funding position of the scheme—

(a)   in the case of the first summary funding statement issued in respect of the scheme, since the last actuarial valuation in respect of the scheme under regulation 30 of the Occupational Pension Schemes (Minimum Funding Requirement and Actuarial Valuations) Regulations 1996 (ongoing actuarial valuations), or, if no such valuation was obtained, since the last actuarial valuation under the rules of the scheme, and

(b)   in the case of any subsequent summary funding statement, since the date of the last summary funding statement.

19   The actuary's estimate of solvency contained in the last actuarial valuation under section 224 of the 2004 Act received by the trustees.

20   A summary of any recovery plan prepared under section 226 of the 2004 Act which is currently in force.

21 Whether the scheme has been modified under section 231(2)(a) of the 2004 Act, is subject to directions under section 231(2)(b) of that Act or bound by a schedule of contributions imposed under section 231(2)(c) of that Act, and if so an account of the circumstances in which the modification was made, the direction given or the schedule of conditions imposed.

22 Whether any payment has been made to the employer under section 37 of the 1995 Act (payment of surplus to employer)—

(a) in the case of the first summary funding statement issued in respect of the scheme, in the 12 months preceding the date on which it is prepared, and

(b) in the case of any subsequent summary funding statement, since the date of the last such statement,

and, if so, the amount of the payment.".

3 (1) Until the trustees or managers of a scheme have prepared a schedule of contributions under section 227 of the 2004 Act (in accordance with regulation 9(1) of, or paragraph 5 of Schedule 4 to, these Regulations), the Disclosure Regulations have effect in relation to a scheme to which Part 3 of the 2004 Act applies as if—

(a) the amendments in paragraph 2 of this Schedule had not been made;

(b) those Regulations included the requirement in sub-paragraph (2) of this paragraph, and

(c) regulations 1(2) (so far as material), 10 and 11 of those Regulations applied in respect of that requirement.

(2) The requirement referred to in paragraph (1)(b) is that, before 22nd September in 2006 and each subsequent year the trustees or managers of the scheme furnish all members and beneficiaries (except excluded persons) with the following information, in the form of a summary funding statement—

(a) a summary, based on the last actuarial valuation under regulation 30 of the Occupational Pension Schemes (Minimum Funding Requirement and Actuarial Valuations) Regulations 1996 ("the MFR Regulations") received by the trustees or managers or, if no such valuation was obtained, the last actuarial valuation under the rules of the scheme, of the extent to which the assets of the scheme are adequate to meet its liabilities as they fall due;

(b) an explanation of any change in the funding position of the scheme—

(i) in the case of the first summary statement issued in respect of the scheme, since the last actuarial valuation in respect of the scheme under regulation 30 of the MFR Regulations, or, if no such valuation was obtained, since the last actuarial valuation under the rules of the scheme, and

(ii) in the case of any subsequent summary funding statement, since the date of the last summary funding statement;

(c) any estimate by the actuary of the solvency of the scheme, or, if the actuary has made more than one estimate of solvency, the latest such estimate;

(i) whether any payment has been made to the employer under section 37 of the 1995 Act—in the case of the first summary funding statement issued in respect of the scheme, in the 12 months preceding the date on which it is prepared, and

(ii) in the case of any subsequent summary funding statement, since the date of the last such statement,

and, if so, the amount of the payment.

(3) The trustees or managers of a scheme are not required to comply with the requirement in sub-paragraph (2) in any year if the scheme had fewer than 100 members during the 12 months ending on 31st August in that year.

(4) A summary funding statement furnished under sub-paragraph (2) must be accompanied by a written statement that further information about the scheme is available, giving the address to which enquiries about it should be sent.

Occupational Pension Schemes (Scheme Administration) Regulations 1996

4 (1) The Occupational Pension Schemes (Scheme Administration) Regulations 1996 are amended as follows.

(2) In regulation 1(2) (interpretation), after the definition of "the 1995 Act" insert—

""the 2004 Act" means the Pensions Act 2004;".

(3) In regulation 16A(2) (circumstances in which notice of an employer's failure to make payments to trustees or managers need not be given), for sub-paragraph (b) substitute the following—

"(b)   where the scheme is exempt from the requirement to prepare, review and if necessary revise a schedule of contributions under section 227 of the 2004 Act, by virtue of any of sub-paragraphs (a) to (i) and (k) to (m) of regulation 17(1) of the Occupational Pension Schemes (Scheme Funding) Regulations 2005; or".

Occupational Pension Schemes (Transfer Values) Regulations 1996

5   (1) The Occupational Pension Schemes (Transfer Values) Regulations 1996 are amended as follows.

(2) In regulation 1(2) (interpretation), after the definition of "the 1995 Act" insert—

""the 2004 Act" means the Pensions Act 2004;".

(3) In regulation 7 (manner of calculation and verification of cash equivalents)—

(a)   insert the word "and" at the end of paragraph (3)(b)(ii);

(b)   omit the word "and" at the end of paragraph (3)(b)(iii), and

(c)   omit paragraphs (3)(b)(iv) and (4).

(4) In regulation 8 (further provisions as to calculation of cash equivalents)—

(a)   in paragraph (4), for "section 56 of the 1995 Act (minimum funding requirement)" substitute "Part 3 of the 2004 Act (scheme funding)";

(b)   in paragraph (4B), omit "then, subject to paragraph (4D)";

(c)   omit paragraphs (4D) to (4I), (4K) and (4L);

(d)   in paragraph (5)—

    (i)   for "section 61 of the 1995 Act" substitute "section 232 of the 2004 Act";

    (ii)   for "section 56" substitute "Part 3", and

    (iii)   for "paragraphs (4), (4A) and (4G)" substitute "paragraphs (4) and (4A)", and

(e)   omit paragraph (6).

Personal And Occupational Pension Schemes (Pensions Ombudsman) Regulations 1996

6   (1) The Personal and Occupational Pension Schemes (Pensions Ombudsman) Regulations 1996 are amended as follows.

(2) In regulation 4(2) (compliance with particular requirements excluded from ombudsman's jurisdiction), after sub-paragraph (g) add—

""or the requirements under Part 3 of the Pensions Act 2004.".

Occupational Pension Schemes (Winding Up) Regulations 1996

7   (1) The Occupational Pension Schemes (Winding Up) Regulations 1996 are amended as follows.

(2) In regulation 12(3) (winding up of sectionalised schemes etc)—

(a)   for "Schedule 5 to the MFR Regulations" substitute "Schedule 2 to the Occupational Pension Schemes (Scheme Funding) Regulations 2005", and

(b)   for "section 56" substitute "Part 3 of the Pensions Act 2004".

(3) In regulation 13 (hybrid schemes), omit paragraphs (6) and (7).

Occupational Pension Schemes (Contracting-out) Regulations (Northern Ireland) 1996

8   (1) The Occupational Pension Schemes (Contracting-out) Regulations (Northern Ireland) 1996 are amended as follows.

(2) In regulation 49(4)(a)(i) (determination of cash equivalent of rights under a scheme which is not a money purchase scheme)—

(a)   for "Article 56 of the Order applies (minimum funding requirement)" substitute "Part IV of the 2005 Order applies (scheme funding)", and

(b)   for "Article 56(1)" substitute "Article 201(1) of that Order".

Pension Sharing (Valuation) Regulations 2000

9   (1) The Pension Sharing (Valuation) Regulations 2000 are amended as follows.

(2) In regulation 1(2) (interpretation), after the definition of "the 1999 Act" insert—

""the 2004 Act" means the Pensions Act 2004;".

(3) In regulation 4 (calculation and verification of cash equivalents)—

(a)   insert the word "and" at the end of paragraph (3)(b)(i);

(b)   omit the word "and" at the end of paragraph (3)(b)(ii), and

(c)   omit paragraphs (3)(b)(iii) and (4).

(4) In regulation 5 (further provisions as to calculation of cash equivalents)—

(a)   in paragraph (3), for "section 56 of the 1995 Act" substitute "Part 3 of the 2004 Act";

(b)   in paragraph (3B), omit "then, subject to paragraph (3D)";

(c)   omit paragraphs (3D) to (3I), (3K) and (3L);

(d)   in paragraph (4)—

   (i)   for "Schedule 5 to the Occupational Pension Schemes (Minimum Funding Requirement and Actuarial Valuations) Regulations 1996" substitute "Schedule 2 to the Occupational Pension Schemes (Scheme Funding) Regulations 2005";

   (ii)   for "section 56 of the 1995 Act" substitute "Part 3 of the 2004 Act", and

   (iii)   for "paragraphs (3), (3A) and (3G)" substitute "paragraphs (3) and (3A)", and

(e)   in paragraph (5), for "paragraphs (3) and (3F)" substitute "paragraph (3)".

Pension Sharing (Implementation and Discharge of Liability) Regulations 2000

10   (1) The Pension Sharing (Implementation and Discharge of Liability) Regulations 2000 are amended as follows.

(2) In regulation 1(2) (interpretation), after the definition of "the 1999 Act" insert—

""the 2004 Act" means the Pensions Act 2004;".

(3) In regulation 16 (adjustments to the amount of pension credit)—

(a)   in paragraph (2), for "section 56 of the 1995 Act" substitute "Part 3 of the 2004 Act (scheme funding)";

(b)   in paragraph (2B), omit "then, subject to paragraph (2D)";

(c)   omit paragraphs (2D) to (2I), (2K) and (2L), and

(d)   in paragraph (3)—

   (i)   for "Schedule 5 to the Occupational Pension Schemes (Minimum Funding Requirement and Actuarial Valuations) Regulations 1996" substitute "Schedule 2 to the Occupational Pension Schemes (Scheme Funding) Regulations 2005";

   (ii)   for "section 56 of the 1995 Act (minimum funding requirement)" substitute "Part 3 of the 2004 Act", and

   (iii)   for "paragraphs (2), (2A) and (2G)" substitute "paragraphs (2) and (2A)".

Pension Sharing (Pension Credit Benefit) Regulations 2000

11   (1) The Pension Sharing (Pension Credit Benefit) Regulations 2000 are amended as follows.

(2) In regulation 1(2) (interpretation), after the definition of "the 1999 Act" insert—

""the 2004 Act" means the Pensions Act 2004;".

(3) In regulation 24 (calculation and verification of cash equivalents)—

(a)   insert the word "and" at the end of paragraph (3)(b)(ii);

(b)   omit the word "and" at the end of paragraph (3)(b)(iii), and

(c)   omit paragraphs (3)(b)(iv) and (4).

(4) In regulation 27 (increases and reductions of cash equivalents)—

(a)   in paragraph (4), for "section 56 of the 1995 Act" substitute "Part 3 of the 2004 Act";

(b)   in paragraph (4B), omit "then, subject to paragraph (4D)";

(c)   omit paragraphs (4D) to (4I), (4K) and (4L);

(d)   in paragraph (4M), for "paragraphs (4J) and (4K)" substitute "paragraph (4J)", and

(e)   in paragraph (5)—

    (i)   for "Schedule 5 to the Occupational Pension Schemes (Minimum Funding Requirement and Actuarial Valuations) Regulations 1996" substitute "Schedule 2 to the Occupational Pension Schemes (Scheme Funding) Regulations 2005";

    (ii)   for "section 56 of the 1995 Act" substitute "Part 3 of the 2004 Act", and

    (iii)   for "paragraphs (4), (4A) and (4G)" substitute "paragraphs (4) and (4A)".

Stakeholder Pension Schemes Regulations 2000

12   (1) The Stakeholder Pension Schemes Regulations 2000 are amended as follows.

(2) In regulation 19 (requirement for trustees of a stakeholder pension scheme established under a trust), omit "except the reference to section 56 in section 35(2) and 35(5)(b) of that Act".

Occupational Pension Schemes (Republic of Ireland Schemes Exemption) Regulations 2000

13   (1) The Occupational Pension Schemes (Republic of Ireland Schemes Exemption) Regulations 2000 are amended as follows.

(2) In regulation 1(3) (interpretation), after the definition of "the 1995 Act" insert—

""the 2004 Act" means the Pensions Act 2004;".

(3) In regulation 2 (exemption of Republic of Ireland schemes – general provision), after "the 1995 Act" insert "or the 2004 Act".

(4) In the Schedule, at the end insert—

Provision of the 2004 Act	Purpose of provision
Part 3	Scheme funding

Occupational Pension Schemes (Administration and Audited Accounts) (Amendment) Regulations 2005

14   (1) The Occupational Pension Schemes (Administration and Audited Accounts) (Amendment) Regulations 2005 are amended as follows.

(2) In the substituted regulation 16A of the Occupational Pension Schemes (Scheme Administration) Regulations 1996 set out in regulation 4(5) (circumstances in which trustees or managers do not need to notify failure to pay contributions), for paragraph (d) substitute the following—

"(d)   the scheme is exempt from the requirement to prepare, review and if necessary revise a schedule of contributions under section 227 of the 2004 Act, by virtue of any of sub-paragraphs (a) to (i) and (k) to (m) of regulation 17(1) of the Occupational Pension Schemes (Scheme Funding) Regulations 2005.".

NOTES

Initial Commencement

Specified date

Specified date: 30 December 2005: see reg 1.

SCHEDULE 4
Transitional Provisions and Savings

Regulation 20(2)

PART I
TRANSITIONAL PROVISIONS

1   Paragraphs 2 to 7 of this Schedule apply to a scheme which—

(a)   is either—

      (i)   subject to section 56 of the 1995 Act (minimum funding requirement), or

      (ii)   exempted from the application of that section by regulation 28 of the Occupational Pension Schemes (Minimum Funding Requirement and Actuarial Valuations) Regulations 1996 ("the 1996 Regulations"),

    immediately before the commencement date, and

(b)   becomes subject to Part 3 of the 2004 Act (scheme funding) on that date.

2   Section 224 of the 2004 Act (actuarial valuations and reports) applies to the scheme as if—

(a)   it included a requirement for the trustees or managers of the scheme—

      (i)   to obtain an actuarial valuation ("the first valuation under the 2004 Act"), in accordance with the requirements specified in paragraph 3 of this Schedule, and

      (ii)   to ensure that the first valuation under the 2004 Act is received by them within the relevant period specified in paragraph 4 of this Schedule;

(b)   neither paragraph (a) of subsection (1) nor subsection (4) applied in relation to the first valuation under the 2004 Act, and

(c)   paragraph (a) of subsection (3) were omitted.

3   (1) Except where sub-paragraph (3), (5) or (7) applies, the trustees or managers of the scheme must obtain the first valuation under the 2004 Act by reference to an effective date not more than one year after the commencement date.

(2) Sub-paragraph (3) applies where—

(a)   the trustees or managers received, before the commencement date, in accordance with any provisions of section 57 of the 1995 Act (valuation and certification of assets and liabilities) and the 1996 Regulations, or receive—

      (i)   on or after the commencement date, and

      (ii)   within one year of its effective date,

    in accordance with any such provisions which continue in force under Part 2 of this Schedule, an actuarial valuation by reference to an effective date on or after 21st September 2002, and

(b)   neither sub-paragraph (5) nor sub-paragraph (7) applies.

(3) Where this sub-paragraph applies, the trustees or managers must obtain the first actuarial valuation under the 2004 Act by reference to an effective date which is—

(a)   no earlier than 22nd September 2005, and

(b)   not more than three years after the effective date of the last valuation they received under the 1995 Act.

(4) Subject to sub-paragraph (8), sub-paragraph (5) applies where—

(a)   immediately before the commencement date, the trustees or managers were required under section 57(2)(a) of the 1995 Act to obtain an actuarial valuation by virtue of a certificate in the terms set out in that provision, or

(b)   on or after the commencement date, the trustees or managers receive a certificate in the terms set out in section 57(2)(a) of the 1995 Act in consequence of the requirements saved by paragraph 15 of this Schedule,

and the trustees or managers have determined before that date, or determine subsequently, that the valuation should be obtained by reference to an effective date which is no earlier than 22nd September 2005 and not more than three years after the effective date of the last valuation they received under the 1995 Act.

(5) Where this sub-paragraph applies, the trustees or managers must obtain the first valuation under the 2004 Act by reference to the effective date they have determined.

(6) Subject to sub-paragraph (8), sub-paragraph (7) applies where—

(a)   immediately before the commencement date, the trustees or managers were required under section 57(2)(b) of the 1995 Act to obtain an actuarial valuation by virtue of the occurrence of an event of the kind described in regulation 13 of the 1996 Regulations (section 75 debts in multi-employer schemes), and

(b)   they have determined before that date, or determine subsequently, that the valuation should be obtained by reference to an effective date which is no earlier than 22nd September 2005 and not more than three years after the effective date of the last valuation they received under the 1995 Act.

(7) Where this sub-paragraph applies, the trustees or managers must obtain the first valuation under the 2004 Act by reference to the effective date they have determined.

(8) In a case where, but for this provision, sub-paragraph (5) would apply, by virtue of the receipt by the trustees or managers of a certificate in the terms set out in section 57(2)(a) of the 1995 Act, and sub-paragraph (7) would also apply, by· virtue of the occurrence of an event of the kind described in regulation 13 of the 1996 Regulations, sub-paragraph (5) applies only if the certificate was received before the event occurred and sub-paragraph (7) applies only if the event occurred before the certificate was received.

4   The trustees or managers must ensure that the first valuation under the 2004 Act is received by them—

(a)   where paragraph 3(1) applies, or where paragraph 3(3) applies and the trustees or managers obtained that valuation by reference to an effective date which is after 29th December 2005, within 15 months after its effective date;

(b)   where paragraph 3(3) applies and the trustees or managers obtained that valuation by reference to an effective date between 22nd September and 29th December 2005, within 18 months after its effective date;

(c)   where paragraph 3(5) applies, within 18 months after the date on which the certificate referred to in paragraph 3(4) is signed, and

(d)   where paragraph 3(7) applies, within 18 months after the date on which the event referred to in paragraph 3(6) occurred.

5   Section 227 of the 2004 Act (schedule of contributions) applies to the scheme as if it included a requirement for the trustees or managers of the scheme to prepare a schedule of contributions ("the first schedule of contributions under the 2004 Act") within the same period as that within which they are required by paragraph 4 to ensure that they receive the first valuation under the 2004 Act.

6   In the circumstances described in paragraph 4(b), (c), and (d), regulation 6(2) of these Regulations (first statement of funding principles) applies to the scheme, and regulations 8(1)(a) and 13 apply in relation to the first valuation under the 2004 Act, as if the period there referred to were the same period as that within which the trustees or managers are required by paragraph 4 to ensure that they receive the first valuation under the 2004 Act.

7   References in sections 224 to 231 of the 2004 Act to actuarial valuations or schedules of contributions shall be taken to exclude any such valuation or schedule of contributions under the 1995 Act as in force before the commencement date or as continued in force by paragraphs 9 to 16 of this Schedule.

NOTES

Initial Commencement

Specified date

Specified date: 30 December 2005: see reg 1.

PART 2
SAVINGS

8   Paragraphs 9 to 19 of this Schedule apply to a scheme which—

(a)   is subject to section 56 of the 1995 Act immediately before the commencement date, and

(b)   becomes subject to Part 3 of the 2004 Act on that date.

9   Sections 56 and 58 to 60 of the 1995 Act, regulations 15 to 17 and 19 to 27 of the 1996 Regulations and Schedules 2 and 4 to those Regulations continue to apply to the scheme from the commencement date until the date on which the first schedule of contributions under the 2004 Act comes into force.

10   Where—

(a) immediately before the commencement date, the trustees or managers of the scheme were required under section 57(1)(a) of the 1995 Act and regulation 10 of the 1996 Regulations (time limits for minimum funding valuations) to obtain an actuarial valuation within a period ending on or after the commencement date, and

(b) they have determined before that date, or determine subsequently, that the valuation should be obtained by reference to an effective date before 22nd September 2005,

those provisions apply to the scheme on and after the commencement date in respect of that valuation.

11 Where—

(a) immediately before the commencement date, the trustees or managers of the scheme were required under section 57(2)(a) of the 1995 Act to obtain an actuarial valuation within the period specified in section 57(4)(a) of that Act, and

(b) they have determined before that date, or determine subsequently, that the valuation should be obtained by reference to an effective date before 22nd September 2005,

those provisions apply to the scheme on and after the commencement date in respect of that valuation.

12 Where—

(a) immediately before the commencement date, the trustees or managers of the scheme were required under section 57(2)(b) of the 1995 Act to obtain an actuarial valuation by virtue of the occurrence of an event of the kind described in regulation 13 of the 1996 Regulations, and

(b) they have determined before that date, or determine subsequently, that the valuation should be obtained by reference to an effective date before 22nd September 2005,

those provisions apply to the scheme on and after the commencement date in respect of that valuation, subject to the modification that the valuation must be obtained within the period of six months beginning with the date on which the relevant event occurred.

13 Where—

(a) immediately before the commencement date, the trustees or managers of the scheme were required under section 41(1)(a) and (2)(c) of the 1995 Act and regulation 30 of the 1996 Regulations (ongoing actuarial valuations and statements) to obtain an actuarial valuation within a period ending on or after the commencement date, and an accompanying statement in the form set out in Schedule 6 to those Regulations, and

(b) they have determined before that date, or determine subsequently, that the valuation should be obtained by reference to an effective date before 22nd September 2005,

those provisions apply to the scheme on and after the commencement date in respect of that valuation and statement.

14 Where a requirement to obtain a valuation is preserved by any of paragraphs 10 to 13 of this Schedule, section 57(5) to (7) of the 1995 Act, regulations 3 to 9 of the 1996 Regulations and (except in the case to which paragraph 13 applies) regulation 14 of and Schedule 1 to those Regulations apply in respect of that valuation.

15 Where, immediately before the commencement date, the trustees or managers of the scheme were required under section 57(1)(b) of the 1995 Act and regulation 18 of the 1996 Regulations (occasional and periodic certification of adequacy of contributions) to obtain annual certificates as to the adequacy of contributions payable towards the scheme, those provisions, sections 57(5) to (7) of that Act and Schedule 3 to the 1996 Regulations apply to the scheme until the effective date of the first valuation under the 2004 Act relating to the scheme.

16 Section 61 of the 1995 Act (supplementary), regulation 2 of the 1996 Regulations (interpretation) and regulation 29 of, and Schedule 5 to, those Regulations (modifications) apply, so far as material, on and after the commencement date in relation to the provisions of the Act and Regulations saved by paragraphs 9 to 15 of this Schedule.

17   Where any provision of the 1995 Act or the 1996 Regulations applies to the scheme on or after the commencement date by virtue of this Schedule, any reference to that provision in the Occupational Pension Schemes (Contracting-out) Regulations 1996 ("the Contracting-out Regulations") applies in relation to the scheme on and after the commencement date as if—

(a)   in the case of a provision of the 1995 Act, the repeal of that provision by the 2004 Act had not come into force on that date in accordance with the Pensions Act 2004 (Commencement No 8) Order 2005 ("the Commencement Order");

(b)   in the case of a provision in the 1996 Regulations, those Regulations had not been revoked by regulation 21, and

(c)   the amendments of the Contracting-out Regulations in paragraph 1 of Schedule 3 to these Regulations had not come into force.

18   Where any provision of the 1995 Act or the 1996 Regulations applies to the scheme on or after the commencement date by virtue of this Schedule, regulation 4(2) of the Personal and Occupational Pension Schemes (Pensions Ombudsman) Regulations 1996 shall be taken to include a reference to that provision notwithstanding its repeal by the 2004 Act in accordance with the Commencement Order or the revocation of the 1996 Regulations by regulation 21.

19   Any reference to the 1995 Act or the 1996 Regulations in—

(a)   the Occupational Pension Schemes (Winding Up) Regulations 1996;

(b)   the Occupational Pension Schemes (Deficiency on Winding Up etc) Regulations 1996, or

(c)   the Occupational Pension Schemes (Employer Debt) Regulations 2005,

applies to the scheme on and after the commencement date as if, where the reference is to a provision of the Act, the repeal of that provision by the 2004 Act had not come into force on that date in accordance with the Commencement Order, and, where the reference is to a provision in the 1996 Regulations, those Regulations had not been revoked by regulation 21.

NOTES

Initial Commencement

Specified date

Specified date: 30 December 2005: see reg 1.

SCHEDULE 5
Revocations

Regulation 21

(1)	(2)	(3)
Regulations revoked	*References*	*Extent of revocation*
The Occupational Pension Schemes (Minimum Funding Requirement and Actuarial Valuations) Regulations 1996	SI 1996/1536	The whole Regulations
The Occupational Pension Schemes (Investment) Regulations 1996	SI 1996/3127	Regulation 12
The Personal and Occupational Pension Schemes (Miscellaneous Amendments) Regulations 1997	SI 1997/786	Paragraph 8 of Schedule 1 and the entry relating to SI 1996/1536 in Schedule 2
The Personal and Occupational Pension Schemes (Miscellaneous Amendments) (No 2) Regulations 1997	SI 1997/3038	Regulation 4
The Personal and Occupational Pension Schemes (Miscellaneous Amendments) Regulations 1999	SI 1999/3198	Regulation 8
The Occupational Pension Schemes (Miscellaneous Amendments) Regulations 2000	SI 2000/679	Regulation 3

The Pension Sharing (Consequential and Miscellaneous Amendments) Regulations 2000	SI 2000/2691	Regulation 4
The Occupational Pension Schemes (Minimum Funding Requirement and Miscellaneous Amendments) Regulations 2002	SI 2002/380	Regulation 2
The Occupational Pension Schemes (Minimum Funding Requirement and Actuarial Valuations) Amendment Regulations 2004	SI 2004/3031	The whole Regulations
The Occupational Pension Schemes (Employer Debt) Regulations 2005	SI 2005/678	Paragraph 1 of Schedule 2
The Occupational Pension Schemes (Winding up etc) Regulations 2005	SI 2005/706	Paragraph 9 of the Schedule
The Occupational Pension Schemes (Employer Debt etc) (Amendment) Regulations 2005	SI 2005/2224	Regulation 6

NOTES

Initial Commencement

Specified date

Specified date: 30 December 2005: see reg 1.

Appendix 16

The Occupational Pension Schemes (Cross-border Activities) Regulations 2005

SI 2005 No 3381

Occupational Pension Schemes (Cross-border Activities) Regulations 2005

Made 8th December 2005

Laid before Parliament 9th December 2005

Coming into force 30th December 2005

1 Citation and commencement

These Regulations may be cited as the Occupational Pension Schemes (Cross-border Activities) Regulations 2005 and shall come into force on 30th December 2005.

NOTES

Initial Commencement

Specified date

Specified date: 30 December 2005: see above.

2 Interpretation

(1) In these Regulations—

"accrued European rights" means—

    (a)   in relation to a European member of the scheme—

        (i)   any rights which have accrued to or in respect of that European member to future benefits under the scheme rules, or

        (ii)   any entitlement to the present payment of a pension or other benefit under the scheme rules,

to the extent that those rights or entitlement result from the periods when that European member was—

        (aa)   both employed by a European employer and a qualifying person, or

        (bb)   a qualifying self-employed person, and

    (b)   in relation to a European survivor, any entitlement to benefits, or right to future benefits, under the scheme rules in respect of a European member to the extent that that right or entitlement results from the periods when that European member was—

        (i)   both employed by a European employer and a qualifying person, or

        (ii)   a qualifying self-employed person;

"the Act" means the Pensions Act 2004 (unless the context otherwise requires, any reference to a numbered section being to the section so numbered in that Act);

"the 1993 Act" means the Pension Schemes Act 1993;

"the 1995 Act" means the Pensions Act 1995;

"the 1999 Act" means the Welfare Reform and Pensions Act 1999;

"actuarial valuation" shall be construed in accordance with section 224 (actuarial valuations and reports), and includes an actuarial valuation obtained by the trustees or managers of a scheme for any purpose, including that of making an application under section 288 (general authorisation to accept contributions from European employers) or section 289 (approval in relation to particular European employer);

"the commencement date" is the date referred to in regulation 1;

"cross-border scheme" means a scheme which applies to European members or in relation to which there are European survivors;

"the effective date" shall be construed in accordance with section 224(2);

"employment" includes any trade, business, profession, office or vocation and "employed" shall be construed accordingly;

"European employer" has the meaning given in regulation 3(1);

"European member" means a member of a scheme who is, or was,—

    (a)   a qualifying person in respect of whom contributions were made to the scheme by a European employer, or

    (b)   a qualifying self-employed person who has made contributions to the scheme;

"European survivor" means a survivor of a European member of the scheme who is entitled to benefits, or has a right to future benefits, under the scheme rules in respect of that European member;

"host member State", in relation to a European employer, has the meaning given in regulation 3(5);

"multi-employer scheme" shall be construed in accordance with section 307(4) (modification of this Act in relation to certain categories of schemes);

"new scheme" means a scheme—

    (a)   which does not have any members—

        (i)   in relation to whom there are any rights which have accrued to or in respect of the members in question to future benefits under the scheme rules, or

        (ii)   who have any entitlement to the present payment of a pension or other benefit under the scheme rules, and

    (b)   in relation to which there are not any survivors of any members of the scheme who are entitled to benefits, or have a right to future benefits, under the scheme rules in respect of those members;

"new section" means a section of a segregated multi-employer scheme—

    (a)   which does not have any members—

        (i)   in relation to whom there are any rights which have accrued to or in respect of the members in question to future benefits under the scheme rules, or

        (ii)   who have any entitlement to the present payment of a pension or other benefit under the scheme rules, and

    (b)   in relation to which there are not any survivors of any members of the scheme who are entitled to benefits, or have a right to future benefits, under the scheme rules in respect of those members;

"notice of intention" shall be construed in accordance with section 289(1);

"pay-as-you-go scheme" means an occupational pension scheme under which there is no requirement for assets to be set aside in advance for the purpose of providing benefits under the scheme (disregarding any requirements relating to additional voluntary contributions);

"pre-23rd September 2005 scheme" means an occupational pension scheme—

    (a)   which—

        (i)   has its main administration in the United Kingdom, and

        (ii)   is not a pay-as-you-go scheme; and

    (b)   in relation to which—

        (i)   the trustees or managers were accepting contributions on 22nd September 2005 from any person who, had section 287(6) been in force at that date, would have been a European employer, or

        (ii)   any such person was under a liability to pay contributions to the trustees or managers on 22nd September 2005;

"qualifying person" means a person who is employed under a contract of service and whose place of work under that contract is sufficiently located in a member State other than the United Kingdom so that his relationship with his employer is subject to the social and labour law relevant to the field of occupational pension schemes of that member State, but, for the purposes of this definition, a seconded worker is not to be regarded as being so sufficiently located in a member State other than the United Kingdom;

"qualifying self-employed person" means a self-employed person whose place of work is sufficiently located in a member State other than the United Kingdom so that his employment in that member State is subject to the social and labour law relevant to the field of occupational pension schemes of that member State;

"registrable information" shall be construed in accordance with section 60(1) (registrable information);

"scheme" means an occupational pension scheme;

"seconded worker" means a person—

    (a)   who—

        (i)   is employed under a contract of service by an employer established in the United Kingdom and whose habitual place of work under that contract is located in the United Kingdom, or

        (ii)   immediately before the commencement of the period of secondment was employed under a contract of service by an employer established in the United Kingdom and whose habitual place of work under that contract was located in the United Kingdom,

    (b)   who—

        (i)   was posted before the commencement date for a limited period which had not expired before that date, or

        (ii)   is posted on or after the commencement date for a limited period,

to a member State other than the United Kingdom for the purpose of providing services on behalf of his employer, and

    (c)   who—

        (i)   at the time when that posting began expected to return to the United Kingdom to work for the employer described in (a)(i) or (ii) after the expiry of that period, or

        (ii)   expects to retire from employment immediately after the expiry of that period;

[…]

"segregated multi-employer scheme" means a multi-employer scheme which is divided into two or more sections where—

    (a)   any contributions payable to the scheme by an employer in relation to the scheme or by a member are allocated to that employer's or that member's section, and

    (b)   a specified part or proportion of the assets of the scheme is attributable to each section of the scheme and cannot be used for the purposes of any other section;

"statutory funding objective" shall be construed in accordance with section 222 (the statutory funding objective); and

"the survivor" in relation to a member of a scheme means a person who—

    (a)   is the widow, widower or surviving civil partner of the member, or

    (b)   has survived that member and has any entitlement to benefit, or right to future benefits under the scheme in respect of that member.

(2) In these Regulations, "employer" in relation to a scheme which has no active members includes every person who was the employer of persons in the description of employment to which the scheme relates immediately before the time at which the scheme ceased to have any active members in relation to it.

(3) Where a scheme is a segregated multi-employer scheme, these Regulations, except regulations 4 to 8, apply as if each section of the scheme were a separate scheme.

    NOTES

    Initial Commencement

    Specified date

    Specified date: 30 December 2005: see reg 1.

    Amendment

    Para (1): definition "section 615 scheme" (omitted) inserted by SI 2006/467, reg 9(1), (2).

    Date in force: 20 March 2006: see SI 2006/467, reg 1(1).

    Para (1): definition "section 615 scheme" (omitted) revoked by SI 2006/925, reg 2(1), (2).

Date in force: 28 March 2006: see SI 2006/925, reg 1(1).

3 Meaning of "European employer" and "host member State" in Part 7 of the Act

(1) Subject to paragraphs (2) to (4), in Part 7 of the Act "European employer" in relation to a scheme means a person who—

(a) either—

(i) employs qualifying persons, or

(ii) is a qualifying self-employed person, and

is making (or proposes to make) contributions to that scheme either in respect of a qualifying person or in respect of himself as a qualifying self-employed person.

(2) But an employer is not to be regarded as a European employer in relation to any persons whom he employs who are not qualifying persons.

(3) Where—

(a) the Regulator has approved the trustees or managers of a scheme in relation to a European employer, and

(b) benefits are, or will become, payable under the scheme rules to or in respect of any member who is or was a qualifying person in relation to that European employer, or to or in respect of any member who is or was a qualifying self-employed person,

"European employer" shall include the persons specified in paragraph (4).

(4) The persons referred to in paragraph (3) are—

(a) in a case where the approval was granted in relation to a body corporate which has since ceased to be an employer of qualifying persons, that body corporate,

(b) in a case where—

(i) the approval was granted in relation to a European employer who is not a body corporate, and

(ii) that European employer has ceased to be an employer of qualifying persons,

the person who was the employer of qualifying persons who were, in accordance with that approval, members of the scheme immediately before the time at which the scheme ceased to have any such active members, and

(c) in a case where the approval was granted in relation to a qualifying self-employed person who has ceased to be such a person, that person.

(5) In Part 7 of the Act, "host member State", in relation to a European employer, means—

(a) where that European employer is specified in a notice of intention, the member State or States other than the United Kingdom where—

(i) that European employer has employees who are qualifying persons, or

(ii) that European employer is a qualifying self-employed person, or

(b) where the Regulator has approved the trustees or managers of a scheme in relation to that European employer, the member State or States other than the United Kingdom where—

(i) that European employer has or had employees who are or were members of the scheme, or

(ii) in the case of a self-employed person who is or was a member of the scheme, that self-employed person is or was a qualifying self-employed person.

NOTES

Initial Commencement

Specified date

Specified date: 30 December 2005: see reg 1.

4 Applications for general authorisation to accept contributions from European employers: established schemes which are not carrying on cross-border activity

(1) This regulation applies to all schemes other than—

(a) a scheme which is a new scheme on the date on which the trustees or managers make an application for authorisation under section 288, or

(b) a scheme which is a pre-23rd September 2005 scheme.

(2) Where the trustees or managers of a scheme apply to the Regulator for authorisation under section 288, the application shall be made—

(a)   in the case of a money purchase scheme, in a form which provides the information described in paragraphs 2 and 3 of Schedule 1, or

(b)   in the case of a scheme which is not a money purchase scheme, in a form which provides the information described in paragraphs 2 and 4 of that Schedule.

> **NOTES**
>
> **Initial Commencement**
>
> *Specified date*
>
> Specified date: 30 December 2005: see reg 1.

5   Applications for general authorisation to accept contributions from European employers: established schemes which are carrying on cross-border activity

(1) This regulation applies where—

(a)   a scheme is a pre-23rd September 2005 scheme, and

(b)   the trustees or managers of that scheme apply, within the period of three months beginning on the commencement date, to the Regulator for authorisation under section 288.

(2) [Subject to paragraph (3),] such an application shall be made—

(a)   in the case of a money purchase scheme, in a form which provides the information described in paragraphs 2 and 3 of Schedule 1, or

(b)   in the case of a scheme which is not a money purchase scheme, in a form which provides the information described in paragraphs 2 and 5 of that Schedule.

[(3) Where—

(a)   the trustees or managers of a [pre-23rd September 2005] scheme make such an application on or before 29th March 2006;

(b)   that application is made in a form which—

   (i)   includes the full name of the scheme; and

   (ii)   in the case of—

      (aa)   a money purchase scheme, provides as much of the information specified in paragraph (2)(a) as is readily available to those trustees or managers on the day on which the application is made; or

      (bb)   a scheme which is not a money purchase scheme, provides as much of the information specified in paragraph (2)(b) as is readily available to those trustees or managers on the day on which the application is made; and

(c)   those trustees or managers provide all of the remaining information specified in paragraph (2)(a) or (b), as the case may be, on or before 15th May 2006;

that application shall be deemed to have been made on the day on or before 29th March 2006 on which the application was first made.]

> **NOTES**
>
> **Initial Commencement**
>
> *Specified date*
>
> Specified date: 30 December 2005: see reg 1.
>
> **Amendment**
>
> Para (2): words "Subject to paragraph (3)," in square brackets inserted by SI 2006/467, reg 9(1), (3)(a).
>
> Date in force: 20 March 2006: see SI 2006/467, reg 1(1).
>
> Para (3): inserted by SI 2006/467, reg 9(1), (3)(b).
>
> Date in force: 20 March 2006: see SI 2006/467, reg 1(1).
>
> Para (3): in sub-para (a) words "pre-23rd September 2005" in square brackets substituted by SI 2006/925, reg 2(1), (3)(a).
>
> Date in force: 28 March 2006: see SI 2006/925, reg 1(1).

6   Applications for general authorisation to accept contributions from European employers: new schemes

(1) This regulation applies to schemes which are new schemes on the date on which the trustees or managers make an application for authorisation under section 288.

(2) Where the trustees or managers of a scheme apply to the Regulator for authorisation under section 288, the application shall be made—

(a)   in the case of a money purchase scheme, in a form which provides the information described in paragraphs 2 and 3 of Schedule 1, or

(b)   in the case of a scheme which is not a money purchase scheme, in a form which provides the information described in paragraph 2 of that Schedule.

NOTES

Initial Commencement

Specified date

Specified date: 30 December 2005: see reg 1.

---

7   Conditions for general authorisation to accept contributions from European employers

(1) Where the Regulator receives an application for authorisation under regulation 4, 5 or 6, it shall, before granting the authorisation, be satisfied that the applicant meets the conditions described in paragraph (2).

(2) The conditions to be met under paragraph (1) are—

(a)   that the scheme is registered in the register,

(b)   the matters set out in Article 9(1)(b) to (f) of the Directive are satisfied,

(c)   that the trustees or managers of the scheme have ensured that the scheme will be operated in a way which is consistent with the requirements of the law relating to schemes, and

(d)   in the case of a scheme which is not a money purchase scheme—

    (i)   where the application is made under regulation 4, that the scheme meets the statutory funding objective, or

    (ii)   where the application is made under regulation 5, that the scheme will, in the opinion of the Regulator, meet the statutory funding objective by 22nd September 2008, or

    (iii)   where the application is made under regulation 6, that the scheme will, in the opinion of the Regulator, meet the statutory funding objective by the expiry of the period of two years beginning on the date on which the application was made.

NOTES

Initial Commencement

Specified date

Specified date: 30 December 2005: see reg 1.

---

8   Criteria for revocation of general authorisation to accept contributions from European employers

(1) The Regulator may revoke an authorisation granted under section 288 where it is satisfied by the trustees or managers of that scheme that—

(a)   the scheme does not have any European members who have any accrued European rights, and

(b)   there are not in relation to the scheme any survivors of a European member of the scheme who have any accrued European rights.

(2) The Regulator may revoke an authorisation granted under section 288 where it is satisfied that any of the criteria described in paragraph (3) are met in relation to the scheme.

(3) The criteria to be applied by the Regulator in reaching any decision relating to the revocation of an authorisation under paragraph (2) are the seriousness, frequency and persistence of any failure—

(a)   by the trustees or managers of the scheme to ensure that the scheme is operated in a way which is consistent with, or

(b)   by the scheme to comply with,

any of the requirements described in paragraph (4).

(4) The requirements for the purposes of paragraph (3) for the purposes of any decision by the Regulator relating to the revocation of an authorisation are—

(a)   the provisions of the Directive other than Article 16(3),

(b)   the condition described in regulation 7(2)(c), and

(c)   in the case of a scheme which is not a money purchase scheme and to which—

(i)   regulation 4 applies, the condition described in paragraph (5),

(ii)   regulation 5 applies, the condition described in regulation 7(2)(d)(ii) or, after 22nd September 2008, the condition described in paragraph (5), or

(iii) regulation 6 applies, the condition described in regulation 7(2)(d)(iii) or, after the expiry of the period of two years beginning on the date on which the application for the authorisation of the scheme was made, the condition described in paragraph (5).

(5) The condition to be met under paragraph (4)(c)(i), (ii) or (iii) is that the scheme—

(a)   meets the statutory funding objective, or

(b)   where—

(i)   the trustees or managers of the scheme have obtained an actuarial valuation, and

(ii)   it appears to them that the statutory funding objective was not met on the effective date of that valuation,

the scheme will, in the opinion of the Regulator, meet the statutory funding objective within two years after that date.

NOTES
Initial Commencement
Specified date
Specified date: 30 December 2005: see reg 1.

9   Applications for approval in relation to particular European employer: established schemes which are not carrying on cross-border activity

(1) This regulation applies to all schemes other than—

(a)   a scheme which is a new scheme on the date on which the trustees or managers make an application for approval under section 289,

(b)   a scheme which is a pre-23rd September 2005 scheme, or

(c)   where the trustees or managers of a segregated multi-employer scheme have stated in the notice of intention relating to an application for approval under section 289 that any contributions payable to the scheme by the European employer specified in that notice of intention will be allocated to a new section, that section (to which these Regulations apply as if that section were a separate scheme in accordance with regulation 2(3)).

(2) Where the trustees or managers of a scheme apply to the Regulator for approval under section 289 in relation to one or more European employers, the information to be contained in the notice of intention, in addition to the information specified in section 289(1)(a) to (c), shall be determined—

(a)   in the case of a money purchase scheme, in accordance with the provisions of paragraph 6(1), (2), (3) and (7) of Schedule 1, or

(b)   in the case of a scheme which is not a money purchase scheme, in accordance with the provisions of paragraph 6(1), (2), (4) and (7) of that Schedule.

NOTES
Initial Commencement
Specified date
Specified date: 30 December 2005: see reg 1.

10   Applications for approval in relation to particular European employer: established schemes which are carrying on cross-border activity

(1) This regulation applies where—

(a)   a scheme is a pre-23rd September 2005 scheme, and

(b)   the trustees or managers of that scheme make an application for approval under section 289 in relation to one or more European employers within the period of three months beginning on the commencement date.

(2) [Subject to paragraph (3),] the information to be contained in the notice of intention relating to such an application, in addition to the information specified in section 289(1)(a) to (c), shall be determined—

(a)   in the case of a money purchase scheme, in accordance with the provisions of paragraph 6(1), (2), (3) and (7) of Schedule 1, or (b)　　in the case of a scheme which is not a money purchase scheme, in accordance with the provisions of paragraph 6(1), (2), (5) and (7) of that Schedule.

[(3)　Where—

(a)　　the trustees or managers of a [pre-23rd September 2005] scheme make such an application on or before 29th March 2006;

(b)　　that application is made in a form which—

　　　　(i)　　includes the information specified in section 289(1)(a) to (c); and

　　　　(ii)　　in the case of—

　　　　　　　(aa)　　a money purchase scheme, provides as much of the information specified in paragraph (2)(a) as is readily available to those trustees or managers on the day on which the notice of intention is given; or

　　　　　　　(bb)　　a scheme which is not a money purchase scheme, provides as much of the information specified in paragraph (2)(b) as is readily available to those trustees or managers on the day on which the notice of intention is given; and

(c)　　those trustees or managers provide all of the remaining information specified in paragraph (2)(a) or (b), as the case may be, on or before 15th May 2006;

that application shall be deemed to have been made on the day on or before 29th March 2006 on which the notice of intention was first given.]

NOTES

Initial Commencement

Specified date

Specified date: 30 December 2005: see reg 1.

Amendment

Para (2): words "Subject to paragraph (3)," in square brackets inserted by SI 2006/467, reg 9(1), (4)(a).

Date in force: 20 March 2006: see SI 2006/467, reg 1(1).

Para (3): inserted by SI 2006/467, reg 9(1), (4)(b).

Date in force: 20 March 2006: see SI 2006/467, reg 1(1).

Para (3): in sub-para (a) words "pre-23rd September 2005" in square brackets substituted by SI 2006/925, reg 2(1), (3)(b).

Date in force: 28 March 2006: see SI 2006/925, reg 1(1).

11　Applications for approval in relation to particular European employer: new schemes and new sections of segregated multi-employer schemes

(1)　This regulation applies to—

(a)　　a scheme which is a new scheme on the date on which the trustees or managers make an application for approval under section 289, or

(b)　　where the trustees or managers of a segregated multi-employer scheme have stated in the notice of intention relating to an application for approval under section 289 that any contributions to the scheme by the European employer specified in that notice of intention will be allocated to a new section, that section.

(2)　The information to be contained in the notice of intention relating to such an application, in addition to the information specified in section 289(1)(a) to (c), shall be determined in accordance with the provisions of paragraph 6(1), (2), (6) and (7) of Schedule 1.

NOTES

Initial Commencement

Specified date

Specified date: 30 December 2005: see reg 1.

12　Conditions for approval in relation to particular European employer

(1)　Where the Regulator receives an application made under regulation 9, 10 or 11 for approval in relation to one or more European employers specified in the notice of intention it shall, before granting the approval in relation to any such European employer, be satisfied that persons giving the notice of intention meet the condition described in paragraph (2) in relation to that specified European employer.

(2)　The condition to be met under paragraph (1) is that the Regulator has no reason to doubt that—

(a)　　the administrative structure of the scheme,

(b)   the financial situation of the scheme, and

(c)   the repute and professional qualifications or experience of the persons running the scheme,

are compatible with the proposed operations of the scheme in the specified host member State.

NOTES

Initial Commencement

Specified date

Specified date: 30 December 2005: see reg 1.

13   Revocation of approval in relation to particular European employer

(1) In this regulation, "notified" in relation to a requirement means a requirement which was included in information which was received by the Regulator from the competent authority in the host member State in pursuance of Article 20(5) or (8) of the Directive and was forwarded by the Regulator—

(a)   in accordance with section 290(1) (notification of legal requirements of host member State outside the United Kingdom) to the person who gave the notice of intention, or

(b)   in accordance with section 290(2) to the trustees or managers of the scheme,

as the case may be.

(2) Where the Regulator has granted approvals under section 289 to the trustees or managers of a scheme in relation to one or more specified European employers it may revoke any or all of those approvals where it is satisfied by the trustees or managers of the scheme that—

(a)   the scheme does not have any European members who have any accrued European rights, and

(b)   there are not in relation to the scheme any survivors of a European member of the scheme who have any accrued European rights.

(3) Where the Regulator has granted approvals under section 289 to the trustees or managers of a scheme in relation to more than one specified European employer it may decide under paragraph (4) or (5) to revoke those approvals in relation to one or more such European employers.

(4) Where the Regulator has granted approvals under section 289 to the trustees or managers of a scheme in relation to one or more specified European employers and those European employers are all located in the same host member State, the criteria to be applied by the Regulator in reaching any decision relating to the revocation of any such approval are the seriousness, frequency and persistence of any failure—

(a)   by the trustees or managers of the scheme to ensure that the scheme is operated in a way which is consistent with, or

(b)   by the scheme to comply with,

any of the requirements described in paragraph (5).

(5) The requirements under paragraph (4) for the purposes of any decision by the Regulator relating to the revocation of an approval are—

(a)   the notified requirements of the social and labour law of that host member State,

(b)   the notified information requirements imposed by that host member State in pursuance of Article 20(7) of the Directive, or

(c)   the conditions described in regulation 12(2).

(6) Where the Regulator has granted approvals under section 289 to the trustees or managers of a scheme in relation to more than one specified European employer and not all of those European employers are located in the same host member State, the criteria to be applied by the Regulator in reaching any decision relating to the revocation of any such approval are the seriousness, frequency and persistence of any failure—

(a)   by the trustees or managers of the scheme to ensure that the scheme is operated in a way which is consistent with, or

(b)   by the scheme to comply with,

any of the requirements described in paragraph (7).

(7) The requirements for the purposes of paragraph (6) are—

(a)   the notified requirements of the social and labour law of any of the host member States,

(b)   the notified information requirements imposed by any of those host member States in pursuance of Article 20(7) of the Directive, or

(c)   the conditions described in regulation 12(2).

14 Modifications of pensions legislation in relation to European members of cross-border schemes

(1) Where a cross-border scheme is not a pre-23rd September 2005 scheme, the provisions of the 1993 Act and the 1995 Act which are listed in paragraph 2, 3 or 4 of Schedule 2 shall be modified in their application to that scheme as if—

(a)   the European members of that scheme, and

(b)   any European survivors,

were excluded from the application of those provisions in respect of any accrued European rights.

(2) Where a cross-border scheme is a pre-23rd September 2005 scheme, the provisions of the 1993 Act and the 1995 Act which are listed in paragraph 2 or 4 of Schedule 2 shall be modified in their application to that scheme as if—

(a)   the European members who were such members of that scheme on the commencement date; and

(b)   any European survivors of such European members,

were excluded from the application of those provisions in respect of any accrued European rights.

(3) Where a cross-border scheme is a pre-23rd September 2005 scheme, the provisions of the 1993 Act and the 1995 Act which are listed in paragraph 2, 3 or 4 of Schedule 2 shall be modified in their application to that scheme as if—

(a)   the European members who became such members of the scheme after the commencement date, and

(b)   any European survivors of such European members,

were excluded from the application of those provisions in respect of any accrued European rights.

15 Ring-fencing of assets

(1) For the purposes of this regulation, the assets and liabilities of a scheme shall be determined in accordance with Part 3 of the Act and regulations made under that Part.

(2) Where the trustees or managers of a scheme receive contributions to the scheme from a European employer, the Regulator may issue a notice ("a ring-fencing notice") to the trustees or managers of that scheme where it has reasonable grounds for believing that—

(a)   a person has done or will do any act which constitutes a misuse or misappropriation of the assets of the scheme, or

(b)   a situation exists which amounts to a material threat to the interests of the members of the scheme who are or have been qualifying persons or qualifying self-employed persons in relation to any European employer.

(3) A ring-fencing notice may direct the trustees or managers of the scheme—

(a)   to notify the Regulator, within three months of the date of the issue of the notice, of the details of the assets and liabilities of the scheme attributable to each European employer—

    (i)   from whom the trustees or managers have received or are receiving contributions, and

    (ii)   in relation to whom the ring-fencing notice is given, or

(b)   for so long as the Regulator has reasonable grounds for believing that there is a material threat to the interests of the members of the scheme who are or have been qualifying persons in relation to any such European employer or who are or have been such a European employer, to divide the scheme into two or more sections and ensure that—

    (i)   any contributions payable to the scheme by any such European employer in relation to the scheme or by any such member are allocated to a separate section, and

> (ii) a specified part or proportion of the assets of the scheme is attributable to that section and cannot be used for the purposes of any other section.

NOTES

Initial Commencement

Specified date

Specified date: 30 December 2005: see reg 1.

16 Relevant legal requirements for the purposes of section 293

Where a UK employer has made, makes, or proposes to make, contributions to a European pensions institution in respect of persons who are not qualifying persons, the relevant legal requirements for the purposes of section 293 are, in relation to such persons and their survivors, those requirements of the law relating to schemes as it applies in Great Britain which are listed in paragraph 2, 3 or 5 of Schedule 2.

NOTES

Initial Commencement

Specified date

Specified date: 30 December 2005: see reg 1.

17 Manner of applying to the Regulator under regulations 4 to 6 and 9 to 11

(1) In this regulation, "electronic communications network" shall be construed in accordance with section 304 (notification and documents in electronic form).

(2) An application to the Regulator by the trustees or managers of a scheme for authorisation under section 288 or for approval under section 289 shall be made in writing, or, where any requirements imposed by or under section 304 are complied with, may be made by transmitting it to the Regulator—

(a) by means of an electronic communications network, or

(b) by other means but in a form that nevertheless requires the use of apparatus by the Regulator to render it intelligible.

(3) A notification by the Regulator under section 289(2)(a)(i) or (b) to the persons who gave a notice of intention shall be made in writing, or, where any requirements imposed by or under section 304 are complied with, may be made by transmitting it to those persons—

(a) by means of an electronic communications network, or

(b) by other means but in a form that nevertheless requires the use of apparatus by those persons to render it intelligible.

NOTES

Initial Commencement

Specified date

Specified date: 30 December 2005: see reg 1.

18 Consequential amendment

(1) The Occupational Pension Schemes (Trust and Retirement Benefits Exemption) Regulations 2005 are amended as follows.

(2) In paragraph (2) of regulation 1, after the definition of "relevant statutory scheme", add—

""scheme undertaking cross-border activities" means a scheme in relation to which the trustees or managers are—

(a) authorised under section 288 of the 2004 Act (general authorisation to accept contributions from European employers), or

(b) approved under section 289 of the 2004 Act in relation to a European employer.".

(3) After regulation 1, insert—

1A "Application

With the exception of regulation 2(a), these Regulations do not apply to any scheme undertaking cross-border activities.".

NOTES

Initial Commencement

Specified date

Specified date: 30 December 2005: see reg 1.

SCHEDULE 1
Additional Information to be Contained in Applications for Authorisation or Approval

Regulations 4 to 6 and 9 to 11

1   In this Schedule—

"minimum funding valuation" means an actuarial valuation required by section 57(1)(a) or 57(2) of the 1995 Act (valuation and certification of assets and liabilities);

"payment schedule" shall be construed in accordance with section 87 of the 1995 Act (schedules of payments to money purchase schemes);

"schedule of contributions" shall be construed in accordance with section 227 (schedule of contributions), and includes a schedule of contributions prepared by the trustees or managers for any purpose, including that of making an application under section 288 or 289;

"statement of funding principles" shall be construed in accordance with section 223 (statement of funding principles), and includes a statement of funding principles prepared by the trustees or managers for any purpose, including that of making an application under section 288 or 289.

2   The information about the scheme to be provided in an application for authorisation in accordance with regulations 4(2), 5(2) and 6(2) is—

(a)   the pension scheme registration number which is allocated to that scheme in the register,

(b)   a statement signed by the trustees or managers of the scheme that they have provided to the Regulator all the registrable information with respect to the scheme,

(c)   a statement signed by the trustees or managers of the scheme that the scheme complies with the requirements of section 252(2) and (3) (UK based scheme to be trust with effective rules),

(d)   a statement signed by the trustees or managers of the scheme that any requirements made by or under—

    (i)   section 113 of the 1993 Act (disclosure of information to members of schemes etc),

    (ii)   section 35 of the 1995 Act (investment principles), and

    (iii) section 36 of the 1995 Act (choosing investments),

have been complied with, and

(e)   a statement signed by the trustees or managers of the scheme that—

    (i)   where section 247 (requirement for knowledge and understanding: individual trustees), and section 248 (requirement for knowledge and understanding: corporate trustees) are in force on the day on which the application is made, any requirements made by or under those sections have been complied with, or

    (ii)   where section 247 and section 248 are not in force on the day on which the application is made, any requirements made by or under those sections, or in any instrument made under either or both of those sections, will be complied with once those sections are in force.

3   The information about a scheme to be provided in an application for authorisation in accordance with regulations 4(2)(a), 5(2)(a) and 6(2)(a) is the most recent payment schedule for the scheme.

4   The information about the scheme to be provided in an application for authorisation in accordance with regulation 4(2)(b) is—

(a)   a statement signed by the trustees or managers of the scheme that the scheme complies with the requirements of section 222,

(b)   a statement signed by the trustees or managers of the scheme that any requirements imposed by or under—

    (i)   section 224 (actuarial valuations and reports),

    (ii)   section 225 (certification of technical provisions), and

    (iii)   section 227 (schedule of contributions),

    have been complied with,

(c)   the most recent statement of funding principles for the scheme, and

(d)   an actuarial valuation for the scheme the effective date of which is within the period of 12 months ending on the date of the application.

5   The information about the scheme to be provided in an application for authorisation in accordance with regulation 5(2)(b) is the most recent minimum funding valuation for the scheme.

6   (1) In this paragraph—

(a)   except in sub-paragraph (2)(c), references to the European employer are references to the European employer specified in the notice of intention, and

(b)   references to the provision of information in relation to one European employer shall include the provision of that information in relation to each European employer so specified.

(2) The additional information about the scheme and its existing activities to be contained in the notice of intention in accordance with regulations 9(2), 10(2) and 11(2) is—

(a)   where—

    (i)   the application for approval is not made on the same day as the application for authorisation, and

    (ii)   the trustees or managers have not satisfied the Regulator that there has not been any material change in the information described in paragraph (2)(a) to (e) above since the application for authorisation was made,

    the information so described in so far as there has been any material change in that information,

(b)   where the trustees or managers of the scheme have been authorised by the Regulator under section 288, the date on which such authorisation was granted,

(c)   where the trustees or managers of the scheme are already accepting contributions from a European employer, the name and address of that employer and the host member State of that employer, and

(d)   a copy of the scheme rules.

(3) The additional information about the scheme and its existing activities to be contained in the notice of intention in accordance with regulations 9(2)(a) and 10(2)(a) is the most recent payment schedule for the scheme.

(4) The additional information about the scheme and its existing activities to be contained in the notice of intention in accordance with regulation 9(2)(b) is—

(a)   where—

    (i)   the application for approval is not made on the same day as the application for authorisation, and

    (ii)   the trustees or managers have not satisfied the Regulator that there has not been any material change in the information described in paragraph 4(a) to (d) since the application for authorisation was made,

    the information so described in so far as there has been any material change in that information, and

(b)   the most recent schedule of contributions for the scheme.

(5) The additional information about the scheme and its existing activities to be contained in the notice of intention in accordance with regulation 10(2)(b) is the most recent minimum funding valuation for the scheme.

(6) The additional information about the scheme to be contained in the notice of intention in accordance with regulation 11(2) is a statement signed by the trustees or managers of the scheme showing—

(a)   the rates of contributions which will be payable towards the scheme by or on behalf of the employer and the active members of the scheme, and

(b)   the dates on or before which such contributions are to be paid.

(7) The additional information about the future activities of the scheme when it is approved in relation to the European employer to be contained in the notice of intention in accordance with regulations 9(2), 10(2) and 11(2) is—

(a)   the names of any member States other than the United Kingdom where the scheme already has members who are qualifying persons or qualifying self-employed persons,

(b)   where the scheme has established, or is intending to establish, a branch in the host member State, the address, e-mail address, telephone number and fax number of—

    (i)   that branch, and

    (ii)   all persons authorised to represent the scheme for the business of that branch,

(c)   the address, e-mail address, telephone number and fax number in the host member State of the European employer,

(d)   a description of the type of scheme to be offered to the European employer (including whether it will be defined contribution only, defined benefit, final salary, salary related or some form of hybrid),

(e)   the conditions to be met before benefits are, or will become, payable,

(f)   the types and rates of contributions to be paid towards the scheme by or on behalf of the European employer and those active members of the scheme in the host member State who are—

    (i)   qualifying persons in relation to that European employer, or

    (ii)   qualifying self-employed persons,

(g)   a description of any guarantees and additional coverage offered by the scheme,

(h)   a description of the categories of persons who are employees in the host member State of that European employer who cannot become members of the scheme, and

(i)   whether the assets or liabilities (or both) of the scheme which correspond to the activities carried out in the host member State will be ring-fenced.

NOTES

Initial Commencement

Specified date

Specified date: 30 December 2005: see reg 1.

SCHEDULE 2
Modifications of Pensions Legislation, and Relevant Legal Requirements for the Purposes of Section 293

Regulations 14 and 16

1   (1) In this Schedule, a reference to a section of an Act includes a reference to any subordinate legislation made or having effect as if made under that section.

(2) In this Schedule, "the 2000 Act" means the Child Support, Pensions and Social Security Act 2000.

2   For the purposes of regulations 14 and 16—

(a)   the provisions of pensions legislation which are modified in their application to European members and European survivors of cross-border schemes, and

(b)   the relevant legal requirements for the purposes of section 293,

are the provisions listed in Column 1 of Table 1—

Table 1	
Provision of the 1995 Act	*Description of provision of the 1995 Act*
Section 50(1) to (5) and (7)	Resolution of disputes

3   For the purposes of regulations 14 and 16—

(a)   the provisions of pensions legislation which are modified in relation to European members and European survivors of cross-border schemes, other than European members of a cross-border scheme which is a pre-23rd September 2005 scheme who became members of that scheme before the commencement date and European survivors of such members, and

(b)   the relevant legal requirements for the purposes of section 293,

are the provisions listed in Column 1 of Table 2 set out below—

Table 2

Provisions of the 1993 Act	Description of provisions of the 1993 Act
Sections 69 to 76 and 81 and 82	Preservation of benefit under occupational schemes
Sections 83 to 86	Revaluation of accrued benefits (excluding guaranteed minimum pensions)
Sections 93 to 98, 99(1) to (4A), (7)(a) and (8), 100 and 101	Transfer values
Sections 101AA to 101AI	Early leavers: cash transfer sums and contribution refunds
Provisions of the 1995 Act	Description of provisions of the 1995 Act
Sections 51 to 54	Indexation
Sections 91 to 94	Assignment, forfeiture, bankruptcy etc

4   For the purposes of regulation 14, the other provisions of pensions legislation which are modified in their application to European members and European survivors of cross-border schemes are the provisions listed in Column 1 of Table 3 set out below.

Table 3

Provisions of the 1993 Act	Description of provisions of the 1993 Act
Section 99(7)(b)	Trustees' duties after exercise of option
Provisions of the 1995 Act	Description of provisions of the 1995 Act
Section 50(6)	Resolution of disputes

5   For the purposes of regulation 16, the other relevant legal requirements for the purposes of section 293 are the provisions listed in Column 1 of Table 4 set out below.

Table 4

Provisions of the 1993 Act	Description of provisions of the 1993 Act
Sections 9 and 10	General requirements for certification
Sections 12A to 12D	Requirements for certification of occupational pension schemes
Sections 13 to 21 and 23	Requirements for certification of occupational pension schemes providing guaranteed minimum pensions
Sections 27 to 33	Requirements for certification of occupational and personal money purchase schemes
Sections 37 and 39	Alteration of scheme rules after certification
Section 45B	Money purchase and personal pension schemes: verification of ages
Sections 50 and 51	Approval of arrangements for scheme ceasing to be certified
Sections 52 to 54	Supervision of formerly certified schemes
Sections 55 to 58 and 61 to 63	State scheme premiums
Sections 68A to 68D	Safeguarded rights
Sections 87 to 92	Protection of increases in guaranteed minimum pensions ("anti-franking")
Section 93A(1) to (3)	Salary related schemes: right to statement of entitlement
Sections 109 and 110	Guaranteed minimum pensions
Sections 129 to 132	Relationship between requirements and scheme rules
Section 159	Inalienability of guaranteed minimum pension and protected rights payments

Provisions of the 1999 Act	Description of provisions of the 1999 Act
Sections 11 to 13	Pensions and bankruptcy
Section 40	Other pension schemes

NOTES

Initial Commencement

Specified date

Specified date: 30 December 2005: see reg 1.

Appendix 17

The Pension Protection Fund (Provision of Information) (Amendment) Regulations 2006

SI 2006 No 595

Pension Protection Fund (Provision of Information) (Amendment) Regulations 2006

Made 7th March 2006

Laid before Parliament 13th March 2006

Coming into force 6th April 2006

1   Citation, commencement and interpretation

(1) These Regulations may be cited as the Pension Protection Fund (Provision of Information) (Amendment) Regulations 2006 and shall come into force on 6th April 2006.

(2) In these Regulations "the principal Regulations" means the Pension Protection Fund (Provision of Information) Regulations 2005.

> NOTES
>
> **Initial Commencement**
>
> *Specified date*
>
> Specified date: 6 April 2006: see para (1) above.

2   Amendment of regulation 3 of the principal Regulations

(1) Regulation 3 of the principal Regulations (information to be provided by the Board) shall be amended in accordance with the following provisions of this regulation.

(2) In paragraph (2), for "within the period of 28 days beginning with its receipt of that notice", substitute "within the period specified in paragraph (12)".

(3) After paragraph (2) insert—

"(2A) This paragraph applies where the Board receives a notice under section 120(2) from an insolvency practitioner that an insolvency event has occurred in relation to an employer, and—

(a)   the scheme to which the notice relates is not an eligible scheme; or

(b)   the section of the segregated scheme to which the notice relates is not an eligible section.

(2B) Where paragraph (2A) applies the Board shall within the period specified in paragraph (12) inform—

(a)   the Regulator;

(b)   the trustees or managers of that scheme or section of a segregated scheme; and

(c)   that insolvency practitioner,

that the scheme is not an eligible scheme or, as the case may be, the section is not an eligible section.".

(4) After paragraph (8) add—

"(9) Where the Board receives—

(a)   an application under section 129(1) (applications and notifications for the purposes of section 128) from the trustees or managers; or

478

(b)   a notice under section 129(4) from the Regulator,

it shall provide the information specified in paragraph (10) to the persons specified in paragraph (11) within the period specified in paragraph (12).

(10) The information to be provided under paragraph (9) is—

(a)   where the scheme is not an eligible scheme, that the scheme is not such a scheme;

(b)   where the scheme is an eligible scheme, that the scheme is such a scheme and the date on which the assessment period began;

(c)   where the section of the segregated scheme to which the application or, as the case may be, the notice relates is not an eligible section, that the section of the segregated scheme is not such a section; or

(d)   where the section of the segregated scheme to which the application or, as the case may be, the notice relates is an eligible section, that the section of the segregated scheme is such a section and the date on which the assessment period began.

(11) The persons specified in this paragraph are—

(a)   the Regulator;

(b)   the trustees or managers of that scheme or section of a segregated scheme;

(c)   the employer who is the employer in relation to that scheme or section of a segregated scheme; and

(d)   the insolvency practitioner in relation to that employer.

(12) The Board shall provide the information specified in paragraph (3) or (10) within the period of 28 days beginning with—

(a)   the date it receives the notice under section 120(2);

(b)   the date it receives the application under section 129(1);

(c)   the date it receives the notice under section 129(4);

(d)   where the Board requires the—

      (i)   Regulator,

      (ii)   insolvency practitioner, or

      (iii)   trustees or managers,

to produce a document or provide information in connection with a notice given under section 120(2) or 129(4) or, as the case may be, an application under section 129(1), the date on which the document is produced to, or the information received by, either the Board or a person authorised by the Board for the purposes of section 191(2)(b) (notices requiring provision of information); or

(e)   where a person is required to produce a document or provide information in connection with a notice given under section 191(1), the date on which the document is produced to, or the information received by, either the Board or a person authorised by the Board for the purposes of section 191(2)(b).

(13) This regulation does not impose any duty on the Board to provide any information to the trustees or managers of a scheme where the address of the trustees or managers has not been provided by the person who referred the notice or application to the Board.".

NOTES

Initial Commencement

Specified date

Specified date: 6 April 2006: see reg 1(1).

3   Amendment of Schedule 1 to the principal Regulations

In the first column of the table in paragraph 1(2) of Schedule 1 to the principal Regulations (information to be provided by the Board), in the tenth row, for "party to matrimonial proceedings or who is contemplating such proceedings", substitute "party to matrimonial or civil partnership proceedings or who is contemplating such proceedings".

NOTES

Initial Commencement

Specified date

Specified date: 6 April 2006: see reg 1(1).

4 Amendment of Schedule 2 to the principal Regulations

(1) Schedule 2 to the principal Regulations (information to be provided by trustees or managers) shall be amended in accordance with the following provisions of this regulation.

(2) In paragraph 1(1), in the definition of "notification date", for "in accordance with regulation 3(3)(b)", substitute "in accordance with regulation 3(3)(b), (10)(b) or (d)".

(3) In the second column of the table in paragraph 1(2), in the first row, at the end of that row in that column add—

"(e)   if applicable, the date he left the employment of the employer in relation to that scheme; and

(f)   a statement containing a brief description of his illness or injury.".

(4) After the first row insert—

"The Board	The number of ill health pensions awarded each year for the previous six years immediately before the assessment date.	The period of 28 days beginning on the notification date.".

NOTES
Initial Commencement
Specified date
Specified date: 6 April 2006: see reg 1(1).

5 Amendment of Schedule 3 to the principal Regulations

(1) Schedule 3 (information to be provided by members and beneficiaries) to the principal Regulations shall be amended in accordance with the following provisions of this regulation.

(2) In the second row in the table—

(a)   in the first column, after "whose marriage ends in divorce", add "or whose civil partnership is dissolved";

(b)   in the second column, for "divorce and a copy of the decree of divorce", substitute "divorce or dissolution of the civil partnership and a copy of the decree of divorce or dissolution of civil partnership"; and

(c)   in the third column, after "decree became absolute", add " or the civil partnership was dissolved".

NOTES
Initial Commencement
Specified date
Specified date: 6 April 2006: see reg 1(1).

The Occupational Pension Schemes (Trustees' Knowledge and Understanding) Regulations 2006

SI 2006 No 686

Occupational Pension Schemes (Trustees' Knowledge and Understanding) Regulations 2006

Made 9th March 2006

Laid before Parliament 16th March 2006

Coming into force 6th April 2006

1 Citation, commencement and interpretation

(1) These Regulations may be cited as the Occupational Pension Schemes (Trustees' Knowledge and Understanding) Regulations 2006 and shall come into force on 6th April 2006.

(2) In these Regulations—

"the 2004 Act" means the Pensions Act 2004;

"the 1995 Act" means the Pensions Act 1995.

> **NOTES**
> **Initial Commencement**
> *Specified date*
> Specified date: 6 April 2006: see para (1) above.

2 Exceptions for trustees of small schemes

(1) The requirements imposed by sections 247(3) and (4) of the 2004 Act (requirement for knowledge and understanding: individual trustees) shall not apply to trustees of schemes with fewer than twelve members where all the members are trustees of the scheme and either—

(a)   the provisions of the scheme provide that all decisions which fall to be made by the trustees are made by unanimous agreement by the trustees who are members of the scheme, or

(b)   the scheme has a trustee who is independent in relation to the scheme for the purposes of section 23 of the 1995 Act (power to appoint independent trustees), and is registered in the register maintained by the Authority in accordance with regulations made under subsection (4) of that section;

(2) The requirements imposed by section 248(3) and (5) of the 2004 Act (requirement for knowledge and understanding: corporate trustees) shall not apply to trustees of schemes with fewer than twelve members where a company is a trustee of the scheme and all of the members of the scheme are directors of the company and either—

(a)   the provisions of the scheme provide that any decision made by the company in its capacity as trustee is made by the unanimous agreement of all the directors who are members of the scheme, or

(b)   one of the directors is a trustee who is independent in relation to the scheme for the purposes of section 23 of the 1995 Act and is registered in the register maintained by the Authority in accordance with regulations made under subsection (4) of that section.

NOTES

Initial Commencement

Specified date

Specified date: 6 April 2006: see reg 1(1).

3 Individual trustees: period of grace

Section 247(3) and (4) of the 2004 Act shall not apply to any individual who is a trustee of a relevant scheme for a period of six months beginning with the date of his appointment as such a trustee, unless—

(a)   he is an independent trustee who meets the requirements of section 23(1) of the 1995 Act; or

(b)   he was appointed as a consequence of holding himself out as having expertise in any of the matters listed in section 247(4) of the 2004 Act or in any regulations made under paragraph (c) of that section.

NOTES

Initial Commencement

Specified date

Specified date: 6 April 2006: see reg 1(1).

4 Corporate trustees: period of grace

Section 248(3) and (5) of the 2004 Act shall not apply to any individual, who exercises any function which a company has as trustee of a relevant scheme, for a period of six months beginning with the date of his appointment to the company, unless—

(a)   he is an independent trustee who meets the requirements of section 23(1) of the 1995 Act; or

(b)   he was appointed as a consequence of holding himself out as having expertise in any of the matters listed in section 248(5) of the 2004 Act or in any regulations made under paragraph (c) of that section.

NOTES

Initial Commencement

Specified date

Specified date: 6 April 2006: see reg 1(1).

The Occupational Pension Schemes (Member-nominated Trustees and Directors) Regulations 2006

SI 2006 No 714

Occupational Pension Schemes (Member-nominated Trustees and Directors) Regulations 2006

Made 13th March 2006

Laid before Parliament 16th March 2006

Coming into force in accordance with regulation 1(1)

1   Citation, commencement and interpretation

(1) These Regulations may be cited as the Occupational Pension Schemes (Member-nominated Trustees and Directors) Regulations 2006 and shall come into force on 6th April 2006, immediately prior to the coming into force of Article 2(6) of the Pensions Act 2004 (Commencement No 8) Order.

(2) In these Regulations—

"the Act" means the Pensions Act 2004;

"the 1995 Act" means the Pensions Act 1995;

"associated" shall be construed in accordance with paragraph (4);

"church legislation" means—

    (a)   any Measure of the Church Assembly or of the General Synod of the Church of England; or

    (b)   any order, regulation or other instrument made under, or by virtue of such a Measure;

"connected" shall be construed in accordance with paragraph (4);

"direct payment paid-up insurance scheme" means a scheme under which—

    (a)   no further contributions are payable;

    (b)   the benefits that may be provided in respect of an individual are determined by reference to the value of the whole or a specified part of the rights under a contract of insurance; and

    (c)   the benefits in respect of any member are, in accordance with an agreement made between the insurer and the trustees of the scheme (or a subsequent agreement made with any person for the provision of those benefits in respect of the member, by that person), to be paid by the insurer (or that person) directly to the member or to a person entitled to benefits in respect of that member;

"former old code scheme" means a registered pension scheme which was formerly approved under section 208 of the Income and Corporation Taxes Act 1970 (approved superannuation funds) and under the provisions of which—

    (a)   no further contributions are payable; and

    (b)   the entitlement in respect of each member is to a benefit consisting of a specified fixed amount which may not be altered unless—

        (i)   the member retires otherwise than at his normal pension age; or

        (ii)   another person becomes entitled to a benefit in respect of him;

Appendix 19

"independently selected" in relation to a trustee of a scheme or a director of a company which is a trustee of a scheme, means selected as a trustee (or, as the case may be, a director)—

(a)　by some or all of the members of the scheme (otherwise than wholly or mainly by members who are directors of companies which are employers in relation to the scheme); or

(b)　by an organisation which represents some or all of the members of the scheme (other than wholly or mainly members who are such directors);

"insurer" (subject to paragraph (5), means—

(a)　a person who has permission under Part 4 of the Financial Services and Markets Act 2000 (permission to carry on regulated activities) to effect or carry out contracts of long-term insurance; or

(b)　an EEA firm of the kind mentioned in paragraph 5(d) of Schedule 3 to that Act (EEA passport rights), which has permission under paragraph 15 of that Schedule (grant of permission) (as a result of qualifying for authorisation under paragraph 12 of that Schedule) to effect or carry out contracts of long-term insurance;

"registered pension scheme" has the meaning given in section 150(2) of the Finance Act 2004 (meaning of pension scheme);

"relevant centralised scheme" means a scheme in which—

(a)　membership is open to employees of more than one employer under a single scheme;

(b)　at least two of the employers are not associated or connected; and

(c)　in the case of a scheme which has one or more trustee and in which each trustee is a company—

(i)　the scheme rules do not provide that the power to appoint or remove all the directors is exercisable solely by one employer; and

(ii)　at least one-third of the directors of the company or each of those companies are independent or independently selected; or

(d)　in the case of a scheme where at least one of the trustees is not a company, either—

(i)　the scheme rules do not provide that the power to appoint or remove all the trustees is exercisable solely by one employer; or

(ii)　at least one-third of the trustees are persons who—

(aa)　have no legal or beneficial interest in the assets of any of the employers or of the scheme (otherwise than as trustees) and are neither connected nor associated with, any of the employers; and

(bb)　have been independently selected;

"relevant executive pension scheme" means a scheme—

(a)　in relation to which the company is the only employer and the sole trustee; and

(b)　the members of which are either current or former directors of the company and which includes at least one-third of the current directors;

"relevant small occupational pension scheme" means—

(a)　a scheme with fewer than twelve members, where all the members are trustees of the scheme, and either—

(i)　the rules of the scheme provide that all decisions are made only by the trustees who are members of the scheme, by unanimous agreement; or

(ii)　the scheme has an independent trustee who is independent in relation to the scheme for the purposes of section 23 of the 1995 Act (power to appoint independent trustees) and is registered in the register maintained by the Authority in accordance with regulations made under subsection (4) of that section; or

(b)　a scheme with fewer than twelve members where all the members are directors of a company which is the sole trustee of the scheme and either—

(i)　the rules of the scheme provide that all decisions are made only by the members of the scheme by unanimous agreement; or

(ii)   one of the directors of the company is independent in relation to the scheme for the purposes of section 23 of the 1995 Act and is registered in the register maintained by the Authority in accordance with regulations made under subsection (4) of that section;

"relevant wholly insured scheme" means a scheme under which there is a sole trustee and all the benefits are secured by contracts of insurance or annuity contracts, some or all of which are with an insurer who—

(a)   is, or is connected, with the sole trustee of the scheme; but

(b)   is not, and is not connected, with the employer;

"section 615(6) scheme" means a scheme with such a superannuation fund as is mentioned in section 615(6) of the Income and Corporation Taxes Act 1988 (exemption from tax in respect of certain pensions);

"small insured scheme" means a scheme—

(a)   with fewer than twelve members; and

(b)   in which all the scheme benefits are secured with an insurer under a contract of insurance or annuity contract.

(3) For the purposes of paragraph (2), a director is independent in relation to a scheme only if he—

(a)   has no direct legal or beneficial interest in the assets of any of the employers or of the scheme; and

(b)   is neither connected, nor associated with, any of the employers.

(4) For the purposes of these Regulations—

(a)   sections 249 and 435 of the Insolvency Act 1986 (connected and associated persons) shall apply as they apply for the purposes of that Act; and

(b)   section 74 of the Bankruptcy (Scotland) Act 1985 (associated persons) shall apply as it applies for the purposes of that Act.

(5) The definition of insurer in paragraph (2) must be read with—

(a)   section 22 of the Financial Services and Markets Act 2000 (the classes of activity and categories of investment); and

(b)   any relevant order under that section; or

(c)   Schedule 2 to that Act (regulated activities).

(6) References to "employer" and "employers" in paragraphs (c)(i) and (d) of the definition in paragraph (2) of "relevant centralised scheme" and in paragraph (3) do not include companies which carry on the business of acting as trustee of, or providing administrative services to, the scheme and no other business.

NOTES

Initial Commencement

Specified date

Specified date: 6 April 2006: see para (1) above.

2   Exemptions from requirement to have member-nominated trustees

For the purposes of section 241(8)(c) of the Act (requirement for member-nominated trustees) a scheme is of a prescribed description, if the scheme—

(a)   has fewer than two members;

(b)   is a scheme to which section 22 of the 1995 Act (independent trustees – circumstances in which following provisions apply) applies;

(c)   is an occupational pension scheme within the meaning given by section 1 of the Pension Schemes Act 1993 (categories of pension schemes), but if it is not a registered pension scheme;

(d)   is a relevant small occupational pension scheme;

(e)   is a relevant centralised scheme;

(f)   is a direct payment, paid-up insurance scheme;

(g)   is a former old code scheme;

(h)   is a section 615(6) scheme;

(i)   is set up under section 2 of the Parliamentary and other Pensions Act 1987 (power to provide for pensions for Members of the House of Commons etc);

(j) has been modified under Schedule 5 to the Coal Industry Act 1994 (pension provision in connection with restructuring);

(k) is a scheme where the sole trustee, or all the trustees are independent within the meaning given by section 23(3) of the 1995 Act;

(l) is a stakeholder pension scheme within the meaning of section 1 of the Welfare Reform and Pensions Act 1999 (meaning of "stakeholder pension scheme");

(m) is a small insured scheme;

(n) is independent of the employer by virtue of the employer having been dissolved or liquidated prior to 6th April 2005; or

(o) is a scheme where the trustee is a body governed by church legislation.

NOTES
Initial Commencement
Specified date
Specified date: 6 April 2006: see reg 1(1).

3 Prescribed exemptions from requirement to have member-nominated directors of corporate trustees

For the purposes of section 242(10) of the Act (requirement for member-nominated directors of corporate trustees) a scheme is of a prescribed description if the scheme—

(a) has fewer than two members;

(b) is a scheme to which section 22 of the 1995 Act applies;

(c) is an occupational pension scheme within the meaning given by section 1 of the Pension Schemes Act 1993, but if it is not a registered pension scheme;

(d) is a relevant small occupational pension scheme;

(e) is a relevant centralised scheme;

(f) is a direct payment, paid-up insurance scheme;

(g) is a former old code scheme;

(h) is a section 615(6) scheme;

(i) is set up under section 2 of the Parliamentary and other Pensions Act 1987;

(j) has been modified under Schedule 5 to the Coal Industry Act 1994;

(k) is a stakeholder pension scheme within the meaning of section 1 of the Welfare Reform and Pensions Act 1999;

(l) is a scheme which is a relevant executive pension scheme in relation to the company;

(m) is a scheme where the sole director, or all the directors are independent within the meaning given by section 23(3) of the 1995 Act;

(n) is a small insured scheme;

(o) is independent of the employer by virtue of the employer having been dissolved or liquidated prior to 6th April 2005;

(p) is a scheme which is a relevant wholly insured scheme; or

(q) is a scheme where the trustee is a body governed by church legislation.

NOTES
Initial Commencement
Specified date
Specified date: 6 April 2006: see reg 1(1).

4 Transitional

In relation to a scheme which has alternative arrangements for the appointment of trustees or directors approved under section 17(1) (exceptions), or 19(1) (corporate trustees: exceptions) of the 1995 Act immediately prior to the date those sections were repealed, the approval of such arrangements shall cease to have effect—

(a)   on the date the approval under regulation 20 of the Occupational Pension Schemes (Member-nominated Trustees and Directors) Regulations 1996 (cessation of approval of appropriate rules and alternative arrangements) would cease to have effect but for the revocation of those Regulations; or

(b)   on 31st October 2007,

whichever is the earlier.

NOTES

Initial Commencement

Specified date

Specified date: 6 April 2006: see reg 1(1).

5   Modifications of sections 241 and 242 of the Act

(1) Sections 241 (requirement for member-nominated trustees) and 242 (requirement for member-nominated directors of corporate trustees) of the Act are modified in their application to the cases prescribed in paragraphs (2) to (6).

(2) In relation to a scheme where the scheme rules contain provisions requiring that there be more than one-third member-nominated trustees or directors as the case may be, sections 241 and 242 of the Act are modified as if—

(a)   in section 241(1)(a) for "at least one-third of the total number of trustees" there were substituted "the nomination and selection of member-nominated trustees at least in a proportion not less than that proportion set out in the scheme rules";

(b)   section 241(4) were omitted;

(c)   in section 242(1)(a) for "at least one-third of the total number of directors of the company" there were substituted "the nomination and selection of member-nominated directors at least in a proportion not less than that proportion set out in the scheme rules"; and

(d)   section 242(4) were omitted.

(3) In relation to a scheme where the scheme rules provide that trustees of the scheme may be removed by a vote of the membership, then in relation to any application of that scheme rule, section 241 shall be modified as if subsection (6) were omitted.

(4) In relation to a scheme which has member-nominated trustees or, as the case may be, directors appointed under section 16(1) (requirement for member-nominated trustees) or section 18(1) of the 1995 Act (corporate trustees: member-nominated directors) immediately prior to the date those sections are repealed, sections 241 and 242 of the Act are modified as if—

(a)   in section 241 after subsection (2) there were inserted—

"(2A) In the case of a scheme which has member-nominated trustees appointed under section 16(1) of the Pensions Act 1995 immediately prior to the date that section was revoked, "member-nominated trustees" includes any member-nominated trustees appointed under that section for the remainder of their term of office under section 16(5)."; and

(b)   in section 242 after subsection (2) there were inserted—

"(2A) In the case of a scheme which has member-nominated directors appointed under section 18(1) of the Pensions Act 1995 immediately prior to the date that section was revoked, "member-nominated directors" includes any member-nominated directors appointed under that section for the remainder of their term of office under section 18(5).".

(5) In relation to a scheme which has arrangements for the appointment of member-nominated trustees or directors approved under sections 17(1) or 19(1) of the 1995 Act, immediately prior to the date those sections are repealed, sections 241 and 242 of the Act are modified as if—

(a)   in section 241 for subsection (3)(a) and (b) there were substituted—

"(a)   the date the approval under regulation 20 of the Occupational Pension Schemes (Member-nominated Trustees and Directors) Regulations 1996 (cessation of approval of appropriate rules and alternative arrangements) would cease to have effect but for the revocation of those Regulations; or

(b)   31st October 2007,

          whichever is the earlier."; and

(b)   in section 242 for subsection (3)(a) and (b) there were substituted—

"(a)   the date the approval under regulation 20 of the Occupational Pension Schemes (Member-nominated Trustees and Directors) Regulations 1996 (cessation of approval of appropriate rules and alternative arrangements) would cease to have effect but for the revocation of those Regulations; or

(b)   31st October 2007;

        whichever is the earlier.".

(6) In relation to a scheme which has no active or pensioner members section 241 and 242 of the Act are modified as if for subsection (2)(a) in both sections, there were substituted—

"(a)   are nominated as the result of a process in which at least such deferred members as the trustees determine are eligible to participate, and".

NOTES

Initial Commencement

Specified date

Specified date: 6 April 2006: see reg 1(1).

6   Revocations

The subordinate legislation specified in column 1 of the Schedule to these Regulations are revoked to the extent specified in column 3.

NOTES

Initial Commencement

Specified date

Specified date: 6 April 2006: see reg 1(1).

SCHEDULE

Regulation 6

Column 1	Column 2	Column 3
Regulations revoked	*References*	*Extent of revocation*
The Occupational Pension Schemes (Member-nominated Trustees and Directors) Regulations 1996	SI 1996/1216	The whole of the Regulations
The Personal and Occupational Pension Schemes (Miscellaneous Amendments) Regulations 1997	SI 1997/786	Paragraph 5 of Schedule 1, and Schedule 2 to the Regulations (in so far as it relates to the Occupational Pension Schemes (Member-nominated Trustees and Directors) Regulations 1996)
The Personal and Occupational Pension Schemes (Miscellaneous Amendments) Regulations 1999	SI 1999/3198	Regulation 7
The Stakeholder Pension Schemes Regulations 2000	SI 2000/1403	Regulation 30
The Financial Services and Markets Act 2000 (Consequential Amendments and Repeals) Order 2001	2001/3649	Article 524
The Occupational Pension Schemes (Member-nominated Trustees and Directors) Amendment Regulations 2002	2002/3227	The whole of the Regulations

NOTES

Initial Commencement

Specified date

Specified date: 6 April 2006: see reg 1(1).

Appendix 20

The Occupational Pension Schemes (Levy Ceiling) Order 2006

SI 2006 No 742

Occupational Pension Schemes (Levy Ceiling) Order 2006

Made 13th March 2006

Coming into force in accordance with article 1

I Citation and commencement

This Order may be cited as the Occupational Pension Schemes (Levy Ceiling) Order 2006 and shall come into force on the day after the day on which it is made.

> **NOTES**
> **Initial Commencement**
> *Specified date*
> Specified date: 14 March 2006: see above.

2 The levy ceiling

For the purposes of section 177 of the Pensions Act 2004 (amounts to be raised by the pension protection levies), the levy ceiling for the financial year beginning on 1st April 2006 is £775,000,000.

> **NOTES**
> **Initial Commencement**
> *Specified date*
> Specified date: 14 March 2006: see art 1.

Occupational Pension Schemes (Modification of Schemes) Regulations 2006

SI 2006 No 759

Occupational Pension Schemes (Modification of Schemes) Regulations 2006

Made 14th March 2006

Laid before Parliament 16th March 2006

Coming into force
regulations 6 and 7 30th March 2006
remainder 6th April 2006

1 Citation, commencement and interpretation

(1) These Regulations may be cited as the Occupational Pension Schemes (Modification of Schemes) Regulations 2006.

(2) Regulations 6 and 7 shall come into force on 30th March 2006 and all other regulations shall come into force on 6th April 2006.

(3) In these Regulations—

"the 1993 Act" means the Pension Schemes Act 1993;

"the 1995 Act" means the Pensions Act 1995;

"the 2004 Act" means the Finance Act 2004;

"the 2006 Regulations" means the Registered Pension Schemes (Modification of the Rules of Existing Schemes) Regulations 2006;

"protected rights" has the same meaning as in section 10 of the 1993 Act (protected rights and money purchase benefits);

"public service pension scheme" has the same meaning as in section 1 of the 1993 Act (categories of pension schemes);

"registered pension scheme" means a scheme which is a registered pension scheme for the purposes of Part 4 of the 2004 Act (pension schemes etc);

"scheme" means an occupational pension scheme;

"the scheme administrator" has the same meaning as in section 270 of the 2004 Act (meaning of scheme administrator);

"the transitional period" has the same meaning as in regulation 1(2) of the 2006 Regulations;

"unauthorised member payment" has the same meaning as in section 160(2) of the 2004 Act (payments by registered pension schemes).

NOTES

Initial Commencement

Specified date

Specified date (for the purposes of regs 6, 7): 30 March 2006: see para (2) above.

Specified date (for remaining purposes): 6 April 2006: see para (2) above.

2 Schemes exempted from the subsisting rights provisions

For the purposes of section 67(1)(b) of the 1995 Act (the subsisting rights provisions), a scheme of a prescribed description is—

(a)   a scheme with fewer than two members; or

(b)   a scheme which is not a registered pension scheme.

NOTES

Initial Commencement

Specified date

Specified date: 6 April 2006: see reg 1(2).

3 Non-application of the subsisting rights provisions

For the purposes of section 67(3)(b) of the 1995 Act, the prescribed manner of the exercise of any modification power in relation to a scheme to which the subsisting rights provisions do not apply, is any modification of a scheme—

(a)   which provides for any or all of a member's or survivor's subsisting rights to—

    (i)   be assigned;

    (ii)   be commuted;

    (iii)   be surrendered;

    (iv)   be charged;

    (v)   have a lien exercised in respect of them; or

    (vi)   have a set-off exercised in respect of them,

provided that a modification in such a manner is not prohibited under section 91 of the 1995 Act (inalienability of occupational pension), any other enactment or other rule of law;

(b)   which provides for any or all of a member's or survivor's subsisting rights to be forfeited provided that a modification in such a manner is not prohibited under section 92 of the 1995 Act (forfeiture), any other enactment or other rule of law;

(c)   to provide for the revaluation of an earner's earnings factors in accordance with section 16(1) or (2) of the 1993 Act (guaranteed minimum pensions: revaluation of earnings factors for purposes of section 14: early leavers etc);

(d)   which provides for the rate of pension or annuity provided in respect of subsisting rights which are protected rights—

    (i)   to be calculated on the basis that the member will not, in the event of his death, be survived by a widow, widower or surviving civil partner, and

    (ii)   provides that the member must consent to the calculation of his pension or annuity being on that basis;

(e)   which provides for the transfer of a member's or survivor's subsisting rights—

    (i)   with his consent; or

    (ii)   without his consent in accordance with the conditions specified in regulation 12 of the Occupational Pension Schemes (Preservation of Benefit) Regulations 1991 (short service benefit: transfer of member's accrued rights without consent);

(f)   which ensures that any payment made by the scheme, relating to rights which accrued on or after 6th April 2006, is not an unauthorised member payment;

(g)   which ensures that the scheme administrator can pay—

    (i)   any short service refund lump sum charge or special lump sum death benefits charge under sections 205 and 206 of the 2004 Act (short service refund lump sum charge and special lump sum death benefits charge) for which it is liable;

    (ii)   any lifetime allowance charge for which, under section 217 of the 2004 Act (persons liable to charge), it is jointly and severally liable with the individual (to whom the charge relates);

(h)   which has the same effect as any or all of the modifications in regulations 3 to 8 of the 2006 Regulations (modification of rules of existing schemes), but without limitation to the transitional period; or

(i)   which provides in relation to all or part of a member's subsisting rights that after his death—

    (i)   a surviving civil partner is treated in the same way as a widow or widower, and

(ii)   the rights of any other survivor of the member are determined as if the surviving civil partner were a widow or widower.

NOTES

Initial Commencement

Specified date

Specified date: 6 April 2006: see reg 1(2).

4   Qualifications or experience required for a person providing an actuarial equivalence statement

For the purposes of section 67C(7)(a)(ii) of the 1995 Act (the actuarial equivalence requirements), a person with the prescribed qualifications or experience is a—

(a)   Fellow of the Faculty of Actuaries; or

(b)   Fellow of the Institute of Actuaries.

NOTES

Initial Commencement

Specified date

Specified date: 6 April 2006: see reg 1(2).

5   Calculation of the actuarial value of affected member's subsisting rights

(1) The prescribed requirements with which any calculation of the actuarial value of an affected member's subsisting rights must conform, for the purposes of the actuarial value requirement in section 67C(5) of the 1995 Act, are those specified in paragraph (2).

(2) The actuary—

(a)   shall calculate the value of the subsisting rights of an affected member by adopting methods and making assumptions which—

    (i)   have been notified to the trustees of the scheme;

    (ii)   are consistent with methods and assumptions used by the trustees as at the date of the modification to calculate a cash equivalent transfer value in accordance with regulation 7(3)(b) of the Occupational Pension Schemes (Transfer Values) Regulations 1996 (manner of calculation and verification of cash equivalents); and

    (iii)   exclude any provisions relating to a reduction in the value of an affected member's cash equivalent transfer value due to the funding position of the scheme;

(b)   shall ensure that the calculation of the actuarial value of an affected member's subsisting rights is made in accordance with any guidance that is prepared by the Faculty and Institute of Actuaries which is current on the date that the actuarial equivalence statement is obtained by the trustees;

(c)   shall exclude from the subsisting rights calculation—

    (i)   the value of any subsisting rights that have been surrendered, commuted or forfeited before the date on which the modification of the scheme takes effect;

    (ii)   the value of any amounts paid, or due to be paid, in respect of any pension or other benefit in payment to an affected member in respect of a period prior to the date on which the modification takes effect;

    (iii)   the value of discretionary benefits that have not been awarded to an affected member or are not in payment on the date on which the modification takes effect;

    (iv)   any subsisting rights which consist wholly or partly of rights to money purchase benefits where—

        (aa)   those benefits are not valued in a manner which involves making estimates of the value of the rights, and

        (bb)   the modification has no effect on the value of those rights.

NOTES

Initial Commencement

Specified date

Specified date: 6 April 2006: see reg 1(2).

6   Modification of schemes: Finance Act 2004

(1) The trustees of a trust scheme may by resolution passed before 6th April 2011 modify the scheme for the purposes of—

(a)   achieving the same effect as all of the modifications in regulations 3 to 8 of the 2006 Regulations, but without limitation as to the transitional period; and

(b)   amending the scheme rules so that the 2006 Regulations no longer apply in relation to the scheme with effect from the date on which the modifications referred to in sub-paragraph (a) take effect.

(2) Modifications made by resolution under paragraph (1) may have effect from a date before the date the resolution is passed but not before 6th April 2006.

(3) Modifications made under paragraph (1) shall have effect from any date on or after 6th April 2006.

(4) Without prejudice to section 67 of the 1995 Act, modifications made by resolution under paragraph (1)(a) may be modified by exercise of any power conferred on any person by a scheme to modify the scheme.

> **NOTES**
> **Initial Commencement**
> *Specified date*
> Specified date: 30 March 2006: see reg 1(2).

7   Modification of schemes: surviving civil partners

(1) Subject to paragraph (2), the trustees of a trust scheme may by resolution modify the scheme in relation to all or part of a member's subsisting rights so that after his death—

(a)   a surviving civil partner is treated in the same way as a widow or widower, and

(b)   the rights of any other survivor are determined as if the surviving civil partner were a widow or widower.

(2) A modification under paragraph (1) which confers rights on surviving civil partners which are in excess of what is required to comply with the relevant requirements of the Civil Partnership Act 2004 shall not be made unless—

(a)   the employer in relation to the scheme consents; or

(b)   in the case of a scheme where there is more than one employer—

    (i)   a person nominated by the employers, or otherwise in accordance with the scheme rules, to act as the employers' representative (the "nominee") consents; or

    (ii)   where there is no such nominee, all of the employers in relation to the scheme consent other than any employer who has waived his right to give such consent.

> **NOTES**
> **Initial Commencement**
> *Specified date*
> Specified date: 30 March 2006: see reg 1(2).

8   Modification of schemes: prescribed schemes

For the purposes of section 68(6) of the 1995 Act (the power to modify schemes by resolution does not apply to trust schemes within a prescribed class or description), the prescribed class or description of trust schemes is any scheme—

(a)   in respect of which any Minister of the Crown has given a guarantee or made arrangements for the purposes of securing that the assets of the scheme are sufficient to meet its liabilities; and

(b)   which is a public service pension scheme.

> **NOTES**
> **Initial Commencement**
> *Specified date*
> Specified date: 6 April 2006: see reg 1(2).

9   Revocations

The enactments listed in the Schedule are revoked to the extent specified.

Appendix 21

NOTES
Initial Commencement
Specified date
Specified date: 6 April 2006: see reg 1(2).

SCHEDULE

Revocations	Reference	Extent of revocation
The Occupational Pension Schemes (Modification of Schemes) Regulations 1996	SI 1996/2517	The whole of the Regulations
The Personal and Occupational Pension Schemes (Miscellaneous Amendments) Regulations 1997	SI 1997/786	Paragraph 16 of Schedule 1
The Personal and Occupational Pension Schemes (Miscellaneous Amendments) Regulations 1999	SI 1999/3198	Regulation 9
The Occupational and Personal Pension Schemes (Contracting-out) (Miscellaneous Amendments) Regulations 2002	SI 2002/681	Regulation 5
The Civil Partnership (Contracted-out Occupational and Appropriate Personal Pension Schemes) (Surviving Civil Partners) Order 2005	SI 2005/2050	Paragraph 35 of Schedule 2
The Civil Partnership (Pensions, Social Security and Child Support) (Consequential, etc Provisions) Order 2005.	SI 2005/2877	Paragraph 6 of Schedule 2

NOTES
Initial Commencement
Specified date
Specified date: 6 April 2006: see reg 1(2).

The Occupational Pension Schemes (Payments to Employer) Regulations 2006

SI 2006 No 802

Occupational Pension Schemes (Payments to Employer) Regulations 2006

Made 16th March 2006

Laid before Parliament 16th March 2006

Coming into force 6th April 2006

PART I
CITATION, COMMENCEMENT AND INTERPRETATION

I Citation and commencement

These Regulations may be cited as the Occupational Pension Schemes (Payments to Employer) Regulations 2006 and shall come into force on 6th April 2006.

> **NOTES**
> **Initial Commencement**
> *Specified date*
> Specified date: 6 April 2006: see above.

2 Interpretation

(1) In these Regulations—

"the 1995 Act" means the Pensions Act 1995;

"the 2004 Act" means the Pensions Act 2004;

"earmarked scheme" means a money purchase scheme under which all the benefits are secured by one or more insurance policies specifically allocated to the provision of benefits to or in respect of individual members;

"effective date" means the date by reference to which the scheme's assets are valued and liabilities calculated by the person specified in Regulation 6;

"excluded person" means a deferred member or pension credit member whose current address is not known to the trustees or managers of the scheme, and in respect of whom correspondence sent to the last known address of such a member, by the trustees or managers, has been returned;

"freezing order" has the meaning given in section 23(3) of the 2004 Act (freezing orders);

"insurance policy" means—

(a) in relation to an earmarked scheme a contract on human life or a contract of annuity on human life; and

(b) in any other case, a contract on human life or a contract of annuity on human life, but excluding a contract which is linked to investment funds;

"money purchase benefits" means benefits the rate or amount of which is calculated by reference to a payment or payments made by the member or by any other person in respect of the member and which are not benefits the rate or amount of which is calculated by reference to the average salary of a member over the period of service on which the benefit is based;

"money purchase scheme" means a pension scheme under which all the benefits that may be provided, other than death benefits, are money purchase benefits;

"regulatory own funds scheme" means a scheme in which the scheme, and not any employer in relation to that scheme—

(a)   underwrites any liability to cover against biometric risk;

(b)   guarantees an investment performance; or

(c)   guarantees a level of benefits;

"relevant accounts" for the purposes of identifying and valuing the assets of a scheme are audited accounts for the scheme which—

(a)   comply with the requirements imposed under section 41 of the 1995 Act (provision of documents for members); and

(b)   are prepared in respect of a period ending with the effective date of the valuation; and

"valuation certificate" means a valuation certificate which complies with regulation 7.

(2) In the application of—

(a)   section 37 of the 1995 Act (payment of surplus to employer); and

(b)   these Regulations,

to a scheme which has no active members, references to the employer have effect as if they were references to the person who was the employer immediately before the occurrence of the event after which the scheme ceased to have such members.

NOTES

Initial Commencement

Specified date

Specified date: 6 April 2006: see reg 1.

PART 2
SCHEMES NOT IN WIND UP

3   Schemes not in wind up

(1) Subject to paragraph (2) and regulations 12 to 14, the prescribed requirements for the purposes of section 37(3)(b) (payment of surplus to employer) are that the scheme is not in wind up, and—

(a)   it is a scheme which—

(i)   is subject to Part 3 of the 2004 Act (scheme funding); and

(ii)   is not a regulatory own funds scheme; or

(b)   it is a scheme that is an earmarked scheme.

(2) A scheme to which—

(a)   paragraph (1)(a) applies must also comply with regulations 4 to 7 and 9 to 11; or

(b)   paragraph (1)(b) applies must also comply with regulation 8.

NOTES

Initial Commencement

Specified date

Specified date: 6 April 2006: see reg 1.

4   Schemes that are subject to Part 3 of the 2004 Act—determination of assets and liabilities

(1) In the case of a scheme to which regulation 3(1)(a) applies, where the trustees propose to make a payment to the employer, either—

(a)   the written valuation of the scheme's assets and liabilities required under section 37(3)(a) of the 1995 Act shall be prepared in accordance with this regulation and regulations 5 and 6; or

(b)   where—

    (i)   an actuarial valuation has been prepared for the purposes of Part 3 of the 2004 Act; and

    (ii)   this valuation is valid for the purposes of regulation 9,

the trustees may use this valuation for the purposes of regulation 7(1) and section 37(3)(a), ("a Part 3 valuation").

(2) Where trustees use a Part 3 valuation—

(a)   the value to be placed on the scheme's liabilities shall be the value placed by the actuary on the scheme's liabilities for the purposes of the actuary's estimate of the solvency of the scheme included in that valuation, in accordance with—

    (i)   regulation 7(6)(a)(i) and (ii); or

    (ii)   regulation 7(6)(b),

as the case may be, of the Occupational Pension Schemes (Scheme Funding) Regulations 2005 (actuarial valuations and reports); and

(b)   the value to be placed on the scheme's assets shall be the value placed by the actuary on the scheme's assets for the purposes of the actuary's estimate of the solvency of the scheme included in that valuation.

(3) Subject to paragraph (7), the assets of the scheme to be taken into account for the purposes of the written valuation specified in paragraph (1)(a) are the assets attributed to the scheme in the relevant accounts, excluding—

(a)   any resources invested (or treated as invested by section 40 of the 1995 Act) in contravention of section 40(1) of the 1995 Act (restriction on employer-related investments);

(b)   any amount treated as a debt under section 228(3) of the 2004 Act (failure to make payments) which is unlikely to be recovered without disproportionate cost or within a reasonable time; and

(c)   where it appears to the actuary that the circumstances are such that it is appropriate to exclude them, any rights under an insurance policy.

(4) Subject to paragraph (6), the liabilities of the scheme to be taken into account for the purposes of the actuarial valuation specified in paragraph (1)(a) are any liabilities—

(a)   in relation to a member of the scheme by virtue of—

    (i)   any right that has accrued to or in respect of him to future benefits under the scheme rules; or

    (ii)   any entitlement to the present payment of a pension or other benefit which he has under the scheme rules; and

(b)   in relation to the survivor of a member of the scheme, by virtue of any entitlement to benefits, or right to future benefits which he has under the scheme rules in respect of the member.

(5) For the purposes of paragraph (4)—

"right" includes a pension credit right; and

"the survivor" of a member is a person who—

    (a)   is the widow, widower or surviving civil partner of the member; or

    (b)   has survived the member and has any entitlement to benefit, or right to future benefits, under the scheme in respect of the member.

(6) Where rights under an insurance policy are excluded under paragraph (3)(c), the liabilities secured by the policy shall be disregarded for the purposes of paragraph (4).

(7) Where arrangements are being made by the scheme for the transfer to or from it of accrued rights and any pension credit rights, until such time as the trustees or managers of the scheme to which the transfer is being made ("the receiving scheme") have received assets of the full amount agreed by them as consideration for the transfer, it shall be assumed—

(a)   that those rights have not been transferred; and

(b)   that any assets transferred in respect of the transfer of those rights are assets of the scheme making the transfer, and not the receiving scheme.

NOTES

Initial Commencement

Specified date

Specified date: 6 April 2006: see reg 1.

5   Schemes that are subject to Part 3 of the 2004 Act—valuation of assets and liabilities

(1) In the case of a valuation specified in regulation 4(1)(a) and subject to paragraph (2), the value to be given to the assets of a scheme for the purposes of section 37(3)(a) of the 1995 Act (payment of surplus to employer) is the value given to those assets in the relevant accounts, less the amount of the external liabilities.

(2) The value to be given to any rights under an insurance policy not excluded under regulation 4(3) is the value the actuary considers appropriate in the circumstances of the case on the effective date.

(3) The value to be placed on the liabilities of the scheme shall be the actuary's estimate of the value of the liabilities of the scheme on the effective date.

(4) In paragraph (3), "estimate of the value of the liabilities of the scheme" means—

(a)   an estimate by the actuary of the cost of purchasing annuities, of the type described in section 74(3)(c) of the 1995 Act (discharge of liabilities by purchase of annuities satisfying prescribed requirements) and on terms consistent with those in the available market, which would be sufficient to satisfy the liabilities taken into account under regulation 4(4); and

(b)   other expenses which, in the opinion of the actuary, would be likely to be incurred in connection with the winding up of the scheme.

(5) Where the actuary considers that it is not practicable to make an estimate in accordance with paragraph (4)(a), he shall make an estimate of the value of the liabilities of the scheme on the effective date, in such manner as the actuary considers appropriate in the circumstances of the case.

(6) Where the actuary's estimate of the liabilities of the scheme is made under paragraph (5), the valuation must include a brief account of the principles adopted in making the estimate.

(7) In paragraph (1), "the external liabilities" of a scheme are such liabilities of the scheme (other than liabilities within regulation 4(4)) as are shown in the net assets statement in the relevant accounts, and their amount shall be taken to be the amount shown in that statement in respect of them.

(8) The assets of the scheme shall be valued, and the amount of the liabilities determined, by reference to the effective date.

NOTES

Initial Commencement

Specified date

Specified date: 6 April 2006: see reg 1.

6   Prescribed persons for the purposes of section 37(3)(a) of the 1995 Act

The classes of prescribed person for the purposes of section 37(3)(a) of the 1995 Act are in the case of a scheme that is subject to Part 3 of the 2004 Act (scheme funding)—

(a)   where the scheme is a scheme for which an actuary is required to be appointed under section 47(1)(b) of the 1995 Act (professional advisers), the actuary appointed under that section; or

(b)   where it is a scheme which is exempt from the application of section 47(1)(b) of the 1995 Act by virtue of regulations made under subsection (5) of that section—

(i)   a Fellow of the Faculty of Actuaries; or

(ii)   a Fellow of the Institute of Actuaries.

NOTES

Initial Commencement

Specified date

Specified date: 6 April 2006: see reg 1.

7   Schemes that are subject to Part 3 of the 2004 Act—valuation certificate and amount of payment to employer

(1) Where a written valuation prepared in accordance with regulation 4(1) shows that the value of the assets of the scheme is greater than the value of the scheme's liabilities, the prescribed person shall prepare a valuation certificate in the form prescribed in Schedule 1.

(2) Where paragraph (1) applies, the maximum payment that may be made to the employer is, in the case of a valuation prepared in accordance with—

(a)   regulation 4(1)(a), the amount by which the value of the scheme's assets exceeds the value of the scheme's liabilities at the effective date of the valuation; or

(b) regulation 4(1)(b), the amount of the excess of the scheme's assets over its liabilities specified in the actuary's estimate of the solvency of the scheme prepared in accordance with regulation 7(4)(b) of the Occupational Pension Schemes (Scheme Funding) Regulations 2005.

NOTES
Initial Commencement
Specified date
Specified date: 6 April 2006: see reg 1.

8 Earmarked schemes

(1) In the case of a scheme to which regulation 3(1)(b) applies, a payment may only be made to the employer where all liabilities accruing in respect of a member, beneficiary or his estate have been—

(a) secured by the purchase of one or more insurance policies; or

(b) paid in full.

(2) Where paragraph (1) applies, the maximum payment that may be made to the employer is a payment no greater than the excess of the scheme assets in relation to that member after all the liabilities accruing in respect of that member have been secured or paid in full.

NOTES
Initial Commencement
Specified date
Specified date: 6 April 2006: see reg 1.

9 Period for which a valuation certificate is to remain in force

A valuation certificate shall remain in force—

(a) in the case of a scheme that falls within regulation 3(1)(a) for fifteen months where the valuation is prepared pursuant to Part 3 of the 2004 Act; or

(b) twelve months in all other cases,

from the effective date of the valuation.

NOTES
Initial Commencement
Specified date
Specified date: 6 April 2006: see reg 1.

10 Notification to members

(1) Where the trustees of a scheme to which regulation 3(1)(a) applies propose to make a payment under section 37(1)(a) of the 1995 Act, the prescribed requirements in accordance with which the notice referred to in section 37(3)(g) of the 1995 Act must be given are—

(a) that the trustees of the scheme must make a written statement that they have decided to make such a payment;

(b) that the amount of the proposed payment must be stated;

(c) that the date that the payment is to be made which is—

(i) not later than the last day on which the valuation certificate is valid for the purposes of section 37(4)(e) of the 1995 Act; and

(ii) at least three months after the day the information is sent to the members or survivors,

must be stated; and

(d) that the notice must provide that the member may, within one month of the date of the notice, request a copy of the relevant valuation certificate prepared in accordance with regulation 7(1).

(2) Where a member requests a copy of the relevant valuation certificate under paragraph (1)(d), the trustees of the scheme shall provide this information within one month from the date that the request is received by them.

(3) A notice under section 37(3)(g) of the 1995 Act does not have to be given to any excluded person.

11   Notification to the Regulator

Where the trustees of a scheme to which regulation 3(1)(a) applies have made a payment in accordance with section 37(1)(a) of the 1995 Act, they shall notify the Regulator that the payment has been made by no later than one week after the day on which the payment was made.

PART 3
EXEMPTIONS, TRANSITIONAL PROVISIONS AND MODIFICATIONS

12   Exemptions

(1) Sections 37 and 76 (excess assets on winding up) of the 1995 Act shall not apply to a scheme where—

(a)   a Minister of the Crown has given a guarantee or made any other arrangements for the purpose of securing that the assets of the scheme are sufficient to meet its liabilities;

(b)   arrangements for the payment of any surplus or for the distribution of any excess assets on the winding up of the scheme are subject to the approval of a Minister of the Crown; or

(c)   the scheme does not fall within the description of schemes prescribed in regulation 3(1).

(2) Where such a guarantee has been given as is mentioned in paragraph (1)(a) or (b) in respect of only part of a scheme, sections 37 and 76 of the 1995 Act, shall apply as if that part and the other part of the scheme were separate schemes.

13   Transitional

The prescribed requirements for the notice specified in section 251(6)(a) of the 2004 Act (payment of surplus to employer: transitional power to amend scheme), are that the notice shall—

(a)   be in writing; and

(b)   contain the following information—

   (i)   that the trustees have decided to exercise their power under section 251(3) or (4), as the case may be; and

   (ii)   the date, being a date which is at least three months after the date that the information is sent to the employer and members, from which the trustees' proposed exercise of the power is to take effect.

14   Modifications in relation to earmarked schemes

In relation to a scheme to which regulation 3(1)(b) applies, section 37 of the 1995 Act is modified as if in subsection (3) paragraphs (a) to (c), (f) and (g) were omitted.

PART 4
SCHEMES IN WIND UP

15 Notice of proposal to distribute excess assets to the employer

(1) The prescribed requirements for the notice specified in section 76(3)(d) (excess assets on winding up) are set out in paragraphs (2) to (5).

(2) Where the trustees or the employer propose to exercise the power in section 76(1)(c) of the 1995 Act, the trustees or, as the case may be, the employer, must take all reasonable steps to ensure that each member, except any excluded person, is sent a written notice divided into two parts, of the proposal in accordance with the following provisions of this regulation.

(3) The first part must—

(a)   inform the member as to—

(i)   the trustees' estimate of the value of the assets remaining after the liabilities of the scheme have been fully discharged and the persons or class of person to whom, and in what proportions, it is proposed that they should be distributed; and

(ii)   whether the requirements of section 76(3) of the 1995 Act are satisfied;

(b)   invite the member, if he wishes, to make written representations in relation to the proposal to the trustees or, as the case may be, to the employer, before a specified date (which is not earlier than two months after the date on which the first part is given); and

(c)   advise the member—

(i)   that the second part of the notice will be sent to him if the trustees or, as the case may be, the employer intend to proceed with the proposal to exercise that power; and

(ii)   that no excess assets may be distributed to the employer in accordance with the proposal until at least three months after the date on which the second part is sent to him.

(4) The second part of the notice must be given after the date specified in accordance with paragraph (3)(b) and at least three months before the power is exercised and must—

(a)   contain the information referred to in paragraph (3)(a), including any modifications to the proposal; and

(b)   advise the member that he may make written representations to the Regulator before a specified date (which is not earlier than three months after the date on which the second part of the notice is sent to him) if he considers that any of the requirements of section 76(3) of the 1995 Act are not satisfied.

(5) The parts of the notice under paragraphs (3) or (4) shall be treated as having been given to a member where it has been sent by post to either—

(a)   the address at which he was last known to be living; or

(b)   in the case of a person who was an active member, immediately before the commencement of the winding up of the scheme, an address at which he is currently known to be employed.

16 Circumstances in which the Regulator must be satisfied that requirements of section 76 of the 1995 Act are met

(1) For the purposes of section 76(2) of the 1995 Act the prescribed circumstances are that—

(a)   subject to paragraph (2), in relation to any proposal to which that section applies, the Regulator receives—

(i)   written representations from a member to the effect that any requirements of section 76(3) of the 1995 Act are not satisfied; or

(ii)   information from any source sufficient to raise a doubt as to whether all the requirements are satisfied; and

(b)   the Regulator notifies the trustees or, as the case may be, the employer in writing that the power should not be exercised until the Regulator has confirmed in writing that it is satisfied that those requirements are satisfied.

(2) Where notice has been given to a member in accordance with regulation 15(3), paragraph (1)(a)(i) shall only apply in the case of representations received by the Regulator from the member before the date specified in accordance with regulation 15(4)(b) (expiry date of the second part of notice).

NOTES
Initial Commencement
Specified date
Specified date: 6 April 2006: see reg 1.

17   Additional requirement for purposes of section 76 of the 1995 Act

Where—

(a)   the date specified in accordance with regulation 15(4)(b) (expiry date of the second part of the notice) has passed; and

(b)   the trustees or, as the case may be, the employer have not received notification from the Regulator in accordance with regulation 16(1)(b),

the trustees or, as the case may be, the employer shall obtain written confirmation from the Regulator that it has not received any representations or information referred to in regulation 16(1)(a) and that section 76(4) of the 1995 Act accordingly, does not apply.

NOTES
Initial Commencement
Specified date
Specified date: 6 April 2006: see reg 1.

PART 5
MULTI-EMPLOYER SCHEMES

18   Schemes with more than one employer

(1) Where—

(a)   a scheme in relation to which there is more than one employer is divided into two or more sections; and

(b)   the provisions of the scheme are such that they meet conditions A and B,

these Regulations shall apply as if each section of the scheme were a separate scheme.

(2) Condition A is that contributions payable to the scheme by an employer, or by a member in employment under that employer, are allocated to that employer's section (or, if more than one section applies to the employer, to the section which is appropriate in respect of the employment in question).

(3) Condition B is that a specified part or proportion of the assets of the scheme is attributable to each section and cannot be used for the purposes of any other section.

(4) In their application to a scheme—

(a)   which has been such a scheme as is mentioned in paragraph (1);

(b)   which is divided into two or more sections, at least one of which applies only to members who are not in pensionable service under the section;

(c)   the provisions of which have not been amended so as to prevent conditions A and B being met in relation to two or more sections; and

(d)   in relation to one or more sections of which those conditions have ceased to be met at any time by reason only of there being no members in pensionable service under the section and no contributions which are to be allocated to it,

sections 37 and 76 of the 1995 Act and these Regulations apply as if the section in relation to which those conditions have ceased to be satisfied were a separate scheme.

(5) For the purposes of paragraphs (1) to (4), any provisions of the scheme by virtue of which contributions or transfers of assets may be made to make provision for death benefits are disregarded.

(6) But if paragraph (1) or (4) applies and, by virtue of any provisions of the scheme, contributions or transfers of assets to make provision for death benefits are made to a section ("the death benefits section") the assets of which may only be applied for the provision of death benefits, the death benefits section is also to be treated as if it were a separate scheme for the purpose of sections 37 and 76 of the 1995 Act and these Regulations.

(7) For the purposes of this regulation, any provisions of a scheme by virtue of which assets attributable to one section may on the winding up of the scheme or a section be used for the purposes of another section are disregarded.

(8) In the application of section 37(3) of the 1995 Act to a scheme in relation to which there is more than one employer, paragraph (e) of that subsection has effect as if for the words "employer has asked", there were substituted the words "person whom the employers nominate to act as their representative for the purposes of this paragraph has asked, or, if no such nomination is made, all the employers have asked".

NOTES
Initial Commencement
Specified date
Specified date: 6 April 2006: see reg 1.

PART 6
REVOCATIONS

19   Revocations

The Regulations specified in column 1 of Schedule 2 to these Regulations are revoked to the extent specified in column 3.

NOTES
Initial Commencement
Specified date
Specified date: 6 April 2006: see reg 1.

SCHEDULE 1
Actuary's Certificate—Valuation of Assets and Liabilities

Regulation 7

Actuarial Certificate Given for the Purposes of Regulation 7 of the Occupational Pension Schemes (Payments to Employer) Regulations 2006

Name of scheme

Date on which valuation is made

1 Comparison of value of scheme assets with amount of scheme liabilities

In my opinion, at the above date the value of the assets of the scheme was greater than the amount of the liabilities of the scheme.

The value of the assets of the scheme was

The amount of the liabilities was

The amount of the difference (being the maximum amount of payment that may be made to the employer) was

2 Valuation principles

The scheme's assets and liabilities are valued in accordance with section 37 of the Pensions Act 1995 and the Occupational Pension Schemes (Payments to Employer) Regulations 2006

Signature

Date

Name

Qualification

Address

Name of Employer

Note

The valuation of the amount of the liabilities of the scheme may not reflect the actual cost of securing those liabilities by the purchase of annuities if the scheme were to have been wound up on the date as at which the valuation is made.

NOTES

Initial Commencement

Specified date

Specified date: 6 April 2006: see reg 1.

SCHEDULE 2
Revocations for the Purposes of Regulation 19

Regulation 19

Column 1	Column 2	Column 3
Regulations revoked	*References*	*Extent of revocation*
The Occupational Pension Schemes (Payments to Employers) Regulations 1996	SI 1996/2156	The whole of the Regulations
The Personal and Occupational Pension Schemes (Miscellaneous Amendments) Regulations 1997	SI 1997/786	Paragraph 14 of Schedule 1 and Schedule 2 to the Regulations (in so far as it relates to the Occupational Pension Schemes (Payments to Employers) Regulations 1996)
The Occupational Pension Schemes (Payments to Employers) Amendment Regulations 1997	SI 1997/2559	The whole of the Regulations
The Occupational Pension Schemes (Winding up etc) Regulations 2005	SI 2005/706	Regulation 14 (in so far as it relates to the Occupational Pension Schemes (Payments to Employers) Regulations 1996) and Paragraph 11 of the Schedule to the Regulations

NOTES

Initial Commencement

Specified date

Specified date: 6 April 2006: see reg 1.

The Occupational Pension Schemes (Levies) (Amendment) Regulations 2006

SI 2006 No 935

Occupational Pension Schemes (Levies) (Amendment) Regulations 2006

Made 28th March 2006

Coming into force 1st April 2006

1 Citation, commencement and interpretation

(1) These Regulations may be cited as the Occupational Pension Schemes (Levies) (Amendment) Regulations 2006 and shall come into force on 1st April 2006.

(2) In these Regulations "the Levies Regulations" means the Occupational Pension Schemes (Levies) Regulations 2005.

> **NOTES**
> **Initial Commencement**
> *Specified date*
> Specified date: 1 April 2006: see para (1) above.

2 Amendment of the Levies Regulations

(1) The Levies Regulations shall be amended in accordance with this regulation.

(2) In paragraph (4) of regulation 4 (liability for the levies)—

(a)   for "year" substitute "years"; and

(b)   after "31st March 2006" insert "and 31st March 2007".

(3) In regulation 5 (the reference day)—

(a)   in paragraphs (2) and (3), in both places—

    (i)   for "years" substitute "year"; and

    (ii)   omit "and 1st April 2006"; and

(b)   in paragraph (4), for "1st April 2007" substitute "1st April 2006".

(4) In paragraph (2) of regulation 6 (the amount payable)—

(a)   for "year" substitute "years"; and

(b)   after "31st March 2006" insert "and 31st March 2007".

(5) In regulation 13 (meaning of "the levies" in Part 4)—

(a)   in paragraph (1), after "the administration levy," insert "the pension protection levy,"; and

(b)   in paragraph (2), after "14(3)" add "or, as the case may be, 15(7)".

(6) In paragraph (3) of regulation 14 (attribution of payments in respect of levies), omit "any pension protection levy and".

(7) After paragraph (6) of regulation 15 (multi-employer schemes) add—

"(7) This regulation does not apply to any pension protection levy.".

(8) In paragraph (4) of regulation 18 (avoidance of double liability: schemes in Northern Ireland)—

(a)   in sub-paragraph (b), for ", and" substitute ";"; and

(b)   in sub-paragraph (c), after "regulation 9" insert—

"; and

(d)   in the case of the pension protection levy, if it is imposed under any equivalent provision to section 175 of the 2004 Act".

NOTES

Initial Commencement

Specified date

Specified date: 1 April 2006: see reg 1(1).

Table of Statutes

Table of Statutory Instruments

Paragraph references printed in **bold** type indicate where the Statutory Instrument is set out in part or in full.

Table of
European Legislation

Index